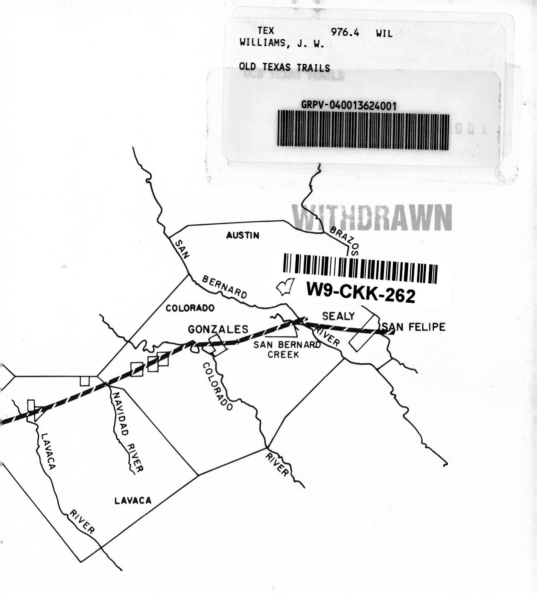

W9-CKK-262

N ANTONIO-SAN FELIPE ROAD

OLD

TEXAS

TRAILS

AUTHOR J. W. WILLIAMS.

OLD

TEXAS

TRAILS

By J. W. Williams

Edited and Compiled by Kenneth F. Neighbours

EAKIN PRESS   *   *Burnet, Texas*

i

Published in the United States of America
By Eakin Press, P. O. Box 178, Burnet, Texas 78611

FIRST EDITION

Second Printing

Library of Congress Catalog Card No. 79-56554

ISBN 0-89015-232-2

ACKNOWLEDGMENTS

The author, Jesse Wallace Williams, would have wanted to give credit and thanks to a vast cloud of helpful souls who assisted him in the course of more than forty years on his study of Texas trails. Many of these he mentioned in the text.

Others that he would have thanked include the Rockefeller Foundation which in 1942 gave him a grant to finish the book. Particularly helpful were the staffs of the Texas General Land Office, the Texas State Archives, and the archives of the University of Texas, Eugene C. Barker Texas History Center. Every author of a Texas historical work of any significance in the last fifty years is indebted to Miss Winnie Allen of the latter depository. Among other things, she furnished Mr. Williams a large collection of photostats of historic maps.

He would have spoken highly of the late H. Bailey Carroll, another noted trails historian; the late R. Ernest Lee, Senior; and Rupert Norval Richardson, his classmate and later director of his Master's Thesis on trails. He would have mentioned his niece and her husband, Mr. and Mrs. L. B. Cosper, who accompanied him on tracing Cabeza de Vaca's trail, as well as Anthony Brollier, a former student. I would join him in thanking Arturo Villareal, Father Martinez, David Quintero, and Cesareo Nañez Garza of Monclova who were helpful to us. To the host of others who unknown to me assisted the author I extend on his behalf a most hearty expression of appreciation.

I must personally thank those who helped me in finishing the book, especially the brother, Mr. Robert H. Williams, and his son, Don, who edited the chapter on Cabeza de Vaca, and who encouraged and sustained me. R. Ernest Lee, Junior, as a labor of love, transcribed the maps for the trails of Cabeza de Vaca, the San Antonio roads, La Bahia Road, The San Antonio-San Felipe Road and Texas Trails 1716-1886. Mr. and Mrs. Lewis A. Parr of La Pryor ex-

iii

tended me the hospitality of their beautiful home, made available valuable pictures of sites now inaccessible, while he transplated a Rose of Saint John in a valiant effort to get me a picture of it in bloom.

The Ross O. Sculls made me welcome as their house guest for extended periods while I gathered pictures and worked on the book. The J. E. Piries also of La Vernia were hospitable and helpful. Mr. Joe Moore dropped his work and took me, a total stranger, several miles through his ranch for me to take a picture of the mouth of Little River. Mrs. Jane Duggan typed the scribbled manuscript for me and expressed a lively and encouraging interest in the manuscript which she found exciting. The editors of the *Southwestern Historical Quarterly* and the *West Texas Historical Association Year Book* kindly granted permission to reproduce the articles and maps published in them.

To all the wonderful people who helped over the years, we express our heartfelt thanks.

IN MEMORIAM

Jesse Wallace Williams

Jesse Wallace Williams, the son of Robert H. and Mary L. (Ely) Williams was born in Cross Plains, Callahan County, Texas, on June 3, 1891. After graduating from high school, he attended Simmons College (later Hardin-Simmons University), majored in mathematics, participated on the debate team with Rupert Norval Richardson, and received his bachelor of arts degree in 1911. In 1938 he received his master of arts degree from Hardin-Simmons University with a major in history. In the meantime he had attended the University of Texas where he completed graduate courses in economics.

He varied his career by serving as an oil scout for Magnolia and Texas oil companies, and then engaged in oil production on his own for a time in Wichita County. He also worked briefly for Wilson Manufacturing Company.

His first love, however, was teaching. He taught a rural school near Merkel, 1911-1912; taught mathematics in the Big Spring High School, 1915-1916; in the Burkburnett High School, 1921-1923; and in the Wichita Falls Senior High School from 1916 to 1918 and from 1923 to 1960 when he retired.

On the college level, he taught at Midland Junior College for the years 1913-1915; and at Howard-Payne University at Brownwood, Texas, in the summer of 1960. He taught an advanced course on Southwestern Trails at Midwestern University in the summer of 1957. One of his students published a paper in the West Texas Historical Association *Year Book.*

His consuming interest was the tracing of Southwestern trails from the Spanish period through the American occupation. He published many scholarly articles in the West Texas Historical

Association *Year Book* and the *Southwestern Historical Quarterly.* He brought to bear on his trails studies such diverse disciplines as mathematics, astronomy, botany, and zoology. He received a Rockefeller grant in 1942 to publish his book on trails and was still at work on it at the time of his death.

He was the author of three books: *The Big Ranch Country; Sizzling Southwest Football;* and *Great Moments with the Coyotes.* The reprint of the *Big Ranch Country* is a current publication of Nortex Press.

He was the president of the West Texas Historical Association for the years 1952 and 1953, and continued to serve on its executive council until his death. He also served on the executive council of the Texas State Historical Association from 1961 to 1971.

He married on August 11, 1915, Miss Ruth Elizabeth Veazey who died on September 26, 1955. On November 22, 1964, he married Mrs. Agnes McCarty who died on December 12, 1975. He had no children. His last wife's son and daughter were as his own. After a series of accidents and illnesses in his last year, Jesse Wallace Williams died at Bethania Hospital, Wichita Falls, Texas on February 22, 1977, and was buried on February 25, 1977, in Crestview Memorial Park, Wichita Falls, Texas.

He was a Baptist, a member of the Southwest Rotary Club, the Wichita County Historical Commission and the scholarly associations mentioned above. He served for a time on the staff of the Texas Historical Commission. As a member of the Wichita County Historical Commission, he sponsored markers for the Van Dorn Trail and the Buffalo Road. His intimate contemporaries called him Jake. I always winced for fear lightning would strike such irreverence.

Jesse Wallace Williams's life was an inspiration to others. He was a man of integrity in his daily life and in his scholarship. He lived his Christian faith. His speech was clean and his habits pure. Through his long life he avoided the use of alcohol and tobacco. He was of a cheerful and generous nature. He did enjoy the innocent pleasure of contriving on occasion a situation which he knew would make me use intemperate language at which he would laugh merrily. He spent his life in the service of others. He will not need to await canonization. He was a living saint.

Kenneth Franklin Neighbours
Midwestern State University

IN APPRECIATION

My brother Jesse, a little older than I, was one of a family of eleven children. For the four of us who survive him I take this means of thanking Dr. Kenneth F. Neighbours for getting Jesse's last book into shape for publication.

Though in his eighty-sixth year and finally too weak to walk, Jesse evidently never gave up the notion that he himself would finish *Old Texas Trails:* so he left us no instructions, other than, at my guarded request, an oral outline indicating the sequence of the chapters. He did mention, however, from time to time the fact that his close friend, Dr. Neighbours, had gone with him on numerous trips to research old trails on the scene, and we all knew that Dr. Neighbours was familiar with much of his work.

When Jesse was no longer with us and I asked Dr. Neighbours if he would be willing to take over the editing of the book, he must have been appalled. For, though virtually all the material had been reduced to writing and some of it typed and revised, only the first chapter was put together in unified order, the others having been written in separate sections as discoveries were made over a period of forty years. Each of these sections would have to be examined in relation to other sections and fitted into its proper place, with overlapping of sections minimized.

We fortunately found footnotes for the first chapter, in handwriting but legible. The rest of the manuscript had not been annotated. And the reference material consisted of tons of notes, books, maps, magazine articles, interviews, data dug out of old surveys and county records across Texas—a forty-year accumulation stacked high on a platform my brother had built in his carport above the level of his car, plus shelves and boxes in various parts of his house. He just needed a few more months in which to streamline the manuscript and add the footnotes. He carried the reference material in his memory—and took it away with him.

Dr. Neighbours had hardly had time "to recuperate," as he put it, from his own extensive work on the biography of Major *Robert Simpson Neighbors* (published under that title). Nevertheless, he agreed to take over the editing of the book. In addition to countless hours of desk work he has made several trips across Texas to gather bits of data and get some photographs which he knew Jesse had hoped to get. We will never be able adequately to express our gratitude to him.

We also want to add our thanks to all those persons cited by him in his *Acknowledgment,* and to any and all others whose identity we cannot know. We are especially grateful to Ernest Lee, Jr., Jesse's friend and neighbor, for adapting many maps for publication, an exacting and time consuming contribution.

—Robert H. Williams

EDITOR'S FOREWORD

I have a right to be a rebel—or put it more mildly—I
have a right to be a dissenter. That is, I have a right to dis-
sent as long as I can furnish substantial reasons for my objections. This time I am objecting to some long held opin-
ions about some of the old Spanish roads that led to San
Antonio.

Thus wrote Jesse Wallace Williams in an unpublished manuscript
which he probably meant to use in a talk never made before the West
Texas Historical Association. Making use of many disciplines such as
mathematics, astronomy, botany, and zoology, years of field work
and analysis, the author did beg to differ with other studies of Texas
trails. His background and temperament eminently fitted him for his
self appointed task. R. Ernest Lee, Senior, often quoted Rupert Norval Richardson as saying that only one J. W. Williams comes along
every thousand years.

No one else could have persevered and have brought to bear so
many talents to bring forth this book. Only one who has spent years
tracing ancient trails knows the difficulty of matching vague descriptions, directions and distances with the topography and understands
that the book will touch off lively discussions of various points. He
saw the book as a study of the role of transportation in the development of Texas. His preeminent contribution was tracing the first San
Antonio Road by Domingo Ramón in 1716.

Many of us eagerly anticipated for years the appearance of this
book. Heavy responsibilities and his high standards of research
prevented the author from publishing all his trails studies in book for-
mat. He had published a large part as articles in scholarly periodicals
which are reproduced here. He left in manuscript Chapters I, V, VI
and VII. He had projected but not commenced writing other trails
studies.

On June 18, 1956, the author told me that he had in his will made me the legatee of his books, maps, notes, and other data in order for me to finish his book on trails. At the time I thought there was little likelihood that he would not finish it himself. His circumstances and wills changed. Near the end he designated his brother, Mr. Robert H. Williams, to see that the book was finished and stated that I would know most about it. After the author's death, the brother, the author's step children, Mr. Alan McCarty and Mrs. Don Pearson requested me to finish the book.

One of the main problems was that no one had ever seen any of the author's unpublished manuscripts, and he requested that not a word be changed. He had a justifiable fear of plagiarism particularly after another person contracted to publish my major manuscript but failed. (Mr. Williams assisted me in saving my book.) In order not to miss anything, Alan, his sister, Mrs. Beverly M. (Don) Pearson, their spouses, and I sifted through tons of material in the house and I sifted through other tons in the garage.

The author had a highly individualistic but laudable style of writing. The injunction not to change a single word was followed as far as possible. It was not always possible. There were gaps that had to be reconstructed, and great amounts of puzzling duplications had to be cut out that had crept in through the years of writing and rewriting. I was awed at the thought of touching his manuscript and appalled at the immensity of the task which I had hoped against hope not to have to do. I only wish that the book had come out in his time. I am greatly honored and humbled by the confidence reposed in me by the author and his family.

The author and I spent many happy years discussing the book and exploring some of the trails together. I even served as his *Dolmetscher* in Mexico as he knew no Spanish. I have since obtained some of the long list of desired pictures he had postponed taking. I had planned to drive him to the sites during the summer of 1977 but time ran out. It gives me great pleasure and pride to send forth this work of my dear and precious friend which will forever remain a classic.

KENNETH F. NEIGHBOURS
Blue Bird Hollow
June 18, 1979

CONTENTS

Page

FRONTISPIECE: Picture of Jesse Wallace Williams, 1891-1977 .
ACKNOWLEDGMENTS iii
IN MEMORIAM v
IN APPRECIATION vii
EDITOR'S FOREWORD ix
CHAPTERS
I. The Route of Cabeza De Vaca In Texas 1
II. Coronado: From The Rio Grande To The Concho 44
III. New Evidence On Moscoso's Approach To Texas 77
IV. Moscoso's Trail In Texas 89
V. Spanish Exploration Preliminary To Texas Settlement 111
VI. Spanish Road System: Ramon's Road to San Antonio 126
VII. Spanish Road System: Ramon's Road From San Antonio
     To Nacogdoches 141
VIII. New Conclusions On The Route Of Mendoza 1683-84 181
IX. The National Road Of The Republic Of Texas 201
X. Marcy's Road From Doña Ana 219
XI. Marcy's Exploration To Locate The Texas Indian
    Reservations in 1854 245
XII. Military Roads Of The 1850's In Central West Texas 271
XIII. The Van Dorn Trails 288
XIV. Journey Of The Leach Wagon Train Across Texas, 1857 312
XV. The Butterfield Overland Mail Road Across Texas 365
XVI. Some Northwest Texas Trails After Butterfield,
     Mrs. Virgil Johnson and J. W. Williams 384
XVII. Robson's Journey Through West Texas in 1879 412
      Bibliography 427
      Index 434

ILLUSTRATIONS AND MAPS

Number   Description   Page

1. Route of Cabeza De Vaca 8
2. Coronado's Visit To Texas 48
2b. Coronado's Journey into Texas and the Army's Return 56
3. Flood Map Of The Mississippi 78
4. Route of Moscoso in 1542 104
5. The San Antonio Roads 128
6. Route Of Mendoza 1683-84 182
7. La Bahia Road .... back end sheet
8. San Antonio-San Felipe Road .... front end sheet
9. Map Of The Central National Road Of
     The Republic of Texas................................202
10. A Partial Map Of Dallas Showing The Route
     Of The National Road And The Old Preston-Austin Road .. 214
11. Marcy's Road Fron Doña Ana..........................220
12. Picture section
13. Map Of Marcy's Exploration To Locate The Texas
     Indian Reservations 1854 248
14. Military Roads Of Central West Texas 1849-60 272
15. Van Dorn's Trails 1858-1859 289
16. Route Of The Leach Wagon Train Across Texas 328
17. The Butterfield Mail Route In Texas 366
18. A Concord Coach Used On The
     Butterfield Overland Mail Route 383
19. Some Historic North Texas Trails......................392
20. Texas Trails 1716-1886 ....Foldout

I

THE ROUTE OF CABEZA DE VACA IN TEXAS[1]

The miraculous story of Alvar Nuñez Cabeza de Vaca is well known to a Texas audience—and this study expects to add only a single significant fact to the sources of the story that come from Spain and Spaniards. It is not the exciting narrative that is to be undertaken here though—rather, a cold fact-finding effort to trace the trail of these Spaniards across the map of the Southwest.

But even this becomes an intriguing game of hide-and-seek. Though far more than a dozen others have attempted this same thing, the present writer proposes to add some very material evidence that seems never to have been explored or understood in any previous effort. In Texas there is another island of pines besides that at Bastrop; only this second little forest was made up of nut-bearing pines called piñons, just as Cabeza de Vaca described them. Let us

1. Cabeza de Vaca published the account of his journey, known as the *Naufragios*, in 1542 and again in 1555. The two accounts were almost identical. The 1542 edition was translated by Mrs. Fanny Bandelier and published in 1905 and again in 1922. The 1922 edition is the publication referred to in this article. It is entitled *The Journey of Alvar Nuñez Cabeza de Vaca and His Companions From Florida to the Pacific, 1528-1536*. For the sake of brevity this source of information will be referred to hereafter as Bandelier, *Cabeza de Vaca*.

The 1555 edition was translated by Buckingham Smith and published in *Spanish Explorers in the Southern United States*, edited by Frederick W. Hodge and Theodore H. Lewis, published in 1907 by Charles Scribner's Sons, New York, hereafter referred to as Hodge, *Cabeza de Vaca*. In addition to these two sources the joint account by Cabeza de Vaca, Alonzo del Castillo and Andrés Dorantes has survived in the publication known as *Historia General y Natural de las Indias* by Gonzalo Fernandez de Oviedo y Valdez. It was published in four volumes by the Royal Academy of History at Madrid, 1851-1855. This joint account is found in Vol. III:582-618. It was translated by Harbert Davenport and Joseph K. Wells. Edited by Davenport, it was published in the *Southwestern Historical Quarterly*, Vols. XXVII: 2-4 and XXVIII: 1, 2 (1923-24), hereafter referred to as Davenport, *Quarterly*. (Davenport gives credit to Bernardo Calerio for the original translation, which Davenport and Wells revised.)

return to this strange bit of timber later in the story.

Meanwhile, may we go back to this remarkable Spaniard and his three companions who made such a seemingly impossible trip across the North American continent some four and a half centuries ago.

Actually there were not just four but in fact about 600 Spaniards who, in June 1527, left the port of San Lucas de Barrameda at the mouth of the Guadalquivir River on the southwest coast of Spain. The expedition was headed by Pánphilo de Narváez, who had spent much time as an important official in the West Indies.

The party reached Santo Domingo as the first point of contact in the new world. Here they purchased horses and took on some supplies. Some of the original party of 600 quit the expedition and stayed in Santo Domingo. Next, Narváez moved to Cuba, where he spent the remainder of the winter (1527-28). Two of the ships were sent to the south coast of Cuba. A storm battered these ships to splinters and took the lives of sixty of the men. But Narváez bought more ships and made ready to move ahead.

The newly constituted party of Spaniards numbering about 400 made contact with the west coast of present-day Florida on April 15, 1528. Some 300 of the men struck inland in a northward direction from this point. Without any carefully made plans, Narváez sent the ships ahead to explore the coast, expecting to make contact with them later. Cabeza de Vaca protested this indefinite arrangement, but he was overruled. The land party never saw the ships again; provisions were soon exhausted and, largely because of this failure to replenish food and other supplies, the expedition failed. Many of the men died of hunger, exposure and Indian fights.

Some five months after the ships and the land party had separated, Narváez and about 240 survivors embarked in five small poorly made boats in an effort to reach Pánuco, the nearest of the settlements of Mexico. They set sail on the Gulf Coast somewhere to the west of Florida, September 27, 1528, and reached the coast of Texas in early November of the same year.

Cabeza de Vaca and the men in his boat landed on an island[2] on November 6. Andres Dorantes had landed only three or four miles away the day before. Both boats capsized and the men had to spend the winter on this small body of land, which they named Malhado Island.

2. For these introductory facts leading up to the study of the route of Cabeza de Vaca see Hodge, *Cabeza de Vaca*, 14-44.

Here we arrive at the first problem in determining the route of Cabeza de Vaca. On what island did these first two boatloads of Spaniards make a landing? Further study of the accounts left by the Spaniards reveals that this island was just east of some large river that flowed directly into the Gulf of Mexico.[3] More than a half century ago Brownie Ponton and Bates H. McFarland, then undergraduate students of the University of Texas, pointed out that the Brazos was the only such large stream between the Mississippi and the Rio Grande that flowed directly into the Gulf.[4] This fact, now generally accepted as basic in the study of Cabeza de Vaca's route, greatly narrows the search for the island.

Actually, on first sight the answer seems simple. On the Texas coast of today, Galveston Island is the only outright island that by any stretch of the imagination is large enough to qualify as Cabeza de Vaca's Malhado for much more than 100 miles east of the Brazos. Each of the several small islands along that more than 100 miles of seacoast is only a small fraction as large as the dimensions which the Spaniards gave for Malhado Island.

But when we closely examine the facts about Galveston Island, our study runs into real difficulties. Malhado Island was reported to be five leagues long and one-half league wide;[5] Galveston Island is eleven leagues long and more than a league wide. When the Spaniards traveled from Malhado Island to the river that is now identified as the Brazos, they first went to the mainland, then walked two leagues west to the first stream and from there three additional leagues[6] to the Brazos. If one now attempts to travel from the mainland opposite Galveston Island westward to the Brazos, he must cross not one but at least two streams—Bastrop and Oyster bayous—and in so doing he must travel not just a succession of two leagues and then three leagues. Rather he must travel a succession of at least six leagues across Bastrop Bayou to Oyster Creek and then some three leagues to the Brazos.[7] Plainly, Galveston Island is too wide, too long, too many leagues away from the Brazos and across too

3. Davenport, *Quarterly*, XXVII: 235, 236.

4. See Miss Brownie Ponton and Bates H. McFarland, "Alvar Nuñez Cabeza de Vaca: A Preliminary Report on His Wanderings in Texas," *The Quarterly of the Texas State Historical Association*, I (January 1898): 175.

5. Hodge, *Cabeza de Vaca*, 54.

6. Davenport, *Quarterly*, XXVII: 235.

7. See United States Geological Survey maps of Texas: *Christmas Point Quadrangle* and *Freeport Quadrangle*.

many bayous to qualify as Malhado Island.

To put it bluntly there is no island east of the Brazos that can qualify as Malhado, but some historians—notably Harbert Davenport and Joseph K. Wells[8]—have offered a solution. They suggest that San Luis Peninsula, just east of the Brazos, probably was an island 400 years ago and that it was the body of land that de Vaca called Malhado.

Surely, their solution offers the most probable answer. Inland from San Luis Peninsula one can walk westward to the Brazos and in so doing cross just one bayou (Oyster Creek). The distances of two leagues to the bayou and then three leagues on to the Brazos can very well fit the terrain here. The width of the peninsula conforms well to Malhado's half a league.

As to length, of course the answer would depend on where the immense loads of silt that have floated down Oyster Creek have closed the gap between the original island and the remainder of present-day San Luis Peninsula. An examination of United States Geological Survey maps[9] of this area makes it plain that San Luis Peninsula is almost an island until this good day. The part of the peninsula between Swan Lake and San Luis Pass is completely surrounded by water except the marsh some two miles in extent that lies between Swan Lake and Drum Bay. Certainly this area that is still almost submerged has been built up by the loads of silt deposited in this whole area of marshland near the lower part of Oyster Bayou. According to the maps there is not even a neck of solid ground between San Luis Peninsula and the mainland. These facts seem to argue strongly for the conclusion that San Luis Peninsula was an island 400 years ago, especially when one considers that there is no other body of land that can answer the description of Malhado Island.

The peninsula from Swan Lake to San Luis Pass, it is true, is fifteen per cent short of the five leagues ascribed to Malhado Island but it is unlikely that any of the Spaniards stepped its length. A man on foot is very likely to overestimate distances and his error is likely to increase if the land traversed is sandy or mountainous. Only an actual

8. See Harbert Davenport and Joseph K. Wells, "The First Europeans in Texas, 1528-1536," *The Southwestern Historical Quarterly*, XXII (October 1918): 121-23. Hereafter the two-part article by Davenport and Wells will be referred to as Davenport and Wells, "First Europeans." The first part, cited here, holds that Malhado Island was San Luis Peninsula.

9. See footnote 7.

count of steps could have approached accuracy in this or any of the other distances traveled by Cabeza de Vaca. There is not the slightest evidence left by the Spaniards that any such careful methods were employed. The whole journey across the continent was an effort to survive, not to take notes.

Still another significant fact about San Luis Peninsula is its distance from the mainland. In the widest place (across Christmas Bay and Bastrop Bay) it is approximately two leagues from the mainland. This again conforms to the distance as told by Cabeza de Vaca.[10]

This explanation of the reasons for identifying San Luis Peninsula with the island of Malhado is not new. Most of these same facts were presented by Davenport and Wells[11] in their study published in 1918, but since a later writer[12] has attacked their conclusion, this review of their logical statements is presented and elaborated a bit in order that the reader may better determine the true answer.

The winter of 1528-29 was one of disaster for the Spaniards on Malhado Island. Of the eighty or more who survived the first few days after landing, only sixteen[13] were still alive in the spring. Disease, exposure and starvation had all but wiped them out.

Four of the party—all good swimmers—had been sent ahead in the fall[14] of 1528 to try to reach Mexico and summon aid for the others, but they failed either to reach Mexico or to return to Malhado Island. In the spring of 1529 Andres Dorantes assembled thirteen of those who survived the winter (for the other three including Cabeza de Vaca were seriously ill) and moved down the coast.[15] Dorantes and his men saw the wrecked boat commanded by Alonzo Enriquez, probably at the mouth of the San Bernard River.[16] Later, they learned that a fourth boat with Narváez and two others of his party was swept out to sea (and all of them undoubtedly drowned) probably from

10. Davenport and Wells, ''First Europeans,'' 116.

11. See footnote no. 8.

12. See Cleve Hallenbeck, *Alvar Nuñez Cabeza de Vaca, the Journey and Route of the First European to Cross the Continent of North America, 1534-1536* (Glendale, Calif., 1940), 119-29, 289-90. Hereafter this work will be referred to as Hallenbeck, *Cabeza de Vaca*. Hallenbeck attacked the Davenport-Wells thesis that Malhado Island was the same as San Luis Peninsula.

13. Davenport, *Quarterly*, XXVII: 235-36; Hodge, *Cabeza de Vaca*, 55.

14. Hodge, *Cabeza de Vaca*, 49.

15. *Ibid.*, 55.

16. Davenport, *Quarterly*, XXVII: 236.

Cavallo Pass[17] at the mouth of Matagorda Bay.

Figueroa was the only survivor of the four good swimmers who had been sent ahead to try to reach Mexico. Figueroa had learned the facts about the men from the third and fourth boats from Esquivel, the only one who lived long enough to tell the story.

It is doubtful if any of Dorantes' little band of thirteen ever reached beyond the Corpus Christi country. Death by drowning, starvation, and murder reduced their ranks, and the Indians enslaved all the survivors. By 1534 only three of the party, Alonzo del Castillo, Estevánico the Moor, and Dorantes himself, remained alive.[18]

Meanwhile, back at Malhado Island two of the three sick men lived. The two were Cabeza de Vaca and Lope de Oviedo. Cabeza de Vaca had slipped away from his Indian masters and had taken up residence with the Charruco Indians on the mainland. Each year he went back to the island and tried to persuade Oviedo to join him in an attempt to escape to Mexico. But Oviedo could not swim and was further handicapped by fear. Finally, in 1534, Oviedo consented to go[19].

17. *Ibid.*, 236-38. This reference tells the story of the loss of the boats of Enriquez and Narváez.

18. Hodge, *Cabeza de Vaca*, 59-60.

19. *Ibid.*, 57. Here Cabeza de Vaca tells the story of his and Oviedo's departure and journey westward from Malhado.

20. Davenport and Wells, "First Europeans," 123-33. Note that Davenport and Wells (pp. 132, 133) give James Newton Baskett credit for originating the very logical theory that the route followed by Dorantes in 1529 and by Cabeza de Vaca and Oviedo a few years later passed along Matagorda Peninsula and across Cavallo Pass, etc. See James Newton Baskett, "A Study of the Route of Cabeza de Vaca," *The Quarterly of the Texas State Historical Association*, XX, 257-59. Hereafter the Baskett articles will be referred to as Baskett, *Cabeza de Vaca*.

The article written by Baskett and by Davenport and Wells show (as do the Spanish sources) that Dorantes in 1529 found the overturned boat commanded by Enriquez at the mouth of the third river, which was undoubtedly the San Bernard River. Certainly this is proof that Dorantes was following the coast. But let us engage in a chain of reasoning that will vastly increase the probability that the Dorantes party followed the Texas coast almost to Corpus Christi.

Dorantes and his party (1) spent four days along the land (Matagorda Peninsula) and (2) crossed a pass a league wide and very deep, (3) next traversed an island twelve to fifteen leagues long, (4) came to a pass so narrow that they could talk across it, (5) walked the length of another island six leagues long and (6) came to a pass probably of medium width, but references are not definite. Now, let's put the present-day names for six bodies of land or water along the Texas Coast: 1. Matagorda Peninsula, 20 leagues long; 2. Cavallo Pass, one league wide; 3. Matagorda Island, 14 leagues

Cabeza de Vaca managed to assist Oviedo across to the mainland and across four streams—probably Oyster Creek, the Brazos River, the San Bernard and Caney Creek. The exact route by which Cabeza de Vaca and Oviedo traveled is in dispute. Davenport and Wells[20] trace the route very near the coast and along Matagorda Peninsula and across Cavallo Pass at the mouth of Matagorda Bay to the mainland near present Port O'Connor. From here the Davenport-Wells route extends inland to a point a short distance up the Guadalupe River.

A more recent study by Cleve Hallenbeck[21] traces the route of the two Spaniards across the same four streams, but on the mainland side of Matagorda Bay to the Colorado River. Here one arrives at an important difference in the two studies.

The coastal Indians of four centuries ago knew a point on one of these rivers where pecans were so plentiful that for more than twenty leagues around these red men gathered at the pecan groves[22] at the proper season of the year for a great part of their food supply. Hallenbeck believes that this river was the Colorado;[23] Davenport and Wells believe it was the Guadalupe.[24]

---

long; 4. Cedar Bayou, narrow; 5. St. Joseph Island, 7 or 8 leagues long; 6. Aransas Pass, of medium width.

Note that the lengths of the three bodies of land in the Spanish accounts correspond very closely to the three bodies of land on the Texas coast mentioned above. The number of days required to travel the length of the first body of land makes it plain that it is longest of the three, and actual measurements given show that the second body is next in length and that the third body of land is shortest. Matagorda Peninsula, Matagorda Island, and St. Joseph Island are in that exact order of magnitude. The first pass in the Spanish accounts is unquestionably the widest of the three passes. In the example given above, Cavallo Pass, which is first, is by all odds the widest of the three passes given.

Now, if one wishes to calculate the number of possible combinations—that is, the shortest body of land could have come first or second or the widest pass could have come second or third—the order of these physical facts might be scrambled into eighteen different possible combinations. Strangely, the order of magnitude of these physical dimensions in the Spanish accounts is exactly the same as the order of dimensions of the bodies of land and water to be found on the Texas coast. Mathematically—unless the Spaniards were talking about this very piece of the Texas coast—the chance for the order of magnitude to be identical in these two cases was only one out of eighteen.

But if we pursue the facts still further the law of probability will give us a much stronger case than that. The Spaniards applied the name Espiritu Santo to the map at the first pass. They identified it by a high point of sand. Now there is (according to the topographical map) just such a high point at Cavallo Pass. No such point is shown

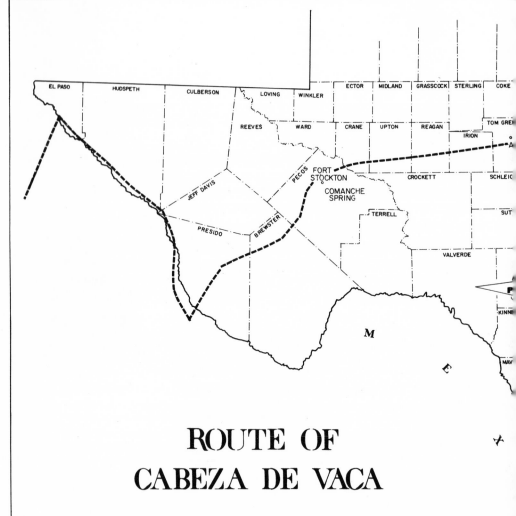

ROUTE OF
CABEZA DE VACA

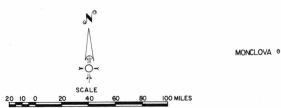

SCALE

20 10 0   20   40   60   80   100 MILES

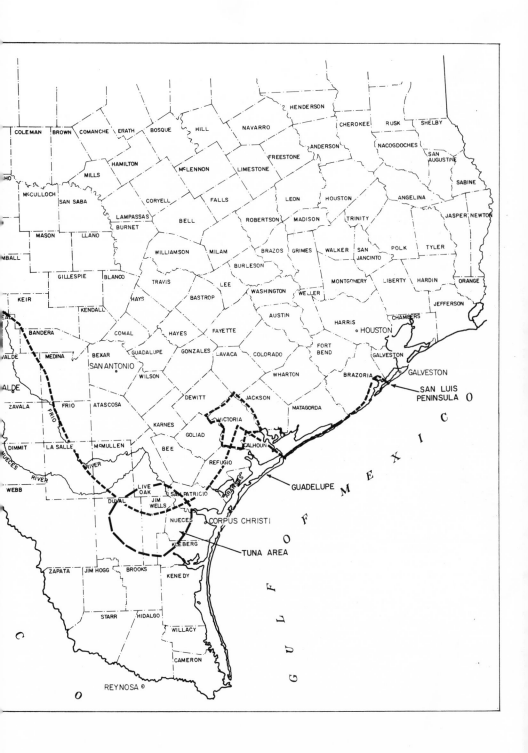

Here the issue is sharply drawn. If this "river-of-nuts" is the Colorado, then the Cabeza de Vaca route must have followed the mainland side of Matagorda Bay. Otherwise, the Colorado would not have been on the route. On the other hand, if the "river-of-nuts" is the Guadalupe, the Cabeza de Vaca route would have crossed five or six rivers (and if all the creeks are counted the total is thirteen) instead of four in reaching that stream, unless the two Spaniards followed the Matagorda Peninsula on the Gulf side of Matagorda Bay.[25]

Hallenbeck supports his conclusion by citing J.H. Burkett to the effect that the Colorado has the greatest pecan growth of all Texas rivers. Burkett is correct as to the total, but only a small percent of the pecan trees on the Colorado (or its branches) can be found below Austin. The Davenport-Wells conclusion appears to be supported by first-hand evidence, but is hardly specific enough to be a complete answer. What we need is an actual count of trees.

---

either at Cedar Bayou or Aransas Pass. Note that according to the law of chance this coincidence of high point at the first pass known to the Spaniards and the high point at Cavallo Pass is only one out of three. Now the possibility of coincidence in the details of the Spanish story and the selected part of the Texas coast becomes only one in fifty-four. But if we continue to examine details the odds become much greater than that. The Spaniards crossed four rivers immediately after they left the island of Malhado. They gave statistics which show that the distance between the first two of these rivers was less than the distance between any of the others. They also showed that the distance between the second and third rivers was greater than that between the first two and that the distance between the third and fourth rivers was greater than any of the others. Now, the spaces between Oyster Creek, the Brazos River, San Bernard River and Caney Creek are in exactly that same order of magnitude. Mathematically there is only one chance in six that the order of magnitude in this spacing should be the same in the account related by the Spaniards as with these four named Texas rivers. And finally it was the second of the four rivers in the Cabeza de Vaca accounts that forced its current far out beyond the coast. Now, note that in the above four named rivers that flow into the Gulf of Mexico, the Brazos, which is by far the most powerful of the four, is the second in order of the four streams. This coincidence had only one chance in four to exist.

Now, in the final calculation what is the chance that the order of the spacing of the rivers, the order of the length of the islands, the order of the magnitude of the passes and all the other facts should be the same in the Cabeza de Vaca story as along the Texas Coast? If left to chance, just one in 1,296! And yet all of these dimensions and other facts coincide all the way from Oyster Creek to Aransas Pass. Surely, the sheer mathematics of the problem removes all reasonable doubts about the route of Dorantes in the spring of 1529. But since the joint account shows that Cabeza de Vaca's journey passed the point where the name Espiritu Santo was applied, it means that he and Oviedo followed this same route as far as Cavallo Pass. Even so, this study will develop another very powerful fact that confirms this conclusion.

Fortunately, we have that very thing. The 1910 United States census shows the number of pecan trees in each Texas county. If we total the number of these trees in all Texas counties from the Brazos to the Rio Grande and extend that count inland two counties deep from the coast we find a rather remarkable answer to the problem at hand. Sixty-six per cent of all the pecan trees in all this coastal area are in Victoria County[26] alone. If we eliminate the bitter pecan belt on the lower Brazos and otherwise cover the same coastal area as above, we find that Victoria County has about eighty per cent[27] of all the pecan trees. Victoria County is on the lower Guadalupe and even though the statistics are of 1910 instead of 1530 they weigh powerfully toward accepting the route as outlined by Davenport and Wells.

---

21. See Hallenbeck's *Cabeza de Vaca*, 133-36. Hallenbeck points out that Caney Creek does not now flow directly into the Gulf of Mexico. Davenport and Wells hold that Caney Creek was one of two channels of the Colorado in the 16th century and flowed into the Gulf, which it must have done if Dorantes crossed four rivers before he came to Cavallo Pass. Hallenbeck agrees that Dorantes did cross Cavallo Pass.

22. Davenport, *Quarterly*, XXVII: 281.

23. Hallenbeck, *Cabeza de Vaca*, 136-40. Hallenbeck overlooks both Live Oak Creek and Cottonwood Creek, which are between Caney Creek and the Colorado River. These two streams would have brought the number of "rivers" up to six, which Cabeza de Vaca must have crossed before reaching the Colorado.

24. Davenport and Wells, "First Europeans," 132-42. The Davenport and Wells article presents this discussion very thoroughly and convincingly.

25. See the map of the *State of Texas* by the United States Department of Interior Geological Survey, A.F. Hassan, cartographer. The map was compiled in 1922. It is in four large sections.

The thirteen rivers and creeks on this map, beginning with Oyster Creek and extending westward to the Guadalupe, are as follows: Oyster Creek, Brazos River, San Bernard River, Caney Creek, Live Oak Creek, Cottonwood Creek, Colorado River, Tres Palacios Creek, Carancahua Creek (two branches), Keller Creek, Lavaca River, Garcitas Creek, and Placido Creek.

26. Abstract of the 1910 census, 728-50. The number of pecan trees in 1910 in each of these coastal counties was as follows: Brazoria 6,834; Fort Bend 1,091; Wharton 2,990; Matagorda 427; Jackson 164; Calhoun 3; Victoria 28,006; Goliad 1,597; Refugio 1,112; Bee 7; San Patricio 2; Live Oak 24; Nueces 0; Duval 0; Cameron 110; Hidalgo 0; Starr 0. Victoria County on the Guadalupe River had 66 percent of the total number of trees in the above counties. Excluding Brazoria and Fort Bend counties, Victoria County had 81 percent of the total. Since the 1910 census was taken this coastal area has been further subdivided by the addition of six counties. These are Aransas, Jim Wells, Kleberg, Kenedy, Brooks, and Willacy. Victoria County (on the lower Guadalupe) had eight times as many pecan trees as had both Wharton and Matagorda counties (on the lower Colorado).

27. *Ibid.*

Surely the "river-of-nuts" was the Guadalupe where more than four-fifths of the pecan trees of this Gulf Coast region were concentrated. With that statement goes the further probability that Cabeza de Vaca traveled the Matagorda Peninsula-Port O'Connor route in order to reach the Guadalupe, for by no other route could he have reached the pecan groves of Victoria County without crossing more than four rivers.[28]

When Cabeza de Vaca and Oviedo reached the mainland near Port O'Connor, they discovered that the Indians of that area were hard and brutal masters. Oviedo was afraid to go on and (in company with some Indian women) turned back[29] toward Malhado Island.

Cabeza de Vaca went on and contacted Dorantes at the pecan groves on the Guadalupe.[30] Cabeza de Vaca became the slave of one of the local Indians,[31] but fortunately he, Dorantes, Castillo and Estevanico did not at any time during this period belong to more than two different tribes.[32]

Their real opportunity to escape was not at the pecan groves but in the prickly-pear country to the west. Food was scarce among the coastal Indians most of the year and the meeting in the pecan groves was usually a time of feasting, but the coming together in the prickly-pear belt was an even greater time of feasting.[33] Many of the tribes of Indians gathered in the prickly-pear country in mid-summer each year and left that section by about the end of September.

Mid-summer was a number of months after the nut season, but the Spaniards agreed to wait to escape until that time of the year when their tribes would come together in the prickly-pear country. Unfortunately in the summer of 1533 the two tribes of Indians who held the Spaniards as slaves had a quarrel[34] and separated before the escape plans could be carried out. But the prickly-pear season of 1534 gave the four men their opportunity and they made a hasty retreat at the time of the full moon in September.[35]

---

28. See the United States Geological Survey map of Texas as cited in footnote 25.

29. Hodge, *Cabeza de Vaca,* 59.

30. *Ibid.,* 59, 60.

31. *Ibid.,* 61.

32. The Marians (or Mariames) and the Yguaces (also called the Yguazos or Iguaces). See Hodge, *Cabeza de Vaca,* 61, 65.

33. Hodge, *Cabeza de Vaca,* 66, 67.

34. *Ibid.,* 70, 71.

35. *Ibid.,* 71-73.

It was their first real break for freedom. If it failed—if the Indians overtook them—they were sure to die at the hands of their savage masters. But the attempt did not fail. As we have noted previously, the escape plans had been made with great care. The habits of the Indians were carefully appraised and undoubtedly the Spaniards tried to plan a route ahead that would lead through friendly bands of red men.

The experience of half a dozen years had made it possible for the white men to draw a mental picture of the area of greatest hostility. So far as is known, none of the Spaniards had been murdered east of Matagorda Bay, and the Indians on Malhado Island had given both food and shelter to the white men when such hospitality meant the difference between life and death.[36] But this climate of tolerance (and in some cases of outright friendliness) changed on the west side of Matagorda Bay. On the west side of Cavallo Pass—the entrance to Matagorda Bay—both Cabeza de Vaca and Oviedo had been slapped and beaten by the Indians as a kind of crude introduction to their customs.[37] Oviedo was afraid and turned back, but Cabeza de Vaca had the courage to go on.

However, Cabeza de Vaca soon heard about the atrocities of the Indians in the country immediately ahead. He heard the various accounts from Andres Dorantes. Piecing these accounts together we can compile the names of a total of fourteen men who lived among the Indians as slaves west of Matagorda Bay. Nine of the Andres Dorantes party who went west from Malhado Island in the spring of 1529 lived to reach the west side of Cavallo Pass. The four swimmers went west in late 1528. All of them seem to have gone well beyond this pass. Hernando de Esquivel, the sole survivor of the Narváez and Enriquez boats, brings the total up to fourteen who were enslaved by Indians west of Matagorda Bay. At least five of the fourteen were murdered by Indians.[38] Certainly these grim statistics weighed heavily in the thinking of the Spaniards who were planning an escape route.

The hostility of Indians increased toward the west. Dorantes, Castillo, and Estevanico had been the servants of Indians who probably lived as far west as present-day Corpus Christi. All three of them at one time or another escaped from these cruel Indians because life was unbearable among them: all three of them moved eastward

36. *Ibid.*, 46-48.
37. *Ibid.*, p. 59.
38. *Ibid.*, 58.

and became the slaves of other Indians among whom life was a little less dangerous.

All of these facts were known to the Spaniards when they made their break for freedom in September 1535. But only a short while before this escape, they had heard about the worst of all the Indian atrocities. The Camoles, a tribe that lived farther down the coast than any of the others (probably well beyond Corpus Christi), had killed all forty-eight of the men who landed (probably on Padre Island) from the boat commanded by Peñalosa and Tellez.[39] The Lanegados Indians had given this account of the murdered Spaniards and produced articles of clothing to prove their story. This narrative accounted for the fifth and last of the little boats in which Narváez had attempted to bring his stranded men to Mexico, but also it served as a grim warning to Cabeza de Vaca and his party to chart their course well away from the Gulf Coast ahead of them. Surely these four men who were running for their lives would not go in the direction of the boatload of murdered Spaniards.

Certain historic facts seem to furnish the background for this zone of Indian hostility that increased in intensity toward Mexico. First of these were the injustices which the Spaniards had heaped on Indians in the country not far south of the Rio Grande. After the Pánuco area was subjugated, the Spanish authorities captured some nine to ten thousand Indians and sold them into slavery.[40] One of these Spanish expeditions went forty leagues northward from Pánuco.[41] Earlier than these slave-hunting movements (in 1520) Camargo and 150 men had gotten into trouble with the Indians on the Rio de las Palmas, which authorities believe was the Rio Grande.[42] Camargo had anchored his three ships up the river probably in the neighborhood of present-day Brownsville. After a time hostilities broke out and the Indians in hundreds of little boats inflicted heavy

39. *Ibid.*, 72.

40. Carlos E. Castañeda, *Our Catholic Heritage in Texas, 1519-1936*, 1 (Austin, 1936): 35.

41. *Ibid.*, 36, 37. Under the rule of Nuño de Guzmán at Pánuco, slave-hunting expeditions had caused the Indians to desert their pueblos. An expedition sent by Guzmán in 1528 found the Indians in hiding and hostile as the explorers travelled at least 40 leagues north of Pánuco.

42. *Ibid.*, 16-17.

casualties on the Spaniards and drove them out of the mouth of the river.[43]

Certainly the battle on the Rio Grande (if the identity of the river is correct) could have been the cause of a zone of intense hostility both up the Rio Grande and along the Texas coast. Just as certainly the slave hunting that went on south of the Rio Grande must have set up a zone of hostility not only along the coast of Mexico but far into the back country.

It seems very doubtful that four Spaniards without an escort could have penetrated this hostile zone in Mexico even if they had tried. By their own admission they were greatly afraid of the hostility along the Texas coast.[44] It would have been the part of prudence for Cabeza de Vaca and his three companions to have detoured toward the north or northwest to avoid almost certain trouble that lay ahead of them along or near the coast.

There is good evidence that the four men were planning to go in a northward direction. The first red men whom the Spaniards contacted after their break for freedom were the friendly Avavare Indians who were in the prickly pear country probably not far inland from Corpus Christi. After a short stay with these Indians, Cabeza de Vaca and his men inquired about the country "farther on." They were told that the country in question was "very cold,"[45] which was a statement not easy to misunderstand by anyone conversant with the extreme south Texas climate. Undoubtedly the Indians were not pointing south or southwest into the Lower Rio Grande Valley when they referred to the country as "very cold," for that area has the mildest winter climate to be found in all of Texas. What else could the language have meant except that the Spaniards had planned to go in a northward direction?

Certainly a warning that a country is "very cold" means that it is colder than the present location. The four Spaniards evidently so interpreted the meaning of the words for they spent the winter with the Avavares Indians rather than to go "farther on" where it was "very cold."

It was a winter of hardships for both the Indians and the Spaniards. They were in an area where there were neither nuts nor

---

43. *Ibid.*, also see J. Lee Stambaugh and Lillian J. Stambaugh, *The Lower Rio Grande Valley of Texas* (San Antonio, 1954), p. 3.

44. Davenport, *Quarterly*, XXVII: 296.

45. Hodge, *Cabeza de Vaca*, 74.

acorns[46]—in a land without pecans or oaks. Pecans are not native to the country southwest of the San Antonio River and south of Frio County.[47] But there are many live oaks in the country south of Falfurrias. The writer passed through this area in mid-April, 1961, and found a veritable forest of live oaks some ten miles across. Certainly it could have provided ample food for the Spaniards and their Indian friends during the winter of 1534-35. This region of live oaks in the heart of the southernmost part of Texas furnishes strong evidence that Cabeza de Vaca and his associates did not spend the winter in that area—and Cabeza de Vaca said, as noted above, that the Avavare lived in a section that was without acorns. The prickly pear area extends both to the north and for a short distance to the northeast of this country below the Nueces.[48]

It was in the prickly pear country that the Spaniards first contacted the Avavares Indians, but it was the end of the prickly pear season. Food was not to be had, so both the Indians and their four guests set out on a hunt for something to eat. After five days of searching they found a section where the fruit of prickly pears was still available.

At the end of October, 1960, the writer made a field trip from Uvalde southward to Freer, then to San Diego, Robstown, Mathis, Tynan and Beeville. The prickly pear crop was completely gone in the Uvalde area and far to the south, but the writer began to find a scattering few to the north of Freer. However, this fruit was much more plentiful in and near southern Bee County. Some varieties of the prickly pear had already matured and dropped their fruit crop just as in the area farther north, but other types of this cactus plant (not markedly different in appearance) were just well into their ripening season. Still others, somewhat fewer in number, were not yet ripe. This preponderance of late ripening prickly pears north of Corpus Christi and east of the Nueces (in and near southern Bee County) may

46. Bandelier, *Cabeza de Vaca*, 111.

47. Abstract of the 1910 census, 728-50. The number of pecan trees (in 1910) was given for each Texas county. Refugio County, which borders the San Antonio River, had 1,112 pecan trees; Cameron and Hidalgo counties, which front on the Rio Grande, had 110 and 21 trees respectively. All the eleven other counties of this area listed a total of only 33 pecan trees.

48. A personal inspection of this area was made by the writer, October 31 and November 1, 1960.

offer a suggestion about where Cabeza de Vaca and his hosts, the Avavares, satisfied their hunger.

The next answer to this strange quest for food was the "product of certain trees which is like peas."[49] This kind of tree was found along a river. Now the hackberry grows along the streams over most of Texas including the prickly pear belt described above.[50] The fruit of this tree matures in the fall and can quite accurately be described as "like peas."

After leaving the Avavares, the Spaniards passed from one group of Indians to another three or four times until at length they lost their way in a large wood of small trees. Only a short while later they crossed a river that was apparently 100 to 150 yards wide and very swift but shallow enough to wade. Some twenty to twenty-five miles farther on these four European travellers came to a village where the Indians had fairer skins and some of them were blind. Then after a short day of travel the four men began a long trek parallel to a chain of mountains.

Do all of these facts[51] seem to spell out a route for the Spaniards with any degree of certainty? Did they after all move down to and across the Rio Grande where the Indians held murder in their hearts for any white man? Or did they move in some other direction where the winters were very cold? Is there some distinct marker on the trail ahead that will give a positive answer to these questions?

This much is certain: the Spaniards soon came into some country where the Indians ate the nuts from the piñon tree. Cabeza de Vaca's own account[52] of his journey mentioned that at one place the Indians ate these nuts (the seeds of pines) and he went on to state that the trees were little pines. Let us check the various piñon belts and if possible identify the spot over which Cabeza de Vaca actually walked.

To single out these little pine trees has been the stumbling block that has wrecked more than one involved effort to trace the route of Cabeza de Vaca. Mind you, stumbling block is not too strong a term; for if the author who traced the Spaniards almost to Monterrey, Mexico, and on to the mountains near Monclova in order to find piñons,

49. Hodge, *Cabeza de Vaca*, 74.

50. See note No. 48.

51. For an account of this part of the journey see Davenport, *Quarterly*, XXVII, 287-96.

52. Hodge, *Cabeza de Vaca*, 96, 97.

is right, then the author who traced those same Spaniards up the Colorado River of Texas and far up into New Mexico in order to find piñons is wrong. Or if the second author is right, then likewise the first author must be wrong. These are the two extreme views about this route. In between them, Frederick W. Hodge, for instance, seems to pay little attention to piñons and suggests that the route passed through Mason County.[53] Dr. Robert T. Hill,[54] who wrote extensively for *The Dallas Morning News* in 1933 and 1934, traced Cabeza de Vaca through the Uvalde country. The Hill route is defended by Carlos E. Castañeda.[55] Judge O. W. Williams,[56] who knew much about the flora of Texas, found piñons on the Dry Devils River north of Del Rio and designated it as a point on the route of Cabeza de Vaca.

The present writer intends to present evidence that points to a route not vastly different from that suggested by Judge Williams. There is a piñon belt in the hill country about 100 miles northwest of San Antonio, despite the fact that one of the writers referred to above states positively that there is no such thing east of the Pecos River in Texas. The writer has spent several weeks in this hill country both observing these piñons and interviewing people who know about this unique island of little pines that is almost totally unknown anywhere away from that part of the hill country. This belt of nut-bearing pines begins just west of the Frio River and extends westward some sixty miles[57] almost to the Dry Devils River. More accurately the east boundary line of this piñon area is a straight line beginning some twenty miles north of Uvalde and extending about thirty miles north of that point. There are still thousands of trees in this irregular belt that extends to the west of that line, but a few decades ago the trees could have been numbered in tens of thousands. The cedar post industry that has laid bare a vast acreage of the hill country has made many inroads in this belt of little pines. Originally piñons were especially numerous in the high hills west and northwest of the little town of

53. *Ibid.*, 92-93n, 95n.

54. The Robert T. Hill map of the route of Cabeza de Vaca was published in *The Dallas Morning News*, Nov. 19, 1933.

55. Castañeda, *Our Catholic Heritage*, I: 75-78.

56. O. W. Williams, "Route of Cabeza de Vaca in Texas," *The Quarterly of the Texas State Historical Association*, III, 54-64.

57. (Tell my personal story about the piñons here.) [We did not find this K.F.N.]

Leakey. This belt extended west across the head branches of the Nueces River. West of the Nueces where the destruction of timber has been less pronounced, hundreds of small piñons are sold for Christmas trees each year.

The testimony of a number of local ranch owners establishes beyond doubt that this area of nut-bearing pines could have been an important source of food[58] for early-day Indians. But certainly this bare fact is not enough to prove that this belt of little pines was the particular one visited by Cabeza de Vaca.

Actually there are some five spots on the map of the Southwest (including Mexico) one of which almost certainly was the piñon belt visited by Cabeza de Vaca. Let us discuss the reasons why each of these five localities might or might not have been on Cabeza de Vaca's route.

One of these areas of little pines lies in the mountains of New Mexico beyond Roswell. The distance of this mountain country from the Texas coast is over 600 airline miles. The Oviedo account of the Cabeza de Vaca trek across the continent reveals that the piñon country is some 150 leagues[59] from the place where the Spaniards began their journey. But the same account shows that about forty leagues[60] of the distance were directly parallel to the coast, leaving the actual journey from the coast to the piñons only 110 leagues or 290 miles. As will be shown later, the Cabeza de Vaca estimates of distance uniformly overstate the mileage. But whether 290 miles or less is the correct amount, it is plain that the Roswell country 600 miles away is vastly too far to conform to the piñon country told about by Cabeza de Vaca.

The same reasoning would eliminate any other area of nut-bearing pines in New Mexico. Also it would eliminate from consideration a second piñon belt found in the mountains of the trans-Pecos part of Texas.

In a third area the nut-bearing pines seem to be plentiful. This belt is in the high mountains of Mexico west of Eagle Pass, Texas. Here again it seems impossible to correlate a piñon belt and the other known data of the Spanish journey. As the Cabeza de Vaca party progressed from the piñon country toward the west coast, the next stream

58. See footnote 57.
59. Davenport, *Quarterly*, XXVII: 298.
60. *Ibid.*, 282.

mentioned was a river that came down from the north. Now if one moves westward from this piñon area of Mexico, the first river which he encounters is the Rio Conchos. This stream, contrary to what it must be to fit the known facts of the Spanish journey, flows down from the south and not from the north. The only other river at hand is the Rio Grande, which in this sector flows from the west—or even from the southwest.

The fourth spot of nut-bearing pines is that mentioned in the very excellent study made by Davenport and Wells.[61] They point to an area of these trees in the mountains near Monclova, Mexico. This suggested route traces the path of the Spaniards almost to Monterrey, then northward and finally westward over a local mountain to the banks of the Nadadores River at Monclova. Davenport and Wells call attention to the piñons, the volcanic iron rocks and the "beautiful" river in this area. Now all of these things were mentioned by Cabeza de Vaca in whatever place it was that he found piñons. But Cabeza de Vaca found all of these things in a single day's journey of seven leagues[62]—or eighteen miles. The difficulty in trying to fit his description to the Monclova area is that the iron rocks according to local mining engineers are not nearer to the town than forty miles—and none of these rocks are on the mountain east of town.[63] Also, the piñons are eight miles back in the mountains[64] and as if adding insult to injury, many local people say the Nadadores is far short of a "beautiful river."

Not only do these three essentials of the Cabeza de Vaca account fail to team up together at Monclova; there are other things equally contradictory to the Spanish accounts near this place. After leaving the piñon belt by the "beautiful river," Cabeza de Vaca reported that his party " . . . travelled through so many sorts of people of such diverse languages the memory fails to recall them."[65] The language

61. Davenport and Wells, "First Europeans," 111-42.

62. Hodge, *Cabeza de Vaca*, 95-96. Also Bandelier, *Cabeza de Vaca*, 139-40.

63. Jesús de la Fuente is a prominent citizen of Monclova and has been so for many years. His many-sided local experiences include mining engineering. The information about the iron rocks was given the writer by him and confirmed by others.

64. The Jesús de la Fuente interview.

65. Hodge, *Cabeza de Vaca*, 97. Also Bandelier, *Cabeza de Vaca*, 142. The Bandelier translation has the same meaning as the Buckingham Smith translation as cited from Hodge above. The Bandelier translation follows: " . . . we travelled among so many different tribes and languages that nobody's memory can recall them all . . ."

plainly infers that the Spaniards travelled a long distance for which no details are given. At length they came to a river that flowed from the north,[66] and after crossing the river the party walked across thirty leagues of plains.[67] But the Davenport-Wells study has the Spaniards begin this walk of thirty leagues of plains almost immediately after leaving Monclova[68] without any allowance for the distance " . . . travelled through so many sorts of people . . ." Next they have the Spaniards cross the Sabinas River at the end of the thirty leagues.[69] This is a reversal of the Cabeza de Vaca account, which tells that the river from the north comes first and the thirty leagues of plains come afterward.

The Monclova area plainly does not meet the requirements of Cabeza de Vaca's account of the journey. The long distance "through so many sorts of people . . ." is not there. The thirty-league spread of plains country is there, but it is on the wrong side of the river that flows from the north.

A third checkup that would seem to eliminate the Monclova route (and with it the Monclova piñon belt) concerns the mountains of Mexico and the Rio Grande. Cabeza de Vaca and his companions forded a river that was compared in width to the Guadalquivir[70] at Seville, Spain. In the Davenport-Wells study this river was supposed to be the Rio Grande. Now the Cabeza de Vaca party according to the Spanish accounts crossed this river that was compared to the Guadalquivir, passed two Indian villages and came to a third village where there were some blind Indians.[71] At this third village the Spaniards began to see mountains.[72] A part of the distance from the river to the village of the blind Indians was seven and a half leagues.[73] The whole distance from the river is not exactly known, but apparently it was

---

66. Hodge, *Cabeza de Vaca*, 98-99. Also Bandelier, *Cabeza de Vaca*, 144.

67. Hodge, *Cabeza de Vaca*, 99. Also Bandelier, *Cabeza de Vaca*, 144.

68. Davenport and Wells, "First Europeans." See map between 258 and 259.

69. *Ibid.*

70. Bandelier, *Cabeza de Vaca*, 129. Also Hodge, *Cabeza de Vaca*, 90. Also Davenport, *Quarterly*, XXXVII: 291.

71. Davenport, *Quarterly*, XXVII: 291-95. Also Hodge, *Cabeza de Vaca*, 92. Also Bandelier, *Cabeza de Vaca*, 133.

72. Davenport, *Quarterly*, XXVII: 295. Also Hodge, *Cabeza de Vaca*, 92. Also Bandelier, *Cabeza de Vaca*, 133.

73. Davenport, *Quarterly*, XXVII: 291, 293. Only the joint account gives the distances between villages at this point of the journey.

some twenty to twenty-five miles.[74]

Thus the Monclova route and also the Monclova piñon belt fail to stand the test.

By contrast the fifth piñon belt, the area of little pines north of Uvalde, seems to comply remarkably well with all of the specific details described in the old Spanish accounts of Cabeza de Vaca's journey. Let us suppose that these four survivors of the Narváez expedition walked north up the Sabinal River valley to the "ridge" country above the head of that stream near the northwest corner of Bandera County. At this point, let us suppose that they turned west some eighteen miles past the Prade ranch to a beautiful branch of the Nueces River known as Bullhead Creek some fifty miles north of Uvalde. Will this supposed route comply with the exact things known about the land through which these Spaniards travelled?

Note how well it does comply. The many leagues up the Sabinal River valley follow a course almost due north—and north was just what the old Spanish manuscripts said[75] (and this route skirts mountains all of the way).[76] Again it meets a specific requirement of the Spanish sources. Turning west a day's journey of about eighteen miles, the path of the four Europeans entered the best of the piñon belt and, after a few miles, reached a beautiful river.[77] Both the piñons and the beautiful river are the exact meaning of Cabeza de Vaca's own language.

Also, this day of westbound travel could well have passed the iron rock deposits on the Frank Powers ranch.[78] Here in plain contrast

---

74. The whole distance from the river that was compared to the Guadalquivir to the village of the blind Indians was the seven and a half leagues accounted for in footnote 73 and in addition an unknown distance walked late one afternoon from the river to the first village. Both the joint account (see Davenport, *Quarterly*, XXVII: 290) and Cabeza de Vaca's personal account (see Hodge, *Cabeza de Vaca*, 90) indicate that this late afternoon walk was probably only a small fraction of a day's journey. If this part of a day's journey amounted to as much as five miles it would make a total of twenty-five miles from the river to the village of the blind Indians.

75. Davenport, *Quarterly*, XXVII: 297.

76. *Ibid.*

77. Hodge, *Cabeza de Vaca*, 95-96. Also Bandelier, *Cabeza de Vaca*, 139-40.

78. The writer was escorted over the Frank Powers ranch, some 20 miles northwest of Leakey, during August, 1960 by Mr. Powers himself. The iron rocks referred to were not commerical iron ores but were made up of chert with a noticeable iron content. A Mr. Udden of Corpus Christi sent some of these rocks to his son, a chemist, who tested the specimens and reported the iron content. The rocks were

to the whole countryside of white limestone are three distinct areas of
large boulders, colored yellow or red or brown with iron ores such as
hematite and lucite. These boulders are basically made of the almost
unworkable rock called chert but the iron ores give the boulders their
distinct appearance and color. The three chief areas of these large
stones lie in an east-west direction and stretch out some two miles in
extent. Iron rocks do not completely fill the gaps between these areas
of big boulders, but broken fragments have tumbled down the slopes
until the smaller stones at least partly fill the spaces between the three
areas of larger stones. The whole path of these iron rocks is not very
wide, perhaps not much more than a hundred yards. But the fact that
these stones contain red ochre, a commodity much sought by red
men, would have caused the Indians to have paid special attention to
the small but unique rock formations. Why should we believe that
these iron rocks were on the route of the Spaniards? Cabeza de Vaca
when referring to this day of westbound travel said, "The stones are
scoria of iron,"[79] or "iron slags."[80]

The writer has spent several weeks searching the area along the
east edge of this Uvalde piñon belt trying to find other deposits of
iron rocks. There are three or four other small deposits but none of
them approach the size of the iron rocks on the Frank Powers ranch.
This was also the experience of a local rock collector who has lived at
Leakey for more than a dozen years.[81]

Surely this piñon belt north of Uvalde meets the requirements of
the Cabeza de Vaca manuscripts in a satisfactory manner, such as do
none of the other areas of nut-bearing pines. If so we can now go back
down the trail where we left off and attempt to trace the route of
Cabeza de Vaca's little party all the way up from the Gulf coast to this
small forest of little pines.

Careful study of the facts as related by the Spaniards makes it
seem very probable that these men of the Narváez Expedition did not
move directly toward the site of present-day San Antonio. When they

variously colored brown, red or yellow by the different types of iron compounds.

The deposits followed a path of about a hundred yards in width that stretched
out intermittently for some two miles. Some of the rocks much have weighed several
tons each.

79. Hodge, *Cabeza de Vaca*, 94.

80. Bandelier, *Cabeza de Vaca*, 139.

81. Lewis Casey of Leakey has collected the rocks of his area for a number of
years. He seemed to have no doubt that the iron rocks on the Frank Powers ranch
constituted an aggregate of vastly greater proportions than existed in any other area.

left the Avavare Indians just before the prickly pears ripened in the summer of 1535, they passed through a large wood of small trees.[82] Here the Indians in fact ate the seeds of two kinds of trees.[83] More than once in this part of the journey the Indians gave them food prepared from mesquite beans,[84] which tells what kind of small trees were meant. But what else besides mesquite trees? Evidently huisache, which also has a bean growth.[85] Both kinds of beans—mesquite and huisache—ripen in the late summer.[86] The mesquite trees are more plentiful but the huisache are found in sufficient numbers to be noticeable.

The place where the mesquite trees predominate is quite a bit farther west than the Corpus Christi-San Antonio road. Northwestward from the country inland from Corpus Christi, across Duval and McMullen counties and on to the Frio River northeast of Cotulla, in the present LaSalle County, is perhaps the best guess at the route of the Spaniards through the mesquite country.[87]

If so, then the Frio River almost certainly must qualify as the stream that "might be as wide as the Guadalquivir." One may ex-

---

82. Davenport, *Quarterly*, XXVII: 288-289; Hodge, *Cabeza de Vaca*, 82; Bandelier, *Cabeza de Vaca*, 155.

83. Davenport, *Quarterly*, XXVII: 288.

84. Hodge, *Cabeza de Vaca*, 89. Bandelier, *Cabeza de Vaca*, 126-27. Davenport, *Quarterly*, XXVII: 291.

85. The writer travelled through the country between San Antonio and Laredo several times from August 1960 to April 1961. The mesquite is the principal kind of tree, especially to the east and northeast of Cotulla. But the huisache is much in evidence in that area.

86. Mrs. Thelma Lucas, who carried the mail for some years in the area to the east and northeast of Cotulla, states that the fruit of both the mesquite and the huisache ripens in that area in August.

87. See *The Texas Almanac* (Dallas), 1925. This issue of *The Texas Almanac* obtains its data on the various Texas counties from well-informed local sources. The reports on Duval (272-73) and La Salle (309-10) counties leave no doubt that mesquite timber at that time predominated in those counties. The fact that McMullen County at the time was much excited about new railroads and an oil discovery seems to have diverted the interest of the local informant for such assets as trees but an earlier *Texas Almanac* (1904) did give prominent mention to mesquite timber. The writer's personal examination of these several counties confirms the earlier reports about mesquite timber. Also, to a lesser extent the writer observed the existence of huisache in the area. It is the writer's observation that such timber as post oaks and live oaks becomes much more prominent in the country immediately southwest of San Antonio and bordering the above counties on the north and east. The *Texas Almanac* of 1925 mentioned both post oak and live oak timber in addition to mes-

pect a multitude of objections here. The river here is little more than a glorified irrigation ditch but it has an extensive watershed. Very much rainfall above will certainly cause the seemingly small stream here in the relatively flat country northeast of Cotulla to overflow its banks. Certainly it can become 100 yards wide and even more. Recent measurements on the old channel of the Guadalquivir at Seville, Spain, show that it is about 148 yards wide.[88] The Spaniards at some point in their journey in or near Texas waded a stream that was compared in width to the Guadalquivir. The water of the stream was first knee deep, then thigh deep, and for twice the length of a lance it was breast deep.[89] The current was "very swift." If one tried to describe a small stream in a flat country that overflowed its banks, surely the above language paraphrased from the translations of the Cabeza de Vaca manuscripts could well serve his purpose. The sluggish stream that is the lower Rio Grande when its channel carries enough water to become "very swift" is far too deep to wade. The same thing is probably true of the other large rivers of Texas.

If one remembers that the Spaniards began to see mountains only about twenty to twenty-five miles after they had crossed a river[90]

---

quite in Atascosa county (244). It mentioned no other timbers in Live Oak County except "the live oak groves" that gave the county its name (312-13). The same volume mentioned both live oak and mesquite timber in Jim Wells County (302). The above county reports in a measure serve to guide one to the area in which Cabeza de Vaca subsisted largely on mesquite beans.

88. Mrs. Maurice McCall of Wichita Falls wrote to a friend of hers living in Madrid, Spain, for information about the width of the Guadalquivir river at Seville. Through her own knowledge and that of those who assisted her, the Madrid friend made a map of the Guadalquivir at Seville showing the old original channel of the river and also a new channel constructed to prevent floods. The three bridges on the old channel were shown on the map. Their lengths varied only between the narrow limits of 130 and 135 meters. The width of the river at the upper bridge (a pontoon bridge in Cabeza de Vaca's day) was 135 meters or 148 yards. This old bridge was said to be the only crossing in Cabeza de Vaca's day. Mrs. McCall made the map available to the writer. Her information was confirmed by the port director of Seville.

89. Davenport, *Quarterly*, XXVII: 291. Also Hodge, *Cabeza de Vaca*, 90. Also Bandelier, *Cabeza de Vaca*, 129.

90. Hodge, *Cabeza de Vaca*, 92. Bandelier, *Cabeza de Vaca*, 133. Both translations show plainly that the Spaniards began to see mountains when they were at the village of the blind Indians. The joint or Oviedo account also first mentions the mountains at the village of the blind Indians. The Cabeza de Vaca accounts translated by Hodge and Bandelier, above, mentioned the extensive chain of mountains that extended toward the North Sea (the Atlantic) while the Oviedo account mentioned another "cordillera" that extended to the north. Hence it becomes quite

that was compared (in width) to the Guadalquivir, he must realize that the Frio in the area mentioned is about the only river that can qualify. It is at the right distance from the hill country. None of the rivers near San Antonio are in the country where the mesquite and huisache supplement each other in extensive woods.

Twenty miles or more north of this supposed crossing on the Frio would have placed Cabeza de Vaca and his companions somewhere to the north of Pearsall. Here they could have seen mountains to the north that stretched out toward the east far beyond the range of eyesight. The Spaniards seem to have believed (probably by misunderstanding the Indians) that these mountains extended to within fifteen leagues of the Atlantic Ocean (the "North Sea"). It is only natural that they should have so misunderstood, for they must have gone far enough north when they travelled inland from Florida to have learned about the Appalachian Mountains. Apparently they believed that this hill country that lies to the north and west of San Antonio was an extension of the same mountains. They had no accurate knowledge of the size and topography of the southern United States. Also the Spaniards were in sight of a low chain of hills east of the lower Sabinal River that at a distance appeared to be mountains. At most these hills reach a height of 300 feet. De Leon (in 1669) referred to the hills that lie some fifty miles east of the site of Laredo as mountains.[91] None of these hills east of Laredo is as high as 300 feet.

This small chain of hills which Cabeza de Vaca saw between the lower parts of Hondo Creek and the Sabinal River extended to the north. Oviedo says of this chain (if we are correct in identifying it): There was a cordillera of them [mountains] which appeared to traverse the land directly to the north.[92]

It was at a village where some of the Indians were blind that the Spaniards saw this chain of hills that ranged toward the north, and apparently at the same time they saw the other chain of hills (north of them) that extended toward the Atlantic Ocean. They were at this village of the blind Indians (probably north of Pearsall) where they "began to see mountains."[93]

It was here at this village at the time when they first viewed the

---

clear that both ranges of mountains were visible at the village of the blind Indians.

91. De Leon called the hills 20 leagues east of Laredo "mountains."

92. Davenport, *Quarterly*, XXVII: 295.

93. See footnote 90.

mountains that they saw what their reports called "the point of the ridge."[94] The "point of the ridge" must have been either the end of the chain of low hills mentioned above or some outlying spur with a "point" at the top. Pilot Knob, some 300 feet high, is an outlying spur across the Frio River south of this low chain of hills, about a half dozen miles to the south of Frio Town. The point of the low chain of hills is a half dozen miles north of Frio Town.

If the village of the blind Indians lay to the north of Pearsall, "the point of the ridge," whichever of these it may have been, lay across a river from this Indian village. This is in keeping with the Spanish manuscripts of the Cabeza de Vaca journey.

At this point it is possible to make a mathematical calculation that will give a correct conception of the height of these mountains (or hills) which Cabeza de Vaca saw from the village of the blind Indians, whether north of Pearsall or elsewhere. It was five leagues (thirteen miles) from the village to the river. The mountain was across the river. If the distance to the top of the mountain was sixteen miles (allowing three miles beyond the river), then the mountain would have been visible if it had been only 170 feet high. This result comes from a fairly simple calculation based on the earth's curvature.[95] By a

94. Hodge, *Cabeza de Vaca*, 93: [point of the ridge]; Bandelier, *Cabeza de Vaca*, 134-35; Davenport, *Quarterly*, XXVII: 295.

95. The simple formula from which this result is obtained is based on the mathematics of a circle. If a tangent and a secant are drawn from an outside point to a circle the square of the tangent is equal to the product of the secant and its segment that lies outside the circle. Let us represent the tangent by the letter "t", the secant by the letter "s", and its external segment by the letter "e." Then the formula becomes $t^2 = se$. Hence $e = t^2/s$. In the present case $t = 16$ miles, and s, which is only slightly more than the diameter of the earth, is nearly 8000 miles. If we let $s = 8000$ miles the error in the result is negligible. Hence, the formula $e = t^2/s$ becomes $e = 256/8000$. The result is that $e = .032$ miles or $e = 168.96$ feet. In round numbers let us call this 170 feet. This means that the mountain, or in this case the hill, must be 170 feet high.

Now, if we employ the same formula and calculate the height of a mountain that can be seen from a distance five leagues greater than the above examble, or from a total distance of about 28 miles, we find that the mountain must be, in round numbers, 520 feet high.

Calculating from the same formula, a mountain 1056 feet high can be seen 40 miles; one 2112 feet high can be seen 56½ miles. If (as is the case with the highest of the Cerralvo mountains in Mexico) a mountain is 4800 feet high it can be seen 73 miles.

These results, of course, will become greater if a river valley (and no additional similar calculation, had the mountain been 520 feet high it could have been seen ten leagues back from the river instead of five. In an area where the surface is not very irregular, it is highly probable that local terrain would have permitted such a mountain (520 feet high) to have been seen the entire ten leagues as derived from the mathematical formula above, or at least far before the Spaniards reached the village of the blind Indians.

The two calculations indicate that the mountains that Cabeza de Vaca saw across the river from the village of the blind Indians were only a chain of hills, somewhere from 170 to 520 feet high. It is quite plain that these hills between Hondo Creek and the Sabinal River (which are at their greatest elevation 300 feet high)[96] meet the requirements of the manuscripts of Cabeza de Vaca's trip across Texas. Also it is just as plain that the mountains of Mexico that are thousands of feet high run afoul of the Spanish accounts when we employ such earth curvature calculations as listed above.[97]

Now the Spaniards had become great healers even before they had reached the village of the blind Indians. For this reason they were highly regarded and the red men had learned to extract many gifts each time they passed these paleface miracle men from one village to the next. The more Indians in a village the more gifts, was the obvious formula for profit making.

The blind Indians passed the Spaniards to a village somewhere toward the mountains. The members of this second village tried to get the white medicine men to go toward the point of the ridge in the direction of the coast because there were many Indians that way.[98] In fact the Indians near the coast seem to have been moving inland toward the point of the rise. The white men were afraid to risk any contact with these coastal Indians; possibly they were the murderers

---

obstruction) lies between the observer and the mountain. Local terrain may interfere with these results and obscure or black out a mountain, but if the mountain is high, as are the Cerralvo mountains, these blackout areas are only local.

96. [U. S. Geological Survey map, Sabinal quadrangle (1970), shows the highest elevation as under 1020 and the lowest as about 850 feet above sea level. Adjoining quadrangles on the east, south, and southeast (D'Hanis, Irishman Hill, and Frio Town) show elevations of about 690 to 1110 feet, but these extremes are in widely separated parts of the surveys.]

97. See footnote 95.

98. Davenport, *Quarterly*, XXVII: 296; Bandelier, *Cabeza de Vaca*, 134-35; Hodge, *Cabeza de Vaca*, 93.

of the boatload of Spaniards on Padre Island.

For this reason Cabeza de Vaca and his companions travelled up some river *north*, away from the coast. Probably it was Seco Creek.[99] The three streams at hand are the Hondo River, Seco Creek and the Sabinal River. The fact that the channel of the stream was dry at the time would lend some weight to the assumption that Seco Creek was the stream they followed.[100] However, it is almost certain that if they were not in the Sabinal, they moved over into the valley of that river not far to the north of the town of Sabinal.[101]

Why the Sabinal? Because it is the first river east of the piñon belt. To have moved west from the head of the Sabinal past the iron rocks on the Powers ranch and on through the piñon country to a beautiful river was possible in a day's journey of seven leagues. Any other river except the Sabinal was vastly too far away. In passing up the Sabinal valley, the Spaniards skirted mountains all the way. This is in keeping with the accounts of the journey.[102]

But here we meet with one of the difficulties in making the manuscript fit the map. Cabeza de Vaca reported that this northward journey skirting mountains was more than fifty leagues.[103] Oviedo stated that it was about eighty leagues.[104] Map measurements show that from the country north of Pearsall up the rivers to the head of the Sabinal was about ninety miles, which is less than forty leagues. But there is fairly good evidence that the Spaniards continually over-estimated the distances which they walked. In every case where we

99. Hodge, *Cabeza de Vaca*, 94; Bandelier, *Cabeza de Vaca*, 136; Davenport, *Quarterly*, XXVII: 296-97. These references show not only that Cabeza de Vaca (at a distance of two leagues or five miles from the last Indian village) was going upstream but that the river which he ascended at that point was dry. Several Indian women were carrying water. "Seco" creek in English means "Dry" creek. This fact lends some weight to the assumption that Cabeza de Vaca was ascending Seco Creek.

100. See footnote 99.

101. It is in keeping with local topography to suppose that Cabeza de Vaca's route here passed up Seco Creek near the town of D'Hanis and also to assume that it continued up that creek some ten to twelve miles north of that point before it turned westward through a saddle in the hills and reached the Sabinal River in the John Rodswall survey. An early Comanche Indian trail that passed down the Sabinal turn-ed eastward away from the river in the Rodswall survey at just the right point to have passed through this saddle.

102. Davenport, *Quarterly*, XXVII: 297; Bandelier, *Cabeza de Vaca*, 135, 138; Hodge, *Cabeza de Vaca*, 95.

103. Bandelier, *Cabeza de Vaca*, 138; Hodge, *Cabeza de Vaca*, 95.

104. Davenport, *Quarterly*, XXXVII: 297.

can check the distances reported by the four surviving Spaniards, they have greatly over estimated the actual number of leagues travelled. If we scan the Oviedo account we find that the distances across the four south Texas rivers from Malhado Island westward make a total of from eleven to thirteen leagues.[105] Now we may be reasonably sure that the "rivers" were Oyster Creek, the Brazos River, the San Bernard and Caney Creek. Map measurements show that from the first to the last of these four streams was not eleven or thirteen leagues but only nine leagues.

Cabeza de Vaca says that he went "along the coast forty or fifty leagues." Close study of the manuscripts shows that he travelled along the coast from San Luis Peninsula to Cavallo Pass,[106] an actual distance of thirty leagues. In the spring of 1529 Dorantes travelled westward from Malhado Island (San Luis Peninsula) and met Figueroa at a point which we can almost certainly identify as Cedar Bayou.[107] Dorantes said the journey was sixty leagues, but the map shows that it was only forty-four leagues. Note that the exaggerations in these cases were in one case 22 percent and 44 percent, in another 33 percent and 66 percent, and in the last case 36 percent. In each instance the estimate was too large—and the average error was 40 percent. Now in each of these instances the false estimate was made along the coast and coastal islands where the route was almost a straight line. Probably it would have been much worse following a winding stream through the mountains. The fifty leagues or eighty leagues which the Spaniards said they walked are very probably overestimated.

105. The distance from Oyster Creek to the Brazos (surely the identity of the streams is correct) is 3 leagues; from the Brazos to the San Bernard was 3 or 4 leagues, and from there to Caney Creek was 5 or 6 leagues (See Davenport, *Quarterly*, XXVII: 235, 236). The total distance was 11 to 13 leagues.

106. Davenport, *Quarterly*, XXVII: 233. There can be little doubt that Cabeza de Vaca had come to Cavallo Pass (which the Spaniards called Espiritu Santo) for the third time where he made his final trip west to join Dorantes, Castillo and Estevanico. It was only 30 leagues from San Luis Peninsula but he said that he traveled along the coast 40 or 50 leagues—plainly an overestimation.

107. See Hodge, *Cabeza de Vaca*, 61. Dorantes and his party ". . . proceeded until they crossed the bay [Cavallo Pass]—and fifteen leagues thence they came to another [Cedar Bayou]. By the time they reached this, they had lost two companions in sixty leagues . . ." Thus, Cabeza de Vaca reproduces information given him by Dorantes. In footnote 20 it is shown beyond a reasonable doubt that the Dorantes party had crossed Cavallo Pass and had reached Cedar Bayou when they had finished traveling the above sixty leagues (44 leagues by present-day maps).

From some point near Pearsall to the ridge country above the head of the Sabinal River, as mentioned before, is about ninety miles by the nearest roads. For obvious reasons the present-day paved roads are nearly always shorter than the old trails that preceded them. It is not improbable in the present case that the route of the Spaniards zig-zagged to some extent in order to pass from one Indian village to the next. If all of these reasons combine to make the actual path of the four European travelers as much as 20 percent longer than present-day pavement, they must have walked more than forty leagues in this northbound leg of their journey. Hence, it is not at all surprising that Cabeza de Vaca estimated the distance at more than fifty leagues. The very fact that he suggested fifty leagues and that Oviedo (or the joint account) suggested eighty leagues is very good evidence that neither of them knew with any great degree of accuracy how far the four of them did actually walk.

Two writers on this subject disregard the statement of Oviedo that the Spaniards travelled north while they skirted these mountains. Dr. Robert T. Hill[108] and Dr. Carlos E. Castañeda[109] both trace the route of these four men along the south side of this San Antonio hill country all the way from San Marcos to Del Rio, which is 197 miles by paved highways. Certainly this solution answers, in fact over-reaches, the requirement of distance. But such a route runs into insurmountable difficulties. In referring to the direction of this part of the journey that parallels mountains, Oviedo specifically says "north."[110] Both Cabeza de Vaca and Oviedo say "inland,"[111] which of course is away from the coast, which is also north. Both accounts show that at least a part of this journey was upstream,[112] which again is north.

The Hill-Castañeda route takes the Spaniards west instead of north. It takes them across rivers all the way and not upstream anywhere. Equally as contradictory to the facts of the two Spanish ac-

108. Robert T. Hill, *The Dallas Morning News*, Nov. 19, 1933. The route is shown on a map with this article.

109. Castañeda, *Our Catholic Heritage*, I: 75-77.

110. Davenport, *Quarterly*, XXVII: 297.

111. Davenport, *Quarterly*, XXVII: 297; Hodge, *Cabeza de Vaca*, 95; Bandelier, *Cabeza de Vaca*, 138.

112. Davenport, *Quarterly*, XXVII: 297; Hodge, *Cabeza de Vaca*, 94; Bandelier, *Cabeza de Vaca*, 136.

counts, this route misses the entire piñon country.[113] Surely the route up the Sabinal River, as outlined in this paper, although a few leagues short of Cabeza de Vaca's estimate, more nearly meets all of the requirements than does the Hill-Castañeda route.

Here let us enumerate the details of a check-list of essential facts of this leg of Cabeza de Vaca's journey as preserved by the accounts of the Spaniards themselves:

(1) the distance was estimated at from fifty to eighty leagues;
(2) the route ran parallel to mountains;
(3) the direction was north;
(4) the route ran upstream;
(5) it was inland and away from the coast;
(6) the route turned west for seven leagues (or eighteen miles);
(7) it passed some kind of iron rocks;
(8) it entered the piñon belt from the east;
(9) it reached a beautiful river.

Now the Hill-Castañeda route complies with only the first, second, and seventh of these facts and misses all the other six. The route as outlined in this chapter specifically meets all these nine requirements except the first and last. And considering how greatly the Spaniards overestimated the number of leagues they travelled, the first item above, that of distance, very probably meets the requirement if the exact mileage could be known. The last item, the beauty of the river, of course, is a matter of opinion. Surely the many thousands of tourists who visit this hill country above Uvalde each year have rendered by their presence an affirmative testimonial to the beauty of the rivers.

But in addition to the facts of the above checklist, the route up the Sabinal was a known Indian trail.[114] In 1848 much of the land up

113. The piñon country as previously outlined lay west of the Frio at a distance of twenty to fifty miles north of Uvalde. It extended westward of this east boundary some sixty miles. It consisted of much scattered growth but nowhere did it cover any part of the country near the San Marcos-Del Rio road.

114. This old Indian trail is shown on the Texas General Land Office maps, one of Bandera County and another of Uvalde County, both dated 1862. The trail was called "Comanche Trail." Land records at Bandera show that surveyors collected the information about this "Comanche Trail" in 1848

the Sabinal River valley was surveyed. Indians had so plainly beaten a path up this stream that the surveyors showed some thirty miles of their trail in the old land plats. The early route in 1848 was called "the Comanche Trail" but the same natural conditions that made it a road of importance for the Comanches had very probably made it a road of importance for all Indians who preceded them. In fact one may project this old Indian trail into a route that once reached many hundreds of miles to the north and northwest. Granted that this trail reached westward to the headwaters of the Nueces River, as discussed above, it connected at that point with very early roads that led all the way to the high plains of Texas and across westward to the pueblo country of northern New Mexico. That these first roads of white men followed to a great extent the old trails of red men is easy to understand when one remembers that for the most part the wagon roads were made under the directions of Indian guides.

We can still trace the old wagon roads from the Nueces to New Mexico without great error. In fact Col. R. S. Mackenzie's wagons at one time or another followed nearly all of this route. These are the details: First, the old road extended from the head of the Nueces to old Fort McKavett at the head of the San Sabá River. Next, it reached northwest to Fort Concho inside present-day San Angelo.[115] From there it followed the North Concho River to a point two miles east of Sterling City. Here the road turned north past the present-day Spade Ranch, Colorado City, Snyder, and on to Mackenzie's supply camp[116] in Blanco Canyon, ten miles southeast of Crosbyton. From the old supply camp this early road passed northwest up Blanco Canyon into Floyd County, then across southern Hale County and on past modern Portales, New Mexico, to Fort Sumner, four miles down the Pecos River[117] from the present-day town of Fort Sumner. This was the ex-

115. These military roads even predated Mackenzie's activities in Texas. Also they predated Fort Concho. From the head of the Nueces to and beyond the forks of the Concho (at present-day San Angelo) these old roads are shown on Pressler's Travelers Map of 1867, which can be found in the Texas General Land Office.

116. See map of the State of Texas by Charles W. Pressler and A. B. Langermann, General Land Office (1879), Austin. See also *Southwestern Historical Quarterly*, XXXXXXIII (1959-60): 212, fn. 67.

117. [A map showing Mackenzie's route across the plains is in Cartographic Records Division, RG75, National Archives. A small map, together with an itinerary, is in Ernest Wallace, *Ranald S. Mackenzie on the Texas Frontier* (Lubbock: West Texas Museum Association, 1964), 65-73.] Also, in order to fix Mackenzie's route more exactly, see the following county maps at the Texas General Land Office: Bailey

treme western point reached by Mackenzie's wagons, but old wagon roads and cart trails[118] extended from there up the Pecos and across to the Santa Fe area in the Rio Grande valley which was in the heart of the pueblo country.

Most of Mackenzie's road to New Mexico was in use long before his day. The entire route was one of choice topography with water available at frequent intervals. There is little doubt that Indians had long passed that way.

Perhaps the reader is curious to know why we thus outline an early route to New Mexico. Simply because it makes understandable several statements given in the old Spanish accounts of Cabeza de Vaca's journey. Let us quote from the joint account of the Spaniards to illustrate this point. When the four Europeans had reached the point at which this route was to turn west into the piñon belt, they came upon a small Indian village "at the foot of the mountain." It consisted of "four ranches of another nation and tongue, who said they were there from more inland, and that they went by *that road* to their home. There they gave the Christians a rattle of brass, and certain shawls of cotton. They said that these came from the north, [and] across the land toward the Sea of the South [the Pacific Ocean]."[119] With the road to New Mexico in mind this quotation is not difficult to interpret. Plainly the cotton shawls had come from the pueblo country of New Mexico, the one and only place toward the northwest where cotton shawls were produced.[120] It was a correct description of this route to the pueblo country to say that it extended to "the north" and "across the land toward" the Pacific Ocean.

The statement of the Spaniards may also mean that the rattle of brass (which was really made of copper) came down this road from New Mexico. Cabeza de Vaca's own account makes possible a slightly

County (1884), Cochran County (1884), Lamb County (1884), and Hale County (1879).

118. Many photostats in the writer's possession of township plats taken from the plat books in the Federal Land Office at Sante Fe, New Mexico, will confirm this statement.

119. Davenport, *Quarterly*, XXVII: 297-87.

120. See Herbert Eugene Bolton, *Spanish Exploration in the Southwest, 1542-1706* (New York, 1916), 177. In Espejo's journey of 1582 he found cotton shawls at one point on the Rio Grande not a great way above present-day Presidio, Texas, but plainly stated that the shawls were produced elsewhere. However, when he came to the Pueblo country in northern New Mexico the immense amount of cotton cloth which he mentioned leaves no doubt that cotton goods were local products.

different interpretation. Cabeza de Vaca said, "Among the articles given us, Andres Dorantes received a hawkbell of copper. They told him they had received it from others, their neighbors; we asked them whence the others had obtained it, and they said it had been brought from the northern direction, where there was much copper . . ."[121] Possibly the hawkbell came from New Mexico or it may have come from Archer County or Knox County, Texas, or from some of the nearby areas where free copper could be found. Thus the source of the copper may be in doubt but the cotton shawls were not produced by the Plains Indians and must have come from New Mexico down the road described above—or down alternate routes that served the same traffic.

But this road across the Plains was in fact two roads. One of these led west from the High Plains into New Mexico; the other reached southward from the Plains to the hill country above Uvalde. Another road extended northward, possibly as far as Kansas, and still another of these long distance thoroughfares connected the High Plains with the deep woods of East Texas.[122] The fact is that all of these roads were routes from important portions of the Indian population into the buffalo country. Buffalo meat was the one source of food that was even greater than the Indians needed. The Indian population that covered the present-day United States and Canada has been estimated at about 1,000,000 souls[123] while the buffalo herds of the Plains country have been estimated at from 4,000,000 to 12,000,000 animals.[124] So there were from four to twelve of these big shaggy beasts to every Indian in North America. Since only a fraction of the above million Indians lived near enough to the Plains to avail themselves of buffalo meat, there must have been as many as twenty or thirty or forty of the big animals to every Indian who lived in reach of the buffalo country. By contrast, the beef supply in present United States is less than half a cow per person,[125] which means that the average Indian who once lived in or near the western plains had

121. Hodge, *Cabeza de Vaca*, 95.

122. See Frederick W. Hodge, ed., *Spanish Explorers in the Southern United States 1528-1543* (New York, 1907), 362.

123. Encyclopedia Britannica (14th ed.), XVI: 506.

124. Walter Prescott Webb, *The Great Plains* (Boston, New York, Chicago, London, 1931), 44.

125. J. W. Williams, *The Big Ranch Country* (Wichita Falls, Texas, 1954), 280-81.

perhaps fifty times as much buffalo meat at his disposal as the supply of beef available to the average American today.

This overshadowing fact of Indian economy supplied the compelling urge that must have worn deep the trail to the High Plains of Texas. Where Cabeza de Vaca and his party entered the piñon country high up in the hills above Uvalde, they were presented with buffalo robes.[126] Here the Spaniards were evidently travelling the long Indian trail that led from the Sabinal River valley across to the pueblos of New Mexico where cotton shawls were made. They were moving up the big road that led to the land of the buffalo. The fact is, Coronado in 1541 found Indians at the east edge of the plains who had seen Cabeza de Vaca down in South Texas six years earlier.[127]

How far did the Spaniards continue to travel northward toward the Texas plains? At what point along the trail did they bend their route toward the west coast? Soon we must turn attention to these important problems, but for the moment we must turn backward down the Sabinal and beyond to discuss certain details that we have as yet left undone.

When the Spaniards were walking up one of the streams near the Sabinal (or it may have been the Sabinal) the Indian women gave them some cornmeal and told them there was plenty of that meal farther up the river.[128] Here it seems probable that the Spaniards misunderstood the Indians whose language they did not know. Evidently, the conversation was in sign language. The Indians, while pointing up the river, were, it seems, also pointing up the trade route to New Mexico. It is not improbable that the cornmeal had come down the same road as had the cotton shawls. The buffalo robes had come down the part of the same road that had led from the Plains.

At this point it is possible to offer an explanation about some gourd rattles[129] which the Indians gave to the Spaniards. The gourds came down in the floods of the river that was compared to the Guadalquivir. These gourds were first given to the Spaniards near this river but more of the gourds were given to them farther up toward the piñon country.

Even now there is a small wild gourd that grows in the Sabinal

126. Hodge, *Cabeza de Vaca*, 96.
127. Hodge, *Spanish Explorers*, 332.
128. Hodge, *Cabeza de Vaca*, 94; Bandelier, *Cabeza de Vaca*, 136.
129. Hodge, *Cabeza de Vaca*, 90, 95; Bandelier, *Cabeza de Vaca*, 129, 138.

River valley at Utopia.[130] Some of the gourds have "handles"; some of them do not. Surely it was not the present-day well-known large gourd with a handle a foot to two feet long from which the Indians made the famous gourd rattle. These little gourds that now grow at Utopia could have floated down the Sabinal River, which flows into the Frio, and from the junction of the streams on down the Frio to where the Spaniards crossed. The route of Cabeza de Vaca as suggested now—across the Frio and later up the Sabinal—is thoroughly consistent with the present known facts about the little wild gourd that grows at Utopia. This little gourd of today adds its own bit of evidence toward the probable correctness of the theory that Cabeza de Vaca's route four and a quarter centuries ago travelled across the Frio and up the Sabinal on his way to the piñon country.

Thus far we have discussed the route of Cabeza de Vaca and his party from its beginning point on the Texas coast just east of the mouth of the Brazos River to the piñon country at a head branch of the Nueces River some fifty miles north of present-day Uvalde. Now let us attempt to find the route of that strange party of Spaniards on the next leg of their journey.

We are fortunate to be able to locate a point on the route of this party almost with certainty many miles ahead. Surely they reached the Rio Grande at or very near the present-day town of Presidio, Texas. The evidence comes from a source outside of the Cabeza de Vaca manuscripts.

Another Spaniard, Antonio de Espejo, travelled along this part of the Rio Grande forty-six years later than Cabeza de Vaca. Espejo travelled down the Conchos River (in Mexico) to its mouth opposite the point where Presidio is now located. Continued northward expansion of the settlements of Mexico by that time had added to geographical knowledge until there is no doubt about the location of this part of the Espejo route. There were numerous Indians living in the area who had been there in Cabeza de Vaca's day. These Indians told Espejo about three Christians and a negro who had travelled through their country a long time ago. Certainly this identification of the Cabeza de Vaca party is not to be doubted. In identifying these four Spaniards so perfectly, these Indians met by Espejo have remov-

130. Mrs. L. L. Tubbs, who teaches Texas history in Utopia High School, has told the writer of the small gourd that grows wild in the Sabinal River valley at and near Utopia. In general the gourd is cut out of gardens there as are weeds, but it is also used as a decoration at student Halloween parties.

ed all reasonable doubts that the Cabeza de Vaca party actually came to the area near Presidio.[131]

But this fact leaves us another problem to solve. If Presidio is a point on the Cabeza de Vaca trail and Bullhead Creek, fifty miles north of Uvalde, is another point, how can we trace the route between these points? Actually there are no data for a sure answer to this question. Any attempted solution must lie not in the realm of certainty but in the realm of probability. Here the joint account left us by the Cabeza de Vaca party becomes vague and confusing and Cabeza de Vaca's own account summarizes great lengths of the journey in a few words.

Cabeza de Vaca does make a statement which is some assistance to us here. He mentions a great river "coming from the north,"[132] which the Spaniards crossed. Now if one moves either southwest, west, or northwest from Bullhead Creek the next important river in his path is either the Rio Grande or the Pecos. The Rio Grande flows from the west or southwest in the country ahead of Bullhead Creek except in the sector immediately above Eagle Pass. A look at the map reveals how unlikely that the Eagle Pass sector of the Rio Grande can qualify as the river that flows "from the north." Surely the Spaniards who had just walked some fifty leagues due north did not turn at Bullhead Creek and walk almost as many leagues to the southwest in order to cross the Rio Grande!

Perhaps the most probable answer to the problem is to assume that Cabeza de Vaca and his party followed a natural route of travel. As mentioned earlier the Spaniards were following, at this point, an important Indian trail that led northward toward the Texas Plains. This route would have led them northward to the head of the San Sabá River near Fort McKavett and from there northwestward to the San Angelo country. From here the natural (and much travelled) route westward would have followed the middle Concho River. This

131. Bolton, *Spanish Exploration*, 172-73.

132. Bandelier, *Cabeza de Vaca*, 144; Hodge, *Cabeza de Vaca*, 98-99.

133. See Sen. Ex. Doc. No. 64, 31st Cong., 1st sess., 24-25. This reference includes a road log (furnished by Lt. Francis T. Bryan of the Topographical Engineers) of the newly made (in 1849) road from San Antonio to El Paso which passed through the San Angelo country as we know it now. Part of this road as shown by the log passed up the Concho River, through the Castle "Mountain" and on to the Pecos River.

was the one early-day route from the San Angelo country to the Pecos River.[133]

There was another route from San Angelo westward to the Pecos,[134] but the Spaniards had already crossed it and were some fifty miles north of it at Bullhead Creek. The middle Concho route was the only way left (so far as the writer knows) by which the Spaniards could reach the Pecos River without great inconvenience.[135] In 1848, before Texans were well informed about these routes, Captain Samuel Highsmith of the Texas Rangers led a detachment of men from the Pecos eastward between these two natural trails, but his route was evidently subject to great objections, as it was not used as a route of travel thereafter.[136]

Cabeza de Vaca's own accounts of his journey tell about certain Indians who were hunting jackrabbits with clubs. Those of the Indians who had bows and arrows hunted deer in the ridge.[137] Cabeza de Vaca crossed the river flowing from the north (probably the Pecos) in company with these Indians.[138] Immediately beyond the river they traversed thirty leagues of plains.[139]

These details about the terrain—a ridge on one side of the river and thirty leagues of plains on the other side—describe the Pecos River country in the area from McCamey north to Crane.[140] South of

134. *Ibid.*, 28-29, 51-52. This more southerly route passed near the present-day towns of Uvalde and Del Rio and reached the Pecos near the present town of Sheffield.

135. *Ibid.*, see map opposite p. 250. Only the two early roads referred to in footnotes 133 and 134 are shown on this old map. The writer has examined many such early maps of Texas. None of them show more than these two routes in the area referred to.

136. See the *Austin Democrat*, Jan. 28, 1849, for an account of the Highsmith journey. It was sixty miles from the Pecos to the head of Devils River and two days on horseback from there to the Concho.

137. Bandelier, *Cabeza de Vaca*, 142-43; Hodge, *Cabeza de Vaca*, 98.

138. Bandelier, *Cabeza de Vaca*, 144; Hodge, *Cabeza de Vaca*, 98-99.

139. Bandelier, *Cabeza de Vaca*, 144; Hodge, *Cabeza de Vaca*, 99. Both of the translations here tell of a multitude of several thousand Indians that had been following the Spaniards but apparently the number was greatly reduced before approaching the river that came from the north. In the plains country beyond the river there is no further mention of the multitude. Plainly the accounts which summarized great lengths of the journey in general terms became specific at the river. Here they described the rabbit hunt and told that the Spaniards crossed the river "in company with these" Indians.

140. Here the river is crossed first and the thirty leagues of plains afterwards, just as the Cabeza de Vaca narrative states. Those accounts of the Cabeza de Vaca journey

McCamey there is no plain west of the river; north of Crane there is no ridge east of the river.

The two facts limit the probable crossing on the Pecos to the McCamey area and about twenty miles north of it. The ridge that lies some ten miles east of the Pecos at this point is rather difficult to cross except at two points. McCamey is in the flat country just south of this ridge and of course offers no obstruction to traffic; old Castle Gap is a narrow break in the ridge some ten miles north of McCamey. This latter gap was a natural pass through the ridge—in fact the one most used by pioneer westbound travelers. Also it can be said that Castle Gap lay in the direct course of travel that had come up the middle Concho. Furthermore, perhaps the best-known crossing on the Pecos (Horsehead Crossing) lay just ahead.

All of the foregoing facts seem to indicate that the Pecos was the river that flowed "from the north" and that McCamey and Castle Gap were the two most likely breaks in the ridge through which the Cabeza de Vaca men could have approached the Pecos. But we run into more trouble at this point. The Pecos River in the McCamey-Crane sector was in early days usually at least ten feet deep and neither Castillo nor Estevanico could swim.

This blunt fact leaves certain possibilities. The information about the depth of the river is almost, if not all, confined to the late spring and early summer when the snows in the mountains at the head of the Pecos were melting at a very rapid rate. By the fall of the year when the Cabeza de Vaca party crossed the river (assuming that it was the Pecos) the snow was largely melted, and any snow not melted would probably by that time of the year begin to freeze again. The reduced flow of snow water may have made the river shallow enough to wade—but this conjecture is without a direct report to confirm it. Another possibility is that the Spaniards went upstream a few miles to Grand Falls where the river, though undoubtedly very swift, may have been shallow enough to wade. As a third possibility, Cabeza de Vaca may have assisted the nonswimming members of his party across the river as he had done on some of the streams of south Texas. Unfortunately, the accounts left us by the Spaniards leave us

---

which map his route by Monclova and northeastward across the Sabinas River must place the thirty leagues of plains first and the river afterward. This direct violation of the order of Cabeza de Vaca's own account seems to this writer a fatal defect in the Monclova route.

no details at all about crossing the "great river coming from the north."

But after all of these objections have been mentioned, the Spaniards did cross some river that flowed from the north, and the Pecos is the one such river on the natural route from Bullhead Creek north of Uvalde to Presidio on the Rio Grande. From the Pecos (if the assumption be correct) the early trails led by present Fort Stockton, Alpine, through Paisano Pass and down Alamito Creek to Presidio.[141] Again this route is suggested because it was the route first known to white men.

A good look at the map may cause one to ask why the route of Cabeza de Vaca made this great rainbow—from the Texas coast northward near San Angelo, then westward to Fort Stockton and finally southwest to Presidio. The existence of rugged mountains in the Big Bend of the Rio Grande on the Texas side of that river and a much more rugged mountain system on the Mexican side offer the best explanation. From 1849 to about 1880 an extensive trade was developed between San Antonio, Texas, and Chihuahua, Mexico. When it would have saved many miles to have made a road straight from one of these cities to the other, the great wagon trains of those early days made almost the same rainbow in their route of travel as mentioned above. Their road, which became known as the Chihuahua Trail, passed near the present-day towns of Uvalde, Del Rio, Sheffield, Fort Stockton, and Presidio; but without adding much to their mileage, they could have passed near the site of San Angelo on their way to the Pecos River, instead of choosing the Uvalde-Del Rio route—if we may so call it. The San Angelo route was the road chosen by a great part of the South Texas traffic to the California gold fields in 1849.[142] Certainly Cabeza de Vaca could have chosen the Uvalde-Del Rio route, but fear of the hostile Indians on the Texas coast apparently caused him to travel the more northerly route. But whether he had happened to travel by Del Rio or San Angelo, the great mountain chains on both sides of the Rio Grande would have

141. This route from Fort Stockton to Presidio became the great trade route known as the Chihuahua Trail. See Walter Prescott Webb, "Chihuahua Trail," *The Handbook of Texas*, 1 (Austin, 1952): 337-38.

142. *The Texas Democrat*, June 16, 1849. Also Kenneth F. Neighbours, "The Expedition of Major Robert S. Neighbors to El Paso in 1849," *Southwestern Historical Quarterly*, LVIII (July 1954): 36-59.

been sufficient reason for the northward bend in his route of travel. Not only did the Chihuahua Trail make approximately this same bend but no other important road or trail until this good day has cut across the rugged mountains on the Mexico side of the Big Bend. Of course modern engineers can make a road across those forbidding mountains—in fact such a way has been proposed—but until now nature set the pattern of travel in such a way that all previous generations avoided those rugged mountains. This same fact of topography probably dictated a northward bend in Cabeza de Vaca's route between the piñon country that lies north of Uvalde and the trans-Pecos town of Presidio.

This suggested San Angelo route offers an explanation for a mystery of long standing about the Cabeza de Vaca journey. Somewhere not long after leaving the piñon belt the four Spaniards, because of their reputation as healers, were followed by as many as 2000 to 4000 Indians—great multitudes like those that were fed beside the Sea of Galilee. If the location was a semi-desert like the country north of Monclova or in much of semi-arid West Texas, how would that many Indians have found food and water?

Both answers are easy if you accept the route of Cabeza de Vaca as outlined in this chapter. The four Spaniards were travelling up the great Indian trail toward the buffalo plains of Texas. It was late summer. The buffalo had migrated north to avoid the heat, and of course the buffalo hunt was over for the year. Great crowds of Indians were returning southward on down the trail. They were undoubtedly well fed and well supplied with buffalo meat. Also the pecan groves in the country from San Angelo southeastward are now, and probably were then, vastly greater than any to be found near the Texas coast. In 1920 the three counties, Tom Green, Menard, and Kimble, had 15 percent of all the pecan trees in Texas—more than 150,000 trees.[143] It is true that by late summer when the Spaniards had reached this area it was probably long after the pecan crop had fallen; but when Coronado came this way in 1541 he found pecans as late as June. This would seem to indicate that pecans in the area (whether on the ground or still on the trees) were so numerous that the Indian population had not been able to consume them all. Also some varieties of wild plums ripen in late summer and the small varieties of wild grapes are at their best at the end of August. But whether or not these and

143. *Abstract of the 1910 Census,* 740, 742, 748.

other types of vegetation could have furnished a sizable supplement for the meat that the Indian had brought along with him, buffalo meat alone could have answered the whole problem of hunger. As to water, the Llano, San Sabá and Concho are great spring-fed rivers and can supply the needs of tens of thousands of people at all seasons of the year. Not only does the route of Cabeza de Vaca as suggested here explain how as many as 4000 Indians might have found food and water, but it also explains why there might have been such a great number of Indians in the country in the first place. How could so many people have assembled in the sparsely populated, sparsely provisioned and sparsely watered areas of northeastern Mexico and extreme western Texas? Most studies have completely ignored the problem. It would seem most difficult to find a complete answer to this problem other than the suggestion that Cabeza de Vaca was following the great Indian trail to the buffalo country on the part of his route that reached from the head of the Nueces to present-day San Angelo.

The writer has not attempted to trace the route of the four early-day Spaniards beyond Presidio, but the many writers who have done so are in fairly close agreement on the rest of the trail. Nearly all of these writers trace the journey of Cabeza de Vaca up the Rio Grande to the El Paso area and westward across southern Arizona (or nearby northern Mexico) and finally to make contact with the Spanish settlements on the west coast of Mexico.

As a revelation of the interior of the North American continent, this journey was the inspiration of much future exploration. As a story of miraculous adventure it has few parallels in the annals of mankind, and caused the Expedition of Francisco Vasquez de Coronado.

II

CORONADO

FROM THE RIO GRANDE TO THE CONCHO

To fit the all-but-ancient story of Francisco Vásquez de Coronado to the modern map of Texas involves a type of detective work almost without a parallel. If one unravels the case, there is no criminal to break down and confess. If one touches basic truth toward a correct solution, there is no ancient jurist who can come back across four centuries and lend a knowing nod.

In such a search, not descriptions of terrain that may be subject to varied interpretations, but facts that cannot de denied or altered must weigh heavier than all else. The flora of the land—pecans, mulberries, the date of ripening of wild grapes, and the like—things that have been almost totally ignored in prior studies, are to be made the chief guidelines of this strange trail hunt.

Almost as completely as the flora, some of the prior studies of Coronado's route ignored the simple facts of arithmetic.

Thus far it has been assumed that almost everyone knows something of the story of Coronado, who was appointed to explore the country northward of Mexico. In 1540 he assembled an army and materials at Culiacán on the west coast of Mexico. Then with one eye looking for lost souls and the other scouting for gold, he moved toward his objective. Northward in southern Arizona and northeastward in central New Mexico his search for gold was disappointing. Likewise his search for lost souls was hardly what it might have been. He had to force the Indians whom he contacted to submit to his will—if not to his religion—at gun point. With force and bloodshed he dominated the Pueblo Indians of the Albuquerque-Santa Fe country.

In the late spring of 1541 he moved from a point some twenty miles north of present-day Albuquerque[1] across to the pueblo near

---

1. The place called Tiguex here was, according to Herbert Eugene Bolton, the pueblo of Alcanfor. "It was the southernmost of the Tiguex group, and stood on the

the present town of Pecos,[2] then traveled down the Pecos River for four days[3] according to one account. He stopped there for four days and built a bridge over which he crossed the Pecos. He then spent some eighteen days[4] in travel eastward across the high flat plains of New Mexico and Texas. At the east edge of the High Plains he dropped down into a deep canyon with steep walls like those of Colima in New Spain.[5]

Thence he traveled four days[6] and arrived at the encampments of Teyas Indians, whose permanent homes lay in the direction of Florida (probably in East Texas).[7] This place was called Cona. For three days[8] his party moved ahead among these Indians of Cona. Then for not less than four days[9] the Spaniards traveled forward again before Coronado finally decided that his party which had set out for Quivira had been led in the wrong direction by his Indian guide.[10]

At this point the expedition had reached a large ravine with a little bit of a river at the bottom of it.[11] From this ravine Coronado with

---

west bank of the river (Rio Grande) near the site of the present-day Bernalillo.'' See Herbert Eugene Bolton, *Coronado on the Turquoise Trail: Knight of the Pueblos and Plains* (New York, 1949), 193. Other accounts of the Coronado Expedition are in substantial agreement with the location given in the above quotation.

2. This was the large and powerful pueblo of Cicuye two miles south of the present Pecos, New Mexico. See W. C. Holden, ''Coronado's Route across the Staked Plains,'' West Texas Historical Association *Year Book*, XX, 3.

3. *Fourteenth Annual Report of the Bureau of American Ethnology* (Washington, 1896), Part I, 504. Hereafter this report will be referred to as *Bureau of Ethnology Report*. The translated account by the Spanish historian Castañeda who accompanied Coronado is given in pages 470-544 of the above report. Castañeda's arithmetic of time and distance so accurately fits the map of Texas and New Mexico as shown by this article that it is accepted here whenever there is a conflict with other accounts. Other accounts in this matter of the arithmetic of travel vary widely from Castañeda. Jaramillo, for instance, often uses such indefinite expressions as eight or ten days.

4. *Bureau of Ethnology Report*, 504, 505. Coronado traveled ten days from his bridge on the Pecos until he reached the Querecho Indians on the Plains. He then traveled two days with the Querechos. Next Coronado sent a scouting party to travel hurriedly two days to the east and return. The army halted for a day and then started eastward to meet the scouts, which undoubtedly means that the scouts returned westward for only one day until they met the army. Thus the army apparently traveled two days while the scouts were in transit. After the return of the scouts, Coronado spent four days in travel and reached a canyon at the east edge of the Plains. These details of time are ten days, two days, two days, and four days, or a total of eighteen days.

5. *Ibid.*, 505.

6. *Ibid.*, 507.

thirty of his best horsemen went north,[12] while he left his army at the encampment to hunt buffalo and build up its meat supply before turning back to New Mexico.

At this terminal point of the Coronado journey in Texas the trail detective's problem becomes acute—and blooms with excitement. If this large ravine can be located with certainty—and this paper will present strong evidence that it can—the entire puzzle of finding the Texas segment of the Coronado route is more than half solved. Historians have nailed down one end of this route at a point some twenty miles north of Albuquerque, New Mexico. If in this article the other end can be nailed down, the problem of fitting intermediate points into place becomes far simpler.

Here, though it may seem fantastic, this study will begin the search for the place to drive that nail in the map of Texas by the aid of simple arithmetic. Though there be skeptics, there is abundant evidence that at least one historian's statistics of the Texas leg of the Coronado journey are remarkably accurate.[13] For thirty-seven days these Spaniards moved eastward (or southeastward) until they reached the above mentioned large ravine. The distance was 250 leagues or

7. *Ibid.*, 527. Castañeda here tells that the various Indians return from the Plains to their homes for winter. He tells that each group of Indians goes back for the winter to the settlements that are nearest, "... some to the settlements at Cicuye, others toward Quivira, and others to the settlements which are situated in the direction of Florida. These people are called Querechos and Teyas." The order of the language seems to indicate that it was the Teyas who went in the direction of Florida. Certainly the Teyas were the Indians nearest East Texas if they were in the Upper Brazos Valley as explained in this paper.

8. *Ibid.*, 507.

9. *Ibid.*, 504-508, 580-584. Coronado's letter to the King dated on October 20, 1541, indicates that there were seventeen days of travel from the Rio Grande to the place where the Spaniards met the Querecho Indians on the Plains. Footnote 4 shows that there were eight days travel from there to the east edge of the plains which is a total of twenty-five days of travel from the Rio Grande to the east edge of the Plains. Discrepancies in accounting for time between the Rio Grande and Coronado's bridge amount to one day—which may mean that it required twenty-six days travel from the Rio Grande to the east edge of the Plains. Add to this four days of travel to Cona and three days through Cona and the total becomes either thirty-two or thirty-three days. Thus thirty-seven days were required on the outgoing journey—which means that either four or five days were left from Cona to the end of the journey in Texas.

10. *Ibid.*, 507.

11. *Ibid.*

12. *Ibid.*, 508. This study does not propose to delineate Coronado's northward march.

657½ miles.[14] Eyebrows may be raised at any attempt to rely on these figures—but it should be remembered that one man counted his steps[15] and that his count of leagues, wherever it can be checked, will stand the test of modern scientific measurements.

One example of his accuracy is his reported distance from Tiguex (twenty miles north of Albuquerque) to the Pecos pueblo. This Spaniard who counted his steps measured the distance between those two known points and found it to be twenty-five leagues.[16] If one struggles with that same problem on a modern map, he must reach the same conclusion.[17]

Applying the distance of 250 leagues to the present Texas-New Mexico map, one finds that a straight line of 250 leagues eastward from the Rio Grande near Albuquerque would reach Dallas or Waco. But admittedly the Coronado Expedition did not follow a straight line on the trip into Texas. The account of the army on its return to New Mexico reveals, however, that a straight course was followed as nearly as topography would permit. The return trip required only twenty-five days.[18] At the same rate as the eastward journey, therefore, these twenty-five days of travel amounted to only 444 miles.

Next measure 444 miles eastward from the Rio Grande near Albuquerque. From Albuquerque to Farwell, Texas, the distance is 234 miles by the nearest highway. Add a few miles and call it 244 miles from Tiguex on the Rio Grande (near Albuquerque) to the Texas line near the salt lake southeast of Portales, New Mexico. This lake is (as will be explained later) almost certainly a point on the route

13. Castañeda, who was a part of the Coronado Expedition, gives the distance traveled in leagues and the number of days of travel. Thus a daily rate of travel (17.77 miles per day) may be arrived at. The number of days required for the army to return to New Mexico (actually it was twenty-five days) multiplied by this rate gives a total of 444 miles from the Rio Grande to the end of Coronado's journey in Texas. As shown later in this presentation, Coronado reached the pecan country in Texas which at its nearest points was some 440 to 450 miles from the Rio Grande near Albuquerque.

14. *Bureau of Ethnology Report*, 507-508.

15. *Ibid.*, 508.

16. *Ibid.*, 503.

17. Frederick W. Hodge and Theodore J. Lewis (eds.), *Spanish Explorers in the Southern United States, 1528-1543* (New York, 1907), 329n.

18. *Bureau of Ethnology Report*, 507-508.

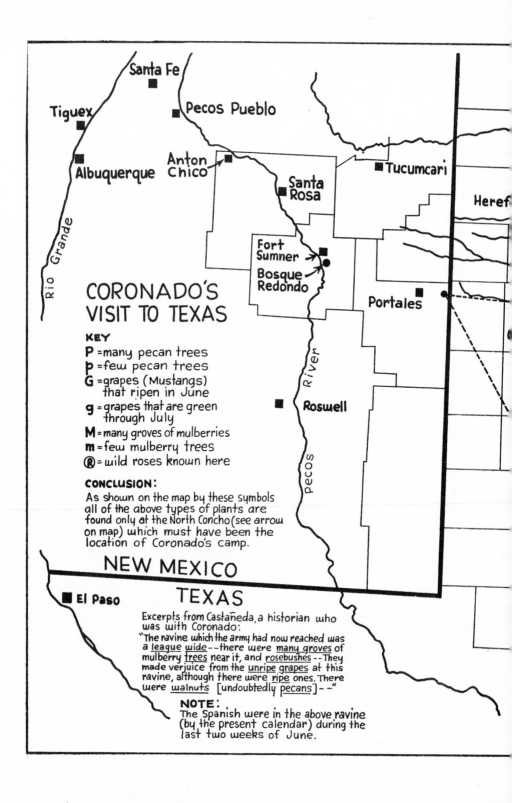

Santa Fe

Tiguex

Pecos Pueblo

Albuquerque

Anton Chico

Tucumcari

Santa Rosa

Heref

Rio Grande

Fort Sumner

Bosque Redondo

Portales

CORONADO'S VISIT TO TEXAS

KEY

P = many pecan trees
p = few pecan trees
G = grapes (Mustangs) that ripen in June
g = grapes that are green through July
M = many groves of mulberries
m = few mulberry trees
® = wild roses known here

CONCLUSION:

As shown on the map by these symbols all of the above types of plants are found only at the North Concho (see arrow on map) which must have been the location of Coronado's camp.

River

Roswell

Pecos

NEW MEXICO

El Paso

TEXAS

Excerpts from Castañeda, a historian who was with Coronado:

"The ravine which the army had now reached was a <u>league wide</u>--there were <u>many groves</u> of mulberry <u>trees</u> near it, and <u>rosebushes</u>--They made verjuice from the <u>unripe grapes</u> at this ravine, although there were <u>ripe</u> ones. There were <u>walnuts</u> [undoubtedly <u>pecans</u>]--"

NOTE:

The Spanish were in the above ravine (by the present calendar) during the last two weeks of June.

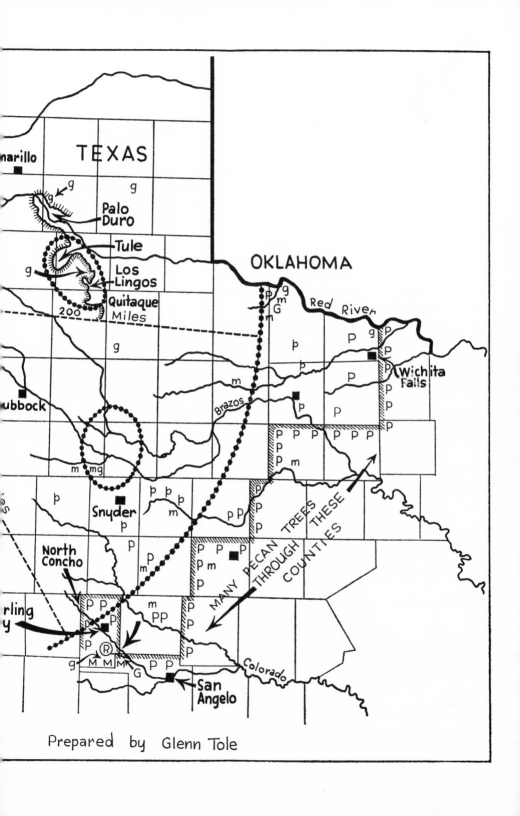

Prepared by Glenn Tole

by which Coronado's army returned to New Mexico.[19]

Using a point on the Texas-New Mexico line near this salt lake as a pivotal point, draw an arc across the Texas map 200 miles to the east. Two hundred and forty-four miles from the Rio Grande to the Texas line and these 200 miles that reach eastward into Texas make up the total of 444 miles mentioned before. This arc passed midway between Chillicothe and Quanah, twenty-five miles west of Seymour, just west of Haskell, Stamford, and Anson, fifteen miles east of Sweetwater, and a half dozen miles southeast of Sterling City.

One is inclined to smile at this use of simple arithmetic in locating the end of Coronado's journey. But actually there is powerful evidence that Coronado's last ravine was situated not far away from this arbitrary line across the map of Texas. What is the evidence? Simply, it is this: Coronado reached the pecan country[20]—and native pecans do not grow in Palo Duro Canyon, or Tule, or Quitaque, or in any of the canyons to the south or, with one minor exception, in any of the counties that border these canyons on the east.[21] Coronado had to journey beyond the High Plains to reach the pecan country.

It is true that the historian, Castañeda, said there were walnuts (according to some translations) in this last ravine, but since walnuts are not natives of West Texas—except a few of the little dime-sized walnuts that grow in the same area as the pecan—how else can one translate the Spanish word "nueces"[22] in this case except to call it a pecan? The Nueces River derived its name from this Spanish word for walnut. But from much personal experience, the writer can testify

---

19. *Ibid.*, 510. The great amount of salt deposits in this lake (visited by the writer on June 14, 1959) offers the best answer to the extremely salty lake referred to by the Spanish historian. South of this salt lake the Plains were almost impassable to early-day travel as shown by expert testimony later in this paper. There are no salt lakes north of this point. This combination of facts makes it all but impossible to escape the conclusion that the Coronado party passed by the Great Salt Lake southeast of Portales, New Mexico. The distribution of the salt lakes on the Texas Plains is quite clearly presented by W. C. Holden. See Holden, "Coronado's Route across the Staked Plains," *West Texas Historical Association Year Book*, XX, 16.

20. *Bureau of Ethnology Report*, 507. Actually the word in the translation of the Castañeda manuscript was walnut, but as shown later it undoubtedly meant pecan.

21. *Thirteenth Census of the United States Taken in the Year, 1910. Abstract of the Census with Supplement for Texas* (Washington, 1913), 728-750. This volume of the 1910 census lists the number of pecan trees in each Texas county. Hereafter the volume will be referred to as *Abstract of the 1910 Census*.

22. *Bureau of Ethnology Report*, 442. The Spanish text of the Castañeda history of the Coronado Expedition is given in the above report on pages 414-468.

that the Nueces is the river of pecans—not walnuts. One of the accounts of the De Soto Expedition told of a "walnut" found in the western part of the Southern States, but the words of explanation clearly described a pecan.[23] Even if the historian of the Coronado trek could have referred to the dime-sized walnut, it should be pointed out that it does not grow in the canyons mentioned—Palo Duro and the others—or in the area that borders them on the east. The dime-sized walnut—except for a few trees on the creeks of Scurry County and a small mott of three trees west of Quitaque—does not reach westward beyond the pecan country. Thus, whether the word means pecans or the small degenerate variety of the Western walnut, the conclusion must be the same—to have reached the area of native nut production, either walnuts or pecans, Coronado must necessarily have gone some distance eastward of the Cap Rock of the High Plains.

One is consequently faced with the task of outlining the western limit of the pecan country. If Coronado's army camped on some stream within this area of native pecan production, then exactly *where is* pecan country? The United States census of 1910 supplies the answer handsomely in this regard.[24] In that year the census listed the number of pecan trees in each Texas county. Although this record did not distinguish between native trees and those that were planted, it did, by the sharp dropping off of numbers, draw its own line across the map of Texas. In reconstruction one may draw the line at the western boundary of the counties in which, according to this census,

23. Edward Gaylord Bourne, *Narratives of the Career of Hernando de Soto in the Conquest of Florida: As told by a Knight of Elvas and in a Relation by Luys Hernandez de Biedma* (2 vols.; New York, 1904), I, 222. Here the contemporary Spanish account described the walnut found in the western part of the Southern States as having a "form like an acorn." Hereafter these narratives will be referred to as Bourne, *De Soto*.

24. *Abstract of the 1910 Census*, 728-750. The number of pecan trees given by this census in the Texas counties that have a possible relation to this study of the route of Coronado are as follows: Clay 19,549; Jack 2,731; Young 9,149; Throckmorton 9,895; Stephens 8,829; Shackelford 31,975; Taylor 2,126; Callahan 17,040; Runnels 4,893; Coleman 24,923; Concho 8,798; Tom Green 54,909; and Sterling 9,230. These constitute the last tier of Texas counties where one would find thousands of pecan trees if he were traveling westward toward New Mexico. Just above or west of these counties the number of pecan trees falls off suddenly. Here are the statistics: Wichita 154; Archer 0; Baylor 1; Knox 1; Haskell 4; Jones 813; Nolan 106; and Coke 730. Above this thin layer of counties, the figures on pecan trees follow: Wilbarger 2; Hardeman 0; Foard 0; Childress 0; Hall 1; Motley 0; Cottle 0; King 0; Dickens 4; Garza 0; Kent 2; Stonewall 0; Borden 0; Scurry 5; Fisher 34; Howard 2; Mitchell 0;

there were thousands of pecan trees. That line began on Red River at the northwest corner of Clay County. From there it extended fifty miles southward to the northeast corner of Young County, then west sixty miles to the northwest corner of Throckmorton County, and there it turned south thirty miles, then ten miles west, and then south another thirty miles to the northeast corner of Taylor County. At this point the line turned west for thirty miles and then with a small variation sixty miles south to the line of Tom Green, a county with more than 50,000 pecan trees. Then the line turned west thirty-five miles, north twenty, and west thirty to follow the boundaries of Tom Green and Sterling counties.

This broken line across the Texas map extends from a point twenty miles northeast of Wichita Falls to another point sixty miles northwest of San Angelo. Every county that touches this line on the east or south had, according to the 1910 census, thousands of pecan trees. No county west of the line had as many as one thousand trees and only four counties had more than one hundred. All of these counties join the line on the west. They were Wichita County with 154 trees, Jones County with 813 trees, Nolan with 106, and Coke

---

and Glasscock 1. The fact that only 51 trees were found in these eighteen counties indicates that the hand of man had begun to extend the pecan country by his own planting. There is a widely held opinion that no native pecan trees grow in the upper valleys of the Brazos, the Wichita, the Pease, or the principal branch of Red River. Persons well acquainted with the plant growth in their respective areas who hold this opinion are many. Interviews with Wayne Williams of Garza County, W. T. Cathey and T. M. McFadin of Kent, Walter S. Barclay of Dickens, Kenneth H. Grant of Cottle, and Charles E. (Dock) Wallace of Silverton confirm this statement. Probably the one tree in Hall County, the four in Dickens, the two in Kent, and two in Howard, and the one in Glasscock were planted. Personal investigation by the writer has revealed that a few native pecan trees have grown or are growing in a small part of these eighteen counties in addition to those given in the census report. A few trees grow on Wanderers Creek above and below Chillicothe; some pecans grow or have grown on both Beaver Creek and the Wichita River south of Vernon; pecans are found on Holliday Creek in Archer County; some pecans are found on the Brazos River below Seymour; a single large pecan grew eight miles east of Gail in Borden County; and a grove of pecans grew on Champion Creek to the east of Colorado City. These facts obtained from many personal interviews and hundreds of miles of travel change the complexion of the census report so little that references are omitted here.

West of these eighteen counties and on the High Plains (originally treeless), the census lists Lubbock County with 4 trees; Hale with 21; and Floyd with 60. Obviously these planted pecan trees have no bearing on this Coronado study. There were nineteen other counties on the Llano Estacado and extending west to the New Mexico line that listed no pecan trees in the 1910 census.

with 730. In Jones and Coke counties nearly all of the pecans are grown in the east part of the county. Hence, with only a little bending, the line already mentioned (from near Wichita Falls to sixty miles northwest of San Angelo) outlines the actual pecan country.

Above this line (that is, farther west of it) only a few pecan trees were found by the census takers of 1910. Thirty-four of these trees were in Fisher County—probably all of them along the Clear Fork of the Brazos. Other than Fisher County there are more than twenty counties between what has been outlined as pecan country and the Cap Rock of the Plains. In all this large area combined, the census reported only sixteen trees. Probably all of the sixteen were planted, but if one assumes that there were a like number in Coronado's day it would have been a rare coincidence had he found any of them while on his journey. Quite by contrast with this area in which pecan trees were so few, Sterling County in 1910 had 9,230 trees—all on the North Concho River.[25] This county with its principal river is the only place in West Texas where large pecan production lies within 200 miles of the selected point on the New Mexico line southeast of Portales. In other words, the arc which has been drawn across the map 200 miles within Texas touches nothing more than the thin fringe of pecan country until it crosses the North Concho near Sterling City.

Obviously, from the proven facts derived from the 1910 census, Coronado could not have reached the pecan country unless he did travel some 200 miles east of the New Mexico line. Thus the conclusion earlier deduced from simple arithmetic is abundantly supported by the facts about the locale of pecan production in West Texas. Not only does the outline of the pecan country cause one to look far to the east of the Cap Rock of the High Plains for Coronado's last ravine, it also brings into sharp focus the North Concho River in Sterling County as the probable point at which he and his army came to the end of their journey in Texas. Other facts to be presented shortly about the flora of the land will make it possible for this study to drive a nail in the map of Texas at that point.

Castañeda, the recorder, told what the Indians at this last ravine did with the green grapes. Also, Castañeda added, "But there are ripe ones."[26] This significant statement makes it plain that the grapes

25. A number of personal interviews with Elton Mims of Water Valley, Texas (who is especially well informed on the Concho country), has helped to clarify this study of the flora of Sterling and adjoining counties.

26. *Bureau of Ethnology Report*, 507.

were beginning to ripen, or probably that there were two varieties of grapes, one of which was beginning to ripen. Where in West Texas do the wild grapes begin to ripen by the time of Coronado's encampment in the last ravine?

This question makes it necessary to check the month of the year and also the days of the month when the Spaniards were in this ravine. According to Coronado's letter to the King, his army left the Rio Grande on April 23.[27] Castañeda gives the date as May 5.[28] Probably Coronado's letter is correct since it was written only a year after the event, whereas the Castañeda account was written some years later.[29] If one accepts the date of April 23, then Coronado's army was in the last ravine from about June 7 to June 21.[30] But it must be remembered that the Gregorian calendar, which was not yet adopted, moved up all dates ten days. Thus by the present calendar, the Spaniards were in the last ravine from about June 17 to July 1.

Where could grapes have begun to ripen this early in the summer? Certainly not anywhere in the Texas Panhandle or in any of the

27. *Ibid.*, 580.

28. *Ibid.*, 503.

29. *Ibid.*, 504-511. In order to show that the date, April 23, is consistent with so much other evidence, one should examine the following data from Castañeda's account. First (p. 507) the historian says that the expedition traveled thirty-seven days from the Rio Grande to the end of the journey (in Texas). Second (p. 504) that the party was delayed four days while building the bridge on the Pecos. Third (p. 505) that, out on the Plains, the army waited a day while Coronado's fast-moving scouts traveled eastward. Fourth (p. 506) that Coronado and his army rested in the first ravine (the ravine like those of Colima) for a time which because it is consistent with later evidence is here arbitrarily called three days. Fifth (p. 508) the army stayed in the last ravine (and hunted buffalo, and the like) for fourteen days (a fortnight). Sixth (p. 510) that it returned from this ravine to the Rio Grande in twenty-five days. The total of all of these amounts of time (37 + 4 + 1 + 3 + 14 + 25) is 84 days. Now if one adds these 84 days to the date of April 23, he reaches the result that Coronado's army returned to the Rio Grande on July 16. This is consistent with the seventh reference (p. 511) above in which Castañeda states that the army "reached Tiguex, about the middle of July . . . " Thus the cumulative references from Castañeda are consistent with the date of April 23 given by Coronado in his letter to the King instead of Castañeda's own date of May 5. Even here the greater body of Castañeda's statistics proves to be accurate, as did his time and distance data.

Obviously the arbitrary statement that Coronado and his army rested three days in the first ravine fits to a nicety, but the time could have been a day or two more than that without violating any of the remaining statistics.

30. As shown in the preceding footnote, the total time involved in Coronado's march from the Rio Grande to the last ravine was approximately forty-five days.

counties east of the Cap Rock and south of it. Examples pile convincingly high to show that the date of ripening of wild grapes in that area is late August and September.

United States army scouts for Colonel Ranald S. Mackenzie located an Indian village on McClellan Creek in Gray County by tracing the grape peelings that the Indians had dropped. The date was September 29.[31] The Abert Expedition of 1845 crossed the Texas Panhandle between August and October. The members found ripe grapes at six different places as they moved across and near that part of Texas.[32] G. W. Williams of Snyder told of an immense amount of ripe grapes which he once saw in late August on Dixon Creek not a great distance from the present-day city of Borger.[33] Mrs. J. H. Patton of Wichita Falls, who once taught school in Palo Duro Canyon, gave the information that wild grapes in that canyon ripened in late September.[34]

Probably the most exact information about wild grapes is that left by the Marcy Expedition of 1852. This party reported particularly

31. Robert G. Carter, *The Old Sergeant's Story* (New York, 1926), 82-83.

32. H. Bailey Carroll, *Gúadal P'a: The Journal of J. W. Abert* (Canyon, 1941), 45, 50-51, 57, 62, 88, 103.

33. From a telephone conversation with G. W. Williams. The information was obtained in March, 1952.

34. Ray Patton of Wichita Falls interviewed his mother, Mrs. J. H. Patton, for the writer.

35. *Senate Executive Documents*, 33rd Cong., 1st Sess. (Serial No. 666) Document No. 54, pp. 35, 36, 38, 39, 250.

36. It has not been possible to make for this study a scientific classification of the wild grapes in West Texas. Popularly the "Possum" grape (or little grape) and the Mustang grape (or big grape) are the two well-known varieties. There is much evidence that only the small grape (of whatever number of varieties it may be) grows in the Panhandle or in a large strip of country north of Snyder and east of the High Plains. Some of those who confirm this statement, each in his local area, are William Collins of Chillicothe, Mrs. W. R. Harris of Hedley, Walter S. Barclay of Spur, Mr. and Mrs. W. M. Walker of Kermit (formerly of Dickens County), and Wayne Williams of southeast Garza County. As an exception, Miss Lena McKee reports that a grapevine was found on Holliday Creek near Wichita Falls which appeared to be a mustang. All of these observers have had long acquaintance with their respective local areas.

The first six of the above named persons (all who expressed an opinion) testify that the wild grapes in their several areas do not ripen until after June—in fact all of the six except the first named placed the time of ripening from the last of July through September. Perhaps enough evidence has already been presented to show that at least many of the grapes of this Panhandle and near-Panhandle area do ripen in late August and September (see footnotes 31, 32, and 33).

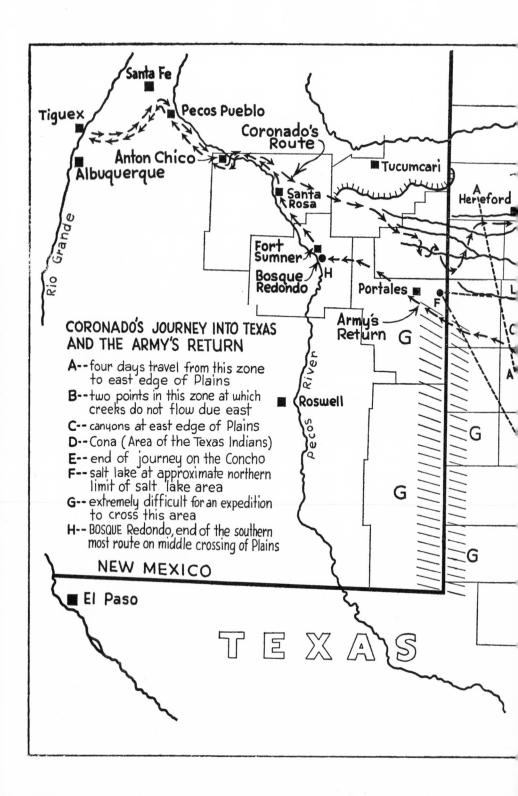

CORONADO'S JOURNEY INTO TEXAS AND THE ARMY'S RETURN

A-- four days travel from this zone to east edge of Plains

B-- two points in this zone at which creeks do not flow due east

C-- canyons at east edge of Plains

D-- Cona (Area of the Texas Indians)

E-- end of journey on the Concho

F-- salt lake at approximate northern limit of salt lake area

G-- extremely difficult for an expedition to cross this area

H-- BOSQUE Redondo, end of the southern most route on middle crossing of Plains

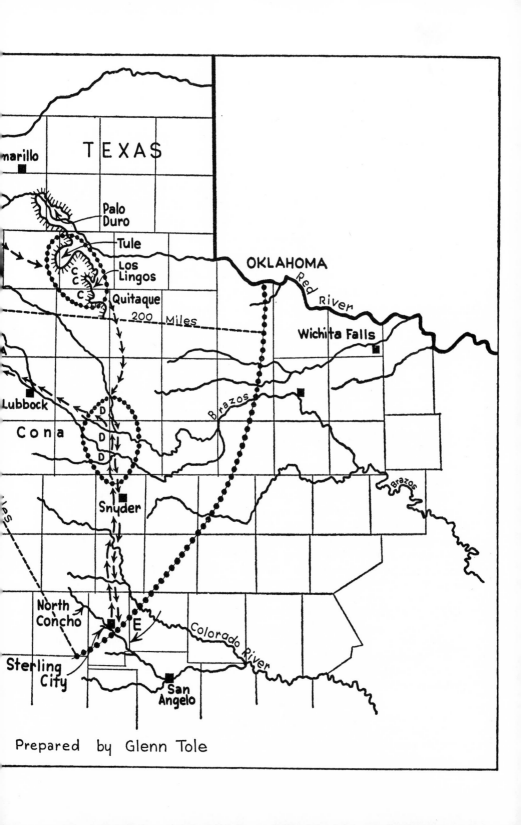

Prepared by Glenn Tole

on wild grapes between the Wichita Mountains and Red River. Actually the Marcy Expedition was almost directly across the river from the 200-mile arc which has been drawn across a portion of West Texas. Marcy and his party were in this area from July 9 to July 18. They reported that the grapes were immature at that time.[35] But even in this summer of 1959 (from June 26 to July 8), the writer has (personally or through the aid of others), inspected the wild grapes from the Panhandle and Palo Duro all the way south to Snyder—and has without exception found them all green. Surely Coronado's last ravine must been much farther south than any of the country in or near the Texas Panhandle for his army found ripe grapes at that place sometime in late June (by the Gregorian calendar).

On the other hand, present-day observers and observations reveal that wild grapes do ripen in the vicinity of the North Concho as early as late June. Thus it is that the date of ripening of the tell-tale grape lends its evidence to eliminate the whole Panhandle and North Plains area as the possible point at which Coronado's army came to

------

Obviously it remained to find by investigation whether or not some of the wild grapes of this part of the country do ripen in June. In order to carry on this investigation the writer arranged to visit personally wild grapevines wherever possible and to obtain, by long-distance telephone, reports from others who have made similar visits. The time of this investigation was June 26, 1959, to July 8, 1959. The report follows: On June 26 the wild grapes on the Wayne Williams Ranch were reported green by Wayne Williams; on June 30 the writer found the wild grapes green at the Roaring Springs in southwestern Motley County; on July 1 Ed Gardner found the wild grapes on the Perkins Reservation in northeastern Wichita County; on June 5 Mrs. W. R. Harris found the wild grapes green some four miles northeast of Hedley, Texas (in Donley County); also on June 5 Kenneth H. Grant was unable to find any grapes on a large old grapevine on the Pease River north of Paducah. On July 7, the writer found that the grapes were green in Palo Duro Canyon, and on July 8 he also found that the grapes were green on the banks of South Polecat Creek between Los Linguish (*Las Lenguas*) and Quitaque canyons. In each of these instances there were no ripe grapes. In addition it should be remembered that scientists with the Marcy Expedition in 1852 found the wild grapes green in mid-July near the Wichita Mountains northeastward of present-day Vernon, Texas (see footnote 35). Also an observer with the Coronado Expedition in 1541 found that the wild grapes were green near the middle of July on the Pecos in about the same latitude as Plainview (see *Bureau of Ethnology Report*, 510).

Thus in all available instances (with a near exception given at the end of this footnote), the wild grapes of the Panhandle and near-Panhandle country when observed before mid-July were green. Certainly this combined evidence makes it highly improbable that Coronado's last ravine—the one in which ripe grapes were found—was anywhere near the Texas Panhandle.

the end of its forward march in Texas.[36] Also that same tell-tale grape helps to confirm the suspicion that the North Concho River could have been the place where this army of Spaniards came to a halt.

The North Concho might well have been the last ravine, not only because it was the lone point within the pecan country near enough to the Rio Grande to satisfy the known arithmetic of Coronado's journey, but is was far enough south to have been the place where this party of Spaniards could have found ripe grapes.

A study of the distribution of wild mulberries in West Texas tends not only to confirm the North Concho as the site of Coronado's camp but at the same time to point out almost the exact spot, if not the exact one, which his party occupied.

Castañeda, the historian, called attention to the fact that ''many groves of mulberries''[37] were located near the camp of the Spaniards. At several places east of the Cap Rock of the High Plains, one currently finds evidence that at one time or another a few wild mulberry trees could be found. This was true southeast of Post,[38] at a point on

---

On the other hand, J. R. Mims of Water Valley, Texas (a resident of the Concho country for seventy years), tells positively of having seen wild grapes in that area that were ripe by the last week in June. His observation is corroborated by testimony from Mrs. Ella Bugg Ligon of Puyallup, Washington, and her sister, Mrs. Laura Bugg Green, both of whom lived on the North Concho nine miles southeast of Sterling City more than sixty years ago. They well remembered having gathered great quantities of wild grapes from the banks of the Concho—both the small grape and the larger mustang. The mustang grape ripened quite a bit earlier than the smaller grape, although the women did not remember the exact time during the summer when this large grape became ripe. Surely it was the same grape that according to Mims ripened during the last week in June. It must have been the same mustang grape as that discussed on pages 62 and 63 of *The Botany of Western Texas* by John M. Coulter (Washington, 1891-1894). Coulter says that this is a mustang grape that ripens in June. It grows, according to Coulter, from the Colorado to the Rio Grande and west to the Pecos. It must have been the grape which was ripe at the last ravine while Coronado's army was engaged in its two weeks' buffalo hunt. This hunt, it will be remembered, took place—by the Gregorian calendar—during the last two weeks of June. After a diligent search, as shown in the details of this footnote, the writer has been unable to find any wild grape north of the Concho that ripens so early. A case that is almost an exception is that of two wild grapevines in the yard of Doyle Adams at Odell, Texas. These were transported from the banks of near-by Wanderers Creek by Homer Johnson and his father some twenty-five years ago. The writer inspected the grapevines on July 15, 1959. Some of the grapes were ripe. Mrs. Adams, who believes that these are mustang grapes, reports that a few of the grapes had begun to change color by the end of June.

37. *Bureau of Ethnology Report*, 507.

Mulberry Creek in Hall County,[39] at a point a few miles northwest of Truscott in Foard County,[40] on a tributary or two of the Clear Fork of the Brazos,[41] and in somewhat greater number on Wanderers Creek in Wilbarger County.[42] Also far to the south the same is true in Nolan and Coke counties, but nowhere in all this area of some twenty or thirty counties can one find what might be described as "many groves of mulberries."

For some reason, the soil, the climate, or possibly some other thing or combination of circumstances has not permitted the growth of mulberries over any extensive area in all this country east of the Cap Rock. There is an exception to this rule, however, in the eastern part of Sterling County. There, on Mulberry Creek, slightly more than ten miles southeast of Sterling City, was once an extended area covered with groves of mulberry trees. J. R. Mims of Water Valley, Texas, who has lived in and near the Concho River Valley for seventy years and whose duties took him over a wide area covering many counties, says that in earlier days Mulberry Creek contained " . . . the largest concentration . . ." of mulberry trees which he encountered in West Texas. To confirm Mims's statement, the *Texas Almanac of 1925* still at that late day listed mulberry wood as a timber asset of Sterling County.[43]

According to Mims, so many of the trees were cut down for fence posts that the extensive use for this purpose did much to deplete the large groves of mulberries. But before the axe had done its work, the valley of Mulberry Creek had a greater growth of this kind of timber than could be found elsewhere for many miles in any direction.[44] Like

38. Interview with Wayne Williams, who owns a ranch of considerable size that lies in southeast Garza County and adjoining areas. Probably several dozen wild mulberry trees once grew on the Williams Ranch. None of them is left at present.

39. *Senate Executive Documents,* 33rd Cong., 1st Sess. (Serial No. 666), Document No. 54, p. 65. Randolph B. Marcy camped on Mulberry Creek on July 6, 1852, and gave the stream its name. Marcy explained why he so named the stream. It had "a few mulberry trees, which being the first we have seen for several weeks, has suggested the name."

40. Interview with C. H. Laquay of Truscott, Texas, 1959.

41. Interviews in 1952 with William B. Halbert of Throckmorton, Texas, and A. E. Hilburn of Roby, Texas.

42. Interview with Paul Robinson, Route 3, Vernon, Texas.

43. *Texas Almanac, 1925* (Dallas, 1925), 347.

44. Mrs. Laura Bugg Green of Puyallup, Washington, and her sister, Mrs. Ella Bugg Ligon, members of a pioneer family that lived on the Concho nine miles southeast of Sterling City, confirm Mims's testimony about the large growth of

a "pointer" dog, it stood within four miles of the North Concho in the right position to call attention to the probable camp site of Coronado's army. Certainly it could have been said of a point ten miles down the North Concho from Sterling City that ". . . there were many groves of mulberry trees near it." These are the same words that Coronado's contemporary applied to Coronado's camp site in the last ravine—only the recorder's statement was made 400 years ago.

But in addition to the great groves of mulberries and all the other flora, the Spaniards found some type of wild rose growing at this last ravine. Mrs. Ella Bugg Ligon and her sister, Mrs. Laura Bugg Green (see footnote 36), suggest that the Spaniards may have seen and made reference to the algerita bush which grows on the Concho. This plant has a small yellow bloom and produces a red berry. But the two long-time residents also mention a wild rose which they as girls saw quite often in the hills just south of the Concho. This rose, pink in color, grew on a shrub and was about two inches in diameter. Apparently goat ranching has exterminated this colorful plant of earlier days for it seems to have vanished from the hills near the Concho.

But even the wild rose does not conclude all of the details wherein the North Concho resembles the last ravine in which Coronado's army camped.

Herewith is Castañeda's contemporary description of the place where the Spaniards camped at the end of their journey in Texas: "The ravine which the army had now reached was a league wide from one side to the other, with a little bit of a river at the bottom . . ."[45] The valley of the North Concho is bounded on each side by a broken chain of hills. The width of the valley between these hills is about a league or slightly more. It is 1.2 leagues wide some four miles southeast of Sterling City. The width is about the same down the valley at Broome and it is almost exactly a league wide two miles below.[46] Plainly the generalization that "the ravine . . . was a league

------

mulberries. Walter Gressett of Forsan, Texas (while driving sheep), camped on Mulberry Creek in 1916. He reports that numerous motts of mulberries, one to two acres each, grew up and down Mulberry Creek and its valley at that time.

45. *Bureau of Ethnology Report,* 507.

46. The first two of these measurements were made on the aerial maps of the valley in the Sterling County Courthouse. These measurements were checked in the field against the contour map of the area printed by the army map service corps of engineers. The third measurement was made in the field, also on the same map. Ob-

wide . . ." can very well describe the valley of the North Concho.

Another physical fact about Coronado's last ravine may be arrived at by inference. One method of assisting the hunters in finding the way back to camp at night was by building great fires in the valley.[47] This method would have been useless in such a canyon as Palo Duro, for almost anywhere about this deep gorge one cannot even see the canyon a few hundred yards away from its rim—much less could he see a fire hundreds of feet deep inside the canyon. On the other hand in such a valley as the North Concho, with its more gradual, sloping sides and with its many breaks between the hills that form its boundaries, a fire by the river's edge could have assisted many of the hunters in finding the camp at night.

To recapitulate briefly, the writer realizes that it is not impossible that pecans could once have grown all the way west to the Cap Rock of the Plains and that some stroke of nature could have exterminated them. Also nature could have wiped out some kind of wild grape near or east of the Plains—a grape which ripened in June; and further, mulberries, which presently grow sparingly or not at all, could once have grown in great groves in the counties bordering the High Plains. But that nature should have destroyed all of these at the edge of the Plains—or to the east of them—and have preserved all at the Concho seems rather remote. Certainly the physical makeup of canyons at the edge of the Plains and elsewhere probably has not changed much in 400 years.

Thus with so many types of evidence mounting toward the probable conclusion that Coronado ended his journey in Texas southeast

---

viously such measurements are only an approximation, since one must arbitrarily select the points that represent the sides of the valley.

The physical fact that Coronado's last ravine was a league wide positively eliminates Wanderers Creek as a possible answer for that point on Coronado's route. From the standpoint of vegetation, Wanderers Creek makes a strong bid for one's consideration as the above-mentioned last ravine. Its growth includes pecans, a number of mulberry trees, a little grape that ripens in August and September, and it also includes the larger (probably mustang) grape that ripens in early July—possibly some seasons it may ripen in late June. The thing that eliminates this creek is the fact that it flows through a flat country. It has no sides as does a canyon. It cannot be described as "a league wide" or of any other definite width, but of the several dozen creeks and canyons (except for this physical fact) within the possible range of Coronado's journey, it comes nearer to the right answer than any of the others except the North Concho.

47. *Bureau of Ethnology Report,* 508.

of Sterling City, the writer proposes to drive a nail there in the map of Texas and to turn back to discuss intermediate points along the proposed trail.

The beginning of this trail heading toward Texas was a point on the Rio Grande some twenty miles north of Albuquerque. For more than 150 miles eastward of that beginning point, the route of the Coronado party as outlined by W. C. Holden in 1944 seems most accurate to the present writer.[48] From the beginning point, Holden traces the expedition through Glorieta Pass (the only mountain pass available) to the Pecos Pueblo two miles south of the present-day Pecos, New Mexico. From here Holden describes the route as following the west side of the valley of the Pecos River to Anton Chico, New Mexico, where the Spaniards built a bridge and crossed the river. Continuing, the Holden route extends in an east-southeast direction paralleling the river on its east side, most of the way to Santa Rosa, New Mexico. A little short of Santa Rosa, the Pecos turns more to the south but the Holden route continues its course and reaches the High Plains not far east of Santa Rosa. Once on the High Plains this route soon reaches Frio Draw to the south of Tucumcari, New Mexico.

The writer wishes to borrow this part of the route from Professor Holden with due acknowledgments and thanks. Beyond the Frio, however, this study expects to delineate the Coronado route over a different course.

In carrying forward from the Frio, it is highly important that one should know with some certainty which of the limited number of possible routes Coronado followed across the High Plains. These possible crossings of the Plains are few. The location of permanent watering places is the all-important first consideration in determining those few routes. This was true not only in Coronado's day but continued to be true for some 350 years afterwards. The locations of those permanent watering places were well known to many of the Indians, and it was perfectly logical that expeditions from Coronado in 1541 to Mackenzie in 1871-1874 should have been guided either by Indians or other native guides. Probably there were expert guides during all of those three and a half centuries, but the guides whose advice can currently inform most are those who lived during the last century. They began to call places by names that are still in use; hence they speak in terms of present-day geography.

48. Holden, "Coronado's Route across the Staked Plains," West Texas Historical Association *Year Book*, XX.

Probably no guide of last century was better versed in plains-craft than Manuel, the Comanche, who guided Josiah Gregg along the Canadian River in 1840. With high praise Gregg said that Manuel knew the plains like a landlord knew his premises.[49] Randolph B. Marcy, whom Manuel guided across the South Plains in 1849, recommended the Indian as "the best guide that can be found in New Mexico."[50]

Manuel informed Marcy that there were only three places where the party might begin at the Pecos River and travel eastward across the High Plains.[51] The Canadian River route was undoubtedly one of the three, but since Marcy had just traveled that way, the Indian did not call it by name since the reference was obviously superfluous. The Comanche guide, however, did mention the crossing of the Plains east of El Paso—in fact he guided Marcy that way near the present-day towns of Pecos, Odessa, and Big Spring.

The third crossing of the Plains was the one which Manuel most strongly recommended. This began on the Pecos at the Bosque Redondo[52] four miles downstream from present-day Fort Sumner and extended eastward near Portales and on southeast-ward to the east edge of the Plains.

When Marcy, in the expedition of 1849, reached the Pecos, near the present Texas-New Mexico line, he wished to go directly east across the Plains. His Comanche guide, Manuel, somewhat dramatically told about the almost impossible barrier that lay ahead. "Not even an Indian ever undertakes to cross that way," he explained. The guide told Marcy that he must either go sixty miles down the Pecos before he crossed the Plains, or else he must go eight days upstream to the Bosque Redondo to cross.[53] The Indian was plainly warning Marcy to stay out of the strip of country—some 175 miles in its north-south dimension—that lies between Monahans, Texas and Portales, New Mexico. The joint Texas-United States commission of 1859-1860 tried and failed twice to complete the survey of the Texas line between these points.[54] The gap left in the Texas line was not

49. Josiah Gregg, *Commerce of the Prairies* (Dallas, 1933), 312.
50. *Senate Executive Documents,* 31st Cong. 1st Sess. (Serial No. 562), Documents No. 64, p. 209.
51. *Ibid.,* 196.
52. *Ibid.*
53. *Ibid.,* 204.
54. *Senate Executive Documents,* 47th Cong. 1st Sess. (Serial No. 1987), Document No. 70, pp. 296-305.

surveyed until a half century later. The Comanche guide, in warning Marcy to stay out of that vast area of many sand dunes and little water, was surely passing on to him the accumulated experiences of many generations of Indians.

But what Manuel failed to tell Marcy about this middle crossing of the Plains was that it was wider than just a single trail. The Fort Sumner-Portales route which Manuel so strongly recommended became an early wagon road. The old road branched near the Texas line, the south fork passing through present-day Lubbock while the north branch (probably the older one) passed at least twenty miles north of there. This road near Portales was at the south edge of this middle crossing of the Plains. Other roads and branches of roads lay to the north, proving that this part of the Plains—sometimes called the shallow water belt—had watering places enough to permit passage over quite a spread of country. This belt in which there were early roads (and Mexican cart trails) was about sixty miles wide at the state line from Portales northward.[55] It was about a hundred miles wide from Lubbock northward. This entire belt was what should be properly considered the middle crossing of the Plains. Most likely any well-informed High-Plains Indian could have zigzagged about almost at will among the watering places which dotted this part of the High Plains.

Which of these three crossings of the Plains did Coronado follow? The southern crossing—by Pecos, Odessa, and Big Spring—may be eliminated in short order. This route began more than 350 miles down the Pecos River from the Pecos Pueblo, while the arithmetic of the Coronado Expedition—four days travel below the Pecos Pueblo downstream to the bridge and about thirty leagues beyond that point—plainly shows that the southernmost point at which the Spaniards traveled the Pecos was less than 150 miles below the old pueblo.

The Canadian River route may be eliminated almost as quickly as the southern route. The Canadian River when chosen as a crossing

---

55. Since a full listing and explaining of the maps and land plats necessary to show the various roads of this area would be of such great volume, most of the details are omitted here. Much of the detail of roads and road fragments may be obtained from the following General Land Office maps: Deaf Smith County (1881), Bailey County (1884), Cochran County (1884), Lamb County (1884), Lamb County (1914), Hockley County (1884), Hale County (1879), Briscoe County (1879).

of the Plains was followed because of the many streams that served as watering places. To pass from one of these streams to another from day to day, one constantly encounters broken country. Only once did Marcy in his 1849 journey along the Canadian River travel out onto the High Plains as much as a whole day. The Coronado party on the other hand spent day after day upon the high flat prairies. Wherever the Spaniards came to a small creek the descriptions plainly showed that the land all about continued as monotonously level prairies.[56] To have continued upon such flat terrain south of the Canadian would have meant to miss all of the watering places. Obviously the Canadian River route does not at all fit the description of Coronado's journey.

If one thus discards both the southern crossing of the Plains and the Canadian River route, he is forced, as was Holden, to accept the middle crossing. At one point on the Plains, which proved to be just four days of travel from the east edge or outcropping of the Cap Rock, Coronado came to one of those small creeks that traverse the flat surface of the Plains. He had sent a scouting party east toward the sunrise, hoping to find a place called Haxia which the Indians had described. The scouts were due to be back about the time Coronado came to the small creek. He also was traveling east in order to follow the course of his scouting party. When he reached the creek, he sent six Spaniards upstream and another six downstream to see whether either party could discover (at the creek) signs of the returning scouts.[57]

Careful study here reveals that the creek must have run in a north-south direction across his course, otherwise it would have been foolish to spread out searchers except that upstream and downstream meant to his right and left—which would have meant north and south.

Thus finding some segment of a creek that runs in a north-south direction gives a clue to Coronado's location at the time he reached this small stream. Remembering that he was at this time four days travel distant from the east side of the High Plains, one may draw a north-south line across the map in Lamb and adjoining counties some fifty miles from the east edge of the Plains. Then project another such line about twenty-five miles farther west. Obviously Coronado was somewhere between these two lines, for four days travel was between

56. *Bureau of Ethnology Report*, 505.
57. *Ibid.*, 505.

fifty and seventy-five miles. All the creeks between these lines flow from west to east with two exceptions. In central Lamb County, almost due west of Plainview, for about ten miles Sod House Draw flows from north to south. Also to the south and southeast of Hereford, Frio Draw for fully as many miles flows toward the northeast. Here the spotlight points out the two possible locations of Coronado's camp—for only Sod House Draw in central Lamb County and Frio Draw near Hereford can qualify.

There is another fact which tends to confirm this two-headed conclusion. Neither of the searching parties found the returning scouts, but the scouts were discovered by some of the Indians from the army who were out looking for fruit.[58] Certainly the word fruit must have meant wild plums for no other kind of native wild fruit grows on the High Plains, and even these do not grow except at certain favored spots. There are many wild plums along the great sand belt that extends in an east-west direction across central Lamb County, and none is to be found for a good many miles on either side of this belt. The fact that this long narrow streak of sand intersects the same ten miles in which Sod House Draw flows toward the south adds considerable strength to the conclusion that Coronado's camp was in that part of Lamb County.[59]

But the fact is that wild plums once grew at least in the area of Frio Draw.[60] In addition the further fact that Coronado in his last four days of travel had moved northward[61] then eastward makes it much easier to find the route to the Hereford country consistent with the flat terrain over which the Spaniards had just passed than to try to find a similar approach to central Lamb County. Perhaps the Hereford area should have the more favored conclusion.

The next movement of Coronado's army was a continuation of his eastward journey—this time to the edge of the High Plains. Apparently Coronado was still trying to find Haxia, which according to

58. *Ibid.*

59. Local study presents some difficulties with this conclusion. Hardly could Coronado have reached the intersection of this sand belt with Sod House Draw except that he had slipped through the sand belt to the west of central Lamb County. This could have been possible in the somewhat less sandy stretches near the Sudan-Muleshoe road or seven miles north of Sudan.

60. Thomas Falconer, *Letters and Notes on the Texan Santa Fe Expedition, 1841-1842* (New York, 1930), 112.

61. *Bureau of Ethnology Report,* 504.

the Indians lay in the direction of the sunrise. For four days his party pushed forward and at last reached not Haxia but a canyon at the edge of the plains.[62] The canyon must have been deep with precipitous walls, for the advance party had to send guides back to Coronado's principal army to help it find the way. At this camp site, after a day or more of rest, the Spaniards suffered great damage from a severe hailstorm. Tents were knocked down, dishes were broken, and nearly all of the horses broke loose from their hitching places and would have run away except that the walls of the canyon prevented.[63] It was with great difficulty that some of the horses were brought down from the sides of the canyon. Thus the evidence mounts toward the conclusion that this *first ravine* visited by the Spaniards was a deep cut at the east edge of the Plains. Probably it was neither Yellowhouse Canyon nor Blanco Canyon.[64] Horses in wild flight could have escaped from either. Canyons immediately to the north of these—Quitaque, Los Linguish (Las Lenguas), and Tule—have high steep walls that most likely would have stopped the horses in their efforts to escape.[65]

Up to this point the Spaniards had traveled some twenty-six[66] days (possibly it was only twenty-five days) in their journey from the Rio Grande. Thus of the thirty-seven days consumed in the whole outgoing journey, only eleven days (or possibly twelve) remained. How far could the Spaniards have traveled in eleven days? The answer is 195 miles—that is at the same rate as that established for the entire thirty-seven days. Then the question remains: "How far is it from Quitaque (or Las Lenguas) Canyon to a point ten miles down the Concho from Sterling City?" By straight-line map-measurement, the distance is just short of 180 miles. But certainly it is highly im-

62. *Ibid.*, 505.

63. *Ibid.*, 506.

64. Edward McMillan to J. W. Williams, March 10, 1959. It was McMillan's opinion, after an investigation, that horses could have escaped from Blanco Canyon. The writer has crossed both Blanco and Yellowhouse canyons in a number of places and found no place in either canyon from which a frightened horse might not have escaped.

65. In company with Kenneth F. Neighbours of Midwestern University, the writer visited Quitaque Canyon on March 21, 1959. Interviews with Raymond Upton of South Plains and Charles E. (Dock) Wallace of Silverton, Texas, on the same date made it quite clear that all three of these canyons were deep, with quite abrupt walls—and that each has an abundant supply of permanent water.

66. See footnote 9.

probable that any such expedition should have followed an exact straight line for 180 miles.

Colonel Ranald S. Mackenzie established a wagon road which, with only the slightest variation, connected these same two points.[67] Obviously Coronado's army did not follow Mackenzie's wagon road 330 years before the road was opened. But just as Mackenzie followed the advice of guides who were thoroughly familiar with the well-established routes of Red Men, so Coronado in his day was confronted with nearly the same problem in transportation. Both men faced the same topography and most likely followed about the same route.

Mackenzie in one of his Indian campaigns in the early 1870's made an old wagon road up the North Concho to within two miles of present-day Sterling City, then north to a point just west of Colorado City, then north across the Colorado River a few miles upstream and on past the site of modern Snyder. From the Snyder area he entered present Kent County, three and a half miles east of its southwest corner, and then moved northward and finally a little northwestward to his supply camp in Blanco Canyon, ten miles southeast of Crosbyton. More of this old Mackenzie Trail extended still farther up Blanco Canyon and on completely across the High Plains of Texas and New Mexico, but that branch of the old road does not concern the present study. From Mackenzie's base camp in Blanco Canyon his supply wagons made another road that passed northward in the western part of Dickens County and continued northward across Motley County, some eight or ten miles west of Matador, and on across Quitaque Creek near the northwest corner of Motley County.

To extend Mackenzie's road further is again beside the point, for it was up Quitaque Canyon (or the branch known as Las Lenguas) that was the most likely site of Coronado's first camp—at the east

67. For the route of Colonel Mackenzie as given in the next paragraph of this paper, see Map of the State of Texas by Charles W. Pressler and A. B. Langermann, General Land Office (1879), Austin, Texas. This old time-worn map shows most of Mackenzie's route by land surveys even though the scale of the map is so small that it must be magnified and compared with later maps of larger scale. The Mackenzie Trail is not named on the Pressler and Langermann map but part of the same old road is shown on the Texas General Land Office map of Mitchell County (July, 1880) by Louis C. Wise. On the Wise map the road is identified as "McKenzie's Trail." For the extension of the road to the Quitaque Canyon area, see W. F. Cummins, "Report on the Geography, Topography, and Geology of the Llano Estacado or Staked Plains," *Third Annual Report of the Geological Survey of Texas, 1891* (Austin, 1892), 144-145.

edge of the Plains. Coronado could have followed in reverse this route that was later used by Mackenzie. This route that passed from eight to fifteen miles west of Matador, Dickens, and Spur, and on south through Snyder, and nearly through Colorado City and Sterling City, could have served Coronado as well as it did Mackenzie. Because of extremely rough terrain in parts of Dickens, Kent, and Sterling counties, the old route could hardly have been much farther east. Also the bad water belt paralleled the old road along the east for a good many miles. These physical facts left little choice in the route open either to Mackenzie or to Coronado.[68]

If one arbitrarily assumes that Coronado was camped ten miles up Quitaque Canyon above the point where his route turned south toward the Concho, one may make an estimate of the distance from Quitaque Canyon to the North Concho at somewhere between 190 and 200 miles. Note that this is the distance which Coronado made in an average eleven days of travel. If one changes and assumes that the first ravine at the edge of the Plains in which the Spaniards camped was Tule Canyon, the distance to the Concho from that point amounts to about 225 miles; or if one goes to greater lengths and assumes that this first ravine was Palo Duro, he is stretching the last eleven days of Coronado's outgoing journey far beyond reasonable limits.

Plainly from their camp in the first ravine the Spaniards must necessarily have changed their direction to the south if they were to reach the North Concho. If from this camp site at the east edge of the Plains Coronado reached and followed the route later marked by Mackenzie's supply road across the western parts of Motley and Dickens counties and finally turned down into Blanco Canyon near the later site of Mackenzie's supply camp (ten miles southeast of Crosbyton), his journey would have required about sixty-five miles (or four days) of travel. Note that it *was* four days of travel from the first ravine to the next important point on Coronado's route.[69] Here, in an area known as Cona, Coronado met the Teyas Indians and traveled (southward) among them for three days.[70] This would have

68. Wayne Williams, who has lived near Snyder, Texas, for many years, says that, because of the availability of water and the rough terrain on each side of it, the Mackenzie Trail was the best route through the country. Obviously the same conditions made it the best route in Coronado's day.

69. *Bureau of Ethnology Report,* 507.

70. *Ibid.*

taken him down the spring-fed White River that flows at the bottom of Blanco Canyon and then across the Salt Fork of the Brazos and on across the Double Mountain River. Here in southwestern Kent County, he must have ascended Mackenzie Creek until he passed out of Kent and into Scurry County.

This area across the headwaters of the Brazos was a land of wild grapes and wild plums,[71] much as one of the Spanish historians describes Cona.[72] It remained so until civilization had cast its modifying influence—and even in 1959 a few of the wild grapes are left, and wild plums still grow extensively. This expanse of well-watered valleys and canyons on the Upper Brazos was the area into which the first cattlemen rushed[73] in 1878, 1879, and 1880 just after the great herds of buffalo had been cut down to a small bewildered remnant. Nature had set this section of country apart from all the rest of West Texas—had sealed off this Upper Brazos Valley, so to speak, between the Cap Rock of the Plains on the west and the bad water belt forty miles to the east of it. It was not a land of milk and honey, but for those who indulged in camp life as did cattlemen or Indians, it was about the best substitute that semi-arid West Texas had to offer. It was a godsend to the vanguard of open-range cattlemen; it must have been equally so to the prehistoric East Texas Indians who each year poured by hundreds and even thousands up the Brazos River toward the buffalo country when the change of seasons called them.

It fits exactly into the geography of this trail study to assume that this Upper Brazos Valley was the land of the Teyas—the land known as Cona. Four days of travel from Quitaque Canyon would have reached Cona in Blanco Canyon in southeastern Crosby County. three days of travel through Cona would have reached across the headwaters of the Brazos almost to Snyder, and four more days would have reached past Colorado City and on down to the North Concho just as has previously been pointed out in outlining the probable route of Coronado.

71. *Texas Almanac, 1925*, p. 305. Wayne Williams tells of an immense wild plum thicket that once grew near the junction of the two branches of the Double Mountain Fork of the Brazos River in western Kent County. Picnicking at this point became an annual event on the Fourth of July. Grapevines also grew up the tall trees in the valley. Castañeda refers to the wild grapes of Cona as "Tall Vineyards."

72. *Bureau of Ethnology Report*, 507.

73. C. L. (Kit) Carter came to the Upper Brazos area in August, 1879, for the purpose of selecting his range but was already too late to find a choice location and had to go elsewhere. See the Fort Griffin *Echo*, August 2 and November 1, 1879.

Not only would the designation of the Upper Brazos as Cona have satisfied the arithmetic of this trail study, but it would have harmonized with the known route by which East Texas Indians approached the Plains. Undoubtedly that route came up the Brazos. It was approximately 200 years ago that De Mézières followed an Indian trail up the Brazos[74] to the semi-permanent village of certain East Texas Indians near this same area. That was after Europeans had unintentionally covered the Plains with wild horses, and the consequent aggression of such Indians as the Comanche had probably made it more difficult for the East Texas Indians to occupy the hunting grounds of their choice. Even additional evidences as to the location of Cona are available.

On the Wayne Williams Ranch, along the canyon walls of Grape Creek, Indian pictographs are still to be seen and a whole piece of Indian pottery was found near by. Surely these things are evidences of an early Indian culture. Grape Creek is a tributary of the Double Mountain Fork of the Brazos River, in the heart of the area that this article has designated as Cona.[75]

In 1541 the Teyas (when Coronado came) occupied not just one village but were spread out for some fifty miles—for it required three days for the Spaniards to pass through their country. They may have occupied most or all of the good camping places in the Brazos Valley above the bad water belt. Be that as it may, the great spread of country which they occupied indicates that they were probably on the buffalo range by the thousands. Thus it fits both the arithmetic of this trail study and the known habits of East Texas Indians to assume that Cona was the Upper Brazos River Valley (with possibly some additions to the south).

There is, however, at least one unsolved mystery about the plant life that grew in Cona. These Teyas Indians, who lived in Cona, had plenty of kidney beans.[76] Certainly the phrase "kidney beans" does not describe mesquite beans. Hardly does it describe the beans that grew on the native catclaw. The mystery would have been equally great to have assumed that Cona was anywhere else in West Texas.

---

74. Herbert Eugene Bolton, *Athanase de Mézières and the Louisiana Frontier, 1768-1780* (2 vols.; Cleveland, 1914), I, 294. The first roads (they were military roads) came up the Brazos near present-day Weatherford, Graham, Throckmorton, Aspermont, and on to the mouth of Blanco Canyon.

75. The writer visited the Wayne Williams Ranch on June 13, 1959.

76. *Bureau of Ethnology Report*, 507.

Might it have been that East Texas Indians brought their own dried beans to the Upper Brazos and did a little gardening while on these extended buffalo hunts? Capable biologists who are intimately acquainted with the plant life of this area are at a loss to know what else could have been properly described as "kidney beans."[77]

For the present, however, the mystery may rest and the account will return to the North Concho, from which point the Spanish army began its return journey to New Mexico. First, though, one must remember that Coronado, with thirty picked horsemen and a half dozen footmen, separated from his main army at the Concho (if this interpretation be correct) and went north perhaps to Kansas in further search of Quivira. Meanwhile his army remained on the Concho and hunted buffalo in the flat country near by until its efforts extended over fourteen days, netting some five hundred of the shaggy beasts to replenish the meat supply.

About the first of July, reckoned by a present-day calendar, the march back to the Rio Grande began.[78] First the Spaniards went back to Cona—by Colorado City and Snyder, and on into Kent County by the same route which they had followed to the Concho.[79] Here they found the Teyas Indians willing to furnish guides[80] for the whole journey to the Pecos and perhaps beyond. The Spanish accounts do not leave any doubt but that the return route was as near a straight line as topography would permit.[81] It extended from Kent County through the north part of Garza, across the southwest part of Crosby, and on past present-day Lubbock to the Yellowhouses in northwest Hockley County. It continued westward from there to the large salt lake southeast of Portales, and on past Portales—all of the way almost in a straight line—to a spring near present Taiban, and on to the Pecos River just south of modern Fort Sumner. All of the route from Kent County to the Pecos was almost identical with the line across the turf of the Plains that became known as the Fort Sumner-Fort Griffin Road a little more than three centuries later.[82] From the Yellowhouses

---

77. The mysterious kidney bean was discussed with W. T. Fall, a biologist of many years' experience. Fall has observed the plant growth of the Snyder country for several decades but does not know of any wild plant life that answers the description.

78. See footnote 29.

79. *Bureau of Ethnology Report,* 509.

80. *Ibid.*

81. *Ibid.,* 509-510.

82. This was the most probable route. If Cona extended southward into the up-

west it was the same road as that which Manuel the Comanche had recommended to Marcy in 1849. It was at the southern edge of the middle crossing of the Plains for the salt lakes do not extend further to the north. Extended toward the east, the route crossed the counties of Stonewall, Haskell, Throckmorton, Young, and Palo Pinto. It was the "big road" from New Mexico across the Plains and down the Brazos and on to East Texas. In this same year, 1541, Moscoso and his party found in East Texas turquoise and cotton shawls that came from the direction of the sunset.[83] The odds are heavy that these articles of commerce had passed down this same trail. Also it is entirely likely that the Teyas had come up the road from somewhere in East Texas and that later in the summer they traveled back down the road to their homes.[84]

The thread of this account, however, left Corondao's army on the Pecos River. The army must have reached the Pecos at the Bosque Redondo (Round Grove) four miles south of the present-day town of Fort Sumner. Manuel, the great Comanche guide on the 1849 expedition, told Marcy, it will be remembered, that the expedition which Marcy guided could not cross the Plains south of that point. Accepting Manuel's statement as correct, it would not make sense to place the Spaniards' approach to the Pecos anywhere below the Bosque Redondo.

From this place on the Pecos the Coronado army traveled thirty leagues up the river where the members crossed on Coronado's bridge.[85] Converted into modern units of measurement, this places the significant bridge seventy-nine miles above Bosque Redondo. By present-day roads the distance up the Pecos from old Bosque Redondo to Anton Chico is eighty-eight miles. But a three-mile elbow just east of Santa Rosa and another much longer such right angle turn just west of the same town account for all of the difference in the two

---

per valley of the Colorado, however, the return route could have been from the headwaters of the Colorado to the Yellowhouses and west by present-day Portales to the site of Fort Sumner.

83. Bourne, *De Soto*, I, 818.

84. It seems probable that these Indians lived in the Fort Worth or Waco country or near by between the Brazos and Trinity rivers just as did the Indians of De Mézières' time. This was the nearest point from which the agricultural type of Indians could have moved up the Brazos to hunt buffalo.

85. *Bureau of Ethnology Report*, 510.

distances. One cannot presently follow the exact path made by Coronado's army up the east side of the Pecos, but careful map measurements between Bosque Redondo and Anton Chico make it quite plain that, in round numbers, the distance was thirty leagues. Surely Holden's statement that Coronado's bridge was at Anton Chico suggests the most accurate location yet offered for this crossing of the Pecos.

The remaining part of the journey up the west side of the Pecos at the Pecos Pueblo and back through Glorieta Pass to Tiguex on the Rio Grande was merely a retracing in reverse of Coronado's steps as he started out to Texas.

Next one should go back and pick up another thread of the story which is understandable in the light of the facts of this paper. When Coronado's army came near the Pecos, an Indian woman slipped away from her Spanish hosts, hid in one of the ravines, and returned to her people[86]—probably these same Indians at Cona. She spent nine days in flight, but the Spanish recorder fails to tell where she went. Some three months later the De Soto Expedition, then headed by Moscoso, found her somewhere in East Texas. She even told the De Soto party the names of some of Coronado's captains, which is rather strong evidence that her story is not fictitious. But the story poses a problem in time and distance. How could she have gone all the way from the Pecos River to East Texas in nine days—an average of more than fifty miles a day?

Herewith is a possible solution: the woman did not go all the way to East Texas in nine days; she was a Teya Indian from Cona who fled not to East Texas but merely hurried across the Plains to Cona in the Upper Brazos Valley. The distance from Fort Sumner on the Pecos River to Lubbock at the east edge of the Plains is, by present-day highways, 163 miles, and the distance by the old Fort Sumner-Fort Griffin wagon road was even shorter than that. Add another possible twenty or thirty miles down Yellowhouse Canyon below Lubbock and the total distance of the Indian woman's nine-day flight back to her people in Cona was some 180 to 190 miles. On an average she traveled twenty to twenty-one miles a day which was only about three miles per day faster than Coronado's army was moving.

To go on with the suggested solution—when warm weather drove most of the buffalo out of the Brazos Valley northward, when

86. *Ibid.*

the Teyas Indians had gathered the best of the lush wild plum crop of Kent and adjoining counties, and when the mysterious kidney bean crop had served its purpose and the wild grapes had turned temptingly ripe on the vine, the Indians of Cona folded up their tents and started home. They harnessed their dogs travois-fashion and took the long trail back down the Brazos to East Texas. Following near the roads that were later opened by Mackenzie and other military personnel, they were back in their own matured corn fields in September and October. The Indian woman who had escaped on the Pecos was with them ready to tell her story to the De Soto party. Probably because of language difficulties the De Soto followers misunderstood her, but once these Spaniards were safely in Mexico where they could compare notes with the Coronado party, they realized that the Indian woman had correctly given the names of Spanish captains, and that a great opportunity to learn of other Europeans and the land of the pueblos to the west was tragically lost.

Does this suggested explanation about the Indian woman seem fantastic? If so, how can it be explained that the Indians in her neighborhood had turquoise and cotton shawls that had come from the direction of the sunset (New Mexico)? Probably they too had been west in the buffalo country where they had obtained these articles in trade. Obviously the woman's story depends on the supposition of this paper that Cona was in the Upper Brazos Valley, but hardly can the geography or arithmetic of this paper be true at all if Cona was somewhere else. This paper offers an explanation of the Indian woman's story; also her story in a measure helps to confirm the geography as set out in this study.

Surely this solution of the Coronado tangle that places the East Texas Indians in the choice camping places of the Upper Brazos suggests a more peaceful co-existence among the Indians 400 years ago than that known to have existed after the advent of the horse had implemented the aggressiveness of certain of the northern tribes. If so it may suggest a basis for further study among the real students of the North American Indian. This paper refrains from attempting to classify either by tribes or linguistic stock any of the Indians which Coronado met in the Plains. If this effort has in a measure helped to satisfy the curiosity of those who wish to follow the route of Coronado, and if at the same time it has added any facts of geography which may be useful to the scholars, it has served its purpose.

III

NEW EVIDENCE ON MOSCOSO'S APPROACH TO TEXAS

That the study of De Soto's journey near the Mississippi River can add anything to the knowledge of Texas history may appear to be a very unlikely statement. However, when one remembers that it was from the place of De Soto's death—somewhere on the Mississippi—that the surviving Spaniards of his expedition set out for Texas, the statement begins to have meaning. During the summer and fall of 1542 these Spaniards under Luys de Moscoso made the first known visit of white men to the northeast portion of Texas.

From what direction did they approach? Prominent historians are divided on the answer to this question. Some eminent scholars claim that the party of Spaniards came from the mouth of the Arkansas River, while others with equal sincerity believe that they came from near the mouth of Red River. Evidence toward a solution of the problem that seems not to have entered previous discussions will be offered in this chapter.

The writer became keenly interested in this subject when his next-door neighbor, Ernest Lee, returned from a short sojourn in Mississippi. Lee and his family had visited Natchez to see its highly colorful azalea show and to spend a day or two reviewing the feudal splendor of the Old South. Neighborly conversation about the recent journey flowed back and forth across the back yard fence—and then the discussion moved into the living room. Pictures of old pre-Civil War mansions were exhibited and finally state road maps were produced.

At length Lee mentioned the bluffs that border the east side of the Mississippi. He had just traveled through the high country that lies east of the river and remembered how it had appeared in sharp contrast to the bottom land that lay to the west of the age-old watercourse. On the west side that mighty stream had periodically overflowed covering many hundreds of square miles of rich land—but the hill country to the east had always remained high and dry above

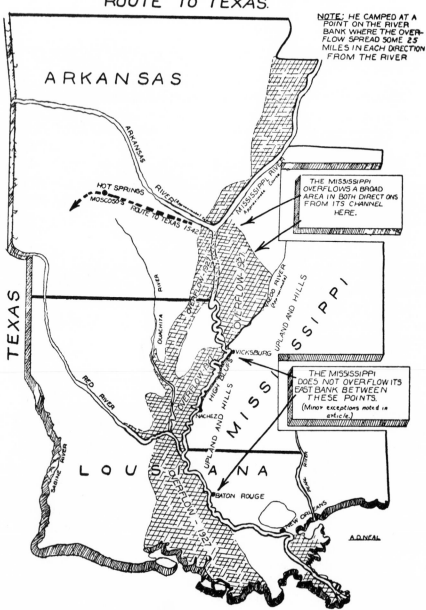

FLOOD MAP OF THE MISSISSIPPI THROWS NEW LIGHT ON MOSCOSO'S ROUTE TO TEXAS.

the flood level. The one hundred and sixty miles of this countryside between Vicksburg, Mississippi, and Baton Rouge, Louisiana, had for all these centuries defied the giant river, while on the other hand the river had constantly cut away millions of tons of earth from the little upland empire—forming the well-known bluffs at Vicksburg and other points.

This talk of topography and floods turned the conversation to De Soto's journey and the later itinerary of his Spanish explorers. The Spaniards under Moscoso had gone to Texas, but after several months had returned to an Indian village near the place on the Mississippi where De Soto was buried. They found and conquered an Indian village a few miles away where they decided to spend the winter. The village was about a half mile west of the river bank at what seemed a safe distance from overflow.[1] But in the spring following (in 1543) the Mississippi staged its first great flood known to written history. It spread all over the country where the Spaniards were camped and extended some twenty-five miles west of the river. It even reached the Indian village of "nine leagues off."[2]

But the mighty Mississippi was not content to limit its overflow to the west side of its valley. "The Indians said that on the opposite side it also extended an equal distance over the country."[3] This language quoted from the best existing account of the later stages of the Spanish expeditions means that the river at Moscoso's camp was some fifty miles wide, spreading into a veritable inland sea both to the east and west of its channel.

With this fact gleaned from the account of the Spanish journey, the little living room party settled down to some earnest research. Where could the Mississippi have overflowed its valley twenty-five miles on each side of its normal stream bed? More maps both ancient and modern were brought forth and even a few volumes of encyclopedias were put into play. The living room was now as cluttered as a carpenter's work shop. The answer to the query about the Mississippi's flood plain was not found in an obscure work of ancient lore but in a schoolboy's encyclopedia. A map of the great floods of 1927 published in that schoolboy's reference book showed how the

1. Edward Gaylord Bourne, *Narratives of the Career of Hernando De Soto in the Conquest of Florida*, as told by a Knight of Elvas and in a relation by Luys Hernandez de Budma (2 Vols., New York, 1904), I, 186. Hereafter cited as Bourne, *De Soto*.

2. *Ibid.*, 189.

3. *Ibid.*

mighty Mississippi had broken its levees as an angry imprisoned giant might choose to snap his chains.[4] The flood reached from Missouri to the Gulf of Mexico.

Below New Orleans, during the flood of 1927, the river had inundated its delta for miles both to the right and left of the levees. There were no breaks in the levees between New Orleans and Baton Rouge, but great rifts near the mouth of Red River had turned loose the full fury of the flood on the west side of the Mississippi. It raged all the way from Red River to the Gulf, and at one place ranging southwestwardly across the river from Baton Rouge it was seventy-five miles wide.[5]

Still higher up—above the mouth of Red River—the flood was also serious,[6] but it spread with slight exceptions only to the west side of the channel. This condition was true up the river all the way from Baton Rouge to Vicksburg. Certainly the overflow could not have climbed the bluffs or the hills to the east where the Lees had so recently traveled. The azaleas and old southern mansions of Natchez and the country far to the north and south of it—including the country east of the mouth of Red River—were safe from the frothing torrents of the angry river. Lee estimated the bluffs at Vicksburg and Natchez at perhaps one hundred feet high, and the east bank of the river far down at Baton Rouge is more than thirty feet above the water level. According to the map (of the 1927 flood) in the child's encyclopedia there was no levee on the east side of the river between Baton Rouge and Vicksburg.[7] Indeed, for the most part none was necessary, for water cannot flow uphill.

A flood map in the *Encyclopedia Brittanica*[8] varies only slightly from the map shown in the child's reference work. The Brittanica map does not portray any particular flood but indicates the area that is at all subject to overflow—including at places a narrow ribbon of

4. Michael V. O'Shea, Editor-in-Chief, "Mississippi River," *The World Book Encyclopedia* (Chicago, 1941), XI, 4547. The map here shows the Mississippi Flood of 1927. The maps (especially the state maps) found in this school-age encyclopedia are in general superior to those found in other encyclopedias.

5. *Ibid*.

6. *Ibid*.

7. *Ibid*.

8. Edgar Jadwin, "Mississippi River," *The Encyclopedia Britannica*, 14th edition, XV: 606. Major-General Jadwin, who wrote the encyclopedia article of which the map was a part, was Chief of Engineers for the United States Army and had supervision of the flood control work on the Mississippi River.

flood plain on the east side of the Mississippi between Baton Rouge and Vicksburg.

One of these flood points about twenty miles below Natchez needs closer examination. The area in question is the lower valley of the Homochito River on the east side of the Mississippi. Here according to the *Brittanica* the flood plain extends somewhat arrow-point fashion up the Homochito Valley some thirteen miles (by map measurements) from the east bank of the Mississippi. Careful check against a topographical map of the state of Mississippi[9] shows that the upper limit of this Homochito flood plain is roughly a contour line

9. William D. McCain, "The Story of Mississippi," *The World Book Encyclopedia* (Chicago, 1941) XI, 4535. A colored Mississippi state map (between pages 4534 and 4535) shows the country that is less than 100 feet above sea level—also the country between 100 feet elevation and 500 feet and the area above 500 feet. On the extreme southwest corner of Mississippi the terrain rises above 500 feet within about five miles east of the Mississippi: it rises to the same height 25 miles east of Natchez. Except the area mentioned in the Homochito Valley and a very narrow margin of two to four miles along the east bank of the Mississippi, all of the area within the state and not more than 50 miles from its southwest corner is more than 100 feet above sea level. At a bend of the river some 20 miles above Natchez the 100 foot contour recedes to about six miles from the river. Otherwise the area below the 100 foot level is negligible for a full 80 miles north of the southwest corner of Mississippi. All of the country extending many miles west of the Mississippi (in the state of Louisiana) according to the map, was less than 100 feet above sea level.

10. *Louisiana: A Guide to the State* (New York: Hastings House, 1945), 466. Vadalia on the west bank of the Mississippi opposite Natchez is 63 feet above sea level. Morgazania some 60 air line miles south and also on the west bank of the river is 35 feet above sea level. That the flood of 1927 inundated both of these villages simultaneously together with all the country between them along the west side of the levee, indicates clearly that the southward slope of the flood plain here is uniform (else there would have been spots of dry land in evidence). Assuming that the slope is uniform the west bank of the Mississippi opposite the Homochita River, which is a point between Vadalia and Morgazania, is approximately 55 feet above sea level.

11. Jadwin, *op. cit.*, 608. A statement from Jadwin's article which applies to the entire river below Cairo recites in part " . . . the confinement of the river between levees has caused large increases in flood heights . . ." If without the levees the Mississippi during the flood of 1543 had risen high enough to inundate the Homochito flood plain (as it did in fact inundate the country across the river from Moscoso's camp) it in so doing must have risen to a depth of some 40 feet above its west banks. Obviously Moscoso's camp could not have been located under such a depth of water—and even if imperfect maps result in an error of 10 or 20 feet here the result is essentially no different. It is true that so far as the writer knows no historian places Moscoso's camp at this exact point on the river or anywhere below it but since this paper is not primarily in the nature of refutation it is felt that all possibilities should be explored with the available evidence.

one hundred feet above sea level—or in plain language that the water in the Mississippi at this point must rise until it is one hundred feet above sea level in order to reach thirteen miles up the Homochito Valley. The west bank of the Mississippi here is only about sixty feet above sea level[10]—meaning that the river must flow forty feet deep over its west bank in order to push thirteen miles up the Homochito flood plain. Obviously it is only because of the man-made levees on the west side of the Mississippi (necessary, of course, because of their function in the greater flood control plan) that the Homochito flood area is ever large enough to warrant attention. Without the levees the river in Moscoso's day could not seriously have overflowed its east bank in this section.[11] At no other point between Vicksburg and Baton Rouge did the Brittanica map show a possible flood plain on the east of the Mississippi that even approached a width of thirteen miles. Above this Homochito area and for some distance above Natchez, overflows along the east side of the river, according to the map, are not at all possible.[12] All other exceptions to this rule found elsewhere between Baton Rouge and Vicksburg are minor and almost reach the vanishing point when one remembers that, as in the case discussed, the floods that do occur are largely due to manmade levees on the west side of the river.

Above Vicksburg, however, the map shows that (except for an island of dry land protected by the levees, about twenty-five miles wide and fifty miles long in northeast Louisiana) the floodwaters spread broadly both to the east and the west of the river as far up as the mouth of the Arkansas.[13] Shortly above the Arkansas the floods do not extend east of the river but continue up the west side all the way into southeast Missouri. The levee extends up the east side of the river perhaps fifty miles above the mouth of the Arkansas.

12. It is in this area approximately opposite Natchez that the United States De Soto Expedition commission mapped the site of Moscoso's camp (at the Indian village of Aminoya) of the winter and spring of 1543. Surely they have not taken due cognizance of the statement that the Mississippi overflowed its flood plain broadly in both directions at Moscoso's camp (see footnote No. 2). The map made by the Commission was published in *The Southwestern Historical Quarterly* of October, 1942. (Albert Woldert, "The Expedition of Louis De Moscoso," *The Southwestern Historical Quarterly*, XLVI, opposite page 162.

13. The flood maps in both encyclopedias previously cited are in agreement here as they are in the main throughout the river valley. Both maps show that the valley from Vicksburg to well above the mouth of the Arkansas is subject to overflow on both sides of the river channel (see footnotes No. 4 and No. 8).

Here then from Vicksburg to possibly fifty miles above the mouth of the Arkansas is the only part of the Mississippi above Baton Rouge where the river overflows its flood plain both to the east and the west of the normal channel—*here is the only place where Moscoso's camp could have been waterbound with floods reaching some twenty-five miles on each side of the river.*

That this segment of the Mississippi covers a span of some one hundred fifty air line miles need not add to the researcher's worries for there is yet another fact that limits the area in which the Spaniards were encamped. In 1542 these bold explorers had followed some large river down from the west to its junction with the Mississippi near their present encampment.[14] Since the Arkansas is the only river that intersects this one hundred fifty mile span of the Mississippi's flood plain from the west, the answer to our search is rather definite. Moscoso was encamped near the mouth of the Arkansas—and his march into Texas in 1542 originated from that point. This was the conclusion of the little living room party before it adjourned—for the high country east of the Mississippi that extends many miles both above and below the mouth of Red River offers a near insurmountable argument against the supposition that Moscoso's camp was anywhere opposite the Vicksburg-Natchez-Baton Rouge segment.

There is yet other evidence to confirm this conclusion. Moscoso and his Spaniards broke camp in June, 1543, and sailed down the river en route to Mexico. After a few days they came to the bluffs[15] along the stream—and one should keep in mind that the pronounced bluffs lie between Vicksburg and Natchez well downstream from the mouth of the Arkansas but well above Red River.

Even the known facts of mileage along the crooked Mississippi channel confirm the Arkansas site as the location of Moscoso's camp. An old map of Arkansas[16] published in 1850 lists the steamship mileage from the mouth of the Arkansas to New Orleans as 673 miles. From New Orleans to the Gulf is approximately one hundred fourteen miles,[17] thus making a total of 787 miles from the mouth of

14. Bourne, *De Soto*, I, 150, 179, 182, 183; II, 38.

15. *Ibid.*, 196.

16. Thomas Cowperthwait & Co., *A New Map of Arkansas* (Philadelphia, 1850). The distance by river from the mouth of the Arkansas to the Gulf is about 100 miles shorter according to present-day information than as shown in Cowperthwait's old map (see John W. Woerman and W. G. Burroughs, "Mississippi River," *The New International Encyclopedia*, second edition, XVI, 14).

17. Jadwin, *Op. cit.*, 607.

the Arkansas to the Gulf of Mexico. The Gentleman of Elvas who wrote the chief account of Moscoso's travels called the distance 250 leagues[18] down the river—or 660 miles, which is about 19 per cent less than the steamship mileage. The steamship mileage from the mouth of Red River to New Orleans as given by the old map was 223 miles or a total to the mouth of the Mississippi of 337 miles. This is hardly more than half of the 250 leagues estimated by the Gentleman of Elvas and obviously is at far greater variance with it than the 787 miles between the mouth of the Arkansas and the Gulf.

The fact is that the drift of the current of the Mississippi even without the aid of oars would have floated the boats of the Spaniards down stream from the mouth of Red River in much less time than they actually spent in transit. The Spaniards spent seventeen days on the Mississippi, according to the Elvas account[19] and nineteen days according to Biedma.[20] During at least three days, because of continued attacks by Indians, they traveled day and night.[21] On two different days the party did not travel at all. For the remaining twelve (or fourteen) days, travel seems to have been limited to daylight. Thus it is easy to calculate that a total of more than 200 hours[22] were spent in actual movement down the river. If the current flowed only 1.9 miles per hour, it would have drifted them from Red River to the Gulf within that 200 hours.[23] Proof (offered below) is rather definite that only at low water does the Mississippi flow so slowly. And proof is equally definite that Moscoso and his men were traveling when the water was considerably higher than normal. A secondary flood came down the Mississippi in June (1543) overflowing its banks enough to float the sailing vessels made by the Spaniards on dry land into the main river channel.[24] Shortly thereafter the Spaniards set sail toward

18. Bourne, *De Soto*, I, 201.
19. *Ibid.*
20. *Ibid.*, II, 39.
21. *Ibid.*, I, 200, 201.
22. The Spanish were hard pressed by Indians during the greater part of their journey down the river and made all the speed possible. Three days and nights of travel alone amounted to 72 hours. Travel during only 75 per cent of daylight during twelve additional days will add enough time to make a total of 200 hours. Probably they traveled more than 200 hours.
23. It is only 337 miles down the Mississippi from Red River to the Gulf. Two hundred hours of travel at 1.9 miles per hour would amount to 380 miles or enough to allow for a supposed journey from more than forty miles above the mouth of Red River.
24. Bourne, *De Soto*, I, 191-192. The secondary flood of June, 1543, caused the

the Gulf of Mexico. Numerous passages in the accounts of the expedition refer to the swiftness of the current.[25] At one time eleven Spaniards who were cut off and surrounded by the Indians in their canoes were abandoned by Moscoso because "the force of the stream" would not permit his men to row against the current to aid their comrades in distress.[26]

The facts about the speed of the current of the Mississippi are these—at low water the current flows from .7 miles to 1.75 miles per hour, while in its lower course the river at high water races along at from 4.1 to 5.5 miles per hour.[27] If one strikes an average of these rates the result is approximately three miles per hour—and all the evidence indicates that the flow of the river during Moscoso's journey was more than average. However, basing the calculation on just three miles per hour, the drift of the current alone during 200 hours would have resulted in 600 miles of progress down the river. In addition the Spaniards expended much energy on their oars. Certainly one does

---

Mississippi to overflow its banks.

According to present-day information such a flood requires a flow of at least 1,000,000 cubic feet of water per second. At low water the river flows less than one-tenth of that amount. Aside from references from old accounts of Moscoso's river voyage, present information causes us to know that the Mississippi had not had sufficient time to even reach its normal state between the June flood and the 18th or 19th of July when Moscoso reached the Gulf—that is unless the river had fallen abnormally fast. Expert information points out that a rapid drop in the river channel leaves sand bars that are "most disastrous" to river navigation. On the other hand "if the river falls slowly, say 0.2 or 0.3 foot per day, the current will have time to cut down the bars fast enough to maintain a good channel." (For these several facts about the Mississippi see John W. Woerman and W. G. Burroughs, "Mississippi River," *The New International Encyclopedia*, second edition, XVI, 11, 14, 15).

It is evident that the flood of June, 1543, did not subside rapidly else the Spaniards would have encountered much difficulty with sand bars. Let us assume that the river level fell 0.3 foot per day—the maximum mentioned in the article quoted above. The low bank of the Mississippi opposite Natchez, for instance, is 63 feet above sea level (footnote No. 10) and the normal height of the river at that place is 40.5 feet above sea level (see Forrest Morgan, "Mississippi River," *The Encyclopedia Americana*," 1943 edition XIX, 248). Thus we have at Natchez a fall of 22.5 feet from flood stage to normal which at 0.3 foot per day would have required 75 days. At this rate the flood that began in June could not have fallen to normal until at least the middle of August or a whole month after Moscoso had entered the Gulf of Mexico. Hence it is an easy deduction that the Spaniards traveled on the Mississippi when it was between normal and flood state—probably about midway—and that near the beginning of the journey when they traveled day and night it was not far below flood height.

not assume a realistic viewpoint toward these physical facts of time and river current when he concludes that Moscoso traveled no farther tha' the 337 miles between Red River and the Gulf of Mexico. Nor does it materially change the concept to assume that the Spaniards journeyed from forty or fifty miles above the mouth of Red River.

Still another and even more specific fact is contained in the summary to one of the lost chapters in the Ranjel account of this Spanish expedition. According to that summary, this missing chapter which detailed Moscoso's journey to Texas told of "hot streams and salt made from the sand."[28] Surely the reference was to the present-day resort place widely known as Hot Springs, Arkansas, which is well in line between the mouth of the Arkansas River and the northeast corner of Texas. Certainly it does not even approach any point on the

25. Bourne, *De Soto*, I, 195, 198, 199; II, 39.

26. *Ibid.*, I, 198; II, 39.

27. John W. Woerman and W. G. Burroughs, "Mississippi River," *The New International Encyclopedia*, second edition XVI, 14. At low water the current in the lower course of the Mississippi flows at a rate varying from 1 to 1.5 feet per second: at high water it flows from 6 to 8 feet per second.

These rates are translated into miles per hour in the above discussion. Mark Twain estimated the rate of the current at 5 miles per hour during high water (see Mark Twain, *Life On the Mississippi*, New York, 1917, 156).

With these facts in mind concerning the rate of the current, one may more intelligently attack one of the problems of distance presented by the accounts of Moscoso's river journey, viz: "How far did the Spaniards travel down the Mississippi from their beginning point until they reached the bluffs?" The Indians said it was "three days' journey down the river" to Quigualtam (Bourne, *De Soto*, I, 195), and a careful reading of the Elvas account of the expedition reveals that "a town near the river's bluff" was in the province of Quigualtam (Bourne, *De Soto*, I, 153), but the Spanish scoured the country for "fourteen or fifteen leagues" down the river and found neither of these places. Either the Spanish had misunderstood the Indians or else in the wake of the June flood—and there is no sure way of knowing how much longer—before he reached the bluff, should dispel all doubt that the distance intended by the Indians was three days' travel and not three leagues (Bourne, *De Soto*: I, 195-196).

The question still remains, however, "How far did the Indians normally travel down the Mississippi in three days?" Some assistance can be had from Joutel's *Journal of La Salle's Last Voyage* (Henry Reed Stiles, ed., Joutel's *Journal of La Salle's Last Voyage*, 1684-7, Albany, 1906, 183-185). In August, 1687, five survivors of La Salle's expedition, in a canoe rowed by four Indians, traveled up the Mississippi from the mouth of the Arkansas to the Chickasaw Bluffs, a distance of some 200 miles. (It was 202 miles according to Cowperthwaite's map cited in footnote No. 16) in seven days of actual rowing time. This was an average of 29 miles per day. It is true that the supposed route of Moscoso from the mouth of Red River to northeast Texas.

All in all the facts of topography including the area where it was possible for the Mississippi to overflow both directions from its channel, the location of the river bluffs with reference to that area, the known river mileage downstream as compared with estimates made by the Spaniards themselves and the fact that the location of the known "hot streams" does not harmonize with the supposed more southerly route—these facts forge a chain of evidence, largely new, that should cause several eminent authorities to restudy Moscoso's approach to Texas. To conclude with Bolton[29] and with Lewis[30] that this Spanish journey to northeast Texas in 1542 came from the mouth of the Arkansas seems abundantly justified. The *Report of the United States De Soto Expedition Commission* mapped the route of the Spaniards with the mouth of Red River as one of its anchor points. To change the anchorage to the mouth of the Arkansas would require the abandonment of at least a thousand miles of the route as mapped by the De Soto Commission. It would require a re-study of the whole De Soto-Moscoso journey west of the Mississippi with the possibility

Chickasaw Bluffs were not called by name in Joutel's account, but a result not very different may be had by following the journey of this canoe up to the mouth of the Huabache River (the Ohio) or on up to the Missouri—only in these latter instances the length of stop-overs is less certain.

This average of 29 miles per day was made against the current, which let us estimate at two miles per hour (probably a little too low) or say 25 miles per day. The result would have been 54 miles per day in still water. Now let us add another 25 miles per day in order to represent the speed of a canoe traveling down stream with the aid of the current and we have the result of 79 miles per day. At this rate three days downstream would amount to 237 miles. Actually the distance by river from the mouth of the Arkansas to the bluffs at Vicksburg in 1850 was 284 miles (according to the Cowperthwait map referred to in footnote No. 16) which would also have been the result of the above calculation if we had supposed the rate of the current in the case cited were 2⅔ miles instead of two miles per hour. This segment of the Mississippi above Vicksburg seems to have been abnormally long in 1850, and during the next 20 or 30 years without the aid of engineers it materially shortened its course.

Some of the elements may be wrong in this attempt to determine what the Indians meant by three days' travel down the river. The La Salle party in the example given above did not travel upstream against the swiftest of the current, but to avoid doing so they zigzagged their course and probably added enough mileage to make the result here about the same as if they had met the current squarely. Thus the elements of river current, the rate at which the Indians could row a canoe, and the practical problems of river navigation are dealt with above at so nearly their actual of a revision of the route in Texas. Even some rather careful studies of more recent date by Dr. Albert Woldert[31] and Dr. Rex Strickland[32] based on the mouth of Red River as an anchor point should require a new approach.

The writer, who contributed an article published in the same journal with those of Woldert and Strickland, based his study on the mouth of the Arkansas as a beginning point for the Moscoso journey to Texas. He does not intend this study as a continuation of a debate with those two excellent gentlemen, but rather as an addition to the discussions published at that time and previously. Let the evidence as published then and now stand on its own feet. Certainly there is yet plenty of room for careful on-the-ground study of the route of Moscoso. It is hoped that the facts of Mississippi River topography as presented herein may throw some new light on the solution of the greater problem.

---

values as to make it seem entirely probable that it was in fact three days' travel from the Arkansas river to the Vicksburg Bluffs. By the same token it seems all but impossible to find any place near or even 100 miles above the mouth of Red River from which Moscoso might have begun his journey such that in three days' travel his brigantines might have reached any noticeable river bluffs—for the pronounced bluffs on the lower Mississippi are confined to the 100 miles of shoreline between Vicksburg and Natchez.

28. Bourne, *De Soto*, II, 150.

29. Herbert E. Bolton, *The Spanish-Borderlands*, (New Haven, 1921), 69.

30. F. W. Hodge and Theodore H. Lewis (eds.), *Spanish Explorers in the Southern United States, 1528-1563* (New York, 1907), 226-227.

31. Albert Woldert, "The Expedition of Louis De Moscoso in Texas in 1542" *The Southwestern Historical Quarterly*, XLVI, 158-166.

32. Rex W. Strickland, "Moscoso's Journey Through Texas," *Ibid.*, 109-137.

IV

MOSCOSO'S TRAIL IN TEXAS

Seeming now as if they had come from the pages of an ancient story book, a party of Spanish adventurers, headed by Luys de Moscoso, made the first *entrada* of Europeans into the northeast corner of Texas just four hundred years ago. To connect the journey of these archaic figures—some of whom were clad in the armor of mediaeval knights—with the Southwest of today presents a field for no little interesting speculation. An attempt to follow the actual route of these Spaniards, which is the chief problem of this paper, holds some of the intriguing aspects of dragging a bit of mythology into the plain daylight of Texas history. A brief review of the background of the expedition will prove helpful.[1]

The expedition originated in Spain under the official stamp of the king, and included several persons of noble birth, chief of whom was the leader of the party, Hernando de Soto. With a will of iron, and courage that knew no fear, De Soto conducted his party from Spain to Cuba, from Cuba to Florida, and from there across most of the area that is now the southern United States. His long-drawn-out journey was, in the main, a search for gold. With his curiosity in microscopic focus looking for that precious element, he crossed the present states of Georgia, South Carolina, North Carolina, Tennessee, Alabama, Mississippi, Arkansas, Missouri, and probably parts of Kansas and Oklahoma. After three years of such wandering, De Soto turned back to the mouth of the Arkansas.[2] Somewhat broken in spirit, he sickened and died, leaving his followers to work out their own salvation.

---

1. Edward Gaylord Bourne, *Narratives of the Career of Hernando de Soto in the Conquest of Florida*, as told by a Knight of Elvas and in a relation by Luys Hernández de Biedma (2 vols.; New York, 1904). Hereafter cited as Bourne, *De Soto*. The introduction to this article is based chiefly on these narratives.

2. Herbert E. Bolton, *The Spanish Borderlands* (New Haven, 1921), 69.

Indian fights and long exposure had taken a toll of nearly half of his six hundred men, and only about forty of his two hundred and forty horses still survived.[3] The search for gold had proved to be a disappointment; these men who had been fired by visions of immense riches had worn out their European clothes and were now dressed in the skins of animals.[4] Probably their morale had suffered as much as their raiment.

After De Soto's death the luxury-loving Moscoso was selected as leader. After due consultation with the ranking Spaniards of the group, he decided to turn the course of travel toward the settlements in Mexico. Thus the frayed-out remnant of the well trimmed De Soto expedition came into the land that we now know as Texas. Slowed to a snail's pace by the lack of horses and further impeded by a train of captured Indian slaves and burden-bearers, the party was able to travel little more than an average of six miles per day.[5] For four months this strange party of white and red-skinned humanity moved westward and southwestward under the convoy of the few mounted men who still faintly resembled Spanish cavalry. Then fear seized them, fear of starvation if they went ahead, and the party returned to the mouth of the Arkansas, hoping to escape by water.

But details of the journey are not the purpose of this paper. Chiefly, this effort is concerned with the route which the Moscoso party followed in Texas. Difficult as that task may be, the writer has employed evidence not previously emphasized in attempting its solution.

To begin the search for a trail at the very end of it, is an odd, and doubtless novel procedure, but that is the method to be employed in this research. Like raveling an old stocking by beginning at the toe, that journey of four hundred years ago seems easier to understand when first approached from the "wrong end." Here, at the final point of that long, crooked trail—on the bank of some Texas river—this unique party of Spaniards gave up the idea of crossing the North American continent by land. That stream beside which

3. Bolton, *The Spanish Borderlands,* 69.

4. Bourne, *De Soto,* I, 214.

5. A study of the actual time traveled from the mouth of the Arkansas to the river Daycao (Bourne, *De Soto,* I, 166-180) reveals that about seventy days were so spent. This does not include the detour at Guasco. Accepting the estimate of 150 leagues (Bourne, *De Soto,* I, 182) as something near the correct distance traversed in those seventy days, the result is an average near six miles per day.

Moscoso's party stood in early October, 1542, most authorities believe, was the Brazos, but agreement ends just there. As to the exact place on that great river, those same authorities disagree by half the width of Texas.

Why should one believe that the Brazos was the actual stream upon which that journey ended? First, because it is the one Texas river that is almost exactly one hundred and fifty leagues southwest from the mouth of the Arkansas, the exact distance given by accounts as to this last leg of the Spaniards' journey.[6] Next, this Texas watercourse was the second large river mentioned on the route southwest from the mouth of the Arkansas. Finally, the river beside which the Spaniards ended their journey was a stream so large that certain of the East Texas Indians could see other Indians on the opposite bank, but apparently had no communication with them, and did not know what people they were.[7] Certainly no Texas river other than the Brazos seems to fit all these descriptions.

The big puzzle, however, still remains: at what place on the Brazos did Moscoso's Spaniards halt and face eastward? The writer has attempted the task of hunting down the answer to that question only because a great length of that important river is within easy range of the family car and a modest-sized tank of gasoline.

Clues that throw light on any part of Moscoso's trail are extremely scarce. Accounts of this expedition have dropped a few specific phrases or sentences that are probably due more attention than they have previously received. Most prominent among such expressions is part of a sentence used by the Gentleman of Elvas. The Spaniards, in an unfruitful search for other white men, finally reached an Indian village called Guasco. The natives of this village told the Spaniards of other Indians who might be of assistance. " . . . ten days journey . . . toward sunset was a river called Daycao [probably the Brazos] whither they sometimes went to drive and kill deer and whence they had seen persons on the other bank but without knowing what people they were."[8] Moscoso and his followers did as directed and pushed westward to the river Daycao, where these Guasco Indians went to *drive* and *kill* deer. It was the end of their long journey previously referred to.

6. Bourne, *De Soto*, I, 182.
7. *Ibid.*, I, 179.
8. *Ibid.*, I, 178, 179.

It is evident that the Spanish explorers came to a final halt in the heart of the deer country, a fact which brings us immediately into a search for the habitat of the north Texas deer of four centuries ago. Facts about deer that were true only one century ago will probably yield the required truth. Josiah Gregg, one of the keenest observers of frontier conditions during the last century, said that deer did not inhabit the high plains. These animals, he observed, were to be found farther east, in and near the timbered belts and along certain timber-lined streams that arose to the west of those wooded areas.[9] Marcy, in 1849, crossed West Texas from the Big Spring to near the site of Denison. His party did not kill any deer until they had crossed to the east side of the Brazos in present Young County.[10] Kendall, with the Texan Santa Fe Expedition in 1841, found deer scarce in the prairie country to the east of the Brazos, some miles above present Waco;[11] he apparently found them plentiful in the upper Cross Timbers,[12] and found one large herd on the Wichita River, not a great distance from the location of Seymour.[13] This appears, however, to have been near the west edge of the deer country. Meat became scarce with the Texans and a special party of experienced hunters were detailed to keep them supplied. Kendall reported only one more deer killed.[14]

Thus far, the accounts of Gregg, Marcy and Kendall seem to show a cross section of the deer country with those fleet-footed little animals most numerous in the upper Cross Timbers, and less numerous in the prairies to the east and west of that wooded belt. Other experiences confirm this picture. In 1840 Colonel William G. Cooke and his Texas soldiers found game so scarce in the open country between the sites of Waxahachie and Dallas that they were forced to kill their mules for food.[15] Certainly they were not in the heart of

9. Josiah Gregg, *Commerce of the Prairies* (Dallas, 1933), 369.

10. Grant Foreman, *Marcy and the Gold Seekers* (Norman, 1939), 385. This volume contains the diary of Randolph B. Marcy made in 1849 on his expedition across the Texas plains and return. Marcy observed that the deer had probably been driven out of the area just west of the Brazos by Indian hunters, but that fact does not materially change the evidence as to their habitat.

11. George Wilkins Kendall, *Narratives of the Texan Santa Fe Expedition* (Austin, 1935), I, 107.

12. *Ibid.*, I, 111.

13. *Ibid.*, I, 167.

14. *Ibid.*, I, 199. The hunting party on this Texan Santa Fe Expedition, unable to find deer, killed a mustang and, in true Texas fashion, made a joke of it, allowing it to be eaten before explaining that the delicacy was horse meat.

15. Mattie Davis Lucas and Mita Holsapple Hall, *A History of Grayson County,*

the deer country. It should be added that the game on which they did subsist between the Waco Village and Waxahachie did not seem to include venison.

Sixty-eight years earlier, De Mézières crossed this same prairie that lies to the east of Waco. He reported that the Quitsey Indians, who lived east of the Trinity, traded the skins of buffalo and deer to the people of Natchitoches. He also reported that the "Tancagues" traded these same commodities to the Tuacana Indians, whose principal village was located in the prairies west of the Trinity.[16] In each case the supply of deerskins came from the west. Certainly these statements are not to be construed as meaning that deer were not found in the timber of East Texas, but that they were far more plentiful somewhere to the west. Thoroughly consistent with the fact is the statement of the Indians of Guasco [in 1542] that the place where they hunted deer was ten days' travel toward the sunset.[17]

The Coronado expedition came past the east edge of the Staked Plains only one year before Moscoso came to Texas. Coronado's men found deer, so says the account of Castañeda but the description left of those animals plainly shows that what they found were not deer but antelope. Castañeda's statement "the deer are pied with white"[18] contains its own tell-tale evidence. The pronghorn, or prongbuck, that lived west of the Cross Timbers and in the high plains, which is popularly called an antelope, was undoubtedly "pied with

Texas (Sherman, Texas, 1936), 45. Colonel Cooke's Report is copied in full in this volume, pp. 44-47.

16. Herbert Eugene Bolton, *Athanase de Mézières and the Louisiana Frontier, 1768-1780* (Cleveland, 1914), I, 286, 290, 294. Hereafter cited as Bolton, *De Mézières*.

17. Here it is not essential to find the entire deer country, but only the part of it that lay on the Brazos River. Since deer were not numerous in open prairies, and since the only timbered belt that intersected the upper Brazos was the upper Cross Timbers, it is logical to suppose that the deer country known to the Indians of Guasco was in that timber-belt. The lower Cross Timbers, it will be noted, did not reach the Brazos River. Probably the hill-country northwest of San Antonio, with its natural water supply and numerous hiding places, was a great deer country in 1542, as well as now. Cabeza de Vaca found deer more numerous inland from the coastal plain. The Palo Pinto mountain country in the upper Cross Timbers has the same natural advantages for deer as has the San Antonio hill-country. Probably it was a good deer country in 1542.

18. F. W. Hodge and Theodore J. Lewis (eds.), *Spanish Explorers in the Southern United States, 1528-1543* (New York, 1907), 363.

white.''[19] The deer of Central Texas were not so colored. All of which confirms Gregg's statement that deer did not inhabit the high plains, for the kind of deer that Coronado saw obviously were not deer at all. Gregg's statement of one hundred years ago tells plainly that the high plains was the antelope country and that the timbered area to the east was the deer country.[20] Castañeda's statement of four hundred years ago tells part of the same story. That the upper Cross Timbers were the heart of the deer country on both of these widely separated dates seems to be borne out by such straws of evidence as present themselves.

A further fact helps to limit the terminal point of Moscoso's journey. The Indians of Guasco sometimes went west to wherever that terminal point was in order to *drive* and kill deer. In what kind of country could Indians, on foot, successfully drive and kill deer? Certainly not in a wide open prairie, say the best modern deer hunters whom the writer has been able to contact.[21] The type of terrain where the drive method of hunting deer was most likely to have succeeded must have included canyons and, possibly, open places in the timber. The one place where the upper Cross Timbers are cut with canyons and at the same time where that timbered area intersects the Brazos River ranges some sixty to ninety miles west of Fort Worth, chiefly in Palo Pinto County. Quite by coincidence, a few wild deer are still at large in that section. It offers something better than a guess as to where Moscoso ended his journey in Texas. The nearest landmark for identification is Possum Kingdom Dam.

Tentatively allowing the end of Moscoso's trail to rest at this place beside the Brazos, we turn, for additional evidence, to another animal. De Soto brought a herd of hogs from Cuba and drove them the entire journey across the present Southern States.[22] That herd of

19. H. E. Anthony, *Animals of America*, 35; also photographs on pp. 36, 37; see also Gregg, *Commerce of the Prairies*, 369.

20. Gregg, *Commerce of the Prairies*, 369, 370.

21. The most successful deer hunter with whom the writer has discussed this subject is Mr. L. T. Cowden of Wichita Falls, Texas. Having hunted deer in Texas during each of the last eighteen years, and in New Mexico almost all of these years, he has killed forty-six deer during those seasons, almost the total number which was permitted by law. Mr. Cowden regards it as highly improbable that any drive method of deer hunting could have succeeded, except where timber or canyons—preferably the latter—aided the hunter. To this he adds, ''You don't find deer in open prairie, unless they are near 'cover' anyway.''

22. Bourne, *De Soto*, I, 14, 21, 163, 192; II, 12, 23, 63, 93, 95, 139.

swine was nurtured by him as something very precious. Indications are that at night the hogs shared the camp site with the Spaniards.[23] De Soto kept them as a kind of insurance policy against starvation.[24] According to accounts, it seems that only once did he issue pork to his followers. At the death of De Soto this moving hog ranch had grown to seven hundred swine.[25] These animals were auctioned among the surviving Spaniards and driven into Texas.[26] Very likely some of them strayed off into the woods of East Texas, and furnished a beginning for the strange species known to pioneers as "razorbacks." The writer has labored diligently to discover whether or not these thin-backed swine inhabited the upper Cross Timbers; the evidence is overwhelmingly in the affirmative, and some of that evidence pre-dates the first Anglo-American settlements by almost one hundred years.[27] But the whole effort loses point when one continues the search and finds that wild hogs, at least similar to razorbacks, ranged the surface of Texas almost wherever there were acorns, from the shinnery of Motley County to the Sabine River bottom, and even to the Gulf of Mexico.[28] If these were truly De Soto's hogs, some of the breed is still left in Jasper County, perhaps to offer a humble grunt in celebration of the four hundred-fiftieth anniversary of the first Spanish expedition in northeast Texas. Possibly there is some slight confirmation of the theory that Moscoso came to the end of his trail near Possum

23. *Ibid.*, II, 23. When Indians burned De Soto's camp at night, 300 hogs were killed in the fire.

24. *Ibid.*, I, 95

25. *Ibid.*, I, 163.

26. *Ibid.*, I, 163-164.

27. Bolton, *De Mézières*, II, 202.

28. That wild hogs ranged through the timbers of East Texas is well known; they were numerous far down the coast of Texas (J. Frank Dobie, *A Vaquero of the Brush Country*, 35). They were along the wooded stream bottoms near modern Belton in 1841. (Kendall, *The Texan Santa Fe Expedition*, I, 87). They were numerous in the woods of southwest Jack County in 1885. (Interview with W. J. Ribble of Graham, Texas). Also, many wild hogs were in the timber of Montague County in 1856 (Interview with Cash McDonald near Bowie, Texas). They were along the Red River in northeast Fannin County in 1875 (Interview with W. G. Bralley of Wichita Falls, Texas). They were in the same area as early as 1803 (Sibley's Report, *No. 4, Original U. S. vs. Texas*, 755). A strange herd of some seventy-five wild hogs lived in the tall grass covering a flat on Soap Creek, seven miles southwest of Midlothian, Texas, in 1877. They apparently subsisted on roots and acorns that grew nearby, and made their bed for winter protection of the tall grass (Interview with George F. Smith, Wichita Falls, Texas). Pioneer citizens in Erath and Eastland Counties rounded up the wild hogs on Armstrong Creek, in the autumn of 1877. The hogs were

Kingdom Dam in the fact that the razor-backs were once unusually numerous from a point southward of Desdemona (commonly called Hog Town) northeastward across Young and Jack Counties.[29]

Leaving this statement on its own merits, or demerits, let us turn to a certain consideration about De Soto's hogs that drives home an important fact, almost with sledge-hammer blows. The route of the Spaniards was limited to the country where there was food for the hogs. Could these explorers have crossed vast stretches of prairie accompanied by their moving pork supply? Obviously not, unless Moscoso had seen fit to conscript an additional seven legions of Indians to carry the necessary corn and acorns. The Spaniards were, plainly, unable to camp in the prairie for very long, unless acorn-bearing or nut-bearing trees were close at hand.

Applying this simple fact to the route of the explorers, one is almost forced to the conclusion that Moscoso did not go west of the upper Cross Timbers, since the prairies beyond would have meant starvation for the hogs.

From the Indian village of Guasco to the end of their trail the Spaniards were forced to carry corn on their backs for their food supply.[30] They camped on the banks of the river Daycao and waited for ten horsemen to return. Meanwhile, no more corn was in sight and the party faced uncertainty if they went ahead, or ten days without an additional supply of corn until they could march back to Guasco. Under such circumstances surely the Spaniards did not divide their corn with the hogs. Or, put another way, surely this last point on

---

vicious—formed themselves in a protective circle, with noses pointed outward. Only by cautious and persistent efforts, and the use of many dogs, could this circle be broken and the drive continued (Interview with R. H. Williams, Abilene, Texas). In the 1870's, local citizens of Young County had a regular camping place on Salt Creek northeast of modern Newcastle, where they hunted wild hogs each year (Interview with Henry Williams, Newcastle, Texas). In 1880, wild hogs were numerous in the shinnery of Dickens County (W. C. Holden, *Rollie Burns*, 80). Wild hogs were found in the shinnery of Motley County in 1881 (Holden to Williams). In 1882, a wild unbranded hog was killed near the northwest corner of Jack County (Interview with Paul Christian, Antelope, Texas). However, it appears that no wild hogs lived in the bottoms of the Little Wichita River, on the east fork of that stream; or on the several thousands of acres of oak timber adjoining. George Cunningham of Henrietta, Texas, hunted over this area as a boy as early as 1874, and makes this report.

29. See footnote 28. The usual testimony of the many persons interviewed about wild hogs was that they were numerous in the parts of the upper Cross Timbers nearest Desdemona, and Young and Jack Counties.

30. Bourne, *De Soto*, I, 179; II, 38.

Moscoso's journey was, at least, near timber that bore either nuts or acorns. The upper Cross Timbers, which provided a haven of security for the deer could, at the same time, have furnished food for Moscoso's hogs.

One may glean still further evidence from the study of the range of another animal. Apparently the Moscoso party never did enter the country in which buffalo grazed in immense herds.[31] It is unthinkable that the Spaniards could have encountered these most distinctive animals of the plains in mass and that both of the two narrators of the journey should have overlooked the fact; this consideration has, no doubt, been a major element in many previous discussions of the route of Moscoso. But part of the import of that statement seems to have been overlooked. The buffalo country was, of course, west of the Cross Timbers and on the high plains, but it did not stop there. On the plains to the west, southwest and to the east and northeast of Waco, great herds of the bison grazed, by the hundreds and even by the thousands. In 1841, Kendall found them very numerous from Austin to a point westward of Waco.[32] Once, near modern Salado, he remarked that one could see " . . . nothing in any direction save the immense animals . . ."[33] For at least three days' travel to the north, Kendall observed that buffalo continued to be numerous. In the prairie that lies west of Cleburne, he stated that " . . . the buffalo had evidently been driven to the south."[34] No more buffalo were encountered until Kendall and his party had passed through the upper Cross Timbers, probably near the east line of Clay County.

Some ten months earlier, Colonel Cooke, with a military detachment, passed over a route near the present towns of Belton, Waco, and Waxahachie. He found buffalo "in abundance" from Belton to Waco, and again on the prairie to the southwest of the site of Waxahachie.[35] However, northward of this area game became so scarce that Colonel Cooke's soldiers were forced to eat their dogs, mules, and horses.[36] Supplementing Cooke's experiences, the diary of a Tennesseean who traveled through Texas in 1846 tells of some five hun-

31. Bolton, *Spanish Borderlands*, 75.
32. Kendall, *The Texan Santa Fe Expedition*, I, 79, 80, 87, 90.
33. *Ibid.*, I, 80.
34. *Ibid.*, I, 107.
35. Lucas and Hall, *History of Grayson County*, 45. The reference is to Colonel Cooke's Report.
36. *Ibid.*

dred buffalo in the prairie north of the site of Corsicana.[37]

Almost seventy years earlier, De Mézières made a journey that extended from the Trinity River westward and up the Brazos from the site of present-day Waco. He observed that the number of wild cattle was "incredible."[38] He passed over the same ground on other occasions and, with less definiteness of statement, seems to have found somewhat the same situation. De Mézières, at a later date, journeyed to the southwest of the Waco Village. His observations about buffalo in that area confirmed the statements of both Cooke and Kendall.[39] Also, this early-day Frenchman found buffalo along the San Antonio road, between the Colorado and Brazos rivers.[40] Probably these observers have left us something like the true limits of the portions of the buffalo country that are essential here.

Apparently the upper Cross Timbers served as a barricade to prevent the large herds of buffalo from ranging to the east. With a minor exception, to be noted later, those animals were very scarce, to say the least, from Red River south to the prairie about Waxahachie. However, coming from the plains of West Texas down the Colorado, and extending east to Waco and even far toward the Trinity, there was almost continuous prairie. Along this line, and over many millions of acres extending to the south and far down between the Colorado and Brazos, was once the range of the buffalo. More extended research would, doubtless, paint the picture in finer detail, but the present information will lend material assistance toward completing this study.

If one accepts the thesis that Moscoso did not enter the buffalo country, then it must follow: first, that he and his Spaniards did not reach the Colorado River;[41] second, that he did not reach the Brazos near Waco, or that he did not traverse the country east of Waco and south of Waxahachie; and third, that he did not go north of the Cross Timbers.

37. A copy of the diary of G. W. Day of Tennessee was furnished the writer through the courtesy of A. W. Neville of Paris, Texas. The diary was published in a 1930's copy of the *Paris News*. The date is not available.

38. Bolton, *De Mézières*, I, 293.

39. *Ibid.*, II, 279-280.

40. *Ibid.*, II, 188.

41. Almost the entire length of the Colorado River was either in the buffalo country, or so located that Moscoso must have passed through a portion of the buffalo range to have reached it.

From the above discussion it becomes apparent that to avoid the buffalo country entirely one is limited to two areas in which he might approach the Brazos. One of these begins some miles below Waco and extends to the Gulf of Mexico, a section properly termed the lower Brazos. It is difficult to believe that Moscoso's Spaniards entered an area so near the coast because all of the Indians contacted by these explorers on this last part of their journey displayed an utter lack of knowledge of the sea.[42]

The other area in which one might approach the Brazos and still avoid the buffalo country as delimited above is the span of that river west of Fort Worth that extends from a little above Graham to a little below Weatherford, a span of perhaps seventy miles by direct line measurements. This section cuts through the upper Cross Timbers and the Palo Pinto Mountains and includes the large, government-built Possum Kingdom Dam already referred to. It is the same area in which a few deer are still running wild, and is also the section previously noted beyond which natural food for Moscoso's hogs would have reached the vanishing point.

Plainly these studies of game-ranges throw the spotlight of probability on the Palo Pinto Mountains as the final point reached by the De Soto expedition. A careful observer may travel across the countryside and find in the Texas corn fields another bit of information that is perhaps equally illuminating, i. e., an imaginary line that divides the good corn country from the poor corn country which runs just west of Fort Worth. East of the line there is from three to ten times as much corn grown per county as just west of it, and corn production thins out to nearly nothing a hundred miles up the Brazos.[43]

42. Bourne, *De Mézières*, I, 174, 181.

43. According to the 1928 *Texas Almanac*, 222-224, corn production figures for 1924, in a block of fourteen counties that lie just east of the 98th Meridian and from Waco on the Brazos, northeast to Red River, showed an average of 650,000 bushels per county. The three westernmost of those counties were Montague, Wise and Parker, with a production of 442,000, 434,000, and 372,000 bushels, respectively.

Following the Brazos River upstream to the west of the 98th Meridian, corn production by counties was as follows: Palo Pinto, 128,000; Young, 82,000; Stephens, 40,000; Throckmorton, 10,000; Baylor, 40,000; Haskell, 30,000; Knox, 52,000; King, 2,800; Stonewall, 7,300; Dickens, 15,000; and Kent, 9,500. Obviously the west line of Parker County, which is almost identical with the 98th Meridian, was the point at which corn production made its sudden drop.

Figures for 1934 (which was a very poor corn year in Texas) show a similar line of contrast in corn production, except that the west boundary of the corn belt in that

Up the Red River, corn production is moderately successful almost to the hundredth meridian. Pioneer farmers tried industriously to raise corn in the country west of the "good corn belt" but the result was largely failure, and other feed crops were substituted.

One hundred and seventy years ago De Mézières found the villages of corn-producing Indians west of the Trinity, near present-day Waco, and a short distance up the Brazos from that point. But these villages stopped at the same imaginary line that now lies at the west edge of the good corn country.[44] Later the pressure of white population drove these Indians upstream into the upper Cross Timbers and finally into a reservation near the site of Graham, Texas. However, they must have had their difficulties with farm production, for a white agricultural expert was furnished[45] them throughout most of the history of the reservation.

The corn belt, probably the same as shown, both by modern statistical tables and by a glance at Indian geography of one hundred and seventy years ago, appears to have presented a very real problem to the Moscoso expedition of four hundred years ago. These Spaniards found corn in some measure wherever they went until they reached the village of Guasco; here there was enough corn to supply them on at least two occasions. At last, loaded with corn from this Indian village, they began the final ten-day march west toward the river Daycao. Apparently neither corn nor Indians were found along the route, and even though ten horsemen scoured the country ahead, there was no more corn to the west.[46] The Indians found west of the river did not farm at all, and were not even able to speak the language of any of the numerous captives which the Spaniards had collected from a vast range of corn-producing villages.[47] Between Guasco and

---

year was some thirty miles east of the 98th Meridian (see *The Texas Almanac for 1939-40*, 177-179).

44. Bolton, *De Mézières*, I, 283-297. The village of the Ouidsitas in 1772 was up the Brazos in a very dry area, beyond the corn belt. De Méziéres explains that the plentiful supply of meat was the reason why the village had not been abandoned.

45. *Record*, 1894, *No. 4, Original United States vs. The State of Texas*, 592. Dr. J. J. Sturn of Waco went among the Indians of the lower reservation near the site of Graham, Texas, in 1857. His capacity was that of farmer. He continued his stay among them as long as they were in Texas and moved with them to Fort Cobb in Indian Territory in 1859. Dr. Sturn married a Caddo Indian woman and continued to live among the people of that tribe.

46. Bourne, *De Soto*, I, 179.

47. *Ibid.*, I, 179; II, 37. Less than a peck of corn was found among these In-

the river Daycao, Moscoso and his men had evidently stepped over an economic boundary line. They had passed out of the corn belt and away from Indians who lived on corn into the area where red men lived on "flesh and fish."[48]

Such a boundary line, by all the standards which we are able to muster, lay just west of the site of Fort Worth and, by the same reasoning, the village of Guasco was not a great distance from Fort Worth itself, and the crossing on the river Daycao must have been a place on the Brazos somewhere to the west in the region of the Palo Pinto Mountains. In no other section of Texas does the Brazos enter the corn belt, and to assume that either the Trinity or the Colorado was the stream approached by the Spaniards leads one into difficulties that can hardly be explained away. The Trinity west of the corn belt is only a creek and the Colorado above that belt is so far into Central Texas that it is beyond the estimated range of Moscoso's journey.

Accepting the Palo Pinto Mountains area on the Brazos as the terminal point of the Spanish expedition, one may anchor one end of the Moscoso trail at that point and begin to study the route of that journey in reverse.

Indian villages were scattered along some portions of that route, and furnish the key to part of the search for the trail. Within the corn belt the Indian's plan of economy limited him to small portions of the vast acreage now cultivated by white men. He could not build his villages in the stream valleys that were subject to overflow, and his failure to obtain water by digging wells, or by other artificial means, prevented him from making use of most of the uplands. Thus, of the whole economic kingdom on which the white race has since waxed wealthy, he was denied all but a few fragments.

One of those fragments was the valley of Village Creek that lies some ten miles eastward and southeastward of Fort Worth. In 1841 it supported a Caddoan Indian population that ran well into the hundreds.[49] It ranges some sixty to ninety miles east of various parts of the Palo Pinto Mountains and, considering the slow speed of Moscoso's footmen, the two places were separated by a distance of about ten days' travel. By all the reckonings of space and direction, it was the

dians, and probably even that small amount was an importation since the Indians "neither planted nor gathered anything."

48. *Ibid.*, II, 37.

49. James T. De Shields, *Border Wars of Texas*, 355-359.

proper site for the community of Guasco. Other known village sites were southward on the Brazos,[50] and near and along another stream eastward of Waxahachie[51] that also is now called Village Creek—all of them miles too far from the Palo Pinto Mountains to blend into the picture left us of Moscoso's trail.

If the real Guasco of four hundred years ago was located on the Village Creek that now skirts the town of Fort Worth, it must have been isolated from similar habitations by a number of miles toward the northeast, for apparently history has not left a record of any large Indian community between that stream and the area near Greenville. That the Trinity River and many of its tributaries are subject to overflow is the probable reason why an area so rich in agricultural possibilities did not support a large population of corn-producing Indians. Immediately west of Greenville are the Caddo Forks[52] of the Sabine River. The name suggests that the area was once habitable for some of these agricultural Indians, and authoritative maps show that such Indians did live nearby at least a century and a half ago.[53]

Eastward of Greenville, the valleys of Sulphur and Cypress Rivers, subject to great inundations, were hardly suitable to the uses of crop-growing Indians. Still further to the east, in the section below Texarkana, is a condition known as the Raft in Red River where that great stream meanders across a flat country, formerly blocking its own course with logs and drift, and making habitation near its wide stream bed all but impossible.

However, to the north of Sulphur River, along the ridge between Paris and Texarkana and northward of that ridge on both sides of the valley of Red River, is an area where corn-producing Indians could supply their full requirements. The best evidence of this is not a review of theory but reference to the well-known historic fact that a whole chain of the villages of such Indians was once located in this section. Nearly two and a quarter centuries ago the Cadodachos lived

50. Bolton, De Mézières, I, 283-297.
51. Sketch Showing the Route of the Military Road from Red River to Austin, Wm. H. Hunt, Engineer, 1840. Drawn by H. L. Upshur, 1841. This old map is in the library of the University of Texas.
52. A plat accompanying the survey of the Central National Road of the Republic of Texas, dated 1844, in the State Land Office, lists these streams as the "Caddo" forks of the Sabine.
53. Fray J. A. Morfi, History of Texas, 1673-1770. Translated with biographical introduction and annotations by C. E. Castañeda (Albuquerque, 1935), map opposite p. 426.

along Red River,[54] above the site of Texarkana, in such numbers as to make it probable that they were the largest population of their kind anywhere near the northeast corner of Texas.

Moscoso came into a land, part of which was called Naguatex, that was very similar to the home of these Cadodacho Indians of known history. The Naguatex Indians were great corn farmers and they lived on both sides of a large river that, to the amazement of the Spaniards, stayed at flood stage for eight days when it had not rained for a whole month.[55] There is no stream except Red River anywhere near the northeast corner of Texas that has a large enough and long enough drainage area to have kept its banks full for so many days without a considerable amount of local rainfall.

Other evidence of similarity can be found between the land of the Naguatex and the land of the Cadodachos. Just four and a half days (say twenty-five to thirty miles of travel) before Moscoso came to Naguatex, he made some salt from a lake. About twenty-five miles north of Texarkana was once a great salt works that employed fifty boilers to turn out its product.[56]

Still another tie has been found between the land of the Naguatex Indians and the valley of Red River. These redmen of Moscoso's day were pottery-making Indians,[57] and such pottery has been found in modern times in the valley of Red River eastward of Paris.[58]

Another of the miscellany of common earmarks between Moscoso's route and the Red River country must be arrived at by indirection. During the two weeks after crossing the large stream (assumed here to be Red River), the Spaniards were several times treacherously led astray by Indian guides into *thickets*.[59] Certainly the inference is that if they had to be led astray into thickets they were normally traveling in a somewhat more open country, which could hardly have been to the south or southwest into the deep woods of East Texas. On the other hand, the ridge westward from Texarkana

54. Bolton, *Texas in the Middle Eighteenth Century*. Attached map.

55. Bourne, *De Soto*, I, 174.

56. Diary of G. W. Day. See footnote No. 37.

57. Bourne, *De Soto*, I, 183.

58. Neville to Williams, February 12, 1942. Mr. A. W. Neville of Paris, Texas, is editor of the *Paris News, author of The History of Lamar County*, and a long-time resident of that area.

59. Bourne, *De Soto*, I, 175; II, 37.

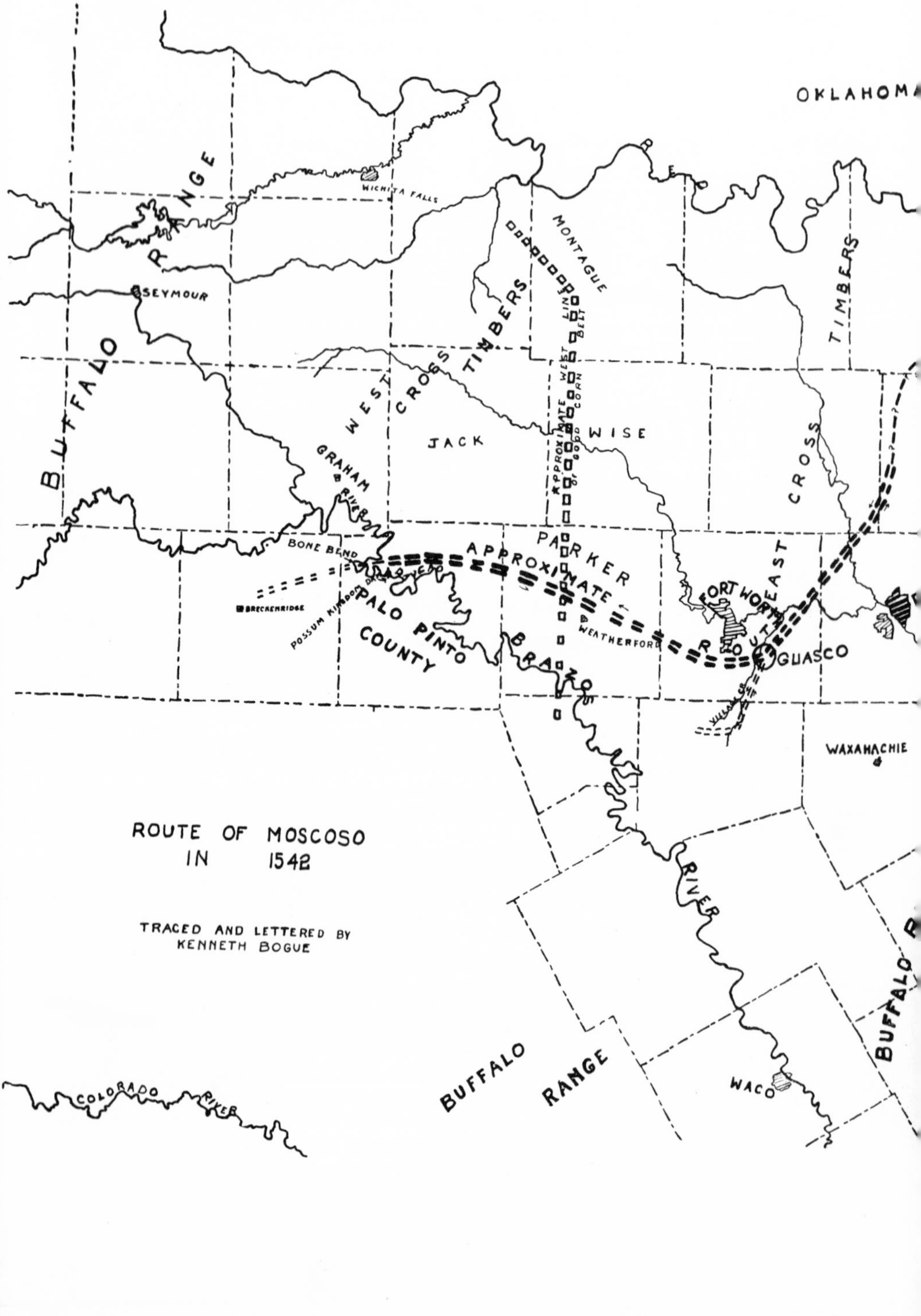

OKLAHOMA

BUFFALO RANGE

WICHITA FALLS

SEYMOUR

MONTAGUE

WEST CROSS TIMBERS

TIMBERS

CROSS

JACK

WISE

APPROXIMATE WEST CORN LINE

GRAHAM RIVER

PARKER

BONE BEND

APPROXIMATE

FORT WORTH

BRECKENRIDGE

POSSUM KINGDOM

PALO PINTO COUNTY

BRAZOS

WEATHERFORD

ROUTE

SOUTHEAST CROSS

GUASCO

VILLAGES

WAXAHACHIE

ROUTE OF MOSCOSO
IN   1542

TRACED AND LETTERED BY
KENNETH BOGUE

RIVER

BUFFALO

BUFFALO   RANGE

WACO

COLORADO   RIVER

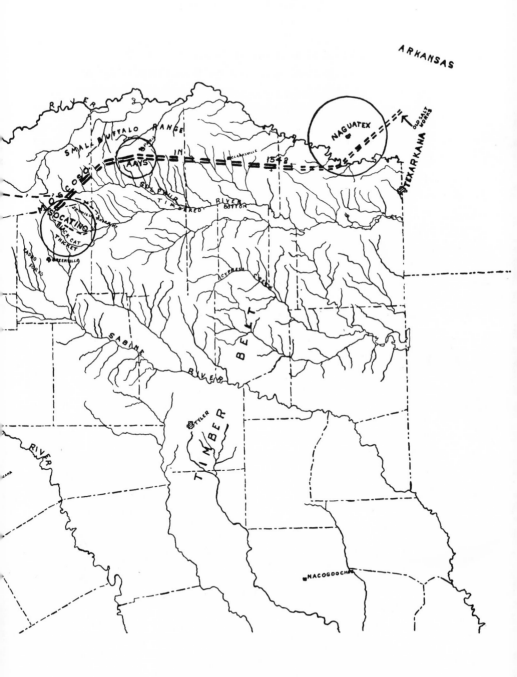

and reaching beyond Paris was a somewhat open country, flanked, however, on the south by the thickly timbered bottom of Sulphur River, which could have furnished thickets equal to the wildest dreams of mischief-making Indian guides.

In this connection, it should be remembered that about ten days' travel (probably from fifty to one hundred miles) after crossing the stream that must have been Red River, the Spaniards saw some buffalo at a place called Aays (or Hais).[60] The evidence is unmistakable that buffalo once grazed along the prairies to the east and west of Paris.[61] If these animals at any time grazed within fifty to one hundred miles in any other direction from the land once occupied by the Cadodacho villages, or say Texarkana for convenience, the writer has been unable to find the evidence. If the heavily wooded section of East Texas that lies to the south and southwest of Texarkana has ever been the range of the buffalo the fact seems not to have been handed down to modern historians.

Assuming that Aays was somewhere near the site of Paris, the route of Moscoso, a little farther along its course, also fits the topography of that part of Texas. Three days' travel from Aays the Spaniards came to a place called Socatino, which was among "close forests."[62] The country to the northeast of Greenville was once covered by the Black Cat thicket and the Jernigan Thicket which, together, made it a veritable jungle.[63] Possibly this was the site of Socatino.

Here it is convenient to call attention to the three phases of Moscoso's journey in Texas and to note, as far as possible, the direction of travel in each case. During the first phase of this journey, from Naguatex to Socatino, the explorers were probably traveling nearly west.[64] A significant statement from the Elvas account informs us that three days after crossing the large river in Naguatex, an Indian guide

---

60. *Ibid.*, II, 36-37.

61. A. W. Neville, *The History of Lamar County,* 68. The Neville history quotes a report of 1849 made by John Barrow and Dr. Edward Smith. The essential part of that quotation is as follows: " . . . buffalo had been plenty about the prairies near Paris, Clarksville and Bonham."

62. Bourne, *De Soto,* II, 37.

63. Personal interview with J. B. Jetter, Wichita Falls, Texas, an early resident of the Greenville area.

64. Bourne, *De Soto,* I, 75.

was hanged for leading the party "east" instead of "west."[65] On the second phase of the journey, stretching from Socatino to Guasco, the Elvas statement indicates that the Spaniards were traveling southward,[66] but Biedma gives the impression that there was a confusion of directions which, during the last six days of this leg of the journey, terminated "in a direction south and southwest."[67] If the two accounts can be taken to mean that the net direction was toward the southwest, they will harmonize with the general observation made elsewhere in the Elvas narrative, namely, that the direction of travel was "always westwardly."[68] A third phase of the journey, after a short side trip, led westward from Guasco to the river Daycao.[69]

These three phases of Moscoso's journey and the direction of travel indicated are in harmony with the route of the expedition as presented in this paper. Briefly stated, and with a few details that have not been previously mentioned, that route, as suggested here, crossed Red River not many miles above Texarkana, passed near Clarksville, Paris and Greenville, and, after some wandering about, reached the eastern edge of the lower Cross Timbers, possibly west of the site of McKinney. From here, following in a southward direction along the margin of this timber belt, the trail reached Village Creek southeast of Fort Worth, at the village known as Guasco. Here there was a detour southward up Village Creek, but the trail returned to Guasco and finally passed toward the west near the sites of Fort Worth and Weatherford. The route continued westward near Possum Kingdom Dam and came to a final halt in Bone Bend (on the Brazos) near the northwest corner of Palo Pinto County.

Certainly this statement of a route contains minute details for which there is no absolute proof, but there is a somewhat plausible reason for each. Passing over the east end of the route as far as the lower Cross Timbers without additional comment, one may ask why the suggestion that the Spaniards followed the edge of this timber belt southward to Guasco. The answer seems to be that Biedma reveals that these explorers were traveling south and southwest when they concluded the second phase of their journey, and it is a physical fact that the eastern edge of the lower Cross Timbers approaches

65. *Ibid.*
66. *Ibid.*, I, 177.
67. *Ibid.*, II, 37.
68. *Ibid.*, I, 182.
69. *Ibid.*, I, 178.

Village Creek in the very direction stated by Biedma.[70] Even the supposed detour up Village Creek is in harmony with the fact of known history that Indian habitations were stretched for miles up that stream in 1841.[71]

From a point on Village Creek southeast of Fort Worth (at the place which seems probable as the location of Guasco) the suggestion here that Moscoso's route extended up the Brazos to a horseshoe curve called Bone Bend, requires additional clarification. Up that very route was a long forgotten horse path over which some of the gold seekers of 1849 traveled to California.[72] Much of the path followed well-beaten Indian trails that led to Bone Bend. The *Northern Standard* of Clarksville recommended it as one of the two routes from North Texas to California.[73] It was undoubtedly a natural path, for no road workers had preceded the California-bound emigrants. Much of this route appears on the *Arrowsmith map* of 1841 as a Comanche Indian trail to East Texas.[74] In the 1940s a very old crucifix and a string of rosary beads were discovered near this trail in the Possum Kingdom Dam area.[75] This discovery may be evidence of early communication between the old missions of East Texas and points up the Brazos.

Even before the period of these missions, La Salle found Comanche Indians in an East Texas village with loot which they had stolen in Santa Fe.[76] But one hundred and fifty years before La Salle, Moscoso himself found turquoise and cotton shawls at Guasco that had come from the direction of the sunset.[77] Guasco, near the west edge of the corn belt and the last town west of all the farming Indians, should

70. The Peters Colony Map of 1852 in the Texas State Land Office shows an early road that branched from the Preston-Austin road, and passed by Bird's Fort on its southwesterly course, missing Village Creek (then Caddo Creek) by less than a mile. This route, as shown by the old map, followed the east edge of the lower Cross Timbers and, in view of this fact of topography, was probably a trail used by Indians and white men alike.

71. De Shields, *Border Wars of Texas*, 355-359.

72. *Northern Standard*, Clarksville, Texas, February 16, 1850.

73. *Northern Standard*, Clarksville, Texas, March 2, 1850.

74. John Arrowsmith, *Map of Texas, compiled from surveys recorded in the Land Office of Texas and other official surveys* (London, 1841).

75. McDonald to Williams, November 27, 1941. A. J. McDonald, formerly of Graham, Texas, discovered these relics. Through his courtesy, the writer obtained a photograph of the crucifix.

76. Francis Parkman, *La Salle and the Discovery of the Great West*, 414.

77. Bourne, *De Soto*, I, 181.

certainly have had first contact with a trade from the area near the turquoise mines of New Mexico. Is it possible that this trade route from Guasco to New Mexico, the Indian trail down the Brazos to East Texas and Moscoso's route from Guasco to—shall we say Bone Bend—were, in part, the same dirt road?

Permitting the question to rest on the information already presented, let us turn for a moment to a consideration of the elements of time and distance involved in the three phases of this journey. From Naguatex to Socatino required about fifteen days' travel; from Socatino to Guasco required twenty days; and from that place to the river Daycao required ten days.[78] These points, as interpreted in this study, were apart by about one hundred and twenty miles, seventy miles and eighty miles, respectively. Plainly, the middle section is out of proportion to the remainder of the journey, but the lack of a consistent direction of travel on this leg of the journey, and the difficulty of obtaining food (corn) at the end of each day offer a reasonable explanation.

Leaving these more minute details of route for whatever they seem to be worth, it should be noted that in this study Moscoso's trail has been studied largely by attempting to eliminate certain portions of Texas from the area visited. To have stayed far away from the sea,

78. From the Elvas account of Moscoso's journey (Bourne, De Soto, I, 169-180) a time table may be constructed without great error. The Spaniards came to a place near Naguatex, either on the 20th or 22nd of July, 1542, and reached the river Daycao " . . . the beginning of October . . . " following. This time interval is about 75 to 80 days. Most of these days are definitely accounted for; it was one day from this first point to Naguatex; then 10 days were spent resting near a river in Naguatex; the horsemen spent an unknown amount of time investigating and forcing their way about Naguatex; for two days Moscoso awaited an answer to his message to the chief of Naguatex; one day later the chief came to Moscoso; four days longer Moscoso waited before he resumed his journey (it is possible this time overlapped the three days during which he awaited and received the Chief of Naguatex); eight days' rise on [Red] River caused further delay; for "some" days he awaited the cacique, but finally he burned the towns and received guides; it was three days' travel to Nissohone; it was two days' travel to Lacane; it was an unknown time (probably but a day or two) to Nondacao; it was five days to Aays; then three days to Socatino; then twenty days to Guasco; an unknown time to Naquiscoca; two days to Nacacahoz; the horsemen hunted Christians possibly one day; possibly two days back to Guasco; then ten days to the river Daycao. The total days accounted for is either seventy-one or seventy-four, depending on the meaning of the language of one of the passages. Obviously it accounts specifically for nearly all the time between July 20 and "the beginning of October."

out of the buffalo country and at the same time not to have exceeded the limits of the section where there was food for the herd of hogs, Moscoso's trail was limited to a relatively small portion of North Texas. This area was almost a rectangle one hundred miles wide by three hundred miles long. It lay north of the site of Waxahachie and east of Graham, and if Moscoso remained within it he could travel no other direction except "always westerly" as stated by the Gentleman of Elvas.

On the positive side of the picture, Moscoso did go far enough toward the southwest corner of this rectangle to reach a river at some place beyond the corn belt and in the heart of the deer country. The translation of the Elvas narrative employed by the United States De Soto Expedition Commission includes language concerning this deer country that hardly leaves any room for one to doubt its location. According to this translation, the Indians of Guasco recommended that Moscoso go to a place on the river Daycao "where they sometimes went to hunt in the mountains and to kill deer."[79] This language can hardly have an ambiguous meaning, for the only place in the northeast half of Texas where there are mountains along a river is in and near Palo Pinto County, west of Fort Worth. Moscoso did as directed and concluded his journey in those mountains. Since the study of his entire trail depends heavily on this western anchorage, perhaps the few significant words of the above translation, when taken with the chief considerations of this study, do much to drag the route of Moscoso into plain daylight.

79. The *Report of the United States De Soto Expedition Commission*, 263.

V

SPANISH EXPLORATION PRELIMINARY TO

TEXAS SETTLEMENT

The real live story of Texas did not begin with Cabeza de Vaca, Moscoso, Coronado or even with Mendoza. It did begin at the Creek of the Crows down in present Maverick County, Texas, in late afternoon April 2, 1689. Here the curtain rose on what was to be—with only short interruptions—a continuous drama throughout the centuries to come. No longer would Texas experience an expedition, then a permanent withdrawal and finally a long period of silence after which some other expedition would appear only to withdraw and be forgotten. Those who camped at the Creek of the Crows on this April afternoon were Spaniards and their aides, just as were those who had composed many previous intrusions into Texas. But this time the campers camped as the embodiment of a new policy which the government of Spain was beginning to formulate. Momentarily we shall need to turn aside to explain the background of this strange episode—but soon we will return to this unusual story that began at the Creek of the Crows.

There was forward movement—and often excitement—in the story of Texas after 1689. Previously, this land to the northeast of Mexico had produced neither gold nor silver. It looked like a poor place to spend the king's money. But, oddly enough, the event that started the hands of the clock in Texas had nothing to do with either gold or silver.

In 1685, the French under La Salle had established a colony (Fort St. Louis) near Matagorda Bay—not far from the coast. Apparently, La Salle had lost his way at sea and made his settlement too far west, but not understanding his (probable) motive the Spaniards were aroused as by a stroke of lightning. Quite obviously, Spain could no longer feel secure in holding Texas as a speculator might hold a vacant lot. Henceforth it would require settlements, forts, missions—any or all of these to assert ownership. Nor would it do to set up these institutions far up in the back country. Spain must guard the gateway both among the pines at the border of East Texas and near the bays and bayous along the coast. It must have saddened Mendoza and Father Lopez to know that their mission San Clemente, up in the land of bubbling springs and singing rivers, must give way to these efforts on the far-flung outlines of Texas. As it turned out, it was more than 150 years later when permanent settlements were brought to the banks of the Llano on which the Mendoza-Lopez mission was built.

But back to the party of Spaniards who were camped on the Creek of the Crows down in present Maverick County, Texas. Alonzo de Leon, governor of Coahuila, was head of the party, with orders from the Spanish government to hunt out La Salle's colony and destroy it. On two previous occasions, de Leon had tried to follow the coast of Texas in his search for the colony, but each time he had encountered large bodies of water which he was unable to cross. This time he had come far inland and crossed the Rio Grande about thirty miles below the site of present day Eagle Pass. Apparently he planned to cross the Texas rivers far up from the coast where he could ford them, and at the proper time turn down between rivers to the coast and La Salle's colony.

De Leon had come from Monclova in the interior of Coahuila southwest of the present Eagle Pass, Texas, and crossed the Rio Grande near where the mission San Juan Bautista was to be located 13 years later. It was on the second of April, 1689, as stated above, that he had come to his first camping place within the present boundaries of Texas. Great flocks of crows—some 3000 in number—settled down in the area near his camp. The creek at that place is still known as Cuervo Creek—which meant the Creek of the Crows. In fact, it is said locally that even now the crows often fly over from Mexico late in the day and roost in the area.

The route of the Spaniards all the way from the Rio Grande to the Gulf of Mexico is of special interest to us here as we are studying the origin of the various Spanish roads in Texas. Did de Leon open one or more of these roads? If not, did his exploration contribute indirectly toward making this early road system? And in this connection, if not de Leon, who did open each of the several old Spanish Roads? Also, as a companion piece to this last question, exactly (or as nearly as is possible to answer) what was the route of each of these old roads? Since transportation in general and roads in particular play such a vital part in the development of any country it appears quite obvious that this study of roads becomes in part a new approach to the history of Texas. So let us return to de Leon's journey into this new country.

It was eighteen leagues from the Rio Grande to de Leon's crossing of the Nueces River, southeast of present day La Pryor, Texas, among the pecan groves from which de Leon gave the river its name. The crossing was at a good pecan grove well above the places where the later old Spanish roads from Mexico to San Antonio were to cross the Nueces. Both the upper and the lower Presidio roads, as we shall learn to call them later, crossed the Nueces below the pecan belt. Other facts about de Leon's journey show that he did not open either of these Presidio roads which are well known to historians.

Continuing with de Leon's journey, it was seven leagues northeastward from the Nueces to the Leona River; the Spaniards called it the Rio Sarco—or in English the Blue River. The Leona flows out of the ground at the south edge of Uvalde, Texas. Its waters are clear and blue just as de Leon reported, and it is the only river down in the flat country and near the Nueces that *is* clear and blue—although at present it is not quite the clear, deep blue that it was some decades ago when the writer first saw it. Earlier this little river was blue almost as far down as the village of Batesville. Obviously de Leon must have crossed the little stream above Batesville—a fact that again shows plainly that this Spanish expedition was travelling well to the north of both of the later Presidio roads. For even the upper Presidio road crossed the Leona some fifteen miles below Batesville and the lower Presidio road passed through the country far to the southeast of the mouth of the Leona—more than fifty miles southeast of Batesville.

De Leon had now travelled four days (and twenty-five leagues) inland from the Rio Grande. On the fifth day he moved five leagues northeastward from the Leona to the Frio. He named this river the Hondo, which was exactly what he should have called it. The banks, so he said, were forty feet high—and remember that in Spanish Hondo means *deep*. Here was a river, set deep down between high bluff banks—a description which makes its identification certain. The Frio from a point southwest of present-day Sabinal all the way down past old Frio Town—a distance of more than twenty miles—flows between bluff banks that are forty, fifty and even as much as sixty feet high. No other stream in this area below the hill country even remotely answers this description.

Some way the names of several of the rivers in this area seem to have been moved one space to the east. The Leona, a stream of cold spring water, was long known to the Indians as the Frio (cold). The name now applies to the next river to the east, the stream with the high bluff banks. The river which we now call the Frio is (near its source) a stream of very cold spring water. But the great volume of clear blue cold water sinks into the earth at the fault-line some twenty miles north of Uvalde and never reaches this area of the high bluff banks. Nevertheless, this stream with the high banks is now known as the Frio. Also, the name Hondo has moved east to the next river. The stream that rises up in the hill country in present Bandera and Medina counties and flows southward into the Frio about ten miles northwest of Pearsall, Texas, is now known as the Hondo. It is the name originally given by de Leon to the river with the high banks.

Now since the Leona is next in order past the Nueces and is the only blue river in the immediate area and since the Frio is the only stream with the bluff banks, we can map this part of the route of de Leon within narrow limits. Remember, it was five leagues from the Leona to the Frio. It is a greater distance than five leagues from the Leona at Batesville across country northeast to the Frio and remember that de Leon went at least four leagues southeastward down the Frio and appears to have crossed there—which would have been near the lower end of the part of the stream where the banks were high. Then he travelled east and sometimes a little to the north of east until he reached a large river which he named the Medina. It was twenty-one leagues from the Frio to the Medina. For the last twelve leagues of that distance the description given in the old Spanish diary points out an area that can hardly be mistaken. First, at a stream which the Spaniards called the ''arroyo del vino'' there were wild grapes, oaks and pecans or walnuts.

The party continued to find the oaks and nut-bearing trees as they travelled the twelve leagues from the *arroyo del vino* most of the way to the Medina River. Here within that twelve leagues they traversed the large sandy and timbered belt that lies mostly in Atascosa County south of San Antonio for there is nothing else near at hand and in line with de Leon's route that can qualify.

More than that, the high point on the west bank at the crossing of the river is fifty to sixty feet high, just as the Spaniards reported. It is about three miles south of Floresville ready to speak for itself. But the thing that ties it all together is some evidence in the ravines a short distance eastward of the river crossing. After de Leon had crossed the river and moved a short distance beyond, he began to cross ravines in which he found exposures of "red and yellow earth." These exposures of red and yellow earth now speak for themselves just southeast of Floresville. Here they lie in a narrow belt not more than three miles wide. This belt is hemmed in on the south by an area of land that ranges from dark to black—and on the north this belt of red earth gives way to a soil that is very sandy. The timber belt from Devine to Poteet and eastward, the high ground west of the San Antonio River and the zone of red and yellow earth exposure south of Floresville are telltale land marks that roughly chart the path of de Leon into the country eastward of Floresville, and that with little room for doubt.

The Spaniards rode on until they reached a stream south of San Antonio which de Leon called the Medina, which is now known as the San Antonio River. The beautiful west branch of the San Antonio that lies west and northwest of San Antonio is still called the Medina River. Apparently, as the site of San Antonio and the city founded there grew in importance, the name, San Antonio, became the name of the river from the city all the way to the Gulf.

A smaller stream that lies east of Floresville was called Leon Creek by de Leon because the Spaniards found a dead lion near by. The name of this creek, which he crossed two or three miles below the bridge on State Highway 97, has been changed to Cibolo, and strangely, the name Leon now applies to a stream within Bexar County that lies east of the present Medina, and just west of San Antonio. Could a misunderstanding of the route of de Leon have brought about this shuffling of names?

But we must return to the job of following de Leon's route. The distance from the river at Floresville to the Guadalupe was slightly more than sixteen leagues if we borrow from the de Leon diary of 1690—for he and his Spaniards travelled this route again in 1690. This data of 1690 is somewhat easier to follow here than that of 1689. It was eleven leagues eastward to a place where the Spaniards camped on a stream of brackish water. It was then five additional leagues to de Leon's camp that was just west of the Guadalupe. Now the place where the Spaniards had to drink brackish water must have been on Salty Creek in west central Gonzales County. There is an extreme westward bend of Salty Creek that just fits the statistics of distance and direction given in the old diary. Had the Spaniards camped very far either above or below this bend on Salty Creek their statistics of distance just wouldn't fit the map.

This places de Leon's crossing of the Guadalupe just west of the village of Hochheim above Cuero where Highway 183 also crosses the Guadalupe. To pinpoint de Leon's old crossing like that sounds too good to be true—but wait just a minute! Let's check the facts and see how near these can be to de Leon's old crossing. First, the line of travel from the river crossing south of Floresville to the bend on Salty Creek continues slightly north of east and strikes the Guadalupe very near this place. Second, the Pressler and Langermann map of Texas dated 1879 shows that an old road forded the Guadalupe at almost exactly the same place and that no other road is shown that crosses near there. Surely the old map pictured the ford where nature had put it—neither had de Leon followed any crew of road workers when he crossed the Guadalupe there in 1689 and 1690.

On his journey of 1690, de Leon with twenty picked men, left his camp near this old ford and during his first day travelled southward fourteen leagues. Next day he continued southward—came to Garcitas Creek, finally down stream to La Salle's old fort, and burned the fort. Still the same day he moved the two leagues down the creek to the mouth of that stream at Lavaca Bay and turned back up Garcitas Creek past the fort after he had completed his second day's travel, which was also fourteen leagues. During de Leon's third day of travel he moved northward twenty leagues back to his camp near the ford of the Guadalupe. Now add his three days' travel down to the bay and back and you find that the total was forty-eight leagues. One way it would have been half of forty-eight or twenty-four leagues. But a little (less than six leagues) of his last day he detoured off of his direct route. If he lost six leagues, in so doing his round trip would have amounted to only forty-two leagues. One way would have been twenty-one leagues.

So it was between twenty-one and twenty-four estimated leagues of travel from de Leon's Camp (near the ford of the Guadalupe) to the mouth of Garcitas Creek on Lavaca Bay. Map measurements show that distance to be about twenty-one leagues!

It should be understood here that in 1689 de Leon made this journey from the Rio Grande to the Guadalupe and then continued down near the Gulf to La Salle's fort, and that he returned by the same route to the Rio Grande. Also it should be understood that a year later he retraced his steps of 1689 to the Guadalupe and also retraced his steps to La Salle's fort. This time he carried out his orders to burn the old fort.

He returned from the ashes of the fort to his camp on the Guadalupe, but he did not return immediately to the Rio Grande. This time he turned northeastward from the Guadalupe and after nearly 100 leagues of travel he set up the first Spanish mission in East Texas, known as San Francisco de los Tejas. It was located in northeast Houston County near the present day village of Weches.

De Leon actually travelled much more than 100 leagues between the Guadalupe and this first mission because of his several detours to contact Indians who might aid in his search for Frenchmen who had strayed off from La Salle's settlement. Most of these side trips seemed to have been completed by the time he had reached the Brazos River. Between the Brazos and the Trinity his log of travel shows 23 leagues which is the actual estimate of distance by his route. Note in this connection that a straight line measured on the map from Navasota near the Brazos to the Robbins Ferry Crossing on the Trinity is an even 20 leagues.

Between this crossing on the Trinity and the mission near Weches is 18 leagues by the de Leon log. Considering that these logged distances were only estimates, this again must be very near the correct distance. But along this 18 leagues between the Trinity and the old mission the de Leon diary gives us a surprise. It was just a little more than seven leagues northeast of the Trinity where de Leon made contact with the first pine trees—or at least that was where he first mentioned pines. This is just as one finds the countryside along Highway 21 between the Trinity River and the town of Crockett today—no pines along or near the road until one approaches Crockett. There are pines, perhaps, two or three miles to the right or left of the road, but none by the roadside until near Crockett. Very likely de Leon in the year 1690 travelled very near this segment of State Highway 21. After several trips through the countryside of Houston County, the writer has not found another such corridor without pines extending northeastward from the Trinity anywhere else in Houston County. This fact should add some weight to the belief that part of de Leon's route follows near Highway 21 at least in southwest Houston County.

It may be interesting to note in this connection that the old La Bahia Road can be found in old land records that reach back to the days of the Republic of Texas. That old road crossed the Trinity at or near the place where Highway 21 now crosses the Trinity. It crossed the Brazos just below the mouth of the Navasota at present Washington-on-the-Brazos.

In other words, the pathway between the pines that helps us to know that de Leon probably travelled near Highway 21 and Midway to Crockett is no help at all in charting his course northeast of Crockett because in that area there are pines almost everywhere. In other words, the kind of trees mentioned will do little to help us determine the route of this Spanish expedition near or beyond Crockett.

But another fact helps us to chart de Leon's route beyond Crockett. He established a mission (San Francisco de los Tejas) near the end of his journey and after he had gone back to Mexico, another mission (Santísimo Nombre de María) was established nearby over northwestward on the west bank of the Neches River. The most exact data from which we might locate these missions did not come from de Leon's diary. [The information comes from the diary of Don Domingo Terán de los Rios, who camped at the second mission on the banks of the Neches in 1691, that we find some mathematical data.] When Terán left the mission on the banks of the Neches he travelled one league down the river valley in a direction south southeast and crossed the river at that point.

Thus, we know that the Neches River flows south southeast for one league from the mission Santísimo Nombre de María. Actually, this is more help to us than it seems, for Highway 21 northeastward of Crockett crosses the river in a bend that is just one league across. Terán could have crossed this bend with his road one league in length and in a direction 30° to 40° east of south and could have crossed the river at the end of the league. Above this river bend the Neches flows almost due east for a number of miles—and below the bend for several miles the meanders of the river are irregular and the one league journey would not fit its course. Thus, many specific measurements make strongly for the conclusion that the bend of the river crossed by Terán was the same as the bend now crossed by Highway 21. The fact that the oldest surveyed road also crossed in this bend almost shuts the door against any other conclusion.

This would place the second of the East Texas missions between a half mile and a mile above the river bridge on Highway 21. At this point let me add that Terán also reported that the first of the missions was a league and a half southwest of the second mission. Another report says two leagues. This would place the San Francisco mission somewhere northward of Highway 21 in the vicinity of the village of Weches in northeast Houston County. This, of course, was the terminal point of de Leon's journey. He travelled many leagues along or near the route of the later road from Nacogdoches to Goliad that was to become known as the La Bahia road. But there seems to be no evidence that his route was used as a road for many decades after his journey.

Next of the Spanish expeditions to the East Texas mission was that of Don Domingo Terán de los Rios only a year after the foregoing journey of de Leon. Terán charted his own course almost completely different from this route of his predecessor. He was not even willing to accept the names that de Leon had applied. As a result, nearly all of the place names given by Terán have fallen by the wayside. However, either the diary of Terán or that of Father Massanet who accompanied him reported a few names from the Indians or from the French that have survived.

De Leon did not open any of the Spanish road system in Texas, but he pioneered a route so close to the old road from LaGrange to the village of Weches that one wishes he might credit the road to that Spanish gentleman.

In somewhat similar fashion Terán was in part the forerunner of those who opened the first (and now almost forgotten) old San Antonio Road to East Texas. That first actual old road to the East Texas missions came twenty-five years later than Terán but it is not impossible that those who made the road fell into Terán's trace at the Navasota River and followed it at intervals all the way to the missions.

Terán must have travelled not far from the later route of one or the other of the two old San Antonio roads part of the way between present day San Antonio and the Colorado River—but it would be difficult to prove that he made as much as a single mile of either of those roads in that area. Not very many pages ahead we shall attempt to explain more thoroughly Terán's relation to the roads across Texas. Also, before the end of this chapter the evidence will be piled rather high to show that there were two old roads from San Antonio to the place that is now Nacogdoches—and that the one of those roads that is almost completely forgotten is much older than the one which we usually call "The Old San Antonio Road."

Now, let us go back briefly and review the events of Terán's expedition all the way from the Rio Grande to East Texas. His score both as to place names and road making will become a little clearer as we review that journey.

Terán seems to have had objections to using any of de Leon's names for Texas rivers. Instead of calling the large river at the west edge of the present map of Texas the Rio Grande as de Leon had called it, he gave it the name Rio del Norte which was actually, even then, another name for the great river. But that was the nearest he came to using de Leon's terminology. He changed the names of all the creeks and rivers as he came to them, but since his new names failed to live, we need not repeat them.

He crossed the Nueces river in the pecan belt and continued northeastward to the Frio, apparently in de Leon's very tracks, but beyond that stream he struck out on his own "travelling in a different direction." He seems to have crossed the Sabinal and thereafter to have stayed far north of de Leon's route to the Medina. Terán called this latter river "San Antonio de Padua" but there is no doubt but that it was actually the Medina. Terán told of the "cypresses" along the banks of the stream—and the Medina is the one and only river in the ninety mile spread between the Sabinal and the Guadalupe that has these trees along its banks.

Five leagues east of the Medina the expedition came to an "intermittent arroyo"—evidently it was Leon Creek—certainly it was not the San Antonio River, a stream that never stops flowing. Four leagues east of Leon Creek, Terán came to "an arroyo with water, which is hot and salty." In this arroyo there was "a rock with an opening from which fine cold water runs." This arroyo, of course, was Salado Creek at a point to the northeast of downtown San Antonio. Now the San Antonio River lies between Leon Creek and Salado Creek and the head springs at this very beautiful ever-flowing stream are in Brackenridge Park which is in San Antonio. How did Terán and his Spaniards miss this showpiece among Texas rivers? The answer is simple. They undoubtedly went a little to the north of it and apparently never saw it! They travelled among the low hills at the south edge of the San Antonio hill country but they saw much higher hills to the north.

This party of Spaniards probably crossed the Guadalupe a few miles below present-day New Braunfels but Terán with four companions visited the Indian villages up at the "head springs." Apparently the head springs are those now in Landa Park at the edge of New Braunfels.

Crossing the river now known as the San Marcos at some point which we shall not attempt to identify, the Spaniards finally reached the banks of the Colorado somewhere between present-day Austin and Bastrop. Down near the Gulf of Mexico, de Leon had called this river the San Marcos, but the diaries of this expedition also made it known that the French called the stream the Colorado.

Terán turned down this river a total distance of some ten or eleven leagues. He crossed the stream where he first touched, it but only a league or two below, he crossed back to the west side of the river again and moved on downstream a half dozen leagues before he made camp. Within this half dozen leagues he passed the little pine belt that is on no other river except the Colorado anywhere west of the Trinity River country. Quite plainly the pines identify this large river as the Colorado of today. Also, the fact that the pines were passed within eight leagues (apparently a little less) below his first contact with the stream would make it certain that he had first touched the Colorado above Bastrop which is a well known point within the little pine belt of the Colorado.

We can be sure that Terán did not blaze the trail for either of the old San Antonio roads between present San Antonio and the Colorado River, for as we have seen, he passed above the site of San Antonio and reached the Colorado between these two old San Antonio roads. As we shall see later one of these old roads crossed the Colorado at Bastrop while the other crossed at the edge of Austin.

That Terán sent a detachment of soldiers with a pack train to pick up supplies which were to be shipped to him from Mexico to Matagorda Bay, that he crossed the Colorado to the east side and camped farther down the river and that the pack train did not stay at the bay long enough to pick up the supplies—all are part of the facts of his expedition but have little bearing on the relation of Terán's journey to the old Spanish road system of Texas.

From his camping place on the east side of the Colorado moving northward Terán crossed the prairie in which the town of Caldwell now holds a central spot. The old trail that is now referred to as the "Old San Antonio Road" passed eastward through the present-day Caldwell and continued in the prairie to the Brazos River. Terán, many years ahead of this famous road, passed northward across its course and moved on out of the prairie into the heavy timber before he turned down to cross the Brazos.

From his crossing of the Brazos, which was, of course, north of the route of the "Old San Antonio Road," he moved to the northeast and crossed the Navasota probably on the west line of present Leon County. Just east of the Navasota, he passed through a narrow belt of timber and camped at a good lake of water. The description is strangely similar to the "Santa Anna" Lake that became a famous camping place on the first old road that led to the East Texas missions.

Continuing his northeastward journey, Terán travelled among the hills and (for a half dozen leagues) through the pines as he came to the Trinity River. Now, both pines and hills are plentiful in Leon County north of the route of the "Old San Antonio Road" but both are missing along that road down in Madison County. Evidently Terán, as he approached the Trinity River, was travelling parallel to the Old San Antonio Road, but his route lay north of it.

Beyond the Trinity Terán moved eastward only eleven leagues until he came to the first of the East Texas missions. This is the shortest approach from the Trinity reported by any expedition. It could not be true unless he crossed the Trinity east of today's town of Centerville (in Leon County) and travelled in a direct line to the old mission. But both the diary of Terán and that of Father Massanet report almost exactly the same distance—and that at a time when the two leaders were acting independently of each other because of strained relations. The segment of the Trinity River east of Centerville and north of Highway 7 is nearer to this first old mission than any other part of the Trinity.

De Leon travelled nearly eighteen leagues from the Trinity to the first old mission as against Terán's eleven leagues. Surely the two went by different routes. Later parties of Spaniards travelled more than eleven but less than eighteen leagues between the two points. From these facts it would seem that Terán followed very little of the path of any later route or road east of the Trinity, but between the Navasota and the Trinity he may have laid out parts of the first Spanish road to east Texas.

Now, let us turn back to a small expedition that explored some of Texas from the Rio Grande to the Colorado in 1709. This was the Espinosa-Olivares-Aguirre expedition consisting of just seventeen men.

The foregoing Terán expedition took place in 1691. In 1693 the East Texas missions were abandoned. Then there was a period of waiting but there were anxious padres all the while. In 1702 the churchmen had established the mission at San Juan Bautista some thirty miles down the Rio Grande from present day Eagle Pass. It was only about five miles west of the river and would serve as the focal point of much that was to take place in Texas in future years.

A little expedition left that mission in 1709 with the purpose of gaining some knowledge of the abandoned mission field in East Texas. Fourteen soldiers headed by two churchmen, Fray Isidro de Espinosa and Fray Antonio de Olivares and Captain Pedro de Aguirre. This little party set out on April 5 for the Colorado River hoping to meet some of the East Texas Indians at that point. The hoped-for meeting of Indians did not take place, but from other Indians some of the desired information was obtained.

But over and above their actual objective this little group of seventeen made for themselves a page in Texas history. They seem to have followed the first part of de Leon's route—across the Rio Grande, the Nueces, the Leona and on to the river that is now the Frio southwest of the present town of Sabinal. They called the Leona the Sarco as de Leon had done, but explained that the Indians called it the Frio. Also, they used de Leon's name, Hondo, for the next river, but as explained earlier, the reader knows the name, Frio, was later applied to the stream then known as the Hondo.

Using present day names, the Espinosa party crossed the Frio on April 9 and went on to camp for the night among the cypress trees of the Sabinal River (which they named the Capa). Two days later they had reached the Medina River. The Payaya Indians who lived on this stream told them the way to the Colorado.

On April 13 the little party of Spaniards discovered and named both the San Pedro Springs and the San Antonio River (San Antonio de Padua they called it). Father Espinosa told about the possibilities and beauties of this newly discovered little wonderland in words that were both simple and eloquent. He found about 500 Indians—Siupans, Chaulaames and Sijames—with a system of irrigation already in operation.

May we move back to one of the problems of the Cabeza de Vaca narrative and view that problem in the light of these irrigation ditches on the San Pedro.

Here is a glowing example of the inaccuracy of those who wish to paint history all white or all black. In the main, the Indians who inhabited the hill country from San Antonio to the north and west were not agricultural Indians and did not irrigate. But the examples are many of the intrusion into this area of Jumano Indians and of others that came from far to the north and west where agriculture by irrigation was widely practiced. The beautiful hill country that lies northwest of San Antonio with its hundreds of springs and dozens of spring-fed streams must have been attractive to the early day Red Men who knew about irrigated agriculture.

Of course, many of these springs and rivers were set too deep in the ground to make irrigation an easy matter. But here at San Pedro Springs the source of water babbled forth right at the surface of the ground. It was easy to cause the water to flow through ditches to the flat country below. There is good reason to believe that other examples of irrigation had existed in the hill country above San Antonio. In like manner the springs that were high up on Seco Creek northwest of present-day Hondo were near the surface. We do not have outright proof that this condition was utilized on the Seco, but a half of an old metate (corn grinding stone) may be seen in that area now, and the broken parts of a piece of Indian pottery have been found nearby.

When Cabeza de Vaca came to the hill country (according to the study made in this volume) he found Indians at the head of the Sabinal River (if we are correct) that had come from far to the north and apparently to the west—possibly from the Pueblo Country of New Mexico or possibly from the West Texas part of the Rio Grande. Did some of these Indians bring gourds or gourd seed from one of these areas? At least gourds grow wild now on both branches of the upper Sabinal.

But we have left Espinosa and some sixteen other Spaniards at the site of the future city of San Antonio with instructions from the Payaya Indians about one of the principal routes that led toward East Texas. In line with those instructions, the Spaniards followed very much the course that was to become part of the "Old San Antonio Road." They went right through the future cities of New Braunfels and San Marcos—across both the four mile long Comal River and across the San Marcos two "Arquebus shots" from its very head. Continuing to go in a northeastward direction they crossed the Blanco (they called it the San Raphael) two leagues beyond the San Marcos.

Six leagues past the Blanco the Espinosa party crossed Onion Creek although they called it the Garrapatas (the river of ticks). It was an additional five leagues to the Colorado River, which they reached a little below the present city of Austin.

After some delay the party of Spaniards contacted the Yojuan tribe of Indians from whom a satisfactory report about the Tejas Indians was obtained. Thus the Espinosa party was now ready to return to the Rio Grande.

Actually the San Antonio Road later when it was opened passed a few miles east of both New Braunfels and San Marcos and from the latter town it turned in a more eastward direction then did Espinosa, toward the present Bastrop. It is quite apparent that the route to East Texas that was known to the Payaya Indians followed a course beyond the San Marcos River that was quite a distance north of the route of the later San Antonio Road.

Not until 1716 did Spain decide to revive her missionary efforts among the Tejas Indians of East Texas. The young audacious Frenchman Louis Juchereau de St. Denis, who came to San Juan Bautista mission and fort in 1714 to establish trade relations with the Spaniards was the trigger that would set the next East Texas move in motion.

St. Denis combined romance with business and temporarily became a part of the next Spanish expedition. He married Manuela Sanchez, the granddaughter of Diego Ramón, the post commander, and was appointed to guide the Spanish force sent to East Texas (to establish missions) in 1716. Domingo Ramón, the son of the post commander, was in charge of the expedition. He commanded twenty-five soldiers but took with him even a greater accompaniment of civilians besides nine priests who were to look after the spiritual welfare of this entire group and as many as possible of the Tejas Indians.

Father Espinosa was to head the religious efforts. The fact that this important priest was in the party may have had some bearing on the route of march. He, it will be remembered, had gone this way only seven years earlier and the route of this expedition of 1716 seems to be identical with that of 1709 all the way from the San Antonio River to the Colorado.

But between the Rio Grande and the San Antonio the Ramón party seemed to have chosen a route different in some particular from any of the previous expeditions.

VI

SPANISH ROAD SYSTEM:

Ramón's Road To San Antonio

Having thus followed in brief the routes of de Leon and Terán and having noted that neither of them made trails that continued to serve as roads, let us settle down to the serious business of developing the story of the old Spanish roads of Texas.

The honor of opening the very first road across Texas belongs to José Domingo Ramón. The year (although it sounds almost like ancient history) was 1716.

Nobody spread a red carpet ahead of Ramón nor of any of those who were soon to travel his road but not many pages ahead we shall see how nature bestowed her own spots of color that even now help to reveal the route of this all but ancient highway.

Ramón and his party began this first Spanish road at San Juan Bautista Mission and Fort (often referred to as the Presidio) some five miles west of the Rio Grande and about thirty miles down the river from the place that is now Eagle Pass, Texas. The road came to an end at Los Adaes about thirty-three miles deep into the present state of Louisiana a mile beyond the little town of Robeline. This was the first of the two old San Antonio-Nacogdoches roads although it passed through the site of San Antonio two years before the place was founded and through Nacogdoches sixty-three years before it became an actual town.

Now do not misunderstand, for there were two old San Antonio-Nacogdoches roads. Both roads passed through the Presidio, through San Antonio, through Nacogdoches, San Augustine and both reached across the Sabine to Los Adaes. Then the two roads nearly followed the same path? Not at all. The later road followed not much more than one tenth of Ramón's original road!

The two roads were roughly parallel and not often more than thirty miles apart. The old route was mostly a trail used by pack trains; the new road was travelled by an increasing number of covered wagons. The old route was mostly Spanish in speech, manners and equipment. It came out of Mexico (New Spain); it faced the East. The new route was largely Anglo-American. It came out of the United States—it faced the West. However, both old roads were opened by Spain.

Then one question should be answered. Why were there no armed conflicts as the two kinds of traffic met in Nacogdoches and other towns where the trails overlapped? The answer is simple. Hardly can it be said that both roads were in use at the same time. Ramón's route served the important expeditions to the missions of East Texas from 1716 until about 1770 when Spain ceased to support those institutions. The Marquis de Rubí travelled the road as late as 1767 when he made his tour of inspection and recommended that East Texas, missions and all, should be abandoned. But one looks in vain to find an expedition that followed Ramón's road as late as 1800. On the other hand, Spain ordered the opening of a mail road between San Antonio and Nacogdoches in 1795 when she began to send troops into East Texas again after the Rubí abandonment. This new road served not only the mail but also completed the second version of the "Old San Antonio Road." The old and the new San Antonio roads served almost altogether in different centuries. In 1821 when Stephen F. Austin came to Texas he travelled the later road and nowhere did his diary even so much as mention the first old San Antonio road. But now let's go out into the open country and follow the details of terrain and in fact the actual story of the party who made this first old road.

Domingo Ramón who opened this history making road crossed the Rio Grande at the Francia crossing on April 20, 1716. He stayed in camp on the east bank of the river for several days and then marched three leagues northward to the Creek of the Crows (Cuervo Creek) on which de Leon had camped twenty-seven years earlier. The creek was almost dry causing Ramón to move westward two leagues and to camp at another crossing of the Rio Grande. A severe wind storm accompanied with some rain struck the party here, but the rain must not have been widespread; water and forage continued to be a problem. Following a course northward of the route that seems to have been a travelled road, Ramón did find both grass and water at Cuervo Creek. But he apparently realized that this detour was too far north to be in line with the route which he wished to follow to East Texas.

Hence, let us leave him (for a short while) here at Cuervo Creek and pick up the part of the road, color and all, which Ramón had missed on the detour.

Two years later Martín de Alarcón came this way. As Ramón had done, Alarcón crossed the Rio Grande at the lower or Francia crossing and also as Ramón had done he went northward to the creek of the crows—but here he was not forced to break away from the road that Ramón had detoured around. This time the spring rains had come—there was water ahead. Just three leagues eastward from the crossing on Crow (Cuervo) Creek, nature had truly put on her "Sunday clothes." Here Alarcón camped at what must have been a well-known camping place. Wild flowers bloomed in profusion. April had spread her own red carpet. No, not truly red, but an extravaganza of pink and orchid that caused the old Spanish diarist not to let us miss it. What was the principal flower of this long forgotten blaze of color? It was known in this country near the Rio Grande as las Rosas de San Juan or the Roses of Saint John. So beautiful were these flowers that the camping place itself became known as las Rosas de San Juan.

History has had its own strange way of preserving the name of this flower and more than that, it has for all of these two and a half centuries that followed preserved the identity of the old camping place itself.

This is the chain of events that has handed down the camp site. First the old road that passed this way enroute to San Antonio (and on to the missions of East Texas) continued to function for many decades. Aguayo in 1721 and Rivera in 1727 both camped there and their diaries called the camp by name. Next (in 1765) while the old road was still in use the king of Spain made a grant of more than 25 leagues of land to Antonio Rivas that had many miles of the Rio Grande for a west boundary and now covers most of the south part of Maverick County beginning nearly 20 miles below Eagle Pass. The old road travelled by the important early expeditions nearly split the Antonio Rivas land in halves. This Spanish grant of 1765 was not actually surveyed as we now survey land but a Spaniard (Miguel San Miguel by name) walked around the large tract of land and described the boundaries and told where the corners were located. One of those corners was the old campsite—the Roses of Saint John.

Antonio Rivas and his heirs continued to hold this great piece of real estate and even now the land maps of Maverick and Dimmit counties have preserved its boundaries including the land corner and

old camping place—still known on the land records as the Roses of Saint John.

This most interesting and colorful point on Ramón's first road across Texas has been visited by the writer. It is about 15 miles westward and 5 miles south of Carrizo Springs, the county seat of Dimmit County.

What were these flowers that grew at this old camping place? In other words what is the name to be found in books of botany or by what common name are these flowers called? It was the contention of the States Attorneys in a land suit (concluded in 1941) that the Mexicans called the white blooms of the button willow the Roses of Saint John. But the States Attorneys must have failed to compare carefully the button willow with the flower that was known to Alarcón as the Roses of Saint John. Alarcón found that this flower made a magnificent display of color with its blooms in early April whereas the button willow does not bloom until June.

Fritz Hoffman in his very praiseworthy volume on the Alarcón expedition falls into a similar error. He cites a botanical authority of Mexico to show that a plant called Houstonia Longiflora was called the Roses of Saint John but a somewhat more careful check of the works of this authority shows that Houstonia Longiflora does not come into full bloom until July (as compared with April when Alarcón found his flowers in bloom). Also, in further checking the works of this Mexican authority (Elna Motts), it is found that she does not actually refer to this flower as the Roses of Saint John but she does tell that the common name of the plant is the Flower of Saint John (Flor de San Juan). Indeed her illustration shows that the plant does not at all resemble a rose. By contrast, all of the diaries of the three Spanish expeditions that camped at Alarcón's colorful camping place give the name as the Roses of Saint John (las Rosas de San Juan). Quite plainly, neither this plant known as Houstonia Longiflora nor the button willow can qualify as the Roses of Saint John found by Alarcón.

But this much of the attempt to establish the identity of the Roses of Saint John is purely negative. Why not hunt a more positive approach to the problem? Why not go down to the very place where Alarcón camped (for even now the old land corner holds that spot) and see what kind of flowers grow there?

The writer did visit the corner of the Antonio Rivas land grant which was known as the Roses of Saint John but unfortunately the visit was made during hot, dry mid-summer weather when almost nothing was in bloom.

However Mr. Lewis Parr of La Pryor, Texas, has made up for the writer's short-comings in this matter. He told me about Earl Shearer, a windmill repairman on the Dolph Briscoe ranch for 30 years in the area near this point that was called the Roses of Saint John. Mr. Parr asked Shearer if he ever saw any wild roses in that area.

This is Mr. Shearer's reply:

"No, there are no wild roses—in fact there are only two flowers there in abundance; one, the Lantana and the other—that's it—that's what they called the wild rose—it blooms from spring to late fall—I'll bring you a blossom."

The old employee of 30 years—a lover of flowers—went home to where he had transplanted this wild flower in his own yard (at La Pryor) and soon returned with some cuttings which included two of the blooms. Lewis Parr pressed these cuttings and sent them to the writer.

Is this flower (called Pavonis Lasiopetala) the actual answer to our search for the Roses of Saint John? In view of the fact that no scientific data were furnished by the old Spanish diaries this cutting taken from the yard of Earl Shearer is surely the most probable answer. This long-time resident not only loved flowers, but he probably knew this land corner where grew Alarcón's roses of St. John as well as anybody else on earth. Alarcón's flower of two and a half centuries ago had all but lost its identity until Earl Shearer with an intense love of wild flowers has now given it back its rightful place in history. Delicate, not a rose but rose-colored, and less than a silver dollar, this bright little witness of the centuries will bloom forth again each April and mark this important campsite on the old Spanish road—the road that was first to cross both the Rio Grande and the Sabine rivers. So now let us leave Alarcón after his diary has so kindly obliged us and let us put Ramón back in charge of his own story—let him make his own road.

It was seven leagues (eighteen miles) northeastward from Las Rosas to Carrizo Creek on which Ramón had camped. Either here or not far to the northeast, all of the remaining early Spanish expeditions of this period were to follow at least part of Ramón's new road. Not only does this attempt to find the old road become a search replete with color, but it directs us into some hard facts that indicate a route which seems not to have been uncovered as a whole in previous historical writings. All of the well known expeditions before

1730—even de Leon—who crossed the Rio Grande in present Maverick County—crossed the creek known as Coramanchel just before they reached the Nueces River. Several of the diaries of these explorers gave the distance from Coramanchel Creek to the Nueces as five leagues. Most of them called attention to the luxuriant growth of pecans along the Nueces. Some translations say walnuts instead of pecans but since the trees along the river are actually pecans and not walnuts that difference in words may be disregarded. The fact that these early Spaniards crossed the Nueces in the pecan belt will shortly render much assistance in finding the rest of their trail.

Another thing will help. All these Spanish expeditions from 1716 to 1727 camped at the same lake just two or three leagues northeast of the crossing of the Nueces. Some of the diaries called the watering place Frog Lake—others called it Turtle Lake. The two accounts of the Ramón expedition of 1716 called this campsite by both names.

Undoubtedly these different parties of Spaniards were all traveling the same road. How can we find the route of that old road? First, where was the pecan belt? The 1910 census helps to answer that question. According to the census takers of that date there were no pecan trees in Dimmit County—the county of which Carrizo Springs is the county seat. But those same census takers reported a number of pecan trees in Zavala County which is just above Dimmit. Certainly the census takers throw some light on the route of the old road.

Also the creeks found on present-day maps can render aid. No Coramanchel Creek appears on the map of either Dimmit or Zavala counties but there is a Comanche Creek (or "Caymanche" Creek) mostly in Zavala County. It is southwest of Crystal City—in fact precisely where it ought to be if an old road from the campsite at the Roses of Saint John ran across it en route northeastward to the pecan belt along the Nueces River in Zavala County. The old road must have passed through Crystal City (of today) or at least very near it.

But how about Turtle Lake (or Frog Lake) two or three leagues east of the Nueces? Today no lake bears that name but at the proper distance east of the Nueces a creek now runs southward parallel to the river. The name of that stream is Tortugas (Turtle) Creek! In other words the creek now bears the name which the old Spaniards of 1716 gave their campsite. This creek flows sluggishly through a flat country and due to silting, early lakes are hardly discernible today. But an early Texas General Land Office map of Zavala County shows four lakes on Tortugas Creek. The northernmost of these lakes—Woodward Lake—is at the proper place to have been two or three leagues northeast of the crossing of the Nueces where pecan trees are numerous.

This old road opened by Domingo Ramón in 1716 should not be confused with the well known Upper Presidio road (opened much later) which crossed the Nueces River in Dimmit County well below the pecan belt.

Beyond Woodward Lake, it was five or six leagues northeastward to the next camping place. Possibly it was on the headwaters of one of the creeks that flow southward into the Nueces. The Alarcón party found more of the little roses of St. John here but passed no compliments on the bad smelling water. Two and a half leagues ahead they crossed a "hill covered with flint, and then the Frio River." Do not misunderstand the name. It is the stream now known as the Leona River. Apparently their crossing of this little river was near the Zavala-Frio county line. The flint covered hills are inside Zavala County here beginning about two and a half miles south of the West Ranch headquarters and extending eastward. But the hill of this chain that one might say is "covered with flint" is five or six miles east of this headquarters and a short distance south of the Leona.

From this crossing near the present-day county line the distance as the old Spaniards put it was about five or six leagues from the crossing of the "Arroyo Hondo"—but again do not let the name deceive you. What de Leon called the Hondo (as did Ramón, Alarcón, Aguayo, and Rivera) we now call the Frio. The above five or six leagues from the crossing of the Leona should strike the Frio (of today) westward of Pearsall. Another fact helps to nail down this conclusion. When Alarcón (in 1718) crossed the Frio he had to travel through a flat bottom covered with heavy timber for a league before he even reached the river. A quarter of a league before he reached the Frio he crossed a creek. Except that the timber in the Frio bottom west of Pearsall is less than a league wide, how could you describe it any better than these old Spaniards did? From a point a little above the place where paved Highway 140 crosses the Frio River northwest of Pearsall to another point a half dozen miles down the river at the mouth of Live Oak Creek the timber is spread out in many places more than a mile wide on the west side of the river. A slough from a few hundred yards to a mile west of the river parallels it most of that half dozen miles. The route of the Spaniards ran northeastward and because of this angle of direction it must have extended nearly a league before it crossed completely out of this timbered bottom. No other place for miles up or down the Frio even remotely meets the description of these Spaniards of two and a half centuries ago. The old Spanish accounts told about the timbered river botton—also the smaller stream in the bottom parallel to the river.

From the Frio, Ramón's road headed directly toward an old Spanish land grant the field notes of which lend a great surprise in our efforts to locate this early road. In 1766—more than two centuries ago—the king of Spain granted a large tract of land to the Indians of the San José Mission. This land began only about sixteen miles west of downtown San Antonio and extended some fifteen miles farther to the west. Its length from north to south was nearly twenty miles and its total area was the greater part of 100,000 acres. Its exact dimensions or its area are not of prime importance here but the thing that does interest us is that fact that its southeast boundary some twelve miles long was an old Spanish road. What was the name of this almost ancient highway? On old land records it was called the Pita Road, evidently because a favored campsite on the road only a few miles southwest of this grant of land was called the Pita camping place.

Almost as strange as if it had come right out of a story book, Ramón's next important camp six leagues or more northeast of the Frio bottom was called the Pita camping place "Charco de la Pita." Not only did one of the Ramón diaries call the place by that name but the accounts of the expeditions under Alarcón, Aguayo, and Rivera all called it by the same name. Each of these important expeditions followed Ramón's road from the Presidio on the Rio Grande to San Antonio—and each of them camped at Charco de la Pita. Most of the diaries made favorable comment on the place and Rivera's diarist liked the place better than any other campsite on the entire road. Quite plainly this camping place in due time gave the entire road its name. It is also important here to mention the fact that the wording of the old Spanish grant told specifically that the Pita Road extended all the way to the Presidio on the Rio Grande, and no other of the old Spanish roads from San Antonio to the Presidio on the Rio Grande passed through this camping place.

Evidently the Pita Road was Ramón's road—but how can we get at the exact location of the southeast boundary of the old grant and thereby find that part of the old road? Had there been no unusual turn of events, the old Spanish grant probably would have faded out of the picture and its wording might have been insufficient to help us locate the old road. The old, old landmarks might have become impossible to locate and of course when San José was secularized the mission Indians must have scattered to the four winds.

But while Texas was a republic one John McMullen tried to pull some of the loose ends together and to acquire title to this valuable tract of land. He had the land surveyed—but the surveyors had their troubles for even they seemed not to know enough about the landmarks. The ever colorful Bigfoot Wallace was called in as a guide and with his aid the surveyors accomplished their task. They made land plats that are now in the Texas Land Office, and we can even now use the plats and find some twelve miles of the Pita Road which undoubtedly was also Ramón's road.

Where was it? It ran parallel to Highway 81—the early automobile road that connects San Antonio with Laredo—and varied from a half mile to more than a mile northwest of a segment of that road. The part of this old Spanish road that is preserved by the land grant begins at Chicon Creek some three miles northeast of Devine, and extends a dozen miles northeastward.

As a strange sequel to the story of this land grant, John McMullen failed (in court, of course) to make good his title and the State of Texas granted the land to others—much of it went to Henry Castro, the colonizer. The town of Castroville twenty-five miles west of San Antonio is not far from the center of this ancient tract of land that once belonged to the San José Indians. For convenience, the land is now known as the John McMullen Grant.

Now let us go back and attempt to locate the Pita camping place. It, according to some of the diaries, was seven and one-half leagues from the Frio and nine leagues from the Medina—or let us say twenty miles from the Frio and twenty-four miles from the Medina. By map measurements the old campsite is thus about two miles west or southwest of Devine, Texas. Francisco Creek is at that place. Apparently Francisco Creek is the stream that Stephen F. Austin called Pita Creek on his map of 1830. On that map Pita Creek was the tributary of Rosalis Creek (Charcon Creek) that lay just west of Rosalis. Now Francisco Creek is in exactly that same relative position with respect to Charcon Creek. There is thus little room to doubt that the Pita camping place was on present Francisco Creek about two miles west or southwest of Devine.

The real reason for this meticulous effort to locate the Pita camping place is to tie together the old Spanish records of the John McMullen Grant and the diaries of the expeditions of 1716, 1718, 1721, and 1727. Also to determine the origin of the word "Pita." Fritz Hoffman in his scholarly account of the Alarcón Expedition (of 1718) defines Pita as a century plant. The Spanish dictionaries seem to bear him out, but plant life in this area southwest of Devine suggests a modification of that definition. The Spanish Dagger once grew in profusion in this area and even now despite the fact that most of the land is in cultivation they are plentiful along fences and roads—but the century plant, the one with a stem fifteen to twenty feet high, is nowhere in evidence. With this fact in mind, if we translate the term Pita Road into the sometimes salty language of the Southwest we can truthfully call it "the trail of the Spanish Dagger." Actually the Spanish Dagger does not in any way resemble a red carpet—but in this strange trail hunt it does add its own bit of color that is much more desirable. Interestingly, Ramón who opened this road camped here May 12, 1716; Aguayo on April 2, 1721; and Rivera on August 13, 1727.

But for the moment the expeditions of Alarcón (the founder of San Antonio) should be of greater interest than any of these. As we have seen, just two years after Ramón had opened the road, Alarcón followed it into this land of Spanish daggers. He camped at the Charco de la Pita on April 20, 1718. Next day he continued his journey traveling only a little more than half a dozen miles to Payaya (Charcon) Creek. Near the half way point of the day's travel he met Fray Miguel Nuñez who had all but starved during the preceding winter and spring. Father Nuñez and four soldiers had taken supplies eastward along Ramón's road intended for the East Texas missions but they found the Trinity River impassable and moved back (west) to the Navasota River (at Santa Ana Lake) where they spent most of the winter. Indians supplied them with corn until the supply was exhausted and then helped them to subsist on roots. The water in the Brazos was also at flood stage and the supplies could not be returned.

Leaving the supplies cached under his tent in a dense wood near the Navasota, Father Nuñez returned westward, evidently down Ramón's road. He may have been the first person who travelled Ramón's road westward. Alarcón met him on the road near the site of present-day Devine and, of course, looked after his needs.

On April 25 Alarcón reached the site of San Antonio and went through the formalities that probably should fix the date for the beginning of San Antonio. Since we know where the southeast boundary of the McMullen Grant was located we can now know that Alarcón's and all the other expeditions mentioned here on recent pages followed Ramón's road almost through Devine and Lytle. Also since we know from land surveys and land maps that both the Upper and the Lower Presidio roads did not follow the same route as did the Pita Road—we now have positive proof that there were three old Spanish roads between San Antonio and the Presidio on the Rio Grande.

Before we continue with Ramón's road to East Texas let us turn aside briefly to outline these other two roads to San Antonio. There is evidence of travel on the lower Presidio Road during the 1730's. The road is so old in fact that it must have pre-dated most of the private ownership of land in Texas so much that very few surveyors noted the road in their work of parceling out any but the very early tracts of land. The old road followed a course slightly west of south from San Antonio into Atascosa County and crossed the Atascosa River some seven and a half miles westward of Pleasanton. But after continuing this course about a mile beyond the river the land maps show no more of the road for almost 100 miles.

Seemingly there are no land maps that show the road any farther southward in Atascosa County, nor in the southeast part of Frio County nor in La Salle County and not even in Dimmit County except at its extreme west line where the road is shown some six miles north of the southwest corner of the county. This skip in the old road is almost a hundred miles long.

The road is shown again about three quarters of a mile a little north of west of this point where it crosses the west Dimmit County line. Here the early road is known to have crossed the boundary of the large tract of land (twenty-five leagues) which the king of Spain granted to Antonio Rivas in 1765. This point on the road was identified (in 1765) as the place where the line of this Spanish grant crossed San Ambrosio Creek. This place on the road (in present Maverick County) can still be located even though the above identification was made more than two centuries ago. This early Spanish road sometimes called the King's Highway (but well known during the last century as the Lower Presidio Road) continued on its course a little north of west (about twelve miles) and reached the Francia crossing on the Rio Grande somewhat more than a league below the mouth of the Creek of the Crows. Testimony included in the official record of this old land grant make it known that this branch of the King's Highway had become the most important road from the Presidio on the Rio Grande to San Antonio by 1765. In other words, by 1765 it had become more important than the Pita Road which had been established by Ramón in 1716.

Before we cease to discuss this Lower Presidio Road, may we call attention to the fact that to find its approximate route is not an impossible task. Elsewhere in this book, the road will be mapped and proper documentation will accompany the map. Father Morfi traveled the road in 1767 and left a diary which is very helpful.

But there is another aid in determining the route that seems to have been overlooked. John Coffee Hays in 1839 (and adjacent years) sent his surveyors down the Frio River in what is now lower Frio and upper La Salle counties. They surveyed a number of tracts of land with frontage on the Frio. They did not map the Lower Presidio Road nor did they include it in their regular land boundary field notes. But what they did do is worth a handful of gold dollars to the person who hunts this ancient trail. When they applied surveying instruments to survey no. 74 of their surveys they said it was "2 miles below the Lower Presidio del Rio Grande road." Survey No. 87 was two miles above the road and the lower corner of survey No. 80 was only a half mile above that old road.

Translated into present day geography, these notes (all consistent with each other) mean that the Lower Presidio Road crossed the Frio River about three and a half miles south of the north line of La Salle County. This old crossing is about ten miles west of the east line of that county.

So here we have a definite point on this old Presidio-San Antonio road far down within the "unknown" skip. Taken with the Morfi diary we may now come nearer to the true route. Now let us block out a brief approximation. The road extended a little west of south out of San Antonio, passed seven and a half miles west of Pleasanton in Atascosa County, cut across the southeast corner of Frio County about a half dozen miles deep and went on to the Frio River crossing just described. From this ford on the Frio in northern La Salle County its course went southwestward and crossed the Nueces River not far from Cotulla; then it ranged only a little south of west. On into Dimmit County it passed a little south of Catarina and stayed in south Dimmit County about a half dozen miles from the south line until it reached Maverick County. Now with little more than a dozen miles (slightly north of west) to go, it reached the old Francia crossing on the Rio Grande nearly thirty miles (as a bird could fly) down the river from Eagle Pass. On the west side of the Rio Grande it was five or six miles still slightly north of west to the old Presidio.

At this point, almost any person who is well informed in Texas history would call attention to the fact that C. N. Zivley ran a survey the full length of this Lower Presidio Road in 1915. And so he did. Granite markers have been set up at about every fifth mile post of his survey and thus the route of the old road was apparently put to rest. But now, even though it may not seem like good manners to criticize after receiving so much help from Zivley's notes let us say that those who assigned this work to Mr. Zivley—that of finding an old road with nearly 100 miles without exact data—gave him all but an impossible task. In La Salle County he admittedly followed the wrong road and was forced to go to the crossing of the Rio Grande and survey eastward in order to correct his mistake. But trouble again dogged at his heels. This time he seemed not to know it but, in part of La Salle County at least, he followed the wrong road again. His survey ran eastward of Cotulla and was a full ten miles south of the place where Jack Hays' surveyors said that the old road crossed the Frio River.

Does this condemn the whole Zivley survey? Not at all. With proper caution much of it can be useful to the research worker. In places where accurate surveyors' field notes are available, his work has been invaluable. After public roads, railroads, and cultivation had played havoc with many miles of the frontier trails, the task of surveying many miles without a few reference points to keep the survey on course—such a task becomes impossible.

With the review of the routes of the Lower Presidio Road and of the still older Pita Road, we are now ready to point out some of the pertinent facts about a third Presidio Road. Five upright and honorable Spaniards in 1838 came before Juan Seguin (chief justice of Bexar County) and testified under oath that Governor Don Antonio Cordera opened the Pita Road during his term of office. Now since Cordera was governor from 1805 to 1810 we have what seems to be an outright contradiction. The old Spanish land grant made to the San José Mission Indians (now called the John McMullen Grant) recites plainly that the Pita Road was at that time (1766) the southeast boundary of the tract of land. It was further recited that the Pita Road extended to the Presidio on the Rio Grande. Obviously the Pita Road could not have been opened between 1805 and 1810 if it was already a going concern in 1766.

A closer look at the testimony of these five Spaniards seems to explain the mystery. Each of them called Cordero's new road the "new" or Pita Road—two of them testified that Don Joachin Menchaca travelled the road long before Antonio Cordero was governor. Thus it appears that each of the five witnesses had in mind both an old and a new Pita road. All of the witnesses mentioned the fact that the road was above the middle (or Lower) Presidio Road; all of them said that it followed a direct or west course. As we have seen the old Pita road followed a direct or west course. Also the road that has long born the name, "Upper Presidio Road" followed that very same course. Simply stated, then Cordero was reopening the old Pita Road. That this new route would come to be called the "Upper Presidio Road" seems not to have occurred either to Cordero or Seguin's witnesses.

But when this new road was opened (in about 1807) Corporal Tobar and his men, who actually did the work, did not follow the exact route of Ramón's old (Pita) road. Probably they were on the same path most of the way across Maverick County and into Dimmit County, but only the old Pita Road crossed Comanche (Coramanchel) Creek near Crystal City—only the old Pita Road crossed the Nueces River up in Zavala County in the pecan belt and in the area where the channel of the river was deep. As we have seen earlier the Upper Presidio road crossed the Nueces below the pecan belt—in fact three miles down in Dimmit County away from the pecan groves of the Nueces Valley.

Most of the route of the Upper Presidio Road was set down by old surveyors and reproduced in the Texas land maps. Much of its route is known exactly. Most of the route of the old Pita road we know from topography, which is not as nearly exact as land surveys, but we can yet follow the paths of the two old roads well enough to compare their routes.

The Pita Road crossed the Nueces some ten miles above the later road. The paths of the two roads crossed about ten miles southeast of Batesville and at the Frio River the two roads were again as much as ten miles apart—but this time it was the Upper Presidio Road that was upstream from the other. As the roads approached San Antonio, the space between them began to gradually decrease. At the Bexar

County line, the two roads were only five miles apart. Here the routes of both roads are known from land records. Observe the accompanying map of the Lower Presidio Road, the Upper Presidio Road, and of Ramón's old Pita Road. Note how the Lower Presidio Road looped far to the south of the other two and in so doing avoided some of the most dangerous of the Indian country. When Antonio Cordero was governor of Texas and for a full decade before, Spain increased her military force in Texas enough to have less fear of wild Indians. Also the increase in transportation that came with an increased army necessitated straightening and shortening the roads.

When the Republic of Texas was a half dozen years old General Adrian Woll of Mexico conducted a raid into Texas that came by the Presidio and penetrated all the way to San Antonio. His thrust into and his withdrawal from Texas both by the same route added yet another road from the Presidio on the Rio Grande to San Antonio, Texas—this last one by a more northerly route than any of the others. Thus, in brief review, let us list the Presidio roads: First was Ramón's road of 1716 that came to be known as the Pita Road translated here as the Trail of the Spanish Dagger. Second came the Lower Presidio Road (about 1730) that curved southward some forty miles off course apparently to avoid Indian conflicts for the many decades during which Spanish forces in Texas were so small. Third came the Upper Presidio Road in about 1807 after the very small Spanish army in Texas had grown to somewhat more than a half a thousand—this increase made partly in fear of the rising tide of westward-bound Anglo-Americans. And fourth, after this push of Americans had formed the Republic of Texas, the Mexican raiding party mentioned above made the last of the Presidio roads (the Woll Road) in 1842. All of these old roads are shown on the accompanying map.

But meanwhile we are following the old road made by Domingo Ramón in 1716. We have traced it from the old Presidio across the Rio Grande from present-day Maverick County, Texas, to San Antonio. Now let us continue with Ramón the road maker as he travelled northeastward to establish a half dozen missions in the great pine belt which is (according to present-day maps) located in eastern Texas and western Louisiana. Not only did Ramón establish a chain of missions but in this journey of 1716 he opened a road all or part of which was travelled by every important Spanish expedition to this mission belt for many decades to come.

VII

SPANISH ROAD SYSTEM:

Ramón's Road From San Antonio To Nacogdoches

Thus Domingo Ramón had opened a road across the part of the present-day Texas that lies between the Rio Grande and San Antonio. This, we repeat was 1716, two years before the actual founding of San Antonio, but Ramón camped in what is now the heart of San Antonio on its strikingly beautiful river and near its highly attractive San Pedro Springs.

However, before continuing to follow Ramón's route, it will be well to clarify two matters that concern his road that are widely misunderstood. First, the frequent statement that the Frenchman, Louis Juchereau de St. Denis, guided Ramón on this expedition is not an exact fact. St. Denis did make this journey across Texas at the same time as did Ramón, but most of the time he travelled far ahead of Ramón and his party, making contact with Indians that lived along the way. How much information the young Frenchman may have contributed to the Spaniards in advance of the journey or at intervals along the way does not seem certain, but it should be noted that one of Ramón's own party had explored part of the route well ahead of this journey. Father Isidro Felix de Espinosa had been one of the leaders of a party of seventeen Spaniards who had made part of the journey in 1709. He had kept a diary at that time all the way from the Rio Grande to the Colorado River before his party turned back to Mexico—and from that diary it is rather plain that he learned something of the remainder of the route to East Texas. Father Espinosa was a member of the Ramón journey in 1716. He again kept a diary from which it is quite clear that the Spaniards of this latter date followed very closely from the San Antonio to the Colorado River the same route that he followed in 1709. Certainly Father Espinosa should share in the credit for having guided this party from the Rio Grande to the missions that were (in 1716) established in East Texas.

The second misconception about Ramón's road had to do with his route. It is widely believed that the part of that old road that lay between San Antonio and Nacogdoches passed through or very near the present-day towns of Bastrop, Caldwell, Normangee, Midway, Crockett, Alto and Douglas. It is to be the major burden of this chapter to show the approximately correct route of Ramón's road, and that it did not pass through any of the seven above-named towns.

Now do not misunderstand—the road through or near Bastrop, etc., was a very old Spanish road. It did connect San Antonio with Nacogdoches, but the evidence of a dozen old Spanish diaries builds mountain-high toward the conclusion that the road was not in existence for many decades after 1716 when Ramón opened his road to the missions which he established in East Texas.

Again do not misunderstand. This old road through Bastrop was known and still is known in memory as the "Old San Antonio Road." It was the principal road in Texas when Stephen F. Austin and his colonists came—as it had been for a few decades earlier.

Not long after Columbus discovered America, Spain began to toy with this land to the north of the Rio Grande. But by 1808 a census showed that only 3,000 had settled here. Thus, for nearly three centuries Spain had failed miserably to develop this land that joins old Mexico. But a short three decades later the population had zoomed to perhaps 50,000, and along with that rise the soul of Texas had been born again. An important part of that rebirth had come with the ox-wagons that followed along this later Old San Antonio Road. But even though the old road was so important in its day, the segment of it between San Antonio and Nacogdoches had no part in the mission period of East Texas history.

Now back to Ramón and his journey. As both travellers and local citizens now enjoy the beauty of the spring-fed San Antonio River, so did Ramón and his party of Spaniards back in 1716. They stayed over an extra day and even then seemed to give up the beauty spot reluctantly. They did move forward on May 16 to Salado Creek, but the distance travelled was only two leagues (five miles) which left them still within the limits of modern San Antonio.

But now after an overnight camp on Salado Creek the party travelled at a more normal pace. Two days and about ten leagues later their camp was pitched within the area that is now the German city of New Braunfels and near the banks of the crystal-clear spring-fed Comal River—sometimes called the shortest river in the United

States. The route of Ramón's road at this point is very definite. His diary says that the distance from the head springs to his road ''is not a greater distance than a shot with a bow and arrow.'' The head springs are in present-day Landa Park, which is a part of New Braunfels. The Spaniards called this little river the Guadalupe, but the fact that when they moved part of a league forward they crossed the other branch of the stream, enables us to know that this second branch is the river that is now called the Guadalupe—the first branch is the Comal, as indicated above.

The journey all the way from the San Antonio River had progressed in a northeastward direction. In fact, the direction of the route had not changed greatly on the whole from the Rio Grande.

Still northeastward, Ramón moved about six or seven leagues to the San Marcos River. Neither the diary of Father Espinosa nor of Ramón gives a perfect answer to the present problem of finding the river crossing. From the Espinosa account we wonder whether the expedition actually crossed the river or travelled in the hills above its source, but Ramón makes it clear that the party did cross the river and that the water at that point was very cold.

With this much a certainty, we may compare Espinosa's diary of the 1709 journey with his diary of 1716 and reach a more accurate conclusion. In the earlier account Espinosa tells almost exactly where he crossed the river—which was just ''two arquebus shots'' below the head spring. That statement is almost like saying that he crossed the river at the same place where one can cross it now—that is, where the old Austin road has crossed that stream for a good many years. But the old diary of 1709 goes on to say that it was about two leagues from that crossing to the intersection of the route with the San Raphael (the Blanco). That would not help so much except that Espinosa's diary in 1716 again shows about two leagues between the two river crossings. Can it be that Ramón's road of two and a half centuries ago passed very near the route of the old Austin road as we know it now? Whether true or not, it is certain that the San Marcos and the present-day Blanco (old San Raphael) are not three miles apart anywhere below San Marcos—and that Ramón's old road could hardly have crossed those two streams where they were two leagues (five miles) apart except by passing through or near the city of San Marcos as we know it today.

Here we should compare the route of Ramón's road of 1716 with that of the Old San Antonio Road that came later in the eighteenth century. Probably both roads followed the same route from San Antonio northeastward for about twenty-five miles, but at that point (about five miles from the Guadalupe) they separated. Ramón's old road, as we have seen, passed through the heart of New Braunfels, but the later road (the old San Antonio Road as it is known today) crossed the Guadalupe below the mouth of the Comal which, of course, was below town. This later road has been preserved by surveyor's records and land maps, and of course we can be sure that the two routes had already begun to spread apart at New Braunfels. They continued to spread with a possible exception between New Braunfels and San Marcos, but at the latter place they were about three miles apart. Here, we have seen that Ramón's road almost certainly passed through San Marcos, but again, land records show that the Old San Antonio Road of popular speech positively crossed the San Marcos below the mouth of the Blanco three miles below town.

Here at San Marcos the two routes had begun to spread apart in earnest—but actually they had just begun to spread! By the time the two old roads had reached the Colorado River they were nearly thirty miles apart! Certainly you, the reader, are entitled to ask for proof—proof that these two old roads between San Antonio and Nacogdoches followed different routes. Not only that, but you are entitled to know the two routes insofar as the facts are available.

Probably it will be easier to present the facts and easier for the reader to follow if we jump ahead to the Brazos River and later come back and fill in the gaps. First then, where did the Old San Antonio Road (the road that came late in the eighteenth century) cross the Brazos? The answer to that question is easy, for the land surveyors have set it down in their field notes, and the map makers have mapped the land from these records of the surveys. The Old San Antonio Road crossed the Brazos just a mile and a half above the bridge on present-day paved highway No. 21.

Not only do we know where the later Old San Antonio Road crossed the Brazos, but we know that for most of the way across Burleson County the land that it traversed was open prairie. By contrast, Ramón made his road of 1716 through some twenty leagues of thick-set brush and trees as he approached the Brazos from the west. The area was known as the "Monte Grande" and was so difficult to penetrate that Alarcón hired a guide to help him find his way through the area as he returned to San Antonio in 1718. Certainly Ramón's road, so heavily set with brush, was not the same as the well-known Old San Antonio Road which approached the Brazos in open prairie.

But even after we have found that the two old roads crossed the Brazos at different places we must still hunt the place where Ramón's road crossed. Actually, besides the fact that the Monte Grande lay just west of Ramón's crossing, we also know that he and his Spaniards crossed not just one stream, but they crossed two—and that both were sizable rivers. Put another way, we can be sure that this old road of 1716 crossed both the Brazos and one of its major tributaries just above the junction of the two streams.

Down near the Gulf of Mexico, the Brazos flows an average of more than 5,339,000 acre-feet per year. The six largest tributaries to this great river are the Double Mountain River that joins the main stream northwest of Haskell, the Clear Fork that joins southwest of Graham, the Bosque just above Waco, the Little River just west of Hearne, Yegua Creek below Bryan, and the Navasota River just below Navasota. The average annual flow in acre-feet of each of these Brazos tributaries is 133,200; 304,800; 143,300; 1,286,000; 200,400, and 340,300 respectively for a total of 2,408,000. Obviously the Little River with an average annual flow of 1,286,000 acre-feet is the only one of these six tributaries that can (on any realistic basis) team up with the main Brazos to make a sizable pair of rivers. The next tributary in order flows just slightly more than 6% as much as the Brazos, but the so-called *Little River* flows 24% as much. Even these twenty-four percentage points do not place the Little River in proper perspective.

The main Brazos at Waco has an average annual flow of 1,835,000 acre-feet. About 100 miles downstream at Bryan, Texas, is the next point at which the Brazos has been gauged. At Bryan it flows 3,941,000 acre-feet—but remember that 1,286,000 of this is contributed by the Little River which enters the main stream at Hearne. Thus the net flow of the Brazos at Bryan (except for the part contributed by the Little River) is 2,655,000 acre-feet. This is a net increase from Waco to Bryan of 820,000 acre-feet. Since most of the creeks that enter the Brazos between Waco and Bryan have not been measured, let us prorate this increase according to distance. Hearne is about 70% of the distance from Waco to Bryan. Seventy percent of this increase, added to the river's flow at Waco, permits us to come up with a total of the main Brazos just above the mouth of the Little River at Hearne of 2,408,000 acre-feet. Not scientific, this answer, but it is something better than a guess. This places the comparison of the main Brazos with the Little River at Hearne in the ratio of 65 to 35. Is this an exact ratio? No. But if we calculate this ratio based on the flow of the Brazos down at Bryan where the main river is certainly some larger than at Hearne, we still obtain the ratio of 67.4 to 32.6. Plainly then if we had the exact flow of the main Brazos just above Hearne, this ratio would be something less than 67.4 to something more than 32.6, and to try to come up with a more accurate answer than the above 65 to 35 ratio is merely splitting hairs where hair-splitting does not change the picture. The plain truth is that the Little River at Hearne teams up with the main Brazos to form two sizable rivers—and that that relationship does not exist at the mouth of any other tributary of the Brazos.

Another fact doubly emphasizes this conclusion. Ramón found some twenty leagues of thickly-set brush and trees which he was forced to penetrate in order to reach the Brazos from the west. Even now there are thousands of acres of such tree growth across the river west of Hearne and not at the mouth of any of the five other tributaries of the Brazos is there a growth of brush and trees that faintly resembles this timbered area in Milam County near the mouth of the Little River.

Ramón's crossing of the Little River and the Brazos (just above their junction) soon acquired a name that became well known. The name was "Brazos de Dios." Neither of the diaries that recorded Ramón's journey mention this name, but only a few years later the name came into use. The expedition of Alarcón in 1718 crossed the two rivers as Ramón had done, but did not yet use the name—that is, it is not in their diary. But the account of the Alarcón journey did say that he came into the "road to Texas" a half-league before he crossed the first of the two rivers. Certainly he, at that point, was entering Ramón's road and even crossed the Brazos above it not far below present Waco. But after crossing the Brazos between that stream and the Navasota he came into "the road to Texas" (certainly Ramón's road) and followed it, as we shall see, all the way to East Texas. The diary of the Aguayo expedition was the first to call Ramón's crossings of the Brazos "Brazos de Dios" but the diaries seem to indicate that one of the two earlier expeditions had called it by that name. Both Alarcón in 1718 and Aguayo in 1721 followed Ramón's road all the way from the missions of East Texas back to San Antonio, including the crossings of the two branches of the Brazos.

After Alarcón, all of the available diaries for over half a century of expeditions from San Antonio to East Texas (or reverse) indicate that the Brazos was crossed at the Brazos de Dios crossings, and each of them (including Rivera in 1727, the Marquis de Rubí in 1767, Father Gaspar José de Solis in 1768, Frenchman Pierre de Pages in 1767, Athanase de Mézières in 1772, and Pedro Vial in 1788, called the river crossing by the name Brazos de Dios).

Two facts are fairly evident at this point. Ramón's crossing of the Brazos was the principal place to cross that stream for most of the eighteenth century. If there was any other crossing of the Brazos on the road between San Antonio and the missions of East Texas from 1716 to 1788, the present writer has been unable to find a diary that says so.

Also, the old Spaniards of the early eighteenth century must have thanked God that He had divided this large river into two branches so that they could ford the streams easier and probably with less delay than would have been necessary to cross the one big river. They named these two branches of this largest river in Texas the "Arms of God," or in Spanish "Brazos de Dios." We still call the principal river the Brazos. The crossings were just west of present-day Hearne, Texas.

Let us again pick up the story of Ramón's road near the site of the present-day city of San Marcos. There is no longer any reason to doubt that Ramón opened a road that (at least between San Antonio and Nacogdoches) followed a different route from that of the popularly known Old San Antonio Road. We now know that Ramón's road cut across country from San Marcos to Hearne. We also can know that the well-known (and later) Old San Antonio Road passed through Bastrop in Bastrop County and through Caldwell in Burleson County and on to the Brazos, a mile and a half above Highway 21.

Now following Ramón's road across country from San Marcos northeastward where did it cross the Colorado River? To answer that question, we need to use the diaries of both the Ramón and the Aguayo expeditions. Both of these Spanish parties of the early eighteenth century crossed the Blanco River (which they both called the San Raphael) and both parties crossed Onion Creek (which they called the Garrapatas, because certain obnoxious ticks, "Garrapatas", attacked the party of 1709 at that stream). Ramón (in his diary) said it was nine leagues between these two streams.

Espinosa, who was with Ramón, said the distance was eight leagues. Aguayo's diarist gave figures from which it can be calculated at eight and a half leagues. Each diary, of course, was giving only an estimate. Surely both expeditions travelled the same road because their road logs indicated that they had done that very thing all the way from San Antonio. The thing that makes it doubly certain that they were travelling the same road (Ramón's road) between the Blanco and Onion Creek is the fact that each of them passed by the San Isidro Spring between these two streams.

Both parties then must have come to the same crossing on Onion Creek. But here there was a difference. In 1716 Ramón apparently crossed the creek where he came to it, but in 1721 Aguayo, due to high water, moved along the creek until he came to a waterfall and crossed on the rocks at this waterfall. Now, since Aguayo's estimated travel for the day was only half a league more than Ramón's, the distance between Ramón's established crossing and the falls must not have been very great.

The important thing, of course, is that there was a waterfall on the creek at all, for one may look for miles up and down the Colorado River here and find that McKinney Falls on Onion Creek is the only place where a waterfall of such magnitude exists. A closer look makes it possible to know that McKinney Falls is just two miles due east of Interstate Highway No. 35, and that the airline distance from the principal one of these two falls is four miles due north to the Colorado River.

But again we seem headed for trouble. Aguayo's diarist reported that this party of 1721 travelled from this waterfall a day's journey to the northeast of three leagues of which it was two and one-fourth leagues to the river. In other words, it was six miles northeastward to the river. The other thing that troubles us here is the fact as reported in the Ramón diaries that it was three leagues northeastward from the creek crossing to the river, and three leagues is equal to eight miles, not just four.

Trouble, you say? No, not at all. Nature took care of the trouble some centuries ago. The Colorado River *is* just four miles due north of McKinney Falls, but a big bend in the Colorado makes it a full six miles to the river in a northeastward direction. Also, if Ramón's crossing was possibly a mile or two up Onion Creek above McKinney Falls, he and his party of 1716 necessarily traveled eight miles (three leagues) northeastward until they came to the Colorado down in the very same bend that lies just northeast of McKinney Falls.

Obviously the facts of local geography just fit the requirements of the old Spanish diaries so that now we may say that on May 24 and 25, 1716, Ramón, while opening his road to East Texas, crossed the Colorado River down in the northeast part of the big river bend that lies some five miles due east of Austin, Texas—that is, about five miles east of Congress Avenue, if you like that better. Also, that in approaching that crossing, he passed only a short distance west of the beautiful waterfalls, now known as McKinney Falls.

North of the Colorado near Austin, this Spanish party of 1716 lost their way for at least part of a day, a fact which renders their diaries for that day all but useless. But even without a diary, by simply checking a map, we can know that the first important stream to be crossed was Brushy Creek and that the next important watercourse was the San Gabriel River. In the old diaries, the first of these they called Las Ánimas and the next one the San Xavier.

It was May 28 before the Spaniards had reached Brushy Creek, and it was June 1 when they reached the San Gabriel. They reached the river near the mouth of a large arroyo. This fact gives us another specific point on Ramón's road, for there is just one large creek that flows into the San Gabriel on its south side for a whole twenty miles above the mouth of Brushy Creek. This stream is Pecan Creek. Rising at least ten miles inside of Williamson County and following a course south of and parallel to the San Gabriel River and almost all of the way within about two miles of the river, this creek flows eastward into Milam County. Once inside of Milam County, Pecan Creek turns sharply toward the north and flows into the river. Here only about a half mile from the west county line is the place described by Father Espinosa as the camping place for the night of June 1, which was near "a large arroyo close to a good-sized river." The mouth of Pecan Creek where the Spaniards camped is five miles north of Thorndale. The fact that the mouth of Pecan Creek, where that "Arroyo" flows into the San Gabriel River, is a point so easy to find makes it also easy for us to backtrack far enough to say that Ramón's road from the vicinity of Austin passed near Rice's crossing on Brushy Creek and on northeastward very near the town of Taylor—in present-day Williamson County.

It rained while the Spaniards crossed this blackland country so they laid over here a short while and fished in the San Gabriel

Let us add that Aguayo, who had crossed the Colorado on

Ramón's road near Austin, did not continue to follow the Ramón road of 1716 but followed a more northerly route here which for the present will take him away from our story.

Now let us remember that Ramón was camped here five miles north of Thorndale by present day maps and just south of the San Gabriel River. He decided to travel again on June 3. The Espinosa diary told that the party traveled a little south of east; Ramón's diary said that the direction was northeast. Surely the Ramón diary should be charged with an inadvertent error, for to have traveled northeast would have required an immediate crossing of the San Gabriel River—which was greatly swollen from the recent rains. Neither diary said anything about an immediate crossing of the river—neither mentioned the great difficulties that necessarily must have been involved in such a crossing. On the other hand, both told of difficulties with the packs that should have been expected at the steep, slick banks of Brushy Creek which lay in their pathway about ten miles southeastward and straight ahead from the mouth of Pecan Creek. The more detailed account by Father Espinosa said that it was Las Ánimas (Brushy Creek) that the party reached and crossed near the end of the day—and that they lost some of the packs in that creek.

Dr. Herbert Eugene Bolton did some very interesting exploring in this ten miles between the mouth of Pecan Creek and Brushy Creek. He found the remains of the old San Xavier missions (of 1745-55), including specifically old irrigation ditches and other details.

The present study now reveals that these missions were established in the San Gabriel River valley along and *near Ramón's road of 1716*. It should be remembered that in 1748, at the time of the beginning of these missions, Ramón's road was the one and only direct road that connected the missions of East Texas with San Antonio. The San Gabriel River was a stream of good water, and its banks were low, such as would make irrigation easy. Why not turn that water on the rich soil of the river valley and thereby solve at least one of the problems of operating a mission? However, there were conflicts among those who operated these missions that soon brought their story to an end. Efforts were made to re-establish one or more of these religious institutions elsewhere on Ramón's road back toward San Antonio between the San Gabriel and San Antonio but each of these lasted such a short time that it occupies a place almost without significance in Texas history.

Here just east of Brushy Creek and possibly some three or four miles northwest of Rockdale, Ramón camped for the night of June 3. He had come to a very thickly set area of trees and brush that would be difficult to penetrate. It would be only a little more than twenty airline miles in a northeast direction to the crossing on the Little River some three or four miles west of the place where the Little River joins the Brazos. But the road across that area of brush and timber would be far from straight and the actual distance would be nearer twenty leagues than twenty miles. In fact, Ramón and Father Espinosa, each of whom kept diaries, each logged more than twenty leagues across this difficult area of trees, brush, timber and grapevines. With knives, hatchets and axes the Spaniards hacked and chopped their way through much of this timbered belt that later became known as the "Monte Grande." The two accounts of this part of the journey were not very consistent. During one day of travel Ramon admitted that he "wandered—without any definite direction."

It may be possible to work out the route of this old road through the "Monte Grande" but it has not been attempted here. What is evident from the map is that the direction straight across this area was a little north of east. The two diaries agree that the party crossed the first river on June 15 which was just twelve days after camp was made east of Brushy Creek. The Spaniards crossed the principal Brazos on the same day—for it was only about one and one-half leagues (four miles) from one river crossing to the other.

Even though both rivers showed evidence of some rain above, Ramón and his party forded both streams. The packs were brought across the Little River on the pack animals with the loss of only one pack. The main Brazos was not crossed by such easy procedure. The packs were crossed on leathern rafts, but the men crossed partly undressed and, of course, went across on horseback.

The fact that these two rivers, even when swollen with rains, could be forded seems to be an important fact in favor of this river crossing.

In summary, from the mouth of Pecan Creek via present Rockdale, the Spaniards reached the Little River some three or four miles above its mouth on June 14. Then, by the end of June 15, the party had crossed the Little River and had moved about four miles eastward and crossed the main Brazos west of Hearne. What travel the Spaniards had done between Rockdale and Hearne was done in twelve days (part-time). The accounts logged more than twenty leagues across this area which included the Monte Grande. The straight-line distance from Rockdale to Hearne is only about half that many leagues, but the exact distance traveled may never be known. It may be possible to work out all or part of that route. No attempt will be made here to detail that very difficult part of the road.

In summary now, it can be said that Ramón's road of 1716 passed through the places where the towns of New Braunfels and San Marcos now stand, that it crossed the Colorado in the big bend some five miles east of the site of Austin, that it passed by the place in Milam County where Pecan Creek flows into the San Gabriel River, and finally that it crossed both the Little River and the Brazos a short distance above their junction. Also it can be said that this was not the same as the road (old San Antonio Road) that crossed the Guadalupe below the junction of the rivers east of New Braunfels and that crossed the San Marcos; and also that Ramón's road was not the same as this lower road (Old San Antonio Road) that crossed the Colorado at Bastrop and that passed through the site of the town of Caldwell on its way to cross the Brazos a mile and a half above the place where Highway No. 21 crosses that river.

But now let us continue the search for the route of Ramón's old road. Up to this point we have followed this route through or near the Texas cities or towns of San Antonio, New Braunfels, San Marcos, Austin, Taylor, and on to cross the Brazos just a short distance upstream from the great river junction five miles west of Hearne.

From the Brazos the Ramón party traveled northeastward past the site of Hearne and on a distance which one account estimated at nine leagues. They had reached a creek which they named Corpus Christi—now known as Cedar Creek. Next day the Spaniards again moved northeastward a distance of either four or six leagues (the diaries do not agree). They had traveled about a league beyond the San Buenaventura River. Their camping place was near a lake known to them and to a number of later expeditions as Santa Ana Lake. Two years later Alarcón followed Ramón's road. He called Corpus Christi Creek, San Buenaventura River, and Santa Ana Lake by the same names as had the Spaniards under Ramón. The Alarcón diary estimated the distance from Corpus Christi Creek to Santa Ana Lake at five leagues. Nine years after Alarcón the diary of the inspection party under Pedro de Rivera estimated this distance at six leagues. The Rivera account called both Corpus Christi Creek and Santa Ana Lake by the same names as those who had preceded but the San

Buenaventura was called the Navasota just as it is called today.

Forty years after Rivera, came the important inspection tour under the Marquis de Rubí. In the diary of this journey, the distance from Corpus Christi Creek to the Navasota was called "a little more than four leagues" and the total distance to Navasota Lake was five leagues. Undoubtedly the Navasota Lake was the same as had been called Santa Ana Lake.

From the foregoing it may be possible to estimate where Ramón's road crossed the Navasota River. The distance between Corpus Christi Creek (Cedar Creek) and Santa Ana Lake as noted above was reported at four, five, and six leagues and from the last of the above diaries the distance from the Navasota River to the Santa Ana Lake was less than a league. Thus it was something more than three leagues in the least of the above estimates from Corpus Christi Creek to the Navasota River. The other estimates would be equal to a little more than four or a little more than five leagues. Probably it is not safe to take these distances and reach a fine-spun answer. Perhaps it is not too far off to suggest that by Ramón's road, it was some ten or fifteen miles between those streams. Thus another clue is available. Malochomy Lake and Baker Lake are just east of the Navasota River and some eight miles north of the south boundary of Leon County. These lakes are a northeastward direction from the junction of the Brazos and the Little rivers just as required in the old Spanish diaries of those who traveled Ramón's road. The Navasota River and Cedar Creek (Corpus Christi Creek) here are about twelve and a half miles apart. No other lakes are near enough to this line northeastward from the river junction to offer a probable solution of our route problem. Thus either Malochomy or Baker Lake seems to offer a reasonable answer to the place where Santa Ana Lake served as a watering place along the old road from San Antonio to the missions of East Texas two and a half centuries ago.

Beyond Santa Ana Lake it was about twenty leagues to the Trinity River. Ramón who opened the road camped halfway to the Trinity at a spring branch which he named Santa Clara. He passed by pine trees and many hills near and beyond Santa Clara. Four leagues northeast of the Trinity, Ramón crossed Santa Efigenia Creek, and continuing in the same direction nine more leagues, he reached the two lakes in a clearing that in a number of later accounts were given as the location of the very first of all East Texas missions, Nuestro Padre San

Francisco De Los Tejas. From this point it was more than three leagues to the Neches River.

Now let us compare this partial road log as reported by the diarists of Ramón's expedition with the details of the route of Alarcón who went that way in 1718, which was two years later. Alarcón travelled ten leagues from Santa Ana Lake to the Santa Clara camping place just as Ramón had done, but his diary reported twelve leagues as the distance on to the Trinity. Recent rains added to his troubles here and may have added to the distance traveled. He splashed his way the last five leagues before he reached the Trinity River. East of the Trinity, Alarcón went toward the northeast without mentioning the Santa Efigenia, but he did report Santa Coleta Creek where he camped twelve leagues from the Trinity. Four leagues past this campsite he came to the two lakes "where the settlement of the year ninety was located." A permanent creek flowed from "west to east" nearby. Obviously, Alarcón had reached the site of the first East Texas mission—the one that was built in 1690. Both Alarcón and Ramón had traveled from Santa Ana Lake to the site of this old mission. Both parties had traveled northeastward every day—in fact both of them had (according to their diaries) traveled northeastward every day from the Brazos to this point. From Hearne near the "Brazos de Dios" crossing to Weches near the San Francisco mission is just a little more than thirty degrees north of due east. In view of the fact that Alarcón reportedly came into Ramón's road near the Brazos surely there is no good reason to believe that he had followed any other course. The routes of the two expeditions were together at the Brazos, they were together at Santa Ana Lake just east of the Navasota, they both camped at Santa Clara and finally they were together at the two lakes near the present little town of Weches.

Now let us pick up the journey of the Marquis de Aguayo and his very large party that came this way in 1721. Aguayo, as we should remember, did not cross the Brazos at the Brazos de Dios crossings but detoured far to the north and finally came into "the old road to Texas" at the Navasota River. He passed near Santa Ana Lake which further shows that he was on Ramón's road. Rains had caused the Navasota River to rise so much that Aguayo had a bridge built across it and, of course, he camped on the west side of the river pending completion of the bridge. From this camp site, it was twelve leagues to Santa Clara. At the end of this distance he camped on the same spot where Alarcón had camped in 1718. He and his party found themselves among the live oak trees on which Alarcón's men had cut crosses three years earlier. Six leagues beyond Santa Clara, Aguayo sent a detachment of men to visit an Indian village. His men had to temporarily leave "the highway" to find the village, and this word "highway" must have meant Ramón's road.

When Aguayo reached the Trinity he solved the very difficult problem of crossing that swollen river by making use of a canoe which the missionaries had hidden up a nearby creek when they had retreated from the French two years earlier. Again, here is evidence that the Aguayo expedition was still following the regular road. Here is more of the evidence: After Aguayo left the Trinity he had traveled just four leagues northeastward to the crossing of Santa Efigenia Creek. Five years earlier Ramón had traveled the same distance and the same direction to cross the same creek. But let us continue. Aguayo moved forward seven more leagues in a northeastward direction to Santa Coleta Creek—this was eleven leagues northeast of the crossing of the Trinity River. Ramón had traveled twelve leagues in the same direction from the Trinity to Santa Coleta Creek on his journey made in 1716. The difference of only one league out of twelve in the estimated distances is surely too small to consider. Aguayo must have traveled on Ramón's road all along.

Thus there seems little reason to doubt that both Alarcón in 1718 and Aguayo in 1721 made use of Ramón's road—the former from the Brazos and the latter from the Navasota—to the mission belt of East Texas. This information if true can greatly aid us a little later in outlining the route of Ramón's road.

With this possible advantage in mind we should briefly relate the routes of two more important expeditions to Ramón's road.

First Pedro de Rivera in 1727 appears to have followed Ramón's road (with one exception) all the way from San Antonio to the missions of East Texas. He traveled as did Ramón from San Antonio, to New Braunfels, to San Marcos and so on past Austin to Brushy Creek (probably at Rice's Crossing). Here he did not cross, but turned downstream on the southeast side of the creek for eight leagues. At this lower point on Brushy Creek (the creek was then called "Las Ánimas"), he camped at a place that he called Lower Las Ánimas. This may have been at Ramón's lower ford on Brushy Creek. Whether this is true or not, Rivera turned southeast and entered the big forest (the Monte Grande) two leagues ahead. He had thus plunged into the dreaded Monte Grande with its thickly grown timber and brush from which he would emerge in less than fifteen leagues. Then, after he had passed through more than a half dozen leagues of open country, he would again enter the ''very dense timber'' as his party approached the Brazos River. His Spaniards crossed at the Brazos de Dios crossings which had been used by every known Spanish expedition for more than a decade.

Eastward of the Brazos he crossed Corpus Christi Creek and the Navasota River (also known then as San Buenaventura) and he, as had nearly all of the East Texas-bound parties, camped at Santa Ana Lake. Rivera passed up the Santa Clara camping place because it had gone dry and later crossed the Trinity apparently at the same place where all the other parties since 1716 seem to have crossed. Two of these preceding expeditions had crossed the Trinity and camped four leagues to the northeast on Santa Efigenia Creek. Rivera did not camp until he was seven and a half leagues beyond the Trinity, but the diary shows that he had crossed the Santa Efigenia within that distance. Surely there is no reasonable explanation of the language of the several diaries from 1716 to this diary of 1727 other than to assume that all parties were traveling the same road across these streams. Seven leagues more (still to the northeast) Rivera had crossed Santa Coleta Creek and camped beside San Pedro Creek, a stream that was not known (and crossed) by these Spanish parties of the early eighteenth century, but is well known today. As we have seen, it is on the map of Houston County just a mile northwest of the little town of Weches.

Already we have noted Rubí forded the Brazos and its largest tributary at the now well known Brazos de Dios crossings just west of present day Hearne. Ramón, Alarcón, Aguayo (on his return), and Rivera had all crossed there. Three of these last four Spaniards had gone northeastward, had crossed the Navasota River and gone a short distance beyond past a small wooded area and camped at Santa Ana Lake. Their estimated distances from the Brazos to this lake varied from thirteen to sixteen leagues. The Marquis de Rubí left the Brazos at the same place as the others, traveled northeastward across the Navasota, passed a small wood and camped at Navasota Lake. His distance was fifteen and a half leagues. Surely the only important difference was the very probable fact that the name of the lake over forty years of time had been changed from Santa Ana to Navasota. If so every one of these old Spanish expeditions from 1716 to 1767 had crossed the Navasota River at this same place.

Now let us move forward (northeastward) to the Trinity River. We have noted already that Ramón in 1716 traveled four leagues northeastward from the crossing of the Trinity to Santa Efigenia Creek—also that Aguayo in 1721 went the same distance and direction from the Trinity crossing to this same creek. We have noted further that Rivera in 1727 went seven leagues that reached northeastward from this crossing of the Trinity to a point beyond Santa Efigenia Creek. And now, forty years later, we note that Rubí traveled northeastward six and a half leagues from the Trinity crossing and reached a hill beyond Santa Efigenia Creek. It would be difficult indeed, even if we tried, to say in plainer language that all of these expeditions had crossed the Trinity River at or very near the same place. In other words Rubí like his several predecessors had traveled Ramón's road.

Most of these Spaniards of the early eighteenth century had crossed the Trinity here at anything but low water. Probably they did not know whether the bottom of the river was mud, gravel, or hard rock. Not so with Rubí. He crossed when there was hardly a span of water in the river. He found that the Trinity at that point had a rock bottom all the way across! Certainly a rock bottom in the Trinity can be an identification mark worth looking for.

But there are other marks of identification beside hard rock. Both the diaries of Aguayo and Rivera found chestnuts growing northeast of this Trinity River crossing after they had crossed Santa Efigenia Creek. The Alarcón diary also told about the chestnuts. The diarist had failed to mention Santa Efigenia Creek when he crossed it, but he did mention the chestnuts by the time the party had traveled seven leagues northeast of the Trinity River crossing. At least two of the three diaries said that the chestnuts were small—and again we have something worth searching for. Facts are available so that we can know that seven important Spanish expeditions—beginning with Ramón in 1716 and extending to de Mézières in 1772, all crossed the Trinity at the same place. Not only did they cross at the same place but we also can know the precise location of that very old river crossing.

Ramón himself, in 1716, crossed at this place on the Trinity River, then traveled four and a half leagues to the northeast where he crossed Santa Efigenia Creek. Aguayo, in 1721, crossed the Trinity, and four leagues northeast of it, he also crossed Santa Efigenia Creek. Surely the two expedition leaders crossed the river at or very near the same place—but let us go on. Rivera, in 1727, on his tour of inspection, went seven and a half leagues northeastward from his Trinity River crossing and within that distance he had reached and had gone beyond Santa Efigenia Creek. Forty years later (in 1767) the Marquis de Rubí, on his epoch-making tour of inspection, moved six and a half leagues to the northeast from the place where he forded the Trinity, also crossing Efigenia Creek. Rubí's diarist did not make it clear whether the party of Spaniards camped at the creek or beyond, but he did say that the camp was on a hill which evidently meant that the six and a half leagues reached beyond the creek. Thus the reports of these four expeditions—when we consider that their estimates of distances probably vary—these reports are not necessarily inconsistent. Certainly the reports are so much alike that there should be no reasonable doubt but that all of the parties crossed the Trinity River at about the same place.

In 1768, Father Gaspar José De Solis also made a tour of inspection. His journey concerned the condition of the missions. Probably he was less concerned with distances than were some of the other Spanish parties, since his diarist was inclined to over estimate. But even with this handicap his diarist shows plainly that the route of travel crossed Santa Efigenia Creek, not far to the east of the Trinity. The road log of Athanase de Mézières made in 1772 shows—as do nearly all of the other accounts—that Santa Efigenia Creek was northeast of the crossing on the Trinity and that the distance was only a part of a span of eight leagues which was a day's journey begun just east of the Trinity.

So far we know that all of the seven foregoing Spanish expeditions crossed Santa Efigenia Creek only a few leagues eastward (very probably northeast) of Ramón's crossing of the Trinity River, which should quiet any doubts but that all of them were traveling the same road at this point. As we have seen, they (except Aguayo) were all traveling the same road at the Brazos. Between the Brazos and the Trinity the logs of the journeys of these parties show so many place names in common and such points as Santa Ana Lake, that were on the route of all, that we can be sure that they were following the same road. Quite obviously they were traveling Ramón's road—since each of them followed the road which he opened.

But we have included the principal Spanish expeditions to East Texas from 1716 to 1772—that is, all except one. That one was the Spanish party led by Alarcón in 1718. After he crossed the Trinity

River his diarist did not even mention Santa Efigenia Creek. But Alarcón had already entered "the road to Texas" (Ramón's road) just west of the Brazos; he crossed the two branches of the Brazos there; he crossed the Navasota River and immediately came to the Santa Ana Lake, as did the others; and continued to pass points and to report place names that were in most of the diaries of the other parties. But one fact reported in the accounts of both Alarcón and Aguayo should dispel all doubts about what road Alarcón was traveling. When Alarcón camped at the Santa Clara Spring in 1718, his men cut many crosses on the live oak trees. Three years later, when Aguayo camped there, his diarist said that the party "halted at Santa Clara, also known as Las Cruces, because of the fact that many crosses had been carved on its trees during the previous '*entrada*'."

However completely the foregoing facts may convince the reader that eastward of the Brazos the several important parties of Spaniards were all traveling Ramón's road, we have not yet nailed down on the map the place where Ramón crossed the Trinity River. The clue to the location of that crossing comes from the diary kept for the Marquis de Rubí in 1767. The very simple fact that Rubí crossed the Trinity on a "ledge of rock" is the one specific thing that can point out the crossing of this old, old road—for the rock crossing is still there.

The fact is that, even though the rock ledge was always in the river, many of the parties of Spaniards did not know about it because quite often the channel of the Trinity was well filled with water. Rubí came at a time when there was scarcely a span of water in the river. Certainly the search for that rock crossing calls for field work. The effort to find Rubí's rock crossing began by driving down paved Highway No. 7 eastward from Centerville in Leon County. Why should the search begin in Leon County? Simply because a majority of the several diaries cited above tell about the pines west of the Trinity, which are plentiful in Leon County but are not in evidence at all along the (later) Old San Antonio Road in the county south of Leon. Still more convincing is the fact that high hills are in Leon County and not where we, in due time, expect to show the later road in the area south of it. Most of the diaries of these expeditions of the 1716 to 1770 period mentioned passing among these hills as they approached the Trinity from the west.

These high hills and pines were much in evidence along Highway No. 7. Two or three miles before reaching the Trinity an informal question asked in a roadside store brought forth the first important information. A young teenaged girl told that only a few years earlier—when the river was low—she had crossed the stream on foot. She had crossed the river on the rocks, which meant that the river had a rock bottom. When asked if the rocks had been piled in the river, she laughingly said, "No, they grew there." The place where she had crossed was about a mile or a little more up the Trinity above the concrete bridge where Highway 7 now crosses the river.

The people in the roadside store all recommended an interview with a Mr. Walter Jones, who lived only a short distance down the road. He had worked on a government structure that was built in the river nearby and would know more about the river than anybody else. I did go to see Walter Jones. It was a warm day, and Mr. Jones sat beneath a shade tree in his front yard. The interview took place in that welcome spot of shade. Mr. Jones knew much more about the river than can be told. During a dry season in 1925, he had helped to drive a Model T Ford across the river at the rock crossing where the young girl, at a more recent time, had walked across. He called this old crossing on the Trinity "Kickapoo Shoals" which brings to mind a Texas Land Office map of Leon County (dated 1857) that shows a crossing at or very near this same place. The map indicated that an Indian village was also at the place.

Surely this is the answer. Leon County is northeast from Hearne, and, of course, also from the Brazos de Dios crossings, just as the old Spanish diaries had said. Here in Leon County are the high hills and the pine trees, neither of which are anywhere near the (later) Old San Antonio Road in Madison, the county that joins Leon on the south. But we need not stop so abruptly. Here is a rock crossing precisely where it should be to harmonize with the northeasterly direction from the old Spanish crossing (Brazos de Dios) of the Brazos—along with the pines and the hills. But where is Santa Efigenia Creek? There is no creek at hand that bears that name, but just northeastward of Kickapoo Shoals, at the proper distance, is Little Elkheart Creek, ready-made to fit the description of old Santa Efigenia Creek. Little Elkheart flows westward into a larger stream, also known as Elkheart. This larger stream flows into the Trinity a short distance above Kickapoo Shoals.

Another bit of supporting evidence fits nicely into the research here. After Aguayo (in 1721) had crossed Santa Efigenia Creek—still moving northeastward—he came into an area where chestnuts were plentiful. In 1727, Rivera also found chestnuts northeast from the crossing of Santa Efigenia. But Alarcón, whose diarist never mentioned Santa Efigenia Creek, found chestnuts (1718) within his first day's journey northeast from his crossing of the Trinity. The accounts of two of these expeditions very significantly reported that the chestnuts were small.

Certainly here again was a challenge to do some field work. This time the field trip led to the little town of Grapeland, which is in Houston County twelve miles north of Crockett. Also let us say that Grapeland is northeast something more than a dozen miles from the place where I had talked to Walter Jones. It is also north of Little Elkheart Creek and northeast of Kickapoo Shoals. It was raining, and to have ventured out on the dirt roads of the area would have been the same as asking for trouble. But there was a good Samaritan in Grapeland who had the right solution for the trouble. He furnished a telephone and a chair and his own personal services in looking up the telephone numbers of the people who lived in the nearby countryside. Person after person was asked this question over the telephone "Do you have wild chestnuts growing in the woodland part of your farm?" And person after person gave back the monotonously unwelcome answer "No."

The field trip had reached a crisis and the search for Ramón's very old road had gone on the rocks. But sometimes help can come from the most unexpected sources! This time, from a boy, just out of his teens, the son of the aforesaid good Samaritan. Modestly he suggested "I don't think you are really looking for chestnuts. What I think you are looking for is chinquapins. The chinquapin is encased in a shell that looks like a cocklebur—so is a chestnut. The difference in appearance is that a chinquapin is smaller. In some parts of Illinois people call the chinquapin a chestnut. There are plenty of them growing in the woods between here and Little Elkheart Creek. I don't think they grow south of Little Elkheart. If you'll wait here about fifteen minutes, I'll bring you some of them."

He did that very thing, and in so doing he gave new life to my field trip. The authorities checked (later) about chinquapins and chestnuts do not show that the latter grow in Texas at all. But they do list the chinquapin as a Texas tree. The scholars confirm what the boy told me, and of course make it practically certain that the old Spaniards of 250 years ago, after they had crossed Santa Efigenia Creek (Little Elkheart), moved into this area of chinquapins (not chestnuts) that is found near Grapeland and north of Little Elkheart

Creek. A trapper who had spent years in the county said that chin-quapins grow north of Little Elkheart Creek but nowhere else in the west part of Houston County. A field trip made sometime later by the writer, along with Mr. Grover C. Ramsey of San Antonio, con-firmed what the trapper had said about the locale of chinquapins in west Houston County. Without any question, the chinquapins are numerous north of Little Elkheart Creek.

But even with these several facts that join hands to identify Kickapoo Shoals as the place where Ramón's road crossed the Trinity River, there may yet be questions. Where, for instance, is the place that came to be known as Robbins Ferry with respect to Kickapoo Shoals? The answer—Robbins Ferry was almost exactly where Highway 21 crosses the Trinity. It was on the east boundary line of Madison County, some six miles northeast of the village of Midway. It was the place the later branch of the Old San Antonio Road crossed the Trinity and was about twenty airline miles almost due south of Kickapoo Shoals. In 1821, Stephen F. Austin forded the Trinity at this Robbins Ferry crossing. He reported the river at that place had a hard gravel bottom, which, of course, was different from the rock bottom at Kickapoo Shoals.

From Kickapoo Shoals on the Trinity River, all of the expeditions recorded here, from Alarcón to De Mézières, followed Ramón's road all of the way to the Neches River. All of them, as we have pointed out, crossed Santa Efigenia Creek; some half-dozen leagues beyond, all of them crossed Santa Coleta Creek; and all of them, by one means of identification or another, indicated that they had passed the place where de Leon's mission of 1690 was located. Ramón identified the spot as the place of the "two lakes." He named the place "San Pedro." Alarcón referred to the spot as the place of the two lakes and also told that it was the place where the settlement of the year '90 was located. Rivera called the place San Pedro, and even forty years later Rubí's diarist also called the place San Pedro. But as late as 1772, it bears the same name in the de Mézières diary.

The direction of these various parties of Spaniards was northeastward. The diaries of Ramón, Alarcón, Aguayo, and de Mézières plainly said so. Certainly, those who did not report their direction of travel—certainly, they too were moving nor-theastward—else how could they have passed through the same places as the others? Another fact can be of help here. At San Pedro a creek flowed from west to east, along the border of the two lakes.

But now we still need to know the actual route of this part of Ramón's road. We can draw lines in a northeastward direction across a map of Houston County and thus begin to arrive at some kind of an answer. Let us begin at Kickapoo Shoals and see what lies northeast of that old crossing. Actually some of the diaries seem to distinguish a little better than to report a simple northeast. Some of them give the direction as east-northeast.

A line east-northeast from Kickapoo Shoals—if extended across Houston County—can be drawn parallel to San Pedro Creek as both the line and the creek approach the Neches River. Not only this, but the line (if it is on the south side of San Pedro Creek) can extend across the Neches and at a little more than two miles beyond the river (and across Bowles Creek) it reaches a very prominent single mound. The mound, of course, can be especially significant. In 1767 Rubí crossed the Neches, and one league beyond some of his party climbed on top of a prominent mound. Certainly, for all of these centuries, the mound has had a fixed location. In present-day geographical terms, it stands more than a quarter of a mile north of Highway 21, and a little more than two miles east of the Neches River.

With a mound and Kickapoo Shoals at opposite ends of this line across Houston County, apparently we are beginning to make progress toward finding the route of Ramón's old road in this area. Such a line would cross Little Elkheart Creek, as previously stated, and without any important deviations it would cross Stowe Creek, Cook Branch, and Austin Branch, all of which flow northward into San Pedro Creek. One of these three creeks must have been the Santa Coleta Creek that was mentioned in the several diaries above. Eastward of these creeks the line on the map would pass along the south side of San Pedro Creek and on beyond it to the crossing of the Neches and on to the old mound.

How did San Pedro Creek get its name? This is a possible explanation. The two lakes and the location of de Leon's mission (of 1690) were named San Pedro by Domingo Ramón in 1716. Probably that old mission and the two lakes were beside the stream that we now call San Pedro Creek. Time has erased the mission and also seems to have filled the two lakes with silt. Over the years the name must have been transferred to the creek. Land maps more than a hundred years old call the stream San Pedro Creek.

Since both Kickapoo Shoals and the mound east of the Neches can be so definitely located, the foregoing line across the map of

Houston County must be the approximate answer to the part of the route of Ramón's old road that lies between the Trinity and Neches rivers.

But before we go on let us examine more carefully the crossing of the Neches River. The Texas General Land Office map of Houston County (1841) shows that this oldest road, recorded in the area land records, traversed the Leonard Williams survey and crossed the Neches River at the Williams' Ferry. C. N. Zivley, who surveyed this very old road (in 1915) had access both to the land records and to the physical evidence of the old road on the ground. With the old land map and supporting field notes as a guide, there is no reason to doubt that he correctly located the old crossing, known as Williams' Ferry. With this river crossing correctly located, Zivley added some other landmarks which we may profitably use in locating Ramón's old road in this area. Zivley's plat shows that a "very deep" lake was located just west of Williams' Ferry and at the north side of the old road. His plat further shows that three "prehistoric mounds" lie just south of the old road at what one may calculate to be about nine-tenths of a league east of Williams' Ferry.

Now since a diary of both the Ramón expedition (of 1716) and of the Aguayo expedition (of 1721) called attention to a lake near the west side of the crossing, and since a diary of the Rubí journey (of 1767) mentioned a hill a league east of the crossing, one is inclined to believe that the surveyor in 1915 not only located the place where Williams operated his ferry 140 years ago, but at the same time, cited facts that pointed out the place where Ramón crossed the river 250 years ago.

It should be noted that while Rubí's diarist estimated the distance from the Neches eastward to a certain hill at one league, the "one league" was only an estimate. Zivley actually surveyed a line at this place and made a plat of it. The writer scaled the plat and found that the "mounds" were only a little more than nine-tenths of a league from the river. Only one of the three mounds is prominent enough to be thought of as a hill, and no other hill is in the immediate vicinity. In 1821 Stephen F. Austin called attention to a single mound that stood "at the edge" of Mound Prairie. The writer, in more recent years, walked near a mound that stood at the edge of Mound Prairie. It was probably a little more than two miles (which is almost a league) east of the Neches River, and by my estimate now it was between a quarter and a half mile north of Texas Highway 21.

Surely it is the same mound of earth that was on the route of Rubí in 1767, of Austin in 1821, and of surveyor Zivley in 1915—and since Rubí was undoubtedly traveling Ramón's road, it stands as an eternal signpost that points the way to the river crossing of this first old road that completely spanned Texas.

The crossing was perhaps about a mile up the Neches above the present-day river bridge on Highway 21. It was here that the colorful frontiersman Leonard Williams had acquired a sitio of land and had established a ferry during colonial Texas. He could not write his name, but he was appointed as an Indian agent by Sam Houston in 1842, and was one of the commissioners who took part in the Tehuacana Creek Council in 1844.

By the time that Leonard Williams began to operate his ferry, traffic on Ramón's old road of 1716 may have ceased entirely, but by that time traffic on the later Old San Antonio road—the road by Robbins Ferry and Bastrop—was well underway. Not only did these two old roads cross the Neches at the same place, but they must have followed the same path for at least a half-dozen miles west of the river. Also they followed the same path eastward to the mound. But not far beyond the mound they divided and followed different routes all the way to Nacogdoches. The north road of the two was a continuation of the road from San Antonio by Robbins Ferry. It passed through (or nearly through) the towns of Alto and Douglas and on to Nacogdoches. The other road ran—at most seven miles—south of the road through Douglas. This latter road passed the old ghost town that—140 years ago—was known as Mount Sterling. Mount Sterling was just east of the Angelina River. It was part of a real estate boom that fell on its face while Texas was still a colonial venture. The part of this road that lay between the Angelina and Nacogdoches was known as the John Durst road. The late R. B. Blake (in 1938) proved beyond any reasonable doubt that the old mission Concepción was along the route that much later became known as the John Durst road. From Blake's conclusion about the old mission, it follows that the south road between the Neches River and Nacogdoches was Ramón's road, for, of course, Ramón—in order to have established the mission—undoubtedly traveled to the place there the mission was erected. Of course, we cannot know what minor changes in the road may have taken place during the century that came between Domingo Ramón and John Durst, but at least the John Durst road is an approximate survival of this part of the old road of 1716.

The Southern Loop

Not only were these two different roads, but none of the numerous important and official expeditions (the diaries of which are cited in this chapter) ever traveled the road through Bastrop from 1716 to 1788. None of the diaries of these expeditions have in any way referred to this lower road. Probably it had not yet been opened. Now let us examine a loop from San Antonio to the Brazos de Dios crossing far to the south of both roads.

The Indian menace and the great difficulty of traveling through the Monte Grande caused many of these expeditions between San Antonio and East Texas to bend their routes far down into South Texas and then to turn back northward and finally to enter Ramón's road and to cross the Little River and the Brazos at the "Brazos de Dios" crossings west of Hearne.

Two years later than Ramón's journey Martin de Alarcón (the founder of San Antonio) turned southward to the Texas coast at San Antonio and after some explorations he returned northward and entered Ramón's road a half league westward of the Little River and continued eastward, following Ramón's road across the Brazos and beyond. Five years after Ramón had made his road, the Marquis de Aguayo followed this road of 1716 all of the way to the crossing of the Colorado below Austin before he followed a new route almost as far north as the Waco country before he crossed the Brazos somewhere well above the "Brazos de Dios" crossings. He entered Ramón's road (to East Texas) between Hearne and the Navasota River. Both Alarcón and Aguayo followed Ramón's road all of the way from East Texas back to San Antonio.

In 1767 the Marquis de Rubí, Father Solis, and the French world traveler, Pierre de Pages, all left diaries of journeys to or from East Texas. Each of these parties traveled the Southern Loop (let us call it) between San Antonio and the "Brazos de Dios" crossings. By this time this Southern Loop had become a road. Ramón's road between San Antonio and the Brazos was still open, since we know that Governor Hugo Oconór traveled from the Brazos by the "upper road" to San Antonio in 1767. In fact, the road log left by Athanase de Mézières in 1772 causes us to know that Ramón's road was still open at that date all the way from East Texas to San Antonio. There was no material difference between the logs given in the diaries of the old road in 1716 and this log of 1772. Even in 1788 Pedro Vial, in travelling from East Texas to San Antonio, crossed the Brazos at the Brazos de Dios crossings. If the "Bastrop" route of the Old San Antonio Road had been in existence at that time, it is strange indeed that he should have traveled the extra mileage required to cross at this uppermost crossing of the Brazos and then to have turned far down into South Texas in order to reach San Antonio.

Information about the route of this Southern Loop is not as complete as one could wish, but the diary of the journey of the Marquis de Rubí can furnish enough data to outline the path of the old road without a very great error.

It was August 25, 1767, when Rubí set out from San Antonio on the long journey to Los Adaes, which was at the site of present-day Robeline, Louisiana. His route began down the east side of the San Antonio River, avoiding the crooked turns of that stream that would have added miles to his journey. He camped the first night at the river bank near the place that is now Floresville. His second day took him across Cibolo Creek, very near the place where that important stream flows into Karnes County, and from there he continued and camped near the mouth of Ecleto Creek (Cleto Creek then), from which campsite he would turn (the next day) at right angles away from the San Antonio River.

Up to this point he no doubt had followed the road from San Antonio toward La Bahia (Goliad), but he must now turn to the northeast and follow the Southern Loop across the Guadalupe. As we shall see shortly, the Southern Loop had already become a road, but it was actually a very dim trail as were most of the other Texas roads at that time. It had become a useful road because it had less interference from Indians than had Ramón's road between San Antonio and the Brazos de Dios crossings on the Brazos. Also the Southern Loop seemed to avoid some of the brush and the timber of the Monte Grande. But this route apparently had come to be considered a part of the San Antonio - Los Adaes Road.

The crossing of the Guadalupe on this road must have been south of and near the site of Cuero. Rubí's diarist indicated that the river was crossed at a southeastward turn in its course—and certainly such a turn is just south of Cuero. What doubly emphasizes this probability is the next fact from the diary. Four leagues (ten and one-half miles) north of the Guadalupe the Spanish inspection party crossed Cuervo Creek—and a stream called Cuero Creek is in that very place today. Surely "Cuero" is (and was in 1767) the right name, for the diary of the churchman Solis, who traveled the same route the year after Rubí, called the creek "Cuero."

Ten leagues northward from Cuero Creek, Rubí and his Spaniards reached the Lavaca River, which was already known by that name in 1767. An additional nine leagues of travel brought the Spaniards to the Navidad River, which is still known as the Navidad. Eight leagues beyond Rubí crossed the Colorado River—another stream that has kept its name for much more than two centuries. Probably the crossing of this big Texas river was at or near the site of present LaGrange. The direction which the Spaniards traveled and the distance between the above rivers makes this conclusion seem likely.

The Colorado bottom was heavily timbered and difficult to cross. Tree limbs had even fallen across the "highway" here. This word from the LaFora diary makes it plain that Rubí was following a road. The churchman Gaspar José De Solis was also following a road—in fact, the same road as was Rubí. Both Rubí and Solis crossed exactly the same streams with just one exception from the Gaudalupe to the Colorado, as shown by their diaries.

The LaFora diary (of Rubí's journey) gives the names of nine creeks and rivers which the Rubí party crossed between the Guadalupe and the Colorado. The Solis party undoubtedly crossed all of the nine, but their diary does not list San Estevan Creek because it must have been small and unimportant. Eight of these streams—Cuero Creek, El Rosal, Padre Campa, Los Ramitos, the Lavaca River, Breviario Creek, La Navidad River, and Los Cedritos Creek—all eight of them are given in the diaries of both expeditions, and all of the eight are listed in the same order in the two accounts. The diaries indicate that each of the two expeditions was traveling a road. One can hardly do other than to conclude that both parties were traveling the same road. Six of the nine streams mentioned above are now known by different names than in 1767, but Cuero Creek, the Lavaca River, and the Navidad River kept their names for all of these two hundred years.

The position of these three streams and the distances between them are a great help in finding the route of the road. In complying with the diaries and the geography of the streams, the road must have passed through or near Cuero, Yoakum, Schulenburg, and LaGrange.

Thus far we have moved from the Guadalupe to and across the

Colorado. The Southern Loop continued northward across parts of Fayette, Lee, Burleson, and Milam counties. Hints from the LaFora diary make it very probable that this old road ran west of the large prairie that nearly crossed Burleson County from the Brazos southwestward. Also the fact that this almost ancient highway passed through two small prairies as it drew nearer to the Brazos crossings gives us a good reason to believe that it passed through the northwest part of Burleson County. There was still plenty of timber ahead as this one-time branch of the road from San Antonio to Nacogdoches traversed a part of the Monte Grande as it approached the Brazos de Dios crossings west of Hearne.

Actually this long loop of road seemed to have served most of the traffic between San Antonio and the Brazos in the middle part and well toward the end of the eighteenth century. As we have indicated, this was the route of the inspector Rubí and the churchman Solis as each of them came this way in 1767. The Frenchman, Pages, whose diary fails to give many landmarks must have gone this way also in 1767, for it was he who explained that Governor Oconór, who had a larger force, traveled the upper road (Ramón's road) in that same year.

The Bastrop Cut-Off of the Old San Antonio Road

Having established Ramón's road, we must now describe the beginning of what became known much later as the Old San Antonio Road. In 1767 came the very important inspection tour of the Marquis de Rubí. Events in Europe had caused France to hand over the Louisiana Territory in 1763 to Spain just as completely as if it had been delivered on a silver platter. The French threat to Spanish operations in the pine belt east of the Trinity had hardly lifted a finger for a long time. Now it had ceased to exist. The Spanish soldiers at Los Adaes and other nearby presidios had just as well go home, except that some of them could stay and guard against Indian raids on the missions. But Rubí thought of that possibility too. Rubí reasoned that the missions of East Texas had ceased to be very effective—why not abandon them all and send the clergy to other fields?

The recommendations of Rubí prevailed and not only were the missions discontinued but private individuals were ordered to leave East Texas and move back to San Antonio and possibly other areas that were already protected by armed forces. Hereafter the rather costly Spanish operations in East Texas could be wiped off the royal books and the Redmen unmolested could plant and reap as of old even though their spiritual welfare had to be disregarded.

Contrary to Spain's efforts to abandon East Texas, Gil Ybarbo and a group of other Spaniards obtained permission to return to that part of Texas. Ybarbo made his settlement on the Trinity River in 1774. Most historians believe that his settlement (called Bucareli) was established near the crossing that became known as Robbins Ferry. Journeys of scouting parties appear to have passed Bucareli near present Midway and to have gone westward over a hill called la Tortuga (the Turtle) and on across the Brazos to the Monte Grande. Sugar Loaf Mountain two miles west of Flynn in Leon County may be the hill that the Spaniards called "la Tortuga." If the travel of scouting parties went west from old Bucareli their route must have passed not far from the hill that we now call "Sugar Loaf." Reports handed down from the days when the Spaniards lived in this outpost on the Trinity River indicate that la Tortuga was fifteen leagues west of Bucareli—which is only a little more than the distance from the Trinity to Sugar Loaf.

Settlers of Bucareli must have made and used a road from Ramón's near Weches to their village on the Trinity and on westward near the place thirteen miles south of Centerville now known as Cross Roads and on to Ramón's road again near Sugar Loaf. Continuing westward along Ramón's road across the Brazos west of Hearne they could have reached the Monte Grande just as old reports indicate. If so, then apparently the settlers of Bucareli opened the part of the so-called old San Antonio road southwest of Cross Roads but instead they must have moved westward and joined Ramón's old road again near Sugar Loaf Mountain (la Tortuga).

The Spanish authority yielded somewhat reluctantly to Gil Ybarbo in permitting him to establish a colony on the Trinity River. They had abandoned all settlements and missions in East Texas, and it was without any enthusiasm that they permitted anybody to return. The danger of losing this big area of colorful pines and singing rivers had passed when France handed over the Louisiana territory to Spain. The Spanish king could cut costs if he didn't have to send soldiers to East Texas, so he let Ybarbo and his colonists worry about their own defense.

But this little colony of Bucareli had another matter to worry about. Disastrous floods on the unruly Trinity first caused them great loss and finally forced them to move away entirely. Many of them moved eastward and established (in 1778) the town of Nacogdoches, but Spain still neglected to concern herself about the defense of this small group of self-willed Spaniards.

It was not until 1795 that Spain reversed her policy and sent troops to Nacogdoches—and even then it was not primarily for the benefit of her subjects that had strayed off into the piney wood. Another threat to Spanish control of East Texas had begun to lift its head over on the east bank of the Mississippi. The young and vigorous United States of America was beginning to have growing pains and along with them, aggressive frontiersmen were pushing westward into Texas.

It was in this year of 1795 that Governor Manuel Muñoz sent the first detachment of soldiers to Nacogdoches. Did he send them by way of the old San Antonio-Nacogdoches road? We can be positive that he did not—for a letter from the commanding officer of this little band of armed men that came back to San Antonio was mailed from a camp on the Navidad River. It should be remembered that the Navidad River is far down in South Texas, a fact which probably indicates that these troops were traveling the long detour from San Antonio into South Texas that came all the way up to the Brazos de Dios crossings and from there reached eastward by Ramón's old road to Nacogdoches. Apparently these Spanish troops were traveling the long route from San Antonio to Nacogdoches that was traveled by Rubí in 1767 and (traveled in reverse) by Vial in 1788.

This long tortuous route was not shortened during the several decades that Spain paid so little attention to East Texas. But now that there were troops to be supplied and mail to be dispatched, something had to be done about it. It no longer made sense to send the mail or gunpowder or other supplies over these 200 extra miles of road from San Antonio to Nacogdoches.

Something *could* be done about it. It was only about 300 miles from San Antonio to Nacogdoches if a road could be made nearly straight across. The Brazos River was almost exactly halfway between these two old Spanish towns if the road between could be made to cross that large river fifteen miles east of the place where the town of Caldwell now stands. Much of the part of the road that lay east of the Brazos must have been traveled for a full twenty years before 1795. There is little doubt that the road from Nacogdoches by present-day Weches, Crockett, Robbins Ferry (Bucareli) and Cross Roads was opened soon after Gil Ybarbo and his friends established Bucareli. Another fifty miles would extend this road to the Brazos east of the site of Caldwell. Most of that fifty miles was either open country or outright prairie where herds of buffalo seem to have attracted Spanish hunters even at that early day.

West of the Brazos the country through which this direct road would pass was not quite so well known. Near San Antonio such a route was not so difficult. It could follow Ramón's old road for more than twenty-five miles northeast from San Antonio but about a half dozen miles short of today's town of New Braunfels it had best turn a little to the right and cross only one river (the Guadalupe) instead of crossing both the Comal and the Guadalupe as Ramón's road did. The same advantage could be had near San Marcos if a new route crossed the San Marcos River just below the mouth of the Blanco three miles downstream from the place that is now downtown San Marcos. But beyond the San Marcos and for a hundred miles northeastward past the present towns of Bastrop and Caldwell and on to the Brazos the route was almost unknown.

It was just eight months after the first troops were sent to Nacogdoches that such a road as the above was opened. Circumstantial evidence strongly suggests that it was the road described above. At first it was used as a mail route. One party set out from Nacogdoches westward and carried the mail to the Brazos. On the same day another party left San Antonio and carried the mail eastward and met the first party at the Brazos. This last party had to have a guide to find the way. Certainly the road was new else a guide would have been unnecessary. The fact that the same number of days were required for the San Antonio mail carriers to reach the Brazos that were required for the Nacogdoches carriers makes it quite plain that the Brazos was the halfway point. The road described above—actually the one now called the old San Antonio Road—was divided almost equally at the Brazos. According to Zivley's field notes, it was 153 miles from Nacogdoches to the Brazos by that road and 150 miles from there to San Antonio.

This fact alone almost certainly identifies (as the San Antonio-Nacogdoches road by Bastrop) the road opened by the Spanish mail carriers. The Brazos does not come near to dividing equally any other old Spanish road between San Antonio and Nacogdoches. By Ramón's road log it was ninety-six leagues from the San Antonio River to the Brazos by his old road of 1716. Also by his road log it was sixty two and a half leagues from the Brazos to the Guadalupe mission which was at the place that later became Nacogdoches. By Father Espinosa's diary it was eighty leagues from San Antonio to the Brazos and only sixty-four leagues on to this old mission at Nacogdoches. Both the diary of Ramón and that of Father Espinosa show that it was nineteen days of travel between the San Antonio River and the Brazos and only twelve days from there to the site of Nacogdoches. Certainly the Brazos does not come near to the half way point on Ramón's road. In this connection the Brazos is even much farther from the midpoint for those who traveled from Nacogdoches to the Brazos de Dios crossings and then made the long detour into South Texas before they reached San Antonio. Any careful study of a map of Texas confirms rather than denies the conclusion that this mail road opened in September, 1795, was the old San Antonio-Nacogdoches road which, of course, is another way of saying that the road now called the Old San Antonio Road was opened in 1795.

Historically, the mail carriers, as far as we are able to check, continued to use the same road. Ferries of some type were set up at the important river crossings. Small detachments of Spanish soldiers were, from time to time, stationed at these crossings.

In 1807 when Zebulon Montgomery Pike crossed Texas, he very probably followed this road opened by the Spanish in 1795. He told about the pines at the Colorado River—a very definite evidence that he was traveling the San Antonio road that crossed the Colorado River at the present town of Bastrop. The road, when Pike made his journey, was still being used by the Spanish mail carriers. In fact, Pike met the mail near the Navasota River as he traveled eastward from San Antonio toward Nacogdoches. This road opened by the mail carriers in 1795 had become the important route from San Antonio to Nacogdoches by 1807.

As we have seen earlier, both this road and Ramón's old road followed near present-day State Highway No. 21 on to the Sabine River (which is the present boundary of Texas) and eastward some fifty additional miles near Louisiana State Highway No. 6 to Los Adaes, once the capital of Texas. This extension of Ramón's road beyond the place where Nacogdoches was established soon followed the founding of the missions in present-day Cherokee and Nacogdoches counties in 1716.

Not only did Ramón's road of 1716 extend to the east even beyond the Sabine River, but it came into the present-day boundary of Texas at the Rio Grande some thirty miles below the site of Eagle Pass. This old road that reached Los Adaes fifty miles deep in Louisiana came from far down in the interior of Mexico. It was the first road (made by Europeans) that completely crossed the geographical unit now known as Texas.

Even before there were such towns as San Antonio, Nacogdoches or Goliad this old road was opened by Domingo Ramón. The motive that prompted the Spanish authorities to do this unusual thing was similar to the motive that sent Alonso de Leon into East Texas in 1690. The Spanish Crown was again afraid that Frenchmen were about to intrude on what Spain claimed as Spanish soil.

But this time the story was quite different and far more colorful than the unsuccessful colonizing effort of La Salle. In this case the Frenchman was very romantic and fell in love with a Spanish girl, almost as if some fiction writer had decided to take over the writing of Texas history. It was mid-summer in 1714 when Louis Juchereau de St. Denis came from Fort Saint John the Baptist at Natchitoches westward across Texas and appeared at another Fort Saint John the Baptist (San Juan Bautista) some five miles west of the Rio Grande and about thirty miles downstream from the site of present-day Eagle Pass. He hoped to establish trade relations between the French of Louisiana and the people of Mexico. His efforts to establish trade were not successful, but Manuela Sanchez, granddaughter of the Spanish captain of that place captured his heart and by the summer of 1715 he and this young lady were married. The Spanish authorities, ever suspicious of French intentions, sent the Spanish captain, Domingo Ramón, in 1716, to what is now the Nacogdoches country with authority (and supplies) to open a chain of missions in East Texas. St. Denis went along also and part of the time he may have helped to guide the expedition, but the diaries of the journey do not indicate that he was very important in the role of guide. When the Spaniards got off course a short distance northeast of present-day Austin, it was not St. Denis but the Payaya Indians who set them right again. Father Espinosa and his party (with information from the Payaya Indians) had pioneered Ramón's route in 1709 between the San Antonio and Colorado rivers—some five years before St. Denis appeared on the scene. Seemingly, the whole route from San Antonio to East Texas was known to the Payaya Indians who gave route information both to Espinosa in 1709 and to Ramón in 1716. Surely credit for opening this road across Texas must go to Ramón, not St. Denis.

A Comparison of the Ramón Road
and Later Old San Antonio Road

It is necessary to recapitulate in part the preceding accounts to distinguish clearly between Ramón's road and that later known as the Old San Antonio Road.

Some concrete evidence bearing on this subject comes from the old diary of the Pedro Vial expedition which came this way in 1788. The old diary tells that Vial came westward through Nacogdoches to the Neches on that journey, and between the Neches and the Trinity he camped on Carriso Creek. His camping place was just four leagues from the Trinity. Now Carriso Creek, as it was known on the Creuzbaur map (of Texas) of 1849, or Caney Creek, as it is known now, flows southwestward and enters the Trinity about a mile below the present-day crossing of Highway 21 on that river. The Highway 21 crossing is almost the exact place that was once known as Robbin's Ferry.

The next night past Carriso Creek, Vial camped on the Trinity—very probably near the present highway bridge. The next night after that he camped at Persimmon Lake—which the writer cannot identify. Then his next camping place was on "the Leona," a total distance of ten leagues from his Trinity River crossing. The Leona is shown on the old Creuzbaur map. It is now known as Spring Creek and is southwest of Centerville in Leon County. Ten leagues on his way from the Leona, Vial next camped on Corpus Christi Creek. This stream was first called Corpus Christi Creek by Domingo Ramón on June 18, 1716, when he camped there. It is in Robertson County eastward of Hearne and is now known as Cedar Creek. Vial, in 1788, camped next, after Corpus Christi Creek, at the Brazos de Dios crossings on the Brazos River west of Hearne and then followed the Southern Loop into San Antonio.

Note that Vial left Ramón's road near Weches and passed near Crockett on his way to the Trinity River a half-dozen miles northeast of the present town of Midway. Then he undoubtedly went a little north of west to Spring Creek in Leon County, which in Vial's time, was known as "the Leona."

Here Vial had come back into Ramón's road again after following a "lower road" for possibly as much as seventy miles. Vial's simple—if somewhat abbreviated—diary seems to clear up the difficulty experienced by some historians in explaining what was meant by the phrase the "lower road." If Ramón's road that ran directly from the Brazos de Dios crossings on the Brazos to Kickapoo Shoals on the Trinity and on to the place that became known as Williams' Ferry on the Neches and all the way beyond to Los Adaes, could be thought of as the regular—or perhaps upper Adaes road—then Vial's route that likewise crossed both the Brazos and the Neches at Ramón's river crossings, but crossed the Trinity at the place that became known as Robbins Ferry, which was lower down the Trinity—this route could have been called the lower Adaes road.

This lower road could have been opened by Gil Ybarbo, who established Bucareli in 1774. Certainly Ybarbo and his followers must have made a road, and if Bucareli was built at the Robbins Ferry crossing on the Trinity, Vial's route of 1788 was precisely where they should have built it.

Assuming that Bucareli was located at the place that became known as Robbins Ferry, why didn't Ybarbo take the direct route to San Antonio by Caldwell and Bastrop and save many leagues of travel?

Circumstantial evidence strongly suggests that in 1774 there was not yet any such road as the Bastrop cut-off between San Antonio and Nacogdoches. If the Bastrop cut-off existed in 1767, why did Rubí follow the Southern Loop from San Antonio far down into South Texas and on that road travel back many miles to the north and cross the Brazos at the Brazos de Dios crossings before he turned eastward toward Nacogdoches and Adaes? Or why did Vial, in 1788, after he had crossed the Trinity at the future site of Robbins' Ferry—why did he travel miles out of his way and go up to the Brazos de Dios crossings and down by the Southern Loop if the shortcut Bastrop road had been opened even as late as 1788? Both Rubí and Vial necessarily crossed this Bastrop cutoff, if such a road existed at the time of the journey of each of them, but neither of their diarists said anything about it. The same may be said about the journey of Father Solis and of the Frenchman Pages, who also crossed the Brazos at the Brazos de Dios crossings in 1767. If these different parties had had the convenience of traveling the shorter road (which let us again call the Bastrop cut-off) instead of crossing at the Brazos de Dios crossings and then following the long Southern Loop, surely they would have followed the shorter road—if the shorter road had been opened in their time.

But Rubí, in 1767, made a statement about these roads to deep

East Texas which can answer the uncertainty here. Below is the statement as paraphrased by Professor Herbert Eugene Bolton. This is the Bolton statement: "Here, then, said Rubí, was a stretch of country beyond Bexar, several hundred miles wide, over which Spain claimed dominion, but which was crossed by *only two* rude paths and occupied by only three small garrisons, a handful of impoverished settlers, and four useless missions." What were these "two rude paths?" Rubí, of all people, should have known, for he traveled both roads. He traveled from San Antonio to Los Adaes over Ramón's road, except that he followed the Southern Loop from San Antonio to the Brazos. That was one of the two roads. From Los Adaes, he returned over Ramón's road as far as Nacogdoches. From Nacogdoches he turned south and crossed the Trinity near the Gulf. Then he went westward and crossed the Brazos at the rock crossing near the future town of San Felipe, and on to Goliad (La Bahía) and, in fact, all the way to Laredo. This was the second road referred to, but the area in which Rubí recommended abandonment lay east of San Antonio and east of Goliad. Not only did Rubí recommend abandonment in the area traversed by these two roads, but abandonment was actually ordered and partly accomplished.

Note that Rubí said that there were only two roads. If the road between San Antonio and Nacogdoches by Bastrop had been in existence, surely he would have mentioned four roads. Then why did all of the expeditions either cross the Brazos at the Brazos de Dios crossings at Hearne or at the rock crossing far down at San Felipe? Because only two roads crossed the Brazos in 1767 and one of these crossed at the Brazos de Dios crossings while the other crossed on the rock crossing down at San Felipe. Certainly these two roads were both in existence in 1767—and certainly Rubí traveled both roads. Why did he say that the area had "only two rude paths" if there were any more?

So, indirectly, Rubí's statement makes it plain that the Bastrop cut-off between San Antonio and Nacogdoches did not yet exist, and also that the La Bahía road between Robbins Ferry and La Bahía did not yet exist.

Now the question arises "when was the Bastrop cut-off between San Antonio and Nacogdoches actually opened?" Surely after 1788, for as we have seen, Vial should have traveled that short-cut route had such a road existed. It was 1795 when Spain began to send soldiers to East Texas again. It was in January of that year when the first troops were sent to Nacogdoches. No account that would tell the route of those soldiers has as yet been located, but the fact that a letter was sent by an officer of this detachment, addressed from the Navidad River, is revealing. Now note that the Navidad River was not even near to either Ramón's original road of 1716 nor to the later San Antonio road that passed through Bastrop. But that river was crossed by the Southern Loop. Probably that detachment of soldiers was traveling (in reverse) the road followed by Vial seven years earlier.

But such a roundabout road would be too slow as either a supply route or a mail route for a military force even though that force was not yet large. The answer came in September of the same year. It would speed up mail delivery if a direct route to East Texas—a route that would cut straight across the Southern Loop—could be opened. Even beyond that improvement, it would cut the time in half if the eastbound mail could be sent from San Antonio and on the same morning the westbound mail sent from Nacogdoches, so that the two could meet at a halfway point and exchange. This plan was adopted. The designated half-way point was the Brazos River at a place now called Paige. No longer were the Brazos de Dios crossings on the route. There is no good reason to doubt that this was for the most part a new route, for guides were sent along so that those who carried the mail would not lose their way. Surely this was the branch of the Old San Antonio Road that passed through Bastrop and Caldwell, the road that crossed the Brazos a mile and a half north of Highway 21. By this road the Brazos was indeed near the mid-point. Surveyor Zivley found by this route that Nacogdoches was 153 miles from that river and that San Antonio was 150 miles from it.

Apparently the mail continued to follow this new road. In 1807, Zebulon Pike traveled the road that crossed the Colorado and immediately passed through the pines. Continuing eastward, Pike met the mail at the Navasota River. He was undoubtedly traveling the later branch of the San Antonio-Nacogdoches Road, for no other road between those points passed through the "Bastrop pines."

The east part of this road passed near or through Nacogdoches, Weches, Crockett, and on to the Trinity at the place later known as Robbins Ferry. From this point on the Trinity, it ran about a dozen miles to a point in the north line of present-day Madison County. This much of the Spanish mail route of 1795 (or of Pike's route of 1807) was traveled by Pedro Vial in 1788 and probably by Gil Ybarbo as early as 1774. But westward from this point in the Madison County line, all the way to within about twenty-five miles of San Antonio, the road was opened by the Spanish mail carriers of 1795—or at least we look in vain for any expedition that traveled that part before 1795.

It was not long until ferries were placed at the important river crossings and detachments of soldiers were stationed at those crossings to guard against interference.

Perhaps we should again give (in later place-names) the route of this, the last of the old San Antonio - Nacogdoches roads. Let us begin at San Antonio, then proceed to the junction of the Comal and Guadalupe rivers, just below New Braunfels, then to the junction of the San Marcos and Blanco rivers, three miles below San Marcos, next to Bastrop, and next to Caldwell and on to cross the Brazos a mile and a half above the river crossing on paved Highway 21. The old road then turned a little to the left, soon entering a blacktop road which is even now known as the "Old San Antonio Road." About ten miles from the Brazos this blacktop reaches the Robertson-Brazos county line, just south of the village of Benchley. From that point, following this county line eastward, both the blacktop and the actual Old San Antonio Road continue together all the way to the Navasota River, not far from the place where Pike met the Spanish mail in 1807. East of the Navasota, the old road and the blacktop follow the line between Leon and Madison counties until they reach Normangee, and even beyond to the little village known as Cross Roads some fifty miles from the Brazos. From Cross Roads, the blacktop turns southeastward a dozen miles to join Highway 21 at the small town of Midway. Highway 21 runs northeastward from Midway a half dozen miles to a good concrete bridge across the Trinity at old Robbins Ferry. The San Antonio-Nacogdoches mail road of 1795 did not follow exactly either of these road segments, but it did curve across from Cross Roads to this concrete bridge, passing about two miles north of Midway.

Perhaps we should go back for a moment and explain that this Old San Antonio Road of 1795 was exactly on or very near paved Highway 21, all of the way from San Marcos to the Brazos River. About three miles northeast of San Marcos to the old road and Highway 21, both followed the southeast Hays County line for about twenty miles. Here the old road turned a little to the right of the pavement. It was about two and a half miles south of the pavement at the west Bastrop County line, but was not quite so far away anywhere else in the west part of Bastrop County. Probably the old road passed through downtown Bastrop and followed at least near Highway 21 northeastward all of the way to the county line, but old surveying records are silent for some ten miles of that distance.

Across Lee County, next east of Bastrop, and across Burleson County, the old road and the pavement were together most of the way. The old road was about 500 yards north of Highway 21 in the county seat town of Caldwell, and as previously stated, was a mile and a half north of this pavement at the Brazos River. All other variations were smaller than these.

Now let us return to the concrete bridge across the Trinity at almost the identical spot where Nathaniel Robbins once operated a ferry. From this bridge, Highway 21 passes through Crockett, Weches, Alto, Linwood, and Douglas, on the way to Nacogdoches. The distance from this bridge to Nacogdoches is only slightly more than eighty miles, but for all these eighty miles the old road is nowhere as much as two miles away from the highway.

It is only a mile and a half south at Crockett, less than a mile north (for a stretch of some ten miles) at Weches, and at only two other places is the difference as great as a half mile. An accompanying map will show the two roads in greater detail.

Thus we have noted that Ramón's road from the Presidio on the Rio Grande to Nacogdoches did not stand alone but that in due time the Spaniards opened other roads to serve the same traffic. Within the course of a little less than a hundred years, they had established two other roads between the Presidio and San Antonio, and in 1842 Mexico had opened still another road between those same two places. From San Antonio to the Brazos, the Southern Loop served most of the traffic after only a few decades. The Bastrop cut-off between San Antonio and Nacogdoches came after Spain had abandoned the missions of East Texas and had attempted to bring about a complete evacuation of the area in which the missions were located.

VIII

NEW CONCLUSIONS ON THE ROUTE
OF MENDOZA 1683-84

Into a veritable paradise of spring rivers, into a land where the harvest of pecans was greater than almost anywhere else, into an area where the wild buffalo came in countless thousands—into this fabulous land of nature's bounty came the expedition of Juan Domínguez de Mendoza[1] in the spring of 1684. This statement, which points to a spot in the heart of what we now call the Edwards Plateau country of Texas, is in sharp conflict with the previous findings of historians. Nevertheless this pronouncement supported by evidence not previously used and spelled out into specific details of route and geography is to be the chief conclusion of this chapter.

Mendoza built a mission two stories high on the Colorado River some fifteen miles southeast of Ballinger, Texas—so say the historians who have previously discussed this subject. In sharp contrast, this study proposes to show that Mendoza built his mission not on the Colorado but on one of the great spring-fed rivers about midway between San Angelo and San Antonio. Obviously there must be a presentation of substantial facts if these new answers to the problem of finding the location of Mendoza's mission are to be accepted. Also there must be facts to support other important diversions from the previously accepted route of this Spanish expedition.

With a promise that these facts will be forthcoming, may we briefly point out some of the visits which Europeans had made to Texas before 1684. Piñeda made a crude map of the coast of Texas in

---

1. See Herbert Eugene Bolton, *Spanish Exploration in the Southwest 1542-1706*, 313-343. Bolton has in these pages reproduced in English the day-to-day account of the expedition of Juan Domínguez de Mendoza 1683-1684. For a more detailed explanation of this and related sources special attention is directed to pages 317-319 of the above work of Dr. Bolton. Hereafter this work will be referred to as Bolton: *Mendoza*.

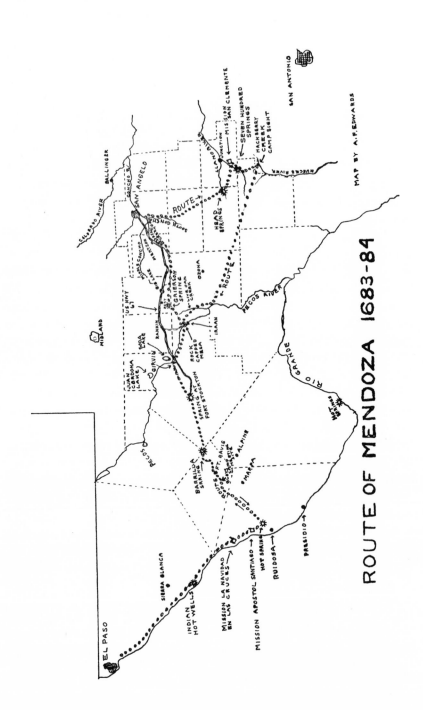

1518. Then Cabeza de Vaca and three companions (sole survivors of the shipwrecked Narváez Expedition) spent a half dozen years as slaves of some Texas Indians from 1526 to 1534. Next, in 1541, came the Coronado party across from the Rio Grande into West Texas and later the same year the worn-out remnant of the De Soto Expedition haltingly marched into East Texas.

There was one important fact that applied to all of those expeditions. None of them found gold in Texas—neither did the several parties who followed during the next 140 years. Thus, without the powerful magnet that had pulled Spaniards into Mexico, Texas had passed the first 150 years (and more) without establishing a single permanent settlement east of the Pecos River. However, the Spaniards by the end of that period had evolved their system for the establishment of missions and had turned their attention more to the spiritual needs of native Indians.

Coupled with this trend toward mission work among the Indians came the Pueblo Revolt of 1680 that drove the Spaniards out of the upper Rio Grande Valley. This combination of forces helped to prepare the way for the Mendoza Expedition toward the center of the area that we now know as Texas. Also Captains Martín and Castillo in 1650 and Guadalajara in 1654 reported the discovery of pearls[2] on a branch of the Concho River—and in addition there was the (purely fictitious) tale in which the Indians claimed to have seen a cross in the sky[3] near the Rio Grande something more than fifty leagues below the site of today's El Paso.

It was December 15, 1683, when Mendoza began his journey.[4] By January 1, 1684, he had followed the Rio Grande from the environs of El Paso to present day Presidio County, Texas. No attempt will be made here to furnish details either of his route or journey until just before January 1.

Omitting any effort to furnish such details, we can at least identify a certain hot spring which was the campsite of January 1.

Probably it will be easier to follow the story of the Spanish party if we begin the more detailed account just four days after Christmas, 1683, and as nearly as possible locate the campsite of each day following.

2. Bolton: *Mendoza*, 314.
3. *Ibid.*, 325 n.
4. *Ibid.*, 320-21.

December 29, 1683. On this date Mendoza and his party reached a point on the Rio Grande which became known as La Navidad en las Cruces[5] from the story previously mentioned of Sabeata (and possibly other members of the Julimes Nation) in which he reported the miraculous appearance of a cross in the sky. Sabeata almost lied his way into literature with the colorful story which even he finally admitted was pure fiction, but his efforts bore fruit. The Spaniards established a mission[6] at the place. The meadows were spacious and the Indians planted corn and knew something of the Mexican language.

The place on the Rio Grande is in west Presidio County, Texas, almost due west of the present-day town of Marfa but here the reader is asked to await the evidence until the campsite of January 1, 1684, is reached.

December 31, 1683. After spending an extra day at the previous camp, the Spaniards moved seven leagues to another point[7] in west Presidio County—probably on Walker Creek to the north of the little village now known as Candelaria. A mission—Apostol Santiago[8] by name—was established at this place.

January 1, 1684. On this day Mendoza reached a hot spring[9] seven leagues from his last camp which must become the real anchor point for our study of this part of his route. Hot springs are very few along the Rio Grande Valley—one is located south of Sierra Blanca in south Hudspeth County; another is seven miles from the river near the village of Ruidosa in southwest Presidio County; and a third is on the Rio Grande southeast of the Chisos Mountains in southeast Brewster County. Surely Mendoza's camp of January 1 was located at one of these three springs, for only the three are to be found north of the Rio Grande[10] in the great span of more than 200 miles from Sierra

5. *Ibid.*, 325.
6. *The Handbook of Texas*, II, 18. The writer reaches a different conclusion about the location of this mission and the Apostol Santiago Mission from that mentioned in *The Handbook*.
7. Bolton: *Mendoza*, 325-26.
8. *The Handbook of Texas*, I, 55.
9. Bolton: *Mendoza*, 326.
10. The writer has made many local inquiries about the location of hot springs on the north side of the Rio Grande in the whole area from the Indian Hot Wells south of Sierra Blanca to the lower turn of the Big Bend of the Rio Grande. Perhaps the most specific interview on the subject was had with Mr. H. Dailey, a life-long resident of Presidio, Texas. Mr. Dailey stated positively that the only hot spring in

Blanca to beyond the Chisos Mountains.

Then which of the three was the site of Mendoza's camp? The account left by the Spaniards is helpful in making that answer. The very next campsite—according to that account—was at the end of a *mesa* "which extends to the north." Here we surely have the answer for none of the three springs are in the vicinity of a *mesa* except the one hot spring near Ruidosa in southwest Presidio County. In fact, the Davis Mountains and those that lie in the Big Bend country to the south and southwest are of the pointed variety—except in the area northward of Ruidosa.[11] Here north of Ruidosa and west of Marfa is a great tableland the edge of which is known as the Rim Rock. Near Ruidosa are several *mesas*.[12]

With this positive bit of topography to confirm the location of the campsite of Jan. 1, then it follows that the missions established at the two previous campsites must be up the Rio Grande Valley from Ruidosa. The Apostol Santiago mission was seven leagues (eighteen miles) up the river valley on a creek that "flows from north to south." Apparently this was Walker Creek. La Navidad en las Cruces mission was somewhere on the Rio Grande seven leagues above.

The locations of these two missions as given here are in conflict with the conclusions usually made by historians but, so far as the writer knows, no historian has previously used the hot spring at Ruidosa as an anchor point of this part of Mendoza's route.

January 2. Another seven leagues of travel took the Spaniards to

---

the area near Presidio was the spring north of the village of Ruidosa which is forty miles or more above (northwest of) Presidio. He mentioned a spring down the valley some miles below Presidio that was slightly warm but emphasized the point that this spring could in no wise be classified as a hot spring. Mr. Dailey's report that the Ruidosa spring was the only hot spring for a great distance up and down the Rio Grande was confirmed by sheriff Ernest W. Barnett of Marfa, Texas.

11. The writer has traveled by highway over the essential part of the Big Bend country except the area near Ruidosa. The Ruidosa area is described in footnote No. 12.

12. Sheriff Barnett of Marfa, who is familiar with the terrain of the Presidio country, described the Rim Rock formation and told about the smaller mesas of southwest Presidio county. Also see B. C. Tharp and Chester V. Kielman (editors), "Mary S. Young's Journal of Botanical Explorations in Trans-Pecos, Texas, August-September, 1914" *The Southwestern Historical Quarterly*, LXV, 528. "All the hills" in the Ruidosa area and near the Rio Grande in southwest Presidio County are said to have "a level top capped by a stratum of rock." Miss Young and Cary Thorp made camp at the hot spring near Ruidosa.

a point at the end of (or alongside of) a mesa[13] probably near Capote Creek west of Marfa. The existence of more than one mesa in the area adds some uncertainty to the location of this campsite.

January 3. Traveling northward again the distance of seven leagues, Mendoza crossed the plain that lies west of Marfa and camped in the southern part of the Davis mountains on ". . . an arroyo which runs toward the west."[14] A number of small streams (normally dry) that flow toward the west cross United States Highway 90 in the span of road to be found from fifteen to twenty-five miles northwest of Marfa, but this area is in a plains country quite by contrast from the campsite of the Mendoza party. The watering place at which the Spaniards were camped was " . . . surrounded by bare denuded rock."[15] There were cedars on the *heights*. These two facts make it quite plain that the campsite was in the mountains. The writer has made a search of the part of the Davis Mountains that lies northwest of Marfa—both on the Texas highway maps and by personal travel and observation. He is able to find only one stream which flows to the west in this area. It is an upper branch of Chispa Creek (the lower part of which flows northwestward parallel to United States Highway 90 between Marfa and Van Horn). This upper branch of Chispa Creek is well within the Davis Mountains, along state highway 166, beginning some fifteen miles southwest of Fort Davis and flowing about five miles to the west before it turns south across the famous Barrel Springs ranch established by Captain James S. Gillett of the Texas Rangers. Surely Mendoza's camp of January 3 was somewhere along this five-mile span of stream bed.

The Spaniards found oaks[16] at their campsite—and sentimentally, one is tempted to place the location at the site at the Bloys Camp-meeting ground which is in the best known grove of oaks (known as the Emory Oak) found anywhere in the Davis Mountains. But factually, this little west-flowing stream on which Mendoza must have camped, begins just over the hill about a mile west of the Bloys Camp-meeting ground. Only a few oaks are now found along the little stream. The Butterfield mail coaches once followed its course as well as modern paved highway 166. But it must be designated as the

13. Bolton: *Mendoza,* 326.
14. *Ibid.*
15. *Ibid.*
16. *Ibid.*

Spanish campsite of January 3, because at the Bloys Camp-meeting ground, beautiful as it is, the drainage *flows to the east.* The distance traveled by the Spaniards on Jan. 2-3 satisfies the actual mileage on the map. The air line distance from the hot spring near Ruidosa to this little upper branch of Chispa Creek is forty miles. This is about eight percent more than the fourteen leagues of travel which the Spaniards reported for the two days' journey, but their miles were not measured—and there is no other west-flowing stream in the mountains that comes within many miles of their estimated distance or that is anywhere near the right direction (north) from the hot spring near Ruidosa.

January 4-7. The next day's journey extended just four leagues[17] (ten or eleven miles) from this campsite in the mountains to a watering place on a creek that flowed toward the north. Several such creeks are branches of Limpia Creek west of Fort Davis and another flows just at the edge of Fort Davis itself.[18] It would be a difficult choice to determine upon which of these north-flowing streams the Spaniards camped. Another day's travel brought the Mendoza party five additional leagues (about thirteen miles) on their way. This camping place was about a mile up a side canyon. To be exact it had ". . . mountains on both sides."[19] Apparently the Spaniards were following Limpia Canyon, for the rough terrain of the area did not permit either the early trails or the modern highway to follow any other route. Turning back from the side canyon the Spanish party must have continued down Limpia Canyon. It was six leagues (about sixteen miles) to their next campsite which was at a spring at the edge of an extensive plain which spread far to the east. Thus, apparently, Mendoza had traveled from his camp near the Bloys Camp-meeting ground by or near Fort Davis, down Limpia Canyon and on to the east edge of the Davis Mountains in an estimated distance of forty miles (by Spanish accounts). This is only three or four miles short of the distance that almost the same span of road later logged on the Butter-

17. *Ibid.,* 327. All distances in this account of the Mendoza Expedition are given in leagues. Constant use of these distances is made in this article, but the many specific references are not made here because of the almost useless addition to the volume of footnotes. Quite obviously the distances in leagues are to be found in the same parts of the Mendoza account from which the other related facts are obtained.

18. See *General Highway Map, Jeff Davis County, Texas,* for 1951.

19. Bolton: *Mendoza,* 327.

field Trail.[20] At the end of these forty miles of mountain travel was the Barrilla Spring well known to travelers on both the Butterfield Stage Coaches and the wagon trains that followed the old San Antonio-El Paso road by the same watering place.

The Barrilla Spring did not entirely lose its significance when the old wagon trails became outmoded. It became the exact west corner of Pecos County[21] (which is also the south corner of Reeves County) when surveyors measured off the county lines. The camping place (also the stage stand) was two miles down a small stream south of the spring.[22] In other words the Barrilla Spring was uphill to the north of the old stage road. Close study of the Mendoza account reveals the same topography. The hills lay to the north of Mendoza's camp—and " . . . a beautiful spring . . . " came down ". . . from the slope of a hill . . ."[23] surely one cannot hope to find closer agreement in the physical facts about an old spring even though the sources of those facts come from different centuries of West Texas history.

January 8-10. During the next three days Mendoza moved across a level plain,[24] first twelve leagues (nearly thirty-two miles) to a spring which must have been at or near Leon Water Hole, and next four leagues (ten or eleven miles) to or below the Great Spring (Comanche Spring) at present-day Fort Stockton. The four mesas that surround Fort Stockton today almost beyond any doubt identify the Comanche Spring as the watering place at which the Spaniards camped. The chief account handed down to us about this journey mentioned the "four high mesas."[25] No other spring in the area can be so identified.

The distance between Barrilla Spring and this great spring at Fort Stockton was, according to the log of the old San Antonio-El Paso road—a total of 42.74 miles.[26] The sixteen leagues reported by the Spaniards for their first three days of travel east of the mountains amount to 42.144 miles which is only a little more than a half mile

20. Randolph B. Marcy, *The Prairie Traveler* (New York, 1859) 289-90. The Butterfield Overland mail road followed the same route here as the San Antonio-Fort Yuma road mentioned in the *Prairie Traveler*.

21. See the map of Jeff Davis County, General Land Office, June 1915.

22. Roscoe P. Conkling and Margaret B. Conkling, *The Butterfield Overland Mail 1857-1869*, 3 Vols. (Glendale, California, 1947), II, 23.

23. Bolton: *Mendoza*, 328.

24. *Ibid.*

25. *Ibid.*

26. Randolph B. Marcy, *The Prairie Traveler*, 289-90.

short of the measurement by this pioneer wagon trail. Surely the above identification by landmarks and by distances can leave little doubt but that Mendoza camped at or very near the site of Fort Stockton on January 10 and that he had approached the place from the old Barilla Spring near the west corner of Pecos County.

January 11-15. During these five days the Spaniards travelled from the place that is modern Fort Stockton to the Salado (or Pecos) River.[27] All the actual travelling took place on January 12 and 13. The party moved first northeastward until they had passed the west end of the long chain of mesas that extend almost due east toward the Pecos River. Next they moved only a little north of east with this long chain of mesas south of them—or to their right. The Spanish account says ". . . toward the east runs a chain of mesas, on the right hand as we came."[28] Surely there is nothing ambiguous about this quotation. The Spaniards travelled to the north of this *chain of mesas* (and parallel to it) until they struck the Pecos River near the little village of Girvin. Previous discussions of Mendoza's route describe this part of his journey as reaching the Pecos River near the little town of Imperial which is north of Fort Stockton, not *east* of it. If one travels from Fort Stockton north to Imperial, the chain of mesas falls behind him—not to his right as the Spanish account describes it in the story of Mendoza's journey.

Pertinent to an understanding of the location of the first camp which the Spaniards made on the Pecos River is an assembling of the essential facts about two salt lakes that lie (each of them about a league) east of the Pecos in this area. The larger of these is Juan Cordona Lake which is located across the Pecos from Imperial. The other is a smaller lake (sometimes called the Soda Lake) directly across the Pecos from Girvin. Just west of the Soda Lake is a high ridge between it and the Pecos River. Just east of the Soda Lake is the very large mesa known as Square Top Mountain.[29] Directly across the Pecos from the Soda Lake and back some three or four miles from the river, is the small Girvin Mesa. By contrast with this Soda Lake the Juan Cordona Lake is some fifteen miles from the nearest mesa. The whole area across the Pecos from Juan Cordona Lake is level prairie for many

27. Bolton: *Mendoza*, 329.

28. *Ibid*. The chain of mesas begins at a point a few miles northeast of Fort Stockton, Texas, and extends eastward almost to the Pecos River.

29. The writer has on several occasions carefully checked each detail of topography mentioned in this paragraph.

miles. The little Girvin Mesa is more than twenty miles south of this large lake—so far away, in fact, that the little mesa blends into the larger chain of mesas until one is hardly conscious of its separate existence.

Now note the significance of these facts when applied to this first camp made by Mendoza on the Pecos River. In describing this first camp the diary of the Spaniards reads "In front there is a little mesa separate from the others."[30] There is no other little mesa except the Girvin Mesa anywhere within the span of eyesight west of the Pecos River at this point. Further note how the Spanish account identifies the camp of the Spaniards with the Soda Lake. The translated words which describe the lake are as follows: "It is about the league on the other side of the Salado River [the Pecos], between a high hill and a mesa which is beyond."[31] Not by any stretching of the facts can one say that the Juan Cordona Lake is between *a high hill and a mesa*. But that, as noted above, is an exact and true description of the Soda Lake. This, of course, locates the camp of the Spaniards just northeast of Girvin on the west bank of the Pecos.

The Pecos was muddy, which evidently told of recent rains upstream, and because of the swiftness and depth of the river (which subsequent history has revealed) we can surmise that the Spaniards had some difficulty in crossing over to view the Soda Lake. This first camp they called San Christóval which must have been suggested by the difficult stream crossing kept by St. Christopher in the legendary story of old.[32]

January 16-23. Apparently it was only a small detachment of Spaniards who crossed to examine the Soda Lake, for Mendoza later continued his journey down the west side of the Pecos River. On the 16th the party moved downstream three leagues, on the 17th six leagues and shortly thereafter an additional league. Within this last league they crossed over to the east side of the Pecos and camped on a hill apart from but near a large assemblage of Jumano Indians.

Here the Indians camped by the river ". . . at the foot of a great rock . . .,"[33] which served as protection against the hostile Apaches.

30. Bolton: *Mendoza*, 330.
31. *Ibid.*, 329-30.
32. This story and its significance in the account of the Mendoza Expedition was pointed out by Mr. Anthony Brollier who traveled with and assisted the writer on one of his several journeys to the Pecos River country.
33. Bolton: *Mendoza*, 331. Obviously the Indians were camped on the Pecos

The writer drove many miles in which he passed over every highway crossing of the Pecos in this area—in an effort to find the *Great Rock.* He also drove down dirt roads that parallel the river and made much local inquiry. The rock as the writer visualized it—a great rock bluff near the river—was not to be found. Not even any prominent hill can be found short of something like a mile east of the river for twenty-five miles below Girvin. But at the end of that twenty-five miles one finds a little mesa with a very massive cap rock just east of the Rankin-Iraan highway (Highway 349). The little mesa slopes from its great cap rock down to the very bank of the Pecos. Had the Jumanos camped up the slope of this mesa against its prominent cap rock—possibly with sentinels above—they would have occupied a very strong position. One looks in vain for anything else that would remotely fit the description of the *Great Rock.* No other hill of any prominence (within twenty-five miles below the Soda Lake) slopes down to the river's edge; no other hill of the few that are within a mile of the river is capped with a rock that approaches the thickness of this great stone cap on the little mesa by the Rankin-Iraan road.

In addition to these peculiarities of the great rock by the above highway the distance factor lends us a helping hand. The distance of this massive stone cap downstream from the above mentioned campsite across from the Soda Lake is as near to ten leagues (26.34 miles) as anyone can expect to determine by map measurements—and ten leagues *was* the distance reported by the Spaniards.

January 25-27. From the campsite near the great rock two days of travel and ten leagues of distance from the Pecos brought the Mendoza party to ". . . a spring of clear and good water."[34] Here indeed is a landmark. The Spaniards spent two days at this important source of water ". . . in order that the horses might recuperate."

Close study of the early roads that spanned the gap from the headquarters of the Concho River (west of San Angelo) to the Pecos makes it highly probable that the watering place where the Spaniards camped was that which later became known as the Grierson Spring.[35]

River—not back from it. The Mendoza account here recites that ". . . we arrived at the rancheria, to the middle of which we crossed the Salado River. . ."

34. Bolton: *Mendoza,* 333.

35. See map of *Reagan County,* General Land Office, Austin, Texas, October, 1915. Also see map of Upton County, General Land Office, Austin, Texas, Jan. 1918. The Grierson Spring is in section 1, Georgetown R. R. Co. lands. It is sixteen

By the Butterfield Stage Road from the head of the Concho through Castle Gap to Horsehead Crossing on the Pecos it was more than seventy miles. Often the whole seventy miles was without water[36]—and at no point along this span of difficult travel was there a spring of any importance whatever. Neither was there an important spring along the later stage road[37] that turned aside from the Butterfield route. Near the west line of Reagan County this new road branched off to the south from the other road, passing near present-day Rankin before it reached the old Pontoon Bridge on the Pecos just two miles up the river from the little rock-capped mesa by the Rankin-Iraan highway. Later the United States Army at least partly solved the water problem by opening a road from near the head of the middle Concho southwest to the Grierson Spring[38] seven miles a little south of west of the small town of Best—or some fifteen miles southwest of present Big lake. From thís important spring the army road extended a little south of west past the little rock-capped mesa to the Pontoon Bridge on the Pecos. Map measurements show that the distance from the little mesa to the Grierson Spring is just less than twenty-five miles, but the terrain was such that the actual road must

---

miles east and six and a half miles south of the town of Rankin, Texas. Or it may be described as three miles north and seven miles east of the southwest corner of Reagan County. As the crow flies it is about seven miles a little west of south of the village of Best. The Grierson Spring must have been a good one for the United States Army to have made the big southward detour in order to reach it. The Spring is still known by name by some of the older settlers in the Big Lake area.

36. J. Evetts Haley, *Charles Goodnight Cowman and Plainsman.* (Norman, 1949), 130-32. Colonel Goodnight's cattle drives along the Butterfield Trail from the head of the middle Concho to the Pecos were made under great stress. There was no water on the entire seventy miles. Men, horses, and cattle all suffered from thirst.

37. There was a spring (apparently not an important one) some four miles east of Rankin. It was known as the Flat Rock Springs (see Roscoe and Margaret Conkling, *The Butterfield Overland Mail,* I, 362). Quite plainly it was an insufficient source of water for United States Army needs, else the army would not have discarded the road near this spring and substituted for it the newer and rougher road by the Grierson Spring. The Ficklin mail authorities do not seem to have considered the spring of great importance. They did not locate a stage stand at that point—although what appears to have been a rock ruin of one of their stations has been found some two or three miles southwest of it. In Rankin (about four miles from the spring) the writer asked several local persons, including early settlers, about this old spring. None of them knew anything about it.

38. The road by Grierson Spring had been opened before 1881. See Grover C. Ramsey, "Camp Melvin, Crockett County, Texas, *West Texas Historical Association Year Book,* XXXVII, 144.

have been slightly more than that distance. Quite obviously this span from the Pecos River to the Grierson Spring fits almost perfectly the ten leagues (26.34 miles) which the Spaniards travelled from the Pecos to the "spring of clear and good water" where they laid over two days to recuperate their horses. It is also quite obvious that frontier travel never found any other important spring at or near the distance of ten leagues east of the Pecos. Hence we may say with reasonable assurance that the Grierson Spring was the watering place where Mendoza camped from January 25th to the 27th.

January 28-February 24. During this period of twenty-eight days the Spaniards travelled only intermittently. On the 28th and 29th of the month they traveled ten leagues (26.34 miles) and camped at a "watering place that runs from a hill."[39] On the 30th and 31st their progress was only four additional leagues to a "gorge which has a pool of good water."[40] It was February 2 when the explorers moved forward six leagues to the "Nueces River."[41] The stream began at some springs and flowed eastward. After laying over until February 5, Mendoza traveled a mere three leagues to what appears to have been the greatest source of water yet encountered east of the Pecos River. It was "a river bearing much water, the source of which is not known because it comes from beneath the earth and issues through some rocks." The Spaniards found their first pecans here.[42] There were many groves of the trees and nuts were plentiful.

This great spring flowing up through rocks is a very good description of the chief spring on Spring Creek, a mile and a half above the town of Mertzon in Irion county. Also it is true that the first pecan trees as one passes down this stream are found only about a mile above this very spring and in great numbers at and below it just as the Spaniards reported.[43] In addition to these facts, the distance from the

39. Bolton: *Mendoza,* 333.

40. *Ibid.*

41. *Ibid.,* 334.

42. *Ibid.*

43. The writer was unable to contact the owners of the land where the head spring of Spring Creek is located, but he did drive along the highway a few hundred yards away. Some of the tree growth was visible from the highway but the more exact details about the spring and pecan trees were obtained from J. A. Boyd and H. F. Sobge of Mertzon, Texas. Also these gentlemen told about a water hole with some springs some six to eight miles upstream above the main spring of the creek. This last information was confirmed in an interview with C. A. Parry of Barnhart, Texas.

Grierson Spring to this great source of water near Mertzon is about fifty-five miles (probably nearly sixty miles by the most practicable route for a frontier trail). The Spaniards reported twenty-three leagues which is equivalent to sixty miles. All of these facts seem to make out a good case for the supposition that Mendoza traveled from the Grierson Spring eastward down Spring Creek.

Now when one tries to fit the road log of the Spaniards to the middle Concho River—the only other route that seems at all possible—he encounters greater difficulties. It is only a little more than thirty miles—instead of sixty—from the Grierson Spring to the head springs of the middle Concho. There is not any such powerful source of water on the middle Concho as that on Spring Creek—neither is there a spring on the Concho that issues up through rocks as does the spring at Mertzon.[44] Examined from a still different viewpoint, the middle Concho fails to qualify. If one measures across the map, from the Grierson Spring a distance of sixty miles to the Concho, he strikes that stream to the north of Mertzon. This is many miles below the place where the first pecan trees grow along the middle Concho.

Obviously, these facts seem to favor Spring Creek as the probable route of Mendoza's Spaniards but other items of the Spanish account tend to cloud any such clean-cut conclusions. Seemingly we have been able thus far to find marks so spaced that we can fit the account of Mendoza's journey to the modern map. But we now approach the point at which this seems impossible. From the great spring near Mertzon to the junction of the Concho rivers south of San Angelo is about ten leagues. The Spanish road log reports the distance from the great spring which they found to the junction of the rivers at eighteen leagues. The discrepancy is great, but to assume that the Spaniards followed the middle Concho instead of Spring Creek can not account for the extra distance. Either route measures some eight leagues less than the Spaniards reported.

Is it possible that those who kept the diary made an error? The expedition was delayed here. The Apaches stole some of the horses. Also the weather threatened and finally it rained.

---

44. The interview with J. A. Boyd (See footnote No. 43), who was a cowboy on the Sugg Ranch along the middle Concho for some twenty years, makes it quite clear that the great spring mentioned by the Spaniards could not have been on the middle Concho.

Regardless of what may be the explanation of the above inaccuracy, there is one thing reasonably certain. The junction of the rivers is a definite point—or shall we say two points, either in San Angelo where the North Concho meets the principal stream or just south of that city where the middle Concho meets the South Concho. The two junctions are not more than a half dozen miles apart which, of course, leaves us little to argue about. Surely it must have been the junction south of San Angelo—if the distinction is worth making—for the Spaniards followed the Nueces River down until it joined the River of Pearls. Then the River of Pearls must have been the South Concho, for indeed it is the river which the middle Concho and Spring Creek meet after they are united some two or three miles above their common junction with the South Concho.

February 24-March 15. It was eight leagues up the River of Pearls—(note the eight leagues again)—from this junction to the point where Guadalajara intersected the stream. Guadalajara must have been near the head springs of the South Concho above Cristoval, Texas. Mendoza apparently was ordered to make some kind of a report on the River of Pearls. He spent three days on this river,[45] but his diary is silent as to details. Surely he did not spend the three days in one place if there was any faint possibility of finding pearls. Surely he did not leave the River of Pearls without ascending it to the place where Guadalajara crossed—else how could he have known that the distance was eight leagues.

A little farther along in this chapter the writer will produce evidence that Mendoza turned south from the junction of the Concho rivers (south of San Angelo) and that he went southward to and beyond the South Llano River. If Mendoza did turn south in order to fit his account to the country in that direction his road log seems to require the addition of about eight leagues which he must have omitted. In his accounting could he have reported eight leagues in one part of his journey when it belonged in another? Did he mean for his reader to infer that he moved eight leagues up the South Concho?

Let us reconstruct his story as later evidence would seem to support. Without proof let us say that Mendoza's party explored the River of Pearls (the South Concho) the approximate eight leagues from his camp at the river junction to the source of the South Concho. Next let us report that he moved six leagues south from that point to a water hole on an upper branch of the San Saba River—for he did move six leagues to a water hole.[46] Also let us add that the following day he moved eight leagues[47] south to the head springs of the north Llano River above the little town of Roosevelt. Here again the distance is as the Spaniards reported and the head springs of the North Llano set down among table-topped hills, as they are, also meet the description of the Spanish campsite.

For seventeen days (February 27-March 15) Mendoza camped at the beautiful head springs of the North Llano where two centuries later the United States Government was to establish Fort Terrett.

March 15-May 1.[48] But on March 15, this Spaniard and his party moved camp some five leagues to the South Llano River about twenty miles southwest of Junction, Texas. Here on this beautiful river, which Mendoza called the "Glorious San Clemente" the Spanish party halted. In fact, they stayed for more than six weeks and erected a two story structure (probably of logs) which was the first mission established anywhere in Texas east of the Pecos River. Nineteen Indian "nations" followed the Spaniards and camped near this mission. Baptism was administered to many of the Indians—undoubtedly from the water of the famous Seven Hundred Springs which constitute the principal source of the river. More than 4000 buffalo were slaughtered while the Spaniards were at this place which makes it clear that the North American Bison originally grazed in great numbers as far south as the Llano River. Such an immense supply of buffalo meat indicates that there were hundreds—or possibly a few thousand—of Indians camped along the Llano.

May 1-25. And now the proof that this mission was probably located on the Llano comes in quite a strange manner. On May 1, the Spaniards left this mission and moved four leagues upstream. Then on the two days following they marched nine leagues to a river that had a growth of both pines and mulberries[49] in its valley.

Now note that the San Clemente River flowed to the east and this other river just nine leagues away (with pines in its valley) flowed to the west. If one sets out from the junction of the Concho rivers near San Angelo and travels in any direction—north, south, east or west—a total distance of any amount near the number of leagues

46. *Ibid.*, 337.
47. *Ibid.*
48. *Ibid.*, 337-40.,
49. *Ibid.*, 341.

reported by the Spaniards, he can find the above combination of rivers and tree growth at only one place, and that place must be at the edge of the belt of nut-bearing pines that is found in the hill country north of Uvalde, Texas. You can not reach this belt of pines if you travel any direction except south from the junction of the Conchos. Moving southward the last river encountered before reaching this belt of pines is the South Llano. This river *does flow to the east.*

This pine belt exists only on the headwaters of the Frio and Nueces rivers and in the hills east of Dry Devils River. Of these rivers in the pine belt only one branch that flows westwardly is within nine leagues of the Llano—and that stream is an upper branch of the Hackberry on the head waters of the Nueces river. The pines grow in the valley of this branch of the Hackberry—so do the mulberries. The writer has visited this stream—also the other upper branches of the Frio and Nueces rivers and both branches of the Llano.[50] Only the South Llano and the east branch of Hackberry can comply with the conditions set out in the account of Mendoza's journey.

It must be admitted that the diary of the Spaniards gives no hint of the direction which these early explorers traveled from the junction of the Concho rivers. But the belt of little pines and the facts about the rivers southward of San Angelo admit of only one conclusion. Obviously Mendoza did travel south—first to the head springs of the South Concho then across the head branches of the San Saba and past the head springs of the North Llano across to the South Llano. Only by traveling south could the Spaniards have reached the pine belt and only the route as herein described seems to fit the details of terrain mentioned by the Spaniards.[50a]

It is apparent that Mendoza and his party had become afraid of

50. The writer has made many visits to this area. With almost exhaustive study on the ground and with much local inquiry he is able to outline the area in which these pines (in this case pinyons) grow. Also, he has intersected and in many cases followed the courses of the various rivers of this part of Texas.

50a. Seymour V. Connor begged to differ at this point and quoted Donovan S. Correll as authority for pines being farther north. Correll, however, stated, "I made no statement regarding pines growing north of the Llano River, except the fact that they may occur in Deaf Smith County, in the Texas Panhandle. The most northeasterly stations that I have seen for piñons are in Real County in canyons along the East Nueces River and in some canyons between this river and the Frio River." Correll to J. W. Williams, Renner, Texas, April 20, 1970. See Connor, *West Texas Historical Association Year Book,* XLV, 22-23.

Indian troubles and that their withdrawal from the Llano on May 1 was really a retreat. They had started home—and home lay to the west. The account left us specifically states that (during one important segment of this leg of their return journey) they *were* traveling west.[51] Also it should be noted that the Pecos (Salado) River lay to the west.

The Spaniards reported their actual distance of travel for only a part of the way between the Hackberry and the Pecos. The part which they reported was twenty-nine leagues, but they traveled three days on this part of their route for which no distances were given.[52] If we estimate these days of progress along their way at seven leagues per day (which was about their average) we arrive at a total of fifty leagues for this distance from the Hackberry to the Pecos. By actual straight line map measurements the distance is about forty-five leagues. Obviously this small discrepancy confirms rather than denies the supposition that the Spaniards had turned south rather than any other direction from the junction of the Conchos near San Angelo. Had the Spaniards continued eastward from San Angelo to the mouth of the Concho River (as historians have generally assumed) the number of leagues back to the Pecos would have been about thirty percent greater than the above measured distance.

Thus, in order to be at all realistic in our mileage and at the same time to give due regard to the fact that the little pine trees grow only in a small area north of Uvalde, there seems to be no other choice of conclusions than that the Spaniards turned south from San Angelo to the Llano and Hackberry and from there westward to the Pecos River.

But where did they reach the Pecos? Again we can arrive at a fairly accurate conclusion, for the Spanish account itself shows that the point of this campsite was fifteen leagues down stream from the place where the Mendoza party had crossed the Pecos on their eastward journey.[53] This fact points to a segment of the Pecos not more than a half dozen miles south of the Ozona-Fort Stockton Highway at a point some thirty miles west of Ozona.

The Spaniards did not cross the river at this place. They moved northward five leagues (thirteen miles) and camped on "a beautiful river"[54]—undoubtedly Live Oak Creek, the stream on which the

51. Bolton: *Mendoza*, 342.
52. *Ibid.*, 341-42.
53. *Ibid.*, 343.
54. *Ibid.*, 342.

United States Government located Fort Lancaster nearly two centuries later. Live Oak Creek is a good stream of good water, as the Spaniards reported, and is the only stream that joins the Pecos within fifteen leagues below the point at which Mendoza had crossed the Pecos on his eastward journey.

On the other hand, the fact that the mouth of Live Oak is nearly fifteen leagues below the massively rock-capped little mesa near which this study has placed Mendoza's first crossing of the Pecos adds another link in the chain of evidence which tends to fix the location of that river crossing. Rather careful measurements on the Texas highway map of Crockett County shows that the above little mesa and the mouth of Live Oak Creek are eleven air-line leagues apart. Certainly no expedition could have made that journey in a perfectly straight line. By any practicable route the distance must have been as much as thirteen leagues. Quite plainly, if this be correct, Mendoza's return crossing could not have been more than two leagues upstream from the little mesa. Since there is no other land mark within the two leagues that at all resembles the description of the rock against which the Jumano Indians camped, surely this new link of evidence doubly confirms our earlier conclusion about Mendoza's crossing. On their return, Mendoza and his party must have crossed the Pecos shortly above the little mesa that stands like a sentinel at the present river crossing of the Rankin-Iraan paved highway. Some two miles above this modern crossing was the early-day Pontoon Bridge built by the United States military forces in 1872.[55] It is not at all unlikely that Mendoza crossed the Pecos at or near this place where the westward surge of early Americans located the Pontoon Bridge.

It is not necessary that we follow the return route of the Spaniards any farther than this crossing of the Pecos. From here westward Mendoza simply followed in reverse the route of his eastbound journey.

Perhaps a few more general remarks will be permissible at this point. It seems to be the accepted opinion of historians that the Mendoza expedition was intended as the beginning of Spanish penetration and settlement of the area that is now near the geographical center of Texas and that the French threat (the expedition of La Salle) diverted the effort to East Texas. In this paper, however, we have seen

55. Roscoe and Margaret Conkling, *The Butterfield Overland Mail*, I, 364.

a little more clearly than previously that the effort was actually begun in the very heart of the land of spring-fed rivers. In view of Spanish history elsewhere, it may not be amiss to assume that some development of agriculture by irrigation may have been a part of the blue print.

As an additional observation it is apparent that, at the beginning, a relatively large population of Indians could and, from time to time, did live in this river country where pecans and buffalo meat were plentiful.

Another strange fact is the great concentration of buffalo as far south as the Llano River. This was not the case in the 1870's when professional hunters slaughtered what was left of the North American bison. Had the frontier settlers depleted the ranks of the buffalo at the southern (and eastern) margin of the range? Or did the Indians themselves become more proficient at hunting after the end of the seventeenth century? Did the red man after that time make increasingly greater use of the horse, and thus implemented, almost wipe out the buffalo in the areas where the Indians themselves were most numerous?

This, of course, is the study of a Spanish route and in no wise an attempt to answer the above questions. If there are herein any new relations brought forth between the seventeenth century story and present-day geography, this effort has not been in vain.

IX

THE NATIONAL ROAD OF THE REPUBLIC OF TEXAS

A long forgotten document, hidden away among the files of the Land Office for nearly a century, now makes it possible to bring into sharper focus certain phases of the history of North Texas. At a time when transportation difficulties were almost the number-one problem, an important old road was laid out by direction of the Texas lawmakers. Its functions among the trails that served pioneer needs, its route, and perhaps even its purpose have been much misunderstood.

This old document, that promises some new data on a certain period of the story of Texas, consists of only a dozen pages of surveyors' notes. It furnishes, nevertheless, a fairly accurate waybill for the route of the "Central National Road of the Republic of Texas,"[1] and through its contribution of an accurate geographical background promotes a better understanding of certain episodes of the development of North and Central Texas. So much confusion has prevailed concerning the course of this road that its route and the way in which it fits into the larger geography of the Southwest will be first considered.

An act of the Texas Congress, finally approved on February 5, 1844, created a commission of five men empowered to select a right-of-way for this road, and to have that right-of-way cleared of obstructing timber, and also to see that the necessary bridges were erected.[2] The commissioners were directed to begin the road on the bank of the Trinity River, not more than fifteen miles below the mouth of the Elm Fork, and to extend it to the south bank of Red River, opposite the Kiamichi—or, in our terms, from central Dallas County to a point approximately one hundred and thirty miles distant in northwest Red

1. The full plat and field notes are given in Promiscuous File No. 3 in the Texas General Land Office. Hereafter this document is referred to as Field Notes.

2. The act was published in full on the front page of the *Northern Standard* (Clarksville, Texas), March 2, 1844.

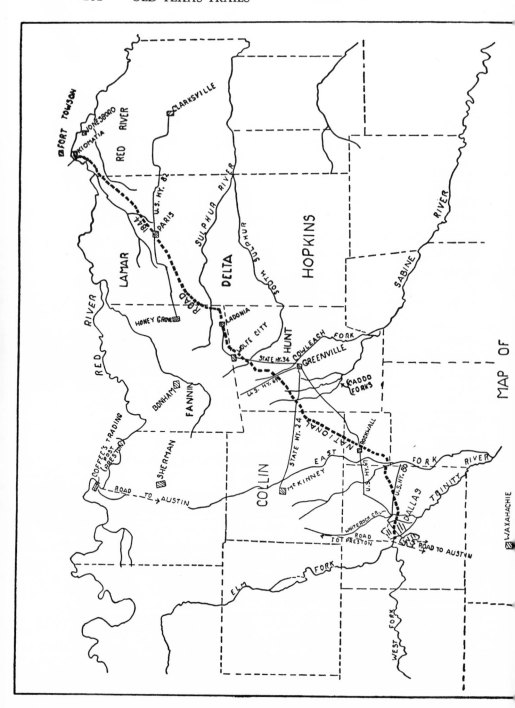

River County. Three of the five commissioners lived less than thirty miles from the new town of Paris,[3] and Paris was also the post office of Major George W. Stell, named by the act to survey the road. The time-worn field notes in the Land Office are in Major Stell's own hand.

Slightly less than two months after the bill was approved, the surveying crew, headed by Major Stell, began its work at the certain cedar tree[4] on the bank of the Trinity River, somewhere in what is now central Dallas County, and thirty days later the enterprise was concluded in the Red River bottom in the northwest corner of Red River County.[5]

In spite of the excellence of the field notes, difficulties are found in following their exact path. In the first place, the cedar tree in Dallas County is gone, and, secondly, there are certain mathematical considerations that make for slight ambiguities in applying the notes.[6] Also, Major Stell admitted the possibility that he had made some minor errors in transcribing his data.

Fortunately, some information within the notes, and some additional facts that have been discovered, limit the possible errors to a relatively small range. A county-line survey, made in 1850, fixes the National Road at a point ten miles and twenty-four chains (or ten and three-tenths miles) south of the north-east corner of Dallas County. A similar survey made of the west Hunt County line in the same year shows that the National Road was nine miles and 74.57 chains (or 9.93 miles) north of the southeast corner of Collin County.[7] Major

3. The commissioners named in the act were Jason Wilson and William M. Williams of Lamar County, John Yeary of Fannin County (who lived four miles south of Honey Grove), Rowland W. Box of Houston County, and James Bradshaw of Nacogdoches County.

4. Field Notes, 1.

5. Field Notes, 1, 5. The surveyor and crew began operations on April 26, 1844, and completed their survey on May 26, 1844.

6. Surveying, as usually practiced, is imperfect to the extent that two surveys begun at the same point and following the same field notes would not likely follow the same exact path for any great distance unless there were recognizable landmarks—stakes, rocks, witness trees, etc.—against which to check the course. The fact that surveying is done on the earth, which is spherical, and platted on maps, which are flat, further complicates one's difficulties in following, on maps, a route surveyed on the earth.

7. Both of these surveys were located among the county-line surveys at the Texas General Land Office. The point at which the National Road crossed the east Dallas County line is further confirmed by the field notes of the near-by Henry D. Banks

Stell's plat shows that this road passed through the town of Paris, and subsequent information identifies it with Bonham street,[8] the important present-day thoroughfare that passes along the north side of the square in modern Paris. The old road came to an end in the northwest part of Red River County, directly opposite the mouth of the Kiamichi River.[9] Obviously these four definite points outline the general course of the National Road; the field notes can be used to fill in details.

A trek across the country, with surveying instruments, in search of this old road might prove to be a first-ranking adventure. The fragments of antique bridges, some of Major Stell's old bois d'arc mileposts—and perhaps a pair of chafing boots, and a little sunburn lotion—might add up to furnish the thrills and attendant miseries of a single day afield. But such an adventure must now wait until less strenuous times.

Instead, this study will proceed by thumb-tacking the necessary county maps[10] to a drawing board and surveying each changing angle of the old road with ruler, protractor, and T-square. For convenience a start is made at the east line of Dallas County, a proven point three and three-quarter miles north of Highway 80. This point on the National Road is slightly more than seventeen miles from the Trinity River and is the place at which that old wagon trail entered the area that is now Rockwall County. At this place the present road runs on almost the same path as the old. Four-tenths of a mile due east, the National Road crossed the East Fork of the Trinity River. The old Mackenzie Ferry[11] was once located there, and in later years the Barnes Bridge[12] was built a half-mile up the stream. Not far across the

survey (Dallas County Surveying Records, Vol. A, 263).

8. A. W. Neville, *The History of Lamar County* (Paris, 1937), 55.

9. Field Notes, 5, 10.

10. Maps, prepared by the Texas Highway Department of Dallas, Rockwall, Collin, Hunt, Fannin, Lamar, and Red River Counties (all dated 1936 but some of them partially revised to 1942) were used in this research; maps of the same counties by the Texas General Land Office were also used. Other maps will be cited specifically at their proper places.

11. Dallas County Commissioners' Court Records, Vol. A, 39.

12. Map of the *Barnes Bridge Quadrangle* by the United States Geological Survey, Oct., 1912.

13. Field Notes, 1, 9. Every mile of the survey, as required by the act creating the National Road, was marked on either a tree or a substantial post. Major Stell's plat and field notes gave the kind of timber or post used at each mile of the road.

East Fork, Major Stell blazed the surface of an ash tree[13] and marked it for his eighteenth mile post. His road next curved southeast, then east, and then northeast around a high hill, and along the north bank of a small creek, which the United States Geological Survey topographical map[14] called Yankee Creek. After a short distance, the road turned more toward the north and finally due north, pointing directly at the future county seat town of Rockwall, and following approximately the route of the present road from Barnes Bridge to Rockwall for several miles. But short of the townsite the old road turned thirty degrees east and crossed the course of a present paved highway about one and one-half miles east of the site of present Rockwall. A little north of the present pavement a cedar post was planted in the ground marking the twenty-seventh mile; the course of the road changed just three degrees more toward the east, and continued in a straight line for eleven miles. In this span of distance, Major Stell passed over the future county line and progressed some seven and a half miles into modern Collin County; a mulberry post was set here to mark the thirty-eighth mile. Cedar posts had marked almost every mile for the past twenty because the route was following a prairie ridge on which there were very few trees.

Observing the map of Collin County for a moment, one finds that this thirty-eighth mile post was about a mile and a half west of a small village called Josephine. Four miles further north the old road survey bent eastward and crossed the line into Hunt County (on land that was part of Fannin County in 1844) at a point two miles south of State Highway 24, between Greenville and McKinney. A few miles to the northeast, Major Stell and his men crossed the route of this present-day State Highway eight and one-half miles west of Greenville, near the village of Floyd.

The land of this area must have appealed to the surveying crew as well as to the Commissioners of the National Road. Each of these early road markers was to receive pay for his work in land, and more than a dozen tracts of this Hunt County real estate were selected by them not far from the village of Floyd. Possibly because of a conflict with the Mercer Colony, most of these parcels of land seem to have been abandoned, but there was at least one exception. John Yeary, one of the commissioners, laid claim to six hundred and forty acres some two or three miles northeast of Floyd.[15] A locust post was set at

14. Map of *Barnes Bridge Quadrangle*.
15. Field Notes, 7, 11.

Yeary's southeast corner;[16] this same piece of timber was also marked as the forty-eighth mile post on the National Road. On current maps of Hunt County there is now a John Yeary survey some seven miles northwest of Greenville,[17] and the method of map surveying employed here places the forty-eighth mile post of the old road near its southeast corner. Apparently this tract of land is identical with the original John Yeary survey, a fact which makes it possible to locate another specific point on the route of the National Road.

Four miles northeast of Yeary's land, the National Road crossed the principal fork of the Sabine River.[18] The bridge on Highway 69, six and one-half miles northwest of Greenville, is almost, if not exactly, identical with the place where the older road crossed.[19] Nearly two miles northeast of this bridge, Major Stell's survey turned due north for three miles, thus avoiding the west part of the dense Black Cat Thicket.

At the fifty-seventh mile post, the northeasterly direction was again resumed, and a little short of the sixty-first marker, the road surveyors crossed South Sulphur near the highway bridge that is now south of Wolfe City. Seven additional miles put the surveying crew a full mile inside the present limits of Fannin County. On this span of road they had missed modern Wolfe City by only a mile, and now

16. *Ibid.*

17. Texas General Land Office Map of Hunt County, of 1894.

18. Field Notes, 2, 11. All of the important streams between the Trinity and Red River are cited in Major Stell's field notes by the names by which they are still called. These are the Bois d'Arc Fork of the Trinity in Rockwall County (more often called the East Fork), the three Caddo Forks of the Sabine in Hunt County, the Cowleach Fork of the Sabine in Hunt County, the South Fork of Sulphur River, also in Hunt County, and Sulphur River itself in Fannin County. The writer has measured the route of the National Road across present-day county maps, as previously mentioned, and in no instance has he found one of the streams out of the place assigned to it in Major Stell's field notes by more than a small fraction of an inch. Even some of the very small streams that did not bear names in the field notes may be identified on present maps. This close correlation between the old field notes and topography is evidence that the route of the National Road as shown in this paper is not greatly in error.

19. Not far below this bridge is the junction of the principal (or Cowleach) fork of the Sabine with Hickory Creek. The National Road crossed above the fork of these two streams (although Hickory Creek was not called by name in the field notes). The crossing on Hickory Creek was 714 varas exactly northeast of the crossing on the Sabine. Obviously, with this specific information at hand, neither map measurements nor actual surveying on the ground can be guilty of more than a very small error in locating the course followed by the National Road at this point.

they were ready to turn twenty-five degrees more toward the east and pass through the south part of the townsite of Ladonia as that town is mapped today.

In 1844, John Loring lived about a mile east of the place that is now Ladonia.[20] The National Road ran a little north of his land and continued eastward some three miles farther before making the abrupt turn northward down into the timbered bottom of the principal branch of Sulphur River. Now a country road runs north to a bridge on Sulphur that is known as the "old Lyday Crossing." Isaac Lyday, who moved to the area in 1836,[21] owned the land just east of the present bridge.[22] He built a frontier fort[23]—perhaps a stockade—that furnished protection to the first settlers. Map surveying traces the National Road across Lyday's old survey about a half mile east of the bridge that now bears his name. There is a creek junction shown in Major Stell's plat that helps to identify this eastward point as the original river crossing.[24]

After passing Sulphur River almost midway of the seventy-

20. The map of Fannin County made by the Texas and Pacific Railway Company c. 1875 shows the J. Loring surveys in the extreme southern part of the county and just east of the site of Ladonia as that town appears on present-day maps. An advertisement in the *Northern Standard* of May 29, 1844, called the attention of prospective bidders to the fact that the contract for opening the part of the National Road between the Trinity and Sulphur rivers would be let at John Loring's house on July 1, 1844. The contract for the remainder of the road was to be opened for bids in Paris on July 10.

21. A. W. Neville, *The History of Lamar County*, 15.

22. Texas General Land Office Map of Fannin County, 1892. A comparison of this map and the present map of the same county by the Texas Highway Department establishes the relative position of the present bridge and the Lyday Survey.

23. R. L. Jones (contributor), "Folk Life in Early Texas: The Autobiography of Andrew Davis," *The Southwestern Historical Quarterly*, XLIII, 332, 333. Apparently Fort Lyday was built by the cooperative effort of the pioneers of the area. The fact that the fort was down Sulphur River some eight or ten miles from the home of Daniel Davis indicates that it was on or near Lyday's land, and the further fact that the buffalo sometimes came down to the fort and mixed with the cattle would cause one to surmise that it was on the prairie north of the Sulphur River bottom.

24. Field Notes, 3, 11. A small creek flows into the Lyday survey and joins Sulphur River on the north side. A short distance below the mouth of that creek (or one at least similarly located) Major Stell's plat shows the crossing of the National Road on Sulphur River. Trigonometric calculations from the field notes do not show the distance from this crossing to the point where the old road crossed Tollett Creek (Early's Creek in the field notes) so exactly as do the measurements on modern maps, but the discrepancy is small.

eighth mile, the old road continued northward, curving more and more toward the east as it reached higher ground. It may have followed a still older road that is known to have connected Fort Lyday with the settlements of Red River County.[25] The survey of the National Road crossed the Fannin-Lamar County line some two miles north of Sulphur River, and passed approximately through the village of Noble, four miles south of present Highway 82 in the west part of Lamar County. It passed midway between the places where the towns of Brookston and Roxton are now located and varied not more than a half-mile to the south of a straight line from there to the railroad depot in the west section of Paris.

The street in Paris running east from the depot, along the north side of the public square and some three or four blocks to the east of that area, is almost identical with the route of the National Road.[26] About half a mile west of the square on that part of the present thoroughfare known as Bonham Street, Major Stell blazed a red oak tree that marked his one-hundredth mile.[27]

The extension of this same street to the east of the square is known as Lamar Avenue. It was from a point probably some three or four blocks down this Lamar Avenue end of the street that the surveyors of the National Road turned forty degrees north of east and continued 1086 feet to their one-hundred-and-first mile post. The angle of direction changed very little during the next twenty miles; from Lamar Avenue to the Red River County line the old road was nearly straight, and followed a general course almost exactly northeast. By several slight changes, it bent to the right of that course at the middle, somewhat like a bow, and even there it was hardly more than half a mile off the direct northeast course.[28]

The present road that extends northeastward from Paris compromises a little with property lines, but follows within a few hundred yards of the old road almost all of the way.[29] At the village of Faught

25. R. L. Jones, "The Autobiography of Andrew Davis," *The Southwestern Historical Quarterly*, XLIII, 335.

26. A. W. Neville, *The History of Lamar County*, 55. Early deeds to town lots on Bonham Street and part of its eastward extension called attention to the fact that they fronted on the National Road.

27. Field Notes, 4, 8.

28. Field Notes, 4, 5, 8.

29. The field notes platted on the current Texas Highway map of Lamar County indicate that parts of the present road are identical with the National Road.

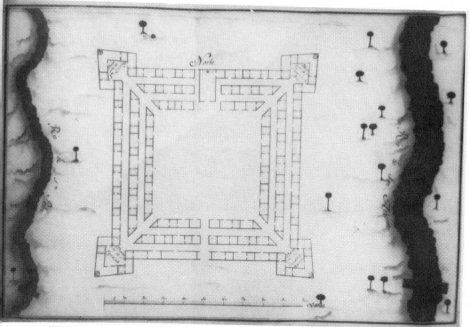

PRESIDIO DE SAN ANTONIO DE BEXAR—Founded by Martin de Alarcón in 1718. —*(K.F.N.)*

PRESIDIO DE NUESTRA SEÑORA DE LOS DOLORES—Founded by Domingo Ramón in 1716.   —*Courtesy Archivo General de la Nación*

PUBLISHER'S NOTE: Photos without credit lines courtesy of Kenneth F. Neighbours.

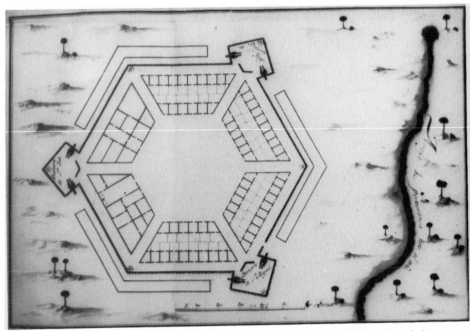

PRESIDIO DE NUESTRA SEÑORA DEL PILAR DE LOS ADAES—Founded by Marques de Aguayo in 1722 near present Robeline, Louisiana. —*(K.F.N.)*

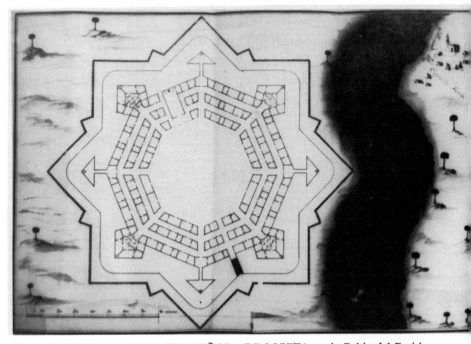

PRESIDIO DE NUESTRA SEÑORA DE LORETA en la Bahia del Espiritu Santo—Founded by the Marques de Aguayo in 1722 presently at Goliad, Texas.   —*Courtesy Archivo General de la Nacion*

CHAPEL AT PRESIDIO de la Bahía (Goliad). —*(K.F.N.)*

MISSION NUESTRA SEÑORA del Espíritu Santo de Zuñiga at present day Goliad. —*(K.F.N.)*

PORTAL OF HOSPITAL of the Presidio San Francisco at Monclova, Coahuila, Mexico. Alonso de Leon set forth from here to explore Texas. —*(K.F.N.)*

RUINS OF WALL OF first Chapel in Monclova, Coahuila, Mexico built by the Franciscans. —*(K.F.N.)*

HOUSE OF ALONSO DE LEON, remodeled, now Banco de Comercio de Coahuila, Mexico. In the background is Iglesia Santiago Apostol-Monclova.
—*(K.F.N.)*

IGLESIA SANTIAGO APOSTOL in Monclova, Coahuila, Mexico. —*(K.F.N.)*

IGLESIA SAN FRANCISCO DE ASISI, Monclova, Coahuila, Mexico. —*(K.F.N.)*

PRESIDIO DE MONCLOVA, 1781 on Hidalgo Sur in Monclova, Coahuila, Mexico. —*(K.F.N.)*

EXCAVATION AT LAST site of Mission San Juan Bautista.
—Courtesy of Harry P. Hewitt

BELIEVED TO BE Commissary Building, San Juan Bautista, Guerrero, Coahuila, Mexico.
—Courtesy L. A. Parr

RUINS OF STABLE at San Juan Bautista. —*Courtesy L. A. Parr*

RUINS OF THE Commandant's House at San Juan Bautista.
—*Courtesy L.A. Parr*

CEMETERY at Guerrero, Coahuila, Mexico.

—*Courtesy L. A. Parr*

MISSION SAN BERNARDO, Guerrero, Coahuila, Mexico.

—*Courtesy L. A. Pryor*

FRANCIA CROSSING of the Rio Grande.

—Courtesy L. A. Parr

SPANISH CANNON wheel found just above the mouth of Cuervo Creek at Paquache crossing of the Rio Grande by Charles Whatley, La Pryor, Texas. —*(K.F.N.)*

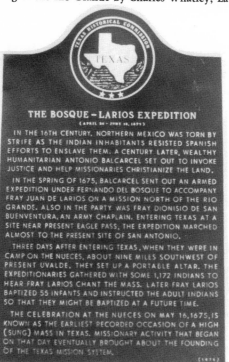

THE BOSQUE – LARIOS EXPEDITION
(APRIL 30 - JUNE 10, 1675)

IN THE 16TH CENTURY, NORTHERN MEXICO WAS TORN BY STRIFE AS THE INDIAN INHABITANTS RESISTED SPANISH EFFORTS TO ENSLAVE THEM. A CENTURY LATER, WEALTHY HUMANITARIAN ANTONIO BALCARCEL SET OUT TO INVOKE JUSTICE AND HELP MISSIONARIES CHRISTIANIZE THE LAND.

IN THE SPRING OF 1675, BALCARCEL SENT OUT AN ARMED EXPEDITION UNDER FERNANDO DEL BOSQUE TO ACCOMPANY FRAY JUAN DE LARIOS ON A MISSION NORTH OF THE RIO GRANDE. ALSO IN THE PARTY WAS FRAY DIONISIO DE SAN BUENVENTURA, AN ARMY CHAPLAIN. ENTERING TEXAS AT A SITE NEAR PRESENT EAGLE PASS, THE EXPEDITION MARCHED ALMOST TO THE PRESENT SITE OF SAN ANTONIO.

THREE DAYS AFTER ENTERING TEXAS, WHEN THEY WERE IN CAMP ON THE NUECES, ABOUT NINE MILES SOUTHWEST OF PRESENT UVALDE, THEY SET UP A PORTABLE ALTAR. THE EXPEDITIONARIES GATHERED WITH SOME 1,172 INDIANS TO HEAR FRAY LARIOS CHANT THE MASS. LATER FRAY LARIOS BAPTIZED 55 INFANTS AND INSTRUCTED THE ADULT INDIANS SO THAT THEY MIGHT BE BAPTIZED AT A FUTURE TIME.

THE CELEBRATION AT THE NUECES ON MAY 16,1675, IS KNOWN AS THE EARLIEST RECORDED OCCASION OF A HIGH (SUNG) MASS IN TEXAS. MISSIONARY ACTIVITY THAT BEGAN ON THAT DAY EVENTUALLY BROUGHT ABOUT THE FOUNDING OF THE TEXAS MISSION SYSTEM.

(1973)

HISTORICAL MARKER —*Photo courtesy L. A. Parr.*

ROSES OF SAINT JOHN found growing at the site of the Domingo Ramón
Road in Texas near the Rio Grande.

—*Courtesy David H. Riskind*

NUECES RIVER near Ramón's crossing. —*(K.F.N.)*

FLINT HILL located on the site of the Ramón Road. —*(K.F.N.)*

FRIO RIVER southwest of Pleasanton, near Ramón's crossing. —*(K.F.N.)*

CAMP SITE of early Spanish expeditions and Ramón's crossing of 1716, present day San Antonio, Texas, Crockett and Navarro Streets. —*(K.F.N.)*

SAN ANTONIO RIVER in downtown San Antonio, 1978, near early Spanish camp sites. —*(K.F.N.)*

COMAL RIVER above Domingo Ramón's crossing in New Braunfels, Texas. Scene is located at the end of Landa Park. Bridge in background is on San Antonio Street. —*(K.F.N.)*

SAN MARCOS RIVER in San Marcos, 1978, near Ramón's crossing of 1716.
—(K.F.N.)

HISTORICAL MARKER for Comal Springs at New Braunfels, Texas, point of Ramón's Road of 1716. —(K.F.N.)

MCKINNEY FALLS on Onion Creek, point on Ramón's Road of 1716.

—(K.F.N.)

OLD RIVER ROAD through the Monte Grande following the Domingo
Ramón's Road of 1716. —(K.F.N.)

OLD RIVER ROAD through the Monte Grande to Domingo Ramón's Brazos
de Dios crossings of Little and Brazos rivers. —(K.F.N.)

BRIDGE OVER LITTLE RIVER on the old River Road at the 1716 crossing of the Domingo Ramón Road. —(K.F.N.)

BRAZOS RIVER at the junction of Little River (left) below Domingo Ramón's crossing of 1716. —(K.F.N.)

BRIDGE ON HIGHWAY 485 (Old 190) over the Brazos River above the mouth of Little River and near Domingo Ramón's crossing of 1716. Located over the line in Milam County from Robertson County. —(K.F.N.)

BRAZOS RIVER above the mouth of the Little River near Ramón's Crossing of 1716 in Milam County just over the line from Robertson County. —*(K.F.N.)*

LOST PINES near Bastrop on the Old San Antonio Road. —*(K.F.N.)*

WICHITA GRASS HOUSE, replica built by Dan Hunt at the Indian village at Anadarko, Oklahoma in the 1950s. This type was built by Caddoan tribes on the Brazos River Indian reservation surveyed by Neighbors and Marcy in 1854.
—(K.F.N.)

SENTINELLA (Gomez Peak) at the tip of the Davis Mountain Range.
—(K.F.N.)

AUTHOR J. W. WILLIAMS and R. Ernest Lee Sr. with metal detector in Haskell County looking for Captain R. B. Marcy's 1849 cache of wagons.

—*(K.F.N.)*

AUTHOR J. W. WILLIAMS at the possible site of Captain Randolph B. Marcy's water hole in the sand hills near Monahans.

—*Courtesy Louise Kelly*

ORIGINAL FORT BELKNAP power magazine. —*(K.F.N.)*

HISTORICAL MARKER dedicated to the Fort-Belknap-Fort Phantom Hill Military Road. —*(K.F.N.)*

ORIGINAL CORN HOUSE at Fort Belknap, left, foreground, restored commisary building in the background. —*(K.F.N.)*

FORT BELKNAP archives on the site of Infantry Quarters No. 4, restored in 1973-74. —*(K.F.N.)*

COTTONWOOD SPRING, a point on the Marcy-Neighbors trail of 1854.
—(K.F.N.)

SMELTER TANKS west of Benjamin, possible site of Marcy's Dripping Springs on 1854 trip to locate resources. Shown above are Kenneth F. Neighbours and R. Ernest Lee. —(K.F.N.)

EL CAPITAN in the Guadalupe Mountains, a point on the route of Major Robert S. Neighbors and Captain Randolph B. Marcy on seperate expeditions in 1849 and on the Southern Overland Mail Route. —*(K.F.N.)*

KIOWA PEAK (Marcy's Round Mountain), a point on the Marcy-Neighbors trail of 1854. —*(K.F.N.)*

HUECO MOUNTAIN, site of Southern Overland Mail Stage stand. —*(K.F.N.)*

EL MUERTO, site of stage stands of Southern Overland mail and Ben Ficklin.
—*(K.F.N.)*

AUTHOR AT Eagle Spring Butterfield Stage Station, pointing at an axle and hounds of a horse-drawn vehicle, September 3, 1959. —(K.F.N.)

CASTLE GAP on the line of Upton and Crane counties. A point on the route of Cabeza de Vaca and the Southern Overland Mail Route. —(K.F.N.)

RUINS OF SOUTHERN Overland Mail Stage stand at Eagle Springs on Eagle Mountain. —*(K.F.N.)*

RELIC AT EAGLE SPRINGS at the Southern Overland Mail Stage stand.
—*(K.F.N.)*

EAGLE SPRING STAGE Stand, point
on the Southern Overland Mail Route.
—(K.F.N.)

MARKER for Pine Spring State Stand,
point on the Southern Overland Mail
Route in the Guadalupe Mountains.
—(K.F.N.)

RUINS OF PINE SPRING Stage Stand, a point on the Southern Overland Mail
Route.
—(K.F.N.)

ten miles from Paris, the road that is traveled today bends sharply to the right and leaves the course of the old road by something like a half mile but shortly swings back across it. The present road is called the Golf Course Road, but it is also known by its older name, the "Pine Bluff Road." The near identity of the present beaten track with Major Stell's survey of 1844 causes one to suspect strongly that both the old and the new are but variations of a single trail. Probably the Pine Bluff Road was included as part of the National Road by the men who laid out the latter thoroughfare.[30]

Beyond Lamar County the surveyors extended their route along Red River for a distance of nine miles. To avoid the bends of that stream their path curved somewhat, resembling a quarter circle until it came to a sudden stop in northwest Red River County, opposite the mouth of the Kiamichi River.[31]

30. *Record, 1894.* No. 4, *Original United States* vs. *The State of Texas,* 1256, 1257, 1321. Hereafter this testimony will be referred to as *Greer County Record.* The testimony of R. H. Burnett and Thomas F. Ragsdale in the Greer County case indicates that the Chihuahua Traders came from Fort Towson by the mouth of the Kiamichi River and by Pinhook (which was just east of the site of Paris). That this party of merchants who came in 1840 found or opened a road through the points mentioned makes it certain that Stell's survey in this area was either along or near a traveled road.

31. The writer checked Major Stell's field notes of the full route of the National Road by trigonometric calculations. Beginning at the point just east of Dallas County where this road crossed the East Fork of the Trinity River, and progressing northeastwardly, the results of these calculations are as follows: From this beginning place to the crossing on the west branch of the Caddo Forks of the Sabine is 20.30 miles north and 13.74 miles east; from this stream to the southeast corner of the John Yeary survey is 2.66 miles north and 3.56 miles east; from here to the Cowleach Fork of the Sabine is 3.02 miles north and 2.80 miles east; from here to the south fork of Sulphur River is 6.85 miles north and 3.72 miles east; from here to Sulphur River is 9.64 miles north and 12.52 miles east; from here to the 100th mile post of the road on Bonham street in Paris is 13.42 miles north and 17.20 miles east; from here to the 121st mile post of the road (where it made the first contact with Red River) is 13.96 miles north and 15.21 miles east, and from here to the point on Red River opposite the mouth of the Kiamichi is 5.89 miles north and 3.56 miles east. These calculations have reduced Major Stell's field notes from varas to miles (rounded off to the nearest hundredth) and have changed and combined the distances and angle data from point to point given in the surveyors' notes into simple statements of the distances north and east from each point to the next. Thus the writer has been able to check total distances across the map against the route of the National Road as he has platted it directly from field notes. No important errors have been discovered, and the line representing the route of the old road made on the maps with drawing instruments has been rather closely confirmed.

A present following of country roads down to this point in the Red River bottom places one at the small village of Kiomatia, one hundred twenty-nine and one-half miles, by the old road survey, northeast of central Dallas County. (Most of the inhabitants of the village were the descendants of slaves who in the early 1940s still chanted weird Negro spirituals and perhaps still believed in ghosts.) There are no shipping facilities at hand, either by land or water, to warrant the construction of a major highway. At first glance, one would be tempted to say that no group other than a whimsical Congress would expend good money to bring a principal thoroughfare to a dead-end in such an out-of-the-way spot.

The facts, however, lead to quite a different conclusion. One hundred years ago steamboats plied the waters of Red River as far up as Wright's Landing,[32] which was in none other than the same bend of the river with the lonely village of Kiomatia and the place where Major Stell completed his road survey. Because of the increased difficulties in river travel above this place, Wright's Landing was generally regarded as the head of navigation on Red River.[33] In addition, one hundred years ago, this same present-day lonely spot in northwest Red River County was just across the river from the end of a United States military highway that was already nearly twenty years old. Fort Towson had been established near the mouth of Kiamichi on the north side of Red River in 1824,[34] and a military highway from

32. The village of Kiomatia joins the George Wright survey (Texas General Land Office map of Red River County of 1905). This old survey became the property of Travis Wright in 1839 (acquired from his brother George) and has remained in his family ever since; [George Travis Wright, a grandson who lived on Bonham Street in Paris, the owner.] Wright's Landing was on the Red River front of this tract of land, opposite the mouth of the Kiamichi River (A. W. Neville, *The History of Lamar County*, 81, 244, 245).

33. In a statement made to the *Northern Standard*, Feb. 23, 1850, Capt. J. Claiborne, agent for the steamboat *Texas*, denied rumors that this boat would not carry cargo above Wright's Landing whenever the depth of the water in Red River made it possible. Great cargoes of cotton and other commodities were transported on Red River as high up as Preston, north of present-day Denison, but this traffic was only possible when the conditions of the river were favorable. It should be borne in mind that river travel below Wright's Landing, while less uncertain than travel above that point, was itself of an intermittent character.

34. *Oklahoma: A Guide To The Sooner State* (Norman, Oklahoma, 1941), 21. This work was compiled by workers of the Writers' Programs of the Works Projects Administration in the State of Oklahoma.

there to Fort Smith and Fort Gibson had become a necessity. Obviously, this out-of-the-way place at the end of the National Road was once well furnished with facilities for both land and water transportation.

As another answer to the reason for a road to the place where the village of Kiomatia overlooks Red River, a survey of North Texas population of one hundred years ago is also revealing. Old Jonesboro—perhaps the first purely Anglo-American town on Texas soil—was only six miles down the river; Clarksville, that had already begun to supersede it, was some twenty-five miles to the southeast. The countryside was, on the whole, well settled, and schools and other requirements of organized society were beginning to appear. Population thinned out to an edge a little more than one hundred miles to the west, but Red River County had become the established center of North Texas.[35]

But full justification for the route of the National Road can hardly be established until one understands more clearly the early transportation routes accessible to North Texans, and the way in which those routes fitted into the geography of the Southwest. Besides the military road facilities available to Fort Towson, other roads connected the Clarksville-Jonesboro area with the settlements of Arkansas. One of these was not very different from the path of the Clarksville-Texarkana road in use today.[36] But all of these facilities for travel and transportation ran northward or eastward, making the citizens of North Texas in reality a part of the economy of the United States.

To the south, however, in their means of communication and exchange with their fellow Texans the North Texans were far less fortunate. The first settlers of Jonesboro had no southward travel facilities except by a few Indian trails and a dim path known to them as the Spanish Trace.[37] An old trail from Jonesboro to Nacogdoches,

35. The counties of Collin, Dallas, Grayson and Hunt were created and organized in 1846 (*Texas Almanac 1939-40*, 400, 404, 416 and 425). There were no county seat towns in Texas west of the present limits of Fannin County in 1844. Grayson County had a population of about 500 when organized in 1846. (Mattie Davis Lucas and Mita Holsapple Hall, *A History of Grayson County, Texas.*)

36. *Greer County Record*, 1339.

37. A. W. Neville, *The History of Lamar County*, 12. The Spanish Trace, evidently a military trail by which the Spaniards reached Red River, was within present Red River County, about three or four miles from its west boundary. Vial, in 1788, found a dim trail that entered the "Natchitoches Forest." Possibly it was iden-

the origin of which is attributed to a certain Mr. Trammell, was blazed about 1820.[38] An older road called Trammel's Trace extending from Arkansas to Nacogdoches and this trail from Jonesboro must have been partly identical, for the Jonesboro trail itself was called Trammel's Trace.[39] At first this route was only a horse path. As late as 1836 some evidence indicates the possibility that there were still no wagon roads connecting North Texas with South Texas.[40] In 1837, Holland Coffee and his bride left Washington-on-the-Brazos for the Coffee Trading Post on Red River, north of present-day Denison. They were forced to make the long, round-about journey eastward by road to Nacogdoches, northward probably by Trammel's Trace to Red River and then westward, perhaps one hundred miles, by road to their new home.[41] In a few years a mail route connected the Red River area with San Augustine,[42] but again the road ran far to the east of a straight line between North and South Texas. Information on just how early the first actual wagon traffic began between Jonesboro and Nacogdoches is not available, but the more direct link that was needed to join the two parts of Texas came in 1840; in that year Colonel Cooke, with a detachment of Texas soldiers, opened a road from Austin to Coffee's Trading Post on Red River.[43] The name of Preston, from one of Cooke's men, was given to the village that grew up at Coffee's Trading Post, and Cooke's road has since been known as the Preston Road. This road passed through the Waco village on the Brazos and by Cedar Springs in central Dallas County. Citizens of Jonesboro or Clarksville could now follow one of the two

---

tical with the Spanish Trace (*Greer County Record*, 908-13).

38. R. L. Jones, "The Autobiography of Andrew Davis," *The Southwestern Historical Quarterly*, XLIII, 323.

39. John Arrowsmith, *Map of Texas Compiled from Surveys Recorded In the Land Office of Texas, And Other Official Surveys* (London, 1841). The full route of Trammel's Trace from Jonesboro to Nacogdoches is shown on this map. Some of the route has been repeated from older records on the later Texas Land Office maps. It is shown on the maps of Rusk County of 1895, of Panola County, 1897, of Harrison County, 1920, and of Marion County, 1920.

40. R. L. Jones, "The Autobiography of Andrew Davis," *The Southwestern Historical Quarterly*, XLIII, 327.

41. Lucas and Hall, *History of Grayson County*, 36.

42. *The Northern Standard*, Feb. 10, 1844.

43. Sketch Showing the Route of the Military Road from Red River to Austin, Wm. H. Hunt, Engineer, 1840. Drawn by H. L. Upshur, 1841. This old map is in the library of the University of Texas.

roads that led westward into present Grayson County until they reached this road, and could then follow it southward into Austin, and to other points of South Texas.

But even this road was not the complete answer to the needs of North Texas. The greater portion of the population, which was still centered in and near Red River County, must travel miles out of the way to reach South or Central Texas. Plainly, the bill that created the National Road corrected this difficulty. That act of Congress made a new, short-cut route available for the inhabitants of the Jonesboro-Clarksville country. These pioneers on far-away Red River could now follow the new road southwest to the banks of the Trinity, and from there drive southward down the Preston-Austin Road into the system of roads and trails then in use in South Texas.

The National Road, instead of beginning at a dead-end on the Trinity and ending at another dead-end on Red River, connected the roads of Texas with the military roads from Fort Towson into the United States. It connected Saint Louis with San Antonio, and was, in fact, an international highway.

The Texas Congress named this new highway the "Central" National Road, even though it led directly into the unsettled frontier. Undoubtedly the Congress was thinking in terms of future development; the great stream of immigrants that soon began to flow justified the undertaking.

Nevertheless, the National Road did not play the glorified role that the Congress may have visualized.[44] The fact that Greenville shortly became a county seat town changed the course of much of the traffic in the middle part of the road, and the swift westward movement of the frontier caused the Preston and other roads to share

---

44. On March 4, 1851, the road from McKenzie's Ferry, via Dallas, to Waxahachie was made 30 feet wide and declared a first class road. All other roads in Dallas County were made 20 feet wide and delcared to be second class (Dallas County Commissioners' Court Minutes, A, 106). Thus it appears that for a few years the National Road (from McKenzie's Ferry to Dallas) was part of the most important thoroughfare in Dallas County. In 1852 the Commissioners of Lamar County granted William Russell and Josiah Ashby a franchise to build causeways closely paralleling the National Road across the three principal creeks between Paris and Pine Bluff; tolls were charged on these causeways. The entire route of the National Road across Lamar County was declared a first class highway (A. W. Neville, *The History of Lamar County*, 95). However, despite these evidences of its early importance, the National Road did not hold the spotlight very long—it does not appear on any of the numerous old maps of Texas that the writer has examined.

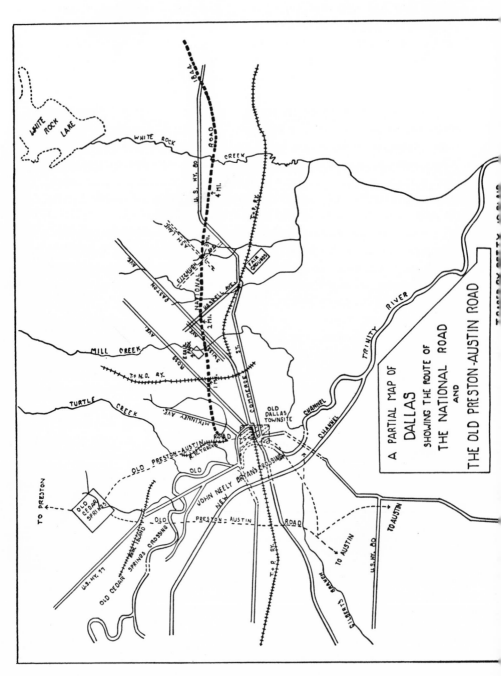

heavily in wagon travel that was soon to double, triple, and quadruple the population of Texas.

One of the best illustrations of this rapid growth came at the very end of the National Road itself. Some study of the early geography of central Dallas County is part of that story, and the route of Major Stell's survey in that area is also an essential factor.

Two old river crossings on the Trinity were destined to witness one of the main currents of immigration into Texas and even to have their moment of opportunity to profit from it. One of these was John Neely Bryan's crossing, just below the site of the Union Station in present Dallas, and the other was the Cedar Spring crossing,[45] some two or three miles upstream. Just how early the rivalry between these places began is probably unknown, but their relations approached the stage of open warfare by 1848. In that year, a man by the name of Collins operated a ferry at the Cedar Springs crossing and Bryan likewise maintained one at the lower crossing. Bryan proposed to the Dallas County Commissioners that, should the people of the county select Dallas as the permanent county seat, he would reward them with five years' free service of his ferry, but there was the further provision (either proposed by Bryan or added by the Commissioners) that Collins' license to operate a ferry should be revoked.[46]

Apparently nothing but intensified rivalry came from Bryan's proposal, but four years earlier, when Major Stell began his survey, it is probable that a more decisive factor in the battle of the river crossings had already begun to operate.

It will be remembered that Stell's survey began on the bank of the Trinity River at a certain cedar tree that has long since disappeared. The only method left us now to discover the site of that old tree is to go northeastward up the path of the early road until a known point is found, then to survey backward to the Trinity River. This plan of approach to the problem takes us back to the east Dallas County line, three and three-quarter miles north of Highway 80. Following Major Stell's field notes in reverse does not prove exceedingly difficult except that possible error increases with the

45. The Peters Colony map of 1852 in the Texas General Land Office shows these crossings, although it does not name them. This map was made from surveying notes and should be far more accurate as to detail than maps not so constructed.

46. Dallas County Commissioners' Court Minutes, A, 17. Bryan was probably prompted to make his proposition because the State Legislature had just passed a law prescribing the method by which the voters of a county might select their county seat.

distance from any positively fixed points on the old survey.

The old road extended almost three miles due west from the county line, then southwest across Duck Creek, then swung more toward the west, passing not far to the north of the present village of New Hope and a few hundred yards north of Buckner's Orphans Home, then turned westward to White Rock Creek between the Texas & Pacific Railway and Highway 80. Here map measurements lead almost to the present city limits of Dallas.

The study should next follow the old road from White Rock Creek directly into the city of Dallas itself. The old field notes reveal that by the National Road it was three and one-tenth miles between White Rock and Mill Creek,[47] that the area immediately east of the crossing on Mill Creek was prairie, and that at the road crossing the latter stream flowed southeast. Correlating the Peters Colony Map of 1852 with present maps of Dallas, one discovers that there was a strip of timber east of Mill Creek in the area south of the Texas & Pacific tracks. These facts recorded in Stell's field notes and the topography of Dallas limit the band in which the National Road could have crossed Dallas to a strip two or three hundred yards wide. The route of that old trail stayed north of the Texas & Pacific railroad all of the way west to the Trinity River. The route was as much as a half-mile north of the Texas State Fair Grounds, yet south of the Ursuline Academy; it crossed Mill Creek just below Exall Park at the place that Mill Creek flows southeast, and it passed about half a mile north of the main business district of Dallas.[48] The last span of the old road

47. White Rock Creek is called by name in Major Stell's field notes. Mill Creek is not. But there is no other stream that can at all qualify.

48. Various types of evidence have been employed in determining the route of the National Road through Dallas. Exhaustive measurements on the Texas Highway Department's map of Dallas were made until the place was found at which Major Stell's field notes almost exactly fitted the space between White Rock and Mill Creek. The writer then went to Dallas, followed the course of Mill Creek on foot as far as obstructions would permit, and had an interview with Henry L. Stokey, who has lived in the immediate area for the past sixty-three years. Stokey reports that the prairie came to the banks of Mill Creek on its east side only between Exall Park and Gaston Avenue and that the present southeasterly course of the stream between these points follows the original stream bed. It should be noted that Stokey's information roughly confirms the Peters Colony map of 1852 as to the distribution of timber and prairie and that the combined evidence leaves no other place for one to locate the crossing of the National Road on Mill Creek except between Gaston Avenue and Exall Park, for Major Stell, according to his notes, entered prairie immediately east of Mill Creek at the place where that stream flowed southeast. To make doubly sure as to the accuracy

turned southwest for about a quarter of a mile, and came to an end, or rather to a beginning, at the railroad tracks a few hundred feet northwest of the intersection of present Lamar Street with McKinney Avenue. Apparently Major Stell's cedar tree, at which he began his survey, was almost 2500 feet north of the Dallas County Courthouse.[49]

Seemingly this was a rather odd place for the location of either end of a national highway, but an examination of the Peters Colony map of 1852 shows that the Preston Road came southward through Cedar Springs and approached Dallas through the area that is now north of the court house. The cedar tree at the beginning of the National Road was evidently at the side of the Preston Road. From this junction point, the two roads must have followed a common roadbed for the half-mile, or a little more, that led down to the river crossing.

Obviously, then, the Central National Road of the Republic of Texas connected with John Neely Bryan's crossing on the Trinity River; equally obviously, the Preston Road from the north and this new road from the northeast converged on this point along the Trinity, ready to serve the great throng of immigrants that was shortly coming, and it is especially important to note that ''a little frontier village called Dallas stood at the fork of the roads.''

---

of this conclusion, measurements were made on the immense map of Dallas that hangs in the Records Building at Dallas (property of the Fidelity Union Abstract & Title Co.). Olen Coats, a draftsman in the Records Building, volunteered to plat the field notes of the old road (to the correct scale) on tracing paper and to find the place where the drawing fitted this large map. Coats' drawing, representing the course of the road from White Rock to Mill Creek, fitted the map without apparent error in the following course:

Beginning on White Rock Creek about 1250 feet south of U. S. Highway 80 (East Pike), then 8780 feet in a direction 6 degrees north of west to a point in Ash Lane about 250 feet northeast of Fitzhugh Street, then due west 5280 feet to a point about 300 feet southwest from the intersection of Junius and Haskell Avenue and then 2300 feet in a direction 10 degrees south of west to Mill Creek at a point about 200 feet north of Swiss Avenue, which is about midway between Exall Park and Gaston Avenue. Mr. W. S. Beesley, head of the Map and Plat Book Department in the Records Building, regards this large map used by Coats as the most accurate map of Dallas to be found, which emphasizes the accuracy of Coats' drawing.

The route of the National Road as platted by Coats is about a quarter of a mile north of the path which that road would assume if Major Stell's field notes were platted without reference to topography. But the old field notes evidently contain a small error, since the plat and field notes do not themselves agree on an eight mile course of the road in east Dallas County. The route as platted by Coats is the only route found by the writer that satisfies all conditions of topography and direction, and it corresponds closely with the exhaustive measurements previously made on the Texas Highway Map of Dallas.

49. This point is at the edge of Cedar Grove Addition (according to the Fidelity Union Map of Dallas) and is in the part of Dallas in which cedar trees originally were numerous.

In the accompanying map of Dallas the route of the National Road was drawn according to the Coats plat. The location of old Cedar Springs, the original townsite of Dallas, and the route of the old Preston Road are made (roughly calculated to scale) from the Peters Colony map of 1852.

X

MARCY'S ROAD FROM DOÑA ANA

The little oil town of Buffalo Springs, is located some forty miles southeast of Wichita Falls, Texas, and only a mile from the site of the old ghost town of Buffalo Springs. Here the emigrant trains of nearly a century ago camped on their way to California's newly discovered gold fields—for in 1849 it was gold instead of oil that fired the imagination of great throngs of Americans. The new wealth of oil and the old trail of the gold hunters now lie side by side at many points across the northern part of Texas. At Muenster in Cooke County, at Olney in Young County, and further west at Rotan and on beyond at Big Spring, and even on the shifting sands of the Pecos River country; these two strangely contrasting efforts at probing for hidden riches have made their marks on the earth only a few miles apart. The new method of wealth production involves miracles of modern machinery and persistent drilling deep into the earth's secrets; the old method required slow plodding for two thousand miles and inexhaustible patience before the relatively crude tools of the miner could operate in pay dirt.

But despite this strange contrast of means of accomplishment, there was and is in a very important respect a remarkable similarity between the two kinds of wealth production—both were the outgrowth of free enterprise and both flourished under a system that did not place a heavy hand on individual initiative.

Quite different had been the story of fortune hunting under the king of Spain. Coronado had been granted a monopoly on much of the western part of the present United States, whereby he could hunt for gold without the least fear of competition. For three hundred years of Spanish and Mexican rule, the manner of search did not undergo any very complete overhauling. However, when the change came—when the strings of monopoly were finally cut and a government came to rule over that part of the land that turned the job of prospecting over to the individual, greater discoveries were made in

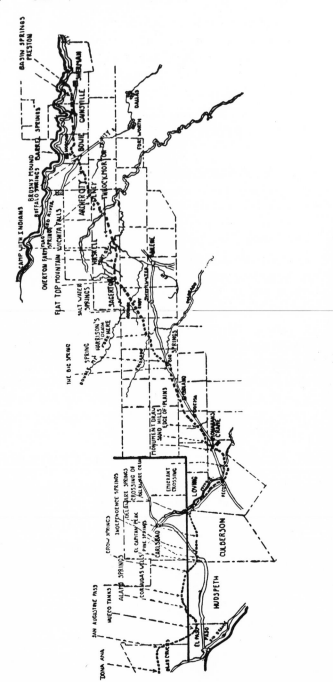

MARCY'S ROAD FROM DOÑA ANA

three years than had been made in the three centuries previous!

In 1848, not long after the west had become United States territory, gold was discovered at Sutters Mill, east of Stockton, California, and the story of America's great gold rush with its every-man-for-himself methods was on in earnest. Prospectors came from the settled areas of the United States; some of them up the North Platte, through South Pass, across Utah and on to California.[1] Others followed the trail from Independence, Missouri, to ancient Santa Fe and west across the south rim of the United States.[2] Still others came to various Gulf ports—chief of which was Indianola, Texas—by way of San Antonio and finally west by El Paso and on to California over the last lap of the same trail which connected Fort Smith, Arkansas, with Santa Fe. It followed the course of the South Canadian River and passed near the site of present day Amarillo, Texas.[4]

Lastly came the trail already mentioned, by old Buffalo Springs and the other towns such as Big Spring, where relatively new oil derricks and the faded path of old wagon ruts even now look at each other across nine decades of American history. This last route, like the old road near Amarillo, was only a tributary of the southern road to California, but the fact that it greatly influenced the course of the first mail route across the United States and contributed to the planning that influenced the construction of a long distance railroad into the west makes it especially worthy of notice.

Like prospecting for gold or oil, the search for the story and the route of this trail has led into somewhat extended effort; but, as a result, at least the route of the old road can be presented here in much greater detail than has been previously published. The physical footprints of the writer have been placed in the dusty roadbed of this early trail at a number of points and its story in Texas land records has been pieced together from many old handwritten volumes.

This particular branch of the southern road to California that crossed north Texas was laid out, strange as it may seem, by an eastbound expedition. Captain Randolph B. Marcy, who had been sta-

1. A. J. Johnson and J. H. Colton, Johnson's *New Illustrated Atlas*. New York, 1864, maps No. 63, 66, 67.

2. *Ibid.*

3. *Ibid* and map, 47, 48.

4. Randolph B. Marcy's Report [on the return from Santa Fe to Fort Smith] 1849; in *Sen. Ex. Doc. No. 64, 31 Cong. 1st Sess.*, 169 ff. Hereafter this document will be cited as Marcy's Report.

tioned at Fort Towson for several years, had been called upon to command a detachment of soldiers over the route from Fort Smith to Santa Fe. The military force under Marcy served as protection for some five hundred immigrants who were enroute to California. With his mission accomplished, Marcy rested his men at Santa Fe and his work animals on a nearby range while he studied available information toward making a new road from southern New Mexico to northeastern Texas.

Upon inquiry he found a Comanche Indian, Manuel by name, who could greatly assist him in his undertaking. Manuel was a citizen of the town of San Miguel on the Pecos River some fifty miles southeast of Santa Fe. This old adobe town was on the Missouri-Santa Fe Trail and was often visited both by bands of Comanche Indians and by American merchants. Manuel apparently could speak the languages of both and his boyhood experiences as a Comanche had taught him both the geography and trails of the plains.[5]

He agreed to guide Marcy on his return journey and at the very outset gave some interesting information. There was a well watered trail that passed near the present day towns of Vaughn and Fort Sumner, New Mexico, and Lubbock, Texas, that Manuel suggested. But Marcy, who knew that several parties from northeast Texas had already found a way to El Paso,[6] rejected Manuel's proposal and led his company of soldiers much farther down the Rio Grande before turning his course eastward. Not until he had reached the town of Doña Ana, New Mexico, about fifty miles above El Paso, did he break away from the old Spanish road along the Rio Grande and begin his return journey to Fort Smith.

From Doña Ana on the Rio Grande to the place where, in modern geographical terms, the Pecos River flows out of New Mexico into Texas—through a country much infested with Apaches—there is little wonder that Manuel was not acquainted with the land to be traversed. A local guide was employed for that leg of the journey and Marcy set out to blaze a new trail that focused public attention on an area that had been little thought of before.

He was to follow very closely the thirty-second parallel of latitude

5. Manuel served as a guide for Josiah Gregg in 1840. Both Marcy and Gregg had high praise for his work as guide.

6. Grant Foreman, *Marcy and the Gold Seekers,* Norman, Oklahoma, 1939, 340. This volume contains Marcy's Report mentioned in footnote No. 4. See the journal of the Thomas Gilbert party in this volume, pp. 153-166.

for some one hundred and fifty miles which later was to become the south boundary line of New Mexico. It is not impossible that those who were to agree on the Texas-New Mexico boundary in 1850 were furnished concrete geographical data for part of their choice by this expedition of 1849.

Marcy's route from Doña Ana took him eastward through San Augustine Pass[7] which is the same gap in the Organ Mountains now traversed by the paved highway from Las Cruces to Alamogordo. Unlike the present highway, however, Marcy's road turned south and shortly entered the old salt trail toward El Paso.[8] This old road along the east base of the Organ Mountains had long served the Mexicans in transporting their requirements of salt. Marcy followed it for seven miles and then turned southeast across the flat, sandy, trackless and waterless prairie. For more than thirty miles he made a new road, finally ending the difficult march at the Hueco Tanks.[9] Here the wagon train passed through a narrow gap between two rugged little mountains where tourists are even now interested in the numerous Indian paintings of ancient origin and the natural rock basin that once stored up a much needed water supply for pioneer travelers. The old camping place is in northeast El Paso County, six miles south of the New Mexico line and only three miles west of Hudspeth County.

From Hueco Tanks eastward to the Pecos River, Marcy followed a course that nine years later was adopted by the Overland mail line as part of their route across the continent.[10] The expedition turned northeast from Hueco Tanks around the south base of Cerro Alto Peak and crossed the future Texas-New Mexico line twelve and one-half miles east of the corner of El Paso County.[11] Continuing

7. *Ibid.*, 344.

8. *Sen. Ex. Doc. No. 70, 1st Sess., 47th Cong.* This is the report of the Texas Boundary Commission of 1859 and 1860 and should be regarded as accurate. Hereafter this document will be referred to as the Texas Boundary Commission Report. Map No. 1 appended to this report shows part of this old Salt trail. Also it shows part of the road to Ojo Solidad which was Marcy's Road. It crossed the present part of the road to Ojo Solidad which was Marcy's Road. It crossed the present Texas boundary northeast of El Paso just eight and one-half miles east of a small village called Newman.

9. Grant Foreman, *Marcy and the Gold Seekers*, 345.

10. The Texas Boundary Commission *Report,* map No. 1. The mail station commonly called a ''stage stand'' was just east of the little mountain that lay north of the road at Hueco Tanks.

11. Grant Foreman, *Marcy and the Gold Seekers*, 346. Marcy passed around the

northeastward across the corner of Hudspeth County into what is now Otero County, New Mexico, the party passed along the northwest base of the Cornudas Mountains. Some ten miles on their road was the Alamo Spring, made conspicuous by three cottonwood trees that served as a guide to travelers. Nine miles beyond were the Cornudas Wells at the northeast extremity of the mountain chain. This strange watering place, standing brimful of pure water,[12] was inside a cavern that had its own natural sky light. It is located some twenty-five miles north of the Carlsbad-El Paso Highway at the mid-point of present day Hudspeth County and is nine miles north of the state boundary.

Marcy's course bent southward again from this point and crossed the future state line some twenty-five miles to the southeast.[13] The next camping place was Crow Spring only half a mile south of the imaginary line that now divides Texas and New Mexico.[14] Crow Springs was on the floor of an immense inland salt basin larger than the state of Massachusetts. Not far south of this camping place were several salt lakes whence the Mexicans of the San Elizario area had for a good many years hauled salt by the cart load.

It was impossible for the exploring party under Captain Marcy to continue directly eastward, for the rugged Guadalupe Mountains, taller than any other peaks in Texas, lay less than fifteen miles to the east. At the southmost tip of these mountains precipitous El Capitan Peak stood some eight miles south of the present New Mexico border. Marcy's wagon train bent its course so as to pass to the right of this barrier. A spring on the southwest slope of the mountain was the next campsite.[15] From here in a short day's journey the explorers circled

south side of Cerro Alto Peak, but the United States Mail passed over the longer but smoother road on the north side of the peak. The two roads joined again in a few miles. The point at which Marcy's Road crossed the state line was measured on Map No. 2 of the Texas Boundary Commission *Report.*

12. Grant Foreman, *Marcy and the Gold Seekers,* 347. The well in the cavern had gone dry by 1854 when Captain John Pope made a survey along the same route.

13. The Texas Boundary Commission *Report,* 302, and map No. 2. In 1859 monuments No. 16 and No. 17 of the series of markers placed by the boundary commission were located on the two sides of this road where it crossed the state boundary back into Texas. The Texas Land Office map of Hudspeth County dated 1917 shows the two monuments on the north line of section no. 1, township 1, block 68, of the Texas and Pacific Railway lands, about nine miles west of the northeast corner of Hudspeth County.

14. *Ibid.*

15. Grant Foreman, *Marcy and the Gold Seekers,* 349.

around the south base of the mountain and camped at Pine Springs, two miles east of the summit of El Capitan.[16] The ruin of a stage stand built for John Butterfield and associates a decade later still identifies this camping place.

The explorers had climbed out of the salt basin through Guadalupe Pass near the present El Paso-Carlsbad Highway, and were now on terrain that for the most part sloped gently toward the Pecos River. Marcy hesitated to move forward as if he enjoyed his stay among the pines. It was afternoon before the wagon train was in motion again and even then the day's forward progress was only the scant five miles required to reach Independence Spring.[17] The course of travel was slightly south of east and lay about eight miles within the present geographical limits of Texas.

In fact the route of this party did not again touch the area that is now New Mexico although it came near doing so just before reaching the Pecos River. Fifteen miles still to the east were the head springs of Delaware Creek.[18] It was the party's next camping place and was a full nine miles from the thirty-second parallel that later was to assume the importance of a state boundary line. Delaware Creek flowed somewhat north of east across this future state border into the Pecos River. Marcy's Road stayed on the north side of this stream for more than twenty miles and crossed it only a mile and a half south of present New Mexico at a point just nine miles west of the Pecos.[19]

Here the route that was later to be used by the overland mail and Marcy's Road parted company. The two routes, with a minor exception, had been identical for the one hundred and twenty-five miles

16. Pine Spring is in the south central part of section 41, township 1, block 65 of the Texas and Pacific Railway lands. (The writer has a copy of the original "map of Texas and Pacific Railway surveys in El Paso County, Texas" surveyed and mapped by Paul McCombs in 1884. Pine Springs is shown on that map.) The summit of El Capitan Peak is shown on the Texas General Land Office Map of Culberson County in section 48, township 1, block 66. The mountain is about two and one-fourth miles west and one-third mile south of the spring.

17. *Map of Texas and Pacific Surveys in El Paso County Texas.* Independence Spring is in section 43, township 1, block 64, Texas and Pacific Railway lands.

18. *Ibid.* The Delaware Spring was in section 9, township 2, block 64 of the Texas and Pacific Railway Lands. It was 373 varas slightly south of east of the northwest corner of that section. An old stage stand was (in 1884) 101 varas nearly east of the spring.

19. *Ibid.* This Texas and Pacific Railway map of 1884 shows a road so nearly like the route reported by Marcy that there can be little doubt that the two roads are identical.

from Hueco Tanks to this crossing on Delaware Creek. Almost all of Marcy's camp sites within this span were to become the location of stage stands for this first great transcontinental mail line in American history.[20] But contrary to an impression that has long held forth and has often been published *the road beds of these two early trails were not identical anywhere else in Texas.*[21] The overland mail road continued eastward and crossed the Pecos River while Marcy's Road turned down the west side of that stream. He passed almost if not exactly through the limits of the town of Pecos of today and continued some twenty miles downstream before making his crossing.

It was probably on section no. 16, block 33, of the lands that were in later years surveyed for the Houston and Texas Central Railway Company that Marcy crossed the Pecos. Even now this place located in south Ward County is known as Emigrant Crossing.[22] Here again near the east bank of the Pecos the road made by Marcy's wagons intersected—but did not follow—the path later used by the Overland Mail. The mail road passed much farther down the east bank of the Pecos before turning away from the river, but Marcy's Road struck out boldly across country from this point. Through present day Monahans, a little north of Odessa, Midland, and Stanton, and on to the Big Spring, notably an area now prosperous through oil production, was roughly the route followed.

The journal of this expedition did not tell what happened to the

20. The Texas Boundary Commission Report maps No. 1, 2. In addition to the mail station at Hueco Tanks, these maps show stations at some of Marcy's other camping places—Alamo Spring and Cornudas Tanks—and at several places the road is called the "mail route." In map No. 2 the mail route extends through Crow Spring. Unfortunately map No. 3 was either lost or destroyed before the report was published but the known stage stands at Pine Springs, and the Delaware Spring complete the required identification.

21. Rupert N. Richardson, "Some Details of the Southern Overland Mail," *Southwestern Historical Quarterly*, July, 1925, 4. A footnote lists the various stage stands along the route of the Overland Mail. A careful study of the locations of these mail stations compared with a study of Marcy's route reveals that the two are not identical in Texas east of the Pecos River.

22. *Reports of Explorations and Surveys to Ascertain the Most Practicable and Economical Route for a Railroad from the Mississippi River to the Pacific Ocean, being House Ex. Doc. No. 91, 33rd Cong., 2 Sess.,* II, 68 also map opposite page 40. Hereafter referred to as Pope's *Report.* The location of the narrows with respect to this crossing and the location of Toyah Creek with respect to it make it seem probable that Pope's reference to "Emigrant Crossing" indicates the same place called Emigrant Crossing today.

guide who was employed at Doña Ana. Probably he turned back at the Pecos River after leading the party through the Apache country. At least Manuel, the Comanche, wise in the topography and trails of the Plains, took the helm at the Pecos. A long chain of sand hills lay parallel to the Pecos and some thirty to forty miles east of it. Marcy sent horsemen ahead to investigate. The sand was so deep that a man on horseback could hardly penetrate it; much less could the wagon train hope to make a passage. But Manuel, who was in the part of the Plains with which he was least acquainted, nevertheless proved equal to the emergency. He guided the party northeastward, probably over the townsite of Monahans and seven or eight miles beyond to the lakes of living water that still lie hidden among the sand hills. Marcy made camp in the deep sand and probably still had some misgivings about his future course, but his Comanche guide revealed the passageway known to red men and the problem was solved. It was five miles due east through the towering little mountains of sand to the edge of this unique desert; but again here was a camp site with water and both firmer and smoother ground lay ahead.

The evidence that this pass in the sand hills was northeast of Monahans is too voluminous and too much involved to present in full, but it does include one interesting angle that should be mentioned. Captain John Pope, who made a survey along this part of Marcy's Road in 1854, found some wagon wreckage in this crossing of the sand hills.[23] Also, a white boy who was captured by some Comanches during the Civil War told the writer how the Indians had taken him on the road through the sand hills.[24] He identified the place as being in the vicinity of the Pecos River "where you scratch down in the sand and get water" and where there were many parts of old wagons. He said that an old trail crossed through the sand hills at that place.

Whatever may have been the origin of the wagon parts, it is significant that Pope found them on Marcy's road through the sand hills and that the boy captive probably found the same things at the same place. In recent years, Arthur E. Hayes of Monahans has collected many parts of old wagons from the sand hills some eight miles

23. Pope's *Report*, 70.

24. The white captive did not wish his name published but he was interviewed under circumstances that would cause one to accept his report.

25. Mr. Arthur E. Hayes of Monahans was interviewed by the writer on April 9, 1938.

northeast of the town near Willow Springs.[25] The fact that these wagon parts were found at the watering places in the sand hills makes it seem probable that the place where Hayes found them is the same place on Marcy's Road where Pope saw them and likewise was the point at which the boy captive acquired some vivid impressions of his new savage masters.

Marcy and his men continued a northeastward course approximately parallel to the present day Texas and Pacific Railway all the way to the Big Spring. So much of the land in that part of Texas is level prairie that one finds it very difficult to trace their route by topography. They camped at a lake eight miles east of the sand hills and passed several more along the route; but shallow plains lakes are so numerous in that section as to puzzle the minds of persons attempting to identify them.

However, there is one great natural land mark other than the sand hills between the Pecos and the Big Spring. Just seventy miles west of the town of Big Spring, the surface plunges down off the Cap Rock of the plains toward the Pecos River. Following the Texas and Pacific Railway over the edge of the Cap Rock, the surface of the earth drops one hundred and twelve feet in two and two-tenths miles.[26] Marcy failed to note this change of elevation, but Captain Pope who made a survey along Marcy's Road in 1854 did show this sudden westward plunge just seventy and seven-tenths miles west of the Big Spring.[27] According to Pope the change of elevation was eighty-nine feet in two and two-tenths miles. From these facts, two conclusions are permissible (1) Marcy's Road did not pass over the edge of the Cap Rock exactly at the Texas and Pacific Railway tracks, and (2) since the edge of the plains along the old road and the Texas and Pacific tracks were so nearly the same distance west of Big Spring one can hardly escape the conclusion that the two roads must have plunged off the Cap Rock near the same point.[28]

Even another bit of topographical information may be helpful. Pope surveyed this span of Marcy's Road to make a profile of the

26. The writer has a copy of the profile of the Texas and Pacific Railway from Big Spring to Pecos obtained through the courtesy of the Texas and Pacific offices at Dallas.

27. Pope's *Report,* 111.

28. Since the edge of the Cap Rock here extends from northwest to southeast, measurements from Big Spring to two widely separated points on the formation would show a considerable discrepancy in distances.

country showing especially the changes of elevation. From a position probably somewhere in present Ward County to a point in the sand hills, he made an observation of a single span that was seventeen and one-half miles long.[29] One who has watched a ship at sea realizes that one cannot see seventeen and one-half miles across water because of the curvature of the earth. Likewise on level prairie an observation of seventeen and one-half miles is similarly impossible. However, if the observer is located on a hilltop of sufficient height or is looking across a valley of sufficient depth, he may see seventeen and one-half miles or even farther. Hilltops of any considerable height were not available in central Ward County, but a valley, Monument Draw by name,[30] is so situated with respect to the probable route of Marcy's Road across that area as to make a long distance view of seventeen and one-half miles entirely within the range of possibilities. Had Pope stood across this draw some ten miles to the southwest of the site of Monahans and looked seventeen miles northeastwardly across that future townsite toward the sand hills, the terrain would have permitted his observation and, notably, it is one of the few points at which eyesight has so long a span.

Farther along the route near the place that is now Midland, a similar long distance observation was made. This time Pope recorded an uninterrupted view of fifteen miles.[31] Such is not possible exactly at the town of Midland, but some four or five miles north there is a junction of two draws whose combined width greatly increases the range of eyesight, probably to fifteen miles or more.[32]

29. Pope's *Report*, 111.

30. Monument Draw is a valley about nine miles wide with the town of Monahans east of its midpoint. The west bank of the valley is seventy feet above the floor. The low point is only three miles from the west bank. The edge of the sand hills is six miles east of the floor of the valley and ninety feet above it. Plainly an observation of seventeen and one-half miles if made at an angle across this draw is a mathematical possibility since the valley need be only forty-five feet deep to offset the curvature of the earth and permit such a view. (This cross section of Monument Draw was obtained from the profile of the Texas and Pacific Railway.) There is specific evidence that a trail passed through Monahans. An early plat in possession of the Texas and Pacific Company at Dallas shows an old Indian trail passing through Monahans in a northeastward direction "to water in the sand hills."

31. Pope's *Report*, 111.

32. The Texas and Pacific profile shows that the valley or depression at the town of Midland is only eleven and one-half miles wide and that beyond at each edge of the valley the earth slopes in the reverse direction making a fifteen mile observation impossible at that place.

All in all, the old wrecked wagons, the known location of the lakes within the sand hills, the position of the west edge of the Cap Rock and even the valleys or draws that permitted Pope's long distance observations combine to make the route through Monahans northeast some eight miles to the sand hills and then parallel to the Texas and Pacific Railway and a few miles north of it, nearly all the way to Big Spring the most probable answer to the route of Marcy's old road. The writer has plotted the course from Marcy's notes across present maps of the Pecos to the Big Spring country and has obtained the same result.

The journal of the Marcy expedition gives one the impression that when the party had arrived at the Big Spring, they had reached an oasis in the desert. Water was abundant and the frontier traffic lanes from various directions led toward it. Here was an important way station for Comanches who raided annually in Mexico and here was a place where conflicting races met and sometimes fought to settle differences. Manuel's own brother had been killed in such a fight, and Manuel himself was back in familiar territory. He had led the exploring party across the dreaded Llano Estacado and had demonstrated very well through his knowledge of the plains that his race was supreme above the Cap Rock. Two more days along the trail and this efficient Comanche guide must turn back to his home and Mexican wife in faraway San Miguel, high up in the Pecos Valley.

Almost on Manuel's last day as guide, Marcy turned across the future townsite of Big Spring and on to a spring in section 5, township one north, block 31 of the Texas and Pacific surveys some twelve miles to the northeast.[33] Soon the party must depend upon other advice to find a route across this little known part of Texas. But the problem of guidance was not difficult, for here, upon the headwaters of the Colorado, they were approaching the hunting grounds frequented by the semi-civilized tribes of Indian Territory. Black Beaver, a Delaware Indian from this area who had guided Marcy on the early part of his long journey was still in his party and was now ready to point the way back to the settlements of North Texas and on toward Fort Smith, Arkansas.

---

33. Grant Foreman, *Marcy and the Gold Seekers*, 364. The spring found by Marcy was in "limestone rock." The spring on section 5 answers that description and there is no other such spring for several miles. To the east of this place there is no more limestone.

After Manuel's departure, the explorers continued northeastward, entering the flat country in and near the northeast corner of Howard County.[34] Much of this level prairie was once the range of the Bush and Tiller Ranch, and it constitutes the only extensive "flat" at the right distance and in the right direction from the Big Spring to comply with the data given in Marcy's journal. Here the exploring party came into the valley of a creek that flowed eastward into the Colorado River. Willow Creek is the only stream that flows in the required direction from the area of the Bush and Tiller Ranch. The party followed this water course and crossed the Colorado near the junction of the two streams.[35] An old bridge across the Colorado some twenty miles south of Snyder and between the villages of Ira and Cuthbert cannot be very far from the crossing. Moving ahead a few miles, Marcy's Company camped on Canyon Creek in south Scurry County.

They rested for a day or two here and suffered the only casualty of their long journey while encamped at this place. Lieutenant Harrison, who evidently did not understand the hatred that existed between wild Indians and white men, was brutally murdered when he went out alone about two miles from camp. According to the guide, Black Beaver, who carefully examined the ground and all possible clues, Harrison had attempted to be friendly with two Kiowa Indians, even going so far as to permit them to take hold of his gun, when the two red men suddenly became hostile and killed him while he was unarmed. Marcy sent a detachment of men to punish the murderers, but too much time had elapsed before the tragedy was discovered and the Indians fled beyond the reach of the soldiers.

Camp was moved three miles to Deep Creek near the present village of Dunn,[36] and then the party moved on across the Colorado-Brazos divide near the site of Hermleigh and continued across the future county line into Fisher County. They camped on Buffalo Creek, a large tributary of the Clear Fork of the Brazos, about a mile south of the Hobbs school if one uses present day place names. It was only thirteen miles northeast from here to the place where the old highway bridge between Rotan and Roby spanned the Clear Fork.

34. *Ibid.*, 365. A flat country of the type mentioned by Marcy can certainly be found in and near the northeast corner of Howard County.

35. *Ibid.*

36. Near Dunn is the only place at which Deep Creek and Canyon Creek are as little as three miles apart.

Some large salt water springs flowed into the Clear Fork at this old bridge.[37] Long before there was such a highway bridge, Marcy in this expedition of 1849 camped at a hole of fresh water about four hundred yards above those salt water springs.[38]

The identification of this last camp site is as nearly certain as one can ask. Marcy was, according to his unmeasured estimate, some ten miles south of the Double Mountains.[39] Also, it was two miles northeast from the Clear Fork at this place to an area of deep sand, and that sand stretched across the course of the old trail in a belt three miles wide. Every one of these land marks may be found even now in Fisher County in the vicinity of the old bridge across the Clear Fork,[40] and surely the salt water springs at that bridge complete a chain of evidence sufficiently strong to make it possible for one to anchor the route of Marcy's trail at this place without serious question.

With the waterhole four hundred yards above the old Roby-Rotan bridge as one end and the Big Spring two miles south of the town of Big Spring as the other end of this section of Marcy's road, the writer has been able in the foregoing account to follow from camp site to camp site and to call the creeks along the way by their present names. The table of distances and directions that accompanies Marcy's report when measured across correctly drawn maps fits so well the actual topography and dimensions of the country that it removes most of the mystery from this part of the early trail.

This old road of the gold prospectors, even in the Big Spring-Roby span, passes through an area of more recent oil wealth in Mitchell, Scurry, and also in Fisher County. From the crossing of the Clear Fork toward the northeast corner of Fisher County,[41] this trail of the "forty-niners" did not greatly miss the area where oil production has equaled in value a total of many fine nuggets of gold—enough in fact to have dazzled the eyes of the pioneer prospectors.

Once out of Fisher County, as present day maps outline it, Marcy

37. Interview with Dr. J. D. Davis of Roby, Texas, April 8, 1938. Also personal observation on the same and succeeding dates. Above this bridge the water in the Clear Fork is fresh. There is an irrigation dam not far above this point but none below—at least not near by.

38. Grant Foreman, *Marcy and the Gold Seekers,* 372.

39. Marcy's road was actually about fifteen miles south of the Double Mountains.

40. Personal observation, principally in April, 1938.

41. Marcy's *Report,* 230. Marcy's direction of travel was north, 52 degrees 30 minutes east.

and his company of soldier trail-blazers crossed the corner of what is now Stonewall County, across the Flat Top Ranch of the Swenson interests, up to the very bank of the Double Mountain Fork of the Brazos River, and then turned away from that stream across the north end of Flat Top Mountain and down into Haskell County.[42] The old road ran a half mile south of Sagerton, and from this point forward, there is little room to question the route for surveyors have set much of it down in their field notes.

From the end of Flat Top Mountain eastward across Haskell, Throckmorton, Young, Archer, Clay, Montague, Cooke, and Grayson Counties, surveyors have preserved so much of Marcy's Road in these exact field notes that an accurate outline of its path is available all the rest of the way. This convenient fact will be used quite often in the following pages.

Trouble again hovered over the explorers as they moved along the flat lands of present Haskell County. It was now mid-October and a cold north wind and rain beat down on them and wrought much damage, especially among the mule teams that had come from southern climates. These animals already thin of flesh were barely able to reach camp on the night of October 13, for the black rain-soaked soil eight miles south of the site of Haskell made the wagons very difficult to move forward. Five of the mules were unable to finish the day and twenty-eight more died before morning.[43] [The party made camp on land that in recent years was the property of Mr. W. H. Overton,][44] a mile and a half northeast of the flag station of Mc-

42. Haskell County Surveyors' Records, I, 188. The F. H. K. Day Survey, established May 30, 1856, shows the route of the California Road across what is now the west line of Haskell County.

43. Grant Foreman, *Marcy and the Gold Seekers*, 373-375.

44. Marcy's *Report*, 230-231. The table of distances and direction of travel given by Marcy has been checked against the map and land of Haskell and nearby counties. The distance by straight line map measurement from the Overton farm back to the Roby-Rotan Bridge is forty-one and one-half miles. By Marcy's distance table it was forty-three and eight-tenths miles from the camp site of October 10, evidently at the site of the bridge, to the camp site of October 13. By map it is seventeen miles back to the point where the Double Mountain River had "high banks." By Marcy's distance table and journal it was eighteen and six-tenths miles from the point of the river to the campsite of October 13. Both comparisons indicate that the Overton land was certainly not far from the camp site.

To run ahead of the story, and measure forward from the Overton farm to a camp site two miles above the mouth of Paint Creek one finds that the distance is twenty miles. From the camp site of October 13-17 to this same point on Paint Creek

Connell. Little Timber Creek lay just east of them and other streams of still greater capacity stretched across their course. It came a veritable downpour of rain all night long and in fact did not cease for fifteen hours. The creeks ahead spread out along the country side as wide as rivers and not for several days did they recede into their sluggish channels.

To Marcy, the outlook was none too bright. Due to the loss of draft animals, he discarded five of the train of eighteen wagons and buried boxes filled with the least essential baggage. Fires were made on the ground above the buried articles, probably so as not to arouse the suspicion of prowling Indians. Directions were written on a nearby tree—possibly a note was pinned on it—telling how to find the things that were buried. Whether or not any of the pioneer travelers ever found the discarded materials is not known. Travelers who came along Marcy's road probably appropriated the discarded wagons part-at-a-time, but since it was too late in the season for California bound emigrants to begin a journey to the west coast, it seems unlikely that the note of instructions on the tree was ever found or that the buried articles have ever been discovered.

Part of an old type wagon hub was found by the writer west of Little Timber Creek at the place on Overton farm where it seems most likely that Marcy camped. Pioneer blacksmiths who have examined the part are positive in the opinion that it came from a wagon of early origin. Whether or not it is part of one of Marcy's discarded wagons,

---

Marcy's distance table shows it twenty-two and three-fourths miles. Hence calculating both forward and backward across the map, one arrives at the conclusion that the camp of October 13-17 must have been almost if not exactly on the Overton farm.

Now note that by surveying records Marcy's trail did cross the Overton Farms. (Young County Deed Records, I, 134.)

Note further that the camp of October 13-17 was just west of a creek and that it is four miles eastward to another creek and that there is such a creek (Little Timber Creek) on the Overton farm, and another just four miles east of it. In addition to these facts note that Marcy crossed four creeks in the next three days' travel of ten and one-half miles after the camp of October 13-17, and that Little Timber Creek, Mule Creek, Paint Creek, and California Creek along the mapped route of his trail are spaced by a total distance of ten and one-half miles. Obviously the assumption that Marcy camped October 13-17 on the Overton farm is supported by so many measurements that fit precisely into the map of Haskell County that one can not escape the conclusion.

it adds a touch of interest to the search for the boxes of buried baggage.

It required three days to reorganize the expedition and to resume the march. On October 1, the party, reduced in equipment and baggage, moved eastward four miles to Mule Creek.[45] The stream was still too high to cross and camp was made. By the next morning the water was low enough to permit a crossing but after moving only two miles it was found that Paint Creek was still too deep to cross. Again the party waited overnight but again by morning the water level had fallen and the wagon train could move ahead. This time they crossed both Paint and California Creeks and camped not far from the latter stream, after a march of four and one-half miles. At this point the expedition had passed through a succession of four creeks now found in south Haskell County and being no longer impeded by the high water were in a position to move ahead with less delay. The next day's travel placed them twelve and one-fourth miles farther on their way. The camp site at the end of this day was in present Throckmorton County. The party was again on Paint Creek, this time only two miles above its junction with the Clear Fork of the Brazos.[46]

It is interesting to observe that here is the point at which Marcy had his one extended conference with wild Indians on his return trip from Santa Fe and that five years later he, in company with Major Robert S. Neighbors, surveyed an Indian Reservation only a few miles down the Clear Fork from this same point. During this night on Paint Creek, Marcy had as his guest Senaco, an important Comanche Chief, and seven of his fellow chieftains. The whole group of Comanches were camped nearby and also a band of Kickapoos with one hundred warriors were in the vicinity. The whole assemblage of Indians was entirely friendly. The Kickapoos had come down into Texas on a hun-

45. Marcy's *Report*, 230-231. None of these creeks were called by name in Marcy's *Report*. The account given here is a reconstruction of the story from Marcy's notes and Haskell County topography. The route through this area can be verified from Cooke County Surveying Records, Vol. C, 54, Vol. D, 586, Vol. B, 593, and Vol. 3, 173. The road passed across Haskell County nearly due east and was an average of about six miles from the south line. The route was seven and one-half miles north of the south county line at the west edge of the county, six and one-half miles at the Overton farm, only four miles at approximately three-fourths of the way across the county and six miles at the east line of the county.

46. Grant Foreman, *Marcy and the Gold Seekers*, 380. Also Throckmorton County Deed Records, M 3, 432.

ting trip and the Comanches were within their native range. Apparently this camping ground near the Clear Fork, like that at the Big Spring, was sort of a crossroad point for the different tribes of red men. Black Beaver, the guide, was well schooled in the ways of Indians in their common hunting grounds and did much on this occasion to make the contact between races such a friendly meeting. At first sight of the Comanches, while Marcy was still two miles or more west of Paint Creek, it was Black Beaver who made the approach. He moved out to a hilltop and at a great distance talked to the strange Indians in the sign language of the Plains. Suspicion shortly gave way and friendly intercourse was soon established.

The exploring party did not linger among their new Indian friends, with the exception of this one overnight stop. It required seventeen days (October 21 to November 6) to reach the old town of Preston on Red River, which was the head of navigation on that stream and the end of their journey in Texas.

The route followed by the expedition during these last seventeen days can best be told by listing specific points along the way:

1. Marcy's camp on Paint Creek was at the southwest corner of Thomas Lambshead Survey, fifteen miles by direct line southwest of Throckmorton and four miles east of Haskell County.[47]

2. The road of this expedition passed what later became the northwest corner of the Comanche Indian Reservation some two miles northeast of the camping place on Paint Creek.[48]

3. The California Road, as the route of this party became known, crossed the place where the paved highway now runs about four miles south of Throckmorton although no land survey fixes the exact spot.

4. This old road entered the Felix A. Richardson Survey four miles east and three and one-fourth miles south of Throckmorton.[49]

5. The road crossed Elm Creek at the northeast corner of Texan Emigration and Land Company Survey Number 2347. This place is nine miles east of Throckmorton and three-fourths of a mile south of the highway leading toward Newcastle.[50]

47. *Ibid.* After an exhaustive study of maps and county archives, Mr. Williams located most of the sites described in the following pages by visiting these localities and looking over the terrain.—The Editor.

48. Throckmorton County surveyors records, B, 178 ff. Marcy surveyed the Comanche Indian Reservation five years later and mentioned the nearby California Road at the northwest corner.

49. Texas General Land Office Map of Throckmorton County, 1898.

50. The Peters Colony map of 1854 found in the Texas Land Office shows the

6. The road crossed the place where the Throckmorton-Newcastle Highway is located, ten miles east of Throckmorton at the northeast corner of Texan Emigration and Land Company Survey Number 2146.[51]

7. Next the California trail crossed the east line of Throckmorton County slightly more than a mile north of the Throckmorton-Newcastle Highway.[52]

8. The crossing of Marcy's road on the Brazos River was three and one-half miles down stream from the Olney-Throckmorton Highway bridge.[53]

9. The old road crossed Rabbit Creek three miles (by direct line) southeast of the village of Padgett, in the north central part of survey Number 338.[54]

10. The road crossed Paint Creek (formerly known as California Creek) in the southeast part of survey Number 46.[55] This point is four miles west and seven miles south of Olney.

11. The California Trail crossed the railroad one-half mile south of the village of Orth.[56] This village is six miles south of Olney.

12. This old trail crossed the east line of survey Number 241, one-fourth mile north of the southeast corner. It crossed the paved highway some six miles south of Olney and almost due east of Orth.[57]

13. This old road of 1849 crossed the Olney-Jean Highway seven miles southeast of Olney in survey Number 1461.[58]

---

route of Marcy's road for about eighty miles. The portion shown in that map extends from Throckmorton County across Young, Archer, Clay, and into Montague County. The Peters Colony surveys are listed on current maps of those counties as Texas Emigration and Land Company surveys. For the sake of brevity these tracts of land will be referred to hereafter simply by calling the survey number.

Numerous references are made to the route of Marcy's Road in the deed records and surveying records of the above counties but since the Peters Colony map of 1854 was compiled from the record of these surveys which were made in 1853, it is obviously useless duplication to make direct reference in this article to more than the map.

51. *Ibid.*
52. *Ibid.*
53. *Ibid.*
54. *Ibid.*
55. *Ibid.*
56. *Ibid.*
57. *Ibid.*
58. *Ibid.*

14. The California Trail was joined by the Preston-Belknap Road in survey Number 1395 some ten miles east of Olney.[59]

15. This old road crossed the present day boundary line between Young and Archer counties in survey Number 1802 about nine miles west of the northeast corner of Young County.[60]

16. Marcy's trail crossed the Trinity River (which in this area is only a creek) in a survey Number 1831 about ten miles south and three and one-half miles east of the location of Archer City.[61]

17. About three miles northeast of this crossing on the Trinity, the old road crossed the common boundary line of surveys Number 1848 and Number 1861.[62] The writer has followed the path of the road at this point. It is visible for more than a half mile.

18. The California Road as used in 1853 divided for a few hundred feet at Flag Springs which were near the mid-point of the common boundary line between surveys Number 1841 and Number 1844.[63] The branch of the road that passes a little north of this line is visible for a short distance. The location of the place is two and one-half miles west of the Wichita Falls-Jacksboro Highway at a point five and one-half miles south of the village of Windthorst.

19. The old road is also visible a mile east of this last place in survey Number 1874.[64]

20. This former road is also visible in survey Number 1872 at a point nearly five and one-half miles south of Windthorst and just over the hilltop west of the paved highway. These last two points on the old road are on the J. S. Bridwell Ranch.[65]

21. The road entered the limits of what later became Clay County three miles north of the southwest corner.[66]

22. Three miles to the east of the county line the road passed through survey Number 2616 one-half mile south of a prominent mount.[67]

59. *Ibid.*
60. *Ibid.*
61. *Ibid.*
62. *Ibid.*
63. *Ibid.*
64. *Ibid.*
65. *Ibid.*
66. *Ibid.*
67. *Ibid.*

23. Nine and one-half miles east of the county line the road passed through survey Number 2695, just a mile north of a hill known in 1854 as Post Oak Knob.[68]

24. A mile and a half east of this hill was Prairie Spring, evidently a watering place on the road. The location was the northeast part of survey Number 2698.[69] The old road is still visible in survey Number 3206, which lies just east of the site of Prairie Spring. Two parallel road channels at least twenty feet apart may be seen here. A mesquite tree some six inches in diameter is growing in one of them.

25. Three miles southwest of the village of Buffalo Springs in the central part of south Clay County, the road is plainly visible in survey Number 3222.[70] Several parallel channels—possibly a foot deep—follow northwestwardly down a gentle slope at this place.

26. The old road passed about one-half mile south of the present village of Buffalo Springs. The direction of the road was northeast through survey Number 3227, Number 3238, and Number 3260.[71] The springs were on the creek that had its source due east of the present village and ran in a direction somewhat east of north. Following the course of this spring branch the road ran nearly two miles before it turned east again.

27. The road then changed its course more toward the southeast and crossed a present day county road one-half mile north of the village of Vashti.[72] Old Grass Springs near the point probably was a watering place on the early trail.

28. In surveys Number 2843 and Number 3844,[73] about four and one-half miles south of the town of Bellevue the old road bed shows very distinctly.

29. It crossed the Clay-Montague County line about two and one-half miles south of the Wichita Falls-Fort Worth Highway.[74]

30. The old road crossed the above paved highway five and three-fourths miles northwest of Bowie and continued northward, passing on the north side of Bushy Mound which is the most prominent hill in the vicinity.[75]

68. *Ibid.*
69. *Ibid.*
70. *Ibid.*
71. *Ibid.*
72. *Ibid.*
73. *Ibid.*
74. *Ibid.*
75. *Ibid.*

31. Continuing its northeast course the old trail crossed the southeast corner of survey Number 3428 and entered a one hundred and ten acre tract of land belonging to J. W. Rhyne.[76] One can see the path of the old road across Rhyne's field. The terraces on this farm are necessarily much higher and broader than elsewhere at the point where they intersect the old road bed. Otherwise erosion would soon carry them away.

32. The old road intersects the path of the paved Bowie-Ringgold Highway about five and one-half miles northwest of Bowie.[77] This point is a little more than a mile northwest of a prominent hill known as Queen's Peak. In 1853 this hill was known as Victoria Peak and was cited as a land mark in many of the Texan Emigration and Land Company Surveys.

33. Marcy's Road crossed the east fork of Belknap Creek near the west corner of the H. Ravestone Survey.[78] This crossing is by direct line nine miles southwest of Nocona.

34. Almost exactly midway between this point and Nocona is the Barrel Springs Rural School. The old roadbed of the California Trail can be seen in the east part of that school yard.[79] The name of the school is taken from the old springs a mile to the southwest, which were once a watering place on Marcy's Road.

35. The California Trail came within less than three miles south of the site of Nocona. The most exact information on this fact is that derived from the field notes of the J. Olabarry league of land surveyed in 1851. The old trail crossed the northeast boundary line of that tract just one mile from the east corner.[80] This place is three miles south and three-fourths mile west of the business section of Nocona.

36. Here for a distance of about eight miles through the upper cross timbers the old trail made a swing to the southeast but apparently land records are silent about its exact route.

37. The old road is recorded again at a point on the northwest

76. *Ibid.* Also Cooke County Surveyors Records, B, 508.

77. Montague County Surveyors Records, I, 188. This point is in the Limestone County School Land—a survey of four leagues—and is so far from the point at which the old road is mentioned that the location is not as definite as in smaller surveys.

78. Cooke County Surveyors Records, A, 76. This survey was made August 1, 1851.

79. The Texas General Land Office map (No. 5) of Cooke District plotted January 30, 1856.

80. Montague County Surveyors Records, I, 247

line of the Calhoun County school land,[81] league Number 12. This place on the road is one-half mile west of the north corner of the league of land and is four and one-half miles slightly north of east of the town of Montague. The southeast course of the trail changed to east and even to a little north of east within less than a mile.

38. It followed the high prairie ridge to the site of Saint Jo, very much as the Montague-Saint Jo road does today and crossed Elm Creek in the A. Kitchens Survey some six or seven hundred yards south of the business district of the old town.[82]

39. Four and one-half miles northeast of Muenster the "military or Chihuahua" road crossed the H. Barnet Survey.[83] The record left by early commissioners of Cooke County called it the California Road, which identified this section of Marcy's road of 1849 with the route of the Chihuahua Traders of 1840. Probably the two routes were identical from a point near Callisburg, northeast of Gainesville, to Brushy Mound, five miles northwest of Bowie. They may have followed the same roadbed for thirty or forty miles west of Brushy Mound.

40. Marcy's road passed about three miles north of Gainesville, a town which was not in existence until 1850. Soon a branch route of the California Trail left the original road six miles northeast of Gainesville,[84] and passed along California Street of that town, again joining the main trail before reaching the "head of Elm" or modern Saint Jo.

41. On the night of November 4 Marcy camped near the plantation of a Mr. McCarty who lived on the head of Big Sandy.[85] The land records have preserved the site of the McCarty Survey and of Basin Springs, an important frontier watering place that was near the center

81. Cooke County Surveyors Records, A, 238.

82. *Ibid.*, 48. The surveyors records of Cooke and Monatague counties list a number of points on Marcy's Road omitted here for the sake of brevity. The map accompanying this chapter has been compiled from the more complete information.

83. Cooke County Surveyors' Records, B, 43. The Chihuahua Trail was elsewhere mentioned in Cooke County Surveyors' Records in Vol. B, 42, also Vol. A, 3 and 269.

84. Cooke County Surveyors' Records, A, 122. The E. D. Webster survey was near the fork of the roads, as the field notes mentioned both the Belknap Road and the Preston-Gainesville Road. The survey of the Peters Colony boundary line made a few miles west of Gainesville in 1853 shows that the Preston-Belknap Road was nearly three miles north of the Belknap-Gainesville Road at that point. (General Land Office "Field notes boundary line Peters Colony" Vol. 18, pp. 54-57.)

85. Grant Foreman, *Marcy and the Gold Seekers*, 391.

of the tract of land.[86] The springs are six and one-half miles northeast of Whitesboro and near it is the Basin Springs rural school that was, in early Grayson County history, the site of an educational center of note. Land records have also preserved the route of the California trail at this point.[87] Probably the old road now visible a few hundred yards north of Dixie (a village just north of Whitesboro) is a point on this early road that ran west from Basin Springs toward the Pacific Coast.

42. From Basin Springs Marcy's road continued in a northeasterly direction to the high ground some seven or eight miles northwest of modern Denison. Then it turned more to the north, passing across the William J. Reeves Survey[88] and crossing Little Mineral Creek not more than a mile above its mouth. It finally turned back toward the east to the town of Preston on the bank of the Red River about a mile northeast of the mouth of Little Mineral. This is the bend of Red River in which Holland Coffee established his trading post some twelve or thirteen years before the California Gold Rush. Much of this bend of the river was submerged as the Denison Lake reached its high water mark.

It is not the intent of this chapter to follow Marcy on to his destination at Fort Smith, Arkansas. He had opened a new road across north Texas that furnished a shorter route to California than the road by Santa Fe. The Comanche Indian Guide, Manuel, had pointed out the route near present-day Lubbock, Texas, and Fort Sumner, New Mexico, that may have been shorter than either, and undoubtedly had fewer streams to cross. However, Marcy made his choice and a comparison of merits with other routes would be of little value here.

Within the chosen course each of Marcy's three guides performed his task of pointing the way with little short of expertness. The guide from Doña Ana to the Pecos knew the springs and mountain passes unerringly and found the most direct route possible within his assignment.

Manuel made the best of a bad situation. The Sand Hills and the Llano Estacado constituted the greatest barrier to traffic on the whole road, but this Comanche guide found the way across them both. During dry seasons permanent springs and lakes were much too far

86. Grayson County Surveyors' Records, A, 444.
87. *Ibid.*
88. *Ibid.*, 228.

apart on this section of the road and the pass through the Sand Hills was always a difficult drive, but the road functioned for some years in spite of such drawbacks.

Black Beaver, who piloted Marcy from the Colorado River back to the settlements of North Texas, apparently followed the route of hunting parties of semi-civilized Indians from that stream to the upper Cross Timbers. From that point there were readymade roads to follow on to Preston that made the rest of the task easy. Beaver especially demonstrated his knowledge of the country by steering the party just to the left of a large arm of the Cross Timbers that extends into Jack and Young counties for more than forty miles.

The old road accommodated travel for some years after it was opened, but it was important, as previously mentioned, more because it focused the attention of the public toward the El Paso country than that it ever served a very great traffic. Quite a little of the road must have disappeared before 1880. The late J. Wright Mooar told the writer that he did not see the old trail when he crossed its route in Fisher County in 1876.[89] B. F. Reynolds of Throckmorton in company with others followed the old road from Throckmorton County well into central Haskell County "before Mackenzie's time." The roadbed was not even then visible at all points and Reynolds said it was not a plain road except in places.[90]

However, this old trail did perform an important service as far west as Archer and Young counties. It was "the road west" to pioneer hunters, cattlemen, and farmers for a long time. The late J. W. McMurtry once stood near his house seven miles southwest of Windthorst in southeast Archer County and pointed out the old trail which the writer had identified by land records as Marcy's Road. "That was the main road when I came to this country fifty years ago," said McMurtry. And well it might have been the "main road" for it consisted of three well beaten tracks some twenty to thirty feet apart and as much as a foot deep—even after it had been pasture land for nearly five decades.

This effort to revive the route of the old road is done on the theory that it was not merely a trail of dirt but an institution in American History. The tracks at McMurtry's house and other points

89. Interview with J. Wright Mooar, April 2, 1938. Mooar hunted buffalo in this section in 1876.

90. Interview with B. F. Reynolds, December 30, 1937.

along the trail were made by the first great surge of free men on their way to develop the West after paternal govenments had failed at that task for three centuries. Like the succeeding generations who discovered oil along the trail, these men were operating after the fashion of American patterns of life. In view of such understandings it is probably not amiss to say that the road of Doña Ana was part and parcel of the American way of life.

XI

MARCY'S EXPLORATION TO LOCATE THE TEXAS INDIAN RESERVATIONS IN 1854

J. W. Williams and Ernest Lee

Randolph B. Marcy probably did more of the detailed exploring of northwest Texas than any other individual. In company with Robert S. Neighbors, he spent the time from July 15 to August 21, 1854, in examining a portion of that part of the state with a view of finding suitable locations for the two Indian reservations that were shortly to be placed in Young and Throckmorton counties. Land adaptable to farming, with suitable camp sites and with plenty of good water were most of the essential features to be looked for.

In the opinion of the two writers Marcy's journey was confined largely to the present Texas counties of Young, Archer, Wichita, Baylor, Knox, Haskell and Throckmorton, and in addition it barely touched southeastern Wilbarger and only a limited area along the east parts of King and Stonewall counties. This view is a little unorthodox and will most likely invite a rather critical examination of some of the footnotes that follow. Such criticism, of course, is welcome.

Marcy wrote his own account of the expedition, the essential parts of which occupy the remaining pages of this article. His account follows:

Chapter VII [p. 170].
INDIAN RESERVATIONS.
Arrival at Fort Belknap.—Troubles of the Small Tribes of Texas.—Jose Maria. Council.—Major Neighbors.—Wolf Dance.—Comanche Visit to the Tonkawas.—Admiration for the Major's Wardrobe.—Enlists in a War Expedition.—Little Wichita River.*—Big Wichita River.—Perilous Position of

*Spelled consistently by Marcy *Witchita*. The present-day spelling—Wichita—is adopted here.

Major Neighbors.—Head of Big Wichita.—Bad Water.—Reach Brazos River.—Head of the Brazos.—Abundance of Game.—Ketumsee.—Clear Fork of the Brazos.—Council.—Location of the Reservations.—Summary.—Double Mountain Fork.—Mesquit Tree.—Mesquit Gum.—Civilizing Comanches.

In 1853,[1] the Legislature of Texas passed an act authorizing the general government to have selected and surveyed, from any vacant lands within the limits of the state, reservations amounting to twelve leagues, for the exclusive use of the Indians inhabiting that Territory.

I was, in 1854, selected by the War Department to go out into the unsettled parts of the state, and, in conjunction with Major Neighbors, special agent for those Indians, to locate and survey these reservations.

I had already explored a great portion of Northern and Western Texas, and was perfectly familiar with the character of the country upon Red River, Trinity, some sections of the Brazos, and Colorado; but up to that time there was no record of any white man having explored the Brazos or the Big Wichita Rivers to their sources. As these streams were included within the limits of Texas, and as I deemed it desirable to locate the Indians as far as possible away from the white settlements, I determined to explore [p. 171] the streams alluded to. Accordingly, after procuring a suitable escort and outfit, I proceeded to Fort Belknap, on the Brazos River, where I was joined by Major Neighbors, with several Delawares for guides, interpreters, and hunters . . .

[p. 180] The following extracts from my journal, giving my impressions of the country as I passed over it, will probably convey a more accurate idea of that section than can be given in any other way.

"On the 15th of July we left Fort Belknap, and traveled back on the Preston road for fourteen miles to the '*Cottonwood Spring,*'[2] [p. 181] upon the large prairie east of that post. Here we encamped, and at an early hour the following morning left the road, striking out into

1. Colonel R. B. Marcy, *Thirty Years of Army Life on the Border* (New York, 1866), 170.

Marcy's narration, repeated here, includes excerpts from pages 170 to 217 of the above publication.

2. The Cottonwood Spring was a regular camping place on the old road from Fort Belknap to the town of Preston in Grayson County. It was located about a mile north of the present day village of Jean in north Young County (one mile west—K.F.N.).

the prairie with a course a few degrees west of north toward the Little
Wichita River, passing over a rolling country covered with groves of
mesquit trees, and intersected by several spring branches (tributaries
to 'Salt Creek'),[3] flowing through valleys clothed with a dense coating
of verdure, and teeming with a multitude of beautiful flowers of
brilliant hues, the aroma from which filled the atmosphere with a
most delicate fragrant perfume.

"We made our camp at a fine large spring near the head of one
of the branches of the west fork of the Trinity.[4]

"Our course the next day was northwest for six miles, crossing
several small tributaries of the Trinity, all of which were wooded with
mesquit, and occasionally a grove of postoak was seen, with here and
there a cottonwood or willow tree along the banks.

"The water in all these branches is clear and palatable, and may
be relied on throughout the season.

"The geological features of this section are characterized by a
predominance of dark sandstone, which in many places crops out or is
laid bare by the action of water, and is covered with detached
fragments of volcanic scoria.

"We are encamped to-night upon a confluent of the 'Little
Wichita,'[5] which is here bordered by high, abrupt, rocky bluffs. The
water stands in pools along the bed of the stream, and, although by
no means good, it is drinkable.[6]

"Our course on the morning of the 18th was nearly west,
gradually deflecting to the southward, for the purposes of avoiding
the numerous branches of the Wichita, but we soon discovered they
would take us too far out of our course, and turned north, crossing
them at right angles.

[p. 182] "Our march this morning led us along a gradual slope
of beautiful and picturesque country, interspersed with mesquit

3. The route in order to continue on the head branches of Salt Creek necessarily
paralleled the railroad from Jean toward nearby Olney and was not far north of the
railroad tracks.

4. Probably northward of Olney some three or four miles.

5. Bluffs are rather numerous on the upper part of the south fork of the Little
Wichita River.

6. The Little Wichita River and its tributaries were—before the drilling of oil
wells—uniformly soft water streams. Any unpalatable features of the water here in
1854 were most likely due to the stagnant condition of the pools and to undesirable
vegetation in the streambed.

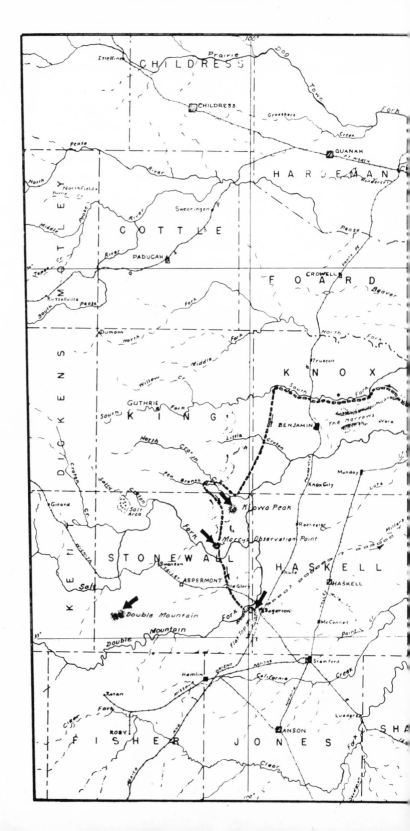

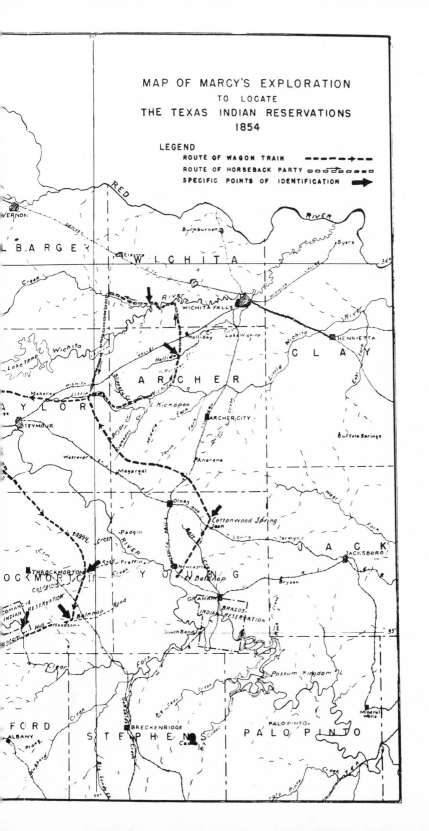

MAP OF MARCY'S EXPLORATION
TO LOCATE
THE TEXAS INDIAN RESERVATIONS
1854

LEGEND
ROUTE OF WAGON TRAIN
ROUTE OF HORSEBACK PARTY
SPECIFIC POINTS OF IDENTIFICATION

glades and prairie lawns, for about eight miles, when we found ourselves, on reaching the crest of the ascent, upon the summit level of three streams, the 'Brazos,' 'Trinity,' and the 'Little Wichita.'[7] Here a most beautiful panorama was opened to our view. On our left, in the distance, could be seen the lofty cliffs bordering the Brazos, while in front of us, toward the sources of the Little Wichita, were numerous conical mounds, whose regular and symmetrical outlines were exhibited with remarkable truth and distinctness on a background of transparent blue sky. On our right, several tributaries of the Little Wichita, embellished with light fringes of trees, flowed in graceful sinuosities among green flowering meadows, through a basin of surpassing beauty and loveliness as far to the east as the eye could reach—all contributing enticing features to the romantic scenery, and producing a most pleasing effect upon the senses.

"We continued the same course on the 19th, crossing several more of the Wichita tributaries, which caused us considerable detention in excavating banks and constructing bridges to cross our train.

"The soil in the valleys of all these streams is a rich mellow alluvion of a highly productive character, and, were it not for the scarcity of timber which begins to be apparent, this would undoubtedly prove a desirable farming locality.

"The adjacent uplands are broken and rolling, but the soil possesses the elements of fertility. Upon the summit of the bluffs, at the head of the streams we are now passing, nothing can be seen toward the west but one unbroken expanse of prairie, spreading out beyond till it is lost in the dim distance.

"In previous communications to the War Department, I [p. 183] have spoken of the great deficiency of building timber where I have traveled west of the 'Cross Timbers.' It may be added here that the same facts are observed in this section; and although mesquit is found sufficient for fuel, yet there is a great scarcity of timber suitable for building purposes. There are, however, many quarries of stone, which might answer as a substitute.

"If this country is ever densely populated by agriculturists, a new era in husbandry must be instituted. Nature seems to demand

7. The expedition was now a few miles east of the present-day village of Megargel, too far west to have been "upon the summit" of the Trinity River, although there was no marked elevation in the country to emphasize that fact. The exploring party was located on the divide between the Brazos and Little Wichita rivers.

this. Instead of clearing up timbered lands for the plow, as in the Eastern States, it will be necessary to cultivate timber; indeed, this has already been commenced in some Western prairies with successful results.

"We find an abundance of game throughout this section, and our hunters are enabled to keep the entire command supplied with fresh meat, so that we have had no occasion to make use of our beef cattle.

"Our noon halt to-day was upon the summit of a hill, where we found a spring of cool, wholesome water, surrounded with a luxuriant crop of grass, which afforded our cattle the very best pasturage.

"After noon we continued on for about eight miles over mesquit glades, when we arrived in a broad lowland valley, through which meanders a stream about twenty feet wide and two feet deep. This proved to be the main trunk of the Little Wichita.[8] Its banks are about ten feet high, very abrupt, and skirted with elm and cotton-wood. The water has a slightly brackish taste, but is palatable.

"We remained in camp on the 20th, making preparations to leave the train and escort at this place, while Major Neighbors and myself proposed to make an excursion toward Red River. As we should, under any circumstances, be obliged to return this way, and could move much more [p. 184] rapidly with pack mules than with our wagons, and as we did not anticipate meeting hostile Indians in this direction, we determined to take with us only our Delawares and three soldiers. Accordingly, on the following morning, we started at

8. Marcy's campsite was on the principal branch of the Little Wichita about a half dozen miles within Baylor County. The possibility that this camp was on the head of Kickapoo Creek northeast of present-day Megargel has been rather critically examined. The theory was discarded because it would have been impossible for Marcy to have ascended the Kickapoo Creek twelve miles from this camp as his journal reports that he later did. On the principal branch of the Little Wichita the channel extends westward a full dozen miles in the exact direction necessary to conform to Marcy's journal on July 25. Also the very short distance between this campsite and the Big Wichita as shown in Marcy's short journey on the morning of July 24 causes one to earmark the supposed Kickapoo campsite as highly unlikely.

9. Slippery Creek joins the Little Wichita on the north at right angles about five miles within Archer County. It is a short stream omitted from most maps, but in appearance it is almost as large as the Little Wichita at the junction of the two streams. The city of Wichita Falls is owner of the land where these two streams meet. When that city's new domestic water reservoir, Lake Kickapoo, was filled to spillway level, this point was submerged.

an early hour in a course nearly due east down the valley of the creek upon which we had encamped, and, after descending fifteen miles, arrived at a point where another large tributary from the north[9] united with the main branch. Directly at the confluence our Indians discovered a swarm of bees, that had taken up their abode in a dry limb of a gigantic old cottonwood-tree.[10] We were anxious to get the honey, but a small hatchet was the only substitute for an axe in our possession; and as chopping down the tree with this was out of the question, I was upon the point of leaving the industrious little insects in quiet possession of the fruits of their labors, when one of the Delawares resorted to the ingenious expedient of climbing a small tree standing near the cottonwood, and, on reaching the top, swung himself within reach of the limb that contained the desired treasure. He was soon seated upon it, and, fastening to it a lariat which was thrown to him, we seized the other end, and with our united efforts broke off the part containing the honey, which afforded us all a bountiful feast. We then resumed our journey down the stream, and traveled thirteen miles before we encamped.

"The character of the country along the valley is similar to that at our last camp. The soil is exceedingly rich, producing a heavy crop of grass, but the valley is subject to inundation, and no woodland is seen except directly along the banks of the stream.

"The valley varies from half a mile to two miles in width, and is shut in by rolling uplands, entirely void of any timber save mesquit.

"There are timbered lands below this point, but they are [p. 185] mostly disposed of by the state, and are not now vacant;[11] we did not, therefore, deem it advisable to proceed any farther in this direction, and on the morning of the following day turned north toward the Big Wichita River, not expecting to find any more tributaries to

10. The timber has been cleared from the junction of these two streams and in fact from the entire Lake Kickapoo basin, but an aerial map in possession of the City of Wichita Falls Water Department showed dense timber bordering both streams at this point. There were cottonwood, elm, ash, hackberry and chinaberry trees, but no pecans. Some of the cottonwoods were as much as forty-eight inches in diameter. Ernest Lee, one of the two writers of this article, served as field engineer on the construction of Lake Kickapoo and in the course of his duties traversed this area almost daily for more than a year.

11. The Texan Emigration and Land Company surveyed their premium lands in 1853. Their surveyed area included great blocks of land in Young and Throckmorton counties and smaller areas in south Archer and in southeast Baylor County. Marcy's route westward of these traversed a country that had not yet been surveyed.

the Little Wichita, but, after traveling about five miles, we crossed another nearly as large as the main branch. This proved to be the most northerly confluent. It was twelve feet wide, the banks high, and lined with large pecan trees, and, as we have seen none of this timber upon the other branches, it occurred to us that it might appropriately be named the 'Pecan Fork.'[12] The water during this dry season stands in pools along the bed of the creek, but it is free from salts and palatable.

"There is more timber along this branch than upon the others, but away from the stream no woodland is seen, the soil here does not appear to be as prolific as upon the other branches.

"Leaving the valley of the 'Pecan Fork,' we continued on in a north course over a very elevated prairie for seven miles, which brought us upon the crest of the ridge dividing the waters of the 'Little' from those of the 'Big Wichita,' from whence we descended by a smooth and regular grade for eight miles, and entered the valley of the latter stream, making our noon halt in a grove of hackberry trees, near a pool of muddy water.

"After dinner we crossed the valley, which was here about three miles wide, and found ourselves standing upon the bank of the Big Wichita, and, ascending about four miles, discovered a large spring of cold pure water bursting out from the bank near the river, and here made our bivouac for the night.

"After a long and tiresome march, through an atmosphere heated almost to suffocation by the intense rays of a [p. 186] southern sun, it is difficult for one who has not experienced the sensation to conceive the exquisite pleasure imparted by a drink of cold water, particularly after being deprived of it for a long time. Such was the

12. This was Holliday Creek (a tributary of the Big Wichita) south of the little town of Holliday. Here on the Reunion Grounds is a dense grove of pecan trees. Pecan timber is found along the banks of the stream throughout most of its course. Pecan timber does not grow naturally west of Holliday Creek. Neither is it found on the Little Wichita or its branches west of the Wichita Falls-Archer City highway or for some distance east of that highway. Hence there is no branch of the Little Wichita located geographically so that it can answer the description of Marcy's "Pecan Fork."

Holliday Creek is the only stream that can qualify and only a small segment of it—the portion south of Holliday—lies within five miles of the Little Wichita River. Ernest Lee's duties as an engineer have taken him many times over much of Holliday Creek at the Little Wichita and his search among land owners to complete his knowledge of the locale of pecan timber makes it possible to locate the pecan groves south of Holliday as a point on Marcy's route.

case with us upon this occasion, and everyone now seemed perfectly happy and contented with himself and all the world.

"The 'Big Wichita' River at this point is 130 yards wide and three feet deep, with a current of about three miles per hour. The water is of a reddish cast, and rather turbid, but does not contain so much sedimentary matter as the water of the Little Wichira. It is so excessively bitter[13] and nauseating to the taste that it can only be drunk in cases of the greatest extremity, and is similar to the water of Red River.

"We are at this place about twenty-five miles above the mouth of the river (one of our Delawares having visited this locality before and estimated the distance), yet the river is wider here than at its confluence with Red River.

"It never rises above its banks, which are from ten to twenty feet high, and although its general direction is nearly east and west, it frequently flows toward all points of the compass within a short distance. Its course is very tortuous, running from one side to the other of a valley about four miles wide, bounded upon both sides by lofty bluffs. The soil in the valley is a dark red and exceedingly rich alluvion, covered with the very best grass; unfortunately, however, the almost total absence of woodland, and the very great scarcity of good water, will render this section unsuited to the purposes of agriculture.

"With the exception of a scanty skirt of cottonwood trees along the course of the river (and even this, in many places, entirely disappears), there is no timber in this part of the valley. These considerations influenced us in rejecting this as a locality suited to the wants of the Indians, except for purposes of hunting.

13. The people of Wichita Falls and vicinity, who some years ago built a large lake (Lake Kemp) up the Wichita River, have found it not an unmixed blessing. The water of this lake, although not as highly charged with mineral matter as is the river at low water such as Marcy found it, had a "hardness" content of 55 grains per gallon and a salt content of 1240 parts per million. This water, so highly charged with mineral matter, had been only a partial success for irrigation and had been very unsatisfactory as an emergency reserve for the city water supply. In view of this fact the city completed the expenditure of some $3,000,000 for its new water facilities in the early 1940s which included Lake Kickapoo with water charges with only four grains per gallon of hardness and a salt content of less than 20 parts per million. Ninety-three years after Marcy's journey, these figures constitute an interesting confirmation of the facts about water in the two Wichita rivers as he found them by the taste method.

[p. 187] "On the morning of the 23rd we reluctantly took our departure from the cold spring, crossed the river and ascended a large tributary which entered from the northwest, about four miles above our camp of last night. This stream is about thirty yards wide and two feet deep, and flows with a lively current over a stratum of rock and gravel, between high banks bordered with cottonwood and hackberry trees. The water is bitter, but not so unpalatable as that in the principal branch.[14] It is clear, and probably issues from the gypsum formation.

"We observed several places where the beavers had left evidences of their industry, and in one spot they had quite recently cut down several large trees. This suggested to us the name we have applied to this pretty stream, 'Beaver Creek.'[15]

"We made our noon halt upon it, about twelve miles above its mouth,[16] and partook of a sumptuous dinner of fish and soft-shell turtle, with which the stream abounds.

"We have been exceedingly annoyed for a few days past with horse-flies. They are enormously large, and their savage attacks upon our animals cause them much acute suffering. A dark blue variety that I saw was nearly, if not quite as large as a small humming bird, and they no sooner light upon an animal than the blood flows copiously.

"We left the creek in the evening and traveled back to the Big

14. The water in Beaver Creek, to which Marcy refers here, was necessarily charged with some mineral matter as its upper branches drain a part of the gypsum belt, but despite that fact the stream until the 1940s was desirable as a supply of "stock water." However, oil field pollution rendered the water of Beaver Creek so salty that cattle will not drink it except after the stream has been flushed out by rainfall.

15. The location of the mouth of Beaver Creek (which stream still bears the name that Marcy gave it) is definitely known and makes it possible to check back over Marcy's route. A careful re-reading of the previous few paragraphs of Marcy's journal will make it evident that he made first contact with the Wichita River eight miles below the mouth of Beaver Creek. This point was some fifteen miles west of present day Wichita Falls. He had gone northward across country twenty-three miles from the Little Wichita to reach this point. Evidently he had turned away from the Little Wichita somewhere to the north of northwest of present-day Archer City. The specific information about the distribution of pecan timber given in footnote No. 12 makes it possible to locate this point south of the village of Holliday. Marcy traveled northward near the site of that present-day village when he crossed over the divide to the Big Wichita.

16. This point is in the extreme east part of Wilbarger County.

Wichita, making our camp upon the north bank, near some pools of fresh water in a ravine.

"In the morning we turned south, and directed our course for camp, where we arrived about twelve o'clock,[17] found every thing quiet, and our animals in fine condition for our onward march.

"An early departure was made on the following morning, and we marched twelve miles[18] along the south bank of the creek, making our camp at some pools of muddy water.

[p. 188] "As we ascended this stream, the timber along the banks diminished in size and quantity, and at this place the few trees that are seen do not average more than fifteen feet in height.

"We are now near the source of the principal branch of the Little Wichita, and as our course from hence will probably lead us along the ridge dividing the Brazos from the Big Wichita, the waters of both of which are wholly unfit for use, we sent our Indians out, soon after we encamped, to search for good water in advance. They returned in the evening and reported a supply fifteen miles distant.

"We resumed our march the next day, in a course a little south of west, along the high prairie 'divide' making our night halt upon the summit of a very elevated bluff[19] bordering the valley of the Big Wichita, and about 400 yards distant from a small spring of water in a deep ravine.

"In our course to-day we passed near a very prominent mound, standing upon the crest of the dividing ridge where it has the greatest elevation. From its anomalous conformation and peculiar outline, it presents an eminently conspicuous landmark, and can be distinguished for many miles in all directions.

"At the base of this mound we discovered some rich specimens of the blue carbonate of copper, and near this we also observed a vein of iron ore, fifteen feet in thickness, of exceedingly rich quality.

"The dwarf red cedar first shows itself upon the bluffs of the Big Wichita, in the vicinity of our camp, and, with the exception of a few mesquit trees, it is the only wood in this section.

---

17. Note the short time required here for Marcy to return from the Big Wichita to his wagon train on the Little Wichita.

18. This campsite was southward of the present-day village of Mabelle in Baylor County.

19. This point is northwest of Seymour. The bluffs in this area are not actually a part of the bank of the river but border the river valley several miles south of the stream itself.

"On the morning of the 27th we again sent our Delawares in advance to search for water, as we were fearful, if we proceeded on with our ox-teams without taking this precaution, we might be obliged to encamp without that most necessary element. As the country in this direction [p. 189] is becoming so exceedingly arid, we have resolved, after going as far as we find water sufficient for all our animals, to leave the train with a majority of the escort, and push rapidly on, with a few mounted men and pack animals, to the sources of the river. Our Indians returned in the evening with their horses much jaded, and reported that they could find no good water within a distance of twenty-five miles, save one small spring, only affording sufficient water for a few men.

"We therefore, on the following morning, found a suitable place to encamp our train, about ten miles south of the Big Wichita, upon a small tributary of the Brazos,[20] where the water was good, and the grass and fuel abundant . . .

[p. 190] "On the following morning, after giving directions to Lieutenant Pearce for moving the camp, Major Neighbors, the doctor, and myself, accompanied by five Indians and four soldiers, all well mounted, with pack mules loaded with the few supplies that were absolutely necessary for a twelve days' trip, including four five-gallon India-rubber water sacks, set out with the firm resolve to see the head of the Big Wichita and Brazos Rivers before our return.

"Although our numbers were small, and we were about to penetrate into the heart of a country infested by Indians of the most lawless propensities, yet the scarcity of water compelled us to adopt this course in order to proceed any further in this direction.

"Our course for the first ten miles was nearly west, along upon the crest of the lofty cliffs bordering the valley of the Wichita, when we turned to the north, and descended by a very tortuous course the precipitous sides of the bluffs,[21] at the base of which we struck the

20. The wagon train was now encamped near the site of the present-day village of Red Springs, west of Seymour. A campsite at this place was well known to travelers along the old wagon trail west from Seymour as early as 1882. W. M. Moore, of Wichita Falls, Texas, camped there often during the early 1880's.

21. This point was below the well known "Narrows" in Knox County, probably not far from the east line of the county. Marcy did not pass through the Narrows else he would have mentioned the broken country that lay southward toward the Brazos as well as toward the Wichita. He also would have mentioned the very narrow passageway between the "bad lands" that slope toward both streams.

trail of a party of Indians traveling to the north with five stolen horses. They had passed about ten days previous, and were moving slowly, all of which was evident from the fact that the whites never visited this section, and that five of the horses whose tracks we saw were shod.

"Continuing on up the valley for fifteen miles, we had the good fortune to discover a small spring of cold pure water near the bank of the river, and here we bivouacked[22] for the night . . .

[p. 191] "As we are now just entering the country where gypsum is the predominating rock,[23] and as we had satisfied ourselves in our former travels that the chance for finding good water in a section where this mineral abounds are but few, we pushed forward as rapidly as possible up the river, crossing several small streams, all of which we tasted, but found the character of the water similar to that in the main river. [p. 192] After traveling twenty-seven miles we found the river reduced to a width of only thirty yards.[24] We continued on for ten miles farther,[25] hoping every turn would disclose to us a fresh-water tributary, but we were disappointed, and encamped upon a small affluent of bitter water, which we were obliged to make use of. Several of the party have been attacked with diarrhoea and cramps in the bowels from drinking the water,[26] and it causes all to feel more or less uncomfortable.

"The portion of the valley over which we have been passing for the last forty miles is barren and sandy, and the only woodland is

22. In Knox County northeast of Benjamin.

23. Gypsum rock is found in the bluffs bordering the valley of the Wichita northeast of Benjamin and for many miles west of that point.

24. The Wichita has become a much narrower stream in middle Knox County than in other counties to the east.

25. Marcy and his men had traveled thirty-seven miles during this day. If one spreads a map before him and measures this mileage straight ahead, he must place the party well into King County at the end of the day. But miles made on horseback through a rough country or along a tortuous stream cannot be so measured. The camp is in Knox County somewhere northwest of Benjamin. The statement will be elaborated in succeeding footnotes.

26. The Texan Santa Fe expedition suffered from the mineral content of the water in this same area (Geo. Wilkins Kendall, *Narrative of the Texan Santa Fe Expedition*, Austin, 1935, I, 188).

27. These cedar bluffs begin in west Knox County and continue into King County for a little more than ten miles. Coon Jeffers, of the Ross Ranch (which encloses the Wichita River on the line between these counties) explained the difficulty with which a horseman can traverse the river breaks at this point.

upon the bluffs,[27] which are covered with dwarf cedar, with an occasional lonely cottonwood or mesquit in the valley. Here and there may be seen a small patch of wild rye or gramma grass, but the principal herbage in the valley is a coarse variety of grass unsuited to the palates of our animals.

"On the following morning we left our salt-water bivouac at an early hour, and traveled rapidly on through the rough and intricate labryinth of cedar bluffs which are closing in near the river bank, and rendering it necessary to pass over them in threading the narrow defile of the valley. A few miles brought us to a point where the river separated into several branches, all having their origin in the valley before us. Taking the principal one of these, we followed it up for several miles through the lofty bluffs bounding the valley, until we reached its source[28] upon the plateau above. We found ourselves here about two hundred and fifty feet above the bed of the stream, and, on turning toward the valley from whence we had just emerged, a most beautiful and extensive picture greeted our eyes—the different confluents of the Wichita dividing as they neared their sources into numerous ramifications, all of which we were enabled from our lofty observatory to [p. 193] trace in their tortuous meanderings to the very heads, and beyond these could be discerned the dim outline of a range of mountains, which stretched away to the south toward the Brazos. All united in forming a landscape pleasing to the eye; but this is the only feature in the country which has left an agreeable impression upon my memory, and I bade adieu to its desolate and inhospitable borders without the least feeling of regret, for it is, in almost every respect, the most uninteresting and forbidding land I have ever visited. A barren and parsimonious soil, affording little but weeds and coarse unwholesome grass, with an inter-mixture of cacti of most uncomely and grotesque shapes, studded with a formidable armor of thorns which defies the approach of man or beast added to the fact already alluded to of the scarcity of wood or good water, would seem to render it probable that this section was not designed by the Creator for occupation, and I question if the next century will see it populated by civilized man. Even the Indians shun this country, and there were no evidences of their camps along the valley, so that the

28. These lofty cedar covered bluffs are on and near the Knox-King County line and a few miles to the west. Both the cedars and the high bluffs disappear above that point. The actual source of the Wichita River is in Dickens County, almost fifty miles west as the crow flies.

bears (which are numerous here) are left in undisturbed possession. On leaving the Wichita, we traveled south toward the Brazos for six miles through mesquit groves, when we were rejoiced to find a miniature spring of fresh water dripping[29] slowly out from under a rock near the crest of the ridge dividing the waters of the Wichita from those of the Brazos. After suffering intensely from thirst for two days, it may be imagined that it made our hearts glad to taste the pure element once more.

"As there was no reservoir to retain the water as it issued from the rocks, we went to work with our knives and tin cups, and in a few minutes each of us had excavated a small hole in the hard clay, which soon filled, and gave us a most refreshing draught. I am not prepared to say that [p. 194] it was equal to Croton water cooled with Rockland ice (being of a deep brown color, and thick with sediment), yet I doubt if the good people of Gotham ever enjoyed their boasted and justly renowned beverage more than we did this. It was free from salts—that was sufficient for us—and we did ample justice to its merits, as numerous cupsful, which disappeared in rapid succession down our parched and feverish throats, abundantly evinced.

"Our course from the spring was nearly parallel with the chain of mountains now distinctly visible, apparently about fifteen miles to our right. The direction of the chain seems to be nearly north and south,[30] and extends off, as far as the eye can reach, toward the Brazos. Our route lay in the direction of one of the most prominent peaks of the chain, which was a very perfect cone,[31] and apparently

29. There is a small fresh water area west of Benjamin and south of the highway. The old Weatherly Spring, a boon to travelers on the old wagon route west, was five miles west and a half mile south of Benjamin. Probably Marcy's source of good water was in the area west of this spring.

30. This chain of low mountains is in the east part of King County extending north and south and ranging from two to five miles within the county. One does not find a similar formation west of this area until he has passed beyond the source of the Wichita River.

31. The writers of this article have searched exhaustively to be sure of the identity of this peak which is according to Marcy "a very perfect cone." One hundred fifty miles of travel both on highways and secondary roads have been devoted to this search in King and Stonewall counties alone, and a number of persons familiar with the area have been questioned. Kiowa Peak in Stonewall County (three miles south and four miles west of the northeast corner of the county) is the only mountain that even approached the answer to that search. It is almost a perfect cone and it can be seen as far as twenty miles in several directions, which later fact meets a second one of the requirements as it was described in Marcy's journal. Moreover this peak lies at the

symmetrical upon all sides. Many of the other peaks, however, were truncated and irregular. Twelve miles' travel brought us to a branch of the Brazos,[32] fifty feet wide and two feet deep, with a rapid current flowing over a bed of quicksand, and the water, as usual, bitter and unpalatable.

"On the 1st of August we continued on toward the conical peak of the mountains for twelve miles, when we struck another branch of the Brazos,[33] which was spread out over a loose sand that absorbs most of the water. We followed up the north bank of this for a few miles, when we encountered still another tributary,[34] of an entirely different appearance. It was shut in by high, abrupt, clay banks, the water clear, deep, and covered with water grasses, very much like one of our northern spring-brooks, and I felt the utmost confidence that we should find the water fresh, but it proved to be, if possible, worse than that in the other branches.

"It is thirty yards wide, from two to fifteen feet deep, and runs through a valley about two miles wide, with no trees upon its banks.

[p. 195] "It was literally alive with a multitude of large cat and buffalo fish, several of which we caught and cooked for our dinner, and can vouch for their good flavor.

"After dinner we crossed the stream, which we called 'Catfish Fork' and in eight miles passed the Round Mountain,[35] making our camp in the mountains five miles beyond.

"We find many spring-brooks issuing from the sides of the mountains, but, unfortunately, the formation here is gypsum, and all the streams are bitter.

"On the following morning we made our way with difficulty over the rugged mountainous region for several miles, when we reached the base of a high peak,[36] which we determined to ascend. Accord-

---

southern extremity of the chain of low mountains in east King county and in parallel-ing this chain one must cross two creeks (Little Croton and North Croton) as he approaches Kiowa Peak. These later facts are also as Marcy described his journey.

If we assume that Kiowa Peak was Marcy's "very perfect cone," the details of topography along the route which the writers have supposed through Knox, King, and Stonewall counties fit to a nicety the description that Marcy gave of the western-most area through which he traveled.

32. This was Little Croton Creek southeast of Benjamin.
33. North Croton Creek in southeast King and northeast Stonewall counties.
34. This was Penn Branch in South King County.
35. Kiowa Peak.
36. Marcy traveled "five miles" after passing Kiowa Peak before he camped and

ingly, leaving our horses in charge of the men, we clambered up the precipitous sides of the eminence, and, on attaining the summit, found ourselves in a position overlooking the surrounding country for a great extent in all directions.

"The principal trunk of the Brazos, which was about two miles to the south, could be traced in its course through the mountains to the west to its very source, and beyond this, after passing a plain of several miles in extent, could be seen another group of mountains[37] much more elevated than those we are now traversing. They seem to be about forty miles distant, and present much the appearance of some of the most elevated spurs in the Wichita range, and fully as elevated.

"The outline of the crest of this group is more deeply serrated and irregular, and the apices of the peaks more acute than those of the range we are now standing upon, having every appearance of upheaval and volcanic origin. If this conclusion is correct, they are probably composed of primitive rocks, and, from their geographical position and the direction of the group, both of which are nearly in the direct line connecting the two primitive ranges of the [p. 196] Guadalupe and Wichita, it has occurred to me that this might be an intermediate outcrop of the same continuous chain. I was surprised to find these lofty mountains at the sources of the Brazos, as I had

---

traveled "several miles" the next morning before reaching this "high peak." This peak was about two miles north of the Salt Fork of the Brazos. The one really prominent peak two miles north of the Brazos in northeast Stonewall County as found by the writers was ten miles south and seven miles west of the northeast corner of the county. This peak stands out in plain view throughout the Brazos valley in northeast Stonewall County. It appears to be the right distance from Kiowa Peak to comply with the distances in Marcy's travel notes. Very probably it is the peak that Marcy climbed.

37. Curiosity to learn what Marcy saw from the top of the mountain caused the writers to climb the peak referred to in footnote No. 36. Actually there was a plain view beyond the broken and mountainous area that bordered the Brazos, and seemingly blending perfectly with the upper Brazos Valley were higher mountains in the distance that resembled the peaks of the Wichita Mountains. Marcy had no means of knowing with the imperfect geographical knowledge available in his day that these prominent peaks—or more accurately, this prominent peak—in the distance was the Double Mountain in southwest Stonewall County some twenty-five miles away. It does not appear "double" from this viewpoint and outranks in size any other mountains in the distance. However, in one particular Marcy's observation from the mountain top was completely wrong. He did not see the source of the Brazos River, which lay several hundred miles west.

before supposed the entire face of the country lying between the Pecos and Red River to be one continuous and unbroken plain, and that the Brazos, like the Red and Colorado Rivers, had its origin in the table lands of the Llano Estacado. On facing to the east, and looking back over the country we had been traveling, it seemed to be an almost perfectly smooth and level surface, without a hill or valley, through which we could trace the several tributaries of the Brazos, as they flowed on in graceful curves, until they finally united in one common receptacle, generally known as the main or 'Salt Fork.' This we followed with our eyes for many miles, when it gradually disappeared in the murky atmosphere in the distance.

"After feasting our eyes for some time upon this rare and magnificent scenery, we reluctantly turned our steps down the mountain, and rode forward to the river.

"It was a broad, shallow stream, very similar to the other branches I have described, about forty yards wide, with a bed of light quicksand, and the water very saline to the taste. We were subsequently told by the Comanches that above this point, upon the plain between the two ranges of mountains, this stream passes over a field of salt[38] (Chloride of sodium), and that above that the water is palatable.

"After traveling ten miles south from the Brazos we left the gypsum formation, and at length discovered a pool of fresh water. We were all much rejoiced at our good fortune, and bivouacked for the night, determined to solace ourselves at this oasis for the privations of the past three days.

"The water was free from salts, but heavily charged [p. 197] with sediment, and we were obliged to boil it for some time, and remove from the surface a very considerable percentage of thick vegetable matter before it was fit for use. . .

[p. 198] "I was very desirous of extending our explorations to the mountains beyond the head of the Brazos, but my associate, Major Neighbors, was unwilling to go farther in that direction, as he had already suffered much from drinking [p. 199] the gypsum water; as moreover, one of the soldiers had become very much debilitated from the same cause, I reluctantly abandoned the project, and contented

38. Twenty miles northwest up the Brazos from the mountain which the writers climbed is "a field of salt" that is much used locally as stock salt. It is shown on the accompanying map.

myself with merely seeing from a distance the position of some of the sources of the river, without visiting the localities 'in propria persona.' I am enabled, however, from the view I obtained upon the summit of the mountain, and from the courses I noted down, with compass in hand, at several different points on our route, to trace the streams with considerable accuracy, and approximate to the distances.

"The next morning we directed our course toward the eastern extremity of a low mountain, nearly south from our last camp, which I recognized as the same I had seen in 1849, from the point where the Doña Ana road strikes a stream which has heretofore been known as the double mountain fork of the Brazos.[39] My Delaware guide (Black Beaver) upon that occasion correctly informed me that this mountain was near the South Fork of the Brazos.

"On reaching the South Fork we found it similar in character to the branch we passed yesterday, and about the same magnitude. Immediately after crossing it we ascended the mountain, which was here composed of sandstone and gypsum, and covered with cedar bushes.

"Upon the summit was an extensive plateau very much resembling the Llano Estacado, and it is highly probable this may be a spur of that plain.

"Toward the east from this elevation nothing could be seen but one continuous mesquit flat, dotted here and there with small patches of open prairie, while in the opposite direction, in a due west course, we discerned the elevated mountains beyond the head of the Brazos. Two peaks presented themselves to the view from this position, the outline of which was similar to the figure on the following page.[40]

"After leading our horses down the mountain, or plateau, [p. 200] we turned our faces toward the train[41] and traveled [A profile of the Double Mountain is inserted at this point] until ten o'clock at

39. The stream was the Double Mountain River. The low mountain was known as Flat Top. It is on the Haskell-Stonewall County line three or four miles southwest of the village of Sagerton. The Doña Ana Road made by Marcy in 1849 crossed the F.H.K. Survey (Haskell County surveyor's records, Vol. 1, p. 163) on the edge of Flat Top not very far from the place where Marcy climbed the mountain. In view of such specific facts the identification of this mountain is hardly open to question.

40. Marcy was again viewing the Double Mountain. The double appearance of the mountain is evident from the direction of Flat Top Mountain.

41. This return of Marcy across parts of Haskell and Throckmorton counties to his wagon train has not been deemed of prime importance in this study.

night, encamping at a pool of despicable water, with which we manufactured a cup of salt coffee, and with a venison steak, cooked by friend Neighbors in his best camp site (which 'by-the-by,' would not bring discredit upon a professional cuisiniére), we managed to make a supper.

"On the following morning we saddled up early and rode rapidly forward, hoping to find some good water for our breakfast. Eighteen miles brought us to some pools of water in the bed of a creek, where we breakfasted, and continued on down the bank of the stream for eight miles, when we encountered a terrific thunder-shower, which called into requisition all our gutta percha and India-rubber habiliments, and those of the party who were not provided with them were thoroughly drenched.

"The country through which we are now passing is gently undulating and covered with mesquit trees. The soil is very rich, producing several varieties of gramma and mesquit grasses, and begins to be watered with streams of fresh water.

"The deer and turkeys are plentiful in this section, and our hunters have no difficulty in supplying us with fresh meat. We now and then see an antelope; I have, however, met with very few during the entire trip, and they seem to have almost disappeared since I was in this country in 1849.

"We encamped upon the creek, where we found a supply of good running water, and the following morning [p. 201] passed another larger stream flowing from the south. We here left the main creek and turned to the left ascending a small spring branch of twelve miles, finding water along the entire distance.

"This stream runs south 20° west, and takes its rise upon the south side of the ridge dividing the Clear Fork from the Salt Fork of the Brazos. It will always afford a sufficiency of good water for the largest trains in the dryest seasons, and I have no doubt that the large creek entering from the south, before mentioned, would supply water for many miles farther in the direction of its course. Had we known these facts before leaving the main body of the escort, we would have had no difficulty in bringing the train much nearer the sources of the Brazos.

"Passing the sources of the spring-creek, in the evening we traveled fifteen miles over mesquit uplands, and encamped at a spring of good water. Our course the next morning was north 20° east for fifteen miles, which carried us to the borders of a valley inclosed

with a barrier of lofty and rugged hills, which shut out the bleak
northers that in the winter sweep across these prairies.

"From the crest of these hills the valley below presented a carpet
of verdant grasses, besprinkled with a profusion of flowers of the most
vivid hues, through the midst of which meandered one of the most
beautiful streams of pure water I have seen in this country.

"We entered this charming valley, and on reaching the banks of
the creek discovered that a large party of Kickapoos, with their usual
good taste, had occupied this locality for a hunting camp. The
skeletons of their lodges (fifty-six in number) were still standing, and,
judging from the piles of deer's hair which we observed in several
places, and the bones scattered over the ground in all directions, they
must have had a successful hunt while here. Our [p. 202] Indians pronounced it four weeks since the camp had been occupied.

"Passing the creek, we continued on for ten miles, when we
again struck the main trunk of the Brazos, and, ascending five miles,
our eyes were once more gladdened by the sight of the encampment
of the escort.

"We joined our comrades, and, after the privations we had
necessarily been subjected to during our excursions, enjoyed exceedingly the few luxuries our remaining stores afforded . . .

"On the morning of the 7th we struck our camp and crossed the
river with our train, descending upon the south side to the old
Kickapoo camp, where we remained on the day following, and examined the creek to its confluence with the Brazos.

"The valley is about a mile wide, the soil productive and well
watered, but, with the exception of mesquit and [p. 203] a few
hackberry trees, there is no timber, which we regard as an insuperable
objection to selecting this as a reserve for the Indians. There are,
however, many quarries of the very best building stone in the valley,
which might serve a white population in lieu of timber, and this may
yet become a superior farming locality. The deep prolific soil would
unquestionably produce bountiful returns of any grain suited to this
latitude, and would, for a long term of years, require no fertilizing
auxiliaries.

"Our course on the following day was southeast, over a mesquit
country for twelve miles, making our camp on a small tributary of the
Brazos, where we found an abundance of good living water.

"Our course the next day was the same, over a very undulating
and, in place, broken country, traversed by several small spring-

branches of good water, between which we passed through groves of mesquit, but possessing little other interest until we reached a large creek running toward the Brazos, which winds through a broad valley inclosed with hills upon either side, and has more timber upon its borders than we have seen above. The water is good, and the high banks have sufficient capacity to contain it all at the highest stage. This valley would be a good position for an Indian reserve, but it is disposed of and not now vacant . . .[42]

[p. 205] "On the morning of the 11th we left our camp before daylight, and traveled ten miles in the same course as the day previous, which carried us into the valley of a fine stream of running water, with several varieties of timber upon its borders. The soil in the valley is arable in the highest degree, and the natural resources of the locality fulfill all the conditions necessary for making good farms. This section is appropriated, and not available for the Indians.[43]

"On the following morning we breakfasted at the very unfashionable hour of one o'clock, and were *en route* an hour afterward in a southeast course toward the high ridge [p. 206] dividing the main Brazos from the Clear Fork, and at ten o'clock crossed the road leading to Doña Ana, encamping near the Fort Belknap and Phantom Hill road, at a point ten miles east of the crossing of the Clear Fork.[44]

"It was our intention to have intersected this road twenty miles farther west, but our guide was in this instance at fault, and although I repeatedly expressed my opinion that our course was leading us too far east, the Delawares believed they were right, and we suffered them to proceed.

"As they have generally been very correct in their judgment regarding courses and localities, this error must be regarded as an exception to the general rule. They, like all their brethren with whom I have been associated, are more perfect in the art of woodcraft than any people I have ever known. They are full of expedients for all

42. This is probably Boggy Creek in Throckmorton County. The Texas Emigration and Land Company had surveyed this area as part of their premium lands in 1853.

43. This was the valley of Elm Creek, an area that was then the property of the Texas Emigration and Land Company.

44. The Texas State Land Office map of Throckmorton County dated 1898 shows the essential part of the Fort Belknap-Phantom Hill Road. This campsite was in southeast Throckmorton County a mile or two west of the village of Woodson.

emergencies, and their great experience upon the prairies renders their services highly valuable.

"Soon after crossing the California road, which I had traveled in 1849, we entered a section covered with large mesquit-trees, beneath which were innumerable large sunflowers, spreading over the entire country as far as we could see, and giving it a brilliant yellow hue.

"These continued as far as the crossing of the Clear Fork of the Brazos, upon the Phantom Hill road, which point we reached the next day about ten o'clock A.M. . . .

[p. 209] "We made our encampment on the bank of the Clear Fork, at a large spring of cold, delicious water, which gushed forth from the bank about half a mile below Stem's ranch. As there is a vacant tract of land of sufficient extent for one reservation lying upon the river above here, we determined to make a halt for the purpose of examining it, and in the mean time send Ketumsee for the other chiefs of the Southern Comanches, who were about seventy miles off.

"On the following morning Major Neighbors and myself ascended the river about eight miles to the confluence of another tributary, called by the Comanches Qua-qua-ho-no, and by the whites, Paint Creek. We ascended this branch to the crossing of the California road, where we bivouacked for the night, and I made my bed under the same tree where I pitched my tent in 1849. It was here that I met Senaco's[45] band of Comanches upon that occasion.

"We turned our steps toward camp at an early hour on the next day, and passed down upon the north side of the river, thus making a careful examination of the tract of country noted as vacant upon the map furnished us from the General Land Office, which we find contains a good share of rich valley land along the borders of the stream, well suited to the culture of grain or plants. The uplands adjoining are undulating, with rich grassy slopes covered with mesquite-trees, well adapted for pasturage . . .

[p. 213] "On the following morning, Major Neighbors and myself, leaving the command upon the Clear Fork, went into Fort Belknap, for the purpose of making a more minute examination of the country below that post than we had been enabled to do previous to our departure upon our expedition up the Brazos.

"We found upon our map a vacant tract of country lying below

45. This point was in southeast Throckmorton County two miles above the mouth of Paint Creek at the southwest corner of the Thomas Lambshead survey.

the junction of the Clear Fork, and as this was the only available locality suited to the wishes of the Brazos Indians, we directed our attention exclusively to it.[46] It is situated on both sides of the river, which divides it into two equal parts of four leagues each, and is in every particular well adapted to the use of the two separate tribes.

"There is a large body of valley land of the most pre-eminent fertility upon either side of the stream, extending throughout the entire length of the tract. This, upon both sides, is bordered by mesquit uplands, covered with luxuriant, gramma grasses, affording the best pasturage, and adjoining this a range of mountains, covered with oak timber, extends upon each side to the north and south lines, bounding the reservations . . .

[p. 216] "Although in our expedition to the sources of the Big Wichita and the Brazos we were unsuccessful in discovering a suitable location for the Indians, yet it is thought that the results of our labors will not be entirely devoid of utility or interest. The geographical knowledge we have obtained of this hitherto unexplored region enables me to complete a sketch of the only tributaries of the Brazos that were before unknown. It will be observed that upon the map accompanying my report, a large stream (the Double [p. 217] Mountain Fork of the Brazos), which has before been noted upon all the maps of this section, is wanting.[47] This imaginary river has heretofore been supposed to enter the main Brazos about thirty miles above Fort Belknap, and is even found delineated upon the surveyor's maps that were sent us from the General Land Office of Texas,[48] with surveys noted upon it. On our return from the headwaters of the Brazos we traveled down the south bank of the stream until we arrived within forty miles of Fort Belknap, when we struck south for the Clear Fork, expecting to cross the Double Mountain Fork before we reached it, but, to our surprise, the Clear Fork was the first stream of magnitude we encountered, so that the Double Mountain Fork has no existence.

"On my return from New Mexico in 1849, I struck quite a large stream running to the east about thirty-five miles west of the crossing of Paint Creek. I was then given to understand by my Delaware guide that this was the 'Double Mountain Fork of the Brazos,' but our observations now prove it to have been Paint Creek."

46. This was a block of land nearly square in shape that lay from the site of present-day Graham southward. It was accepted as the reservation for the Brazos Indians. The upper or Comanche Indian Reservation was located southwest of the site

of Throckmorton on the Clear Fork of the Brazos beginning not far from the mouth of Paint Creek and extending down the Clear Fork. Marcy surveyed this reservation later in 1854. A copy of his field notes can be found in the Throckmorton County surveyor's records Vol. B, pp. 178, ff. Both of the reservations are shown on the accompanying map.

47. Marcy clarified his own knowledge of the geography of Haskell, Stonewall, Knox and Throckmorton counties. He had correctly named the Double Mountain River in the report of his expedition of 1849 but had misunderstood its exact course, even confusing it with Paint Creek. The stream as he understood it ran eastward across both Haskell and Throckmorton counties. In this expedition of 1854 he crossed Haskell County in a northeastward direction and Throckmorton in a southeastward direction, failing to find any such river. What he called the South Fork of the Brazos was actually the Double Mountain River, but contrary to the common belief at the time it ran due north from Flat Top Mountain into the Salt Fork, instead of extending eastward as Marcy and others had believed.

48. There was more accurate information already in the Texas Land Office. The Texas Emigration and Land Company had surveyed much of the east half of Throckmorton County and had surveyed their boundary line northward across the west part of Throckmorton County to the Brazos River striking it in west Baylor County southwest of present-day Seymour. This boundary survey made no mention of the Double Mountain River. The survey may be found in Vol. 18 at the Texas General Land Office. The surveying was done between March 14 and November 1, 1853.

XII

MILITARY ROADS OF THE 1850's IN CENTRAL WEST TEXAS

Perhaps the most important date in many centuries of the transportation history of the country that centers about Abilene was the year 1881. On that date the Texas and Pacific entered West Texas. As the two steel rails of that company's trackage lengthened westward from Fort Worth and Weatherford, a new age was dawning for the Cross Timbers and the prairies of the West. It was to be the age of steam transportation and the age of improved highways. Cities and towns were to rise in short order, and chambers of commerce were to house themselves on the feeding grounds of the buffalo.

But there is another side to the picture. With the beginning of steam railways and graded highways an old chapter in the history of the West was about to be closed—a chapter that will add its color of romance to our literature as well as to our factual history for many generations to come. That old chapter dealt with the age of trails. It began with the coming of mankind on this part of the planet, and closed a few years after 1881. Certain interesting episodes of that age are the subject of this paper.

The first red men—or men of whatever color they may have been—who came to the area that we now call central West Texas moved about from place to place on foot. Their trails were foot paths, probably deepened somewhat by poles dragged about by dogs,[1] which seem to have been their only beasts of burden. The happenings of this age of foot paths are almost totally unknown.

Next, following probably a little less than three centuries ago, came the age of horse-paths. Horses that had strayed from Spanish explorers some four hundred years ago soon covered the plains and, in due time, were domesticated by western Indians. This big animal

---

1. F. W. Hodge and Theodore J. Lewis (eds.), *Spanish Explorers in Southern United States, 1528-1543* (New York, 1907), 362-363.

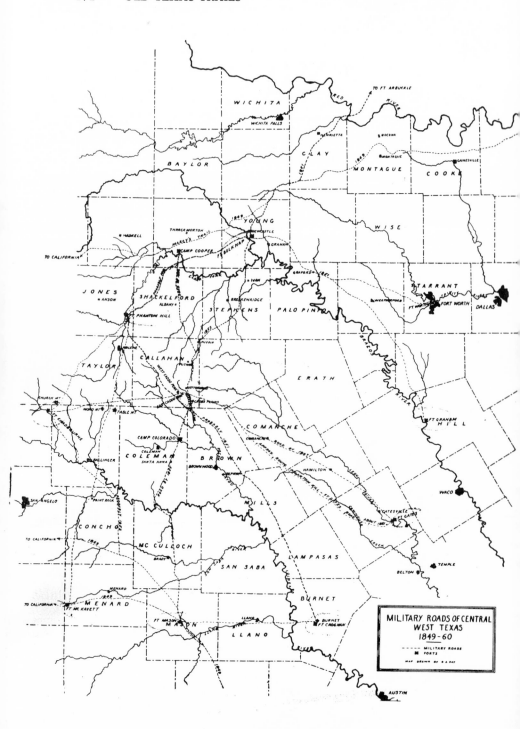

MILITARY ROADS OF CENTRAL
WEST TEXAS
1849-60

- - - - - MILITARY ROADS
■ FORTS

MAP DRAWN BY R A PAY

from the old world revolutionized the lives of these red-skinned pedestrians. With the horse to carry both the Indian and his burdens, the old foot paths began to be deepened and, perhaps lengthened. In some instances, possibly, new trails were routed through less thickly woven timber, or by larger watering holes. In the main, however, west of the ninety-eighth meridian, where water was none too plentiful, the few springs, running streams and permanent water holes that were available probably caused the trails of all generations alike to follow, roughly, the same courses.

A little of the story of that period of West Texas history when red men rode its trails on horseback has filtered through the years. At least one of those old trails was within a day's ride of Abilene and, as will appear later, has some connection with this chapter.

However, it is a third kind of road that concerns us chiefly here. Wagon trails began in central West Texas in 1849,[2] and continued until the age of steam transportation; and soon thereafter men cut across the old trails with wire fences, and finally plowed them under. Only one wagon train is known to have crossed this area before 1849,[3] and that expedition seems to have resulted in nothing more extensive than a local road from the counties of North Texas to the buffalo country above the Cross Timbers.

Quite different is the movement that began in 1849. At that time the United States army took a hand in the history of West Texas, and left fragments of its physical imprint, even to the year of 1942.

It was in 1849 that a very efficient and energetic army captain, Randolph B. Marcy, stationed just across Red River from the settlements of North Texas, led an expedition across the Texas Panhandle and back through central West Texas.[4] He made two wagon roads, both of which served the traffic to the California gold fields. Marcy's return journey passed near the towns of Pecos, Big Spring

2. *Sen. ex. doc. No. 64., 31st Cong., 1st Sess.*

3. Josiah Gregg, *Commerce of the Prairies* (Dallas, 1933), 324, 325: Dr. H. Connelly and a party of traders from Chihuahua, Mexico, crossed West Texas in a northeasterly direction in 1839, and returned to Mexico in 1840. The party, on its return, was equipped with 60 or more wagons that beat out a distinct trail across the prairies, but the route seems not to have been used by other trading expeditions and natural forces erased most of the road.

4. *Sen. ex. doc. No. 64., 31st Cong., 1st Sess.*

5. *Ibid.* Marcy's report, together with a study of the topography of central West Texas and the field notes of numerous early surveys define this route rather accurately.

and Haskell,[5] and entered the older road that connected North Texas with the buffalo country, some thirty to forty miles southeast of Wichita Falls.[6] This was the first actual wagon road that served traffic through the part of West Texas that centers about Abilene.

Shortly more roads were to follow. It was the same army captain who had made these roads toward California who was to open the next road. This time Marcy came from Fort Arbuckle, just west of present-day David, Oklahoma, to the Pecan Bayou,[7] not very far from the site of Brownwood. He crossed the area that has since been made into the counties of Clay, Archer, Young, Stephens and Callahan, and went well into the center of Brown County, before turning back to the north. Much of Marcy's route became a wagon road[8] that at one time helped to span the whole Texas frontier west of the Cross Timbers.

Fortunately, the surveyors of the early 1850's who staked off many thousands of acres of land along the Upper Cross Timbers, preserved quite a little of the route of this road in their field notes. In many places, one can still measure from permanent survey corners and find the path of this once important wagon trail.

It might prove interesting to trace it somewhat more in detail. From Fort Arbuckle this road came southwesterly to the crossing of Red River northeast of Henrietta, and probably about two miles above the mouth of the Little Wichita. The Little Wichita itself was

6. *Sen. ex. doc. No. 64., 31st Cong., 1st Sess.*, 220. Marcy came upon a fresh wagon trail about 5 miles northwest of the site of Bowie, Texas, and followed it through the upper Cross Timbers. His progress through this timbered belt was fast enough to make it certain that little or no road work or cutting down of trees was necessary. By contrast, the Chihuahua Traders who came through this same wooded area in 1840 were obliged to spend much time in cutting out their road. (Geo. Wilkins Kendall, *Narrative of the Texan Santa Fe Expedition*, I, 121). There can be little doubt that Marcy followed this road made by the Chihuahua Merchants. The "fresh wagon trail" found by Marcy is evidence that settlers of North Texas were making use of this path through the Cross Timbers.

7. "Report of Captain R. B. Marcy of the Fifth Infantry, United States Army, on his Exploration of Indian Territory and Northwest Texas," *West Texas Historical Association Year Book*, XIV, 116-136. Hereafter this report will be referred to as *Marcy's Report of 1851*. The introduction to this report is written by R. C. Crane and foot notes are added by the editors of the *Year Book*.

8. *Ibid.*, 122.

9. *West Texas Historical Association Year Book*, XIV, 124 (*Marcy's Report of 1851*).

crossed in a pronounced bend three miles to the west of Red River.[9] This place became known as the Rock Crossing, and served as a ford on that small river for a number of years after Marcy made his journey. An obliging surveyor ran the line of the W. Morse survey in 1854 and gave the location of Marcy's crossing in his field notes.[10] The land became a part of the Stanfield ranch, well known in Clay County history.

The wagon ruts of Marcy's road passed about two miles southeast of Henrietta,[11] and continued to the southwest part of Clay County. Here the old road joined the California trail opened by Marcy in 1849.[12] For about twenty miles, chiefly in Archer County, these two old trails followed a common roadbed.[13] At several places along this twenty miles the trace of this pioneer wagon road is even now very distinct. At one point, on J. S. Bridwell's ranch, some thirty miles south of Wichita Falls, these early wagon ruts are as much as a foot deep.[14]

Nine miles east of modern Olney, Marcy turned to the south of his trail of 1849 and made his way to a point near present-day

10. Cooke County Surveyors' Records, Vol. A, p. 256.

11. Clay County Commissioners' Court Records, Col. 1. A Clay County road survey mentioned "the old G road" at a point about two miles southeast of Henrietta. Probably this "G road" was an abbreviation for government road, and since the Fort Richardson-Fort Sill road is known to have passed through Henrietta itself, there was no other old government road close at hand except Marcy's road.

12. West Texas Historical Association Year Book, XIV, 124 (Marcy's Report of 1851).

13. The Peters Colony Map of 1854, in the Texas State Land Office, shows the route of Marcy's road of 1849 across the present counties of Clay, Archer, Young, and parts of Montague and Throckmorton. This map was drawn from the field notes of Peters Colony surveys made in 1853. Copies of these original field notes, in so far as they apply to Archer County, may be found in the Archer County Surveying Records, Volume I. The remainder of these field notes, with few exceptions, may be found either in the surveying records of embodied in the land patents and recorded in the deed records of the various counties concerned.

14. The writer, supplied with copies of field notes and data from the Peters Colony Map of 1854, has found this part of Marcy's road in four different places as follows; on the Bridwell ranch, in T.E. & L. Co. Block No. 1872; on the same ranch in Block 1874; on the W. J. McMurtry land in Block No. 1842, and on Block 1844. The trace of the old road was also discovered in blocks 1861 and 1845. The Bridwell ranch fronts on the Wichita Falls-Jacksboro highway, some 5 ½ miles south of Windthorst in southeast Archer County. The points at which Marcy's road was discovered ranged to the southwest of that point.

Newcastle.[15] At this place, now recognized as the site of Fort Belknap,[16] this army captain turned his expedition westward and southwestward across the Brazos and on to the Clear Fork.[17] Following a course near the common boundary line of Shackelford and Stephens counties, and crossing the eastern part of Callahan county, Marcy continued his southward journey to Pecan Bayou, near the mouth of Turkey Creek, some ten miles south of the site of Cross Plains.[18] Trees were blazed, stakes were driven, creek banks were cut down, and wagon ruts were made all the way from Fort Arbuckle,[18] which in those days were all the formalities necessary to open a new road. However, the part of Marcy's route southward from Fort Belknap seems never to have been adopted as a military road.[20]

This expedition into Central West Texas and the resulting first military supply road to Fort Belknap came in 1851.[21] It was that same year[22] that another trail gave Fort Belknap a second connecting link in the growing chain of army posts and roads. This was the road from Fort Belknap to Fort Graham. It followed a course that paralleled the Brazos on its northeast side all the way between the army posts. [Some points on this old road are as follows: (1) three miles north of

15. The Peters Colony Map of 1854 shows that Marcy's two roads divided in T.E. & L. Co., Block No. 1395. Both roads are copied on the Texas General Land Office map of Young County, dated 1897.

16. Fort Belknap is about three miles south of Newcastle. Some of the old buildings were restored as part of the Texas Centennial Celebration movement of 1936.

17. *West Texas Historical Association Year Book*, XIV, 125 (*Marcy's Report of 1851*).

18. *Ibid.*, 126. A study of Marcy's Report makes it appear highly probable that he followed Turkey Creek to the Pecan Bayou.

19. *Ibid.*, 122.

20. Marcy's route crossed the Clear Fork of the Brazos 30 miles southwest of Fort Belknap, a fact that makes it certain that he was not following the course of either of the two military roads that were shortly to be laid out from that fort to and across the Clear Fork. One of these military roads crossed that stream 15 miles south of Fort Belknap, while the other crossed it 40 miles to the southwest. Both roads can be definitely traced from land records, as will appear later in this chapter. On Marcy's return from Pecan Bayou, he crossed the Clear Fork 10 miles above this first crossing and in so doing possibly laid out some of the road that later extended from Fort Belknap toward the southwest.

21. *West Texas Historical Association Year Book*, XIV, 116 (*Marcy's Report of 1851*).

22. Joseph Carroll McConnell, *The West Texas Frontier* (Jacksboro, 1933) I, 167.

Graham,[23] (2) three and a half miles east of the southwest corner of Jack County,[24] (3) eight and one-half miles northeast of Possum Kingdom Dam,[25] (4) through the north part of the little town of Graford,[26] (5) seven and one-half miles due north of Mineral Wells,[27]] (6) about three miles southwest of Weatherford,[28] (7) seven and one-half miles east of the Brazos at the south line of Parker County,[29] (8) four and one-half miles east of the tip of De Cordova's Bend on the Brazos at a point eight and one-half miles due west of Cleburne,[30] and (9) at Fort Graham almost on the bank of the Brazos sixteen miles due west of Hillsboro.[31]

[At seven and one-half miles north of Mineral Wells this early road divided.[32] One branch of it turned toward Fort Worth at that point. The old Fort Worth road passed Veal's Station,[33] about six miles north of Weatherford, and crossed the common boundary line of Parker and Tarrant counties less than one-half mile north of the

23. Map of Young County by the Texas General Land Office, March, 1897.

24. Peters Colony Map of 1854, Texas General Land Office. A comparison with modern land maps makes it possible to relate this road to towns and villages established since the Peters Colony survey was made.

25. *Ibid.*

26. *Ibid.*

27. *Ibid.*

28. Presslar's Travelers Map of 1867, in the Texas General Land Office, Austin, Texas. Charles W. Presslar had been connected with the Texas Land Office for nearly two decades when this map was made. Having access to the great mass of information stored in the land office, and understanding the technique of a draftsman, he undoubtedly made one of the best of the general maps of Texas. Nearly all of the important roads of his time are shown on this map. However, one must identify the roads by their terminal points and other available information, since, usually, their names are not listed on the map. Also, it should be noted that a general map covering the entire state cannot possibly be as accurate as county maps and regional maps, such as those made by the Peters Colony surveyors.

29. Parker County Deed Records, Vol. 144, pp. 481-482. The survey of the south boundary line of Parker County, made in 1856, gives the location of the Belknap-Fort Graham road.

30. Texas General Land Office, Austin, Texas, Vol. 18, p. 160. The survey of the south line of the Peters Colony made in 1853, gives the location of the Belknap-Fort Graham road.

31. Map of Hill County, General Land Office, Austin, Texas, June, 1922. Fort Graham was in the Maria Rosa Urrutia survey, 16 miles from Hillsboro, in a direction two degrees south of west. It was about 700 yards from the northeast bank of the Brazos River.

32. Peters Colony Map of 1854.

middle point.[34] Here the road was described by early surveyors as being near the north edge of the Grand Prairie and 1226 varas south of a
"perpendicular bluff" at a large branch of Silver Creek. For obvious
reasons, the road stayed on the prairie as much as possible and
especially avoided the heavy timbers of creek bottoms. In this instance the road curved a little southward as it approached Fort Worth,
keeping well to the south of the area that is now Lake Worth, and
crossing the Clear Fork not far above its junction with the West Fork
of the Trinity River.[35] Exact streets traversed in modern Fort Worth
are not available, but this old army trail followed the ridge on which
Camp Bowie Boulevard is now a prominent thoroughfare and came to
an end not very far from the site of the court house.]

Other events crowded into the same year that saw the completion of the Fort Worth road. Fort Phantom Hill, in Jones County, was
established in November, 1851,[36] and other roads were necessarily
added. A road from Fort Belknap to that new post blazed part of a
trail that has since become famous as the overland mail route, or Butterfield Trail. This old road passed one-half mile north of Woodson,[37]
in Throckmorton County, crossed the Clear Fork about three miles
above the Shackelford County line,[38] ascended the valley of Lambshead Creek to its source, passed through some small mountains in
northwest Shackelford County called the Antelope Hills,[39] and extended southwestward to the well known site of Fort Phantom Hill[40]
in Jones County.

33. Mr. W. J. Webb of Wichita Falls, who, as a small boy, lived at Veal's Station, remembers crossing the "old Fort Worth road" (not then in use) near Veal's
Station on numerous occasions. Scaled on Presslar's Travelers map of 1867, the Fort
Worth-Belknap road was 5½ miles north of Weatherford, thus identifying the road
known to Mr. Webb as the old military road from Belknap to Fort Worth.

34. Parker County Deed Records, Vol. 144, pp. 481-482. The county line survey
of 1856.

35. Presslar's Travelers Map of 1867.

36. McConnell, *The West Texas Frontier,* I, 72.

37. Map of Throckmorton County, General Land Office, November, 1898. The
Military roads shown on this map are repeated from the Peters Colony Map of 1854
which, in turn, was compiled from Peters Colony surveys made in 1853.

38. *Ibid.* The map shows this Military road almost to its intersection with the
Clear Fork.

39. Art Newcomb, born near Fort Griffin in 1869, who owned a store on the
original townsite at that place, gave the writer the above information. The sector of
this old road pointed out by Newcomb connects with other portions of the trail, as
shown from maps and surveying records.

Then, not later than 1852, came an event of unusual significance in the transportation history of West Texas. That event seems to have been buried in a mass of records and not previously made public. It was during the early days of Fort Phantom Hill that the first old army trail cut completely across the West Texas frontier.[41] It connected the old road that Marcy had opened from Indian Territory to Fort Belknap with the army posts of Central and South Texas. That trail that tied together the first complete chain of military wagon tracks west of the Cross Timbers came right by the front door of Abilene. It crossed the ground now submerged by Abilene's new lake at Fort Phantom Hill, and came southward up the valley of Deadman Creek. Just six and one-half miles, by direct line, northeast of the business district of Abilene, this old road crossed the path of the present concrete highway that leads toward Albany.[42]

Full details of the route of this road—if indeed we knew them all—would prove burdensome. However, it may be interesting to note that the complete course of the early trail did not cross a single large creek after it had passed over the site of Phantom Hill Lake. It extended to Fort Croghan, more than one hundred fifty miles to the southeast, along the divide between the Brazos and Colorado rivers, keeping on the heads of the many short streams that flow southwest toward the Pecan Bayou and the Colorado. Following an excellent selection of topography, it just missed the timber three miles west of Clyde,[43] passed a mile and one half southwest of the Caddo Peaks[44] in

40. From the map of Jones County, made by the General Land office at Austin, Texas, May, 1921, Fort Phantom Hill, in Jones County, was centrally located in the Wm. T. Evans survey, about one mile due south of the junction of Elm Creek with the Clear Fork of the Brazos. The remains of the old fort, still easy to identify by some 18 rock chimneys, are about 18 miles northeast of Abilene.

41. A number of land surveys in present Callahan and Brown counties were made in 1852. Several of these were crossed by the road from Fort Phantom Hill to Fort Croghan, a branch of which reached Fort Gates. In none of these surveys was there mention of any road that came southward from any fort other than Phantom Hill. In 1853, however, the notes of numerous surveys contained language that told about a road from Fort Belknap to Fort Croghan, and from Fort Belknap to Austin. Careful study of records reveals that this latter road was identical with the Phantom Hill-Fort Croghan road for many miles. Obviously the Phantom Hill-Croghan road was made first.

42. Jones County Surveying Records, Vol. B, 112, 115, 116, 117, 118, 123, 124.

43. Map of Callahan County, Texas, General Land Office, 1879.

44. *Ibid.*

southern Callahan County, and entered the valley of Turkey Creek at the corner of Brown County,[45] on ground that Marcy had explored a few months earlier. Continuing a southeastward course, this pioneer of West Texas army supply roads came within hailing distance of the present-day town of Zephyr in Brown County[46] and passed not far from the site of modern Goldthwaite.[47] Still following the divide, it passed a little west of Midway, between Lampasas and the Colorado River,[48] and finally reached Fort Croghan, within rifle shot of the county seat town of Burnet.

Fort Croghan was one in the first chain of army posts built across the Texas frontier. Other units of this protective system were Fort Martin Scott near Fredericksburg, Fort Gates in central Coryell County, Fort Graham and Fort Worth, already referred to. A road through all of these military outposts had been opened in 1849, while the California gold rush was still in white heat. That colorful event, more than anything else, had pushed the frontier westward beyond the first chain of forts almost before they were well established. The beginning of Fort Belknap in June of 1851, and Fort Phantom Hill a scant five months later, was a direct answer to the next expansion. The long-forgotten old wagon trail from Phantom Hill to Fort Croghan was more of the same answer.

Other roads across the new frontier came in such rapid succession that nothing less than an exhaustive search of both army records and the field notes of pioneer surveyors would establish their exact order.

In 1849 the road from San Antonio to California had come through Fredericksburg, and across the middle of Mason County before it turned west toward the Pecos River.[49] From central Mason County to the middle Concho, this California trail had two branches.[50] Fort Mason was established in July, 1851,[51] at the point where the trail divided; and Fort McKavett was located at the head of the San Saba River, on the south branch of the trail,[52] the following

45. *Ibid.*

46. Brown County Surveying Records, Vol. A, 180, 184.

47. Estimate from Presslar's Travelers Map.

48. Estimate from Presslar's Travelers Map.

49. *Sen. ex. doc. No. 64., 31st Cong., 1st Sess.* The *Report* of Lieut. Francis T. Bryan, 14-26.

50. *Ibid.* Also see Presslar's Travelers Map.

51. McConnell, *The West Texas Frontier,* I, 71.

52. Footnote eliminated by the author.

March. Both forts were on a well established trail that connected them with points where supplies could be obtained. Seven months later Fort Chadbourne was established,[53] in what is now the northeast corner of Coke County, completely away from beaten trails. Three army roads were made to give this fort the necessary outlet. One of them passed across present Runnels and Concho counties, connecting with the north branch of the California road at a small tributary of Brady's Creek, in southeast Concho County.[54] Another of the three came across the mountains of Taylor County to Fort Phantom Hill.[55] This road was later to become a part of the famous transcontinental stage and mail line begun by John Butterfield and associates. It passed about seven miles northwest of Abilene.[56]

The third road from Fort Chadbourne, the road to Fort Gates, ran eastward, near the south line of Taylor County. Bradshaw was in its course, and both Moro and Table Mountain of Runnels County lay to the south of it.[57] The old wagon trail entered Callahan County some three or four miles north of its southwest corner and made a direct line toward the Caddo Peaks.[58] It passed south of the Tecumseh Peaks, and continuing eastward, crossed the Pecan Bayou about midway across southern Callahan County. Eight miles west of present Cross Plains, or about two miles west of the Caddo Peaks, this road from Fort Chadbourne crossed the Phantom Hill-Fort Croghan road already described.

Here it was not necessary for the first wagon party from Fort Chadbourne to lay out any more of this east bound trail, for that matter had already been attended to by some one from Fort Phantom Hill. A ready-made road, known to surveyors of 1852 as the Phantom Hill-Fort Gates road, branched off to the east.[59] The wagon trains from Fort Chadbourne adopted it as their very own. It ran between the Caddo Peaks, and crossed Turkey Creek three miles northwest of the site of Cross Plains.[60] At this small stream one is back in the land that Marcy had explored in 1851, for Turkey Creek is, most likely, the

53. McConnell, *The West Texas Frontier*, I, 76.
54. Presslar's Travelers Map.
55. Map of Taylor County, Texas General Land Office, 1897.
56. Texas and Pacific Railway Company Map of Jones County, 1874.
57. Presslar's Travelers Map. Also Surveying Records of Taylor County, Vol. A.
58. Presslar's Travelers Map.
59. Brown County Surveying Records, Vol. A, 317.
60. Map of Callahan County, Texas General Land Office, 1879.

stream which he followed southward to the Pecan Bayou.

From Turkey Creek the Fort Gates road curved somewhat to the south and passed very near the common corner of Eastland, Brown, and Comanche counties. Bending its course still more to the south, it passed near the spot where the town of Comanche is now located, and continued down the long, narrow divide between the Leon River and Cowhouse Creek.[61] Old Fort Gates, its terminal point, was on the northeast side of the Leon River, some six miles below modern Gatesville.

All of the network of military roads thus far described seems to have been completed by the early part of 1853. The other principal roads are yet to be mentioned in this study. One of them passed within less than two miles of the city of Abilene. It consisted of a pair of long forgotten wagon ruts that spanned the one hundred forty miles of earth between Fort Phantom Hill and Fort McKavett. This trail followed the same road bed as the Fort Croghan road for the first eight or ten miles, and then branched toward the nearest gaps in the mountains of Taylor County.[62] Across the Texas and Pacific railroad a mile and one-half east of Cedar Creek, just east of Abilene, across the middle of Lytle Lake, and through the Cedar Gap, following that break in the mountains very near the present-day paved highway—these are some of the points along the route of that early trail. The road passed a little east of the place where Tuscola now stands, and continued southward to the area east of Bradshaw.

In Runnels County, this road to Fort McKavett passed between Moro and Table Mountains and followed the east side of Elm Creek

61. Presslar's Travelers Map shows this route. Apparently the first road followed a course somewhat more to the south. See *J. De Cordova's Map of the State of Texas* compiled by Robert Crezbaur, 1858.

62. The Jones County Surveying Records cited in foot note No. 42 shows the northern portion of this old road. A map of Taylor County, made for Canda, Drake and Straus (successors to the Texas and Pacific Railway Company in the ownership of their premium lands, in or about 1894 traces this road, without naming it, southward into Cedar Gap. Presslar's Travelers Map of 1867 shows the entire route of the road from Fort Phantom Hill to Fort McKavett. In tracing this road on the map that accompanies this article, the writer has been guided by its proximity to creeks or mountains on the Presslar map. County lines could not be trusted on a map of West Texas made in 1867, since most of those lines had not yet been surveyed.

The fact that this old road appears on the plates or in the field notes of many surveys made in or about 1856 positively establishes it as a road of the pre-Civil War period.

about half the width of the county. It missed the site of Ballinger and crossed the Colorado River a few miles below. Bending more toward the southwest, this early thoroughfare crossed the Concho River near the much publicized Indian paintings at Paint Rock. Finally, the road passed up the valley of Kickapoo Creek, by the spring at the head of that stream, and extended southward along the west line of Menard County to Fort McKavett, some twenty miles west of present-day Menard.

The exact date when this road was opened is not available. Certainly it came not later than 1854, when Fort Phantom Hill was abandoned. Both this route and the road southward by Fort Chadbourne reached the branches of the California Trail and by that old road connected north Texas with San Antonio.

With a discussion of these units of the system of military roads behind us, the story moved back to Fort Belknap. It will be remembered that Marcy made a road from Belknap to the Pecan Bayou in 1851, but that a sudden westward turn of the chain of forts caused it not to be used. In the middle 1850's the pendulum made a swing back toward the east. The road that Marcy partly made and, perhaps, partly visualized, finally became the "big road" of the West Texas frontier. Probably it came into existence in two stages. The first of these was the road to the Pecan Bayou.

A wagon trail was opened over that span in 1853,[63] but it followed very little of Marcy's route. While Marcy had gone toward the west from Fort Belknap, this road extended due south. In modern terminology, this trail of 1853 passed through the town of Eliasville,[64] five miles east of Breckenridge, and soon curved to the southwest and entered Callahan County, almost at the corner.[65] It went through the wayside village of Pueblo and crossed the Texas and Pacific railroad a mile and one-half of Putnam.[66] From this point, the road continued

63. Many surveys made in 1853 mention this road from Fort Belknap southward, but in no case has the writer found a survey of earlier date that mentioned the road.

64. Map of Young County, Texas General Land Office, 1897.

65. Deed Records of Young County, Vol. 8, pp. 196, 207, 350, 354. The Texas and Pacific Railway Company map of Stephens County made about 1875 shows most of the path of this road across Stephens County. Presslar's Travelers Map shows the entire road from Fort Belknap southward.

66. The Texas and Pacific Railway Company map of Callahan County (made about 1875), and the Texas Land Office map of the same country made in 1879 trace this road completely across Callahan County. The Callahan County Surveying Records confirm the maps.

up the valley of Fish Creek (or Battle Creek) until it passed over the Callahan divide in the gap north of the town of Cottonwood.

South of this low chain of mountains lay the valley of Turkey Creek, probably the stream that Marcy had followed to the Pecan Bayou in 1851. The Phantom Hill-Fort Croghan road had already crossed this creek five miles south of the site of Cross Plains, and the Fort Chadbourne-Fort Gates road has crossed it three miles above that town. Seven miles north of Cross Plains, at the head of a branch of Turkey Creek, were old Cottonwood Springs, and just across the creek west of Cross Plains was a grove of live oak trees that made an excellent camp site. East Caddo Peak was four miles to the west, and her sister mountain was two miles beyond.

The first citizens of Callahan County were well acquainted with these two little mountains, as well as the two camping places in the valley of Turkey Creek. The people of the countryside have collected at the live oak grove, near Cross Plains, for more than half a century to celebrate holiday occasions. Cold drinks and Fourth of July oratory are part of the usual program—and in spite of the swift changes that streamline this age, the old custom still prevails.

In 1853, long before soda water or impromptu oratory were dispensed on Turkey Creek, the United States army made its old wagon road down the valley of this stream. The road came directly by the Cottonwood Springs (now the village of Cottonwood), and passed just west of the picnic spot in the live oak grove at Cross Plains. Five miles further south it joined the road from Phantom Hill to Fort Croghan.

Probably later on, but certainly as early as 1856, this trail was extended southward.[67] The crossing on Pecan Bayou made by this extension was at or near Burkett in Coleman County, and the crossing on Jim Ned Creek was ten miles northeast of the site of Coleman. The road passed just west of the Santa Anna Peaks, and continued almost due south to the site of Mason. Here Fort Mason stood at the junction of the two branches of the California Trail. It was a part of this road

67. All land surveys dated 1853 observed by the writer referred to this road either as the Belknap-Fort Croghan road or the Belknap-Austin road. Apparently it did not continue southward to Fort Mason and San Antonio at that time. However, part of the old Second Cavalry passed over this road to Fort Mason in early 1856. Some time between 1853 and 1856 the road had been extended to Fort Mason. Presslar's Travelers Map has furnished the data relied upon here for the route of this road south of Callahan County.

that had served the gold hunters of 1849 that completed the old military trail from Fort Belknap to San Antonio.

Probably in 1856 a branch of this Belknap-San Antonio road was opened in the area north of the Callahan Divide. This extension turned to the left of the main trail near Putnam and crossed Shackelford County a mile and one-half east of Albany as it approached Camp Cooper from the south.[68] Camp Cooper was established in 1856 and became the scene of much activity for five years after that date.

It was about this same time that Camp Colorado was established in Coleman County. The permanent position of that army post was near the crossing of the Belknap-San Antonio road on Jim Ned Creek.[69] This was the last of the forts to be established along the Texas frontier north of the Llano River and, for the sake of brevity, this study has been limited to that area.

The real live story of the forts and military roads of West Texas began in earnest just after Christmas in 1855, when Albert Sidney Johnston arrived at Fort Belknap with the Second Cavalry from Jefferson Barracks, Missouri.[70] This regiment of cavalrymen, seven hundred fifty strong, with the fire and spirit of college boys, and mounted on fine horses with spirit to match their own, wrote a colorful chapter along the old military trails of the Texas frontier. From the date of their arrival until the beginning of the Civil War, they virtually monopolized the army's activities in Texas.

During this period, their life story revolved about the single military road that connected Fort Belknap with San Antonio, and the short branch that connected this road with Camp Cooper. For the full five and a half years of their stay in Texas their regimental headquarters was always at one of the forts along this road.[71] Fort Belknap, Fort Mason, San Antonio and Camp Cooper were the different places that served as headquarters. North of the Llano River, Forts Mason, Belknap, Cooper and Colorado were the only permanent quarters assigned them.[72] In 1858, Company G was stationed at Fort Chadbourne for four months, and Company A was there a small part of

68. The Texas and Pacific Railway map of Shackelford County, made about 1876, shows the route of this road.

69. Map of Coleman County, Texas General Land Office, August, 1897.

70. George F. Price, *Across the Continent with the Fifth Cavalry*, 32-34.

71. *Ibid.*, 619.

72. *Ibid.*, 619-644.

that time.[73] Fort Phantom Hill had been burned for more than a year before the Second Cavalry came to Texas and, of course, was not in condition to be used. Fort McKavett, for some reason, was never garrisoned by these troops, although they probably used it on scouting trips.

The fact that several of these extreme western forts were little used by the Second Cavalry does not mean that these soldiers were timid and shrank from actual combat. On the contrary, they patrolled the frontier for as much as seven hundred miles, and fought no less than forty battles and skirmishes,[74] ranging all the way from Kansas to Mexico. However, it should be remembered that their real life line was the Belknap-San Antonio road.

Just after these soldiers of the Second Cavalry first came to Fort Belknap they were moved along the military roads to their various stations. On January 2, 1856, after they had rested at Belknap for only six days, six companies of them moved southward to Fort Mason.[75] Even in the day of fine automobiles these cavalrymen would have attracted attention. Their horses were matched in color[76] and must have resembled a parade as they went out of the old south entrance to Fort Belknap. Kirby Smith's company rode sorrel horses; Oakes, Palmer and Brackett's men rode bays, and the remaining two companies were mounted on browns. Southward they rode across the Clear Fork, through the future Eliasville, on through the gap near Cottonwood in Callahan County, down past the live oak grove where Cross Plains holds her traditional picnics, and on southward, past the Santa Anna Peaks. It required twelve days to reach Fort Mason.

It would be interesting to trace these soldiers on their various movements along the old trails, but the story would run into volumes. These seven hundred fifty men included an array of military talent that furnished many of the most prominent figures of Civil War history. It is an interesting fact that no little of their practical schooling for the great struggle came in Central West Texas. Not only did they whet their courage in combat with wild Comanches, but they learned military transportation on Texas rivers. Probably they learned to cross mud holes at the crossing on Turkey Creek and they

73. George P. Price, *Across the Continent with the Fifth Cavalry*, 635-636.
74. *Ibid.*, 650-651.
75. *Ibid.*, 620-644.
76. *Ibid.*, 31.

learned to ford swollen streams on the Colorado and the Brazos.

These men of the Second Cavalry, and the soldiers who have preceded them, opened the networks of the old trails that criss-crossed west Texas. In some instances they actually took over parts of the old Indian trails and made them into wagon roads. That is very probably true of a part of this Belknap-San Antonio road. Just before 1850, a trail much used by Comanche horse thieves passed by the Santa Anna Peaks, by the Caddo Peaks, and crossed the Brazos River northeast of the site of Breckenridge.[77] Apparently this trail crossed the modern paved highway about mid-way between Baird and Putnam in Callahan County.[78] It is entirely in keeping with the changes that occurred if some old Comanche Indian of the 1850's climbed to the top of East Caddo Peak and bemoaned the sad state of the times as he watched military wagons crawling along the trails that he had helped to keep open. Three decades later some old grizzled cowboy could have climbed to the top of the same peak and shared in the same regrets, for the Dodge City cattle trail also passed by the Caddo Peaks, and followed no little of the old San Antonio road. Truly, the iron horse that entered Abilene in 1881 meant new life for a whole empire, but it also plowed under the colorful trails of many generations of pioneers.[*]

*The work done by Miss Llerena Friend and Miss Eva Weber in assisting with this manuscript is gratefully acknowledged.

77. E. B. Ritchie (ed.), "Report of Colonel Samuel Cooper . . . of Inspection Trip from Fort Graham to the Indian Villages of the Upper Brazos made in June, 1851," *Southwestern Historical Quarterly*, April, 1939, 331, and accompanying map.

78. Survey of the boundary line of the Peters Colony, General Land Office, Vol. 18, p. 273.

XIII

THE VAN DORN TRAILS

A small party, including the writer, motored some six miles to the south of Wichita Falls, along the Jacksboro pavement. We stopped the car at a little roadside park near the point where State Highway 66 crosses the south line of Wichita County. It was a beautiful afternoon in mid-September; a clear sun lay to the west and a few scattered clouds floated in the sky.

We turned to look back at the city of Wichita Falls, a picture that the 1940 census takers had only recently reduced to statistical tables. The town had acquired a sky-line of which it felt justly proud, very much as a young boy would take pride in his first coat of whiskers. A large flour mill stood out in the foreground; twelve-story buildings climaxed the business district. A large high school, and a college building that was almost an artist's dream, added distinction to the residential area.

The picture in front of us served to emphasize the changes that eight decades had wrought in northwest Texas history. At almost the very spot where the car was parked the story that led to the first permanent imprint of Anglo-Americans on the soil of the Wichita Falls area began just eighty-two years ago. Two hundred, or more, blue-coated cavalrymen rode fine, well-trained horses over that same hilltop[1] in the fall of 1858. This army detachment consisted of four companies of the old Second Cavalry, led by the somewhat daring Brevet Major Earl Van Dorn.[2] The regimental headquarters from

1. *Deed Records, Archer County, Texas*, Vol. A, 202, 203. The plat of the survey of the north line of Archer County, dated 1881, is recorded on these pages. This plat shows two old trails running in the direction of what we shall later call the Van Dorn Crossing. One of them extended toward the Van Dorn Crossing on the Big Wichita River and is identified by records later in this chapter.

Personal conversations with H. W. Portwood of Seymour, Texas, and R. S. Hillburn of Antelope, Texas, identify these trails as connecting with the Van Dorn Crossing in Clay County. Both men traveled on them in the year 1877.

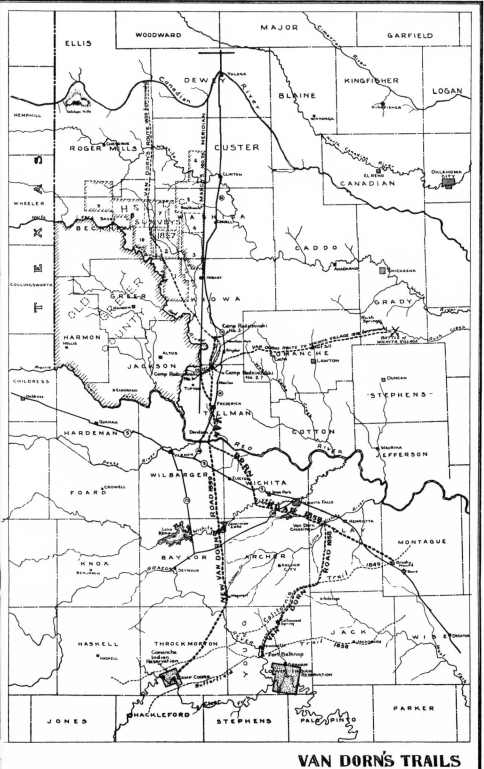

VAN DORN'S TRAILS
1858~1859

which these soldiers had come was old Fort Belknap, located just south of the present-day town of New Castle in Young County. Their objective lay to the northwest in the area that is now Tillman County, Oklahoma, a point from which they expected to carry on an extended Indian campaign.

As they filed over the hilltop that is now decorated by a modern roadside park, perhaps a clear sun shone in the sky and fleecy clouds floated overhead, but the landscape presented a far different picture from the scenery of 1940. These soldiers of 1858 saw no twelve-story buildings, no flour mill, no college. It was forty miles east to the nearest log cabin. Montague County had just been organized, with its county seat at the new village of Montague. Saint Jo (then called Head of Elm) was little more than a country store. Gainesville and Sherman were mere villages, and Dallas, by actual count, had only four hundred and thirty inhabitants.[3] Young County, from which Van Dorn had just moved his little army, had been organized in 1856,[4] with its county seat almost in the shadow of Fort Belknap. Randolph B. Marcy had preceded all settlements west of Gainesville when he opened the California trail midway between the present towns of Wichita Falls and Jacksboro in the gold rush year of 1849.[5]

2. (a) Price, George F., *Across the Continent with the Fifth Cavalry*. Biographies of the old Second Cavalry, later known as the Fifth Cavalry, fill a majority of the pages of this large volume. E. Kirby Smith and Fitzhugh Lee joined Van Dorn later. Robert E. Lee, George H. Thomas, Albert Sidney Johnston and John B. Hood were some of the leading figures of the Second Cavalry who were not part of this particular expedition.

(b) Thorburn, Joseph B., "Indian Fight in Foard County in 1859," *Kansas Historical Collections*, 1911-12.

3. *Texas Almanac*, 1936, 144.

4. *Ibid.*, 455.

5. *31 Cong. 1 sess. Sen. ex. doc. No. 64,* 169-233. Marcy's report details his expedition from Fort Smith, Arkansas, to Santa Fé and return in 1849. His return journey came from the Rio Grande in southern New Mexico, eastward, near the sites of Pecos, Big Spring, Gainesville and Denison. None of these towns were in existence in 1849. Gainesville began as a small village in 1850. The map of the Texan Emigration and Land Company filed in the Texas General Land Office in 1854, shows about eighty miles of the road that resulted from Marcy's journey. This part of the "California Trail" extended from a point about four miles southeast of Throckmorton to Brushy Mound, which is a well known hill some five miles northwest of Bowie. This part of Marcy's trail is shown on the map that accompanies this chapter, for the drawing of which I have to thank the courtesy of Mr. R. W. McClesky of Hardin Junior College. In 1858 John Butterfield and associates established a government mail road to California, through Gainesville and Belknap. Butterfield's road, which was partly

As Van Dorn's soldiers entered Wichita County, an area then devoid of white men, they, perhaps, made a more interesting picture than any scenery around them. They were mounted on good horses, many of them from Kentucky, that had cost the Federal government about one hundred and fifty dollars each.[6] The troop was excellently garbed, even while doing field service. On special occasions they wore dress uniforms trimmed in yellow braid, and presented an array of color that would offer keen competition to a modern college band. "The officers wore silk sashes, brass shoulder scales, and plumed Kossuth hats."[7]

Van Dorn's soldiers were en route to the supposed Panhandle of Texas to mete out punishment to at least one band of Comanche Indians. The military authorities of the United States government probably responded to pressure from Texans in conducting such a campaign. Regardless of the number of peaceful efforts that emanated from Washington, Comanche Indians and frontier Texans continually lived with potential warfare in their hearts. Another factor probably lent weight toward the present venture. Many hundreds of land surveys had been established during 1857 in the very section where it was Van Dorn's purpose to campaign.[8] Such new proprietary interests, added to racial hatred, must have given no little impetus toward the military undertaking.

It later developed that Texas did not own the land which this cavalry expedition set out to patrol. An unofficial observation of the hundredth meridian, made by Randolph B. Marcy and George B. McClellan in 1852,[9] had led to a misconception of the east boundary

---

new, in a large measure supplanted Marcy's road west of Young County. Part of the Butterfield trail is shown on the accompanying map.

6. Thorburn, *op. cit.*, 314.

7. Thorburn, *op. cit.*, 314.

8. *Surveyors' Records of Cooke County, Texas*, Vols. E and H. Many of these surveys that were located in what is now western Oklahoma in 1857 are recorded in these volumes.

An old plat in the Texas General Land Office, signed by J. W. Peery, October 3, 1857, shows more than eight hundred surveys that were made for the H. & T. C. Ry. Co. The land was divided into ten blocks, some of which contained more than one hundred square miles. This H. & T. C. Ry. subdivision from Peery's plat is reproduced in the map that accompanies this chapter. Certain streams shown in Peery's plat have made it possible for us to map these H. & T. C. Ry. surveys in the same area where they were actually located in 1857. They covered about 500,000 acres of land that now lie west and northwest of Hobart, Oklahoma.

9. *House ex. doc. 33 Cong. 1 sess.*, 18.

of the Texas Panhandle. In 1859 it was discovered that the correct position of the hundredth meridian was some fifty miles farther west than these observers had located it, and that the Van Dorn cavalry units were operating almost entirely outside of Texas.

Looking backward, one may wonder whether the campaign would have been launched at all if this fact of geography had been known in advance. However, aside from the motive of those who were responsible for this military thrust into the land of wild Comanches, the expedition had an effect on local history that has heretofore attracted little attention. Van Dorn made a wagon road that extended far beyond the frontier of 1858. This old road did service for some decades of northwest Texas history before changes in transportation methods caused it to fade almost entirely from the hillsides. The facts about this early trail, with special emphasis on its route in terms of modern place names, is the major effort of this chapter.

Laid down in an Indian country the full knowledge of which still lingers on the shadowy edge of written history, the Van Dorn trail offers a study of entrancing interest. The route for this early thoroughfare was not charted by surveyors or men of science. On the contrary, wise old Indians who knew how to profit from a knowledge of topography and the age-old experiences of red men mapped this war trail.

Van Dorn was preceded across Wichita, and other counties, by L. S. Ross,[10] aged twenty, who had just completed his junior year in college. Ross was not a member of the Second Cavalry, but was in command of about one hundred friendly Indians from the reservation in Young County. He was to do scout duty and aid the cavalrymen in actual battle. The members of the Second Cavalry soon learned to respect this Texas boy who could lead a force of semi-civilized Indians in battle, and could, meanwhile, take a full hand in the conflict. Indeed, Ross is none other than the later governor of Texas and president of Texas A. and M. College.

In the selection of a route of travel that ultimately led to the creation of the Van Dorn road, no other held the unique position of the Tonkawa Indian chief, Placedo.[11] He was one of the two principal

10. *Record Supreme Court United States, United States v. Texas in Equity.* Judd and Detweiler, Printers, Washington, D. C. June, 1894, 953 ff. Hereafter called *Greer County Record.* The testimony of L. S. Ross tells of his journey to the Indian Territory in 1858.

11. *Greer County Record,* 953 ff. Ross's testimony tells the names of the Indian

guides relied upon by Ross who paved the way for Van Dorn's journey. Placedo had long been the chief of the friendly Tonkawas, and it would hardly be amiss to refer to him as the greatest single Indian ally that the Texans ever had. He was now about sixty years old and commanded not only the loyalty of his fellow tribesmen but the respect of the Texans.

Ross was not acquainted with the country to be traversed, and Placedo and Ochilas,[12] chief of the Tehuacanas, pointed out his way. Up to the northeast corner of Wilbarger County, north across Red River, and into the northwest corner of what is now Tillman County, Oklahoma, this advance guard of the Second Cavalry made their tracks. The men established a camp on Otter Creek, a few miles from the modern town of Tipton, Oklahoma. And soon they located the band of Comanche Indians—under Chief Buffalo Hump—whom it was Van Dorn's purpose to punish.[13]

Van Dorn probably had little difficulty in following Ross and his friendly redskins. The grass had been burned off all of the way from the Little Wichita to Otter Creek, except about twelve miles in and adjacent to the northeast corner of Wilbarger County.[14]

Following in, or near, the path made by Ross, Van Dorn and his colorful horsemen crossed Wichita County in a northwesterly direction, almost from corner to corner, and crossed Red River a short distance below the mouth of the Pease. They established their supply camp on Otter Creek at the point selected by Ross, and proceeded to make a picket enclosure for defense. The name Radziminski was selected for the new post in honor of a Polish member of the Second Cavalry who had recently died of tuberculosis.[15]

Last of all the expedition to arrive at Camp Radziminski was a plain Mr. Duff,[16] who, unlike some who had preceded him, wore no brass shoulder scales and probably did not even so much as own a

---

chiefs who guided him.

12. *Greer County Record*, 953 ff.

13. Brown, John Henry, *Indian Wars and Pioneers of Texas*, L. E. Daniell, Publisher, Austin, Texas, 112.

14. *35 Cong. 2 sess. Sen. ex. doc. No. 1*, Vol. II, 268. Hereafter called Van Dorn's *First Report*. The report indicates that the twelve miles immediately south of Red River did not have the grass burned off. This was in Wichita and Wilbarger Counties, between China Creek and Red River.

15. Nye, W. S., *Carbine and Lance*, University of Oklahoma Press, Norman, Oklahoma, 1938, 24.

16. Van Dorn's *First Report*.

plumed hat. He was just "the man who had charge of the train of corn wagons" and had no standing in military circles. For our purpose, however, he was the most important figure in the entire expedition. The one and only thing available that would cut deep furrows in the earth and leave a long and lasting trail behind, was a wagon wheel, and Mr. Duff had a monopoly on that kind of equipment.

The characteristic that distinguished the military expeditions of the Federal government from those of the Texas Rangers was their liberal use of supply wagons.[17] The Rangers used pack-mules almost exclusively and hence did not make permanent trails. Thus the field for making new roads was almost entirely left to the Federal government. This was not true, of course, in the settled areas, but out beyond the realm of log cabins the new roads were largely made by army wagons. As an exception to this rule, the Texan Santa Fé expedition crossed this section of Texas equipped with a goodly number of wagons, but it seems unlikely that their trail lasted long enough to make a wagon road. By contrast, Camp Radziminski was in operation for a full year. It was garrisoned by from two to three hundred soldiers, and perhaps at times more. There were at least an equal number of cavalry horses to be fed. It must have made Mr. Duff a busy man with his fifteen wagons[18]—for such was the number—to keep all needs supplied.

Having established the new supply base on Otter Creek, Van Dorn and Ross, accompanied by the cavalrymen and the friendly Indians, hastened to chastise the Comanches.[19] At this very time these hostile Indians were encamped at the Wichita Village at the head of Rush Creek, about twenty miles south of the present site of Chickasha. Eastward, in a course which probably passed near the sites of the towns of Cache and Lawton, the cavalrymen and their allies made their way. The Indian scouts under the command of Ross had located the Comanches near the point at which the town of Rush

17. *Northern Standard,* Clarksville, Texas, June 12, 1858. The report of Ford's expedition to the Antelope Hills shows that he had only two wagons, and both of these were abandoned before he returned to his camp near Fort Belknap.

18. *Northern Standard,* Clarksville, Texas, Aug. 28, 1858. Special Order No. 71 gave the number of wagons and other equipment with which Van Dorn's expedition was to be equipped.

19. *35 Cong. 2 sess. Sen. ex. doc. No. 1,* Vol. II, 272. Hereafter we shall refer to this as Van Dorn's *Second Report.* This report gave an account of the Battle of Wichita Village.

Springs, Oklahoma, was later established, and reported the distance from Radziminski as forty miles. Their failure to understand the white man's units of measure and their inability to recognize the exact site of the enemy delayed Van Dorn's attack to a time slightly later than had been planned.

However, his horsemen swept down upon the half-sleeping Comanches in a complete surprise. Bugles sounded, the attackers set up a deafening cheer, rifles cracked, and the charge was on. The cavalrymen and their Indian allies numbered about three hundred fighting men, and they were not far from evenly matched by their Comanche opponents. The Wichita Indians, at whose village the Comanches were encamped, did not take part in the fight. The Comanches fell back at first, but soon rallied and offered stubborn resistance. The battle lasted more than an hour and a half, resulting in a complete route of the Comanches. Fifty-six of the red warriors lay dead upon the field, and many others escaped in wounded condition. The Comanche retreat was greatly impeded by the fact that the friendly Indians had stampeded and captured some three hundred of their horses.

But the victory was not won without spilling the blood of some gallant white soldiers. Lieutenant Cornelius Van Camp fell dead from the shot of an Indian arrow. He extracted the arrow head from his own heart during the death struggle. Van Dorn fell from his horse with an arrow through his stomach; while he writhed in pain, his fine cavalry horse stood over him like a faithful comrade. Young Ross received a dangerous gunshot wound and came near being killed by one of the Comanches. A total of five cavalrymen lost their lives in the day's encounter and a number of more were wounded. Both Van Dorn and Ross survived their wounds, although their recovery was not immediate.

A feature much to be regretted concerning this fight at Wichita Village is the fact that the Comanches were stolen upon and attacked by the soldiers from Fort Belknap while they were on a peace mission at the request of the authorities at Fort Arbuckle.[20] The government evidently had not let its right hand know what its left hand was doing.

Many other details, some of them colorful, must be omitted, because the chief object of this article is to hunt for the Van Dorn

20. Nye, *op. cit.*, 24, 26.

trails and to relate them to the early life in the land which they served. If the story of the battle of Wichita Village and the events leading
up to it have furnished a background for the investigation, it has served its purpose. Henceforth we are engaged in a kind of Sherlock
Holmes detective story, except that we are hunting out old roads that
created new life rather than finding a murderer who brought about
death. The story of Van Dorn's military campaign which we have
briefly recounted was widely publicized by the newspapers of his day,
and has been repeated often by later writers, but the task of detailing
Van Dorn's route, which we shall shortly undertake, has awaited
some such effort as the present research.

*   *   *

Cash McDonald, who for over three quarters of a century lived
northwest of the site of the present town of Bowie, waved his hand in
a general northwestward direction and mentioned the old Van Dorn
road. That wave of the hand started mental waves of curiosity that in-
itiated the research for this study.

The first discovery was the record of surveys made in 1860 for the
Memphis, El Paso and Pacific Railway Company. These records
revealed that a ''Radziminski Road'' crossed China Creek some five
and a half miles north of the spot where Electra is now located[21] and
not far north of the Magnolia Tank Farm on the same creek. The
surveyors, without doubt, should have known about Camp Radziminski and roads leading to it, since that post had been the center
of great interest only a year before. Moreover, they had probably
traveled the Radziminski—or Van Dorn—Road all the way up from
Fort Belknap to survey for the Memphis, El Paso and Pacific Railway
Company.

It is quite a step to move from the surveying records of Wichita
County to the record of the Greer County case before the Supreme
Court of the United States, but that is the next turn in this particular
detective story. The testimony of L. S. Ross[22] shows that he crossed
Red River below its forks as he preceded Van Dorn into Indian Territory. J. H. Swindells of Fort Worth, Texas, who was with Van Dorn
in 1858, testified, as did Ross, that Red River was crossed below the
forks.[23] Three witnesses estimate the location of a trail crossing on Red

21. *Surveyors' Records of Wichita County, Texas,* Vol. A, 64, 65, 70, 71.
22. *Greer County Record,* 953 ff.

River at from three miles to eight miles below the mouth of the Pease. Horace P. Jones, who was one of the three, and eminently qualified to know the frontier, did not hesitate with the information that the road referred to was none other than the Radziminski-Belknap Road.[24] Hence it seems evident that the old crossing on Red River was north of the point where the town of Harrold now stands and about two or three miles below the Davidson Bridge. The old road passed northward up the west side of Tillman County to the old army post, which was about five miles above the mouth of Otter Creek, the site of which is not far from Tipton, Oklahoma.

The surveyors of the United States government mapped the area that is now Tillman County in 1874 and 1875.[25] They showed a road crossing Red River at the very point mentioned by Jones and other witnesses. That old wagon trail crossed Red River just two miles below the present concrete bridge on the Vernon-Frederick highway, and ascended the east bank of a small creek on the Oklahoma side of the river.[26] At a point a mile and a half east of the present site of Davidson, the old road turned toward the northeast, almost paralleling the present paved highway, until it reached a position some two miles east of that highway and seven miles south of the modern town of Frederick, Oklahoma. Apparently this was a watering place on the upper part of Settles Creek. From here the road turned slightly west of north, passing a mile west of Frederick. At two miles northwest of Frederick the trail divided, one branch extending a few degrees to the east of north, while the other branch turned more to the northwest. This northwestward branch is not completely shown in the records but appears to connect with an old road some three and a half miles east of present Tipton, Oklahoma. The terminus of this trail was the original site of Camp Radziminski, about the location of which the surveyors of 1875 leave very little room for doubt. The old township

23. *Ibid.*, 1126.

24. *Ibid.*, 506.

25. Plat Book in the office of the County Engineer, Tillman County, Okla. These plats are copies of the township plats of the original surveys in the General Land Office at Washington, D. C.

26. (a) Plat Book in the office of the County Engineer, Tillman County, Oklahoma, 34, 27, 28. The road shown in the plats passes between Van Dorn's crossing on the Red River and his camp in Indian Territory. Evidently the road is identical with Van Dorn's trail, or the Radziminski road.

(b) Carter, Robert G., *On the Border with Mackenzie*, 122. Carter says Mackenzie crossed the Radziminski road in this area in 1871.

plat shows an "old post marked 1859" in the northwest quarter of section fifteen, six miles northeast of Tipton.[27] Marion Kelly, owner of this land, found rock ruins in the northwest quarter of section fifteen, and other evidence such as broken champagne bottles, buttons from army uniforms, old style horseshoes and "square nails" a short distance to the northeast of these ruins.[28]

A sketch discovered in the Texas Land Office indicates that Marcy's (incorrect) hundredth meridian also crossed Marion Kelly's land[29] not far from the point at which these remains of army camp life were located. This is not a mere coincidence. Van Dorn reported that his camp was on the south side of Otter Creek, about two hundred yards east of Marcy's meridian.[30] Thus do fragments of army camp life support records from Austin and records from Austin support records from Washington—all to the effect that Van Dorn's camp, or Camp

27. *Ibid.*, 5.

28. Kelly, Marion, Tipton, Oklahoma. Personal observation and interviews, Feb. 24, 1940.

29. This sketch was entitled "Sketch of Triangulation and Surveys North of Red River." It was found in the same envelope with the survey of the east line of the Panhandle, made in 1859. Neither signature nor date was given in the sketch. However, the fact that surveys were made north of the North Fork of Red River indicates that this sketch was made before the Jones and Brown survey of 1859; and the shape of the tracts of land is unmistakable evidence that the work was done by Texas surveyors (unmistakable evidence that the work was done by Texas surveyors, who did not use the township, section and range plan of the U. S. government).

The important feature of the sketch for us here is the fact that it shows a line which must have been intended by Texas surveyors as Marcy's (incorrect) hundredth meridian. The line which appears to represent the meridian began at Otter Creek at "Marcy's Camp," longitude 100° 00′ 45″, and extended north to the Canadian River. Marcy marked exactly that same longitude on an elm tree at one of his camp sites on the south side of Otter Creek in 1852 (See *House ex. doc. 33 Cong. 1 sess.* 18).

Texas surveyors appear to have accepted this camp site of Marcy's as approximating the correct hundredth meridian. Hundreds of surveys were made in 1857 in the area just west of the north-south line shown by the old sketch (see Vols. E and H, *Cook County Surveying Records*), indicating that the line was regarded as the east boundary of the Texas Panhandle. A careful study of the meridian in this Land Office sketch shows that it crossed the North Fork of Red River just half a mile west of the tip of the bend that lies southwest of Snyder, Oklahoma, and that it crossed Otter Creek five and a half miles east of the mouth of that stream. To comply with these measurements Marcy's meridian necessarily crossed the northwest quarter of section 15 that is now the property of Marion Kelly.

30. Van Dorn's *First Report.*

Radziminski, was on the northwest quarter section of Marion Kelly's farm.

With some notion of the northern end of Van Dorn's Road, let us examine the southern end. The long gap between China Creek in northwest Wichita County and Fort Belknap in the heart of Young County leaves much room for speculation. But, presto! The old surveying records of Wichita County again clear up some of the mystery. The Van Dorn Road crossed the east line of the R. J. Scott survey[31] in the east edge of the K.M.A.* oil field. This survey is located on the south side of the Wichita River and extends southward far enough to include the Valley View rural school. This old river crossing was two miles due north of the site of this schoolhouse.[32] The survey was made September 19, 1858, exactly four days after Van Dorn had started north from Fort Belknap to begin his Indian campaign. Apparently the surveyors had accompanied the cavalrymen into Wichita County while military protection was available. Probably Van Dorn was not far north of the Wichita River when the survey was made.

With the gap thus narrowed to less than sixty miles the rest of the search looked easy. A straight line from the east side of the K.M.A. oil field to old Belknap would pass through the middle of Archer County. If some big-league baseball pitcher, endowed with superhuman strength, should stand in the Valley View school yard and throw a baseball all of the distance to old Belknap down in Young County, he would just about throw a strike over one of the flat-topped hills to the southwest of Archer City. With this fact in mind, the scene of the trail hunt moved to Archer City. The old records were dusted off and examined, but they were painfully silent about either the Radziminski road or the Van Dorn Trail. Was it possible that the old road missed the Archer City area entirely? John

31. *Surveyors' Records of Wichita County, Texas,* Vol. A and D, 1. Survey made Sept. 19, 1858. Surveys-723-9501.

32. *Ibid.,* Vol. B, p. 28. Land surveyed in 1859.

*The name ''K.M.A.'' designated a certain oil field in Wichita County is not my abbreviation. It originated from ''Kemp-Munger-Allen,'' the name of the first oil company in the field. In none of the oil publications has the writer been able to find any present day usage of the old original name of the discovery oil company ''Kemp-Munger-Allen.'' A post office was established in this field during 1938. To prevent the usage of a name spelled out with capitals the word ''Kamay'' was coined by the postal department, hence the Kamay post office in the K.M.A. oil field.

Turbeville, who lived in Archer County for more than sixty years, assisted with the information that there was no early road that crossed the heart of Archer County from north to south.[33] The opinion was confirmed by others.

The speculation had to turn to other fields. There was an old Van Dorn crossing on the Little Wichita, five miles south of Jolly, in Clay County, Texas. Everybody in that part of Clay County seemed to know about it. Could it have anything to do with the solution of the problem? Apparently not, because it was a full twenty-five miles too far to the east to be in line with known points on the Van Dorn road. Many publications in the library of The University of Texas were combed;[34] many interesting facts were uncovered about northwest Texas in general and the Van Dorn expedition in particular, but the answer was missing to the crucial question, "Where did the old road run between the Big Wichita and Fort Belknap?" Many pages, biographical and otherwise, about John S. Ford, L. S. Ross, Earl Van Dorn, and others, were read and noted, but the answer was always missing. Finally, notes from which Dr. Walter Prescott Webb wrote *The Texas Ranger* were reviewed[35] and—well, Dr. Webb was downright discouraging. He gave out the very unwelcome information that the route was unknown.

The research was then turned to seeking the route followed by the reservation Indians as they were moved out of Texas—possibly they had followed the Van Dorn road. Major Thomas, Robert S. Neighbors, Leeper, and John Henry Brown all went with the Indians as they left Texas. Anything about their journey might prove to be the essential morsel of truth. Finally the mail brought a copy of the diary made by Robert S. Neighbors as he conducted the Indians out

---

The plat, with Denton County school land adjoining the Scott survey, shows a trail crossing Wichita River on the R. J. Scott Survey.

33. John Turbeville, Archer City, Texas. Interview (made in the early part of 1939). Turbeville has died since this manuscript was prepared.

34. (a) Lacy, Miss Sara, Austin, Texas. Miss Lacy has done much research work in the Library of the University of Texas in securing information used in the preparation of this paper.

(b) Weber, Miss Eva, Wichita Falls, Texas. Miss Weber, of the Hardin Junior College faculty, gave much helpful criticism in the construction of this article.

35. Webb, Walter Prescott. Dr. Webb has placed the notes from which he wrote *The Texas Ranger* in the Library of The University of Texas.

36. Robert S. Neighbors' diary of his journey in moving the Indians from the Texas reservation to the Indian Territory is filed among the *Neighbors Papers* in the Texas University Library.

of Texas—and that diary just about terminated a perfectly enjoyable trail hunt.

Neighbors, according to his diary, followed Van Dorn's road to the Little Wichita.[36] From there he turned northeast and crossed Red River a few miles below the mouth of the Big Wichita. His distance traveled from the Little Wichita to the Red was thirty-six miles—and on that fact hangs much of the answer to our search. A straight line from the Van Dorn Crossing south of Jolly to the mouth of the Big Wichita is twenty-five miles. But Neighbors' crossing on Red River was "a few miles"[37] below the mouth of the Big Wichita.

Also, remember that an old trail across Clay, or any other county, must wind around enough to find water and to miss the rough spots, and the answer is pretty definite. The traditionally known old Van Dorn crossing on the Little Wichita, where Fred Halsell's cows now nip the grass in peace and quiet, is the true spot where Van Dorn, Ross, Neighbors, John Henry Brown—and Mr. Duff—all crossed that stubborn little river when Texas was a younger state.

But before we become too confident, let us consult the one person still living of the adult population that accompanied Neighbors at the time he made the very useful diary above referred to. That unique person is George B. Ely of Clyde, Texas. Ely was one of John Henry Brown's temporary force of Texas Rangers who accompanied Neighbors and his Indians as far as the Little Wichita. In an attempt to identify the Van Dorn crossing by the direct testimony of a living witness, many questions were propounded to George Ely, who was knocking at the door of his hundredth birthday.[38] "It has been so long, I don't remember," was the usual answer. "Did you camp on the mesquite prairie south of the river?" was the next question. "No, we crossed the river and camped in the flat on the north side," said Ely, in words that were positive.

There is an extensive "flat" on the north side of the Little Wichita at the well known crossing in Halsell's pasture south of Jolly.[39] No other combination of a flat and an old crossing could be found.[40] Hence, combining the diary of Neighbors, the testimony of

37. Neighbors to Washington, Lieut. T. A., July 11, 1859.

38. Ely, George B., personal interview. (Ely died in May, 1940—since this manuscript was prepared.) Ely was J. W. Williams's grandfather, K.F.N.

39. The topography of the Little Wichita area south of Jolly in Clay County, Texas, was determined by personal observation of the writer.

40. The only other trail crossing the Little Wichita which might have been confused with Van Dorn's Crossing was located northwest of the present village of Scotland, Archer County, Texas. This trail crossing was considerably more than thirty-six miles from the mouth of the Big Wichita, which would violate the facts

Ely, and the weight of many decades of tradition, the answer seems clear—the old Van Dorn crossing, five miles south of Jolly, or fifteen miles southeast of Wichita Falls, is the genuine article.

The old crossing was plainly visible still. The water still trickled over the sand-rock bottom as it did eighty years hence. The current of the river at flood stage, however, had washed out the south bank so that wagon traffic was no longer possible. The remains of an iron bridge, built by Harry Halsell[41] more than forty years previously, were still seen beside the former crossing.

As to the location of the remainder of the Van Dorn trail, the answer may be brief. A very old road led south from Little Wichita by the village of Halsell, toward Antelope, in the northeast corner of Jack County. It may have been part of our route—though the proof is not positive. However, from a point somewhere near the southwest corner of Clay County to Fort Belknap, there can be little doubt about the course of the old road. Ross, Van Dorn, and Neighbors, all of whom admittedly followed the Van Dorn Road, without exception camped at or passed by the Cottonwood Spring. This spring was just west of the present town of Jean in Young County and was a regular camping place on the Preston-Belknap Road. The course of the Preston-Belknap Road, in so far as it concerns us here, can be marked out almost as definitely as the paved highway from Olney to Graham. Maps from the State Land Office and early surveying records tell the whole story.[42]

For the convenience of those who wish to follow it, we are listing the location of a number of points on the old road from Fort Belknap to Camp Radziminski. Those who do not care to study the route minutely should pass over these details. The route follows:

(1) From old Fort Belknap north, through the east edge of present New Castle in Young County; (2) still northward, passing about one mile west of Jean; (3) next across the Trinity River, about ten miles south of Archer City, in Texan Emigration and Land Company block 1831; (4) northeast, by old Flag Springs in Texan Emigration and Land Company block 1841, and by old Tax Springs in block

---

given in Neighbors' diary, if supposed to be Van Dorn's Crossing. The north side of the Little Wichita at that point is not a flat, as the land at Van Dorn's Crossing is described by Ely. The earliest record of the use of this crossing of which the writer has any knowledge, appears to have been made in 1873 by Alf Green, who lived at Electra, Texas. At that time Green was en route to the Panhandle of Texas to engage in a buffalo hunt.

41. Halsell to Williams.

42. The map of the Texan Emigration and Land Company, dated 1854, is filed in the State Land Office. The trails referred to are shown on that map.

1842; (5) then east, across the ranches of J. S. Bridwell and Lee Underwood, some six miles south of Windthorst in Archer County; (6) then probably northward, following the course of part of the old road from Antelope to the Van Dorn Crossing on the Little Wichita, five miles south of Jolly in Clay County; (7) then northwest near the dam of Lake Wichita, six miles south of Wichita Falls; (8) next, across the Big Wichita, on the R. J. Scott survey, just north of the Valley View school; (9) following from there northwestward, near the Burnett ranch headquarters and passing, probably, about a mile and a half southwest of Sunshine Hill;[43] (10) then across China Creek, five and a half miles north of Electra; (11) northwest from the last point into northeast Wilbarger County, and across Red River, two miles below the Davidson Bridge; (12) and then northward, across Tillman County, Oklahoma, passing a mile and a half east of Davidson and a mile west of Frederick; (13) two miles northwest of Frederick the trail divided, as previously mentioned, one branch extending northwest to the first site of Camp Radziminski in the northwest quarter of section fifteen, six miles northeast of Tipton; while the other branch extended almost due north to both of Van Dorn's other camping places.

After following this route, one is tempted to ask: Why did Van Dorn make the eastward detour into Clay County when his journey's end lay to the northwest? The answer is evidently that he had to have water for men and horses. At the crossing of the Little Wichita, south of the present village of Jolly in Clay County, he found holes of permanent water. Probably Placedo and the other Indian guides who piloted Ross northward are responsible for this big eastward bend in the Van Dorn Trail. Ross, who opened the way for Van Dorn, did not know the country and relied solely upon the judgment of the Indians. Old Placedo and his red-skinned cohorts probably had heard legends of dried-up water holes and failing springs from generations past—and, better still, they knew where to find permanent water. Red men lived along the streams in semi-arid northwest Texas when the nearest white settlers were many moons to the east and south. Indians pitched their tepees or pole huts near the best sources of water; they made trails from one watering place to another. Possibly they were guiding Ross and Van Dorn up an old Indian trail.[44]

43. Marlow, J. B., Wichita Falls, Texas, and Myers, George S. Jolly, Clay County, Texas. Marlow and Myers remember an old road crossing this part of Wichita County. Their information dates as far back as 1882.

44. The Van Dorn trail ran near a course that would have connected some of the early villages of the Wichita and Waco Indians.

The west end of the Wichita Mountains was inhabited by these Indians in 1834 (Foreman, Grant, *Adventure on Red River*, 37). In 1852, Marcy met a band of them

But again it appears that plain Mr. Duff played a role of importance. Not only did the Van Dorn Trail lead from Camp Radziminski in Indian Territory to Fort Belknap in Young County, but a branch of it led eastward across Clay County, joining the old California Trail at Brushy Mound, a few miles northwest of the present town of Bowie. This branch of the trail extended southeast from the Van Dorn Crossing on the Little Wichita, passing some five or six miles south of Henrietta and across the East Fork of the Little Wichita, about fifteen miles southeast of Henrietta and a mile and a half south of the Fort Worth and Denver Railroad at that place. Near this crossing on the East Fork is the old Van Dorn grove of great oaks, and in their shade an inviting spring of fresh water still perpetuates the name.[45] These landmarks are on the Hapgood ranch, and, believe it or not, even the enclosure is known as the Van Dorn Pasture.

The old Commissioners' Court records of Clay County drop a good hint about the location of this early road and remove all doubt as to its existence.[46] Cash McDonald, who lived near the east end of this old trail during the entire eighty-two years of its history, approximately confirms our route across Clay County. Records of the troop movements of the Second Cavalry, however, do not seem to show that the cavalrymen themselves ever used this part of the old road.[47] Hence it is that we give the credit to Mr. Duff and his corn wagons. This early road must have been the route followed by the supply

---

on Otter Creek (*House ex. doc. 33 Cong. 1 sess.*, 17). In 1858, S. P. Ross was accompanied by an old Waco chief who was "born and raised" in the mountains that are north of Altus, Oklahoma (*Greer County Record*, 938).

The area bordering the Wichita River has had a number of Wichita or Waco Indian villages. Before 1800 there was a Wichita Indian village at or near the site of Wichita Falls (Nye, *Carbine and Lance*, 16). There was a Waco village probably near the same place in 1841 (Kendall, Geo. Wilkins, *Narrative of the Texan Santa Fé Expedition*, Vol. I, 135-143). Johnson's map of Texas, 1864, shows a Wichita Indian village near the lower part of Wichita River (Johnson, A. J., *Johnson's New Illustrated Family Atlas*, map No. 48). J. B. Marlow, of Wichita Falls, learned through an early trapper, whose name was Buntin, that some Indians who raised corn lived in the valley above the site of Wichita Falls immediately after the Civil War.

45. Cunningham, George, Henrietta, Texas. Personal interview. Cunningham came to Clay County in 1874 and had lived there continuously since.

46. *Commissioners' Court Records of Clay County, Texas*, I: 227. Road precinct 14 was formed in 1879. It was bounded on the north by the Henrietta-Montague road, on the west by the East Fork of the Little Wichita, on the east by the Clay-Montague county line, and on the south by the "Old Van Dorn Trail."

47. (a) Price, *op. cit.*, 619-651. A complete record of the troop movements of the Second Cavalry makes it appear improbable that the Van Dorn trail in eastern Clay County was ever used by these cavalrymen.

wagons as they journeyed to and from the more thickly populated regions of North Texas. Whether this makes of Mr. Duff, who forced stubborn mules across bad river crossings, a greater contributor to northwest Texas history than it makes of Van Dorn, who crossed swords and lances with wild Comanches, is hardly our function to decide.

The Second Cavalry spent the winter of 1858-59 at Camp Radziminski. L. S. Ross, it will be remembered, returned wounded to Texas. He returned to college, where he completed his senior year.

During the winter and spring Camp Radziminski was moved twice—probably to provide better grass for the cavalry horses. The first move placed the camp several miles up Otter Creek from its original site. This location is not definitely known. The east branch of the Radziminski Road, however, came almost directly north from the junction of the two branches northwest of Frederick. This part of the road itself branched three miles northwest of the little town of Manitou, but the two parts reunited at the crossing on Otter Creek. This crossing was near the center of section six, two and a half miles west and five and a half miles north of Manitou. The second location of Camp Radziminski is known to have been on the south side of Otter Creek.[48] Conjecture would lead one to suppose that this second camp site was near the crossing on Otter Creek, as surveyors' plats do not show any branch road which might have led to any other point.

The last move placed Van Dorn's camp on the location of present section sixteen, two miles north and two miles west of Mountain Park, Oklahoma.[49] On the west side of Otter Creek at this point, the remains of old chimneys and many small objects, such as were found on Marion Kelly's land, give concrete evidence of the site of a military encampment.[50] The mountain to the southeast of this early army post is still known as Radziminski Mountain.

By the spring of 1859 Van Dorn and his command were ready for new conquests. Additional troops had joined them during the winter. The regimental headquarters was moved to Camp Cooper in the southwest part of Throckmorton County.[51] From this point supply wagons or other communications with Camp Radziminski opened a

---

(b) *Texas Almanac*, Galveston, 1861, 189. A note from Clay County says, "His supplies of corn . . . are routed through this county."

48. Nye, *Carbine and Lance*, 31.

49. *Ibid.*

50. Personal observation, December, 1939.

51. Price, *op. cit.*, 619.

52. Neighbors to Washington, July 11, 1859. This letter mentions Van Dorn's new road.

new road.[52] The new route crossed to the northeast corner of Throckmorton County; then northward to join Van Dorn's other road. This road crossed the Brazos southwest of Megargel[53] and extended northward just a slight distance east of the Archer County line. It passed the head springs of Kickapoo Creek in Texan Emigration and Land Company block number 2412 very near the west line of Archer County.[54] It crossed Godwin Creek and the Little Wichita River not far from the Archer-Baylor county line, and crossed the Big Wichita in the middle of present Diversion Lake, two miles west of this common county boundary.[55] From here the route is not so easy to define. Evidently it passed in a northward direction across the east part of Baylor County to Van Dorn's Crossing on Red River, which, as previously stated, was two miles east of the present Davidson Bridge.

In the late spring of 1859 Van Dorn started northward with his combined forces.[56] This time he was accompanied by fifty or more friendly Indians from the Texas reservations. His route led northwest across present Kiowa County and up the valley of Elk Creek to near the present site of Elk City. From here his route was almost due north to the Canadian River, following a course almost, if not quite, identical with the route that later became the Western Cattle Trail. He was accompanied as far as the Canadian by his wagon train, which he left in, or adjacent to, the northwest corner of present Roger Mills County, Oklahoma.[57] Here was the extreme north end of the Radziminski Road. The cavalrymen pushed on to a point about eighteen miles south of present Dodge City, Kansas, where they overwhelmed a force of almost a hundred hard fighting Comanches in what proved

53. *Surveyors' Records of Wichita County, Texas*, 1860, Vol. B, 32. The Radziminski Road crossed the north line of the Allen Hines survey in the northeast corner of Throckmorton County. This volume, which records many surveys in Young and Throckmorton Counties, is on file with the surveyors' records of Wichita County.

54. Portwood, H. W., Seymour, Texas. Personal interview, 1939. Mr. Portwood was in the employ of some of the largest ranches that were located in Wichita, Wilbarger, Baylor, Archer and Throckmorton Counties as early as 1877. He later became a large land owner in this area, and knew much of the topography and early land-marks of the country. He remembered the route of an old trail passing through points which definite records now show to be the Van Dorn Trail.

55. (a) Cummins, W. F., *Notes on the Geology of Northwest Texas*, 224.

(b) Roemer, A. S. Dr. Roemer, of Harvard University, called the writer's attention to the geological literature which establishes this point on the Van Dorn trail of 1859.

56. *Sen. ex. doc. No. 2, 1 sess. 36th Cong.*, 1859-60, Vol. II, 365. The account of Van Dorn's spring compaign (1859) is given in this document.

57. Thorburn, *op. cit.*, 318. A map shows Van Dorn's route north to Kansas.

to be a rather bloody fight. The battle does not concern us here, however. Suffice it to say that this campaign completed the chief accomplishments of the cavalrymen who were stationed at Camp Radziminski.

The counties of Wichita, Clay, Archer, and Wilbarger, and the territory on the north side of Red River saw much in the way of troop movements and their accompaniments in 1858 and 1859. In the spring of 1858 John S. Ford and his Texas Rangers, who together with Indian allies comprised a force of more than two hundred fighting men, followed much the same route that Van Dorn later traveled. As previously mentioned, Ford conducted a successful Indian campaign to the northwest of the point where Camp Radziminski was soon to be established. Accounts seem to indicate that Ford crossed this group of counties in a route at least near the course followed by Van Dorn.[58] Then, in September, came the larger Van Dorn troop movement over the trail which has already been described. Citizens from Grayson County, in pursuit of Indians, crossed these counties again while Van Dorn's tracks were still fresh.[59] Not long after the battle of Wichita Village young Ross returned to Fort Belknap in an ambulance, accompanied by his friendly Indians.[60]

In the fall and winter of 1858-1859, additional troops were sent up the trails to Camp Radziminski. In addition to these, the movements of the supply trains probably did more to keep the new roads open than all else combined. No doubt, at frequent intervals, couriers were sent along the trails between the army posts.[61] Perhaps they had secret camping places along the Red, the Wichita, and the Little Wichita Rivers. The Van Dorn trails were fast becoming the big road of the new frontier.

Then the roads performed the strangest function of all. In 1859 friction between the white settlers and the reservation Indians in Young and Throckmorton counties caused the Indians to be moved out of Texas. Both of these motley appearing caravans, with dogs, poor Indian ponies, papooses and all moved north to the Little

58. (a) Ford and Nelson Report in *Northern Standard*, June 12, 1858. Ford came by the Cottonwood Spring. He also crossed Red River below the mouth of North Fork.

(b) *Greer County Record*, 938, testimony of S. P. Ross. He also passed by Marcy's corner.

(c) Ford, John S., *Memoirs*, Vo. VI, 689-696.

59. *Northern Standard*, Oct. 16, 1858.

60. Wilbarger, J. W., *Indian Depredations*, 331.

61. *Northern Standard*, August, 1858. According to Special Order No. 71, Van Dorn was required to make semi-monthly reports.

Wichita over the Van Dorn trails.[62] More than eight hundred Indians from the lower reservation[63] camped at the Van Dorn Crossing in Clay County, August 4, 1859. From here they turned to the northeast, passing near the site of Petrolia, and camped on Red River, northeast of the present town of Byers. The Comanche Indians, almost four hundred in number, came northeast from their reservation on the Clear Fork, crossed the main Brazos near the northeast corner of Throckmorton County, passed near the location of Megargel in Archer County, and crossed the Little Wichita near the Archer-Baylor county line. They moved northeastward between the Big and Little Wichita Rivers. Soon they joined the other band of Indians in northeast Clay County, and the combined bodies journeyed to their new home to the north of Red River. Major Thomas accompanied the Indian movement with two companies of soldiers. John Henry Brown, with a temporary force of one hundred Rangers,[64] came with the lower group as far as the Van Dorn Crossing on the little Wichita.

In the fall of 1859 the troops were recalled from Camp Radziminski.[65] They returned to Camp Cooper, following a course near the west line of Wichita and Archer counties over the Van Dorn road.

The two years, 1858 and 1859, had witnessed almost a dozen movements of large bodies of men over the new army trails. Hundreds of tracts of land were surveyed in the new counties served by these trails.[66] As to the number of parties of private individuals who followed the wagon-roads out on the fast advancing frontier, there is no basis for estimate. Antelope, in the northwest corner of Jack County, became a village and Henrietta, the county seat of the newly organized Clay County little more than a year afterward.[68]

62. Neighbors to Washington, July 11, 1859. The route, according to this letter, of each of the groups of reservation Indians was northward over the Van Dorn trails to the Little Wichita River.

63. (a) Richardson, Rupert N., *The Comanche Barrier to South Plains Settlement*, 220.

(b) McConnell, Joseph Carroll, *The West Texas Frontier*, I, 282. Population figures are given in a report from Robert S. Neighbors. The population of the Indian reservations varied considerably; about 350 came from the upper reservation, and probably as many as 800 from the lower reservation.

64. Ely, George B., personal interview.

65. Price, *op. cit.*, 619-651.

66. *Surveyors' Records of Wichita County, Texas*, Index Volume. This shows the dates of surveys. Also, the surveying records of Archer, Baylor and Wilbarger Counties show a large number of surveys made during the year 1858 to 1860.

67. *Texas Almanac*, Galveston, 1860, 227.

68. McConnell, *op. cit.*, I, 187.

Then came the Civil War that set back the clock of northwest Texas history for at least a dozen years. In due time, vast bands of wild Indians paraded back into Wichita and adjoining counties.[69] The settlements in Clay County were abandoned.[70] The frontier village of Antelope seems to have lost its post office as well as its inhabitants, and, finally, the Young County organization was given up.[71] The few citizens who lived near Fort Belknap and on the Clear Fork to the west soon huddled together in little colonies, called forts, and weathered out the struggle between the States.[72] Strange Indian signs were marked upon the walls of the abandoned residences of Henrietta, and, a few years later, the old town was burned.[73] Truly the frontier had moved backward. About all that was left of the white man's civilization in Wichita County was Van Dorn's wagon road.

After the war white men again moved northward and westward, up the trails. By 1871 Dan Waggoner had come up from Decatur and was ranching the land to the west and north of the Van Dorn crossing on the Little Wichita River.[74] His range included about fifteen miles of the old Van Dorn Road and extended as far to the northwest as the present site of Wichita Falls. In 1873 Ikard established a ranch on the land later widely known as the K.M.A. oil field. Mount Bare, ten miles west of Wichita Falls, was the dividing point between the two ranches.[75] His headquarters were just northeast of Kadane Corner, at the old V-Bar Springs. This ranch was connected with Henrietta by way of the Van Dorn crossing on the Little Wichita. Ikard's old road passed just north of the site of Holliday and south of the location of Lake Wichita.[76] It crossed the Wichita River very near the bridge on the paved highway from the K.M.A. oil field to Electra.[77] From this

69. *Idem.*

70. *Idem.*

71. Commissioners' Court Records, Young County, Texas.

72. Biggers, Don H., *Shackelford County Sketches.* The diary of Sam Newcomb tells of life in Fort Davis on the Clear Fork, in 1864 to 1866. Numerous references are made to the other so-called forts.

73. Carter, *op. cit.,* 117.

74. McElroy, W. D. (Shinery), personal interview, January, 1940. McElroy, who lived just east of present site of Wichita Falls in 1874, remembered the date, because at that time Waggoner adopted the brand D71, showing the year when he arrived in Wichita County. Several years later, according to McElroy, Waggoner changed his brand to ꓷꓷꓷ.

75. *Ibid.*

76. *Deed Records of Archer County, Texas,* A:202-203. See footnote 1.

77. Banta, Mart, Kamy, Wichita County, Texas. Personal interview, 1938. Dr. Edwards lived on a ranch on the north side of the Wichita River, in Baylor County, in the early eighties.

old river crossing the early road turned westward up the divide between the Wichita River and Beaver Creek.[78] This westward extension was called the Good Creek Road, after a stream it crossed some miles to the west. It became one of the great trails into the buffalo country.[79]

The original Van Dorn crossing on the Big Wichita must have been abandoned, but the part of the original trail north of that point seems to have been used for some years.[80] A road from the Van Dorn Crossing on the Little Wichita extended northwestward and crossed near the falls of the Big Wichita and wound on up the valley to a point southwest of present Iowa Park where it joined the older trail.[81]

By 1880, and perhaps for some years before, the Van Dorn crossing on the Little Wichita had become one of the great cross-roads of early traffic.[82] The three roads above described converged upon this point from the northwest, and others approached it from the southeast. A road from Henrietta approached this early gateway from the east. The old Van Dorn Road, already described, came up from Brushy Mound near Bowie. A road led northwest from old Buffalo Springs,[83] and another came due north from Antelope. Later, perhaps just for good measure, a road came northeast from Archer City. There were minor crossings on the Little Wichita that were used at times, but for at least forty miles southwest of Henrietta there was no other important crossing. In the late seventies great bull wagons, piled high with buffalo hides, en route to Sherman, or herds of cattle headed north and west were not uncommon sights at the Van Dorn Crossing. Whether or not old Placedo was leading young L. S. Ross

---

Edwards lived on a ranch on the north side of the Wichita River, in Baylor County, in the early eighties.

78. Edwards, A. B., Henrietta, Texas. Personal interview, 1938. Dr. Edwards has lived on a ranch on the north side of the Wichita River, in Baylor County, in the early eighties.

79. Williams, O. W., "From Dallas to the Site of Lubbock in 1877," *West Texas Historical Association Year Book,* 1939, 7.

80. Marlow, J. B., Wichita Falls, Texas, and Myers, George S., Jolly, Clay County, Texas. See footnote 43.

81. Maner, "Lige," Jolly, Clay County, Texas. Personal interview, 1938. Maner pointed out the remains of this road to the writer, at a place about four miles slightly west of south of Jolly, Texas.

82. Edwards, A. B., Hilburn, R. S., Portwood, H. W., and many other personal interviews.

83. Hilburn, R. S., personal interview, 1938.

through an ancient Indian gateway when he selected this crossing on the Little Wichita, he was at least making a cross-road for many pioneer trails.

Major Steen crossed at this same point on the Little Wichita in laying out a road north to the Washita River at a time not very far from that of Van Dorn's Indian campaign.[84] In 1855 six companies of soldiers laid out a trail, partly new, from Fort Belknap all the way by the great bend of the Arkansas and north to Fort Riley, Kansas. Apparently they, too, crossed at the Van Dorn crossing.[85]

Other trails crossed and recrossed as the buffalo hunters and the cattlemen took over the development of the country, but Van Dorn holds fairly clear title to having established the first widely used wagon road in the Wichita area to the north and west of the California road. Thus did men, who sometimes wore plumed hats and silk sashes, and who rode fine Kentucky horses, lend greatly to the early transportation facilities of Wichita and her sister counties. Or, perhaps, more to the point, thus did a certain Mr. Duff and his teamsters "cuss" toughmouthed mules across mud holes and swollen rivers that history might record an almost ancient highway leading into the land of new cities.

84. Neighbors to Washington, July 11, 1859. *Neighbors Papers,* University of Texas Library.

85. *Greer County Record,* map opposite, 172.

XIV

JOURNEY OF THE LEACH WAGON TRAIN
ACROSS TEXAS, 1857*

Edited by J. W. Williams

It is difficult to separate the construction or routing of transcontinental wagon roads of the 1850-60 era from politics. The slavery issue overshadowed all else. Abolitionists were inclined to look with suspicion on any extension or improvements in southern wagon roads as a potential extension of slavery, while pro-slavery partisans were most likely to view such extensions with satisfaction. The party in power at Washington had the support of the slave states. Jefferson Davis, Secretary of War, and Jacob Thompson, Secretary of the Interior were in favor of improving a southern route to California. These facts added up to make a favorable political background for laying out roads across the southern rim of the United States. Milder southern winters and easier passes in the southern Rockies were physical factors that argued for the same result.

Senator Thomas J. Rusk of Texas was an ardent advocate of southern road improvement and was one of the central figures in securing the legislation that brought it about. Success came probably as much because of the physical advantages as because of the strong political urges of the day. The establishment of the Southern Overland Mail Line in 1858 across Missouri, Arkansas, Indian Territory, Texas, New Mexico, Arizona, and California, was the greatest victory of the Rusk group.

*The Records of this expedition are in the National Archives and are designated Records of Secy. of Interior Relating to Wagon Roads, 1857-87. Letters Rec'd. El Paso-Fort Yuma Rd., 1857-61. A microfilm copy was secured and was transcribed by Rupert N. Richardson, Jr. In editing the journal Mr. Williams has brought to bear on it knowledge derived from direct observation of the area as well as a study of it through State and County Archives for two decades. The accompanying map is the work and the contribution of Mr. Ernest Lee, Sr.—Editor.

A $200,000 appropriation made in 1857 for the partial rerouting and improvement of a road from the Rio Grande to Fort Yuma across southern New Mexico and Arizona, was secured by the same political forces. The Department of the Interior was placed in charge of the undertaking. James B. Leach was made superintendent of this road-making project and was the person under whose direction the wagons, work animals, and other equipment were assembled at Memphis, Tennessee, to make ready for the road repairing expedition soon to move to the Far West.

The wagon train set out from a point across the Mississippi west of Memphis on July 1, reached Little Rock, Arkansas, on July 19, and camped across Red River from Preston, Texas, August 22. They reached Fort Belknap, Texas, on September 1, Fort Chadbourne on September 12, and Horsehead Crossing on the Pecos River September 29. They reached Fort Davis on October 8 and Franklin, at the site of present day El Paso, on October 22.

They had chosen to follow Marcy's Trail, made on his return from New Mexico in 1849, most of the way from the time they entered Texas, at Preston, until they reached Fort Belknap, some sixty miles south of the future site of Wichita Falls. The shorter road between these points that cut across from Gainesville by Jacksboro to Belknap was not opened until 1858. From Belknap to the Pecos River, the Leach part had followed (with an exception west of of modern San Angelo) the road to be used the following year as the route of the Overland Mail.

At the Pecos they were confronted as they had been at Fort Belknap and at Fort Chadbourne with the choice between a northern and a southern route. From Horsehead Crossing, some forty miles south of the future Odessa, they could have gone up the Pecos River 120 miles to near the New Mexico line and followed Marcy's road near that line west to today's El Paso, a total distance of 306 miles, by the log of the Overland mail as established in 1858. Instead they chose the more southern road through the Davis Mountains, to be used by the Overland mail in 1859-60. This road also adds up to 306 miles. If one adds the 34 miles between Horsehead Crossing on the Pecos and Comanche Springs (Fort Stockton) to the 272.72 miles from Comanche Springs to Fort Bliss, which one may compile from the road logs found in Randolph B. Marcy's *Prairie Traveler** (pp. 289-90), the

*New York: Harpers, 1859.

road through the Davis Mountains reaches the sum of 306.72 miles. Obviously there was no choice as to distance, but the Davis Mountain route followed by Leach was better supplied with water.

That there was inefficiency and even questionable use of funds connected with this road working venture is somewhat beside the point here. Also the fact that the expedition split before it reached Texas allowing the slow ox-train under assistant superintendent D. Churchill Woods to get so far behind that it spent the winter at Fort Belknap is also almost out of the range of this study. In addition to these oddities, the fact that Leach let his paymaster M. A. McKinnon fall behind with the ox-train hundreds of miles away from the place where most of the funds were needed for the road work is a story that cannot be told in this paper. Chiefly to satisfy curiosity, let it be said that the Leach party did engage in road repairs which seem to have fallen short of the full objectives of the $200,000 appropriation. However, the purpose here is to employ the Leach journal chiefly as a study in local history and geography. With that purpose in view, let us now follow the expedition across Texas.**

[1857. Aug. 22nd. Camp No. 36.]***

Camp was pitched on the east bank of Red River, opposite Preston,[1] Texas, at 5 p.m.

N. P. Cook, Asst. Supt., having gone on in advance of the train had procured forage which was awaiting our arrival and which in the somewhat fatigued condition of the animals was of much service to them.

No accidents to note for the day. Health of camp good. For expenditure see voucher Nos. 147, 148 and 149.

[August 23rd. Camp No. 39 9⅓ miles sw of Preston, Texas. Dist. Travel. 9⅓ miles.]

All hands were aroused at an early hour this morning and at half past 6 a.m. the work of crossing Red River was commenced; and having

1. Old Preston was situated on the east side of what was long known as Preston Bend in Red River, upstream to the northwest of the present Denison, Texas. The site is now submerged beneath the waters of Lake Texhoma. Up to 1857 the river crossing and ferry of Preston was the most important in the immediate area. In 1858 the Overland Mail chose to cross the river at Colbert's Ferry, eight miles below. With the added prestige, Colbert's seems to have become the more important of the two.

**For a general account of the various wagon road projects see the very comprehensive and thorough study by W. Turrentine Jackson, *Wagon Roads West; A Study of Federal Road Surveys and Construction in the Trans Mississippi West*, 1846, 1859 (Berkeley and Los Angeles, 1952).

***Marginal notations in the original manuscript are here enclosed in brackets.—Ed.

the advantages of a good boat and skillful ferryman at this point at 12 p. m. the whole train was safely over the river.

A number of mules requiring shoeing the train was detained until two p.m. when the line of march was again taken up.

Preston, Fannin Co.,[2] Texas, bade fair at one time to become a place of considerable importance in a commerical point of view and even now is a well known shipping point during high water in Red River which is navigable up to this point. It has however lost its original promise of increase and is now a place of but little note, a small amount of business only being developed there. As the possible depot however for the supply of very large quantities of forage whether for the subsistence of stationed temporary or fugitive forces or bodies, Preston can present no ordinary claims in her own right. The shipping point of a county, rapidly increasing in wealth, popula-

[1857. Aug. 23rd. Camp No. 37, 9⅓ miles S. W. of Preston, Texas. Dist. Travel. 9⅓ miles.]

tion and agricultural resources, and within convenient distance of other counties . . . it can reasonably be calculated that any legitimate demand which might arise for grain and fodder at Preston could be supplied.

A gentleman residing near this place has the contract for supplying Fort Belknap with corn for this year.[3] The forage for the use of the

2. Originally, Preston was in Fannin County, but in 1846 Grayson County was organized from the immense area that was originally known as Fannin. Grayson County, in 1857 as now, included the site of Preston. The early-day town was the extreme head of the navigation on Red River, but shipping by river boat that far upstream was possible only when the amount of flow of the river was favorable.

3. The corn-wagon trains did much toward keeping the frontier military trails well marked, though they were primitive thoroughfares. In this instance it is evident the supply trains were following the Preston-Belknap road, over which Col. Leach and his train of wagons were to travel. In the main it followed the eastern portion of the road laid out by Randolph B. Marcy in 1849.

Marcy's road connected Preston on the Red River with Doña Ana on the Rio Grande, fifty miles upstream from the present-day El Paso. The eastern portion of it, with which we are here concerned, passed a few miles north of Whitesboro, three miles north of Gainesville (The Preston-Belknap road diverged to pass through Gainesville), and through the town of Saint Jo of today. To the west of this point, the old road traversed Montague County between the towns of Nocona and Montague and crossed the route of the Fort Worth and Denver Railway, west of Brushy Mound and some five miles northwest of the present Bowie.

Dipping into the southern part of Clay County, the early road passed a few hundred yards south of today's cross-road village of Buffalo Springs and, in southeast Archer County, crossed the path of the modern Wichita Falls-Jacksboro highway just

expedition while at Preston was purchased of this gentleman who speaks very intelligently and in the most glowing terms of the, as yet undeveloped but rapidly developing, resources of this section.

Having attempted to describe in this journal, as accurately as possible from day to day, the nature and resources of the Choctaw Nation or at least of that portion of it through which we passed, there remains no reference to be made to it, except to state the probability that in some seasons, portions of the road through which, or rather over which we traveled with ease and comfort will be found extremely bad in wet weather, nor will these difficulties ever be entirely obviated until that great necessity, the Pacific Railroad, shall stretch its length from one ocean to the other.

About to enter as we are upon the ''Plains'' all hearts begin to beat high with the hopes of pure air, better roads and finer times generally.

Leaving Preston our road lay for five miles over a sandy ridge, poorly timbered and badly watered, soil poor. We then entered again upon the Prairie and traveled something over four miles further, when camp was ordered to be pitched at Georgetown, a X roads town nine and one-third miles S. W. of Preston.

While crossing the four mile stretch of Prairie above referred to, a perfect spanker of a ''norther'' came blustering down upon us as if to give expression to its indignant protest against our entering upon the fields which for so long a time it and its bretheren had to themselves. It was a fierce little wind to be sure, its only apparent effect was to frighten the mules and retard for a short time the progress

---

south of the J. S. Bridwell ranch house at a point some five miles south of Windthorst.

Only a mile after entering Young County the Preston-Belknap road—which Col. Leach was following—curved southward away from Marcy's road, passing through the extreme eastern part of present-day Newcastle and terminating at Fort Belknap, three miles to the south. Marcy's road does not further concern us except that it lay to the northward and roughly paralleled Col. Leach's route all the way to the Rio Grande.

The route of the Preston-Belknap as well as this part of Marcy's road, which it follows, may be traced with reasonable accuracy from the old surveying records of Grayson, Cooke, and Montague counties and with great accuracy in Clay, Archer, and Young counties from the Texas Emigration and Land Company map of 1854, located in the Texas Land Office. See J. W. Williams, ''Marcy's Road from Doña Ana,'' *West Texas Historical Association Year Book*, 1934, pp. 128-153.

of the train. Col. Leach had contracted for forage at Preston, which was delivered at the camp.

Plenty of water for the use of the camp was obtained from a well at the house above spoken of, the proprietor of which kindly gave us the use of it. A branch near by supplied an abundance for the stock.

No accident occurred during the day. Health of camp good, several men were discharged to-day; five at their own request, the remainder for worthlessness. For expenditures see vouchers Nos. 150 to 160 incl.

[August 24th.]

The train took up the line of march at an early hour this morning. Our route lay almost entirely through a fertile Prairie country, with a number of settlements scattered along the line of the road, all looking comfortable and prosperous. At 3 p.m. camp was ordered to be pitched near Mineral Creek, where we found an abundance of water and excellent grazing for our stock. No accident nor any incident worthy of note occurred during the day's march.

[1857. Aug. 24th. Camp No. 38. On Mineral Creek, 16 miles East of Gainesville, Cook Co., Texas. Dist. Travel. 15 1/5 miles.]

As a pleasing incident of the evening may be mentioned a visit paid to the Superintendent by several of the neighboring farmers, who were unanimous in there praise of this section of country and spoke enthusiastically of its capacity for raising the smaller grains.

The corn crop is to some extent uncertain owing to the general prevalence of drouth about the time of the forming of the ear. The yield of wheat is from twenty to forty bushels to the acre.

Oats are grown without difficulty and yield readily and plentifully the first year the rich black Prairie soil is ploughed.

One gentleman had planted the Chinese Sugar Cane, which he said had grown finely and gave good evidence of containing large quantities of sacharine matter. He had ordered a mill & was determined to test the merits of the growth and the capacity of the soil & climate for making it a staple production fully. Land in this section of country is cheap & productive, much of it subject to entry & purchase from the State, of Texas, the people intelligent and hospitable inviting emigration & desirous of encouraging it. Mr. W. Wm. Travis the guide employed at Hot Springs in the service of the Engineer Corps reported himself today at this camp his service being no longer required as guide. He was therefore discharged. See voucher no. 161, Mr. N. P. Cook was on yesterday dispatched to Sherman, Texas, to

procure cash on a United States Treasury draft to meet current expenses. He rejoined the camp this evening & presented his account
[1857. Aug. 24th]
for traveling expenses. See voucher No. 162. The health of the camp is generally good. We have found the road today in good order.

[Aug. 25th. Camp No. 39. Dry Fork of Elm 8 miles S. W. of Gainesville, Texas. Dist. Travel. 23¼ miles.]

The train was ordered forward at 6 A.M. For a few miles our route lay through a rolling Prairie Country presenting no new features, when we entered the Eastern and smaller belt of the Cross Timbers. This tract of country is a growth of scrubby Post Oak. Some twelve miles in width interspersed with occasional stretches of Prairie, the soil poor and unproductive and offering few if any inducements to the farmer or grazier. The road passing through it is tolerable good. Passing through the ''Little Belt'' we again entered upon the Prairie & after traveling a few miles along which portion of our route were scattered a number of settlements we reached the town Gainsville the seat of justice for Cook County, Texas, a flourishing village & the center of a considerable trade. Having no occasion to halt here, our march was continued & at Sundown Camp was ordered to be pitched on the banks on the Fork of Elm. Eight miles S. W. of Gainsville we found water in abundance, & fine grazing of the stock.

The crops noticed along the line of today's travel were looking remarkably well. No accident occurred during the day. The health of camp is generally good.

[1857. Aug. 25th. Camp No. 40, On Elm Fork of Trinity, Texas. Dist. Travel. 16 miles.]

The order to move forward was given at an early hour this morning. Our route lay entirely through a high rolling Prairie, destitute of even the appearance of timber. We saw in the early front of the morning several antelope, the first that we have met with. A few hot headed Nimrods gave chase to them but they might, with as much chance of overtaking it, as well have chased the North Wind.

Not a settlement was seen on the line of to-days march until we reached the site of Camp No. 40. The soil had every appearance of fertility. The grazing was fine along the whole route.

After a march of sixteen miles we reached a point on the Elm Fork[4] of the Trinity River. Abundance of water, and fine grazing for

4. Camp No. 40 was at present-day Saint Jo in Montague County. The first name applied to the early village at this place was Head-of-Elm.

the stock, a splendid spring sending up cool streams of limpid water in bountiful profusion and the near neighborhood of the last "settlement" between Gainesville and Fort Belknap were so many inducements to camp that the idea of resisting them was not to be thought of and camp was pitched here.

Here a "squatter" within a few yards of the site of our camp has erected his house of logs and herds his few head of cattle, horses and hogs. He is a true type of that restless class who are always wanting a farm "further west." And to whom this country is indebted for the subjection and opening up to civilization of its frontier wilderness. About one mile from camp No. 40 is an extensive ranch kept up by hired men where are herded large numbers of cattle.

[1857. Aug. 21st. Camp No. 40. On Elm Fork of Trinity, Texas. Dist. Travel. 16 miles.]

This immediate section affords unexcelled advantages to the herder and grazier. We were joined at this point by the detachment of Engineers, who were detailed to survey the Air Line via Hot Springs, Ark. to Preston, Texas on the 8th inst., referred to in the Journal of that date.

The report of Mr. G. C. Wharton, 1st Asst. Eng. to whom the survey was confided, will be made patent to the Dept.

Having preceeded the arrival of the train at this point by several days the gentlemen of the survey have had a fine opportunity to amuse themselves in the pursuit of game which they all agree in saying, more than abounds in the neighborhood. No accident occurred during the day's march. The health of the camp is very good. No expenditures to note for the day.

[Aug. 27th. Camp No. 41. On Belknap Creek, Texas. Dist. Travel. 18 1/8 miles.]

The train was ordered to take up the line of march at ½ past 6 a.m. A march of about four miles brought us within sight of the Western Belt of the Cross Timbers.

They are first seen on this route, by the traveller westward and from the top of a commanding eminence,[5] from which the apparently interminable forests which stretch out as far as the eye can reach North, South and West seem dwarfed to shrubs. This view is general-

5. They were at the west edge of the prairie plateau, four miles west of today's town of Saint Jo and near the present Saint Jo-Montague County road. Just ahead of them for a distance of about eight miles lay the thickly-set belt of dwarf oaks known as the Upper Cross Timbers. It was broken hill country that included Jim Ned's Lookout and other prominent points which were hardly large enough to call mountains.

ly considered a very fine one, a number of mountain peaks seen to the North and South breaking the monotony of the general appearance of the county.

This belt of Cross Timbers is like the "Little Belt," mostly a growth of scrubby Post Oaks and may with propriety be regarded as a

[1857. Aug. 27th. Camp No. 41. On Belknap Creek, Texas. Dist. Travel. 18 1/8 miles.]

waste place affording camping and hunting grounds to several scattered and predatory bodies of Indians and offering no inducement to the farmer or laborer to attempt to make any use of it at least for the present. We travelled today eighteen miles and pitched our camp on Belknap Creek near what are known as Barrel Springs.[6] Here are found plenty of water for stock but very little in the springs for camp use. The springs might however if cleaned out and boxed up made to yeald a fair quanity of good water. We had a slight alarm of Indians from two of the Guard about nine o'clock tonight but as none were found, although a thorough search was made, it was thought to have been a false one. The Kickapoos are the savages of this "neck of the woods." The fresh fine bracing air of the plains seems to have driven all shapes of disease from the Camp. No accidents occurred during the day. No expeditures to note. Forage is plenty & good quality, yet it costs nothing.

[1857. Aug. 28th. Camp No. 42. On Prairie, Texas. Dist. Travel. 19⅓ miles.]

The train was ordered forward at an early hour. The country through which we travelled today was exceedingly rough & broken.

6. The fact that this camp site was at Barrel Springs on Belknap Creek seems to establish the location of this early-day camping place within the H. Ravestone survey a few hundred yards from the extreme west corner of that tract of land and nine airline-miles southwest of present-day Nocona.

Surveying records show that Marcy's road crossed the east fork of Belknap Creek at that point (Cooke County Surveying Records A-76. The H. Ravestone tract was surveyed August 1, 1851). It is approximately eighteen miles, measured by map along this old road from the town of Saint Jo to this point on Belknap Creek. Col. Leach reports his days journey from Elm Creek—Saint Jo by today's map—to Belknap Creek as eighteen miles. The map and Col. Leach's report thus corroborate each other.

However, there is a local tradition to the contrary. A spring on a branch of Salt Creek, some three miles northeast of this old camping place, was pointed out to the writer by residents of Montague County and was called Barrel Springs. A small rural school house (now abandoned) a mile further to the northeast was called the Barrel Springs School. Possibly the name was shifted from Belknap Creek to the spring on the branch of Salt Creek after the old Preston-Belknap road was abandoned.

Mountain peaks[7] of considerable height were frequently seen on either side of the road. The grazing capacities of this Country seem inexhaustible—the whole of today's travel being through as fine a range as the Herdsman could wish for. At 3 p.m. Camp was ordered to be pitched about 2 ½ miles east of Buffalo Springs[8] where water

[1857. Aug. 28th.]

was found in plenty in holes, also fine grazing. No accident occurred during the day. The health of the Camp continues good.

[1857. Aug. 29. Camp No. 43. On Branch of Little Wichita, Texas. Dist. Travel. 22½ miles.]

The train was ordered to take up the line of march at sun up this morning. We found the roads today rather heavy & rough. The country generally seemed well adapted to grazing. The want of Timber for building purposes will prove a serious draw back to the development of the advantages which this county possesses as a home for the Farmer & Grazier. The only timber procurable scraggy Post Oak & Dwarf Mesquite. We have seen nothing of any predatory Indians, although we hear of their occasional forays in this direction. After a march of more than twenty two miles Camp was ordered to be pitched near the branch of the Little Wichita, where we found fine grazing for the stock & good water in abundance. We passed today on the road number of places when water could have been procured. No accident occurred during the day, other than the breaking of the box of one of the wagon wheels which was at once replaced by one of the extra boxes kept on hand for such occurrences. The health of the camp continues generally good.

[1857. Aug. 30th. Camp No. 44. On Branch West Fork of Trinity, Texas. Dist. Travel. 21¼ miles.]

The order to take up the line of march was given at the usual early hour. The country through which we travelled today is much broken & very rough & rocky. Very heavy boulders of stone are scattered in the greatest profusion over the whole surface of this section. Much of the land however is well adapted to grazing, the grass upon it being

7. Queen's Peak, four miles north of Bowie, and Brushy Mound, five miles northwest of the same town, are evidently two of the mountain peaks referred to. The old road passed about a mile northwest of the former and along the north side of the latter.

8. Buffalo Springs in south Clay County was about a mile northeast of the present village of Buffalo Springs. Camp No. 42 was two and a half miles east of the springs.

inferior to some that we have seen. One of the men today killed a very large rattlesnake, the first that we have met with.

About noon we crossed the West Fork of the Trinity River. There was but little water in the bed of the stream & what there was, was very muddy, standing in pools. At 5 p.m. having travelled 21 miles Camp was ordered to be pitched on the branch of the West Fork of the Trinity in the bed of which were a number of pools of fine clear water. We found grazing on the Prairie nearby. Our teams began to manifest some indications of fatigue, several of them having been compelled to halt for an hour or two upon the road not reaching camp until some time after the remainder of the train. No accident occurred during the day. The health of the Camp is good.

[1857. Aug. 31. Camp No. 45. Cottonwood Springs, Belknap County,[9] Texas. Dist. Travel. 3 1/6 miles.]

It was after the usual hour this morning when the train was ordered forward in as much as it was intended to travel but a short distance. Having reached Cottonwood Springs, a point 3 1/6 miles west of Camp No. 44, Colonel Leach ordered camp to be pitched in order that our somewhat jaded animals might have a day's rest.

Cottonwood Springs lies a few hundred yards to the north of the main road at the base of a solitary Cottonwood Tree which has become quite a land mark in this country. We found the spring very unclean & in bad order. Some of our men cleared it out & it will now probably yield a fair supply of water.

One of the Teamsters came into Camp this evening with a fine Buck, the first killed by any member of the Expedition, although game abounds on every side of us. The Camp was visited this Morning by two Indians of the Caddo & two of the Delaware tribe. These tribes have reservations in this Neighborhood & are friendly & peaceful (?) in their relations with each other & the whites. They have considerable trade at Fort Belknap, in skins & articles of Indian

---

9. The cottonwood spring was located in Young County. The site, according to local tradition, was about a mile north of the village of Jean on a minor tributary of Salt Creek. It was beside the Archer City-Graham dirt road that preceded the modern paved highway (greatly changed in route) between those towns. The writer passed by it a number of times on that old road and noted the cottonwood trees but has no recollection of ever having seen water at the place. Evidently silt and sub-surface drainage of water wells has accounted for this drying up of such springs. The distance of this traditional site of the cottonwood spring from Fort Belknap is in accord with the Leach account.

Manufacture, are frequently employed as scouts and Guides by parties unacquainted with localities they may wish to explore. No accident occurred during the day. Health of the Camp good.

[1857. Sept. 1st. Camp No. 46 at Fort Belknap, Texas. Dist. Travel. 14 1/3 miles.]

The early air of this morning had the fine bracing touch of a fall day. The train was on the line of march at 7 a.m.

The face of the country along the line of today's travel is very greatly diversified—Prairie and Post Oak plots, Mezquite thickets and a section of fine rolling wooded lands, offering beautiful sites for farms having come under our observation. About noon we reached the ascent of the hill upon which Fort Belknap is situated. The hill is covered with a scrubby growth of Post Oak and a mixed undergrowth extending to the grounds of the Fort, the grounds of which, are laid off regularly and kept in fine order, present a pleasant contrast to the general appearance of the country.

Passing beyond the Fort and descending the hill to the bottom lands of the Brazos River,[10] which stream skirts the range of hills upon one of which Fort Belknap is situated, Camp was pitched by order of the Superintendent. Fort Belknap is handsomely situated and the old stockade buildings which formerly served the purposes of the garrison are being replaced by handsome buildings of stone which already begin to assume quite an imposing appearance.

The day has been unmarked by accident or incident. Last night however one of the guards detected a man, whether Indian or white man is not known, in the act of leading off a mule belonging to the Expedition. The sentry immediately fired upon the thief who at once dropped the rope and made good his escape. Unluckily for justice, the sentry was not so good a marksman as the exigencies of the case demanded. The animals having been confined to grazing for some time Col. Leach has deemed it expedient to purchase corn for them, for which the contract price at Fort Belknap towit—two dollars and nine cents was paid.

There is some complaint of sickness in Camp.

[Sept. 2. Halt in Camp No. 41.]

The superintendent ordered the expedition this morning to remain in Camp No. 41 for the day. The necessity of giving the animals an opportunity to recruit, of having mules shod and wagons repaired

---

10. The location of Fort Belknap—three miles south of present-day Newcastle in Young County—is well known. It is more than a mile due west from the fort to the Brazos River.

are the reasons for delay. Preliminaries for the exchange of some of the animals belonging to the expedition for some of those belonging to the government stock at Fort Belknap, were entered into between the commanding officer at Fort Belknap and Col. Leach. The men have been busily engaged during the day in unloading the wagons [1857. Sept. 2. Halt in Camp 46.] and spreading out the stores for the purpose of sunning and drying them, pleasant weather with which we are favored, affording fine opportunties for so doing. There are several upon the sick list today. Col. Leach is quite sick.

The expenditures for the day see vouchers Nos. 163 to 169 inclusive.

[Sept. 3. Camp No. 46. 1⅔ miles west of Fort Belknap, Texas. Dist. Travel. 1⅔ miles.]

The exchange of mules referred to in the Journal of yesterday was fully effective today. It was deemed expedient by the Superintendent Col. Leach to employ a man with the yoke of oxen to haul the wagons across the Brazos River there being no ferry privileges at this point. This plan saved the mule trains much severe labor and straining, the bottom of the Brazos being of a quicksand nature, and left them in a much better plight for the prosecution of the long and tedious journey before them. All of the work necessary to be done being completed and all arrangements made for departure, the work of crossing the wagons was commenced at 10 a.m. and at 3 p.m. the entire train was safely over the river and Enroute for Camp which was pitched one and two thirds miles, west of the site of Camp No. 46, in the prairie, [Sept. 3. Camp No. 46. 1⅔ miles west of Fort Belknap, Texas. Dist. Travel. 1⅔ miles.] where we found good grazing for our stock and plenty of water in pools along the bed of a flood water branch near Camp.

The contract which was entered into between Col. Leach on the part of the service of the expedition and J. M. Mire [or Mize] for the transportation of stores, and which went into effect on the 23rd of July, expired today. Mr. Mize was paid off and discharged and four mules and one horse purchased of him. A fine gray mare, one of the animals purchased at Memphis for the use of the Expedition, was today disposed of by the Supt. to one of the officers at Fort Belknap. Although a very fine animal her qualities did not recommend her for the service for which she was purchased. The price obtained was three hundred dollars.

No accident occurred during the day. The health of Camp is good. Col. Leach is still severely indisposed. It was found necessary to leave one of our men, Riley Hooper, at the hospital at Fort Belknap, he not being able to travel further. Col. Leach desires to return his grateful acknowledgments to the officers stationed at Fort Belknap for the courtesies extended by them to the officers of the E.P.& Ft.Y. Expedition during their stay at Fort Belknap. For expenditure see Vouchers Nos. 170 to 177 inclusive.

[1857. Sept. 4th. Camp No. 48. In the Prairie Belknap, Texas. Dist. Travel. 17 1/6 miles.]

The train was ordered forward at an early hour this morning. The face of the county over the whole of today's travel is much diversified, many portions of it offering considerable inducements to the farmer. A number of fine farms are adjacent to the site of Camp No. 47, the crops of which appeared to be doing very well. After a few hours, travel we reached what is known as "12 Mile Creek."[11] Here we found a number of new settlements, of what is known as Peters Colony.[12]

Stock raising is probably the principal object which these people have in view, and the country which they have selected is admirably adapted to the purpose.

After a march of seventeen and one sixth miles Camp was pitched near an arroyo containing water in pools and in the neighborhood of excellent pasturage. The supply of water at this point may it is thought be relied upon except in extraordinarily dry seasons.

The health of the Camp is generally good. Col. Leach remains very much indisposed.

[1857. Sept. 5. Camp No. 49. Two miles west of Camp Cooper, Texas. Dist. Travel. 18 miles.]

11. It was Six Mile Creek—six miles west of Fort Belknap by the Belknap-Phantom Hill military road. The road travelled was a part of the route adopted by John Butterfield and his associates in 1858 for the transport of the Overland Mail. The old road is popularly known as the Butterfield Trail.

12. Col. Leach had been travelling on Peters Colony lands for several days. He had entered this vast spread of land near Brushy Mound some five miles northwest of the site of Bowie in Montague County. Except for a few miles at Fort Belknap he had travelled on these lands across Clay, Archer, and Young counties and was yet to travel half way across Throckmorton County on this same great expanse of the real property. The Peters Colony lands were surveyed in 1853. It is due to the very complete field notes and maps made by their surveyors that we may now trace these old roads with accuracy.

The train was ordered forward at 7 o'clock a.m. Travelled about one mile and reached a wet weather creek which contained an abundance of water for any ordinary purpose in pools.

A man has posted himself here with a small amount of groceries and has had enterprise sufficient to dig a well, which affords a good supply of water, cool but not very pleasant to the taste. Being strongly impregnated with rotten Lime Stone. Beyond this point stretched out before us several miles of high plains covered with dwarf mezquite trees and rotten Lime Stone rock.

About five miles west of the site of Camp No. 48 we crossed a branch with large quantities of water in it. A short distance beyond this point we entered a tract of low Prairie land covered with a growth of small Mezquite timber and curled Mezquite Grass, almost entirely surrounded by a range of low rocky hills, a situation which could not fail to strike the most casual observer at first sight as an unsurpassed location for a ranch. We found upon approaching the defile which led through the western extremity of the range of hills above referred to that the natural advantages so patent to the observation had not been overlooked and that a Mr. Gibbons had established himself at this point from which place the last year supplied Camp Cooper with beef by contract.

At the outer base of the western segment of the range of hills above referred to is a very fine creek which in wet weather becomes a torrent and which in all seasons furnishes an abundant supply of water for all possible uses.

The road from this point westward to the site of our present Camp No. 49 is exceedingly rocky and hilly, the country very poor until we reached the bottom lands of the Clear Fork of the Brazos. We crossed the above mentioned stream about 3 p.m. and proceeding westwardly about two miles pitched Camp in a Cañon, through which our road defiles. Fine pasturage and a bountiful supply of water were close at hand. Near the point at which we crossed the Clear Fork of the Brazos, stand the buildings of one of the Comanche Indian Agencies,[13] a short distance north of this place is the village or

13. The Comanche Indian Reservation of four leagues of land lay on the Clear Fork of the Brazos River in the south part of Throckmorton County. Its northernmost boundary reached some nine miles north of the south boundary of that county, but a part of it extended down the east side of the Clear Fork to within three miles of the county line. The Belknap-Phantom Hill road passed just south of this part of the reservation. One may trace it to this point in the Peters Colony Map of 1854 now in

encampment of the Indians who are at present (or rather this particular tribe or portion of them at peace with the U.S.) and within sight of the Indian town is Camp Cooper a temporary military post established to hold the Indians in awe and subjection. But little reliance is placed in the good faith of these savages. Certainly a more villainous and treacherous looking set than the most of them have not often been seen. No time was allowed for the collection of statistics concerning their number & condition of Camp Cooper was visited during the day by Mr. N. P. Cook, Asst. Supt., who contracted while there with Mr. B. F. Dulingham for the delivery of certain quality of oats in camp & also made the necessary arrangements for having a wagon repaired which had been damaged on the road. No accident occurred during the day.

The general health of the Camp is good. Col. Leach's health is not so good as it has been & the symptoms are regarded as very unfavorable.

[Sept. 6th. Halt in Camp No. 49.]

The condition of Col. Leach's health was found to be precarious this Morning so much so as to preclude the possibility of his travelling without jeopardizing his safety. Orders were therefrom issued for the train to remain in Camp during the day. Col. Leach's complaint is a severe & obstinate case of inflammation of the bowls & stomach, the hitherto unfavorable symptoms and this morning very much agravated. Col. Leach desires to return his thanks to Dr. Sampson of the U.S. Army for professional aid rendered at this important juncture. As well as to Capt. Stoneman, U. S. Army for the proffer of quarters at Camp Cooper until he should have recovered, which offer however Col. Leach was constrained to decline. It was found today upon examination that the wagon which was spoken of in yesterday's Journal as being in need of repairs would require more time to put it

---

the Texas General Land Office. The agency buildings and the Indian village were in this end of the four leagues of land that was nearest the road. Camp Cooper was a little farther up stream.

Another road that indirectly connected Fort Belknap with Camp Cooper (The Camp Cooper-Caddo Agency Road) was opened shortly after the Peters Colony surveys were made and hence does not show on the old Peters Colony field notes. This road passed south of the head of Six Mile Creek in Young County (see Texas Land Office Map of Young County, March, 1897), and was evidently not the road followed by Col. Leach. It is mentioned here because of the usual confusion between the two roads.

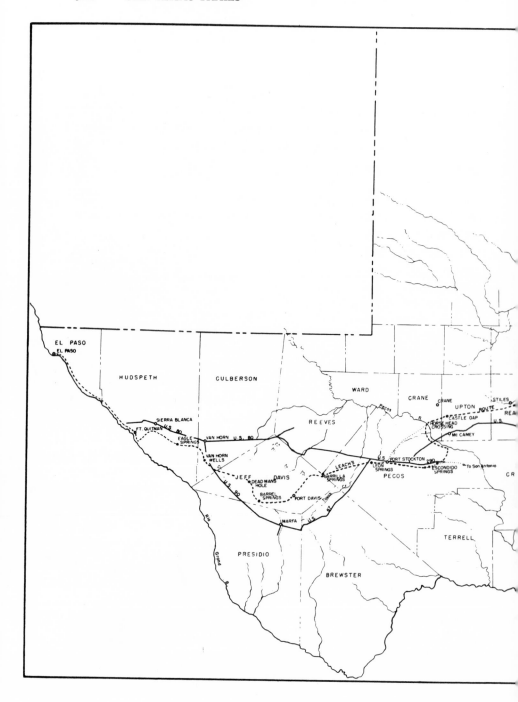

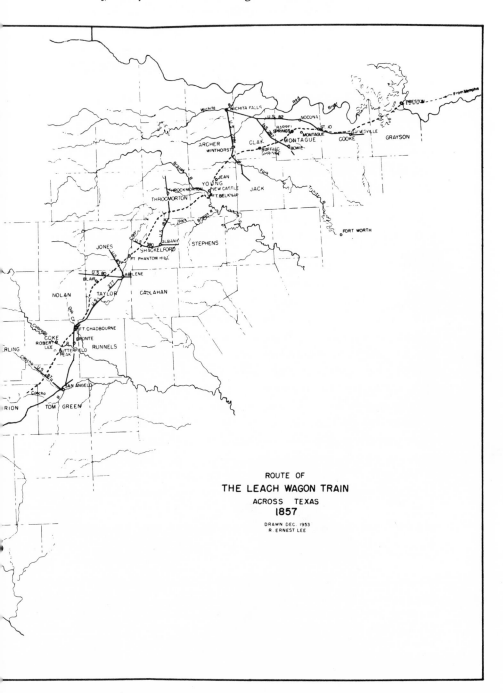

ROUTE OF
THE LEACH WAGON TRAIN
ACROSS   TEXAS
1857

DRAWN DEC. 1953
R. ERNEST LEE

in servicable condition than could be spared from the business of travel. Mr. N. P. Cook, Asst. Supt. therefore applied to Capt. Stoneman commanding officer at Camp Cooper for an exchange which was effected for which accommodation Col. Leach tenders his thanks to Capt. Stoneman. The camp was visited today by a number of Indians of the Delaware and Comanche tribes. The Delaware are regarded as before remarked as altogether friendly & reliable. The Comanche are looked upon with distrust & regarded as vindictive & treacherous, and but little reliance is placed upon their adherence to the disputations to the treaties to which they are parties. No accident occurred during the day. There is tonight a very slight if any improvement in Col. Leach's condition. The general health of the Camp is good. For expenditures see Voucher Nos. 178 and 179.

[1857. Sept. 7th. Camp No. 50. At Comanche Springs, Texas. Dist. Travel. 21 miles.]

Camp No. 49 was vacated at an early hour this morning and our muster and march commenced. Our route lay for several miles over a tedious, monotonous succession of Barren and rocky hills, covered with a short gre[?]en grass of a very poor quality for grazing a more inhospitable unpromising region for grazing one could hardly expect to see. Leaving these barren hills behind us and defiling through a narrow pass between some high hills covered with very heavy boulders of rock, we entered upon an extensive plateau of table land over which we travelled for a considerable distance and about sundown reached a point known as "Comanche Springs,"[14] a point deriving its appellation from the well known fact of its having formerly been a rendezvous for the tribe of Indians from which it takes its name. The tongue of report hath it, that this wild and desolate spot has been the scene of many awful murders, the victims having been travellers over this route at early day. The spring was in bad condition but was cleared out by some of the men and rendered fit for use. An abundance of water was found in pools lying adjacent to the spring which pools will

---

14. "Comanche Springs" must have been some two or three miles east of the Missouri, Kansas & Texas Railroad loading station known as Bud Matthews. This station is between Albany and Stamford in west Shackelford County. The old camp site was, according to the Leach journal, fifteen and a half miles east of Fort Phantom Hill. An Overland Mail stage stand (Smith's Station) was located a year later, twelve miles east of that old fort. The stage stand, according to the late J. A. Matthews, was on Chimney Creek about two miles south of Bud Matthews. These figures would locate Comanche Springs as above indicated east of Bud Matthews.

it should be presumed furnished water at all seasons of the year. They might however fail in seasons of long, excessive drought. The spring it is believed is unfailing.

[1857. Sept. 7th. Camp No. 50 at Comanche Springs, Texas. Dist. Travel. 21 miles.]

Camp was ordered to be pitched at this point, the train having made a march today of twenty-one miles.

Good grazing is found here. No accident occurred during the day. The general health of the Camp continues good. Col. Leach is somewhat improved. One man, Vel Musick, was discharged at this point for idleness and insubordination. He will tomorrow commence his solitary march back to the States.

For expenditures see Voucher No. 180.

[1857. Sept. 8th. Camp No. 51. At Fort Phantom Hill, Texas. Dist. Travel. 15⅓ miles.]

The train was ordered to take up the line of march at 7 a.m.

Leaving Comanche Springs we descended from the arroyo on which it is situated to a high rocky rolling Prairie or Plateau of table land over which our course lay for several miles where we found good water in pools which were in sufficient quantity to answer any ordinary purpose.

The train entered upon a succession of rocky hills & plains covered with a dwarfed Mezquite growth. Here also we found water. Indeed thus far along the whole of our route we have experienced nothing like a want of this great necessity, but have found each day an amount amply sufficient to answer all the purposes of a heavy emigration westward.

The condition of affairs is doubtless to be ascribed in great part to the unusually favorable season which has preceded us, and it may therefore with perfect truth and safety be said that after an ordinarily wet spring the emigrants westward may be well assured of finding an abundance of water along the route we are now travelling.

Proceeding upon our march over a stretch of rolling land very rocky and barren we saw when four miles distant from the spot the remains of the abandoned military Post Fort Phantom Hill, which was built by the U. S. 5th Infantry in 1851-52 abandoned in 1853 and burned and razed by the Comanche Indians almost immediately after its evacuation (such is our information). A curious interest as to the origin or cause of the name "Fort Phantom Hill" is doubtless suggested to the readers mind. Speculation upon the subject had been rife in camp ever since we heard of the post & of our approach to it;

but none of our surmises were correct. It is said that this singular name was given in derision of the locality selected for the Fort.

Nothing now remains of all the life and bustle which once thronged the precincts of Fort Phantom Hill. Bare and mouldering walls blackened and crumbling chimneys[15] and here and there the "fragment of a blade" reveal the site of the Post.

One thrilling memorial of the life that once was meets the travellers' eye as he leaves the ruins behind him. A little tombstone with a touching inscription sculptured upon the cold and passionless marble.

[1857. Sept. 8]

One mile east of the ruins of Fort Phantom Hill we crossed a fine stream of water which was recognized as a branch of the Clear Fork of the Brazos.

Camp was ordered to be pitched a few hundred yards west of the ruins of the old Fort. Water and forage were close at hand in abundance. Health of Camp good. The train was ordered to take up the line of march at an early hour.

Our route all day lay through and over an almost unbroken stretch of table land covered with a struggling growth of scrubby Mezquite. The soil is very poor throughout the whole of the line of today's travel, being a thin reddish clay partially covered with crumbling limestone. We saw however an abundance of water, having passed during the day four deposits of the indispensable requisite of travel, at either of which an amount could have been procured entirely sufficient for any purpose not altogether extraordinary.

It is proper however here to remark not only our reference to the amount of water which we have met with today, but in connection with the generally favorable nature of this report with regard to the great necessary along the route of our travel through Texas to which as

[1857. Sept. 9.]

the probable line of extensive travel and emigration for the future so much anxious attention at present is directed that the present season had been somewhat unusually favorable in regard to rains; and that is in dry season many of the advantages which we have been fortunate enough to meet with might be lacking.

---

15. The location of Fort Phantom Hill may still be identified by the ruins of these old chimneys some fifteen miles north of Abilene. See C. C. Rister, "The Border Post of Phantom Hill," *West Texas Historical Association Year Book*, 1938, pp. 3-14.

This is said in order that the future traveller along the route may fortify himself against surprise and inconvenience by making proper inquiries as to the character of the season in this section which precedes his setting out.

[Camp No. 52. In the Prairie. Dist. Travel. 17⅔.]

Camp was ordered to be pitched[16] about sundown on a small cañon where we found fine water in great abundance but very poor grazing the grass being scrubby and tough.

No accident occurred during the day. The general health of the Camp continued good.

[1857. Sept. 10.]

The line of march was taken up this morning at ½ past 7 a.m.

For ten miles our line of travel lay over a section of country entirely similar to that through which we passed on yesterday, a rolling plateau covered with a spare growth of dwarfed Mezquite.

[Camp No. 53. In the Prairie. Dist. Travel. 15 miles.]

We then entered a cañon lying between a range of rocky sterile hills, and after following its course for about five miles Camp was ordered to be pitched on the banks of a small creek, a spot which is rendered one of considerable interest by the fact that some time during last year the express mail rider between Camp Cooper & Fort Chadbourne, was at this point waylaid by a Camanche Indian, whose intent was murder or robbery; but who found that killing people was a game that two could play at and who lost his own life instead of taking that of another. The place is now called "Camanche Creek."

We find good grazing and an abundance of water at this point.

No accident has occurred during the day the health of the Camp is generally good.

[1857. Sept. 11. Camp No. 54, on Valley Creek, Texas. Dist. Travel. 14 miles.]

The train was En Route at an early hour this morning.

Our line of travel lay for some two miles up and through a gorge[17] between the hills at the base of which our camp of last night was pitched when we ascended an extensive plateau of table land.

The view from the summit was very fine. Far away to the north west and to the south west stretched divergent lines of lofty hills forming the sides of an immense triangular vista the base of which

16. A few miles west or possibly northwest of present-day Abilene.

17. This gorge is known as Mountain Pass in Taylor County, seven miles south of the village of Blair. Blair is a station on the Santa Fe Railroad. A stage stand was located near the north entrance to Mountain Pass in 1858.

was the dim and distant line where the horizon and the billowing prairies seemed to meet and mark the utmost height of human vision.

The soil of this Plateau is of the same sterile sandy clay that has composed the country through which we have travelled for the past two days. We met this morning with a dwarfed and scanty growth of cedar and mezquite.

One mile west of Camp No. 53 we happened upon a village of Prairie dogs, the first that we have seen. The active little denizens of this populous settlement were out of sight in an instant. During the day we passed through a number of these anomalous towns, and in-

[1857. Sept. 11. Camp No. 54, on Valley Creek, Texas. Dist. Travel. 14 miles.]

variably found the little folk living therein wary of the appearance of man retreating at a moments warning to their burrows where they are altogether safe from attack. One or two of these animals were killed by members of our party who remained behind and laid in wait for Stragglers.

We have seen enough of the facts in the case in our "Prairie Dog Experience" to warrant us in accepting as true what may seem to many the apocryphal tradition to the effect that rattlesnakes and owls make common quarters with Prairie dogs in their burrows. Several of these venomous reptiles escaped death by taking refuge in the underground habitations of their guests. One snake over six feet long was killed when half way in the earth.

The Prairie dog resembles in form, color and general appearance the large Fox Squirrel of the States, excepting as regards the tail of the first named animal which is not bushy and long as with the squirrel but stumpty and covered with short wiry hair.

The incisor teeth of the so called Prairie dog are precisely

[1857. Sept. 11. Camp No. 54. On Valley Creek, Texas. Dist. Travel. 14 miles.]

similar to the squirrels as is also his bark, short sharp, saucy and defiant and why the name Prairie Dog is given them is past conjecture.

The food of these animals consists of the grasses of the plains, upon which they grow extremely fat and are esteemed by some when in that condition an agreeable addition to the table.

Continuing our course over the table lands we arrived at Bluff Creek, a very fine stream. Along the meanderings of this water course are many extremely beautiful spots which if accessible to a refined population would be favorite haunts of all the lovers of nature as she appears in her [?] guise.

The general course of this stream is South East. It is a tributary of the Colorado.

Crossing "Bluff Creek" and continuing our march we passed over a hilly rocky country. A short distance west of Bluff Creek is a water course in which there was a very considerable quantity of water standing in pools. Our course then lay for a few miles through an ar-

[1857. Sept. 11. Camp No. 54. On Valley Creek, Texas. Dist. Travel. 14 miles.]

royo lying between a range of low rocky hills, when we crossed another very fine stream of water known as "Valley Creek" also tributary to the Colorado; immediately upon the western bank of which camp was ordered to be pitched.

The character of this stream "Valley Creek"[18] is singular. At the point where its waters cross the road it is but a few feet wide, and not more than six inches in depth. Not more than one hundred yards below the crossing, the stream having fallen in that distance some ten or twelve inches, it widens out into a still dark and deep pool forty or fifty yards deep and from two hundred to three hundred yards wide, the waters of which overhung and shaded by willows and other growth are full of fine fish as we abundantly proved; and following the stream down a short distance, the course of it being marked by a continual descent, we found a mimic lake, through the clear waters of which some eight or ten feet in depth, could distinctly be seen every object at the bottom, while at the same time we noticed several varieties of fish sporting in the limpid element, enough of which

[1857. Sept. 11. Camp No. 54 on Valley Creek, Texas. Dist. Travel. 14 miles.]

were taken to supply the tables of the different messes.

The land in the neighborhood of this camp (No. 54), beautiful as is the location and well calculated as it is to please the eye with the gleam of dancing waters, and the shade of forest trees, as well as the land along the whole of the line of todays travel, is poor and offers

18. Again Col. Leach had selected for his camp the approximate site of a future Butterfield stage stand. This mail line was established in 1858, a year after the Leach journey. The Valley Creek stage stand was located at the crossing of the Phantom Hill-Fort Chadbourne road on Valley Creek, a half mile from the west line of Taylor County. The route of the old road has been followed for this study in Shackelford and Jones Counties from the maps of these counties (Dated 1874) in the original plat book of the Texas and Pacific Railroad Company. The route in Taylor County came from the Texas Land Office map of Taylor County dated 1897. All three of the maps were compiled from old land records that were older than the maps themselves. For an account of the Butterfield Mail and Stage line see Roscoe and Margaret Conklin, *The Butterfield Mail*.

but few inducements to its settlement either by the farmer or grazier.

Game abounds throughout the whole of this section and our tables are plentifully supplied therewith.

No accident occurred during the day. The general health of the camp is good.

[1857. Sept. 12. Camp No. 55. At Ft. Chadbourne, Texas. Dist. Travel. 12 1/5 miles.]

The train was ordered forward at an early hour this morning.

After travelling about two miles we entered a belt of Post Oak, timber running North & South, several miles in width, the road leading through which was very heavy, being a deep fine sand rendering travel exceedingly tedious and difficult.

Leaving the timber we entered upon a plateau or tableland beyond which lay a range of high rocky barren hills, at the base of which we found a water course, known as "Fish Creek" which contained numerous large pools of water.

A few miles west of Fish Creek we reached Fort Chadbourne, a U. S. military post established in 1850 & 1851. The Fort grounds are located handsomely.

Continuing our course we crossed "Oak Creek" a water course lying at the base of the range of hills upon which Fort Chadbourne[19] is situated, when camp was ordered to be pitched immediately upon its western bank.

No accident has occurred during the day. The health of the camp continues good.

The expenditures are on vouchers No. 181 and 185 inclusive.

[1857. Sept. 13. Halt in Camp No. 55.]

Owing to the condition of the health of Colonel Leach it was ordered this morning that the train should remain in Camp No. 55 today.

Live Oak Creek, upon the western bank of which our camp is situated, is a flood water branch in which pools only of standing water are found. Heavy rains during the wet seasons of this country convert it into a roaring torrent. Its waters are tributary to the Colorado.

We were visited last night by a severe storm of wind and rain which sent several of our "Sibley tents" tumbling down upon the heads of the occupants. This was not the fault of the tents which are

19. Fort Chadbourne is within Coke County, three miles south and a mile west from its northeast corner. The rock ruins of the old fort still mark the site. This camp on Oak Creek was a short distance west or southwest of the fort.

admirably adapted to the purpose of which they are intended but of the careless men who pitched them.

No accident has occurred during the day.

For expenditures see voucher No. 186.

[1857. Sept. 14. Camp No. 65 in Pink Valley, Texas. Dist. Travel. 10⅓ miles.] The health of Col. Leach was found this morning to be in such a condition as to render his further progress before recovery entirely dangerous.

It was therefore ordered that the ambulance and team thereto belonging and a detachment of four men be detailed to remain at Ft. Chadbourne until Col. Leach shall be able to resume his journey and it is further ordered that the train proceed without delay under charge of W. P. Cook, Asst. Supt., taking what is known at this place as the Southern Route for El Paso via Fort Davis, Texas.

Note. It has for some time past been on contemplation to take what is known as the Northern route to El Paso from this point, but a careful examination of the relative advantages of the two routes has resulted in the selection of the lower route.

Reason. There is a better and plainer road on the Southern route, there being some seventy miles on the Northern route[20] over which there is scarely even a trail. It is also certain that corn can be purchased at Fort Davis, Texas and the stock is much in need thereof, being unused to heavy work on grazing food.

110[1857. Sept. 14. Camp No. 56. In Peak Valley, Texas. Dist. Travel. 10⅓ miles.]

It is further ordered that the train await the arrival of Col. Leach, or further orders from him at the first camp on Grape Creek a distance reckoned at about thirty two miles west of Fort Chadbourne. Pursuant to the foregoing order communicated to him by Col. Leach, Mr. W. P. Cook, Asst. Supt. ordered the line of march to be taken up this morning at 10 a.m.

Our line of travel today laid over a rolling table land upon which the

---

20. It is not clear exactly what is meant here by the northern route. Probably the Leach party had some notion of turning northwestward to Marcy's road and following it to El Paso. There were direct connections with that road both from Fort Belknap and from Fort Phantom Hill, but Col. Leach was now many miles past those forts. The next connection which he might have made with Marcy's road was by way of the little used route up the north Concho River. This dim trail probably intersected Marcy's road somewhere in the Big Spring country. It is, in round numbers, seventy miles by modern highway from the point where Col. Leach intersected the North Concho to the town of Big Spring.

grazing was tolerably good. The soil was generally poor.

Finding an abundance of good water standing in pools after a slow march of ten and one third miles, Camp was ordered to be pitched in a locality to which the name of Peak Valley[21] has been given. The grazing in the vicinity is good.

Having up to this time neglected to make any particular reference to the element of fire wood it may be remarked that we have experienced no difficulty as yet in obtaining sufficient for our

[1857. Sept. 14.]

purpose from the Mezquite growth of the country. No accident occurred during the day. The health of the camp continues generally good.

[Sept. 15. Camp No. 57, 47½ miles west of Salt Fork of Colorado, Texas. Dist. Travel. 10.6 miles.]

The train was ordered forward at an early hour this morning.

Our line of march lay for some few miles over rolling table land, the grazing upon which was tolerably good, when we entered upon the bottom lands of the Salt Fork of the Colorado River about one mile in width at this place, passing over which we crossed the Salt Fork, which was at a low stage of water and not more than fifteen or twenty yards in width.

At the season of flood water the waters of the Salt Fork are represented as being very brackish and disagreeable. At its present stage, they are not so however.

The train safely over the stream, we entered upon a low marshy prairie which, owing to recent heavy rains, and the character of the soil was in such a condition as to render travel tedious and difficult.

[1857. Sept. 15. Camp No. 51. 4½ miles west of Salt Fork of Colorado Texas. Dist. Travel. 10.6.]

Several of the teams stalled and it became necessary partially to unload the wagons to get them into Camp, which was pitched about 4 P.M. at a point in the Prairie four and a half miles west of the Salt Fork.[22] Some of the best teams were selected to return for the goods left behind over which a competent guard had been placed and it was late in the evening before all were safely in camp. The grazing at this point is good with plenty of good rain water. No supply at this point

---

21. Map measurements place this camp site about four miles northwest of the present-day town of Bronte in Coke County.

22. This camp site was some six to eight miles south of Robert Lee near the Robert Lee-San Angelo highway.

in dry weather can be calculated upon. No accident occurred, during the day. The health of camp good.

[1857. Sept. 16th. Camp No. 58. 3.4 miles.]

Heavy rains fell during the later part of yesterday afternoon and continued through the night rendering it necessary to remain in camp today until 1 o'clock P.M. when camp was ordered to be struck and the train put in motion. The condition of the Prairie, for road there was none,[23] was such as to compel the drivers to double teams, hitching ten mules to each wagon and even then finding it a difficult matter to move the train a distance of four or five miles.

This however was at length accomplished and at 5 P.M. camp was pitched in a [?] gorge at the base of a range of high rocky hills where we found fine grazing and owing to the rains of last night and yesterday a sufficiency of water.

A more eligible situation for a camping ground than we find ourselves in tonight cannot be imagined, if so it were that the water which is abundant now were only permanent. But such is not the case it is believed.

An incident rather laughable in its finale occurred this evening.

The officer of the guard for the night, being a prudent sort of man, and knowing the danger of being caught napping by the

[1857. Sept. 16th. Camp No. 58. 3.4.]

Camanche Indians in the very centre of whose haunts we now are, ordered the guard shortly after dark (without having made any one aware of his intention to do so) to fire off their muskets, fearing lest the damp weather had spoiled their priming and wishing to make assurance doubly sure by reloading.

The order was obeyed, and in an instant the camp was a scene of indescribable confusion, and to the credit of the men be it spoken every man except two stood to his arms and seemed ready for what might follow.

The true cause of the row was quickly explained; but it was discovered afterwards that one person, from whom although nothing else could have been expected, had sought a hiding place in the tall bear grass near the office tent, where he was speedily joined by another, a great tall strapping booby who tremblingly asked in a

---

23. The Leach journal later contradicts this statement that there was no road. The party was following a little-used road. It was in the wrong position geographically to have been used as an important supply route either for Fort Chadbourne or for any other fort.

whisper D—do you think we shall be safe here? The former told the story on the latter but would not divulge the name. Could our knowledge however be as clear as our suspicions are strong containing the identity of the individual, he would not have such an easy time as he might have under different circumstances.

[1857. Sept. 16. Camp No. 58.]

Towering immediately above the site of Camp No. 58 is a lofty hill with a castellated turret crowning its summit[24] the picturesque and massive proportions of which seem as though they might be the results of the labors of giants working out the designs of Titanic architects. The name of Castle Mountain was given to the peak.

No accident occurred during the day. The health of camp continues good.

[Sept. 17th. Camp No. 59 on Grape Fork of Concho River, Texas. Dist. Travel. 7.1.]

The train was ordered to take up the line of march at ½ past 7 A.M.

Corrorborrative of the statement in the journal yesterday to the effect that the site of Camp No. 58 could not be relied on as a regular camping ground it may be remarked that the pools in which last night an abundance of water was to be found barely afforded this morning a supply sufficient for camp uses.

Leaving Castle Mountain and passing through a valley of about one mile in length we commenced the ascent of a remarkably steep and rocky hill[25] the most serious natural obstacle which we have as yet

[1857. Sept. 17. Camp No. 59 on Grape Fork of Concho River, Texas. Dist. Travel. 7.1 miles.]

had occasion to encounter. The ascent however having been ac-

---

24. This must have been Butterfield Peak, nine miles south of Robert Lee. The fact that Col. Leach's party went from Fort Chadbourne thirty miles to Grape Creek, as did the Butterfield stages just a year later, leaves little doubt that his road was the same, or at least nearly the same, as that to be used by the Overland Mail.

Tom Green County surveying records (Vol. C, p. 188) show that the mail line crossed the south boundary of the Caldwell County School Land, and Coke County surveying records (Vol. 2, p. 63) show that it crossed the east line of Survey No. 10, on which Butterfield Peak was located. The Overland Mail ascended Buffalo Creek into the mountains and passed over the divide into the valley of Grape Creek. Col. Leach also went over the divide into the valley of Grape Creek.

25. This steep climb out of the valley of Buffalo Creek is evidently the same point at which the draft animals pulling the first west bound Overland Mail coach stalled at 2 A.M. on September 24, 1858. Ormsby, a New York Herald reporter, was a passenger. He described graphically the delay until morning on this uninviting piece of road. See Hybernia Grace, ''The First Trip West on the Butterfield Stage,'' *West Texas Historical Association Year Book*, 1932, pp. 62-74.

complished we found ourselves upon a lofty plateau of table lands some two or three miles in length from the western extremity of which one of the most beautiful valleys, apart from its only lack of wooded hill sides to make the forming of the picture complete, that one ever looked upon appeared to our view.

Descending the slope and entering the valley we found for the first mile or two a sandy and not very fertile soil the grazing upon which however was excellent.

About three miles from the eastern entrance of the valley to the south of the road, will be observed a heavy ledge of rocks, at the base of which lies a magnificent reservoir of water as clear as crystal and which is probably the first water which will be met with a dry season after leaving the Salt Fork of the Colorado.

On either side of the main valley between the hills which hemmed us in, stretched out smaller valleys all of them beautiful. We momentarily caught glimpses of herds of deer and antelope which as they bounded lightly along at the first sight of their natural enemy, man, lent grace and animation to this lovely scene where nature itself [1857. Sept. 17. Camp No. 59. On Grape Fork of Concho River, Texas. Dist. Travel. 7.1.] seems moved into amorous silence by the charms which the Almighty has lavished upon this favored spot.

At a point about opposite to the reservoir of water above referred to, the road crosses a ravine or arroyo which has the appearance of the bed of a water course during the rainy season.

We found no water in it however. The road crosses this ravine several times between this point and the site of our present camp, No. 59. The beauty of this valley increases as we proceed towards its western extremity. The character of the soil changes and becomes a rich black loam and, if such an expression may be allowed, seems to be of almost fabulous richness. Indeed its fertility seems inexhaustible; groups of umbrageous live oaks whose outspreading branches might serve as a shelter from the noonday heat are disposed picturesquely over the surface of the valley and to the south of this road. Grape Creek either sleeps quietly in deep dark pools beneath overreaching boughs where trout and perch and cat and many other varieties of fish are lying in constant want for a chance to bite, or flashes merrily over a rocky chasm to rest again in another mimic lake, while just over and beyond these beautiful waters or jungles of mat-

[1857. Sept. 17. Camp No. 59. On Grape Fork of Concho River, Texas. Dist. Travel. 7.1 miles.]

ted brush and tangled vines, the watchful ear can catch the echo of the faint footfall of the antlered monarch of the woods, while momentously the piping twit of the wild turkey alternates with the wolfs long howl, and in the stops and pauses of all these sounds the listener can cheat himself into the belief that he heard the music of his native fields in the familiar whistle of the quail.

A little more than six miles west of the point at which we entered the valley, camp was pitched[26] by order of the Asst. Supt.

In less than two hours after camping every mess table was bountifully supplied with fish. Trout, Perch, catfish, and soft shelled turtle were taken in the greatest abundance with ease. Two antelope were brought into camp, all which served to cheer the inner man with something of a better meal than the every day one of camp life.

No accident occurred during the day. The general health of the camp is good. As was intimated in the journal of the 14th inst. the train will await at this point the arrival of orders from the Supt. Col. Leach.

[1857. Sept. 18. Halt in Camp No. 59.]

Pursuant to the hitherto mentioned instructions of the Supt. the train remained in Camp No. 59 today.

The early part of the morning was fair and pleasant and was profitably employed by some of the men in mending Harness, repairing unimportant damages to Wagons, and overhauling and [?] the stores while others were engaged in exacting tribute of the woods and waters; and the condition of the larders of the different messes at night showed that success had attended all their efforts.

About eleven o'clock A.M. Col. Leach rejoined the train much improved in health and of course at once assumed the duties of his position. If the valley of the Grape Fork had its locality in some accessible region, one not so entirely isolated, it could not fail to be the center of a flourishing agricultural community. That it eventually be such, situated as it is, is not at all improbable. The lack of timber for building purposes can be obviated by the use of Stone, of which all of the permanent buildings attached to the military posts on the Texas

---

26. The distance of this camp from the extreme head of East Grape Creek places it down that stream near the common boundary line of Tom Green and Coke counties. It could not have been far from the point at which the Grape Creek stage stand was located a year later.

frontier are constructed, and inexhaustible quantities of which can be procured without difficulty from the hills which form the lateral boundaries of the garden spot.

No accidents occurred during the day. The health of the camp continues good.

[1857. Sept. 19th. Camp No. 60 on Concho River, Texas. Dist. travel 8 miles.]
The order to resume the line of march was given by the Supt. at an early hour this morning.

Our route lay for some two miles down the valley of the "Grape Fork" when the road suddenly deflected to the Northwest, and we wound around the base of a hill of considerable size, gradually ascending as we did so, until having reached the summit of an extended inclined plane, the road suddenly deflected to the West and we entered a tract of bottom land covered with a somewhat dense growth of Mezquite timbers very small however & fit only for firewood.

A march of __ miles brought us without the occurrence of any accident to the Concho River, crossing which without difficulty, camp was ordered to be pitched on the western bank of the stream.

The banks of the Concho are thickly wooded with large Oak & Pecan trees as well as with a very dense under-growth. The lands lying contiguous to the stream seem to be measurably well adapted to the growth of the cereals. The stream at this point is from fifteen to twenty yards in width at present, although it may be presumed that at Flood tide the volume of its waters is much greater than at present. Fish of the same species as that found on Grape Fork abound in this stream.

The health of the camp is good.

[1857. Sept. 20th. Camp No. 61 on Concho, Texas. Dist. travel. 19 miles.]
The morning broke dark & lowering, a fog unusually heavy rendering all the surroundings of the camp obscure in their outline and uncomfortable in fact as well as in appearance. The order to take up the line of march however was passed along the train at an early hour and in a few moments we were en route.

Soon after leaving camp a dull drizzling rain set in which with the fog already spoken of rendered travelling in the vast expanse of Prairie in which we were, absolutely hazardous, so difficult was it to distinguish our surroundings. The road or trail at this point is very indistinct.[27] About two miles West of the site of Camp No. 60 we cross-

---

27. The statement that the road was indistinct is evident that Col. Leach was

ed a ravine containing large quantities of water in pools.

Six and one half miles West of the site of Camp No. 60 we entered a pass between a range of lofty hills, one of which, a conical peak, is a noticable landmark of the route.

This park lies to the north of the road.

Defiling through the pass our route lay through a section of Mezquite flats barren & sterile, upon which we saw an area of several hundreds of acres which had been taken possession of by a luxuriant growth of the two varieties of the Prickly Pear common to this section of country. Both varieties were in fruit bearing season; the fruit of one is as large as the egg of a goose, of a very deep, rich purple color.

[1857. Sept. 20. Camp No. 61, Concho, Texas. Dist. travel. 19 miles.]

The other about the size of a hen's egg and of a vermillion tint. Each variety is armed with innumerable diminutive thorns disposed in clusters on the body of the fruit, and they have the power so as to penetrate through clothes [?], and even through the best buckskin gloves, as to render extreme caution in handling the fruit a matter of necessity, the annoyance arising from the pricking of the thorns being extreme.

The fruit itself is insipid though many profess to like its flavor.

Lizards, centipedes, tarantulas & rattlesnakes find here a favored region, judging from the numbers we meet with every day.

The same description of country prevailed until we reached the __ Concho[28] having travelled a distance of __ miles.

---

following—not opening—a road. It is also evidence that the road served very little traffic.

The Leach journal is proof that a road from Fort Chadbourne across the Colorado River by way of Grape Creek reached across the North Concho before the Overland Mail road was established along the same route. The very thorough work of Roscoe and Margaret Conklin (*The Butterfield Mail, 1857-1869*, I:345, 352) indicates that most of the Butterfield road south of the Colorado was new and company-built. The Leach journal would seem to modify the Conklin statement and indicate that the Leach route and the Butterfield route were probably the same as far as Grape Creek and that they did not vary greatly in the remainder of the route. However, the fact that Col. Leach traveled nineteen miles between the two branches of the Concho would indicate that he reached the Middle Concho near the mouth of Dry Creek several miles west of the probable route of the Butterfield line.

28. This was the Middle Concho, probably near Dry Creek. It is most difficult to trace Col. Leach's exact route from this camp to Horsehead Crossing on the Pecos River, from September 20 to 29. His daily advance during those nine days of travel add up to make a total of 132.5 miles, while the distance between these points by the Overland Mail road of 1858 was a scant hundred miles. The heavy rains that came

This stream has but little to distinguish it from the tributary near which camp No. 60 was pitched.

The adjacent lands are not, judging from general appearance, adapted to farming purposes.

Very large Pecan & Oak trees are numerous in this vicinity and fine fish are abundant in this stream.

No accident has occurred during today. The general health of the camp is good.

[1857. Sept. 21. Camp No. 62 on The Plains of Texas. Dist. travel. 17.]
The train was ordered ahead at an early hour this morning.

Our route lay for some eight or nine miles over an extremely barren plain unmarked by any one feature of interest. When we reached the "False Concho," a stream resembling much in its general characteristics the streams already spoken of in this journal as the "North Concho" and "Middle Concho." Like these streams too the "False Concho" abounds in fish. The character of the country upon which we then entered differed but little from that portion over which we passed between the "North and Middle Conchos," being sterile and arid.

About three o'clock p.m. a storm of wind, rain & hail of great severity overtook us while yet upon the march; such was the quantity of water which fell in the space of about one hour, that it converted the road, which at the commencement of the rain was firm and good, into a quagmire, through which it was a matter of the greatest difficulty to urge the teams. A halt was therefore called and camp ordered to be pitched about 4 p.m. Enough water for cooking purposes was gathered from rain pools, although not without difficulty.

---

must have caused him to travel out of his course part of the time—probably to the south of the Middle Concho. There were well beaten roads that converged on the Middle Concho and extended by a single route across the plains to Horsehead Crossing. This single route was one of the trails followed by the gold-seekers of 1849. Col. Leach traveled on part of this road. He passed through Castle Gap—an unmistakable land-mark—and on to Horsehead Crossing on the Pecos River as had the prospectors of 1849. But the earlier part of this leg of his journey is all but impossible to trace.

The gap through the Castle Mountains is located in sections 91 and 96 in Block Y and were original Gulf, Colorado and Santa Fe Railroad surveys, some twelve miles northwest of the present town of McCamey. Horsehead Crossing is located in Section 37, Block 1, Houston and Texas Central Railroad lands and is twelve miles somewhat south of west of the Gap. See the field notes of surveyor J. W. Armstrong in Vol. D, pp. 123-125, Tom Green County surveying records.

A norther in the meantime came sweeping down upon us, which rendered our situation exceedingly disagreeable.

[1857. Sept. 21. Camp No. 62 on the plains of Texas. Dist. travel. 17.8.]

The cold and wet together made up such a condition of affairs as one might well be glad to escape from. By night however the best disposition was made of everything that could be made, and after such an evenings work as we had had it may well be presumed that camp was soon quiet.

No accident occurred during the day.

The general health of the camp is good.

The road, or more properly speaking, trail at this point is quite indistinct.

[1857 Sept. 22. Camp No. 63 on tributary of Concho, Texas. Dist. travel. 1.67.]

The heavy rains of yesterday afternoon continued through the greater part of last night and the elements were at day-break this morning in every respect a threatening aspect. The clouds fled away however before the morning sun and finding that we were encamped at a distance of only two miles from the "Tribs. of Concho" the Supt. ordered the train forward.

Having reached the bank of the river, camp was ordered to be pitched, it being deemed advisable by the Superintendent to allow the ground to settle after the heavy rains of yesterday and last night, before undertaking a days march.

The Concho at this point differs in no perceptible aspect from the portions already referred to in this journal. The soil of the bottom lands is doubtless susceptible of cultivation, and the Oak & Pecan growth upon the banks is sufficient to afford a very considerable amount of timber. The rock of the adjacent hills would afford an inexhaustible supply of building material.

During the day the men have been employed in overhauling & drying.

[1857. Sept. 21st. Camp No. 63 on Concho, Texas. Dist. travel. 6.7.]

Stores and filling water casks, it being delivered from information which we have received of the country immediately before us, that we will necessarily be compelled to camp tomorrow without water. Fish abound in this portion of the "Concho," as in all the other parts of the "Concho" with which we have been made familiar, and large quantities have been taken through the day. Game is also plentiful.

No accident occurred during the day. But little if any complaint of sickness in camp.

[1857. Sept. 23rd. Camp No. 64 on the Plains, Texas. Dist. travel. 14 miles.]

The morning came over the Eastern hills bright and beautiful: no cloud obscured the horizon. Away to the westward however we saw a faint and filmy vapour as it seemed to be floating lazily above the seemingly interminable prairies that stretched away beyond it. That it was smoke from the watch fires of the Indians no one doubted for an instant. All hands were on the *qui vive*. The order to prepare for marching was given. The water casks were taken from the river in which they had lain over night to secure their hoops and staves. The tents were struck and bundled into the wagons and the word forward given. Following up the course of the stream, upon which we were encamped last night for about three miles at which point a good ford was found, the train was crossed without accident, and at once emerged into the open stretch of ascending table land beyond. Eager looks were at once sent in search of the watch fires, the smoke of which we imagined we had seen, but no such fires were visible. The hazy vapor still was there, and a solution of its cause and nature was now sought for. It was at hand.

[1857. Sept. 23rd. Camp No. 64, on the Plains, Texas. Dist. travel. 14 miles.]

Directly above our heads floated in numbers past all efforts at computation swarm after swarm of the Mormon grasshopper, insects about three quarters of an inch long and of a yellowish gray color. They were migrating, it is supposed from fields and pastures they had already desolated to new fields.

Looking upwards, those immediately above our heads glittered like snow flakes; those in mid air gleamed in the Sunlight like spangles of Silver, while far above those, countless numbers hardly perceptible could be compared only to the motes that people the sunbeam, beyond us. The distant legions floating in the sunlight took the form and hue and indistinct outline of a "morning exhalation," and far off to our extreme right, rising and sinking, dilating and contracting with every breath of wind, immense clouds of these insects floated high above the mountain tops. Wherever they alighted an arid waste of leafless stalks showed their destructive power.

Leaving the river, our course lay up the gradual ascent of an extremely sterile stretch of table land, rocky and almost verdureless.

[1857. Sept. 23rd. Camp on the Prairies, Texas. Dist. travel. 14 miles.]

Proceeding about two miles after a rapid descent we crossed a deep dry ravine, the drainage doubtless of the adjacent mountains. Again ascending, about five and one half miles west of the river we found water in pools (not permanent). Our animals were watered here and after a further travel of about eight miles, Camp was ordered to be pitched in the prairie. Far off to our right (or to the North rather) at what distance it is not known, we saw dimly the outline of the belt of timber, marking the course of the Concho. A fine lot of game was brought into camp during the day.

No accident occurred. The health of the camp continues generally good.

[1857. Sept. 24th. Camp No. 65 On the Plains, Texas. Dist. Travel. 15.5 miles.]

The train was ordered forward at this early hour this morning. Our route lay for some ten miles over a barren plain with nothing to vary the monotony of travel except the crossing of one dry ravine, part of the drainage of the mountainous region surrounding us. Eleven miles west of the site of Camp No. 63, [No. 64?] we crossed the bed of a tributary of the Concho and two miles beyond this point crossed the same stream [?] again. While the train was crossing, a number of the party had fine sport in trout taking, using grasshoppers for bait, at which the fish bit ravenously.

Continuing our course until six p.m. camp was ordered to be pitched on the prairie. A few hundred yards to the south of the camp lay a body of the waters of the "Concho" a natural basin, some twenty or thirty yards in width, several hundred yards long and ten or fifteen feet in depth. Cat fish weighing from twenty to thirty pounds, Eels of an unusually large size and Trout and Perch were taken here in great abundance.

The general character of the country over which we have travelled today was sterile. The hunter and fisher may find all the sport they can desire in this region however.

[1857. Sept. 24th. Camp No. 65 On the Plains, Texas. Dist. Travel. 15.5 miles.]

The grazing at this point is tolerably good.

No accident has occurred during the day. There is very little complaint of sickness in the camp.

[1857. Sept. 25th. Camp No. 65. Near Head Waters of Concho River, Texas. Dist. travel. 7.5 miles.]

The train was ordered to take up the line of march at a very early hour. Our route lay for some miles parrallel to the course of the stream upon which Camp No. 64 was pitched, about four miles from the site of which, we crossed a dry ravine, the road at this point deflecting slightly to the North, the course of the stream at the same time deflecting to the South.

A short distance beyond the ravine above mentioned the road diverged, a well beaten track lying to the South and one equally plain to the Northwest. It was decided to take the Northern tracks. This course led us up the ascent of a precipitious hill from the top which we saw upon the summit of another, several miles distant, a number of what might have been taken for Sibley tents of snow white material, gleaming in the sunlight. A knowledge of the customs and duties of surveyors, in such countries as that through which we are travelling, however, revealed them to us as land marks. Having reached the base of this hill, it was made apparent upon a reconnaisance of our surroundings that the wrong road had been taken by the train. A commission of explorers immediately set out for the purpose of discovering the correct road. This was luckily quickly effected the train turning marched directly to the south at nearly a right angle

[1857. Sept. 25th. Camp No. 65. Near head waters of Concho, Texas. Dist. travel. 7.5 miles.]

was, after a travel of a little more than a mile, again in the right road, and within a short distance of the head waters of the Concho. Camp was now ordered to be pitched (about 3 p.m.) in a small valley at the base of a huge pile of castellated rock, which frowned gloomily and grandly over one of those strange deposits of water, so common are the streams of this section of country. For it frequently happens that at a certain point, say where the train crosses the bed of a stream—the stream is shallow and sluggish, hardly creeping over the bed, while not a hundred yards below will be found a miniature lake, deep and dark, but clear as crystal where the light falls upon it several yards, sometimes thirty or forty yards in width (as in the present case) and several hundred yards in length. The grazing at this point is good. No accident occurred during the day. The general health of the camp continues good. The hill, upon the summit of which are placed the landmarks above referred to, commands a very extensive prospect of the adjacent country and is itself distinctly visible at a great distance. Several of the party climbed to the summit of this hill and left their names with the title of the expedition graven and written on the rocks.

[1857. Sept. 25th. Camp No. 65 Near Head Waters of Concho River, Texas. Dist. Travel. 7.5 miles.]

Skirting the western base of this hill was found a narrow well beaten path or track, which some of the party followed up for a mile or so, finding that it led to a small deposit of water, the residue of a flood season left in the bed of a drain, near which beneath the shelter of a clump of trees they found evidences of the occupation of this spot, on the previous night by a party of Camanche Indians. Among other recent "signs" were found the collar bone of some small animal, upon which were painted in the rudest style of the Indian's rude art two figures, one male, one female, and a part of an ornamented saddle bow. It may be well enough to remark for the benefit of travellers on the plains, that when these landmarks crowning the summit of a hill are seen it may safely be conjectured that water may be found in the vicinity thereof.

[1857. Sept. 26th. Camp No. 66, On the Plains, Texas. Dist. travel. 14 miles.]

The order to prepare for marching was given at an early hour this morning.

Having travelled up the course of the drain of the head waters of the Concho for a few miles, a halt was ordered. At this point the water casks were replenished it being, as it has since proved correctly supposed that we would be forced to halt tonight without finding water.

Eleven miles west of the site of camp No. 65 the road crossed the bed of the draw of the head waters of the Concho, to the north of which we found a pool of water which afforded an ample supply for our animals which, considering the hot weather and dusty roads, was fortunate for us. The bed of the drain up to this time had lain to the South or left hand side of the road. The vivid and peculiar green of the grasses bordering this drain evinced very clearly the presence of a heavy alkaline deposit in the soil. Crossing the ravine the bed of the drain lags to our right or to the north of the road, which skirted the base of a range of hills lying to the South, upon one of which were seen several piles of rock of very peculiar construction. One of the party examined them and gave it as his opinion that they were Indian burial places.

[1857. Sept. 26th. Camp No. 66 On the Plains Texas. Dist. travel 14 miles.]

It may be remarked that to our right between the bed of the drain and the road lay a valley, some half a mile or three quarters of a mile in width, the general appearance of which would seem to indicate fertility of soil. A few miles further on the range of hills above referred to deflected to the south and our road lay through a beautiful valley stretching out a mile in width on either side of us.

Continuing our march we again crossed the head of the drain, the course of which was here marked by merely a slight depression and the peculiar green of the grass above referred to, the unfailing indication as well as consequence of an alkaline deposit in the soil. After a march of ___ miles camp was ordered to be pitched in the valley. Wood was procured with difficulty at this point. The grazing was good. No water.

No accident occurred during the day, the health of the camp continues good.

[1857. Sept. 27th. Camp No. 67 On the Plains Texas. Dist. travel 18.9 miles.]

The train took up the line of march at an early hour. Our route lay for a short distance through the valley where we commenced the gradual ascent of a tract of table land a few miles in breadth; similar in its general characteristics, except in its greater elevation, to the valley through which we had just passed, which being accomplished we again descended and re-entered the drain or valley, and after a march of eleven and one third miles from the site of camp No. 66 we reached the first of these bodies of water, known as "Mustang ponds." A halt was ordered at this point (12 M.). The animals having had no water since yesterday at 2 p.m., after drinking their fill were allowed an hours rest. The water casks were refilled and the train ordered forward at 1 p.m. "Mustang Pond No. 1" lies to the north of the road. The water is ordinarily good.

Proceeding two miles and a fraction further we passed "Mustang Pond No. 2." The approach to this pond is difficult and dangerous owing to the miry character of its banks, and the water is muddy and disagreeable to the taste. "M.P. No. 2" lies to the south of the road. Our route continuing through the valley, we at length passed

[1857. Sept. 27th. Camp No. 68 On the Plains Texas. Dist. travel 18.9 miles.]

Mustang Pond No. 3 lying to the south of the road. The water here is tolerably good although lying in very shallow pools. The grazing in the neighborhood being of the very poorest possible description, and finding no wood nor any substitute for it we were compelled to push on though it was now dark; and about 8 p.m. finding tolerably good grazing and enough wood for camp fires, camp was pitched in the plains.

It is believed by the gentleman composing the Engineering Corps of the expedition that Mustang Pond No. 3 may be considered the real peak of the waters of the Concho; and that it is certain that in rainy seasons the waters gathering at that point flow into and compose part of the drainage of the Concho.

No accident occurred during the day. The health of the camp continues good. Our casks furnished an ample supply of water for camp and cooking purposes. Travellers over this route will subserve their interests in an indispensable particular by availing themselves of the same expedient.

[1857. Sept. 28th. Camp No. 69 On the Plains Texas. Dist. travel 28.6 miles.]

The line of march was taken up at an early hour this morning. Our route lay for a short distance through the western extremity of the valley spoken of in yesterday's journal, passing through which we ascended a plateau of very elevated table land. The extent of which so far as the line of vision was concerned was bounded only by the horizon. This body of land is evidently the divide between the waters of the Concho and the Pecos River. This portion of country we found extremely sterile and desolate, the grass upon it being parched and withered and almost unfit for use. The atmosphere at this elevation is rare and pure, a pleasant breeze obviating what must but for it have been extreme heat. We continued our course over this stretch of desert, for such it may with propriety be termed, until noon, when a halt was ordered. We had made a distance of eleven miles. The animals were turned loose upon the scanty grazing afforded near by and allowed an hours rest. The train was then again ordered forward and travel continued until nine o'clock p.m. in the hope of reaching "Castle Mountain Pass" where it was expected that water could be procured. The Superintendent and chief engineer with several of the party have ridden ahead to discover its locality.

[1857. Sept. 28th. Camp No. 68 On the Plains Texas. Dist. travel 28.6 miles.]

They having fully accomplished the object of their search and finding the distance much greater than had been anticipated, and the position of the water holes such as to preclude the possibility of reaching them with safety to the stock at night, returned and met the train at the hour above mentioned when an immediate halt was ordered by the superintendent and camp was pitched in "the wilderness."

Our animals although giving evidence of exhaustion and want of water were compelled to do without it. The grazing here is poor and scanty, although for the last few miles we have been descending from the extreme elevation of the divide between the Concho and the Pecos and our camp is near the bed of one of the drains.

No accident occurred during the day. The health of the camp continues good.

[1857. Sept. 29th. Camp No. 69 on East Bank of Pecos River, Texas. Dist. travel 10.3 miles.]

All hands were called an hour before day this morning and the train ordered forward as soon as practicable. Our line of travel lay for some four miles through the descent of table land, over which we travelled on yesterday. We then entered the Castle Mountain Pass or Cañon, our road through it lying down an abrupt and in some places almost precipitious descent for some half mile, near which portion of the cañon are situated the pools of water which are the sole dependance of the traveller westward between Mustang Ponds and the Pecos* River and this water is by no means permanent or reliable. There is something of the romantic in the general appearance of this gap or chasm, as Castle Mountain *Cañon* would be called by any one not versed in the nomenclature of those who were once the Spanish proprietors of the vast domain now known as the Lone Star State. Rocky walls some hundreds of feet in height, hem in and overhang the traveller, the shrill war whoop of the "Camanche" has so often echoed through the mazes of the Pass, that almost unconsciously the eye and ear are on the *qui vive* for some such manifestation of the ancient feud which these dusky devils bear to the white race. Nothing of the sort however happened to us.

[1857. Sept. 29th. Camp No. 69 on East Bank of Pecos River, Texas. Dist. travel. 9.3 miles.]

A halt was ordered in due time; the thirsty and tired animals slaked their desires in the muddy reservoir and left to themselves clambered up the rocky steeps which overhang the narrow road and cropped the scanty herbage the mountain sides afforded.

A hasty breakfast was ordered and while the culinary operations were going forward, we had an opportunity to look around us and see that this sterile spot afforded nourishment to some twelve or fifteen different varities of the Cactus family. A number of varieties of flowers were also in bloom, some of them quite pretty. Some of the curious in such matters procured the seed of several species. It is a noticeable fact that almost every shrub tree and bush and indeed every growth of whatever description in this section is armed at all

---

*It is impossible to tell from the script whether the writer spells Pecos with an a or an e.—Ed.

points with innumerable thorns. The economy which nature subserves in this arrangement with us "is past conjecture."

Breakfast being over the train was again ordered forward. "Castle Mountains" with their rugged and inhospitable pass were soon left behind and we saw before us a gradually sloping plain of several miles in extent.

[1857. Sept. 29th. Camp No. 69 on East Bank of Pecos River, Texas. Dist. travel 16 miles.]

We knew that the Pecos River lay before us, but its locality none could determine. Far off to the South West, a gleaming belt of white stretched across the plain, at a point which seemed to be its greatest declination. This was supposed to be the Pecos. Subsequent examination proved it to be only the locale of a heavy and extensive alkaline deposit. A tedious march of __ miles brought us to the Pecos River, which is seen only upon near approach to it, it being a swift and turbid stream about one hundred feet wide, flowing between abrupt precipitious banks, varying from four feet to ten feet in height above the surface of the stream, the waters of which are about ten feet in depth at this point, which is known as the "Horsehead crossing of the Pecos" and is considered one of the most dangerous localities in North Western Texas, it being the regular crossing place of the Camanche Indians when going to and returning from their forages upon the Mexicans, and frequently a place of rendezvous for their hunting parties. Camp was pitched about three p.m. on the eastern bank of the Pecos.

No accident occurred during the day. The general health of the camp continues good. Tomorrow it is expected that the train will cross the Pecos.

[1857. Sept. 30th. Camp No. 70 on West Bank of Pecos River, Texas. Dist. travel crossing river.]

After an early breakfast, all hands were called upon to assist in the work of crossing teams, wagons and stores. Nature not having provided ferry privileges at this point *extempore* arrangements had to be entered into. Per order of Supt. eight barrels were made water tight, two wagons unloaded, the beds taken to the river, four barrels placed in each wagon bed and firmly secured therein and the two wagon beds inverted and launched and then lashed together laterally thus forming a safe and at the same time commodious ferry[29] with a

29. This same type of ferry was improvised by Randolph B. Marcy when he crossed the Pecos River below the present town of Pecos in 1849. It was also used by Dr.

platform about eight or nine feet square. Upon this platform the freight of each wagon was placed successively and safely crossed, the *boat* being drawn from bank to bank by means of ropes in the hands of the crew. Nothing was lost except a solitary _____[?] The wagons and ambulance were then crossed safely in the same manner, all of the labor being accomplished by the hour of 4 p.m. The mules and horses were then driven in, not without some difficulty. They all crossed safely however and before sundown camp No. 70 was fully pitched and quiet as camps usually are.

The general health of the camp continues good. No accident to note for the day.

[1857. Oct. 1st. Camp No. 70 on the Pecos River, Texas. Dist. travel 15.8 miles.]

Camp No. 70 on the west bank of the Pecos was vacated at an early hour this morning. Our line of travel lay directly over the bottom lands of the Pecos, the road through which, although we found it tolerably good, is evidently very bad in wet weather. Capt. Pope's command *en route* for the mouth of Delaware Creek passed this point in wet weather, and their line of march was plainly to be traced by deep gullies and ruts to force their teams and wagons through which must have been a work of extreme difficulty.

After a march of 15.8 miles we again found ourselves upon the banks of the Pecos River and camp was ordered to be pitched. The whole line of to-days travel was marked by the continual recurrence of the alkaline deposits before referred to. The general appearance of the Pecos River at this point differs in no perceptible degree from that presented by it at the "Horsehead Crossing." The grazing along the route is pretty good.

No accident occurred during the day. The general health of the camp continues good.

[1857. Oct. 2nd. Camp No. 72 on the Pecos River, Texas. Dist. travel 6.9 miles.]

The line of travel was taken up at an early hour this morning.

Henry Connelley and associates in 1840. The Pecos River is hardly more than a glorified irrigation ditch in size, but its annual flow is about half as great as the Brazos where Col. Leach crossed it at Fort Belknap. (See the *Texas Almanac, 1952-1953,* pp. 153-154). The water of the Brazos, spread over a bed perhaps fifty times as wide as the bed of the Pecos, is often shallow enough to be forded. By contrast, the Pecos, confined to its narrow channel, seems almost never to have been so shallow. The Butterfield Mail line solved the problem by establishing a ferry at Horsehead Crossing in 1859, when the mail coaches began to cross the river at that place, and the United States Government, in 1872, built a pontoon bridge below the present-day McCamey to meet the needs of all traffic.

The general course of travel which we have pursued yesterday and to-day not agreeing fully with the information concerning the topography of the route which was received at Fort Chadbourne, doubts had arisen in the minds of the Supt. and Chief Eng. as to whether the correct road had been taken after leaving the Horsehead Crossing of the Pecos.

After leaving the site of Camp No. 71 the Pecos River deflected suddenly and very considerably to the South East. To the north of the road showed up a range of hills, more than one of which in the regularity of their sloping ascents and the parapet like battlements which surmounted them bore striking resemblances to Forts and Castles. Between these hills and our road intervened a distance of perhaps two miles, while to the south stretched out the valley or bottom of the Pecos River. This line of travel was pursued for a little more than seven miles, the road deflecting all the while to the South East and leading us in a direction contrary to that which we were satisfied was the correct one.[30] Hereupon the Supt. ordered a halt and a commission consisting of Mr. N. H. Hutton C. E. and several of his party detailed to "spy out the San Antonio and El Paso Road" near which if not altogether wrong in our line of travel, we should now find ourselves. The Pecos River after making a very considerable bend between the site of Camp No. 71 and our present camp, is again rushing sullenly past us.

[1857. Oct. 2nd. Camp No. 73 on Pecos River, Texas. Dist. travel 6.9 miles.]

At about 4 p.m. Mr. Hutton and party returned having been so fortunate as to discover the object of their search about seven miles west of the site of present camp. This news was received with much satisfaction by the entire party.

The day being extremely sultry no further march was ordered.

30. Col. Leach had taken the wrong road at Horsehead Crossing. He should have made the drive directly across the thirty-four miles southwest from Horsehead Crossing to Comanche Springs, a watering place located at present-day Fort Stockton. Instead he had taken a road made by Captain John Pope (who later became General Pope during the Civil War). Pope's supply wagons made or followed roads up each side of the Pecos River to a point near the Texas-New Mexico line. He was drilling (unsuccessfully) for artesian water with the hope of shortening the road across Texas from Preston to El Paso. *Report of the Secretary of War for 1855*, p. 96. This is Senate Executive Document No. 1, 34th Cong. 1st Sess.

For having made the mistake in roads, the Leach party was to travel at least thirty miles more than necessary. Concerning the San Antonio-San Diego Mail, see *The Handbook of Texas*, II, 545.

No accident occurred during the day. The health of the camp continues good. Grazing at this point fine.

[1857. Oct. 3rd. Camp No. 73 at Agua Escondido or The Sinking Springs, Texas. Dist. travel 19.7 miles.]

The train was ordered forward at an early hour this morning. It was thought expedient by the Supt. in view of the character of the report made by the Chief Engineer concerning the character of the country between the site of camp No. 72 and the San Antonio Road to order a direct march across the intervening body of table land. This tract of land we found barren and sterile. After a march of a little more than seven miles we entered upon the San Antonio and El Paso Road, a broad spacious avenue than which there are few better fitted for all the purposes of travel, so far as the mere condition of the road is concerned. The adjacent valleys however extending from each side of the road to the mountains are barren and sterile and the herbage thereupon was poor and scanty.

We met today the San Diego and San Antonio mail coach *en route* for San Antonio.

A little more than seven miles west of the point of our entrance into the road we reached the southern extremity of a watering place known as "Agua Escondido"[31] in the Spanish language. The best translation of the phrase would probably be "Sinking Springs"—the peculiar feature of these waters being that after rising as a spring or

[1857. Oct. 3rd. Camp No. 73 at Agua Escondido or Sinking Springs, Texas. Dist. Travel. 19.7 miles.]

fountain head and feeding therefrom a stream of some size or length sinks or disappears in the ground. Men and animals drank freely of the delicious beverage so bountifully supplied by nature at this point and much refreshed proceeded on their way. This water is strongly impregnated with sulphur but is cool and very palatable.

After a farther march of about 5 miles camp was ordered to be pitched at the head of the waters known as the Agua Escondido.

---

31. This spring is located adjacent to section 1, block 19, University of Texas lands, nearly thirty miles east of Fort Stockton. On the 1917 Texas General Land Office map of Pecos County it is called East Escondido Spring. On the same map about five miles slightly south of west is a second spring called Agua Escondido. Some three miles west of this place the map lists another watering place called West Escondido Spring. All three of them seem to be on the same draw—the draw traversed by the present-day San Antonio-Fort Stockton highway and the same draw up which the old San Antonio-San Diego stage road ran. The stage road was a little south of the modern highway at those watering places.

No accident occurred during the day. The health of camp continues good. The supply of water here is perennial—grazing is good.

[1857. Oct. 4th. Camp No. 74 At Camanche Springs, Texas. Dist. Travel. 23 mile.]

The line of march was resumed at an early hour this morning. A very excellent road than which no macademized one could be better, rendered our days travel over the plains through which it lay easy for both man and beast. Sterility of soil, the absence of timber and total lack of all evidences whatever of the habitation of men were the distinguishing characteristics of the country.

A halt of an hour was ordered at noon, after which the line of march was resumed and about 5 p.m. we reached Camanche Springs[32] a beautiful stream some ten or fifteen yards wide, about ten feet in depth, clear as crystal and running at a mill tail rate a few miles and then losing itself in the earth. Camp was ordered to be pitched here. No accident occurred during the day.

One of the men was this morning discharged for insubordination. See voucher No. 1 report for quarter ending Dec. 31, 1857 favor of J. Wilk date Oct. 3, 1857 amount (75.00) Seventy Five Dollars.

Health of Camp still good. Grazing at this point fine.

[1857. Oct. 5th. Camp No. 75. On the Plains, Texas. Dist. Travel. 17 miles.]

The line of march was taken up at an early hour this morning. Our route lay for some seven or eight miles over an excellent road and through the same barren and sterile description of country as that over which we passed on yesterday. A little more than eight miles from (west of) "Camanche Springs" after descending the slope of a hill we entered a valley and travelling a short distance reached "Leon Springs," which waters form a phenomenon.[33] It may with truth be said that it is difficult to convey any idea of their nature and appearance. They consist of two bodies of water welling up from the bosom of the earth forming two pools the depth of which is considered very great but is not exactly known. The water is clear, impregnated with sulphur and very pleasant to taste. The valley in which they are located is in many places of a very miry nature and

32. This is the great spring on the eastern outskirt of modern Fort Stockton, now well known as a pleasure resort. In 1859 the Butterfield Overland Mail Route was changed so that it came directly across from Horsehead Crossing to this spring. Previously this important mail route had extended up the east side of the Pecos River to near the New Mexico line and thence west along and near that boundary line to the site of present day El Paso.

33. Leon Springs are located nine miles west of Fort Stockton and south of the Fort Stockton-El Paso highway.

there is much danger of losing animals in the bog if suffered to go at large here. The vegetation in the vicinity is extremely rank and plainly indicative of a heavy alkaline deposit. A halt was ordered at "Leon Springs," the stock allowed such grazing as was afforded, a hasty collation partaken of, several of the water casks filled and at 3 p.m. the train was again ordered forward.

[1857. Oct. 5th. Camp No. 76 on the Plains, Texas. Dist. travel 17 miles.]

Leaving "Leon Springs" by a gradually ascending road we were soon again upon the high table lands. At 6 p.m. camp was ordered to be pitched on the plains at a point seven miles west of "Leon Springs." The mariner in mid seas has no more boundless prospect spread out before him than we looked upon from the site of Camp No. 75. No object crossed the line of vision, turn we whithersoever we might until it rested upon the line where the horizon seemed to meet and mingle with the vast expanse of table land upon which we were resting for the night, and when after darkness had fallen like a pall over the scene and silence had flung her mantle over the camp the full orbed moon floated up in resplendent beauty from the depths of space, it was impossible to look unmoved upon the scene so full was it of all the elements of the magnificent and grand in nature.

The grazing at this point, although we found the soil so rocky as to render the selection of a comfortable place for stretching a palate a matter of difficulty, we found unusually fine. No water at this point. No accident during the day. Health of camp good.

[1857. Oct. 6th. Camp No. 77 at Water Holes, Texas. Dist. travel 22 miles.]

Camp No. 75 was vacated at an early hour this morning. The train had proceeded only a little more than two miles west of the site of Camp No. 75 when water was found standing in large pools a short distance to the north of the road.

The animals were watered here and the train proceeded on its way. The country through which our line of travel lay today may be described as poor, rolling and rocky. Twelve miles west of the above referred to pools we met, a small supply of water was found, which however cannot be relied on as permanent.

Shortly after leaving this water a halt of an hour was ordered for the purpose of resting, grazing and watering the stock, we entered a rocky ravine running parallel with the "Dry Bed" of the Lympia River. This ravine is hemmed in on either side by perpendicular rocky cliffs, the character of which was frequently in a high degree picturesque. A few miles west of the water above referred to we crossed the dry bed of the Lympia and after a further march of about two miles camp was pitched near some water holes lying to the south of the trail. No accident occurred during the day.

[1857. Oct. 7th. Camp No. 78 on Lympia River, Texas. Dist. travel 16 miles.]

The train was put in motion at 7 A.M. Our route lay for seven [miles] over a hilly country, the road being difficult to travel. Water was found in abundance in the bed of the Lympia River[34] about seven miles west of the site of Camp No. 76. A short halt was ordered for the purpose of watering the stock at this point leaving which we entered in a short time a beautiful valley. Some mile or two miles in width and several miles in length. The grazing upon it was very fine. About 4 P.M. camp was ordered to be pitched near the Lympia River[35] which at this point is very shallow, rushing madly over a rocky bed and being nowhere in the vicinity of the camp more than a few inches in depth.

No accident occurred during the day. The health of the camp continues good. Grazing at this point excellent.

[1857. Oct. 8th. Camp No. 79 at Davis, Texas. Dist. travel 18 miles.]

The train was ordered forward at an early hour this morning. Our route lay for some few miles parallel with the course of the bed of the Lympia River and through a continuation of the valley referred to in yesterdays journal. We then entered the eastern end, a cañon known as Wild Rose Pass, and which for the beauty and sublimity of the scenery which it affords deserves particular reference. Ordinary language would fail to convey any idea of the beauty of this wild chasm in the rocky hills which hem in the traveler. It must be seen to be appreciated. Leaving the cañon we ascended the most elevated

34. This supply of water must have been at or very near the place where the Barrilla Stage stand was established two years after Col. Leach's journey. The stage stand, although on Limpia Creek, took its name from the Barrilla Spring that marks the southernmost corner of Reeves County, which was two miles north of the station. The spring is shown at the exact corner of Reeves County on the 1915 Texas Land Office map of Jeff Davis County. This corner of Reeves County is on the northeast boundary line of Jeff Davis County.

The road traveled by Col. Leach followed the valley—or canyon—of Limpia Creek all the way up to Fort Davis. So did the El Paso road; so did the Butterfield mail of 1859-60.

35. This camp site on Limpia Creek, according to the Leach journal, was eighteen miles from Fort Davis—also Limpia station, to be established by Butterfield and associates two years later, was eighteen miles down the Limpia from Fort Davis. The modern highway from Pecos to Fort Davis enters Limpia Canyon at this point and follows almost the same route up stream as did the old road.

plateau of table land we have as yet reached in our journey. After a further march of 18.4 miles we reached Fort Davis near which post camp was ordered to be pitched. No accident occurred during the days march. The health of the camp continues good.

[1857. Oct. 9th and 10th. Camp No. 80. Point of Rocks. Dist. travel. 12¼ miles.]

Halt at Fort Davis to shoe mules and repair wagons. This morning the train took up the line of march at 11 A.M. This days march extended over a rolling country possessing a hard gravelly [?] and plenty of grazing. There is very little water until arriving at Point of Rocks 12¼ miles from Fort Davis at which point camp was ordered to be pitched.

No accident happened on the road. The health of the camp is good.

[1857. Oct. 12th. Camp No. 81 on the Prairie, Texas. Dist. travel 20¾ miles.]

This morning the train made an early start and after travelling 10 miles stopped to breakfast at Barrell Springs.[36] After which the train continued its march over a country in every way similar to yesterdays travel for a distance of 10¾ miles when camp was ordered to be pitched on the Prairie at a point where there was no water. No accident happened today. The health of the camp is good.

[1857. Oct. 13th. Camp No. 82.]

This morning the train started at an early hour and proceeded to "El Muerto"—Dead Man's Hole. Here we breakfast and 3 o'clock P.M. orders were given to proceed on our march, the which was put into effect and continued until half past nine o'clock P.M. when camp was ordered to be pitched on the plains at a distance of 16 miles from Van Horns well.

[1857. Oct. 13th. Camp No. 82, on the Plains, Texas. Dist. travel 21 miles.]

The grazing all along the road was good and at this camp was excellent which induced the Supt. to stop here although there was no water. No accident happened today. The health of the camp is good.

[Oct. 14th. Camp No. 83, 6 miles west of Van Horn's Wells. Dist. travel. 22 miles.]

The train took up the line of march this morning before day and proceeded a distance of eight miles to breakfast, after which we continued eight miles more to Van Horn's wells[37] where we filled our

36. The locations of both Barrel Springs and El Muerto (Dead Man's Hole) are made on the accompanying map in accordance with their locations on the 1915 Texas Land Office map of Jeff Davis County.

37. This watering place was some twelve miles south of the present-day town of Van Horn and is less than a mile west of United States highway 90.

water barrels and watered the animals. After a rest of two hours the train again started travelled until dusk when camp was pitched at a point on the plains 6 miles west of Van Horn's wells.

The grazing here is good. There has been no accident today. The health of the camp is good.

[Oct. 15th. Camp No. 84, on the Plains, Texas. Dist. travel. 22 miles.]

The train started early this morning.

The country through which we have passed since leaving Fort Davis has been a rough, rolling prairie, with a mountainous line at each side of the road presenting nothing in any way remarkable for scenic beauty. The grazing all along the road was good.

[1857. Oct. 15th. Camp No. 84, on the Plains, Texas. Dist. travel. 22 miles.]

After a travel of 10 miles we came to a water hole we filled our barrels and proceeded on our march. This water hole is not to be depended on for a supply at all seasons.

At a distance of 5 miles we came to ''Eagle Springs''[38] but did not stop there on account of Indians whose regular stopping place it is reputed to be. Continuing our march camp was ordered to be pitched on the plains 7 miles west of Eagle Springs where we found good grazing. No accident happened today. The health of the camp is good.

[Oct. 6. Camp No. 85 on the Rio Grande, Texas. Dist. travel. 25 miles.]

This morning the Camp was ordered to be struck at an early hour and the train proceeded on its march. The country bears the same aspect as that through which our last 5 days march extended. After travelling 16 miles the train halted & the animals were turned out to grass. This spot is the entrance of ''Eagle Pass Cañon.'' Having rested here some two hours, the train proceeded through the cañon and continued a distance of 9½ miles where we struck the Rio Grande[39] at a point where good grazing is abundant. Here camp was pitched for

38. The location of Eagle Springs is made on the accompanying map in accordance with the location given on the 1917, Texas General land Office map of Hudspeth County. A short portion of the old road is also shown on that map. One should not discount the authenticity of this map because of its more recent date. Land maps include the cumulative information about land and landmarks that is carried forward from the earliest surveys.

39. From a point almost due southwest of Sierra Blanca on the Rio Grande, topography permitted wagon travel up the river all the way to El Paso. A large number of small surveys that cling to the river bank are shown on the 1917 Texas Land Office map at Hudspeth County. They begin at this same point and extend up the river. They appear to be related to the older settlements along the Rio Grande.

the night. The animals were watered and turned out to graze and soon the camp was in quiet.

No accident happened today. The health of Camp is good.

[1857. Oct. 17th. Camp 86 on the Rio Grande, Texas. Dist. Travel. 17 miles.]

After breakfast the order to go ahead was given at 7½ A.M. & the train proceeded on its march up the river.

The road here is very sandy, and on the river side there is an abundance of cottonwood. After travelling 17 miles Camp was pitched on a high clay bluff, right on the Rio Grande. Nothing of consequence happened today. The health of the camp is good.

[Oct. 18th. No. 87 Camp on the Rio Grande, Texas. Dist. travel. 20 1/10 miles.]

The train started at an early hour and continued its march along the river through the same kind of soil as that we passed through yesterday. At a distance of 20 1/10 miles Camp was pitched on a bend of the river opposite San Ignacio, Mexico.

No accident happened today. The health of the Camp is good.

[Oct. 19th. Camp No. 88, on the Rio Grande, Texas. Dist. travel. 14 miles.]

This morning the train started early and proceeded to "Smith's Ranch"—Birchville on the Rio Grande where the order to halt was given for the purpose of purchasing corn. The road was here very muddy and the mules very much worn out.

After making the necessary purchases and a delay of some three hours, the train continued its march through the same kind of road and at a late hour camp was pitched on the banks of the river. No accident happened today. The health of the camp is good.

[Oct. 20th. No. 89 on the Rio Grande, Texas. Dist. travel. 11¼ miles.]

This morning the order to march was given at an early hour and we proceeded on our way.

The day was very disagreeable owing to the heavy rain having made the road so heavy. However the train proceeded as far as San "Elizario," a town on the Rio Grande where camp was ordered to be pitched. The mules were watered and put into corrals for the purpose of being fed as also for safety. No accidents happened today. The health of the Camp is good.

[Oct. 21st. Camp No. 90 on the Rio Grande, Texas. Dist. travel 11 miles.]

The order to take up the line of march was given at 8 A.M.

This morning it still continued raining and the roads were in very bad condition.

The train however proceeded on its way and we soon arrived at the town of "Socorro" or "El Presidio" through which we passed and in a short time came to the town of Isleta in which place we did not make any stay either but went forward to a point about half way between Isleta and El Paso on the banks of the river.

[1857. Oct. 22nd. Camp No. 90 on the Rio Grande, Texas. Dist. travel 11 miles.]

This morning it became necessary to leave some animals in "San Elizario" as they were so fatigued that it was impossible for them to proceed. We also lost one mule which died during the night. Nothing else of consequence happened. The health of the Camp is good.

[Oct. 22nd. Camp No. 91. El Paso, Texas. Franklin Rio Grande. Dist. travel. 12 miles.]

The train started at an early hour this morning and proceeded on its march to El Paso, where we arrived at about 1 o'clock P.M.

XV

THE BUTTERFIELD OVERLAND MAIL ROAD ACROSS TEXAS

Can anything new be said about the old Butterfield Overland Mail Route? This famous route that crossed Texas just before the Civil War has been the subject of many hundreds of pages of published material. Are all the facts already in print? Anyone who wishes may, without extended effort, look up such facts as these:

1. The old dirt road over which the United States government established this first large scale transcontinental mail service was 2,795 miles long.

2. The road began at Tipton, Missouri, a railhead 160 miles west of St. Louis.

3. It extended across the present states of Missouri, Arkansas, Oklahoma, Texas, New Mexico, Arizona, and California and terminated at San Francisco.

4. It passed through the towns or cities of Springfield, Missouri; Fayetteville and Fort Smith, Arkansas; Sherman, Gainesville, Jacksboro, and present-day El Paso, Texas; Tucson and Yuma, Arizona; and Los Angeles, California.

5. Another branch of this mail road extended from Memphis, Tennessee, westward and joined the principal road at Fort Smith, Arkansas.

6. The postal authorities at Washington agreed to pay the mail contractors, John Butterfield and associates, $600,000 per year for their service.

7. These contractors were to furnish semi-weekly mail service, and their mail coaches actually made the 2,795-mile journey in approximately twenty-five days.

8. A total outlay that approaches $1,000,000 was spent by the contractors in preparing to carry out their contract.

9. They purchased about one hundred Concord coaches and many hundreds of horses and mules, to say nothing of the many mail stations that they built.

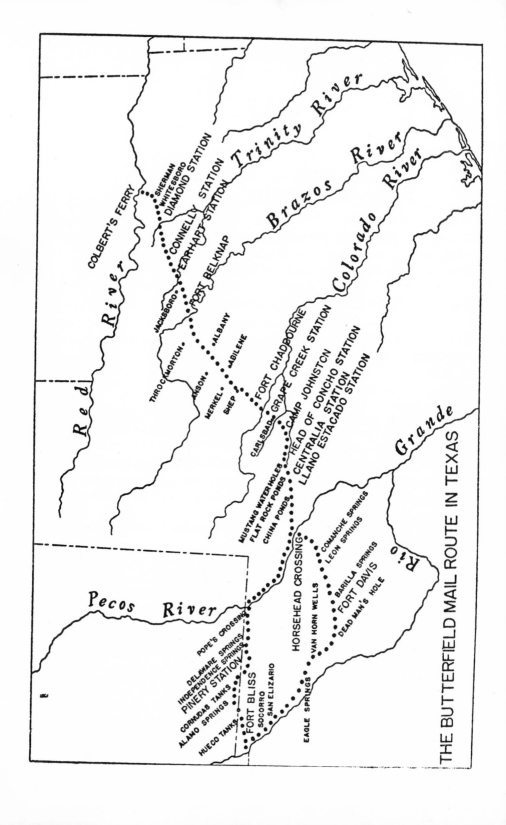

THE BUTTERFIELD MAIL ROUTE IN TEXAS

All of these facts are either well-known or easily accessible. A paper that goes no further has no right to waste either the reader's time or the printer's ink. Actually, the predicament in which the writer finds himself is far worse than even that. The articles written by the twenty-four-year-old reporter of the New York *Herald,* Waterman L. Ormsby, who was the only through passenger to ride the first Butterfield Mail coaches west, have been put into book form and reprinted[1] in 1954. Ormsby's articles were interestingly written and filled with many of the answers that a research worker would want to know. But much more extensive than the Ormsby articles is the three-volume work by Roscoe and Margaret Conkling published in 1947.[2] In nearly one thousand pages, with maps, charts, and photographs, the Conklings tell the story of the Butterfield Overland Mail so near to completeness that certainly no one can hope to compete with them in a short paper.

Obviously the only justifiable course left is to approach this subject from a somewhat different viewpoint than did the Conklings or any of the others. Here, then, is the big detour that this study wishes to make. How can anyone after nearly one hundred years know exact facts about the route of this old mail line? The Conklings seem to have done most of their investigation of this question by personal interviews—and a monumental piece of detective work it was. This paper, however, proposes to supplement that investigation with a somewhat extensive use of land records, and the investigation will be attempted only within the boundaries of Texas. Surveyors crossed the old road many times and often set down in their field notes mathematical data about it that no human memory could hope to retain. The exact nature of these surveyors' notes, wherever they are available, is such that one can know not only the tracts of land over which this early mail road passed but he can know in what part of each of these tracts the old trail may be found.

This statement must be subject to the limitations that surveying records containing the necessary data are not always available. Obviously no notes could have been made where the surveys antedated the Butterfield Mail Route. This is true of nearly all the land traversed

1. Waterman L. Ormsby, *The Butterfield Overland Mail,* edited by Lyle H. Wright and Josephine M. Bynum (San Marino, 1954).

2. Roscoe P. Conkling and Margaret B. Conkling. *The Butterfield Overland Mail, 1857-1869* (3 vols.; Glendale, 1947).

by the road from *Colbert's Ferry,* thirteen miles northeast of Sherman, to Fort Belknap, near the center of Young County. Even here, however, the land records help to establish the route. The log of the mail route, for instance, shows that J. R. Diamond was in charge of the first stage stand fifteen miles west of Sherman. The records show that Diamond's land lay about one mile west of the present Whitesboro, that he was here as early as June 26, 1855,[3] and that his pre-emption certificate was issued on August 18, 1857. Furthermore, the land was patented to Diamond on May 31, 1859.[4] One finds from local inquiry that the Butterfield station stood by the roadside on this land one mile west of Whitesboro. The foregoing land records offer ample confirmation for the conclusion.

Similarly, one may check published statements from some histories misstating that this important mail route missed Montague County entirely. In 1859, however, while John Butterfield and his associates were in full operation of their mail coaches, the east line of Montague County was surveyed. The surveyors' notes show that Butterfield's old stage road crossed this county boundary line just two miles and 1470 *varas* north of the southeast corner of the county.[5]

Land records show that J. J. Connelly (who operated a stage stand forty-one miles southwesterly from Gainesville) was in possession of the land known as the S.E. Clements tract in north Wise County on January 30, 1859, while the old stage line was in operation. This fact puts down another pinpoint on the route of John Butterfield's mail road.[6]

In resume, this early road has been traced across Grayson and Cooke counties and across the southeast part of Montague County. In its southwestwardly course, the road emerged from Montague County

3. Grayson County Surveyors Records (MS. County Clerk's Office, Sherman), B, 408.

4. The old land patent is in the possession of R. V. Dicus of Whitesboro. The date of issue and the date of the pre-emption certificate are both revealed by this instrument. Thus it is certain that J. R. Diamond lived at that place when he had charge of what is known as the Diamond Stage Stand.

5. The 1859 survey of the east Montague County line may be found in the files of the General Land Office at Austin. The *vara,* a Spanish unit of distance, was used in the Spanish and Mexican surveys and land grants in Texas. One *vara* equals approximately thirty-three and one-third inches. See Virginia H. Taylor, *The Spanish Archives of the General Land Office of Texas* (Austin, 1955), 75n.

6. Wise County Surveyors Records (MS., County Clerk's Office, Decatur), A, 98.

and reached Connelly's Station in northern Wise County, some three miles southeast of the present-day town of Sunset. Moving still southwestwardly the road entered Jack County ten miles and sixteen hundred *varas* south of the northeast corner of that county. The veracity of this routing is established by surveying records.[7] The east line of Jack County was surveyed in 1878, some eighteen years after the Butterfield Mail had ceased to function. The surveyors merely called the road the Jacksboro-Gainesville Road. But there is no doubt that this old local wagon route was a part of the Butterfield Trail, for the Jack County commissioners (according to their minutes) accepted this very road and discharged the review committee that laid it out just eleven days before the first Overland Mail coach rolled into Jacksboro.[8] The commissioners noted in their minutes of September 9, 1858, that the road extended eastward from Jacksboro to J. B. Earhart's land and connected with the "over-land mail route at the boundary line of said Jack County in the direction to Gainesville near J. B. Earharts on said county line. . ." The fact that the Earhart Survey is within a few hundred yards of the point at which the county line surveyors of 1878 crossed the Jacksboro-Gainesville Road ought to dispel any doubt about the identity of the road.[9]

Earhart operated a Butterfield station on his land by the present Jacksboro-Decatur Highway near the ten-mile point on the east Jack County line. For some reason the small strip of grassland at Earhart's became known as Hogeye Prairie.[10] After the Civil War, a village by the name of Hogeye grew up on this one-time important road near Earhart's.

The same commissioners court minutes that registered approval of the road to Earhart's recorded other points along the forthcoming mail road. It passed Bean's Crossing (on the West Fork of the Trinity) and crossed "Lost Creek nearly due east of the southeast corner of the public square in the town of Jacksboro . . ."[11] The road also passed by

7. The survey of the east Jack County line, dated May 14, 1878, is recorded in the original Jack County Commissioners Court Records (MS., County Clerk's Office, Jacksboro), III. The part of the survey that reveals the location of the Jacksboro-Gainesville Road is on page 215.

8. *Ibid.,* 49, 55.

9. See the General Land Office map of Jack County, dated 1925, for the location of the Joseph B. Earhart Survey.

10. Apparently because of its shape.

11. Jack County Commissioners Court Records (MS., County Clerk's Office, Jacksboro), I, 55.

B. D. Ham's place, which is identified by a land survey as being six miles west of Jacksboro. This same local road, now famous as the Butterfield Trail, passed into Young County at a point *eighteen miles and 540 varas north of the southeast corner of the county*. The fact comes from the county line survey of 1881.[12] This highway that had by 1881 lost its national significance was called by the surveyors simply the Jacksboro-Belknap Road. Like Cinderella it had been stripped of its finery and had reverted to the level of kitchen maid, but its location on the map was still the same.

The next important point on the road was Fort Belknap in Young County. The commissioners of this county, like those of Jack, had also laid out their part of the new road.[13] Land surveys in Young County east of Belknap made no reference to this thoroughfare because the land surveying was done five years ahead of the road.

Ormsby, one of the first westbound passengers on the mail coaches, declared that the entire stretch of the trail between Gainesville and Belknap was new. Actually the citizenry of this whole area of Texas from Red River to Belknap prepared the way for the incoming stage coaches as if they were unrolling a carpet for the footpath of a bride. Cooke County appointed an overseer exclusively for the overland mail road,[14] and Jack County rushed at the job like a runner out of breath and opened its thirty miles of road less than two weeks ahead of the first stage coaches.[15] The Young County commissioners appropriated $150—a sizable sum in 1858—to cut the new road through both timber and prairie eastward from Belknap.[16]

Grayson County extended a welcome that was indeed unique. The citizens had a champagne supper for John Butterfield himself.[17] The party became quite informal, and one local enthusiast became increasingly more talkative and began to tell about a certain old grey

12. *Ibid.*, III, 380.

13. Young County Commissioners Court Minutes (MS., County Clerk's Office, Graham), I, 25.

14. Cooke County Commissioners Court Minutes (MS., County Clerk's Office, Gainesville), I, 30. Thomas Mackey was appointed county overseer of the overland mail road.

15. Jack County Commissioners Court Minutes (MS., County Clerk's Office, Jacksboro), I, 44, 45.

16. Young County Commissioners Court Minutes (MS., County Clerk's Office, Graham), I, 25.

17. Mattie Davis Lucas and Mita Holsapple Hall, *A History of Grayson County, Texas* (Sherman, 1936), 92-93.

goose that had a nest underneath Sherman's small log courthouse. The story was challenged, and the party moved over to the little courthouse to investigate. Bets were placed on the outcome of the investigation and the party began to tear down the structure, a log at a time. Bets continued as the logs continued to fly. At last the bottom of the small building was reached, and there was found the nest of the old grey goose.

The people of Sherman suffered no great loss in the destruction of their courthouse. Immediately after the coming of the Butterfield Overland Mail, Sherman doubled in population, and without hesitating the residents built one of the finest new courthouses in their part of Texas.[18]

Westward from Belknap, Texas was almost devoid of population. There was no chamber of commerce spirit in that part of the state to welcome the new venture either by an outlay of cash or by an outpouring of champagne. In one particular, however, the trail hunter is blessed for some miles west of Belknap in his search. Strangely enough the surveyors' notes in this new and unsettled part of the state in 1858 give much more data on the route of the Butterfield Trail than in surveys from Red River to Belknap.

The road ahead was not new. For a number of miles westward from Belknap, the Butterfield route followed the military roads that were already in existence before 1858.[19] Fortunately these military roads were opened just before much of the land was surveyed. Thus, in tract after tract of land many of the surveyors laboriously set down in their notes the exact route of the Overland Mail. If these extensive notes were repeated here, the recital would become as monotonous as long-drawn-out quotations from a volume of arithmetic. The map makers at the Texas General Land Office and those employed by the Texas and Pacific Railway Company have made this part of the task much easier than any such recital of field notes. Their county maps, with only short omissions, have traced the Butterfield Trail from Fort Belknap across the remainder of Young County,[20] across the counties of Throckmorton,[21] Shackelford,[22] Jones,[23] and Taylor[24] and on to Fort Chadbourne[25] in Coke County.

18. *Ibid.,* 93.

19. The log of the Overland Mail included Fort Belknap, Fort Phantom Hill, and Fort Chadbourne. Obviously it was necessary to do no more than simply to use the military roads that already connected these forts.

20. See General Land Office Map of Young County, dated March, 1898.

In crossing this tier of counties the old mail road did not pass through any town or village that finally came into being when this area was settled. The mail road missed the future town of Throckmorton twelve miles to the south. It passed ten miles west of Albany. It passed twenty-eight miles east of Anson and missed Abilene by a full seven miles to the north. The road crossed United States Highway 80 just one mile west of the village of Tye and passed along the north base of Castle Peak, the prominent little mountain that sticks up in the sky like a column a half dozen miles south of Merkel. To the southwest of this peak the trail bent its course through the little steep-walled canyon long known as Mountain Pass.[26] From here the stages climbed up on the prairie plateau of west Taylor County and even missed the present-day village of Shep, three thousand yards to the west.[27] Plainly, civilization, when it finally came with its new county seats and its railroads, laid down a pattern entirely different from the old.

At Fort Chadbourne, only three miles deep into northeast Coke County, the problem of the present-day trail hunter again becomes more difficult. The surveyors' records that mention the old road are much less numerous; but few as they are, they do establish certain facts about the route. The first of these is a note taken on the southwest boundary of a tract of school land surveyed for Caldwell

21. See General Land Office Map of Throckmorton, County, dated March, 1898. The early surveying notes and the map of the Peters' Colony land (in the General Land Office), dated 1854, are the sources of the military road information on this map and the Young County map cited in footnote 20.

22. The old Texas and Pacific Railway Company Plat Book, 11. This is a map of Shackelford County not dated but made by the Texas and Pacific land surveys in the 1870's.

23. *Ibid.*, 13. This is a map of Jones County, dated 1874.

24. See General Land Office Map of Taylor County, dated August, 1897. See also the (printed) map of Taylor County made for Charles J. Canada, Simeon J. Drake, and William Strauss, proprietors of the Texas and Pacific lands. Both maps were based on original surveying records.

25. Texas and Pacific Railway Company Plat Book, 16. This map of Nolan County traces the Fort Belknap-Fort Phantom Hill-Fort Chadbourne Road from the Taylor County line across the corner of Nolan County and on to Fort Chadbourne. The road traced from Fort Belknap to Fort Chadbourne on the maps cited in footnotes 20-24 was, of course, also the Butterfield Trail.

26. Mountain Pass, some twelve miles southwest of Merkel, is shown on both of the Taylor County maps mentioned in footnote 24.

County in 1883.[28] This note shows that the Butterfield Trail crossed this boundary line 1,500 yards from the south corner of the survey. The old land line which the surveyors of 1883 were measuring ran parallel to the present-day Robert Lee-San Angelo pavement about a half mile to the northeast of that road. This point is almost twenty miles southeast of old Fort Chadbourne and lies in the flat country three miles south of the Colorado River.

Also the surveyors reported that the trail crossed the east line of the R. H. Harris Survey, which was three and one-half miles southwestward of the Caldwell County school land.[29] Continuing a mile and one-half, the surveyors referred to a land corner as a point in the Butterfield Canyon.[30] These notes plainly outline a course up the valley of Buffalo Creek over a high, steep, rocky hill and down into the valley of Grape Creek. It was at this steep hill that the mules refused to pull the first westbound stage at 2 o'clock on the morning of September 25, 1858. W. L. Ormsby of the New York *Herald* and Nichols, the stage driver, were forced to wait until daylight before they could persuade their stubborn mule team to make the difficult climb up this hill.[31]

The Grape Creek Station near the south line of Coke County on the present-day March Ranch took its name from the creek that was near it.[32] The old mail route *crossed the Concho River just east of the site of Carlsbad* (fifteen miles northwest of San Angelo) and, according to the best information obtainable, it reached the *Middle Concho near the mouth of West Rocky Creek below the site of the old Arden post office.* There appears to have been the location of a stage stand that was in operation soon after the beginning of John Butterfield's transcontinental mail service.

27. The road data traced on a present-day map of Taylor County from these older maps mentioned in footnote 24 make it possible to relate to the path of the old road to points on the map as of today.

28. Tom Green County Surveyors Records (MS., County Clerk's Office, San Angelo), C, 188.

29. Coke County Surveyors Records (MS., County Clerk's Office, Robert Lee), II, 63. The survey was made on June 3, 1879.

30. Tom Green County Deed Records (MS., County Clerk's Office, San Angelo), W, 333.

31. Ormsby, *The Butterfield Overland Mail*, 56.

32. *Ibid.*, 56. Ormsby said it was five miles from the steep hill to the Grape Creek Station.

An interesting side note, meanwhile, proves the later location of a stage stand—apparently the above stage stand moved four miles westward—in Section 59, Block 10, of the Houston and Texas Central Railway Company Surveys. This new site known as Camp Johnston is substantiated in the Probate Minutes of Tom Green County. Volume A of these old minutes was rescued from the flood of 1882 that swept away the former county seat town of Ben Ficklin.[33] The water-stained pages of this volume tell of the sale (by C. Bain and Company who had become the owners) of this stage stand in the above mentioned section in the early 1880's when transcontinental stage lines had become outmoded.

The Butterfield route passed up the north side of the Middle Concho most of the way to the head of the stream.[34] There was a deviation from this course at the mouth of Kiowa Creek where the road crossed to the south side for a short distance.[35] Here at the east river crossing (below Kiowa Creek) the St. Louis *Republican* told of an Indian scare in its issue of January 5, 1859.

Apparently the last permanent water as the stages moved up the Middle Concho was in or near the Nathaniel Gocher Survey No. 1943, a tract of land that is now owned by the Sawyer Cattle Company. Surveyors noted a stage stand in this block on July 29, 1859—when the Butterfield Overland Mail had been in operation for ten months.[36] The date makes it certain that the mail station was the property of the Butterfield interests. This fact puts the writer in the uncomfortable position of being in conflict with the Conklings' study, but there seems to be no way to escape that conflict.

With this station at the head of the Concho established without doubt, supporting evidence can be adduced for locating a station near the early post office of Arden. It was approximately thirty miles down the river from the stand on the Gocher Survey to Arden—which is also the distance given in the original log of the Overland Mail between the head of Concho station and the next mail station to the east. This fact offers strong support to the assumption that the lower stage stand on the Concho was at this site near the one-time post of-

33. Tom Green County Probate Minutes (MS., County Clerk's Office, San Angelo), A, 165.

34. Personal interview with Wade Henderson of San Angelo.

35. Charles William Pressler, *Traveler's Map of Texas*, 1867 revision.

36. Tom Green County Surveyors Records (MS., County Clerk's Office, San Angelo), I, 234.

fice of Arden. There seems to be no doubt that this station was later moved four miles to the west as stated above.

The station at the head of the Concho may be used as an anchor point for study of the route westward just as it has been used in rechecking toward the east. According to the original log of the Overland Mail, it was seventy miles from this point to Horsehead Crossing on the Pecos River. Careful measurements on good present-day county maps show that the road must have been at least three miles longer than that.[37] Perhaps, considering the meanders of the road, seventy-five miles is a more accurate figure for this distance than the mail log gave. But whether seventy or seventy-five miles, the road during most of the year was a waterless drive.

Each point where water might be found, even though temporary, was carefully noted along the route. Eight miles west of the station at the head of the Concho were the Mustang Water Holes, which were often dry. Eleven and one-half miles ahead were the Flat Rock Ponds, shallow basins in the surface rock that sometimes held water.[38] These ponds, according to the Conklings' excellent study, were just west of the former Reagan County seat town of Stiles. Six miles beyond the ponds was old Centralia Station in the San Antonio and Mexican Gulf Railway Company Survey No. 1947. Centralia was built as a way station on Ben Ficklins' mail road established after the Civil War, but all visible evidence indicates that his road at this point was the same as the road used by the Butterfield interests more than a decade earlier. Land surveyors on May 4, 1873, recorded field notes that tie the location of this stage stand to the permanent land records.[39] Confirmation of the fact that the El Paso Road passed by this station is given in the field notes of the adjoining survey some seven years later.[40]

Further exact data are furnished by the map makers of the General Land Office. For twenty miles from Centralia Station

37. A straight line from the station at the head of the Concho across maps of Reagan, Upton, and Crane counties to Horsehead Crossing on the Pecos measures the distance as seventy-three miles. The writer did this experimental job of map surveying across the maps of these three counties by L. C. Heydrick of Wichita Falls, Texas.

38. Conkling, *The Overland Mail*, I, 361-362.

39. Original Transcribed Surveyors Records, Tom Green County (MS., County Clerk's Office, San Angelo), IV, 219.

40. *Ibid.*, XVI, 432.

southwestward to a point near the present-day town of Rankin in Upton County these draftsmen have mapped the mail road.[41] The full twenty miles were used by the Ben Ficklin stage coaches instead of the Butterfield but the part of the road by Centralia Station was also used by the Concord coaches of the Overland Mail. At a mile and a half southwest of Centralia Station the older mail road branched westward toward China Ponds,[42] Castle Gap, and Horsehead Crossing,[43] all of which were known points on the Butterfield Trail. The Conklings discovered the ruins of an old stage stand on the west branch of the trails, two and a half miles west of this point where the roads forked. They named the old depot Llano Estacado and, beyond any reasonable doubt, proved by newspaper items current during the time of the Overland Mail that the man-made and man-supplied oasis was a link in the Butterfield chain of stage stands.[44] The station was undoubtedly established in answer to the urgent need for water on this seventy-five mile stretch of waterless stage road. Ben Ficklin's answer to the same problem on his mail road, which came after the Civil War, was the establishment of Centralia Station.

The General Land Office draftsmen did not map the Butterfield (or westward) branch of these two mail roads even as far as Llano Estacado Station, but they showed it again at China Ponds in central Upton County (called China Lake on some present-day maps) and from there they showed it all the way across the west half of Upton County.[45] These stage station ruins discovered by the Conklings were eighteen and one-half miles from the point where the mail road skirted the north side of China Ponds. It was thirteen and one-half miles from these ponds to the east end of the historic little mountain pass that is known as Castle Gap, which zigzagged a full one and one-fourth miles in a southwesterly direction. Finally, it is twelve miles a little south of west to Horsehead Crossing on the Pecos.[46] The total of

41. General Land Office Map of Upton County, dated, 1918.

42. *Ibid.* China Lake is shown in Block Y, Section 23, Gulf, Colorado, and Santa Fe Railway Company lands.

43. General Land Office Map of Crane County, dated 1902. Horsehead Crossing is shown in Block 1, Section 37, Houston and Texas Central Railway lands.

44. Conkling, *The Overland Mail*, I, 366-369. J. Evetts Haley, *Fort Concho, and the Texas Frontier* (San Angelo, 1952), 90n, discovered authenticity of Llano Estacado name.

45. General Land Office Map of Upton County, dated 1918.

46. Tom Green County Surveyors Records (MS., County Clerk's Office, San

all these miles from the station at the head of the Concho to this crossing on the Pecos River amounts to seventy-four and one-half miles.

Land records establish the route of the road at the Concho Station; land records again establish the route at and near Centralia Station; and again land records chart the course from China Ponds all the way through Castle Gap near the western edge of Upton County. The land maps at Austin locate Horsehead Crossing at the west end of the Houston and Texas Central Railway Survey No. 37, some twelve miles northwest of present-day McCamey in Crane County.[47]

Thus, by land records almost alone, aided only by the known locations of a few towns and old forts, the course of the pre-Civil War Butterfield Overland Mail route can be charted without great error from Colbert's Ferry on Red River to Horsehead Crossing on the Pecos. West of Horsehead Crossing land records are still the major source of information for outlining the route of this old trail all the way west to the Rio Grande at El Paso.

The first of the Butterfield coaches did not actually cross the river at Horsehead Crossing but turned upstream on the east bank fifty-five miles to Emigrant Crossing[48] and yet another sixty-five miles to

Angelo), D, 123-125. J. W. Armstrong of Tom Green County made the survey in 1884.

47. General Land Office Map of Crane County, dated 1902.

48. The search for the location of the Emigrant Crossing Station constitutes a most interesting problem. Roscoe and Margaret Conkling reported in their book, *The Butterfield Overland Mail*, I, 377-378, that the probable location of this stage stand was somewhere in Section 25 or 26, Block 33, of the Houston and Texas Central Railway Surveys. The thoroughness of the Conklings' research methods might cause one to accept their solution to the problem without question. If, however, one studies carefully the notes left by Randolph B. Marcy (*Senate Executive Documents,* 31st Cong., 1st Sess. [Serial No. 562], Document No. 64), he is led to a different conclusion. Marcy's notes are not at all consistent with the physical facts of the river and the topography at Section 25. The Pecos turns sharply to the southeast at Section 25. Marcy traveled 8° north of east from his river crossing and said that he traveled down near the river in so doing. Plainly his crossing could not have been southeast from that point instead of 8° north of east as he reported.

On the other hand, Section 16, which is five miles downstream from Section 25, is a point at which Marcy's notes are thoroughly consistent with the bends of the river. Moreover, this point in Section 16 is well-known locally as Emigrant Crossing. The writer has worked somewhat laboriously studying the bends of the river on the ground and from maps. He has found no other place that is consistent with all of Marcy's notes except the crossing in Section 16 which is locally known as Emigrant Crossing. Apparently the Emigrant Crossing Station was five miles up stream from

Pope's Camp. The writer has not checked this route in land records but the physical path of the river can itself fairly well outline the course of the road between these points. The wagon road which the mail coaches followed had been made by the supply trains of Captain John Pope who had attempted to produce artesian water near the New Mexico line.[49] After his unsuccessful experiment was finished and abandoned, both his road and his camp were taken over by the Butterfield interests. Pope's abandoned camp was on the east side of the Pecos about four miles south of the New Mexico line. Pope's Crossing was some three miles upstream from his camp.[50] It was here, a mile or two below the state line, that the mail road crossed the Pecos and extended due west in its route toward present-day El Paso. Some eight and one-half miles west of the Pecos near the center of Section 11, Township 1, Block 59, of the Texas and Pacific Railway lands, the road crossed Delaware Creek. From here the route of the Butterfield Trail is preserved by Texas and Pacific Railway records most of the way across north Culberson County.[51] The writer has a blueprint from the Texas and Pacific tracing of these lands, showing both Delaware Creek and the road that lay to the north of it. At the crossing of Delaware Creek in Section 11, the road was a mile and one-half south of the New Mexico line. Nineteen and one-half miles west of this creek crossing (somewhat more than that by the road itself) the mail road reached Delaware Springs at a point nine miles south of the New Mexico line. Thus following the general course of Delaware Creek, the Butterfield Trail bore somewhat to the south of its westward objective in order to reach this watering place at Delaware Springs.[52]

Emigrant Crossing itself. There may be, however, some other solution to the problem.

49. "Conclusion of the Official Review of the Reports upon the Explorations and Surveys for Railroad Routes from the Mississippi River to the Pacific Ocean," *House Executive Documents,* 33rd Cong., 2nd Sess. (Serial No. 797), Document No. 91, pp. 16-18.

50. Ormsby, *The Overland Mail,* 72.

51. These lands were first surveyed by Jacob Kuechler in 1879. They were resurveyed and mapped by Paul McCombs in 1884.

52. Most of the road to Delaware Springs is shown on the McCombs map. Notes on the margin of the map show the exact location (in Section 9, Township 2, Block 62) of the springs and the Butterfield stage stand near by. Delaware Springs were south 78°30' east 373 *varas* from the northwest corner of Section 9. The stage stand was south 81°22' 478 *varas* from the same point.

Turning slightly to the north of west from here for fifteen miles the road reached Independence Springs just a little less than eight miles south of the New Mexico line.[53] Five miles to the west the early mail road reached Pine Springs about six and three-fourths miles south of the New Mexico line.[54]

Here the road could not continue in its westward course since El Capitan Peak, two miles to the west, stood across its path. Bending around the south end of this imposing mountain through Guadalupe Pass, as does the present Carlsbad-El Paso Road, the Butterfield Trail soon reached out of Culberson County into the barren land of the Hudspeth County salt flats. In making this curve to the south of El Capitan Peak the old road passed out of the area later surveyed for the Texas and Pacific Railway Company onto Public School Block No. 121, the maps of which did not chart the path of the early mail road.[55]

Near the boundary of Hudspeth County, however, the Butterfield Trail extended northwestward into the Texas and Pacific lands again—into the area where the road is again shown on the land maps. For ten miles, beginning in Section 42, Township 1, Block 67, of the Texas and Pacific Railway Company lands, the mail road extended almost exactly northwest to the Texas-New Mexico line.[56] The road passed out of Texas at this point between two monuments that were erected on the state line by the joint Texas-United States Boundary Commission in 1859.[57]

Actually the mail road was not named on the Texas and Pacific land maps, but the fact that it passed by Delaware Springs and the stage stand at that point, by Independence Springs, and by Pine Springs—all of which are known points on the Butterfield Trail—makes its identification hardly subject to question.

Another group of surveyors in addition to those employed by the

53. The McCombs map shows Independence Springs in Section 43, Township 1, Block 64.

54. The McCombs map shows Pine Springs in Section 41, Township 1, Block 64. Other notes on the map in Section 41, which may refer to the stage stand, are illegible.

55. See General Land Office Map of Culberson County, dated 1908. El Capitan Peak is in Section 48, Township 1, Block 66.

56. See General Land Office Map of Hudspeth County, dated 1917.

57. *Ibid.* These monuments are shown on the map with the road passing between them.

Texas and Pacific Railway Company has rendered material aid at this point. The joint commission appointed by Texas and the United States surveyed this part of the Texas boundary line (which is also the south line of New Mexico) in 1859. Their survey was in progress at the same time that John Butterfield's mail coaches were moving back and forth over this same part of the Butterfield Trail. The surveyors made extensive observations which map makers charted on paper.[58] The result of their work leaves a complete map of the Overland Mail Route from this point that is now northeastern Hudspeth County all the way across a small segment of Otero County, New Mexico, back into northwest Hudspeth County, Texas, and southwestwardly through modern El Paso, and up the Rio Grande to where the old road finally left the boundaries of Texas.

The surveyors camped for some days in northeast Hudspeth County by the side of the mail road just about a mile from the place where the road passed out of Texas between the two monuments previously mentioned. The camp site was called Crow Springs. Later a stage stand was erected at this place—but evidently it had not been built when the surveyors camped at the springs; at least their map omitted it. Some twenty-eight miles northwest of Crow Springs the boundary commission map shows the stage stand at Cornudas Tanks, some half dozen miles north of the Texas-New Mexico line. About ten miles beyond this station the map also shows a stage stand at Alamo Springs. Some seven or eight miles westward from Alamo Springs the road bent back into Texas, probably into Section 6, Block B, of the University of Texas land.[59] Here again the commission erected a monument on each side of the mail road, but the General Land Office map of Hudspeth County does not show these monuments. Another fifteen miles along the mail road is the well-known point in El Paso County known as Hueco Tanks. The mail station was just east of the small mountain that is on the north of the

58. *Senate Executive Documents*, 47th Cong., 1st Sess. (Serial No. 1987), Document No. 70. This is a report of the Texas Boundary Commission of 1859 and 1860. Map No. 1 appended to the report shows the mail road across what is now El Paso County and the west part of Hudspeth County. Map No. 2 joins Map No. 1 on the east and shows the mail road eastward nearly all the way to the east Hudspeth County line.

59. See General Land Office Map of Hudspeth County, dated 1917. This block of the University of Texas lands covers some 450,000 acres. It is the largest tract of the University land holdings.

road at this point. Franklin, a mail station within modern El Paso, was another thirty miles westward.

The trail extended westward across the southern rim of the United States to California where it turned northward and terminated at San Francisco. The part of the route westward from Horsehead Crossing on the Pecos was abandoned after a year of the operation because of the shortage of water. A ferry was established at Horsehead Crossing, and the route was changed to a road that was already in operation through the Davis Mountains.

A review of the cardinal points on this branch of the Butterfield Overland Mail reveals the following facts. From Horsehead Crossing the distance was thirty-four miles southwest to Comanche Springs. The trail from Comanche Springs west followed the San Antonio-El Paso Road which was already well established. Randolph B. Marcy gives the names of important camp sites and the distance from camp to camp as follows: (1) from Comanche Creek to Leon Springs—8.88 miles, (2) from this point to Barela Springs [Barrilla Spring] 33.86 miles, (3) from here to Fort Davis 28 miles, (4) to Barrel Springs 18.42 miles, (5) to Dead Man's Hole 13.58 miles, (6) next to Van Horn's Wells 32.83 miles, (7) to Eagle Springs 19.74 miles, (8) to the mouth of Cañon de los Camenos 32.03 miles, (9) then the road runs up the Rio Grande to San Eluzario [San Elizario] 61.13 miles, (10) then to Socorro 9.25 miles, and (11) finally to Fort Bliss 15 miles.[60]

Without great difficulty, one may find the present-day locations of nearly all of these points from the locations of existing towns or from land records. Comanche Creek (actually the point was Comanche Springs) is at modern Fort Stockton. Barrilla Spring is preserved by land records as the west corner of Pecos County.[61] The stage stand that took the name was on Limpia Creek (principal branch of Barrilla Creek) two miles to the south. Fort Davis was at the present-day town of the same name. Barrel Springs are located in Section 1, Block 1, of the Houston and Texas Central Railway Company lands in Jeff Davis County.[62] Dead Man's Hole is in Section 31, Bock 3, of the Houston and Texas Central Railway Company lands, also in Jeff Davis

60. Randolph B. Marcy, *The Prairie Traveler: A Handbook for Overland Expeditions* (New York, 1859), 289-290.

61. See General Land Office Map of Jeff Davis County, dated 1915. The spring that marks the west corner of Pecos County is shown on this map.

62. *Ibid*.

County.[63] Van Horn's Wells are west of Lobo, nine miles south of the town of Van Horn and less than a mile west of U. S. Highway 90.[64] The site of Eagle Springs is preserved by the 1917 General Land Office map of Hudspeth County. It is Section 9, Township 9 South, Block 68, of the Texas and Pacific Railway Company lands. Cañon de los Camenos is near the Rio Grande, southwest of present Sierra Blanca. From this locality the road went up the Rio Grande past San Elizario and Socorro to Fort Bliss and Franklin, both of which were in what is presently El Paso.

Above El Paso the tracer of the Butterfield Overland Mail Route comes to the border of Texas and this time to the end of this trail hunt. The search has depended heavily on surveyors' notes and on the simple arithmetic of distance. The chief function of this effort has been to correct some of the errors that have crept into the record and to establish more definitely the route of an interesting old trail that still adds its touch of glamour to the story of frontier America.[65]

63. *Ibid.*

64. *Ibid.* The stage stand was in Hudspeth County, but it was on an extension of the Jeff Davis County map that the stage stand was shown.

65. For the sake of accuracy such local errors as the following ought to be corrected. The Texas Highway Department erected an expensive monument on U. S. Highway 281 about five miles northwest of Bowie that purports to mark a point on the Butterfield Trail. There is another marker about seven miles northwest of Bowie on U. S. Highway 287 that also attests to the same misinformation. Both markers are a full twenty miles off the actual Butterfield Mail Route as indicated by the commissioners minutes and surveyors' notes cited in this paper.

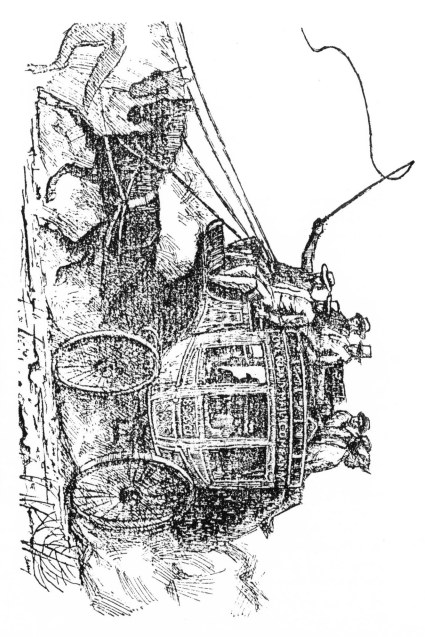

A Concord Coach Used on the Butterfield Overland Mail Route.

XVI

SOME NORTHWEST TEXAS TRAILS AFTER BUTTERFIELD

Northwest Texas does not offer the most spectacular trail migration in American history; perhaps that distinction belongs to California. But the first measurable decade of the northwest portion of our state (1880-1890) in its modest way built up a population one-sixth as great as California during the first decade after the Gold Rush.

West Texas (west of Fort Belknap and north of the 32nd parallel) did not have a gold rush, but it did have what was probably the greatest game hunt in all human history. The trails into this land of the buffalo have furnished some worth-while and colorful writings—but relatively little compared with the immense volume of literature that has come up from the wagon trains and the mail coaches that were inspired by California's dream of gold.

The "Butterfield Trail" and the "Oregon Trail" are words well imbedded in the language of the American people, but how very few are they who ever heard of the old Buffalo Road of West Texas! Who knows with any degree of accuracy the route of the Rath Trail? And who has heard about an old military road (attributed to Colonel R. S. Mackenzie) that directly connected old Fort Griffin with the Texas Panhandle. In this chapter we hope to furnish reasonably adequate information about these particular routes and a few others.

But it is quite obvious that we can only touch a portion of the trails of West Texas. There were military roads, mail roads, buffalo roads, emigrant roads: West Texas had them all.

Let us begin where John Butterfield and his associates left off. Let us briefly explain the changes that railroads brought as they shortened this greatest of trans-continental stagecoach lines and furnished new anchor points from which the mail went west.

The Civil War cut short the operations of the Butterfield or Southern Overland mail, but it was not long after the end of that struggle when responsible management took over, so far as Texas is concerned, the long distance mail service that had been rendered by this first trans-continental stage line. In 1868 Ben Ficklin contracted to carry the mail between Fort Smith and San Antonio[1] and to extend a westward line to El Paso. The hub of his operations was a town known as Ben Ficklin, some three or four miles south of present-day San Angelo. Thus, he took over many of the old station sites and many miles of the very wagon ruts that had been used by John Butterfield. For four years the Ficklin interests continued, and for most of another decade others carried on, but under rapidly changing conditions.

The Missouri, Kansas & Texas railway tracks had reached Denison by 1872[2] and the two roads that ultimately became the Texas & Pacific reached Dallas and Sherman in 1873.[3] From Dallas the steel rails reached across the Trinity River to Eagle Ford in 1874[4] and stretched on to reach Fort Worth on July 19, 1876.[5]

Obviously the mail coaches from Fort Smith, Arkansas, over the long dusty trail to Sherman, Texas, were no longer necessary. The Texas & Pacific Railroad was chartered by the Federal Government, and it was a provision of that charter that the railroad must carry the mail. However, not all of the old Butterfield Trail had yet ceased to function. It will be remembered that that once colorful mail line sent its four and six horse coaches from Sherman to Gainesville, to Jacksboro to Belknap, to Phantom Hill and on to Fort Chadbourne, up the Middle Concho, on across the Pecos and on west to the place that is now called El Paso. That old dirt road had once come down from Tipton, Missouri (160 miles west of Saint Louis) across western Arkansas to Fort Smith and across the corner of Indian Territory to Sherman, Texas.

But the old stage line had seen its days of glory. No longer was the rail head Tipton, Missouri; now (November, 1875) it was Eagle Ford,[6] Texas. Then in 1876, it became Fort Worth, Texas. For a brief

1. See Walter Prescott Webb, ed; *The Handbook of Texas* (Austin, 1952) 1,596 (Hereafter referred to as the *Handbook*. Also see Roscoe P. and Margaret B. Conkling, *The Butterfield Overland Mail*) Glendale, 1947, 1, 309-363 (Hereafter referred to as *Conkling*.)

2. S. G. Reed, *A History of the Texas Railroads* (Houston, 1941), 376. (Hereafter referred to as Reed: *Railroads*).

3. *Ibid.*, 363.

4. *Ibid.*, 364.

5. *Ibid.*, 364.

6. *Frontier Echo* (of Jacksboro, Texas), November 6, 1875.

interval, the United States mail extended west from Eagle Ford and entered the wagon ruts of the overland mail at the little town of Jacksboro. As late as November 6, 1875, the *Frontier Echo* of Jacksboro still referred to the mail line as the "El Paso Stages",[7] but by the end of March following, this early day newspaper indicated that the long distance mail line had ceased to function.[8]

An important change had come to the El Paso mail route. Near the time when Fort Worth became the end of the Texas & Pacific Railway, the El Paso stage line turned southwestward to Granbury, Stephenville, Dublin, Comanche, Brownwood, Coleman, and on to Fort Concho within the present city of San Angelo.[9] Except that it did not pass through Ben Ficklin, this latest edition of long distance mail service followed the tracks traveled by Ben Ficklin himself all the way to El Paso. It was 180 miles from Fort Concho across the Pecos to Fort Stockton, then seventy-nine miles to Fort Davis and 140 miles to Fort Quitman, and a final eighty-four miles up the Rio Grande to El Paso. Thus, if one can trust the United States Postal map of 1878, it was 483 miles from Fort Concho to El Paso.

This road from a point some twenty-five or thirty miles west of Fort Concho followed the route of the old Overland mail all the way to El Paso, with one important exception.[10] From a point some ten miles west of the site of Stiles in Reagan County, the old Overland extended to the west through Castle Gap, and on a dozen miles to ferry the Pecos at Horsehead Crossing, and from there turned southwest to

7. *Ibid.* The *Echo* has this to say, "El Paso stages are being driven by mules between this place and Eagle Ford."

8. *Ibid.*, March 10, 1876. The *Echo* of the latter date says, "The El Paso Stage Co. has thrown up the sponge on the Ft. Griffin mail route."

9. "Post Route Map of the State of Texas, . . ." (1878). Other Post Route maps of Texas referred to in this paper were dated, 1880, 1881, 1884, 1887, 1889. Each of these maps was printed in 8 sections, 18 x 26 inches each. The 4 West Texas, sections of the map of 1884 are missing from the files of the U. S. Postal Department and of the Library of Congress. A "Preliminary Post Route map of the State of Texas . . ." was published in 1874. It was printed in 6 sections. Apparently the above maps mentioned in this footnote are all of the Postal route maps of Texas printed between the Civil War and 1889—Postal route maps of Texas printed between the Civil War and 1889. Photostatic copies of this file of maps are in the possession of the estate of J. W. Williams. Hereafter each map will be referred to as "Post Map," followed by the date.

10. *Conkling.* Maps at end of atlas volume. Also see the Texas General Land Office map of Upton County, dated Jan. 1918. Part of the details by land surveys are shown on this map.

Fort Stockton. To state the route more in detail this latest of the stage lines turned southwest at the point ten miles west of the site of Stiles, passed three miles to the left of present Rankin,[11] and crossed the Pecos two miles above the present highway bridge that crosses that river north of present Iraan.[12] From here the newer lines joined the old Butterfield (or Overland) again at Fort Stockton. In 1872 this crossing near Iraan was bridged by the United States Government.[13] The structure was known as the Pontoon Bridge. The bridge floated high or low according to the depth of the river, and the approaches were so made as to accommodate the traffic at all times.[14]

Was this latest edition of Texas long-distance stages a dull and uninteresting afterthought? Not at all. Judge O. W. Williams, the grand old man of the historical associations, rode this stage in 1880 all the way from Fort Worth to El Paso and beyond. He left us a description of the journey. His party left Fort Worth in a fine mail coach drawn by six spirited horses. After a time, the coach was replaced by a less spectacular vehicle, and the six horses were changed to two wild little mules,[15] but his description causes one to recall the story of Ormsby, the New York correspondent, as he rode west on the first of all the Butterfield stages.

But this new horse drawn and mule-drawn mail service was destined to come to an end in a scant half dozen years. The two great railroads, one from Los Angeles and the other from Fort Worth, met at Sierra Blanca[16] in 1881; and when they met, the reason for the existence of the Southern Overland mail and all of its successors had disappeared.

But even after that chapter was closed, yet a smaller but somewhat similar story remained to be told about Northwest Texas. In 1878 the United States Government mails crossed the Texas Panhandle through Fort Elliott, Tascosa, and on west to Fort Bascomb in New Mexico.[17] Nearer the center of Texas, mail roads came to an

11. The Upton County map as cited in footnote no. 10.

12. O. W. Williams, *In Old New Mexico 1879-1880*, 9. This excellent 48-page pamphlet shows neither the name of the publisher nor the date of publication. Also see *Conkling*, 364.

13. *Conkling*, 364.

14. See O. W. Williams, *In Old New Mexico 1879-1880*, 9.

15. *Ibid.*, 8.

16. Reed: Railroads, 365.

17. Post Map, 1878.

end at Buffalo Gap, Fort Griffin, Spring Creek (twenty-five miles northwest of Belknap), at Archer City, and at Henrietta. These were the five terminal points shown on the Postal map of 1878. There were almost no towns and no mail services northwest of them short of the Fort Elliott-Tascosa Country in the Panhandle. But while the map makers were processing that old spread of postal information, northwest Texas was making ready to change it.

Apparently the people of Fort Griffin, and probably other West Texas towns, had laid it on the hearts of their representatives in Congress to add mail service northwest into the great blank spot that existed westward and northward of this Buffalo Gap-Fort Griffin-Henrietta frontier in early 1879. The answer came in an act of Congress dated March 3 of that year. Many mail routes established by the act were reported in the *Fort Griffin Echo of April 26*.[18] These are the routes reported by the *Echo*:

(1) Fort Sill by Camp Augur (then near Electra, Texas) and Fort Griffin to Fort Concho.

(2) Fort Sill by the Wichita Mountains and the North Fork of Red River to Fort Elliott.

(3) Las Vegas, New Mexico (then probably down the Pecos River and across the plains) by Blanco supply camp, Texas, Old Fort Chadbourne, Old Fort Mason, Old Fort Martin Scott (near Fredericksburg) and on to San Antonio.

(4) Albany to Buffalo Gap.

(5) Albany to Williamsburg (now Throckmorton).

(6) Fort Concho to Fort Chadbourne.

(7) Belknap by Spring Creek and Round Timbers to Oregon. (Oregon was northeast of Seymour and south of the Wichita River).

(8) Belknap to Williamsburg.

(9) Fort Griffin by Williamsburg to Oregon.

(10) Fort Griffin by Simpson's Ranch (just east of Abilene) to Buffalo Gap.

(11) Fort Griffin to Blanco Canyon.

(12) Fort Griffin via California Ranch, Reynolds, Tepee's Store, and Indians Creek to Fort Elliott.

(13) Fort Griffin via Fort Elliott, Camp Supply and Fort Dodge to Leadville, Colorado.

(14) Fort Chadbourne to Fort Griffin.

(15) Sweetwater to Buffalo Gap.

18. The *Fort Griffin Echo*, Apr. 26, 1879.

Obviously there was quite a bit of duplication of routes in this long list. The *Echo* did not report just to what extent these numerous routes may have been combined before putting this new frontier mail service into operation. As reported in the *Echo* of May 20[19] the Postal Department advertised for bids on carrying the mail:

(1) From Fort Griffin by California Ranch (and apparently on to Blanco Canyon), 157 miles, and back once a week.

(2) From Fort Griffin by Phantom Hill to Fort Concho, 150 miles and back once a week.

(3) From Fort Griffin by Throckmorton, Seymour, Hamberg's Store (at Teepee City) and to Fort Elliott, 240 miles, and back once a week.

(4) From Albany by Simpson's ranch (the Hash Knife within the site of Abilene) to Buffalo Gap, fifty miles and back, once a week.

(5) From Albany to Phantom Hill and back once a week. Apparently there was less duplication in this list of mail routes than in the list of routes reported on April 26. Probably other routes were advertised at places other than Fort Griffin, but there was still some delay before anybody actually carried the mail. It was in September before the wheels began to turn.

Monday, September 22 was the date announced by the *Echo* when the first mail (and passengers if any) would leave Fort Griffin for Fort Elliott.[20] A week earlier Colonel DeWitt Clinton Giddings[21] (of Brenham, Texas, and Washington, D.C.), made a statement about the operation of several Northwest Texas mail lines. Giddings and associates had a contract to carry the mails from Fort Griffin to Fort Elliott, from Fort Griffin to Blanco Canyon, and from Fort Griffin to Fort Concho—and in addition from Fort Elliott to Wichita Falls. Giddings said that Concord coaches would serve these lines whenever business justified.

Colonel Giddings was none other than the colorful gentleman from Brenham, Texas, who won an election to Congress from the third congressional district in 1870 but was counted out of his victory by the powers that then controlled Texas. Governor Edmund P. Davis

19. *Ibid.*, May 20, 1879.

20. *Ibid.*

21. *Ibid.*, Sept. 15, 1879. The *Echo* refers to the gentleman who contracted to do this mail service as Col. Giddings of Washington D. C. Evidently the person referred to was DeWitt Clinton Giddings who had just completed his term in Congress.

certified Giddings' Carpetbag opponent, William T. Clark, who was seated by the House of Representatives at Washington. But the ex-Confederate colonel rose to full fighting height, marshalled his evidence of election irregularities, and won back his seat in Congress before that august body—even of opposite political faith.

Who worked the road ahead of Colonel Giddings' mail hacks and stage coaches? In general nobody did. The roads, or more accurately the frontier trails, came about in a different way. The supply wagons of Colonel Mackenzie made some of them, and buffalo hunters and hide haulers added their share to the total. What evidence we have indicates that the actual wagon ruts when they came followed much of the routes that had been used by Indians for centuries before them.

But if the bull wagons and mule teams of the army and the hunters borrowed from the Indians, so did the mail coaches borrow from the mules drivers and bull whackers. Colonel Mackenzie, Charlie Rath, and just plain anonymous John Doe made most of the trails in advance of the United States Mail.

From Fort Griffin westward ran the old military supply route that is so often referred to as "the Mackenzie Trail." Since many miles of this road made the very wagon tracks over which Hank Smith drove the first mail hacks to Mount Blanco, it behooves us to study that route. Much of the route of the Mackenzie Trail has been preserved in land records. It began at the old town of Fort Griffin, which is beside the Clear Fork of the Brazos, hardly two miles south of the north boundary of Shackelford County. It ran a little to the south of due west three miles where it entered the more recent J. H. Nail ranch, about 2¼ miles south of the county boundary line.[22] It continued its course westward for 5½ miles—still in the Nail ranch—at which point it came near the broken country that included the Antelope Hills. Here the Mackenzie Trail turned due north and in fact curved a little toward the northeast for a distance of two miles. In that distance the old road had passed out of the Nail ranch and about a quarter of a mile beyond into land that once belonged to the late J. A. Matthews. Then out of the Matthews ranch and into land that

22. The map of Shackelford County in the original plat book of County maps of the T. & P. RR. Co. (Dallas, Texas) shows a trail across north Shackelford County which the late Phin Reynolds of Albany identified as the Mackenzie Trail. The map bore the following incomplete date, 187-. The estate of J. W. Williams has a photostatic copy of the map.

long belonged to the Reynolds Cattle Company, the early day trail extended due west again for a distance of five miles. In that span of five miles this, Number 1 route of the Mackenzie supply roads, passed almost an even quarter of a mile north of the J. H. Nail pasture fence all the way and then crossed the Clear Fork of the Brazos. The old crossing was fourteen miles west of Fort Griffin as the crow flies or sixteen miles by the Mackenzie Trail.

At the Clear Fork the early trail turned northwest for about a mile and entered Haskell County near its southeast corner. Unfortunately for the researchers—but perhaps fortunately for the reader—land records do not seem to be available for the minute details of the old road in Haskell County. However, there is enough evidence to make it certain that this trail of yesteryear did pass westwardly across the southern part of the county. The late A. J. Swenson[23] of Stamford, Texas, who supervised the fencing of the Swenson Ericsdale ranch in 1883, said that the Mackenzie Trail lay to the north of that ranch. The late R. L. Livengood,[24] who lived in south Haskell County as early as 1886, said that the old trail passed south of his farm. Now the Swenson ranch was two miles south of the Haskell County line while the Livengood farm was five miles north of that line. Hence, it is not at all difficult to see that in this space of seven miles between the two pieces of real estate there was ample room for the old Mackenzie Trail.

Fortunately we have the personal testimony of R. L. Livengood given at his home in south Haskell County near the Mackenzie Trail. "The Mackenzie Trail," he said, "crossed the D. Taylor land three miles south of here. It crossed the Haskell-Stamford pavement on the Ed Rountree[25] land less than a half mile south of Paint Creek. It turned more to the northwest and crossed Paint Creek a half mile or more above the bridge." He said that this crossing was the same as the first Anson-Haskell road crossing on that stream. It was about a half mile below the mouth of Willow Paint Creek. The old road, he said, followed up the northeast side of Willow Paint and crossed that creek

23. A personal interview (at Stamford) with the late A. J. Swenson.

24. A personal interview with the late R. L. Livengood at his home in south Haskell County, Texas.

25. The Livengood interview. Probably the name should have been Ed Jones instead of Ed Rountree. The Ed Jones land is in the position described by Mr. Livengood. The Mackenzie Trail also passed a little south of the L. Dycus survey in southeast Haskell County.

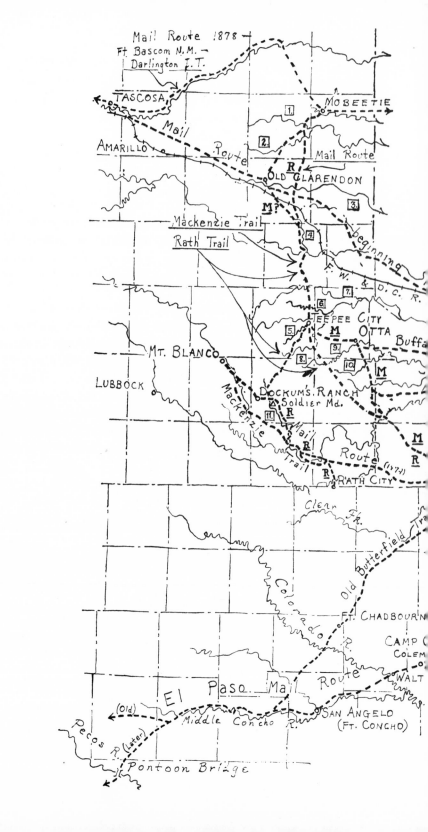

1. North Fork Red River
2. Mc Clellan's Creek
3. Salt Fork Red River
4. Indian Creek
5. Teepee Creek
6. Turtle Hole Creek
7. North Pease River
8. South Pease River
9. North Fork-Wichita River
10. Middle Fork Wichita River
11. Duck Creek

M - Mackenzie Trail
R - Rath Trail

& P. R.R., not shown from Fort Worth West—mapped railways explained in article.

SOME HISTORIC NORTH TEXAS TRAILS

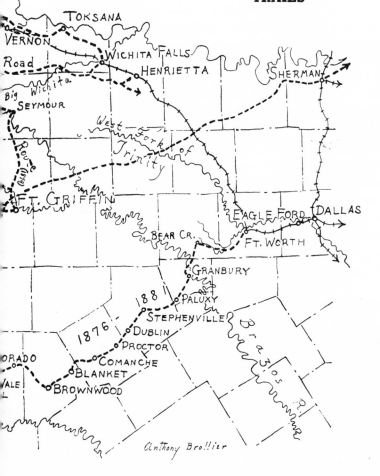

Anthony Brollier

four or five miles above its mouth and went through or at least almost through the site of Sagerton. Perhaps the nearest approach to land records as a source of information at this point is the giant-size map of Texas at the Texas General Land Office, by Pressler and Langermann,[26] which was drawn in 1879. This large map goes so far as to show and dimly identify the great spreads of railroad lands over much of Texas. It even shows the individual sections of land by the tens of thousands of square miles. So small is a single section of land that a good magnifying glass is necessary to identify it. Even then, the old map has deteriorated so much that one is often unable to be certain of his observations.

This old map shows Haskell County as well as most areas of the state. The great spreads of Houston & Texas Central Railway lands can be identified; and a road across the south part of the county, though not named, is undoubtedly the Mackenzie Trail.[27] With a little aid from a magnifying glass one may be reasonably sure that it crossed the Houston & Texas Central sections ten, eleven, and twelve just southeast of Sagerton. Turning again toward the northwest, it skirted the south edge of Sagerton and crossed the Double Mountain Fork of the Brazos in the tip of the principal bend of that river that lies between the present railway bridge and the present highway bridge[28] just west of that little town.

In Stonewall County this one-time useful supply road followed a course nearly due west until it had passed four miles south of Aspermont,[29] and until it had crossed Little Stinking Creek, five miles north of Double Mountains. Here the old road bent a little to the south and crossed the Salt Fork of the Brazos River,[30] some five miles

26. This map in the Texas General Land Office is the last of these large state maps now in that office that were made all or in part by Charles W. Pressler. The other two maps were made in 1858 and 1867.

27. The road on this map conforms with the route of the Mackenzie Trail as shown in Shackelford County, also with the interviews mentioned above.

28. An interview with H. E. Carr of Old Glory, Texas at the Cowboy Reunion at Stamford, Texas about 1947. Carr had lived in the area most of the time since 1880.

29. An interview with John Guest of Aspermont, Texas in 1947. Guest had lived in Stonewall County since 1886. The Mackenzie Trail crossed a tract of his land southeast of Aspermont.

30. The Mackenzie Trail shown on a Texas General Land Office map of Kent County (dated 1895) extends directly toward the old Luzon crossing on the Brazos River. The Luzon Crossing was about 1 ½ miles west of the east line of Kent County. The trail is mapped to within three miles of the crossing.

to the west. The river crossing was a mile or two inside Kent County. Beyond the Salt Fork the trail turned abruptly to the northwest. About four miles southwest of the site of Jayton, it passed near the Salt Fork again. It continued to skirt this principal branch of the Brazos for perhaps a half dozen miles and crossed Duck Creek just above its mouth[31] at a point where Mackenzie, for a while, maintained a supply depot. In all Mackenzie's old freight road ran about thirty miles within Kent County and nearly every one of these miles extended directly toward the northwest. Land records have preserved nearly all of this route in Kent County and in fact nearly all of the route to Mount Blanco in Crosby County.

Mount Blanco was the name applied to the old post office in the west edge of Blanco Canyon, ten miles north of present-day Crosbyton. Hank Smith[32] owned the old rock house there that served both as the post office and as the home of his family. It became a post office, probably, in late September 1879 and continued to be a post office for more than a third of a century. Hank Smith contracted with the Giddings interests and became the first mail carrier from Fort Griffin to this post office in the old rock house.

But this mail route followed the Mackenzie Trail only as far as the mouth of Duck Creek[33] in Kent County. From here it turned off of the Mackenzie Trail and went up Duck Creek past the site of present-day Spur. This part of the mail route followed what the land

---

There is good reason to believe that the Mackenzie Trail followed two different routes for some eight to ten miles in this area. The route as shown on the Pressler and Langermann map of 1879 ran parallel to and about three miles northeast of the route by the Luzon Crossing.

31. The oldest available map that shows this part of the Mackenzie Trail is "Dickens Co. Sk. File A," which was filed in the Texas General Land Office Aug. 13, 1873. This map shows the Mackenzie Trail but does not name it. However, a map by the New York and Texas Land Company not dated but drawn about ten years later identified the trail and extended it. This map is in the same file as the sketch of 1873.

32. See the *Handbook*, 11, 624, for a short biography of Henry Clay (Hank) Smith.

33. See Post Map, 1880. Also see the New York and Texas Land Company map cited in footnote No. 31. A study of the two maps reveals that the early postal route turned away from the Mackenzie Trail, went up Duck Creek to Soldier's Mound where it turned west to Dockum's Ranch and at that point turned northwest to join the Mackenzie Trail again eastward of present-day Crosbyton. The New York and Texas Company Land map shows these old roads by land surveys and corrects an incorrect impression given in the postal map.

records call the road to Tee Pee City.[34] We shall have occasion to refer to this road again. From the Tee Pee City road the mail route turned westward by Dockum's Ranch[35] and joined the Mackenzie Trail again in Blanco Canyon.[36] Perhaps ten miles up this canyon it reached the old Hank Smith rock house.

Another of the Giddings stage routes that began to function at the same time as the Mount Blanco line was the 240-mile mail road from Fort Griffin to Fort Elliott. At six o'clock on Monday morning, September 22, 1879, the first mail bags were due to leave from Griffin for Elliott. The event was foretold by the *Fort Griffin Echo*[37] but the incomplete files of that paper seem not to contain an account of the actual take-off. Only five days later the stage line was advertised in the *Echo*. Apparently the take-off did occur as foretold by the papers, but the advertisement told of a change in the route, from the first announcement. The mail sacks did not go west to California Ranch in Haskell County, then north to Tee Pee City and Fort Elliott as first intended, but instead went north by Throckmorton (then called Williamsburg) to Seymour,[38] northwest by Tee Pee City, and then to Fort Elliott.

What was the route of this new 240-mile stage line? The first leg of this long trail across the frontier could not have been very different from today's road from the crossing of the Clear Fork (north of Albany) by Throckmorton to Seymour. Perhaps the major differences were at the river crossings. Near Fort Griffin the Clear Fork was crossed not far up stream from the present concrete bridge, and at Seymour the Brazos was crossed a mile or two below the present bridge.

West from Seymour the road passed through the "Narrows" past the present site of Benjamin and onto the west line of Knox County. The part of this road beyond the site of Benjamin was surveyed in June, 1881, when the Fort Griffin-Fort Elliott mail line had operated for just twenty months. The surveyors so marked their map as to dispel all reasonable doubts that this was the mail road from Seymour to Fort Elliott.[39] Only the fact that the new mail line

34. See the New York and Texas Land Company map mentioned in footnote No. 31.
   35. *Ibid.*
   36. *Ibid.*
   37. *Fort Griffin Echo* Sept. 20, 1879.
   38. *Ibid.*, May 31, 1879.
   39. This map (or sketch) from the Texas General Land Office was dated June 16,

connected those two distant points could have caused surveyors or any one else to have labeled the road ''From Fort Elliott'' and to have shown by a pointing hand that it extended to ''Seymour.'' With such a label, there is no good reason to doubt that this road in the west part of Knox County was a segment of the new mail line.

But a road turned north near the west line of Knox County. Land records call this northward segment of early-day roads a branch of Mackenzie trails.[40] We shall return to a more complete discussion of that trail at a later time. A land office map shows that this trail crossed the South Fork of the Wichita River just inside of King County and continued northwestward toward the Middle Wichita.[41] With a skip of four miles, the map again showed the road. Here it was called the ''Military Road.'' The Land Office map makers extended this ''Military Road'' northwestward to a point about a mile south of the mouth of Polecat Creek but with a skip of less than a mile another Land Office sketch[42] shows the continuation of the trail in Cottle County.

Here the old road extended to the small willow-picket post office of Otta at the crossing of the North Wichita. This frontier mail station was 9½ air line miles almost exactly southeast of present-day Paducah. Beyond this little post office the Land Office map makers extended their sketch of the road nine miles in a direction only a little north of west, but they left no doubt about the objective of the road in both directions. They called it the ''Seymour and Tee Pee City Road,'' a fact which ties together each of the sketches which this chapter has followed at points all the way from Seymour to Cottle County.

Tee Pee City was fifteen miles west and five miles north of present-day Paducah. The postal maps of 1880 and 1881 both show that it was on the Fort Griffin-Fort Elliott mail road. Those maps also show that Otta was on that road—and here we have the proof that the mail line did turn north on the Mackenzie Trail, for it was the only old road from the middle part of west Knox County to Tee Pee City that passed the post office of Otta.

1881 and was signed by W. C. Roberts of Jack Land District.
    40. See the Texas General Land Office map of King County dated Jan., 1905. The Mackenzie Trail Data on this map comes from the much older surveying records which are recorded in Knox and King counties and at the General Land Office.
    41. *Ibid.*
    42. The Texas General Land Office map of Cottle County dated May, 1883.

In other words, had the mail road continued westward from the vicinity of present-day Benjamin as far as to-day's county seat village of Guthrie, it would have missed Otta; had it turned northward before it reached Benjamin, it could have reached Otta; but it would have missed the place where the surveyors (in 1881) sketched a segment of the road from Seymour to Fort Elliott. Either way, whether by turning northward too soon or too late, it would have violated a very plain bit of documentary evidence.

The facts and the significance of the surveyor's sketch of 1881 told previously is probably clear enough, but the facts of the little post office of Otta need to be explained.

Before the Fort Griffin-Fort Elliott mail went north in September 1879, there was no such place name as Otta. A rancher (actually a hog rancher) whose name was Prewitt lived at the river crossing 9½ miles southeast of the present-day county seat town of Paducah. The mail carriers asked what name to call the new post office at Prewitt's house. Prewitt hesitated for a moment and then suggested his wife's name "Otta."[43] Mrs. Prewitt was a descendant of members of the Ottawa tribe of Indians. The name was adopted and appeared on the very next postal map[44] of the area made in Washington seven months after the first mail left Fort Griffin for Fort Elliott. It was the first post office in Cottle County. Considering the great distance from West Texas to Washington, the slow rate of transportation, and even the time required to draw a map, Otta was undoubtedly on the very first mail line from Fort Griffin to Fort Elliott; therefore the route suggested above from Seymour to central west Knox County and northwestward by the Mackenzie Trail and on by Otta to Tee Pee City[45] is strongly supported by the maps and documents at hand.

North of this frontier post office on Tee Pee Creek, the road passed just east of that stream and continued down the valley of the middle fork of the Pease River almost to the mouth of Turtle Hole Creek. Shortly the road crossed the middle Pease; then it crossed Turtle Hole and continued almost due north to the site of the village of

43. An interview with Mrs. Burk at Crowell, Texas in 1944. Mrs. Burk was Mr. Prewitt's daughter. Also see the West Texas Historical Association Year Book XX, 122 n. Mrs. R. L. Barrister, the granddaughter of Mrs. Prewitt, supplied information about her grandmother.

44. Post Map, 1880.

45. The route between Seymour and Otta may have been shortened a little later.

Northfield.[46] Then this old road that seemed to serve frontiersmen, as well as mail hacks, crossed the North Pease a mile below the mouth of Wind River. Next the route bent a little to the northwest, then to the northeast and crossed Red River partly on an island some three or four miles below the mouth of the little Red River.[47]

There is good reason to believe that the road went up Indian Creek[48] and passed a little west of Memphis. One is on solid ground when he cites land records to prove that this route of travel passed a point in the watershed of Whitefish Creek that is 6 ½ miles west and two miles south of the northeast corner of Donley County.[49] In between Indian Creek and this last point the route probably bent toward the west and passed some of the several lakes or watering places that lie west of Hedley.[50]

The surveyors who found the road in northeast Donley County made no mention of the Fort Griffin-Fort Elliott mail line. They called the road at that place the Rath Trail,[51] but strong circumstantial evidence also makes it appear to have been the route of the United States mail. The first mail route did not bend westward to Clarendon in the segment that ran between Tee Pee City and Fort Elliott. The postal maps[52] show that the mail road ran nearly due north from Tee Pee City precisely as the Rath Trail must have run in order to pass the point in Donley County where the surveyors located it and called it the ''Rath Trail.''[53]

From this place fixed by surveyors the Rath Trail and almost certainly the mail road continued northward skirting to the west of present-day McLean and crossing both McClellan's Creek and the

---

46. An interview with B. F. Simpson of Northfield, Texas in about 1950 (at the Stamford Cowboy Reunion).

47. *Ibid.*

48. *West Texas Historical Association Year Book XX*, 122.

49. See Donley County Sketch File No. 6 at the Texas General Land Office (dated Oct. 27, 1881). This is the field notes of the survey of a connecting line. It shows that a point on the Rath Trail was 1080 varas west of the common corner of sections No. 58, 59, 55, and 61 D & P R R Co. surveys in Block E.

50. These lakes are the natural watering places of the area.

51. See footnote No. 49.

52. Post Map, 1880 and 1881.

53. The B. F. Simpson interview (see footnote No. 46). Mr. Simpson said that everybody called it the ''Rath Trail.'' Mr. Simpson's home at Northfield was on the trail.

North Fork of Red River some three or four miles west of the junction of those two streams.[54] Northward and finally northeastward the old road crossed the west boundary of Wheeler County six or seven miles north of the North Fork.[55] Then it was a half dozen miles only a little north of east to Fort Elliott.

A discussion of the Rath Trail must wait for a short time. It was Colonel Mackenzie, the great road maker of the West Texas Plains, who came to this area near McClellan's Creek just seven years ahead of the mail wagons. He won a signal victory over Chief Mow-way and his Comanches not far from the place where the Rath Trail and the mail road crossed the North Fork of Red River. But he left his supply train some miles to the southwest near the site of old Clarendon.[56] He may have run a few vehicles between the battle site and the supply train. Also he may have sent a few wagons south from the battle site near or along the route that came to be known as the Rath Trail.

Both of those suppositions are mere conjecture, but there are solid facts on which to base the conclusion that he or some of those allied with him in his Indian campaign did send wagon traffic from this part of the Panhandle toward Fort Griffin. Previously we have cited land records to show that a Mackenzie Trail passed northward

54. See J. W. Williams (ed) "Robson's Journey through West Texas in 1879," *West Texas Historical Association Year Book XX* 115, 121. Robson traveled the road from Old Clarendon to Fort Elliott in 1879. He traveled down the north side of Mc-Clellan's Creek, turned northward and crossed the North Fork of Red River above the junction of the two streams but was so little above the junction that he ascended the high hills beside (east of) Cantonment Creek. To have done so he must have crossed North Fork about three or four miles above the mouth of McClellan's Creek. A study of footnotes No. 46 and 54 and of the Robson article indicate that Robson had come into the Rath Trail a short distance before he crossed the North Fork. Hereafter this article will be referred to as Robson: *Year Book*.

55. The Fort Elliott-Clarendon Road crossed the west line of Wheeler County a short distance north of Graham Creek which was some six or seven miles north of the North Fork of Red River. This fact was shown in the survey of the west line of Wheeler County (dated August 18, 1879) to be found in the files of County boundaries at the Texas General Land Office. Beyond any reasonable doubt the Rath Trail and the Clarendon Road (in 1879) were the same from Fort Elliott southwestwardly across the North Fork where the Rath Trail continued southward and the Clarendon Road branched to the right. Had Robson (in 1879), on his return from Fort Elliott, continued southward after he crossed the North Fork he would have reached the point in northeast Donley County which surveyors, in 1881, called the Rath Trail.

56. Ernest Wallace, *Randel S. Mackenzie on the Texas Frontier* (Lubbock, 1964), 78.

near the common boundary of Knox and King counties, that it connected with an old military trail near the middle Wichita in King County, and that it again connected with a road past old Otta in Cottle County and on to Tee Pee City in Motley County.

Now let us add a bit of evidence that this Mackenzie Trail crossed Red River some thirty-five miles due north of Tee Pee City. A. B. Gant ran an advertisement in the *Graham Leader* of March 2, 1877, in which he offered 10,000 acres of land for sale. He said that the land "fronted" on Red River, that it was surveyed by George Spiller in 1874, and that it was on the Mackenzie Trail.[57]

Two years later than the date of this advertisement, George W. Robson, the editor of the *Fort Griffin Echo*, traveled from old Clarendon, where Mackenzie's Supply Train was located (in 1872) and crossed Red River near the mouth of Indian Creek,[58] certainly the approximate site of the Mackenzie crossing, and proceded on due south to Tee Pee City. Thus an old road ran from old Clarendon by Tee Pee City and Otta to the west line of Knox County. Certainly some of it and probably all of it was the road which pioneer surveyors and others called one of the Mackenzie Trails.

This old road ran southward and crossed the Brazos River at Mockingbird Springs,[59] some five miles west of Knox City, continued past the old lake that lay a few miles west of Weinert and extended to the east line of Haskell County on its way to Fort Griffin. Former jurist and attorney, the late W. M. Moore of Knox, King, and Wichita counties said that this was the Mackenzie Trail.

Robson's journey of 1879 followed a road that detoured to the

57. Surveyors, land locators and frontiersmen of the 1870's and 1880's called this road the "Mackenzie Trail." The old road is called by that name in this article because it was the term generally applied to the road. No attempt will be made here to determine exactly what (or whose) military wagons first traveled the road. The proof is positive that an old road (in several places called the Mackenzie Trail) connected the Old Clarendon, near the location of Mackenzie supply train of 1872, with Fort Griffin. John R. Cook (Feb., 1875) found an abandoned military wagon in what is now King County near the Mackenzie Trail. See John R. Cook, *The Border and the Buffalo* (Topeka, 1907), 329-338.

58. Robson: *Year Book,* 114, 115, 120, 121, 122, 123. Some of the road that is known as the Mackenzie Trail is also known as the Rath Trail.

59. The late W. M. Moore of Wichita Falls, Texas (an early resident of Knox and King counties) told about the Mackenzie Trail and other things related to the history of that area in frequent interviews, beginning about 1940 and extending (at intervals) for a period of years following.

west of the above described Mackenzie Trail from Tee Pee City to the Brazos near Knox City. That road passed a little to the west and south of the site of Guthrie[60] and joined the Mackenzie Trail at the Brazos. Robson called all of his route from Tee Pee City to Fort Griffin the "Rath Trail."[61] Most likely Charlie Rath's great wagon trains gave the route its greatest traffic—the route from Fort Elliott to Tee Pee City near Guthrie, Knox City, and Weinert to Fort Griffin. It is not now the custom to call this route the "Rath Trail," but certainly the Fort Griffin editor in 1879 knew better than we do now.

However, if we accept the original mail road from Fort Elliott to Tee Pee City as part of the Rath Trail, we must also give due attention to the branch of that old trail that extended from Tee Pee City to old Rath City near the Double Mountains. In 1876 Charlie Rath,[62] riding horseback and followed by some light wagons, went south from Dodge city to open the road that was soon to bear his name. He marked out the way and may have cut down a few banks, but the great bull train that followed really made the route a very plain road. John Russell with fifty king size freight wagons pulled by a total of 600 oxen brought along the supplies and equipment that made the beginning of Rath City.[63]

The road ran from Dodge City to Fort Elliott[64] and from Fort Elliott to Tee Pee City,[65] but from there it curved a little to the west of the other trails. It went to Tee Pee Creek and crossed over the divide to the South Pease. It crossed that river near the mouth of Sanders Hollow[66] and went up the valley of that stream to Patton Springs[67]

60. Robson: *Year Book*, XX, 121, 122.
61. *Ibid.*, 121.
62. *The Handbook II*, 441.
63. John R. Cook, *The Border and the Buffalo*, 185, 186.
64. *The Handbook II*, 441.
65. The B. F. Simpson interview (see footnote No. 53) and the Donley County sketch from file No. 6 (see footnote No. 49) outline the route of this part of the Rath Trail.
66. An interview with the late Bill Stafford (a little before 1950) at his home near Afton, Texas. Stafford called this part of the trail, the road to Tee Pee City. Bill Stafford had lived in the area since 1883.
67. An interview with F. M. (Frank) Greer of Payson, Arizona. Greer was one of the early day cowboys interviewed at the Stamford Reunion in 1950. He had driven cattle to Patton Springs in 1886. He said that an old trail went northeast from Patton Springs to Tee Pee City. Bill Stafford (see footnote 66) outlined the old trail from Tee Pee City. It crossed the South Pease River, near the mouth of Sanders Hollow, then up Sanders Hollow to Patton Springs and on southwestward to a point on Duck

about 1½ miles east of the village of Afton. Keeping the same southwestward course it passed five miles west of the site of Dickens and down the East Fork of Duck Creek to where the two branches of that stream unite, then on past Soldier Mound and past present Spur and on southeast to the mouth of Duck Creek. Early surveyors mapped this part of the Rath Trail the full length of Duck Creek. As we have seen earlier they called it the road to Tee Pee City,[68] which in fact it was.

At the mouth of Duck Creek, Rath, followed by Russell's great wagon train, turned eastward down the Mackenzie trail until he was three or four miles past the Double Mountains.[69] There he erectd a finger board pointing southward, for it was at that point that this so-called trail blazer, bull train and all, turned a dozen miles south to the Double Mountain River[70] and went three or four miles beyond to establish the trading post known as Rath City.

How do we know that this road from Tee Pee City, near present-day Dickens, down Duck Creek, and east to the Double Mountains was the route of Charlie Rath and his wagon trains? Simply because there was no other way to go. Had Russell tried to cross more directly from Tee Pee City to the Double Mountains, his fifty great wagons could have floundered endlessly in the unspeakably rough Crotan Breaks or other rough terrain to the east. There seems to be no evidence of a major wagon trail straight across that rough country. Light wagons did go across in places, but the big trail went around.

Also, there is direct evidence that the buffalo hunters, even with their lighter wagons, went around when they left the Double Mountain country for the Panhandle in the spring of 1876. John R. Cook, perhaps the chief historian of the buffalo hunt, spelled out some of the details of the routes of travel to the Panhandle[71] after the winter hunt of 1875-76 had come to an end. He told of his own route up the Western Cattle Trail and across into the north Panhandle. He also told about others who left the Double Mountain area. Many went

---

Creek a few miles west of Dickens, Texas.

68. The map (or sketch) of the New York and Texas Land Company, mentioned in footnote No. 31, maps this part of the road all the way from a point five miles west of Dickens to the mouth of Duck Creek. In this old map it is called "the road to Tee Pee City."

69. John R. Cook, *The Border and the Buffalo*, 190.

70. *Ibid.*, 190, 241.

71. *Ibid.*, 157.

"west up the Mackenzie Trail to the Whitefish country,"[72] he said. Now please note that Whitefish Creek—the area to which Cook referred—was not west but almost due north of the Double Mountains. The hunters simply went west up the Mackenzie Trail far enough to by-pass the Croton Breaks, and then they turned north. Cook also makes it quite plain that Russell drove his fifty bull wagons over this same part of the Mackenzie Trail (only eastward instead of westward) as he brought the immense train of supplies down from the Panhandle to establish Rath City.[73] Probably the hunters went west of the site of Dickens and by the place where the frontier village of Tee Pee City[74] was soon to be located. In other words, they probably followed the route of Charlie Rath in reverse all the way from the Double Mountains to Whitefish Creek in present Donley Country.

But this last statement calls for an explanation, for in the spring of 1876, Rath had not yet opened the Rath Trail. The truth is that he probably did not open that trail. There is good evidence, including the above mentioned quotation from Cook, that the hunters, light wagons and all went that way ahead of Rath. Part of the road seems to have been opened by military wagons, but these facts do not in any way discredit Rath. Most likely he gave no thought to the possibility that the road would bear his name. However, in view of the fact that for a short while he made the traffic on the road almost reach the magnitude of the Santa Fe Trail, it seems quite appropriate that the old thoroughfare should be called the "Rath Trail."

The extent to which the Giddings mail route followed the Mackenzie and Rath Trails has been explained. A third mail line that was operated by Colonel Giddings and associates followed a route from Wichita Falls to the Texas Panhandle. This road, almost all the way from Wichita Falls to old Clarendon, lay to the north of the somewhat later route of the Fort Worth and Denver Railway between those points. This mail road probably began in what is now

72. *Ibid.*, 151-152.

73. *Ibid.*, 185-86, 190.

74. Land records do not leave any doubt but that this trail went north from the mouth of Duck Creek to Tee Pee City (see footnote No. 68). Also footnotes No. 53 and 49 show that the trail continued from Tee Pee City to Fort Elliott and surveyors mentioned a point in northeast Donley County, which they said was a point on the Rath Trail. Also this point mentioned by the surveyors was on the watershed of Whitefish Creek or in the language of John R. Cook it was in the "Whitefish Country."

downtown Wichita Falls and crossed the Wichita River near the place where the first bridge was built[75] in the year 1883. This, the Ohio Street bridge, which was still in operation after 83 years of usefulness, was about 100 feet above the old wagon crossing, which in turn was about the same distance above the Falls of the Wichita.

From the river crossing the mail hacks of late 1879 turned northwest across country some thirty five miles to Toksana, the old post office which was northeast of present-day Electra and only two or three miles south of Red River. On to the west beyond Toksana the road passed between Vernon and Doan's Crossing[76] and came to a stage stand just across the creek west of today's Chillicothe.

Beyond Chillicothe the old road passed four miles north[77] of Quanah and then entered Childress County about three miles south of Red River.[78] Then on northwest across that river, the old mail hacks

75. The old bridge (made of iron) is still in use just below the Fort Worth and Denver railway crossing. An iron plate on the bridge shows that the date of construction was 1883. It was a one-way bridge but in 1911 a similar bridge was built just west of it, which since that date has provided for two-way traffic. A slight "rapid" some 200 to 300 feet below the bridge is visible at low water. The rapid marks the location of what was once the "Falls of the Wichita." The water fall poured over a rock ledge that was in the shape of a horseshoe. An old town plat of Wichita Falls dated 1876 (before there was a town) on file at the Wichita County Courthouse shows that the fall was 3.7 feet deep. A flood on the river washed rocks and dirt into the space below the falls and left the slight rapid that can be seen today.

"Shinnery" McElroy, as a boy, lived a mile or two southeast of the falls in 1875. He said (in an interview) that the old road crossed the river just above the falls. Some sign of the approach of the old road (to the river) was visible only a few years ago. McElroy became a Waggoner cowboy about 1880 and spent most of his active life with the Waggoner ranch.

76. The U. S. postal maps of 1880, 1881, and 1884 show Wichita Falls, Toksana, and Doans as post offices. None of them is shown on the maps of 1878. Vernon appears first on the map of 1881 but the mail route to the Panhandle from Wichita Falls and Toksana (according to the maps) did not pass through Doans or Vernon in 1880 or 1881. Probably the maps were several months behind the facts. With no maps available for 1882 or 1883, Vernon first appears on this Wichita Falls-Panhandle mail route in 1884, but it (Vernon) may have been on the route before the end of 1881. A mail line connected Seymour with Doans in 1880. A route between the two post offices passed through Vernon in 1881.

77. An interview with Ed Lutz of Vernon, Texas. Lutz was superintendent of this mail route to the Panhandle for a number of its early years. He said that one of the old stage stands was on Wanderer's Creek just west of Chillicothe and that another such was on Groesbeck Creek four miles north of Quanah.

78. In sketch "A" of the Hardeman County Sketch File in the Texas General

reached the stage stand on Buck Creek almost on the north line of Childress County and about three miles west of the Childress-Wellington highway.[79]

Still continuing to the northwest, the mail passed the head-quarters of the much-publicized Bill Curtis Diamond Trail ranch.[80] Keeping the same course, it missed present-day Memphis perhaps a dozen miles to the northeast and continued to old Clarendon[81] five miles north of the present city of that name.

It is possible that the first mail hacks from Wichita Falls turned north on the Rath Trail ten or fifteen miles east of the Clarendon and reached their terminal point at Fort Elliott; but later the mail bags were taken to Clarendon, where they were relayed to Fort Elliott. At first, both the mail from Fort Griffin and from Wichita Falls term-inated at Fort Elliott, where it made contact with the east-west line across the Texas Panhandle—a line that was already in operation. This east-west mail line served the old Panhandle town of Tascosa.[82]

Later, the mail from Wichita Falls went beyond Clarendon;[83] in

Land Office (dated Oct. 18-27, 1884) shows that a point on the Clarendon Road was 1850 varas west of the northeast corner of section 400. The point is one mile west of the west Hardeman County line and three miles south of Red River.

Childress County sketch file No. 3 (field notes of a connecting line) shows another point on the old road 6.7 miles west and 1.2 miles north of this point.

79.. See Collingsworth County sketch files in the Texas General Land Office. Sketch No. 4 maps about ten miles of the Clarendon-Quanah Road. It began at a stage stand in the southwest part of section 18 (Block 14, H & G N RR Co. lands) and continued to a point 7 miles west and 5½ miles north of that stage stand.

80. The Ed Lutz interview. See footnote No. 77.

81. Post Map of 1880—also of 1881. Both maps show that the mail route reach-ed Clarendon. The Post Map of 1887 also shows the mail road reached Clarendon. From Childress County it appears to have reached Clarendon by the same original mail route to the Panhandle as in the maps of 1880 and 1881. The 1887 map shows that the Fort Worth and Denver railway had reached Quanah by that date and that the mail line continued another seven miles to Kirkland before it turned northward to join the route of the original road.

In the map of 1884 the mail still went by Toksana in Wichita County but it pass-ed through Vernon, Chillicothe and Kirkland before it turned north to the original road.

82. The U. S. Postal map of 1878 shows the east-west mail road across the Texas Panhandle. This route (from Fort Bascomb) passed through Tascosa, Lathrop and Windom on the north side of the Canadian River. Here it turned southeast across the river to Fort Elliott where it turned eastward to Darlington beyond the Texas line.

83. The extension of the mail road from Clarendon to Tascosa is shown in the map of 1887 but since no postal maps of the Panhandle are available between 1881

fact, the Wichita Falls line increased in importance as it became apparent that the Fort Worth and Denver railway would soon furnish fast mail service to the Panhandle. On the other hand, the mail route from Fort Griffin to Fort Elliott was soon discontinued. The post offices of Otta, Tee Pee City, and other points were served by branch lines off what soon became the main mail route, the route from Wichita Falls to the Panhandle.

Shortly after the Griffin-Elliott mail began, a branch line ran from Seymour across the Wichita River (above present-day Lake Kemp) to Pease City, an early village some five miles north of present Crowell, but this arrangement did not last. Not long after the Wichita Falls-Panhandle mail service began, Vernon became a point on the line, and not long thereafter, the point of origin of the Pease City mail was soon changed to Vernon. The new branch line went from Vernon to Pease City.[84] It crossed Good Creek and the North Fork of the Wichita to Otta[85] and for a while on to Tee Pee City.

The Fort Worth & Denver railway reached Wichita Falls in 1882[86] and for a time stopped building.[87] It had completely crossed the Panhandle by January 26, 1888.[88] The old towns and many new ones that were to the right and left of the railroad were served by various short mail routes. But ahead of the railroad for most of a decade the horsedrawn stages (shortening their route as the railway advanced) tramped out their own story as the advance agents of northwest Texas progress. Many interesting frontiersmen are said to have ridden these stages. Perhaps the most colorful of them all was Temple

and 1887 the beginning date of this service to Tascosa can not be known.

84. The route (50 miles long) from Seymour to Pease City is shown in the Postal map of 1880. The map of 1881 shows that mail went (40 miles) north from Seymour to Vernon and west (45 miles) to Pease.

85. In an interview the late Leslie McAdams told about this mail road. The old Route crossed Good Creek at the Boiling Spring in the McAdams pasture. Mrs. Virgil Johnson gives the location of this spring. It is in section 3, block X, T & N O RR Co. lands, 14 miles due west of Crowell, Texas. The springs has met the heavy demands of present-day development and has had water to spare.

86. Reed *Railroads*, 395. The exact date was September 1, 1882.

87. The railway had not built beyond Wichita Falls in 1884 (see Post Map, 1884). It reached Vernon October 15, 1886 (see Reed: *Railroads*, 395) and on May 5, 1885 stopped at Harrold long enough to boom that town. This last information was collected by the Passenger Traffic Department of the Fort Worth and Denver City Railway.

88. Reed: *Railroads*, 395.

Houston, famed orator and prosecutor, the son of the unique Sam Houston of earlier Texas history. Temple Houston, with his professional long-tail coat and his near Beetle-like long hair served as district attorney in a district that included such far-flung outposts as Montague, Tascosa, and Mobeetie. He is said to have used the stages in covering this large assignment.

Quite in contrast with the Fort Worth and Denver, the Texas and Pacific railroad closed the gap across the frontier in a half dozen months more than a single year.[89] Then as if to add insult to injury the Texas Central Railway reached out to Albany in 1882 and cut the dirt out from under the feet of old Fort Griffin,[90] which was a scant sixteen miles away. It no longer made sense to send horsedrawn mail hacks across from Fort Griffin to Fort Elliott; neither did it square with good reasoning to send the mail bags up the Mackenzie Trail from Fort Griffin to Mount Blanco. In fact Hank Smith's Mount Blanco was served by another branch of Mackenzie's trails, a branch that came north from Colorado City by Pete Snyder's store and on up the canyon of the White River to the post office in the old rock house[91] that still stands ten miles north of Crosbyton.

From this old rock house at Mount Blanco mail service was soon extended to Lubbock and a few other points on the plains,[92] but in 1913 when the Santa Fe railroad came all the way across the plains[93] much of this became obsolete.

And now for what may be the climax to this story of Northwest Texas trails, let us go back to the little old willow picket post office to Otta and to Tee Pee City. These were focal points on the Rath and Mackenzie Trails in the movement of buffalo hunters from the north to the south plains. There was another trail that came to the area of these little ghost towns of yesterday. It had several names. The late Dr. A. B. Edwards, whose life span ran farther back into the story of Northwest Texas than all but a very few was the first to call our atten-

89. *Ibid.*, 365.

90. *Ibid.*, 217.

91. Post Map, 1881. Also Post Map, 1887. The 1881 map shows that the mail route west from Fort Griffin terminated at California Ranch just 28 miles away. Surely the route from Colorado to Mount Blanco began at that time but for some reason it is not mapped. No postal maps of West Texas are available between 1881 and 1887. The Colorado-Mount Blanco Route is shown on the map of 1887.

92. See Post Map, 1887. Also see Post Map, 1889.

93. Reed: *Railroads*, 303.

tion to this road that has all but passed from memory.

Dr. Edwards, in fact, told of two old trails to the plains.[94] A road from Buffalo Springs, by Seymour, and on west by the "Narrows," he called the "Great South Road." But he also told about another road that branched from Marcy's California Trail at Brushy Mound, five miles northwest of present-day Bowie. The old road crossed the Little Wichita at the Van Dorn crossing five miles south of Jolly, Texas. It passed about one-half mile north of present Holliday and crossed the Wichita-Archer County line,[95] three miles to the west. On northwest it crossed the Big Wichita River, right where the Electra-K. M. A. concrete bridge[96] is located.

Westward by Guide Mound, the old road went along the divide between Beaver Creek and the Wichita and in places passed near the Baylor-Wilbarger County line.[97] To the west the old trail passed near the head of Beaver Creek, just north of the site of Foard City and went on to the west or northwest of Good Creek.[98] Bending a little southward, this old trail crossed the North Fork of the Big Wichita, probably just inside of Cottle County. It must have crossed this fork of the Wichita again at Otta. Certainly it did so after the Mackenzie Trail went that way and by the Mackenzie route, if not originally, it also reached Tee Pee City.

Dr. Edwards called this more northerly route the "Great North Road." He also called it the "Good Creek Road."[99]

But pioneer cattlemen of Graham in 1877 called the old route the "Buffalo Road."[100] So well did these men of the frontier know this old road that they identified a point on one of their newly made round-up districts as the place where "The Buffalo Road crosses the north fork of the Big Wichita."[101] This point was west of the head of Beaver Creek out near the Foard-Cottle County line, out where the

---

94. In several interviews held in the early 1940's Dr. A. B. Edward gave much information about several old West Texas trails.

95. See Archer County Deed Records, Vol. A, 204. The survey of the north line of Archer County (recorded here) was made in 1881.

96. In several interviews with the late Mart Banta, this and other information was given. Banta lived on Beaver Creek in southwest Wichita County for more than 50 years beginning in 1877.

97. The Banta interviews.

98. The Edwards interviews.

99. The Edwards interviews.

100. The *Graham Leader*, March 9, 1877.

101. *Ibid.*

cattle country of 1877 came to a thin edge; but these men who were assembled in Graham many miles away knew the geography of the old road well enough to understand.

A branch route that began at the Owl Spring in north central Cottle County joined the main trail[102] near today's Foard City. This branch, and in fact the whole trail, was sometimes called the "Henrietta Road."[103] The road must have been old to be so well known. In 1858 when Van Dorn was in or near Wichita County, he made contact with a part of frontiersmen who may have been traveling the Buffalo Road. In 1878 D. L. Dowd[104] with six wagons and thirty-two yolk of oxen came eastward down the old trail.

Had the Henrietta and Cambridge newspaper files escaped destruction, we could doubtless know of many more great wagon trains laden with buffalo hides and much lost history that came down the Buffalo Road.

In the 1870's Mart Banta as a small boy lived near Beaver Creek in southwest Wichita County. His home was beside the Buffalo Road nearly all of his long and interesting life. He was only an infant when the products of the buffalo hunt first came down that old road, but he was soon old enough to remember when the buffalo bone haulers came. Quite often he saw as many as a hundred wagons in a single train winding down the road past Guide Mound, across the Wichita River at the site of today's concrete highway bridge on past the nearby Ikard ranch headquarters, along the north edge of the future village of Holliday, and on to market at Wichita Falls, Henrietta, and other points. These long wagon trains were not the property of some wealthy syndicate. The wagons belonged to the little people,[105] each of whom had gone out and gathered a load of bones to sell and buy groceries or other needed items. They had come from upper Beaver Creek, Good Creek, the upper branches of the Wichita and from near Otta and Tee Pee City.

At nightfall they came together at the well known camping places.[106] What a pity that some present-day expert reporter with

---

102. A survey made by Sam L. Chalk for Baylor Land District May 8, 1883. A plat of this survey may be found in the Cottle County sketch files at the Texas General Land Office.

103. *Ibid.*

104. A personal interview with D. L. Dowd.

105. The Banta interviews.

106. The Banta interviews.

modern recording equipment can not transplant himself backward in time to sit beside one of their camp fires if for just a single night!

When the first freight trains of the Fort Worth and Denver railway reached Wichita Falls, there was a great rick of many hundreds of tons of buffalo bones waiting along Ohio Avenue beside the railroad tracks.[107] A similar pile of bones was stacked at Henrietta. Most of the bones at both places had come down the now long-forgotten Buffalo Road.

107. The Banta interviews.

XVII

ROBSON'S JOURNEY THROUGH WEST TEXAS IN 1879

Almost any carefully made observations on the West Texas frontier in the late seventies would be worth recording. Such observations become doubly valuable if written down at or near the time they were made and of greater worth still if recorded by one skilled in the art of writing.

Such a record was left us by George W. Robson when he was editor of the *Fort Griffin Echo*. Robson, in company with Charlie Meyer and George Guinn, made a trip from Fort Griffin across West Texas in the winter of 1879. It was an 800 mile journey that reached west to within forty miles of New Mexico and north into the Texas Panhandle to within some thirty or forty miles of the Canadian River. The party left Fort Griffin in some kind of a two-horse vehicle on January 19, 1879, and did not return until February 25.

A note about the three travelers is in order here. Almost no information seems to be available about Guinn, but one suspects that since he was the operator of a wagon train and probably knew the roads, he served somewhat unofficially as guide. Meyer owned a general merchandise store at Fort Griffin. Judged by the size and character of his advertisements in the *Fort Griffin Echo,* he was a business man whose local importance was second only to that of F. E. Conrad, who advertised the "largest stock of goods west of Fort Worth."

Robson, who wrote the account of the journey, had been associated with the *Frontier Echo* of Jacksboro since the beginning of that newspaper in 1875, and had been owner most of that time. In January, 1879, he moved the *Echo* to Fort Griffin where it became known as the *Fort Griffin Echo*. He was not a stranger in Fort Griffin, since many of his subscribers were there even while he had published his paper in Jacksboro, and the constant shifting of population between the two frontier towns made for rather numerous acquaintances between them. As a newspaper man, Robson had studied the needs of the cattlemen and kept in close touch with the ever-changing status of the buffalo range. One gains the impression from pioneer citizens of Albany that this early-day editor had put his foot on the rails of Fort Griffin saloons beside that of many a frontier adventurer. He probably knew the West Texas frontier as well as or better than any other person who was specially gifted at writing.

The account of the 800 mile journey made by Robson and his two associates was entitled, "The Modern Anabasis" and was published in the *Fort Griffin Echo* during March and April, 1879. It was divided into as many as five and probably six installments, appearing one per week. All of them except three have been lost from the *Echo* files. Entire pages have been torn from the issue of March 15, and the whole paper of March 22 is gone. With them has disappeared the first chapter, if not the first two chapters of the story—and undoubtedly a valuable record of conditions of that date in the counties of Haskell, Stonewall, Kent, Crosby, and many others has been lost with the missing files.

As to the part of Robson's account that has been preserved, the curtain rises somewhat abruptly at the buffalo camp of the well-known hunter, T. L. Causey. His camp was located at the Yellow Houses some fifty miles northwest of present-day Lubbock. The Causey brothers, T. L. and George, are known to have erected an adobe shack at this place in the winter of 1879.[1] Probably it had already been built by February 3, when the Fort Griffin party arrived. At this point let Robson take over the story.

THE MODERN ANABASIS
(Continued from last week)

For fifty years writers have been describing the chase of the buffalo in the most glowing terms.[2] Some of them basing their descriptions upon actual observation, but most of them drawing largely upon their fancy. The story has generally been the same, viz: A herd

1. J. Evetts Haley, *The XIT Ranch of Texas*, 48. The site of this buffalo camp was near a yellow lime rock formation that under certain atmospheric conditions resembled houses. The peculiar formation was known as the Yellow Houses. It is located in league 697 of the State Capital Lands, seven miles east and about one mile south from the northwest corner of Hockley County. See the Texas General Land Office maps of Hockley County, dated February, 1914.

2. This installment of the story is taken from the *Fort Griffin Echo* of March 29, 1879.

of buffalo making the ground shake with the roar of the bellowing, a daring hunter in buckskin suit, mounted upon his swift footed steed "Flying Wind," dashes upon them, the buffalo fly before him as by "instinct from the human eye," the bold hunter and gallant steed dashes in among them, he selects the largest of the herd which he wounds, the infuriated animal turns, rushes at his horse, when a well directed shot pierces the beast to the heart, and he falls with a thud that is heard miles away.

With some slight variation this story has been current literature in the Eastern States. There has always been the stampeding herd, the daring hunter, the swift footed steed, the wounded bull with distorted nostrils, breathing smoke and dripping blood, turning to charge, a hair-bredth escape, a lucky shot, and a life preserved.

However real or fanciful such pictures may be, such doings belong to the dead past. A hunter now-a-days couldn't earn his rations by such work as that. The romance of hunting buffalo soon vanishes when the reality comes to be known. Hunting them for their hides in Texas became a matter of profitable employment about four years ago, when dealers in hides first began to purchase in large quantities for shipment. The success attending the hunt in the winter of 1875-'76, in which many hunters realized small fortunes, caused thousands of persons to flock to the buffalo range, so that in the winter of 1877-'78 it was estimated that 5,000 hunters were on the range, the main bulk of whom were located along the foot of the plains and from thence Eastward 75 miles, and from the Canadian river on the North to the Pecos river on the Southwest. The slaughter of animals this year was immense, and as the hunt was almost entirely for their hides, it is safe to say that enough choice meat was wasted to have provided every family in Texas with meat for an entire year, and as the business was entirely overdone, it turned out that all the hunters lost money on their ventures, and but few are now left to continue the calling. Among those few is T. L. Causey at whose camp near the Yellow Houses we found ourselves on the morning of the 3rd day of February.

Mr. Causey has the reputation of having killed and marketed as many hides as any hunter in Texas, and a description of his mode of hunting will answer for all.

We will assume that he has his outfit, consisting of two or more wagons and horses or mule teams, one saddle horse for the hunter to ride, a Sharp's rifle, calibre .45 long shell, 16 pounds in weight, ammunition to the amount of 125 pounds of powder, 500 pounds of lead, and 7,000 primers, two to three hands who are expert skinners to each gun, a cook and perhaps one extra hand called a "camp rustler" to do chores. He takes corn and provisions enough to last for sixty days. Thus equipped he moves out to some point where there is a probability of finding buffalo and a good camping ground selected makes his camp there. The hunter leaves camp as early as he can get out in the morning, for if he makes a killing that day it is preferable to do it early, so that the skinners may get through their work by night if possible. We will assume that the buffalo are plentiful and he finds within a couple of miles of his camp a herd of 40 or 50 head grazing. He must now keep away from the windward side, for their smell seems to be their keenest sense, and if the hunter will avoid giving them the wind of him it is an easy matter to ride up to within five or six hundred yards of the herd without alarming them. He will now dismount, and drop his bridle, the horse if he knows his business, will go to grazing and remain where he is left until his master returns for him. The hunter being now on foot can with no great difficulty get within two to three hundred yards of the game. This is near enough with his Sharp's rifle to commence work, and here is where the hunter's instinct with long training comes into play, for if he shoots the right animal, the leader, the rest of the herd will be very apt to stand still until the last one is shot down. This is what they call "killing a stand." But if he picks out the wrong animal, or does not make a lucky shot the herd will run, the hunter pursues on foot and here again long training and hardiness is required. For his foot race may last many miles, but if he understands his business he hangs on and eventually brings them to a stand and gets them all. It is a matter of common occurrence when buffalo are ____ for forty or fifty to be killed on a stand, where they will lie almost touching each other. Seventy to a hundred did not use to be an uncommon number to get, while I have heard of a few instances where as many as one hundred and fifty have been shot down on a space of not over ten acres in area. It speaks well of Causey's skill that this winter, and buffalo being very scarce, he has killed every one that is known to have come within ten miles of his camp.

The gun used must be perfectly adapted for its work. The long range, elevated sights, and thick barrel are necessary. The rapid and continuous firing would heat a thin barrel in a short time so that it would be impossible to use it. The favorite gun is Sharp's rifle of calibre .45 elongated ball. The cartridge shell shoots 110 grains of powder, and the balls run fifteen to the pound. Every hunter prefers to fix his own ammunition, for which purpose he buys with his gun a set of reloading apparatus, and powder and lead by wholesale. So soon as the killing is made the skinners arrive on the ground with wagons, and they go to work to skin the dead animals. This kind of work also required a great deal of practice. The buffalo is usually propped on its back and the hide ripped down the inside of the legs with an ordinary butcher knife and then skinned with a thin bladed knife curved in shape. The Wilson skinning knives seem to be perferred. Some men have been known to skin without help as many as sixty animals in one day. Though from twenty-five to thirty is about the average work for good workmen. When the hide was taken off, formerly the carcass was left where it had fallen, but Causey has this winter been saving all the meat and for that reason has required the use of more transportation and has had with him a train of oxen and wagons. So soon as the skinners have finished, the hides and meat are hauled to camp. The hides are then stretched out on some smooth place, with the flesh side up and made fast with pegs driven into the ground around the edge of the hide, and left there until thoroughly dried, when they are ready for shipment to market. In the warm weather there is a bug about the size of a filbert which is very destructive to hides, and compels the hunter in order to preserve his hides to sprinkle them with a preparation known as the South American hide poison. The meat which is to be preserved is taken from the hump, the hindquarters and the shoulders. The hump of the buffalo is considered the choice part. It is the same thing as sirloin to the domestic beef but much more of it as the hump ribs of the buffalo and the muscle growing to them gives the animal the appearance of carrying his head between his shoulders. The hump is taken off in two strips, the hindquarters and shoulders cut up in chunks by following the seams of the muscles, and the meat preserved free from bone. The meat is thrown into vats improvised from buffalo hides, and salted, it then yields its own brine without adding water. After lying in the vats for ten days it is hung up on scaffolds and smoked. After all this it is now more than two hundred miles to the nearest market, and when all the hardships and exposure are taken into consideration, it will be seen that a buffalo hunter fully earns all that he makes and often extraordinary exertions are called for. For instance, during the snow storm about the first week in January, Causey had made a killing of fifteen head about ten miles from camp. The weather was so cold that the animals had frozen hard before they could be skinned and butchered, so after disemboweling them he loaded them on his wagons, hide, hoof and horns, and hauled them to camp, and when the warm weather returned again and thawed them out he was able to save the hides and meat. Now that is what might be called "rustling."

We remained at Causey's camp during the 3rd and 4th of February, on the 5th we started back to Blanco Canyon, making the distance of one hundred miles in two days. It was on this trip that Meyer showed his skill in driving. He drove two hundred miles over the Staked Plains and never struck a stump on the whole journey. We arrived at the Tasker ranch[3] late at night, February 6th, and next day started for Fort Elliott in the Pan Handle.[4]

(To be continued)

THE MODERN ANABASIS
(Continued from last week)

We arrived[5] at Clarendon[6] in time for dinner and remained there the rest of the day.

This place is known as the "Methodist Colony" also as "Preachertown." The Rev. Mr. Carhart, of the Methodist church, is the chief manager of affairs. His residence is at Sherman, Texas, where he edits a paper in the interests of Clarendon. Clarendon is a quiet little settlement of about a dozen buildings, situated about eight miles from the foot of the plains, and completely land locked with hills. It is located in the fork of two streams where Carroll creek empties into the salt fork of Red River. They are both clear, fresh

3. The Tasker Ranch at the time of Robson's visit was owned and occupied by Henry Clay (Hank) Smith and family. The two-story stone house in which the Smith's lived was built in 1877. The old house still stands in Blanco Canyon ten miles north of Crosbyton. It is owned by a son of Hank Smith and occupied by his grandson.

4. The next installment of Robson's series of articles has been lost from the *Echo* files. It appeared in the issue of April 5, 1879. In this missing chapter the party traveled across Dickens, Motley, and Hall counties and were ready to enter Clarendon.

5. *Fort Griffin Echo*, April 12, 1879.

6. The town of Clarendon in 1879 was on the north bank of the Salt Fork of Red River, 5 miles north and one-half mile west of the present town of Clarendon. See the Texas General Land Office map of Donley County dated 1903.

water streams, and it is hard to understand why this prong is called Salt Fork, for it is not the least brackish and about the only one of the forks of Red River that is not too salty for ordinary use.

They have a good building rock here, a white limestone of base marble, some of the houses in the town are built of it and present a very handsome appearance. Timber, however, is very scarce even for fuel purposes. No intoxicating liquors are allowed to be sold, and any one purchasing a lot in the town must enter into an agreement that in case he should sell liquor upon the premises then his property shall be confiscated for the benefit of a seminary in Clarendon. The boys say that purchasers must also be able to recite the Lord's prayer backwards, but I do not believe this, at least it is not in the printed stipulations. Clarendon is a desirable locality for persons seeking a quiet home, and the county, Donley, in which it is situated will soon organize.

We left Clarendon the next morning, taking the road to Fort Elliott[7] our route this day was over high hills, being near the foot of the plains, crossing several creeks of running water, and reached Mc-Clellan creek near night where we camped. This stream empties into the North Fork, it contains an abundance of clear, fresh water, has wide open bottoms covered with a heavy growth of bottom grass, and more timber than any other part of the Pan Handle. We had a slight fall of snow on us at this camp. Next day our route was down Mc-Clellan creek to North Fork which we crossed above the mouth of the creek, where we stopped at noon, and then up Contentment creek, which comes in from the North side, and after ascending the high hills on head of Cantonment creek we came in sight of Fort Elliott.[8] We crossed the Sweetwater creek, on which the Post is situated, at dark and passing the government corral and Sutler's store we drove on to the town of Sweetwater[9] about three quarters of a mile from the Post. It was dark when we reached the place, and the town was lighted up like a city. Its small size and glaring lights gave it the appearance in a dark night like a first-class steamer on the Mississippi

7. This road is shown on *Pocket Map of Texas* by Charles W. Pressler & A. B. Langermann, 1879. It crossed the course of the present Amarillo Shamrock paved highway (U. S. Highway 66-about 8 to 10 miles west of the site of McLean.

8. Fort Elliott was located in section 55, block number 5, H. & G. N. R. R. lands—4⅓ miles east and 6⅔ miles south of the northwest corner of Wheeler County. See the Texas General Land Office map of Wheeler County dated August, 1899.

9. The name, Sweetwater, was soon changed to Mobeetie.

river. We soon found McKamy, whom everybody knows, and hung up at his ranch. We had been expected for some time as the Fort Griffin Echo had already announced our departure for this place.

Having put up our team at McKamy's corral, and eat supper at his restaurant, we sat down in his store to talk over the news, or "swap lies" as the popular expression now has it. Mac had just got back from a trip across the plains to New Mexico, thence through the Raton mountains to Trinidad, Colorado. He went the route by the Yellow Houses and says that he found plenty of water and good camping places all the way across to Fort Sumner. He further says that New Mexico and Colorado is overflowed with broken down buffalo hunters. And as he was well known to nearly every hunter on the Northern portion of the range, he came in great danger of being talked to death . . .

Mac seems to be driving a miscellaneous business here. He is running a wagon yard, feed stable, restaurant, bar room and family grocery store, and as an out-side trader makes more horse swaps than all the rest of the county. It will thus be seen that he makes an important factor in Sweetwater's social problem. Should they lose him as a stable man, or as a keeper of a lunch house, or in any one capacity the vacancy might be filled, but should he die all over, and all at once he would be a serious loss to that community.

The next morning we took a walk around the town and visited the Military Post, Fort Elliott. The town as yet was but a small affair. It consists of one street about two hundred and fifty yards long. It has ten or twelve buildings on the street and several small ones off the street. All the houses except one are built of pickets and have dirt roofs. There is a good building rock to be found here, and if the town is prosperous, rock buildings will soon replace the pickets which are only intended for temporary purposes. Most of the houses here are intended for saloon purposes, and though it appears at first sight as though the saloon traffic was overdone, yet no one complains of hard times, although the garrison had not been paid off for four months.

We met with many old acquaintances here. Henry Fleming is associated with a Mr. Donally and is doing a good business in his line. We met Gus Bivousette behind the bar in Weed's saloon. This is an elegant saloon, built of dressed lumber, hauled by wagon from Fort Dodge, Kansas, about two hundred miles distant, the bar furniture is new, and a new Brunswick billiard table sits in the room which is amply large for the players. The present town is not more than four months old, but there was an old town about two miles away, which is now abandoned and the inhabitants have moved to the present site. The town and Fort Elliott are about three-quarters of a mile apart, and are situated about seven or eight miles to the Northwest of the center of the county of Wheeler, named for one of the former Chief Justices of Texas. They are located near to a stream called Sweetwater, which crosses the country from a Northwest to a Southeast course. This stream contains an abundance of pure, clear water, it has many deep holes in it, where the water so clear, obtains a marine blue appearance. As to the agricultural prospects of this county it is difficult to form any correct estimate from the limited chances we had, and the season too being winter. And then again no farming has yet been tried to any extent. But from what little seen we think that it bids as fair for farmers as any prairie country in the West. McKamy is opening a farm on Spring creek about six or eight miles from town, the soil of which has not its superior in the State. One man who raised a garden during the last season, brought in some splendid cabbages. This matter of the farming however is prospective.

At present the principal occupations are in the government line, which leads to a description of Fort Elliott and its surroundings. During the year 1873 a cantonment of troops was established on a creek about eight miles West of this place, they were detached from the Fort Sill garrison and stationed here for the purpose of keeping the wild tribes of Kiowas and Comanches (which had that year surrendered), on their reservation in the Indian Territory. Subsequently it was deemed best to establish a permanent Post in this section, the present site was selected and the name of Fort Elliott given to it by the Secretary of War, in honor of a cavalry general of that name. We strode through the Post, which is built on the plan of all frontier outposts. A large parage ground, shaped in the form of a square, with the officers' quarters on two sides, and the soldiers barracks on the two opposite sides.

The Hospital stands off to the North of the parade ground. It is a large commodious building. The Quartermaster and Subsistence store houses are on the East, and the guard house and corral on the South of the parade ground. On the parade ground is a well of water, about sixty feet deep. The water tastes slightly of iron. Another and similar well is at the Hospital. Everything about the Post seems to be well appointed, and in perfect order. Meyer and myself entered one of the buildings used for company barracks to find a barber. We found him, and while Meyer was undergoing the tonsorial operation I had time to take a survey of their quarters. Each company has a separate building, which is erected in shape of an L making two rooms for the men's quarters and the wing for a kitchen and mess hall. In the room we were in were about twenty single iron bedsteads. Each soldier has his bedstead, mattress and blankets, a wooden chest under the foot of the bed contains his clothing, a case of books at the end of the room constituted the company library, composed of Humboldt's Cosmos, Washington Irving's works, and other standard authors of equal eminence. A long table stood near the book case on which were spread the leading newspapers and pictorial journals. Numbers of engravings adorned the walls. A large stove sufficient to warm the entire room occupied the center. Most of the men were engaged in reading. The room presented a neat, orderly appearance. The men were mostly young men, or below middle age, fine looking, manly fellows, neat and clean in their appearance, courteous and gentlemanly in their deportment. Betoking an admirable state of discipline, and a high order of soldiery pride. Uncle Sam seems to be getting very select material now for the rank and file of his army. Under act of Congress called the "Shoo Fly," a worthless soldier may be dropped from the rolls. As a company commander is thus enabled to get rid of the drones in a peremptory manner, the proper exercise of this power serves to create an *esprit de corps* in each company. While in the barracks we heard of a short discussion among the men about one of the company who that morning had been confined in the guard house for some disgraceful conduct, they all seemed interested as though as a body they felt themselves aggrieved by the misconduct of any one of their members. Having finished with the barber we walked down to the Sutler's store. Messrs. Lee and Reynolds are occupying this position. They have several large buildings filled with clothing and groceries and hardware, and almost every species of merchandise in demand by military or civilians.

About the largest stock of goods in the Southwest. Cattlemen come here from a distance of more than one hundred miles to purchase their supplies. These gentlemen also control the government contracts, which amount to a large figure. I suppose that the Government must be disbursing at this point about a quarter of a million dollars annually, and a large slice of this amount passes through the hands of Messrs. Lee & Reynolds. It will thus be seen that they are the bankers of the Pan Handle region. Their disbursements are large, as

they give employment to hundreds of men, on the wool and hay contracts, and to freighters. Fort Dodge being the principal shipping
point. The lumber of which the Post buildings are erected was hauled
from Fort Dodge, Kansas, and has the appearance of Michigan pine.
(To be continued)

THE MODERN ANABASIS
(Continued from last week)[10]

After this short survey to Post we returned to Sweetwater to
discuss with the people the future prospects of their town. Everybody
seems to be enthusiastic in their belief as to its future greatness. The
town is situated in a quarter of an alternate State Select Section of the
Houston & Great Northern Railroad Lands. There is scarcely any
possibility of the title to the land ever being brought into dispute. To
encourage the growth of the town the owners of the property are giving a building lot to any person who will erect a building or tenement
upon it. Taking all things in consideration, this place has a very prom-
ising outlook. Every one who has lived on the frontier knows what
an advantage an Army Post is for the purpose [of] putting money in
circulation. At Fort Elliott there are now stationed five companies of
troops, three of Infantry and two of Cavalry. That this garrison will
remain here a long time is altogether probable, and it is furthermore
a safe conjecture that the [word illegible] of our regular army will be
to guard the boundaries of the Indian Territory. It is the avowed
policy of the general Government to place all the wild tribes upon
reservations, and within the scope of what is called the Indian Territory is ample room for all the Indians East of the Rocky Mountains.
It is likely then that within this territory they will be corralled and
Posts established at convenient distances on the West and South to
enable the troops to keep the Indians on their reservations and prevent their leaving them. And this policy will have to be pursued and
the garrisons kept up until the present generation of Indians have
passed away, and a younger growth has taken place whose savage
nature has been tempered by education. This was the experience with
the Cherokees and Fort Smith and Fort Gibson, which were established for their benefit near fifty years ago, and are still garrisoned with
troops, or were up to four or five years ago. It is quite probable then
that for the next quarter of a century Fort Elliott will contain a large

10. *Fort Griffin Echo*, April 19, 1879.

garrison, and the town of Sweetwater will for the same length of time enjoy an army trade. Many persons in this section have known what the troops did for Jacksboro and Fort Griffin in a financial sense. They know too, how the business of those places went down when the country became settled and the garrisons were moved further West. But such will not be the fate of Fort Elliott. When the garrison at that place is removed, then there will no longer be a need for an army except to garrison the seacoast defenses. There is but one serious drawback to the Pan Handle and that is the scarcity of wood for fuel. But outcroppings of coal are said to have been found in several places, and if that article should be found in sufficient quantities to supply consumers, then there is nothing else needed to make it a desirable country to live in. It is quite probable that coal does exist here in large quantities. Scientific men say so, and it seems to be a fixed law of Nature, that where there is a deficiency in one respect, the want is supplied and replaced in some other manner . . .

We remained two days at Sweetwater, and left on the 17th day of February in the afternoon. It had snowed pretty hard that morning, and the night previous, and the ground was perfectly white, but the chief was determined to go, and go we must. So bidding farewell to everybody we started across the Sweetwater, and the hill to the South of it and struck the head of Spring creek. It is in this creek that McKamy is opening a farm; the creek is a bold running stream of clear water, and strongly impregnated with sulphur. We soon crossed the North fork of Red River, and on the south side there was but little snow. Taking a right hand road we soon entered the bottom land of McClellan Creek, which was very much overflowed, and about one hour after dark reached Norton's sheep ranch, now abandoned, where we camped for the night, which was clear and very cold. The next morning we proceeded on our way up McClellan creek and soon fell into the road we traveled from Clarendon, but we did not succeed in reaching Clarendon that day, for somehow we took a right hand fork, and did not notice our mistake until we reached the edge of the Plains. Our gray horse, whose surname was Cornwallis, at about 9 o'clock that morning began to show symptoms of exhaustion or obstinancy, it was difficult at first to say which. Our chief, who was driving, first commenced with a new black snake whip, but in about five miles the lash wore out, he then tried the butt end but could not reach him well enough, he then got out and thumped his ribs which stirred the horse for about two hundred yards, and then when the slow creeping walk was resumed, the rib pounding process was resumed, but without effect. He then whacked him a few licks on the nose but it was all n.g. Cornwallis had surrendered! Stop and turn out our team to rest, for there was no grazing for them, the grass being all burned off. After a couple of hours rest we retraced our road about three miles, and having got on the right road, we moved on toward Clarendon, but camped for the night on White Fish creek, about five miles from town. Our journey now back to Hamburg's store on Teepe Creek[11] was over the same road already traveled and described. At Teepe creek we took the Fort Griffin road, or better known as the Rath trail, and passed by Mike O'Brien's ranch, situated on Willow creek about twenty-two miles from Hamburg's store. Mike has selected a very fine location for a valley farm. At present he is trying to raise hogs[12] and utilize the mast of the shin oaks which cover the prairie in this region. This was the last house we saw until we reached the neighborhood of Fort Griffin.

Our route took us across the head of the South fork of Big Wichita, and thence Southeast down the main Croton Creek to the Brazos, passing within about five miles of Kiowa Peak, and then by the O'Brien lake across Mule Creek, Miller Creek and Blue Holes to Mr. Tredwell's farm,[13] nine miles from Fort Griffin. There was nothing seen in the last one hundred miles of our journey worthy of

11. The small village of which Hamburg's store was a part was called Tepee City when it became a post office late in 1879. It was located on Tepee Creek some 12 or 15 miles northeast of the site of Matador.

12. Hog ranching on a small scale seems to have preceeded most of the cattle ranching in the patches of shinnery found in the upper valley of the Pease and Wichita rivers and in some of the country to the south of this section. In 1878 or 1879 a Mr. Prewitt of Henrietta built a willow picket shack and started a hog ranch on the North Wichita some 10 miles southeast of the place where Paducah is now located.—Interview with Mrs. Burk of Crowell. Mrs. Burk was Prewitt's daughter. C. V. Cooper of Jack County was operating a hog ranch on the Clear Fork of the Brazos River in January, 1879, probably in Scurry County.—*Fort Griffin Echo*, January 4, 1879. There is incomplete information of a hog rancher who operated in the shinnery of Dickens County as early as 1877. —W. C. Holden, Rollie Burns, 80. There probably were several other such ranches in this area by 1879. The large influx of cattlemen began in this section later in the same year.

13. The exact route of the Rath Trail is not known. From Robson's article, it is evident that it crossed King County southeastwardly near present Guthrie and entered Haskell County near O'Brien. It passed across Haskell County reaching about the midpoint of its eastern boundary before bending southward to Fort Griffin.

description. It was pretty much the same thing, rolling prairie all the way. In fact our party was no longer capable of taking interest in anything. Ever since the surrender of Cornwallis we had lost our vivacity and grown melancholy. Everybody we met sympathized with our unfortunate condition. The Christians at Clarendon sympathized with us, the people at Casner's ranch, and at Hamburg's store sympathized with us, they also sympathized with the horse, said that he was played out, ought to be rested, ought to be swapped off, and wanted to sell Meyer another horse to fill his place. But by a strange coincidence, whenever Cornwallis deteriorated just in the same ratio did other horses increase in value. At Clarendon forty dollars boot was asked on a swap, at Indian Creek seventy dollars, and at Teepe Creek one hundred dollars in cash for a twenty-five dollar pony. So we were compelled to plod along as best we could, walking half the time and riding by turns while gloomy pictures of our party being set afoot in the wilderness, and getting back one at a time to the settlements or perishing on the roadside of starvation to furnish food for the wolves and the buzzards. Every raven flying overhead seemed to croak prophetically of such a fate. A sort of Hypochondria had seized upon the party. Nothing could go right, there was a constant grumbling and disagreement. For instance when we stopped to noon at the water holes on North Pease, one of our party complained of the water as being too salty for any use, that we should have stopped at the Sulphur Springs a few miles back, that the coffee made of the brackish water was nauseating, and more grumbling of that sort. After the meal was over he discovered that when he was putting sugar in his coffee he had dipped his spoon in the wrong sack, and had sweetened his coffee with salt. But he did not tell anybody, for he did not want anybody to know what a blunder he had made; *that was me.* At the Cedar Springs our horses had run away from camp. George Guinn commenced boasting of his skill in trailing, that if he could find their tracks he would soon bring them in; their trail was found which George followed for some distance and came up with a bunch of antelope. He knew that we had lost confidence in him as a guide, he knew too, that we now had good cause to lose confidence in him as a trailer, so he bagged his head in the blankets and slept for twenty-five miles. When we reached the Blue Holes our chief was disappointed. He had expected to find prairie lakes and he found a creek. This dissatisfied him so much that he commenced to abuse the person who had given that name to the creek, and wondered why it had been done. I meekly suggested that perhaps it arose from the Indians camping once at this place with a white captive, that this white captive at the time had the *blues* very badly, hence the term "blue holes." But he would not have this explanation, the disappointment was too great, and like Rachel when weeping for her children, he refused to be comforted . . .

At last on the afternoon of February 25th, we reached Mr. Tredwell's, and having obtained a fresh team we went into Fort Griffin, reaching there early in the night. The spirits of our party rose again when we had got new horses, we had been out thirty-seven days, had traveled over eight hundred miles of new country, and we all felt like heroes returning from the wars. The true hero of the party, Barney [the sound horse that had pulled about all of the load after Cornwallis gave out], we left grazing beside the road near Mr. Tredwell's house, looking as modest as though he had done nothing to deserve notoriety . . .

Having reached Fort Griffin, the members of the expedition disbanded themselves, each returning to his separate vocation. Meyer retiring to the helm of the mercantile business, and George Guinn to the helm of his bull train, while for the Historian of the expedition, who like a broken down wagon wheel, is unfit to be *re-tired,* remains the task of apologizing for the extreme length to which his narrative has been attenuated, by referring to the vast amount of information contained therein. And to those readers who have found an objection to the instructive side of this history it behooves us to explain that it has been more unavoidable than intentional.

This narrative which was commenced with a view principally to recording the fun we had on our trip, has at times unwittingly drifted into the instructive line. That valuable information should grow out of an expedition of such magnitude and importance is just as natural as for the valuable mohair to grow on the back of the wild Mo.

Finis.

BIBLIOGRAPHY

Anthony, H. E. *Animals of America.*

Archer County, Texas Deed Records, Vol. A.

Arrowsmith, John. *Map of Texas, compiled from surveys recorded in the Land Office of Texas and other official surveys.* London, 1841.

Austin Democrat, January 28, 1849.

Baskett, James Newton. "A Study of the Route of Cabeza de Vaca." *The Quarterly of the Texas State Historical Association,* XX.

Biggers, Don H. *Shackelford County Sketches.*

Bolton, Herbert Eugene. *Coronado on the Turquois Trail: Knight of the Pueblos and Plains.* New York, 1949.

Bolton, Herbert Eugene. *Spanish Exploration in the Southwest, 1542-1706.* New York, 1916.

Bolton, Herbert Eugene. *The Spanish-Borderlands.* New Haven, 1921.

Bolton, Herbert Eugene. *Texas In the Middle Eighteenth Century.* Berkeley, 1916.

Bolton, Herbert Eugene. *Athanase de Mèziéres* and the Louisiana Frontier, 1768-1780. 2 vols. Cleveland, 1914.

Bourne, Edward Gaylord. *Narratives of the Career of Hernando de Soto in the Conquest of Florida: As Told by a Knight of Elvas and in a Relation by Luys Hernandez de Biedma.* 2 vols. New York, 1904.

Brandelier, Fanny, trans. *The Journey of Alvar Nuñez Cabeza de Vaca and His Companions From Florida to the Pacific, 1528-1536,* by Cabeza de Vaca. 1905.

Brandelier, Fanny. *The Journey of Alvar Nuñez Cabeza de Vaca and His Companions From Florida to the Pacific, 1528-1536,* by Cabeza de Vaca. 1922.

Brown, John Henry. *Indian Wars and Pioneers of Texas.* Austin: L. E. Daniell, N. D.

Brown County Surveying Records, Vol. A.

Buckley, Eleanor Claire. "The Aguayo Expedition into Texas and Louisiana, 1719-1722," The Southwestern Historical Quarterly, XV.

Callahan County Surveying Records.

Carroll, H. Bailey. *Guadal P'a: The Journal of J. W. Abert.* Canyon, 1941.

Carter, Robert G. *The Old Sergeant's Story.* New York, 1926.

Carter, Robert G. *On the Border with Mackenzie.* New York, 1961.

Castañeda, Carlos E. *Our Catholic Heritage in Texas, 1519-1936. 1. Austin, 1936.*

Census of the United States Taken in the Year 1910. *Abstract of the Census with Supplement for Texas.* Washington, 1913.

Clay County Commissioners' Court Records, Vol. 1.

Coke County Surveyors Records (MS., County Clerk's Office, Robert Lee), II.

Conkling, Roscoe P. and Margaret B. Conkling. *The Butterfield Overland Mail 1857-1869.* 3 vols. Glendale, California, 1947.

Cook, John R. *The Border and the Buffalo.* Topeka, 1907.

Cooke County Commissioners Court Minutes (MS., County Clerk's Office, Gainesville), I.

Cooke County Surveyors' Records, Vols. A, B, E and H.

Cowperthwaite, Thomas & Co. *A New Map of Arkansas,* Philadelphia, 1850.

Crane, R. C. "Report of Captain R. C. Marcy of the Fifth Infantry, United States Army on his Exploration of Indian Territory and Northwest Texas." *West Texas*

Historical Association Year Book, XIV, 116-136.

Crezbaur, Robert, Compiler. *J. De Cordova's Map of the State of Texas.* 1858.

Cummins, W. F. "Report on the Geography, Topography, and Geology of the Llano Estacado or Staked Plains." *Third Annual Report of the Geological Survey of Texas, 1891.* Austin, 1892.

Dallas County Commissioners' Court Records, Vol. A

Dallas Morning News, The. November 19, 1933.

Davenport, Harbert, ed. "*Historia General y Natural de las Indias,* by Gonzalo Fernandez de Oviedo y Valdez." trans. Harbert Davenport and Joseph K. Wells. *Southwestern Historical Quarterly,* XXVII (1923), 2-4.

Davenport, Harbert, ed. "*Historia General y Natural de las Indias,* by Valdez." trans. Harbert Davenport and Joseph K. Wells. *Southwestern Historical Quarterly,* XXVIII (1924), 1 and 2.

Davenport, Harbert, and Joseph K. Wells. "The First Europeans in Texas, 1528-1536." *The Southwestern Historical Quarterly,* XXII (October, 1918), 121-23.

Deed Records of Archer County, Texas, A.

De Shields, James T. *Border Wars of Texas.* Tioga, Texas, 1912.

Dobie, J. Frank. *A Vaquero of the Brush County.* Dallas, 1929.

Echo (Fort Griffin), September 20, 1879.

Echo (Fort Griffin), March 29, 1879.

Echo (Fort Griffin), November 1, 1879.

Echo (Fort Griffin), August 2, 1879.

Encyclopedia Britannica (14th ed.)., XVI.

Falconer, Thomas. *Letters and Notes on the Texan Sante Fe Expedition, 1841-1842.* New York, 1930.

Ford, John S. Memoirs, MS., Vol. VI.

Foreman, Grant. *Marcy and the Gold Seekers.* Norman, 1939.

Foreman, Grant. *Adventure on Red River.* Norman, 1937.

Forrestal, Peter P., translator. "Pena's Diary of the Aguayo Expedition." Copyright by Paul J. Fork, *Preliminary Studies of The Texas Catholic Historical Society,* 1934. Vol. II, No. 7, January 1935.

Frontier Echo (Jacksboro, Texas), March 31, 1876.

Frontier Echo (Jacksboro, Texas), March 10, 1876.

Frontier Echo (Jacksboro, Texas), November 6, 1875.

Grace, Hybernia. "The First Trip West on the Butterfield Stage," *West Texas Historical Association Year Book,* (1932), 62-74.

Grayson County Surveyors' Records, A, B.

Greer County Record.

Gregg, Josiah. *Commerce of the Prairies.* Dallas, Texas, 1933.

Haley, J. Evetts. *The XIT Ranch of Texas.* Norman, 1953.

Haley, J. Evetts. *Charles Goodnight, Cowman and Plainsman.* Norman, 1949.

Hallenbeck, Cleve. *Alvar Nuñez Cabeza de Vaca, the Journey and Route of the First European to Cross the Continent of North America, 1534-1536.* Glendale, California, 1940.

Haskell County Surveyors' Records. "The F. H. K. Day Survey." I (May 30, 1856), 183.

Hatcher, Mattie Austin, translator. *The Expedition of Don Domingo Teran de Los Rios into Texas (1691-1692)*, preliminary Studies of the Texas Catholic Historical Society. Copyright 1932 by Paul J. Foik, Vol. II, No. 1.

Hodge, Frederick W., ed. *Spanish Explorers in the Southern United States 1528-1543*. New York: 1907.

Hodge, Frederick W., and Theodore H. Lewis, eds. *Spanish Explorers in the Southern United States, 1528-1543*. New York: Charles Schribner's Sons, 1907.

Holden, W. C. "Coronado's Route Across the Staked Plains." *West Texas Historical Association Year Book*, XX, 3.

Jack County Commissioners Court Records (MS., County Clerk's Office, Jacksboro), I.

Jack County Commissioners Court Records. "Survey of east Jack County line." May 14, 1878.

Jackson, W. Turrentine. *Wagon Roads West: A Study of Federal Road Surveys and Construction in the Trans Mississippi West, 1846, 1859*. Berkeley and Los Angeles, 1952.

Jadwin, Edgar. "Mississippi River." *The Encyclopedia Britannica*. 14th ed., VX, 606.

Johnson, Mrs. Virgil and J. W. Williams. "Some Northwest Texas Trails After Butterfield." *West Texas Historical Association Year Book*, XLII (October, 1966), 59-89.

Johnson, A. J. and J. H. Colton. *Johnson's New Illustrated Family Atlas*. New York, 1864.

Jones, R. L. "Folk Life in Early Texas: The Autobiography of Andrew Davis." *The Southwestern Historical Quarterly*, XLIII, 332-335.

Jones County Surveying Records, Vol. B.

Kendall, George Wilkins. *Narrative of The Texan Santa Fe Expedition*. Austin, 1935.

Kinnaird, Lawrence. *The Frontiers of New Spain; Nicolas de La Fora's Description 1766-1768*. Berkeley: The Quiviro Society, 1958.

Kress, Margaret Kenney, translator. "Diary of a Visit of Inspection of the Texas Missions Made by Fray Gaspar Jose de Salis in the Year 1767-68," *Southwestern Historical Quarterly*, XXXV.

Louisiana: A Guide to the State. New York: Hastings House, 1945.

Lucas, Mattie Davis and Mita Holsapple Hall. *A History of Grayson County, Texas*. Sherman, Texas, 1936.

"Map of Texas and Pacific Railway Surveys in El Paso County Texas."

Marcy, Colonel R. B. *Thirty Years of Army Life on the Border*. New York, 1866.

Marcy, Colonel R. B. *The Prairie Traveler: A Handbook for Overland Expeditions*. New York, 1859.

"Mississippi River." *The World Book Encyclopedia*, 1941, XI, 4547.

Montague County Surveyors Records, I, 247.

Montague County Surveyors Records, I, 188.

Morfi, Fray J. A. *History of Texas, 1673-1770*. Albuquerque, 1935.

Morgan, Forrest. "Mississippi River." *The Encyclopedia Americana*, 1943, XIX, 248.

McCain, William D. "The Story of Mississippi." *The World Book Encyclopedia*, 1941, XI, 4535.

McConnell, Joseph Carroll. *The West Texas Fontier.* Jacksboro, 1933.

National Archives. "Letters Rec'd.—El Paso-Fort Yuma Rd., 1857-61."

National Archives. "Records of Secretary of Interior Relating to Wagon Roads, 1857-87."

National Archives, Cartographic Records Division. Map RG75.

Neighbors, Robert S. Diary filed among *Neighbors Papers,* Texas University Library.

Neighbours, Kenneth F. "The Expedition of Major Robert S. Neighbors to El Paso in 1849." *Southwestern Historical Quarterly,* LVIII (July, 1954), 36-59.

Neville, A. W. *The History of Lamar County.* Paris, Texas, 1937.

Northern Standard (Clarksville, Texas). 1844-1858: February 10, 1944; March 2, 1844; May 29, 1844; February 16, 1850; February 23, 1850; March 2, 1850; June 12, 1858; August 28, 1858; October 16, 1858.

Nye, W. S. *Carbine and Lance.* Norman: University of Oklahoma Press, 1938.

Original United States vs. The State of Texas. No. 4, Records, 1894.

Ormsby, Waterman L. *The Butterfield Overland Mail,* ed. Lyle H. Wright and Josephine M. Bynum. San Marino, 1954.

Parker County Deed Records, Vol. 144, 481-482.

Parkman, Francis. *La Salle and the Discovery of the Great West.* Boston, 1910.

Plat Book in the office of the County Engineer, Tillman County, Oklahoma.

Ponton, Brownie and Bates H. McFarland. "Alvar Nuñez Cabeza de Vaca: A Preliminary Report on His Wanderings in Texas." *The Quarterly of the Texas State Historical Association,* I (January, 1898), 175.

Pressler, Charles W. and A. B. Langermann. *Pocket Map of Texas.* 1878.

Pressler, Charles W. and A. B. Langermann. Map of the *State of Texas.* Austin: General Land Office, 1879.

Price, George F. *Across the Continent with the Fifth Cavalry.* New York, 1959.

Ramsey, Grover C. "Camp Melvin, Crockett County, Texas." *West Texas Historical Association Year Book,* XXXVII, 144.

Record Supreme Court United States, United States v. Texas in Equity. Washington, D. C.: Judd and Detweiler, June 1894.

Reed, S. G. *A History of the Texas Railroads.* Houston, 1941.

Richardson, Rupert N. *The Comanche Barrier to South Plains Settlement.* Glendale, California, 1933.

Richardson, Rupert N. "Some Details of the Southern Overland Mail." *Southwestern Historical Quarterly* (July, 1925), 4.

Rister, C. C. "The Border Post of Phantom Hill." *West Texas Historical Association Year Book* (1938), 3-14.

Ritchie, E. B., ed. "Report of Colonel Samuel Cooper . . . of Inspection Trip from Fort Graham to the Indian Villages of the Upper Brazos made in June, 1851." *Southwestern Historical Quarterly* (April, 1939), 331.

Rivera, Pedro de. *Diaries.* Mexico, Guillermo Porrae Munoz, 1945.

Sketch Showing the Route of the Military Road from Red River to Austin. William H. Hunt, engineer, 1840.

Stambaugh, J. Lee and Lillian J. Stambaugh. *The Lower Rio Grande Valley of Texas.* San Antonio, 1954.

Stiles, Henry Reed, ed. *Joutel's Journal of La Salle's Last Voyage, 1684-7.* Albany, 1906.

Strickland, Rex W. "Moscoso's Journey Through Texas." *The Southwestern Historical Quarterly*, XLVI, 109-137.

Original Transcribed Surveyors Records, Tom Green County (MS., County Clerk's Office, San Angelo), IV.

Surveyors' Records of Tom Green County, Vol. C, D, I.

Surveyors' Records of Wise County, Vol. A.

Surveyors' Records of Wichita County, Texas, Vol. A, D, B.

Taylor, Virginia H. *The Spanish Archives of The General Land Office of Texas.* Austin, Texas, 1955.

Taylor County Surveying Records, Vol. A.

The Texas Almanac. Galveston, 1860.

The Texas Almanac. Galveston, 1861.

The Texas Almanac. Dallas, 1925.

The Texas Almanac. Dallas, 1928.

The Texas Almanac. Dallas, 1936.

The Texas Almanac. Dallas, 1939-40.

The Texas Almanac. Dallas, 1952-1953.

The Texas Democrat. June 16, 1849.

Texas and Pacific Railway Map. "Shackelford County." 1875.

Texas and Pacific Railway Company Plat Book, 16.

Texas and Pacific Railway Company Map. "Callahan County." 1875.

Texas General Land Office. "Collingsworth County Sketch Files."

Texas General Land Office. "Dickens Co. Sketch File A." August 13, 1873.

Texas General Land Office. "Donley County Sketch File No. 6." October 27, 1881.

Texas General Land Office. "Field Notes Boundary Line Peters Colony." Vol. 18, pp. 54-57.

Texas General Land Office. "Hardeman County Sketch File." October 18-27, 1884.

Texas General Land Office. Plat signed by J. W. Peery, October 2, 1857.

Texas General Land Office. "Survey of east Montague County line." 1859.

Texas General Land Office Maps. "Callahan County." 1879.

Texas General Land Office Maps. "Coleman County." August, 1897.

Texas General Land Office Maps. "Comanche Trail." 1862.

Texas General Land Office Maps. "Cooke District." January 30, 1856.

Texas General Land Office Maps. "Cottle County." May, 1883.

Texas General Land Office Maps. "Crane County." 1902.

Texas General Land Office Maps. "Culberson County." 1908.

Texas General Land Office Maps. "Dallas, Rockwall, Collin, Hunt, Fannin, Lamar, and Red River Counties." 1936.

Texas General Land Office Maps. "Fannin County." 1892.

Texas General Land Office Maps. "General Highway Map Jeff Davis County, Texas." 1951.

Texas General Land Office Maps. "Henry D. Banks Survey." Dallas County Surveying Records, Vol. A.

Texas General Land Office Maps. "Hill County." June, 1922.

Texas General Land Office Maps. "Hudspeth County." 1917.

Texas General Land Office Maps. "Jack County." 1925.

Texas General Land Office Maps. "Jeff Davis County." 1915.

Texas General Land Office Maps. "Jones County." May, 1921.

Texas General Land Office Maps. "Kent County." 1895.

Texas General Land Office Maps. "King County." 1905.

Texas General Land Office Maps. "Pecos County." 1917.

Texas General Land Office Maps. "Peters Colony." 1852.

Texas General Land Office Maps. "Presslar's Travelers Map of 1867."

Texas General Land Office Maps. Promiscuous File No. 3.

Texas General Land Office Maps. "Reagan County." October, 1915.

Texas General Land Office Maps. "Red River County." 1905.

Texas General Land Office Maps. "Taylor County." 1897.

Texas General Land Office Maps. "Texan Emigration and Land Company." 1854.

Texas General Land Office Maps. "Throckmorton County." 1898.

Texas General Land Office Maps. "Upton County." January, 1918.

Texas General Land Office Maps. "Young County." March, 1897.

Thornburn, Joseph B. "Indian Fight in Foard County in 1859." *Kansas Historical Collections,* 1911-12.

Thorp, B. C. and Chester V. Kielman, eds. "Mary S. Young's Journal of Botanical Explorations in Trans-Pecos, Texas, August-September, 1914." *The Southwestern Historical Quarterly,* LVX, 528.

Throckmorton County Surveyors Records, B, 178ff.

Tom Green County Probate Minutes (MS., County Clerk's Office, San Angelo), A.

Tom Green Times, August 26, 1882.

Tom Green County Deed Records (MS., County Clerk's Office, San Angelo), W.

Twain, Mark. *Life on the Mississippi.* New York, 1917.

United States Geological Survey. "Barnes Bridge Quadrangle map." October, 1912.

Unites States Department of Interior Geological Survey, map of *Sabinal Quadrangle,* 1970.

United States Department of Interior Geological Survey, map of *State of Texas,* cartographer, A. G. Hassan, 1922.

United States Geological Survey Maps of Texas: *Christmas Point Quadrangle and Freeport Quadrangle.*

U. S. Congress. House. Executive Document No. 33, 33rd Cong., 1st Sess.

U. S. Congress. House. Executive Document No. 91, 33rd Cong., 2nd Sess.

U. S. Congress. Senate. Executive Document No. 70, 47th Cong., 1st Sess.

U. S. Congress. Senate. Executive Document No. 54, 33rd Cong., 1st Sess.

U. S. Congress. Senate. Executive Document No. 1, 34th Cong., 1st Sess.

U. S. Congress. Senate. Executive Document No. 1, 35th Cong., 2nd Sess.

U. S. Congress. Senate. Executive Document No. 2, 36th Cong., 1st Sess.

U. S. Congress. Senate. Executive Document No. 64, 31st Cong., 1st Sess.

Valdez, Gonzalo Fernandez de Oviedo y. Historia General y Natural de las Indias. 4 Vols. Madrid: Royal Academy of History, 1851-1855.

Wallace, Ernest. *Ronald S. Mackenzie on the Texas Frontier.* Lubbock: West Texas Museum Association, 1964.

Webb, Walter Prescott. *The Great Plains.* Boston, 1931.

Webb, Walter Prescott. "Chihuahua Trail." *The Handbook of Texas.* Austin, 1952.

Webb, Walter Prescott, and H. Bailey Carroll. *The Handbook of Texas.* 2 Vols. Austin, 1892.

Wilbarger, J. W. *Indian Depredations.*

Williams, J. W. *"Coronado, From the Rio Grande to the Concho."* The *Southwestern Historical Quarterly,* LXIII (October, 1959).

Williams, J. W. "New Evidence on Moscoso's Approach." *West Texas Historical Association Year Book,* XXII (October, 1946), 69-80.

Williams, J. W. "The National Road of the Republic of Texas." *The Southwestern Historical Quarterly,* XLVII (January, 1944), 207-224.

Williams, J. W., and Ernest Lee. "Marcy's Exploration to Locate the Texas Indian." *West Texas Historical Association Year Book,* XXIII (October, 1947), 107-132.

Williams, J. W. "New Conclusions on the Route of Mendoza, 1683-84." *West Texas Historical Association Year Book,* XXXVIII (October, 1962), 111-134.

Williams, J. W. "The Van Dorn Trails." *Southwestern Historical Quarterly,* XVIL, 321-343.

Williams, J. W. "Marcy's Road from Doña Anna." *West Texas Historical Association Year Book,* XIX (October, 1943), 128-152.

Williams, J. W. "Military Roads of the 1850's in Central West Texas." *West Texas Historical Association Year Book,* XVIII (October, 1942), 77-91.

Williams, J. W. 'Moscoso's Trail in Texas." *The Southwestern Historical Quarterly,* XLVI, 138-157.

Williams, J. W. *The Big Ranch Country.* Wichita Falls, Texas, 1954.

Williams, J. W. "The Butterfield Overland Mail Road Across Texas." *The Southwestern Historical Quarterly,* LXI (July, 1957), 1-19.

Williams, J. W., ed. "Robson's Journey through West Texas in 1879." *West Texas Historical Association Year Book,* XX (October, 1944), 109-124.

Williams, J. W. "Journey of the Leach Wagon Train Across Texas, 1857." *West Texas Historical Association Year Book,* XXIX (October, 1953), 115-177.

Williams, O. W. " From Dallas to the Site of Lubbock in 1877." *West Texas Historical Association Year Book* (1939).

Williams, O. W. *In Old New Mexico 1879-1880.*

Williams, J. W. "Route of Cabeza de Vaca in Texas." *The Quarterly of the Texas State Historical Association,* III, 54-65.

Woerman, John W. and W. G. Burroughs. "Mississippi River." *The New International Encyclopedia,* 2nd ed., XVI, 14.

Woldert, Albert. "The Expedition of Louis De Moscoso in Texas in 1542." *The Southwestern Historical Quarterly,* XLVI (October, 1942), 158-166.

Writers' Programs of the Works Projects Administration in the State of Oklahoma. Oklahoma: *A Guide to the Sooner State.* Norman, Oklahoma, 1941.

Young County Commissioners Court Minutes (MS., County Clerk's Office, Graham), I.

INDEX

A

AAYS, 106
ABERT Expedition, 55
ADAMS, Doyle, 59 fn 36
AGUIRRE, Pedro de, 122, 123
ALAMOGORDO, New Mexico, 223
ALAMITO Creek, 41
ALAMO Spring, 224
ALARCÓN, Martín de, 129-131, 133-134, 136-137, 147, 155, 167
ALBUQUERQUE, New Mexico, 44, 46-47, 63
ALCANFOR, 45 fn 1
ALLEN, Winnie, iii
ALPINE, Texas, 41
ALTO, Texas 143
AMARILLO, 221
ANGELINA River, 166
ANSON, Texas 50
ANTELOPE, 93
ANTELOPE Hills, 278
ANTELOPE, Texas, 308-309
ANTON, Chico, New Mexico, 63, 74-75
APACHE Indians, 194, 222
APPALACHIAN Mountains, 26
ARANSAS PASS, 7 fn 20, 10
ARCHER County, 35
ARIZONA, 44
ARKANSAS River, 83, 86, 89, 91
ARROYO DEL VINO, 115
ARROYO Hondo (Frio River), 133
ASHBY, Josiah, 213 fn 44
ATASCOSA County, 25, 115, 132
ATASCOSA River, 137
ATLANTIC Ocean, 26
AUSTIN, Stephen F., 128, 135, 143, 163, 165
AUSTIN, Texas, 122
AVAVARES Indians, 15-17, 24

B

BAHIA Road, LA, iii, 119-120
BAKER Lake, 154
BALLINGER, Texas, 181
BANDELIER, Fannie, 1 fn 1
BANDERA County, 22, 115
BANKS, Henry D., 203 fn 7
BANTA, Mart, 309 fn 77, 410
BARCLAY, Walter S., 52 fn 24, 55 fn 36
BARNETT, Ernest W., 185 fn 10
BARREL Springs, 320, 381
BARRILLA Spring, 188, 381
BARRISTER, Mrs. R. L., 398 fn 43
BASKETT, James Newton, 6 fn 20
BASTROP Bay, 5
BASTROP Bayou, 3
BASTROP Cut-off, 177
BASTROP, Texas, 122, 126, 143, 173-174
BATESVILLE, Texas, 114-115, 140
BATON ROUGE, Louisiana, 79-81, 83
BEAN'S Crossing, 369
BEAVER Creek, 52 fn 24, 255, 370
BEE County, 16
BEEVILLE, 16
BELKNAP Creek, 240
BENCHLEY, Texas, 180
BERNALILLO, New Mexico, 45 fn 1
BETHANIA Hospital, vi
BEXAR COUNTY, 116
BIG Bend, 41-42
BIG RANCH COUNTRY, vi
BIG Spring High School, v
BIG Spring, Texas, 64-65, 92, 221, 226
BIG Wichita River, 92, 246, 254, 259
BIEDMA, Luys Hernandez de, 79, 84, 107-108
BIVOUSETTE, Gus, 417
BLACK Beaver, 230-231, 236, 243, 264

BLACK Cat Thicket, 106, 206
BLAKE, R.B., proves there were two San Antonio roads, 166
BLANCO Canyon, 33, 68-71
BLANCO River, 126, 144, 148
BOLTON, Herbert E., 87, 151, 177
BONE Bend, 107-109
BORGER, Texas, 55
BOSQUE Redondo, 64, 74-75
BOSQUE, River, 146
BOWIE, Texas, 241
BOWLES Creek, 164
BOX, Rowland W., 203
BOYD, J. A., 193 fn 43, 194 fn 44
BRADSHAW, James, 203 fn 3
BRAZOS de Dios crossings, 147-148, 172, 174, 176-177, 179
BRAZOS River, 3, 7, 10 fn 20, 11, 30, 37, 71, 76, 91, 94, 98-100, 107-110, 118, 123, 136, 145-147, 152, 173, 246, 250, 261, 263, 324
BRECKENRIDGE Park, 121
BREWSTER County, 184
BRIDWELL, J. S., 303
BRISCOE, Dolph, 131
BROLLIER, Anthony, 190
BROOKSTON, Texas, 208
BROOME, 61
BROWN, John Henry, 300
BROWNSVILLE, Texas, 14
BROWNWOOD, Texas, v
BRUSHY Creek, 150-151
BRYAN, Francis T., 38 fn 133
BRYAN, John Neely, 215
BUCARELI, Texas, 171
BUCKNER'S Orphans Home, 216
BUFFALO, 35, 97-99, 106, 173, 181, 196, 200, 414
BUFFALO Creek, 231
BUFFALO Gap, 388
BUFFALO Hump, 293
BUFFALO Road, 409-411
BUFFALO Road Marker, vi
BUFFALO Springs, Texas 219, 221, 239, 321
BULLHEAD Creek, 22, 38-39, 41
BURKBURNETT High School, v

BURKETT, J. H., 10
BURLESON County, 145
BURNET, Texas 280
BURNETT, R. H., 209 fn 30
BUSH and Tillet Ranch, 231
BUSHY Mound, 239
BUTTERFIELD, John, 281, 365
BUTTERFIELD Overland Mail, 367
BUTTON Willow, 130

C

CABEZA DE VACA, Alvar Nuñez, 1-43 passim, 93 fn 17, 111, 125, 182
CADDO Indians, 100 fn 45, 101, 322
CADODACHOS Indians, 102-103, 106
CADDO Peaks, 279, 281, 287
CALDWELL, Texas, 122-123, 143, 172
CALERIO, Bernardo, 1 fn 1
CALIFORNIA Creek, 235
CALIFORNIA Road, 236, 264, 267-268
CALLAHAN County, v
CALLISBURG, Texas, 241
CAMOLES Indians, 14
CAMARGO, 14
CAMP Cooper, 285, 305, 308
CAMP Johnson, 374
CAMP Radziminski, 293, 305, 307-308
CANADIAN River, 64-66, 306
CANDELARIA, Texas, 184
CANEY Creek, 7, 10 fn 20, 11 fn 21, 30, 176
CAÑON de los Camenos, 382
CAPOTE Creek, 186
CAP Rock, 51, 53, 55, 59-60, 62, 66, 71, 228
CARHART, Rev. Mr., 417
CARRIZO Creek, 131, 175
CARRIZO Springs, Texas, 130, 132
CARROLL, H. Bailey, iii
CARTER, C. L. (Kit), 71 fn 73
CASEY, Lewis, 23
CASTAÑEDA, Carlos de, 18, 31
CASTAÑEDA, Pedro de, 45 fn 3, 46

fn 7, 47 fn 13, 50, 50 fn 22, 53-54, 59, 93 fn 17, 94
CASTILLO, Alonzo del, 1 fn 1, 6, 12-13, 40
CASTILLO, Diego del, 183
CASTLE Gap, 40, 192, 352, 376
CASTLE Mountain, 340
CASTLE Peak, 372
CASTRO, Henry, 135
CASTROVILLE, Texas, 135
CATARINA, Texas, 138
CATHEY, W. T., 52 fn 24
CAUSEY, T. L., 413, 416
CAVALLO Pass, 6-7, 10, 11 fn 21, 13, 30
CEDAR Bayou, 7 fn 20, 10, 30
CEDAR Creek (Corpus Christi), 153, 176
CEDARS, 186
CENTERVILLE, Texas, 123
CENTRALIA Station, 375
CENTURY Plant, 136
CERRO Alto Peak, 223
CHARCO de la Pita, 134, 136
CHARRULO Indians, 6
CHAULAAMES Indians, 124
CHEROKEE County, 175
CHESNUTS (Chinquapins), 158, 161-162
CHICON Creek, 135
CHIHUAHUA, Mexico, 41
CHIHUAHUA Trail, 41-42, 247
CHILLICOTHE, Texas, 50
CHINA Creek, 296
CHINA Ponds, 376
CHINQUAPINS, 162
CHISPA Creek, 186
CHISOS Mountains, 184
CHOCTAW Nation, 316
CHRISTIAN, Paul, 96 fn 28
CHRISTMAS Bay, 5
CHRISTOVAL, Texas, 195
CIBOLO Creek, 116, 168
CICUYE, 45 fn 2, 46 fn 7
CLARENDON, Texas, 401, 417
CLARK, William T., 390
CLARKSVILLE, Texas, 107, 211

CLAY County, 52, 97
CLEAR Fork of the Brazos, 53, 60, 146, 231, 235, 268
CLEBURNE, Texas, 97
CLEMENTS, S. E., 368
CLETO (Ecleto) Creek, 168
COFFEE, Holland, 212
COFFEE Trading Post, 212
COKE County, 52-53, 60
COLLIN County, 203
COLLINS, William, 55 fn 36
COLORADO City, 33, 69-71, 73
COLORADO River, 7, 10, 18, 98, 101, 120, 122, 124, 126, 150, 181, 231, 283
COMAL River, 125, 143, 173
COMANCHE (Caymanche) Creek, 132
COMANCHE Indians, 108, 222, 230, 236, 287, 293, 295, 330, 333, 350
COMANCHE Indian Reservation, 326
COMANCHE Creek, 333
COMANCHE Spring, 188
COMANCHE Springs, 381
COMANCHE Trail, 32 fn 114, 33
CONA, 45, 46 fn 9, 70, 71, 72, 73, 75, 76
CONCHO River, 61-62, 73, 183, 343, 374-375
CONCHOS River, 37
CONNOR, Seymour V., 197 fn 50a
CONRAD, F. E., 412
CONKLING, Margaret, 367
CONKLING, Roscoe, 367
CONNELLY, J. J., 368
CONNELLY'S Station, 369
COOK Creek, 166
COOK, John R., 403
COOK, N. P., 317, 327, 330, 337
COOKE, William G., 92, 97-98, 212
CORAMANCHEL Creek, 132, 140
CORDERA, Antonio, 139-141
CORN, 96, 99-103, 109, 184
CORNUDAS Mountains, 224
CORNUDAS Wells, 224
CORONADO, Francisco Vásquez, 42-46, 50-51, 53, 61, 63, 65, 70,

73, 94, 111
CORPUS Christi, 6, 13-16
CORRELL, Donovan S., 197 fn 50a
COSPER, Mr. and Mrs. L. B., iii
COTTON Shawls, 35-36, 74, 108
COTTONWOOD Spring, 246, 322
COTULLA, Texas, 24, 138-139
COWDEN, L. T., 94 fn 21
CRANE, Texas, 39-40
CRESTVIEW Memorial Park, vi
CREUZBAUR'S Map, 176
CROCKETT, Texas, 118-119, 143
CROSBY County, 71, 73
CROSBYTON, Texas, 33
CROSS Plains, Texas, v, 284
CROW Spring, 224, 380
CRYSTAL City, Texas, 132, 140
CUBA, 2, 89, 94
CUERO, Texas, 117, 137, 168
CUERVO Creek (Creek of the Crows),
    111-112, 128-129
CULIACÁN, Mexico, 44
CUNNINGHAM, George, 96 fn 28,
    304 fn 45
CYPRESS River, 102

D

DAILEY, M., 184 fn 10
DALLAS County, 204
DALLAS *Morning News,* 18
DALLAS, Texas, 92
DAVENPORT, Harbert, 1 fn 1, 4-5, 6
    fn 20, 7, 10-11, 20-21
DAVIS, Edmund J., 389
DAVIS, J. D., 232 fn 37
DAVIS, Jefferson, 312
DAVIS Mountains, 186, 314, 381
DAY, G. W., 98 fn 37
DEAD Man's Hole, See El Muerto.
DE CORDOVA'S Bend, 277
DEER, 91-94, 97, 99, 110
DELAWARE Creek, 225, 378
DELAWARE Indians, 246, 252, 254,
    257, 267, 322, 330
DE LEON, Alonso, 26, 112, 114-120,
    123, 127-128

DEL RIO, 18, 31, 39 fn 134, 41
DE MÉZIÈRES, Athanase, 72, 93, 98,
    100
DENISON, Texas, 92
DESDEMONA, 95
DE SOTO, Hernando, 51, 77, 89-90,
    94-95
DEVINE, Texas, 116, 135-136
DIAMOND, J. R., 368
DICKENS County, 69-70, 96 fn 28
DICUS, R. V., 368
DIMMIT County, 129-130, 132-133,
    137-138, 140
DIVERSION Lake, 306
DIXIE, Texas, 242
DIXON Creek, 55
DOCKUM'S Ranch, 396
DONLEY County, 399
DORANTES, Andrés, 1 fn 1, 2, 5-6,
    11 fn 21, 12-13, 30, 35
DOUBLE Mountain, 232, 262 fn 37
DOUBLE Mountain Fork of the
    Brazos, 71-72, 146, 233, 269
DOWD, D. L., 410
DRUM Bay, 4
DRY Devils River, 18, 196
DUFF, James, 293, 304
DUGGAN, Mrs. Jane, iv
DULINGHAM, B. F., 327
DUNN, Texas, 231
DURST, John, 166
DUVAL County, 24

E

EAGLE PASS, Texas, 19, 38, 112, 124,
    127, 129, 139, 175
EAGLE Springs, 362, 382
EARHART, J. B., 369
EDWARDS, A. B., 370 fn 78, 408
EDWARDS Plateau, 181
EL CAPITÁN Peak, 224-225, 379
ELECTRA, Texas, 296
ELIASVILLE, Texas, 283
ELK CITY, Oklahoma, 306
ELM FORK of Trinity River, 318
EL MUERTO, 361

EL PASO, Texas, 64, 365
ELY, George B., 301
EMIGRANT Crossing, 226, 377
ENRIQUEZ, Alonzo, 5, 6 fn 17
ESCONDIDO Spring, 357
ESPEJO, Antonio de, 37
ESPINOSA, Isidro de, 124-126, 142, 144, 148, 150-152, 174
ESQUIVEL, Hernando de, 6, 13
ESTEVÁNICO, 6, 12-13, 40
EUGENE C. Barker Texas History Center, iii

F

FALFURRIAS, 16
FALL, W. T., 73 fn 77
FICKLIN, Ben, 375, 385
FIGUEROA, 6, 30
FISHER County, 53, 231
FLAG Springs, 238
FLAT Rock Ponds, 375
FLAT Top Ranch, 233
FLEMING, Henry, 417
FLORESVILLE, Texas 115-117
FLORIDA, 89
FLOYD County, 33
FLOYD, Texas, 205
FORD, John Salmon, 300, 307
FORT Arbuckle, 274, 296
FORT Belknap, 246, 276, 278, 283, 286, 290, 311, 313-315, 323, 370
FORT Chadbourne, 280-281, 313, 337
FORT Concho, 33, 43, 386
FORT Croghan, 279-280
FORT Davis, 313, 361
FORT Elliott, 387, 396, 399, 418 fn 8, 420-421
FORT Gates, 280
FORT Gibson, 211
FORT Graham, 276
FORT Griffin, 278 fn 39, 396
FORT *Griffin Echo,* 388, 396, 401
FORT Lyday, 208
FORT McKavett, 33, 38, 280, 282-283
FORT Martin Scott, 280

FORT Mason, 280, 286
FORT Phantom Hill, 278-279, 281-282, 331-332
FORT Saint John the Baptist, Nachitoches, Louisiana, 176
FORT St. Louis, 111, 117-118
FORT Smith, 211, 221
FORT Stockton, Texas, 41, 188
FORT Sumner, New Mexico, 33, 64, 73, 75
FORT Terrett, 196
FORT Towson, 210-211, 222
FORT Worth, 277
FORT WORTH, Texas 94, 99, 101-102, 107-108, 110
FORT Yuma, 313
FRANCIA Crossing of the Rio Grande, 128-129, 137-138
FRANCISCO Creek, 135
FRANKLIN, Texas, 381
FRANK Powers Ranch, 22, 29
FREDERICKSBURG, 280
FREER, 16
FRIEND, Llerena, 287
FRIO County, 16, 137-138
FRIO Draw, 63, 67
FRIO River, 18, 24, 26-27, 37, 114-115, 121, 124, 133-134, 138-140
FRIO Town, 27, 30, 114
FROG Lake, 132
FRONTIER Echo, 386, 412
FUENTE, Jesús de la, 20

G

GAINESVILLE, Texas, 241, 318
GALVESTON Island, 3
GANT, A. B., 401
GARCITAS Creek, 117
GARDNER, Ed, 58 fn 36
GARZA County, 60 fn 38, 73
GENTLEMAN of Elvas, 84, 91, 110
GIDDINGS, DeWitt Clinton, 389
GIRVIN, Mesa, 190
GIRVIN, Texas, 189
GLORIETTA Pass, 63, 75

GLORIOUS San Clemente, 196
GODWIN Creek, 306
GOLIAD, Texas, 120
GONZALES County, 116
GOURDS, 36-37, 125
GRAFORD, Texas, 277
GRAHAM *Leader,* 401
GRAHAM, Texas, 99-100
GRAND Falls, 40
GRANT, Kenneth H., 52 fn 24
GRAPE Creek, 72, 373
GRAPES, 44, 53-55, 58-59, 71, 76, 115
GRAY County, 55
GREAT Moments with the Coyotes, vi
GREEN, Mrs. Laura Bugg, 59 fn 36, 60 fn 44, 61
GREENVILLE, Texas, 102, 106-107
GREER County Case, 209 fn 30, 296
GREER, F. M., 402 fn 67
GREGG, Josiah, 64, 92, 94
GREGORIAN Calendar, 54, 58, 59 fn 36
GRESSETT, Walter, 61 fn 44
GRIERSON Spring, 191
GUADALAJARA, Diego de, 183, 195
GUADALUPE Mountains, 224
GUADALUPE River, 10, 116-118, 122, 173
GUADALQUIVIR River, 2, 21, 24-26, 36
GUASCO Indians, 91, 93-95, 100-102, 108-110
GUINN, George, 412, 426
GULF of Mexico, 3, 10, 11 fn 21, 83-86, 95, 99, 112, 116, 118, 122
GUZMAN, Nuño de, 14

H

HACKBERRY Creek, 197
HALBERT, William B., 60 fn 41
HALE County, 33
HALL County, 60
HALLENBECK, Cleve, 5, 7, 11 fn 21
HALSELL, Fred, 301
HAM, B.D., 370

HAPGOOD Ranch, 304
HARRIS, Mrs. W. R., 55 fn 36
HARRISON, M. P., 231
HASKELL County, 74, 233
HASKELL, Texas, 50
HAXIA, 66-68
HAYES, Arthur E., 227-228
HAYS County, 180
HAYS, John Coffee, 138
HEARNE, Texas, 146, 148
HEDLEY, Texas, 399
HENDERSON, Wade, 374
HENRIETTA, Texas, 308-309
HEREFORD, Texas, 67
HIGHSMITH, Samuel, 39
HIGHWAY 21, 180
HILBURN, A. E., 60 fn 41
HILL Country, 125, 197
HILL, Robert T., 18, 31
HOCHHEIM, Texas, 117
HOCKLEY County, 73
HODGE, Frederick W., 1 fn 1, 18
HOFFMAN, Fritz, 130, 136
HOGEYE Prairie, 369
HOGS, 94-96, 99
HOG TOWN, 95 fn 28
HOLDEN, W. C., 63, 66, 75
HOLLIDAY Creek, 55 fn 36
HONDO Creek, 26, 28
HONDO River, 28, 115
HONDO, Texas, 125
HOOPER, Riley, 325
HORSEHEAD Crossing, 40, 313, 354, 376, 381
HOT Spring, 184
HOT Springs, Arkansas, 86
HOUSTON County, 118-120
HOUSTON, Sam, 166
HOUSTON, Temple, 408
HOUSTONIA Longiflora (Flor de San Juan), 130
HOWARD-PAYNE University, v
HUDSPETH County, 184, 379
HUECO Tanks, 223, 380
HUNT County, 203

I

INDEPENDENCE Spring, 225
INDIAN Creek, 399
IRRIGATION, 124-125, 151

J

J. S. BRIDWELL Ranch, 238, 276
JACK County, 96
JACKRABBITS, 39
JASPER County, 95
JEFFERS, Coon, 258 fn 27
JERNIGAN Thicket, 106
JETTER, J. B., 106 fn 63
JIM NED Creek, 284
JIM WELLS County, 25
JOHNSON, Homer, 59 fn 36
JOHNSTON, Albert Sidney, 285
JOLLY, Texas 300
JONES County, 52-53
JONES, Horace P., 297
JONES, Walter, 161
JONESBORO, Texas, 211
JOSEPHINE, Texas, 205
JUAN Cordona Lake, 189
JULIMES Indians, 184
JUMANO Indians, 125, 190-191, 199

K

KANSAS, 35, 73
KELLY, Marion, 298-299, 305
KENDALL, George W., 92, 97-98
KENT County, 69, 71, 73
KIAMICHI River, 204, 209 fn 30
KICKAPOO Creek, 306
KICKAPOO Indians, 235, 266, 320
KICKAPOO Shoals, 161, 177
KIMBLE County, 42
KIOMATIA, Texas, 210-211
KIOWA Creek, 374
KIOWA Indians, 231
KIOWA Peak, 260 fn 31
KNOX County, 35

L

LACY, Sara, 300 fn 34
LANDONIA, Texas, 207
LA GRANGE, Texas, 120, 169
LAMAR Street, 217
LAMB County, 67
LANDA Park, 122, 143
LANEGADOS Indians, 14
LANGERMANN, A. B., 33 fn 116
LA PRYOR, Texas, iv, 114, 131
LAQUAY, C. H., 60 fn 40
LAREDO, Texas, 26, 135
LA SALLE County, 24, 137-138
LA SALLE, Réne Robert, le Sieur de,
    108, 111, 175
LAS CRUCES, 160
LAS CRUCES, New Mexico, 223
LAVACA Bay, 117
LA VERNIA, Texas, iv
LEACH, James B., 313, 322, 324-325,
    327, 331, 337
LEE, Junior, R. Ernest, iii
LEE, Senior, R. Ernest, iii, 177, 245,
    312 fn 1
LEEPER, Matthew, 300
LEON County, 123, 171
LEON Creek, 116, 121
LEON River, 282
LEON Water Hole, 188
LEONA River, 114-115, 124, 133
LIGON, Mrs. Ella Bugg, 59 fn 36, 60
    fn 44, 61
LIMPIA Creek, 187, 360
LITTLE Elkheart Creek, 161
LITTLE River, 146-147, 152, 250
LITTLE Wichita River, 247, 251, 254,
    256, 274
LIVENGOOD, R. L., 391
LIVE OAK Creek, 133, 198
LLANO Estacado, 230
LLANO Estacado Stage Stand, 376
LLANO River, 42, 195
LORING, John, 207
LOS Adaes, 127, 175
LOS Linguish (Las Lenguas), 68
LOST Creek, 369

LOUISIANA, 127, 141
LOWER (Eastern) Cross Timbers, 93 fn 17, 107, 318
LOWER Presidio Road, 137-141
LUBBOCK, Texas, 65, 73, 75
LUCAS, Thelma, 24
LUTZ, Ed, 405 fn 77
LYDAY Crossing, 207
LYDAY, Isaac, 207
LYTLE, Texas, 137

M

McADAMS, Leslie, 407 fn 85
McCAHEY, Texas, 39-40
McCALL, Mrs. Maurice, 25
McCARTY, Agnes, vi
McCARTY, Alan x
McCLELLAN Creek, 55, 399
McCLELLAN, George B., 291
McDONALD, A. J., 108 fn 75
McDONALD, Cash, 296, 304
McELROY, W. D., 309 fn 74
McFADDIN, T. M., 52 fn 24
McFARLAND, Bates H., 3
McKAMY, a Mr. 417, 420
McKEE, Lena, 55 fn 36
MACKENZIE, Ferry, 204
MACKENZIE, Ronald S., 33, 55, 63, 69-70, 400
MACKENZIE'S Road, 34, 69, 390, 394, 396-397, 400-401
MACKENZIE'S Supply Camp, 33, 70
McKINNEY Avenue, 217
McKINNEY Falls, 149
McKINNEY, Texas, 107
McKINNON, M. A., 314
McMILLAN, Edward, 68 fn 64
McMULLEN County, 24
McMULLEN, John, 135, 137
McMURTRY, J. W., 243
MADISON County, 179
MAGNOLIA Oil Company, v
MALHADO Island, 3-6, 10 fn 20, 13, 30
MALOCHOMY Lake, 154

MANER, "Lige," 310 fn 81
MANUEL, the Comanche, 64-65, 74, 222, 224, 230-231, 242
MARCY'S Meridian, 298
MARCY, Randolph Barnes, 60 fn 39, 64-65, 74, 92, 221-222, 224-225, 245, 257, 268, 273, 279, 283-284, 290-291, 313
MARFA, 186
MARIAMES Indians, 12 fn 32
MARLOW, T. B., 303 fn 43, 304 fn 44
MARQUIS de Aguayo, 129, 134, 136, 147, 150, 155-156
MARQUIS de Rubí, 128, 147, 154, 178
MARTÍN, Hernán, 183
MARTINEZ, Father, iii
MASON County, 18
MASSANET, Damian, 120, 123
MATADOR, Texas, 69-70
MATAGORDA Bay, 6-7, 10, 13, 111, 122
MATAGORDA Peninsula, 6 fn 20, 11
MATAGORDA Island, 6 fn 20, 11
MATHIS, 16
MATTHEWS, Bud, 330 fn 14
MATTHEWS, J. A., 330 fn 14, 390
MAVERICK County, 111-112, 129, 132, 137-138, 140
MEDINA County, 115
MEDINA River, 115, 121, 124
MEGARGEL, 306
MENARD County, 42
MENCHACA, Joachin, 140
MENDOZA, Juan Domínguez de, 181, 183, 190, 195, 199
MERKEL, Texas, v
METHODIST Colony, 417
MEXICO, 5, 76, 83, 114, 119, 122, 128
MEYER, Charlie, 412
MÉZIÈRES, Athanase de, 148
MIDDLE Concho River, 38-39, 194
MIDLAND Junior College, v
MIDLAND, Texas, 226
MIDWAY, Texas, 119, 163, 171

MILAM County, 147, 150
MIMS, Elton, 53 fn 23
MIMS, J. R., 59 fn 36, 60
MIRE, J. M., 324
MISSION Apostol Santiago, 184-185
MISSION La Navidad en Las Cruces, 185
MISSION Nuestro Padre San Francisco de Los Tejas, 155
MISSION Nuestra Señora de Guadalupe de los Nacogdoches, 174
MISSION Nuestra Señora de La Purísima Concepcion, 166
MISSION San Francisco de Las Tejas, 118-120
MISSION San José de San Miguel y Aguayo, 134-135, 139
MISSION San Juan Bautista, 112, 124, 126-127
MISSION Santísimo Nombre de María,
MISSISSIPPI River, 3, 77, 79-80, 83-85, 88
MOBEETIE, 408, 419, 423
MOCKINGBIRD Springs, 401
MONAHANS, Texas, 226
MONCLOVA, Mexico, iii, 17, 20-21, 42
MONTE Grande, 145, 152
MONTERREY, Mexico, 17, 20
MOOAR, J. Wright, 243
MOORE, Joe, iv
MOORE, W. M., 257 fn 20, 401
MORFÍ, Augustín, 138
MORMON Grasshopper, 347
MOSCOSO, Luys de, 75, 79, 83, 85-89, 93-95, 97-98, 103, 108, 110-111
MOTLEY County, 69-70, 95
MOTTS, Elna, 130
MOUND Prairie, 165
MOUNTAIN Pass, 229, 372
MOUNT Bare, 309
MOUNT Blanco, Texas, 405
MULBERRIES, 44, 59-60, 196
MULBERRY Creek, 60

MULE Creek, 235
MUÑOZ, Manuel, 172
MUSICK, Vel, 331
MUSTANG Pond, 351
MUSTANG Water Holes, 375
MYERS, George S., 303

N

NACHITOCHES, 93
NACOGDOCHES County, 174
NACOGDOCHES, Texas, 120-121, 127-128, 172, 174
NADADORES River, 20
NAGUATEX, 109
NAGUATEX Indians, 103
NAIL, J. H., 391
NAÑEZ GARZA, Cesareo, iii
NARROWS, 396
NARVÁEZ, Pánphilo de, 2, 5, 6 fn 17, 13, 22
NATCHEZ, Mississippi, 81, 83
NATIONAL Road, 201, 203-204, 207, 211, 213
NAVASOTA River, 119-120, 123, 136, 146, 174
NAVASOTA, Texas, 118
NAVIDAD en Las Cruces, LA, 184
NAVIDAD River, 169, 172, 177
NECHES River, 119, 155
NEIGHBORS, Robert S., 41 fn 142, 235, 245-246, 251, 257, 265, 268, 300-301
NEIGHBOURS, Kenneth Franklin, 41 fn 142, 68
NEVILLE, A. W., 98 fn 37
NEW BRAUNFELS, Texas, 122, 125, 143, 173
NEWCOMB, Art, 278 fn 39, 309 fn 72
NEW MEXICO, 36, 44, 109, 125
NEW ORLEANS, Louisiana, 80, 83-84
NOLAN County, 52, 60
NORTH Concho River, 33, 53, 58-59, 61, 69-71, 73
NUECES River, 16, 19, 22, 33, 37, 43, 114-115, 121, 124, 132-133, 138, 140
NUÑEZ, Miguel, 136

O

OAKS, 186
O'BRIEN, Mike, 424
OCHILAS, 293
OCONÔR, Hugo, 167, 170
ODESSA, Texas, 64-65, 226
OLD Grass Springs, 239
OLD Salt Trail, 223
OLD San Antonio Road, 120-123, 125-128, 142, 173, 176, 180
OLIVARES, Antonio de, 122, 123
OLNEY, Texas, 219, 233
ONION (Garrapatas) Creek, 126, 148-149
ORGAN Mountains, 223
ORMSBY, Waterman L., 367, 373
ORTH, Texas, 237
OTERO County, New Mexico, 224
OTTA, 397-398, 401, 408
OTTER Creek, 293-294
OVIEDO, Lope de, 6-7, 11, 13
OVIEDO y Valdez, Gonzalo Fernandez de, 26, 29-31
OYSTER Bayou (Creek), 3-4, 7, 10 fn 20, 11 fn 25, 30
OZONA, Texas 198

P

PACIFIC Ocean, 34
PADGETT, Texas, 237
PADRE Island, 14
PAGES, Pierre de, 147, 177
PAIGE, Texas, 179
PAINT Creek, 235, 391
PAISANO Pass, 41
PALO Duro Canyon, 50-51, 55, 62, 70
PALO Pinto County, 74, 94, 107, 110
PALO Pinto Mountains, 99, 101-102
PÂNUCO, 2, 14
PAYAYAN Indians, 124-125, 175
PAPAYAS (Charcon) Creek, 136
PARIS, Texas, 102, 106-107, 203, 208-209
PARR, Mr. and Mrs. Lewis A., 131
PATTON, Mrs. J. H., 55

PATTON, Ray, 55 fn 34
PATTY, C. A., 193 fn 43
PEARCE, N. B., 257
PEARLS, 183
PEARSALL, Texas, 26-27, 29, 115, 133
PEARSON, Mr. and Mrs. Don, x
PEASE River, 398
PECAN Bayou, 274, 281
PECAN Creek, 150-151
PECAN Fork, 253
PECANS, 12, 12 fn 26, 16 fn 47, 42, 44, 50-53, 114-115, 121, 132-133, 140, 181, 193-194, 200, 253
PECOS, New Mexico, 44, 47, 63
PECOS Pueblo, 63, 65, 75
PECOS River, 18, 38-39, 41, 44-45, 63-65, 73-75, 189-190, 198, 222, 226, 354
PECOS, Texas, 64-65
PEÑALOSA, 14
PETERS Colony Map, 216, 325
PIKE, Zebulon Montgomery, 174, 179
PILOT Knob, 27
PIÑEDA, Alvarez de, 181
PINES, 122-123, 174, 179
PINE Spring, 225
PIÑONS, 18-23, 32 fn 113, 37, 42, 196-198
PIRIE, Mr. and Mrs. J. E., iv
PITA Road, 134-135, 137, 139-141
PLACEDO, 292, 363, 370
PLAINVIEW, Texas 67
PLEASANTON, Texas, 137-138
PLUMS, 71, 76
POLECAT Creek, 397
PONTON, Brownie, 3
PONTOON Bridge, 192, 199, 387
POPE, John, 227-228
POPE'S Crossing, 378
PORTALES, New Mexico, 33, 47, 50 fn 19, 53, 64-65, 73
PORT O'Connor, 7, 11
PORTWOOD, Henry W., 306 fn 54
POSSUM Kingdom Dam, 94-95, 99, 107-108, 277
POST, Texas, 59
POTEET, Texas, 116

PRADE Ranch, 22
PRAIRIE Dog, 334
PRESIDIO County, 184
PRESIDIO San Juan Bautista, 126-127, 134, 139, 141, 175
PRESIDIO, Texas, 37-38, 40, 43
PRESSLER, Charles W , 33 fn 116, 117
PRESTON Road, 212, 217, 246
PRESTON, Texas, 236, 313, 315, 319
PREWITT, Mr. and Mrs. 398
PUEBLO Indians, 44

Q

QUANAH, Texas, 50
QUEEN'S Peak, 240
QUERECHO Indians, 45 fn 4, 46 fn 7
QUINTERO, David, iii
QUITAQUE Canyon, 50-51, 68, 70-71
QUITAQUE Creek, 69
QUITSEY Indians, 93
QUIVIRA, 45, 73

R

R. J. SCOTT Survey, 299
RABBIT Creek, 237
RADZIMINSKI Road, 296-297
RAFT, The, 102
RAGSDALE, Thomas F., 209 fn 30
RAMÓN, Diego, 126
RAMÓN, José Domingo, 126-129, 133, 138, 141, 143, 147, 174-175
RAMÓN'S Road, 127-128, 130-131, 133, 141-142, 174, 177
RAMSEY, Grover Co., 163
RATH, Charles, 390
RATH Trail, 399-400, 402-403
RED River, 58, 80, 83-84, 86-88, 98, 100, 102-103, 106-107, 203, 293, 399
REYNOLDS, B. F., 243
REYNOLDS Cattle Company, 391
REYNOLDS, Phin, 390 fn 22
RHYNE, J. W., 240
RIBBLE, W. J., 95 fn 28
RICE'S Crossing, 150

RICHARDSON, Rupert Norval, iii
RIM Rock, 185
RIO GRANDE, 11, 14-15, 17, 20-21, 25, 37-38, 40, 43, 46 fn 9, 47, 50, 54, 63, 68, 73, 75, 112, 114, 118, 121, 124-126, 128-129, 131-132, 137, 141-142, 175, 362
RIO Sarco (Blue River), 114
RIVAS, Antonio, 129-130, 137
RIVERA, Pedro de, 129, 134, 136
ROBBINS Ferry, 118, 163, 171, 177, 179
ROBBINS, Nathaniel, 181
ROBELINE, Louisiana, 127
ROBINSON, Paul, 60 fn 42
ROBSON, George W., 412
ROBSTOWN, 16
ROBY, Texas, 231
ROCK Crossing of the Little Wichita River, 275
ROCKDALE, 152
ROCKEFELLER Foundation, iii
ROCKWALL County, 204
ROSALIS (Charcon) Creek, 135
ROSALIS, Texas, 135
ROSAS de San Juan, las, (Pavonis Lasiopetala), See Picture Section, 129-133
ROSS, Lawrence Sullivan, 292, 296, 305, 307
ROSWELL, New Mexico, 19
ROTAN, Texas, 231
ROUNTREE, Ed, 391
RUIDOSA, Texas, 184-185
RUSH Creek, 294
RUSK, Thomas J., 312
RUSSELL, William, 213 fn 44

S

SABEATA, 184
SABINAL River, 22, 26, 28, 31, 35, 121, 124-125
SABINAL, Texas, 114, 124
SABINAS River, 21, 40 fn 140
SABINE River, 95, 102, 131, 174, 206
ST. DENIS, Louis Juchereau de, 126,

142, 175
SAINT JO, Texas, 241
ST. JOSEPH Island, 7 fn 20
SALADO Creek, 121, 143
SALADO, Texas, 97
SALT, 223-224
SALT Flat, 379
SALT Fork of the Brazos, 71
SALT Fork of the Colorado, 330
SALT Springs, 232
SALTY Creek, 116-117
SAN AMBROSIO Creek, 137
SAN ANGELO, Texas, 33, 39, 41-43,
    52-53, 120, 195
SAN ANTONIO River, 16, 41, 116,
    124, 126, 143, 173
SAN ANTONIO-San Felipe Road, iii
SAN ANTONIO, Texas, 18, 23, 26,
    114-116, 121-122, 125, 127-128,
    135-137, 140-142, 174
SAN AUGUSTINE, Texas, 127, 212
SAN BERNARD River, 5, 7, 10 fn 20,
    30
SANCHEZ, Manuela, 126, 175
SAN DIEGO, 16
SAN ELIZARIO, Texas, 224
SAN FELIPE Rock Crossing, 178
SAN GABRIEL (Xavier) River, 150
SAN MARCOS River, 122, 126, 144,
    173
SAN SABA River, 38, 43, 195
SAN XAVIER Missions, 151
SAN ISIDRO Spring, 150
SAN LUIS Peninsula, 4-5, 30
SAN MARCOS, Texas, 31, 125
SAN MIGUEL, Miguel, 129
SAN MIGUEL, New Mexico, 222
SAN PEDRO Creek, 157, 164
SAN PEDRO Springs, 124-125, 142
SANTA ANA Lake, 123, 136, 154-155
SANTA ANNA Peaks, 284, 287
SANTA Clara Spring, 160
SANTA Coleta Creek, 155
SANTA Efigenia Creek, 154
SANTA FE, New Mexico, 222
SANTA ROSA, New Mexico, 63, 74
SANTO Domingo, 2

SCHULENBURG, Texas, 169
SCULL, Mr. and Mrs. Ross O., iv
SCURRY County, 51, 71, 231
SECO Creek, 29, 125
SECOND United Cavalry Regiment,
    285-286, 288
SEGUIN, Juan N., 139
SHEARER, Earl, 131
SHEFFIELD, Texas, 41
SIBLEY tent, 349
SIERRA Blanca, 184
SIJAMES Indians, 124
SIMMONS College (Hardin-Simmons
    University), v
SIMPSON, B. F., 399 fn 46 and 53
SIUPANS Indians, 124
Sizzling Southwest Football, vi
SMITH, Buckingham, 1 fn 1
SMITH, George F., 95 fn 28
SMITH, Hank, 395
SMITH, Kirby, 286
SNYDER, 33, 55, 69, 71, 73
SNYDER, Pete, 408
SOBGE, H. F., 193 fn 43
SOCATINO, 106, 109
SODA Lake, 189
SOD House Draw, 67
SOLDIER Mound, 403
SOLIS, Gaspar José de, 147, 169, 177
SOUTH Concho River, 195
SOUTHERN Overland Mail Line, 312,
    365
SOUTHWEST Rotary Club, vi
Southwestern Historical Quarterly, iv
SPADE Ranch, 33
SPAIN, 143
SPANISH Dagger, 136, 141
SPANISH Mail Route, 179-180
SPANISH Trace, 211
SPILLER, George, 401
SPRING Creek, 176, 193-194
SQUARE Top Mountain, 189
STAMFORD, Texas, 50
STANFIELD Ranch, 276
STELL, George W., 203-205, 208
STERLING City, 33, 50, 53, 60-61, 63,
    68-70

STERLING County, 52-53
STILES, Texas, 375
STONEMAN, George, 327
STONEWALL County, 74, 233
STOWE Creek, 164
STRICKLAND, Rex, 88
STURM, J. J., 100 fn 45
SUGAR Loaf Mountain, 171
SULPHUR River, 102, 106, 206-208
SUMMIT Level of Three Streams, 250
SWAN Lake, 4
SWENSON, A. J., 391

T

TABLE Mountain, 281
TAYLOR County, 52
TAYLOR, Texas, 150
TAX Springs, 302
TAYLOR, D., 391
TECUMSEH Peaks, 281
TEE PEE City, 396-398, 401, 408
TEE PEE Creek, 398
TEHUACANAS Indians, 293
TEJAS Indians, 126
TELLEZ, 14
TERÁN de Los Rios, Domingo, 119-123, 127
TEXAN Santa Fe Expedition, 92
TEXARKANA, Texas, 102-103, 107
TEXAS Historical Commission, vi
TEXAS Oil Company, v
TEXAS Rangers, 39, 294
TEXAS, Republic of, 141
TEXAS State Archives, iii
TEYAS Indians, 45, 46 fn 7, 70-76
THOMAS, George H., 290 fn 2(a)
THOMAS Lambshead Survey, 236
THOMPSON, Jacob, 312
THORNDALE, Texas, 151
THROCKMORTON County, 52, 74
TIABAN, New Mexico, 73
TICKS, 126, 149
TIGUEX, 45 fn 1, 47, 75
TOBAR, a Corporal, 140
TOKSANA, Texas, 405
TOM GREEN County, 42, 52

TONKAWA Indians, 292, 293
TORTUGAS Creek, 132-133
TORTUGA Hill, 171
TRAMMELL, Nicholas, 212
TRAMMELL'S Trace, 212
TRAVIS, W. Wm., 317
TRINITY River, 99, 101-102, 118-119, 123, 136, 171, 203, 250
TUACANA Indians, 93
TUBBS, Mrs. I. I., 37
TUCUMCARI, New Mexico, 63
TULE Canyon, 50, 68, 70
TURBEVILLE, John, 300
TURKEY Creek, 282
TURQUOISE, 74, 108
TURTLE Hole Creek, 398
TURTLE Lake, 132
TYNAN, 16

U

UNDERWOOD, Lee, 303
UNIVERSITY of Texas, The, 3
UPPER (Western) Cross Timbers, 92-95, 97-99, 243, 274, 319-320
UPPER Presidio Road, 133, 137, 140-141
UPTON, Raymond, 68 fn 65
URSULINE Academy, 216
UTOPIA, Texas, 37
UVALDE, Texas, 16, 18, 22, 32, 39 fn 134, 41, 114-115

V

VAN CAMP, Cornelius, 295
VAN DORN Crossing, 300, 301, 302
VAN DORN, Earl, 288, 295
VAN DORN'S New Road, 306
VAN DORN Pasture, 304
VAN DORN Trail Markers, vi
VAN HORN'S Wells, 361
VASHTI, Texas, 239
VEAL'S Station, 277
VEAZEY, Ruth Elizabeth, vi
VIAL, Pedro, 148, 168, 176, 179
VICKSBURG, Mississippi, 79-81, 83